DISSIDENT RABBI

DISSIDENT RABBI

THE LIFE OF JACOB SASPORTAS

YAACOB DWECK

PRINCETON UNIVERSITY PRESS

PRINCETON AND OXFORD

Published by Princeton University Press
41 William Street, Princeton, New Jersey 08540
6 Oxford Street, Woodstock, Oxfordshire OX20 1TR

press.princeton.edu

Library of Congress Control Number: 2018963247
ISBN 978-0-691-18357-2

British Library Cataloging-in-Publication Data is available

Editorial: Fred Appel and Thalia Leaf
Production Editorial: Lauren Lepow
Text and Jacket Design: Leslie Flis
Jacket Credit: Oil portrait of Jacob Sasportas, attributed to Isaac Luttichuys, ca. 1670.
Photo © The Israel Museum, Jerusalem by Elie Posner
Production: Erin Suydam
Publicity: Nathalie Levine and Kathryn Stevens

This book has been composed in Linux Libertine, Estilo, and ScalaSans

Printed on acid-free paper. ∞

Printed in the United States of America

10 9 8 7 6 5 4 3 2 1

FOR HARRY AND EMMA

One must fight for one's truth while making sure not to kill that truth with the very arms employed to defend it: only if both criteria are satisfied can words recover their vital meaning. With this in mind, the role of the intellectual is to seek by his own lights to make out the respective limits of force and justice in each camp. It is to explain the meaning of words in such a way as to sober minds and calm fanaticisms, even if this means working against the grain.

—Albert Camus, *Algerian Chronicles*

CONTENTS

ILLUSTRATIONS

~

MAPS

FIGURES

ABBREVIATIONS

AHR   *American Historical Review*

BT   Babylonian Talmud

Carlebach, *Pursuit of Heresy*   Elisheva Carlebach, *The Pursuit of Heresy: Rabbi Moses Hagiz and the Sabbatian Controversies* (New York: Columbia University Press, 1990)

Emden, *MS*   Jacob Emden, *Megillat sefer*, ed. David Cahana (Warsaw, 1897)

Franco Mendes, *Memorias*   David Franco Mendes, *Memorias do estabelecimento e progrosso dos Judeos Portuguezes e Espanhoes nesta famosa citade de Amsterdam*, ed. L. Fuks and R. G. Fuks Mansfeld, special issue of *Studia Rosenthaliana* 9 (1975)

Fuks-M., *EH*   L. Fuks and R. G. Fuks Mansfeld, *Hebrew and Judaic Manuscripts in Amsterdam Public Collections*, vol. 2, *Catalogue of the Manuscripts of Ets Haim/Livraria Montezinos Sephardic Community of Amsterdam* (Leiden: Brill, 1975)

Fuks-M., *Ros.*   L. Fuks and R. G. Fuks-Mansfeld, *Hebrew and Judaic Manuscripts in Amsterdam Public Collections*, vol. 1, *Catalogue of the Bibliotheca Rosenthaliana University Library of Amsterdam* (Leiden: Brill, 1973)

Fuks-M., *Typography*   L. Fuks and R. G. Fuks-Mansfeld, *Hebrew Typography in the Northern Netherlands, 1585–1815: Historical Evaluation and Descriptive Bibliography*, 2 vols. (Leiden: Brill, 1984–1987)

HUCA   *Hebrew Union College Annual*

Israel, *Diasporas*   Jonathan I. Israel, *Diasporas within a Diaspora: Jews, Crypto-Jews and the World Maritime Empires (1540–1740)* (Leiden: Brill, 2002)

JHI   *Journal of the History of Ideas*

JQR   *Jewish Quarterly Review*

JSJT   *Jerusalem Studies in Jewish Thought*

Kaplan, *An Alternative Path*   Yosef Kaplan, *An Alternative Path to Modernity: The Sephardi Diaspora in Western Europe* (Leiden: Brill, 2000)

Kaplan, *Orobio de Castro*   Yosef Kaplan, *From Christianity to Judaism: The Story of Isaac Orobio de Castro*, trans. Raphael Loewe (Oxford: Littman Library and Oxford University Press, 1989)

KS   *Kiryat Sefer*

Levie Bernfeld, *Poverty and Welfare*   Tirtsah Levie Bernfeld, *Poverty and*

Welfare among the Portuguese Jews in Early Modern Amsterdam (Oxford: Littman Library, 2012)

P&P *Past and Present*

PT Palestinian Talmud

REJ *Revues des Études Juives*

SAA Stadsarchief Amsterdam

SAH Staatsarchiv Hamburg

Sasportas, *Kitzur,* ed. Emden Jacob Sasportas, *Kitzur zizath novel zvi*, ed. Jacob Emden (Altona, 1757)

Sasportas, *Ohel ya-akov* Jacob Sasportas, *Ohel ya-akov*, ed. David Meldola (Amsterdam: Hertz Levi Rofe, 1737)

Sasportas, *ZNZ* Jacob Sasportas, *Zizath novel zvi*, ed. Isaiah Tishby (Jerusalem: Bialik Institute, 1954)

Scholem, *Mehkarim* Gershom Scholem, *Mehkarim u-mekorot le-toledot ha-shabtaut ve-gilguleha* (Jerusalem: Bialik Institute, 1974)

Scholem, *Mehkere shabtaut* Gershom Scholem, *Mehkere shabtaut*, ed. Yehuda Liebes (Tel Aviv: Am Oved, 1991)

Scholem, *Sabbatai Sevi* Gershom Scholem, *Sabbatai Sevi: The Mystical Messiah*, trans. R. J. Zwi Werblowsky (Princeton, NJ: Princeton University Press, 1973)

SR *Studia Rosenthaliana*

TJHSE *Transactions of the Jewish Historical Society of England*

Yerushalmi, *Isaac Cardoso* Yosef Hayim Yerushalmi, *From Spanish Court to Italian Ghetto: Isaac Cardoso; A Study in Seventeenth-Century Marranism and Jewish Apologetics* (New York: Columbia University Press, 1971)

DISSIDENT RABBI

INTRODUCTION

~

"It is broken in the middle, irreparably broken, and at the end of it, after the revolutions, men can hardly recognize the beginning."[1] Thus Hugh Trevor-Roper described the seventeenth century. War, revolution, famine, plague: Europe tore itself apart over the course of many decades. A century that began with the Spanish Habsburgs at the height of their imperial power saw the rise of the Dutch Republic out of Iberian ruins and the synchronous emergence of the British Empire.

This book is about a man who lived through nearly the entirety of this broken century. Around 1610 Jacob Sasportas was born in Oran, a garrison town at the edge of the Iberian Empire on the Mediterranean coast of North Africa in present day Algeria. The scion of a rabbinic family, Sasportas served the Jews of Oran and nearby Tlemcen as a rabbinic judge for several decades. In his early forties, he was exiled from North Africa for reasons that remain unknown, and fled to Amsterdam. For almost half a century, Sasportas lived among the Portuguese Jews of the Sephardic Diaspora. In 1665 he emerged as one of the few opponents to the provocative persona of Sabbetai Zevi, the self-proclaimed Messiah who became the center of a mass movement.[2] Jews everywhere from the eastern fringes of the Ottoman Empire to the edges of the Atlantic greeted the news of redemption with undisguised jubilation. For the better part of a year, many abjured the traditional laws of Judaism and adhered to new norms established by the Messiah and his prophet Nathan of Gaza.[3] With great speed, this enthusiasm became a widespread phenomenon, as no less a historian than E. J. Hobsbawm observed: "Again, it may not be wholly accidental that the greatest messianic movement of Jewish history occurred at this moment, sweeping the communities of the great trading centers—Smyrna, Leghorn,

---

[1] "The General Crisis of the Seventeenth Century," *P&P* 16 (1959): 33–34; reprinted in *The Crisis of the Seventeenth Century: Religion, the Reformation and Social Change* (Indianapolis, IN: Liberty Fund, 1999), 46.

[2] Scholem, *Sabbatai Sevi.*

[3] Matt Goldish, *The Sabbatean Prophets* (Cambridge, MA: Harvard University Press, 2004); Ada Rapoport-Albert, *Women and the Messianic Heresy of Sabbatai Zevi: 1666–1816* (Oxford: Littman Library, 2011).

Venice, Amsterdam, Hamburg—off their feet with special success in the middle 1660s as prices reached their lowest point."[4]

Sasportas spent considerable time in three of these great trading centers—Livorno, Amsterdam, and Hamburg—as well as in a fourth, London. After his departure from North Africa at midcentury, he occupied rabbinic positions in all four major cities of the Sephardic Diaspora in western Europe.[5] His response to Sabbatianism should give pause to Hobsbawm's economic reductionism. At the moment of the messianic outbreak, he was living in poverty among the Portuguese Jews of Hamburg. From his temporary home, he conducted a vigorous campaign first to challenge and later to undermine the messianic claims of Sabbetai Zevi and Nathan of Gaza. He kept a meticulous record of Sabbatianism as it was occurring. He edited this Hebrew book, which consisted of letters, journal entries, and public circulars, and entitled it *Zizath novel zvi* (Heb. The fading flower of the Zevi). In a phrase characteristic of Sasportas's allusive style, the title simultaneously referred to the object of his vitriol, Sabbetai Zevi, and to the Messiah's failure to fulfill the prophetic promise of the biblical verse from which the title derived: "And the glorious beauty shall be a fading flower" (Isa. 28:4).[6]

Sasportas was the primary critic of Sabbetai Zevi. His own writing and Gershom Scholem's later reconstruction in *Sabbatai Sevi: The Mystical Messiah* indicate that most Jews, including the rabbinic elites, believed, that Sabbetai Zevi was the Messiah prior to his conversion to Islam at the behest of the Ottoman sultan. This period lasted for about a year, depending on where one lived and how long it took for confirmed reports of the Messiah's conversion to arrive. Other Jews may have doubted Sabbetai Zevi's messianic claims prior to his conversion—Samuel Aboab in Venice and Jacob Hagiz in Jerusalem serve as the closest analogues—but no one else wrote about his confusion, his doubt, and his opposition at such length and with such eloquence as Sasportas. Sabbatianism was a genuinely popular movement. It cut across deeply entrenched divisions within Jewish life: Sephardic and Ashkenazic, lay and clergy, rich and poor. Sabbetai Zevi and the movement he initiated brought a wave of piety and repentance among the Jewish

---

[4] "The General Crisis of the European Economy in the 17th Century," *P&P* 5 (1954): 36–37.
[5] Matt Goldish, "Hakham Jacob Sasportas and the Former Conversos," *SR* 44 (2012): 149–172.
[6] Sasportas, *ZNZ*.

laity. Many of Sasportas's colleagues challenged his criticism, and some even begged him to keep quiet. After all, Jews had begun to attend synagogue in droves and repent with fervor. As rabbis, they reasoned, they should support precisely this kind of behavior and these sorts of activities. In his responses, Sasportas effectively argued that his own doubt was a better means to attain genuine repentance than their certainty. This book asks a question: Why would a single individual oppose a messianic movement as it was taking place? What was the source and the substance of Sasportas's opposition? In other words, this book explores the truth-value of doubt within the rabbinic tradition as it was expressed by one man living in the midst of a maelstrom.

PROVINCIALIZING EUROPE

The question is much easier to articulate than it is to answer. The first half of Sasportas's life poses a problem. Extremely little evidence, either in his own hand or in the records of the Iberian powers, survives from his first four decades in Oran and Tlemcen. Sasportas came from beyond Europe and entered the historical record only when he arrived in Europe. This gaping lacuna in knowledge of his life presents both a challenge and an opportunity. The difficulty is relatively obvious: given the choice between more and less evidence, a historian would always prefer more. Nothing is known about Sasportas's childhood, his first wife, or his teachers. Even the structure of rabbinic life in North Africa can be discerned only in its most basic outlines.[7] At the same time, the fact that Sasportas arrived in Europe from North Africa presents an opportunity. Sasportas's writing offers a view of the Sephardic Diaspora in western Europe that has few parallels in the seventeenth century. This diaspora, one of the best-documented and most carefully studied Jewish populations in the early modern world, emerges in a different perspective when viewed through Sasportas's life.[8]

In order to understand the northern Sephardic Diaspora during the Sabbatian crisis and Sasportas's place within it, one must go back all

---

[7] H. Z. Hirschberg, *A History of the Jews in North Africa* (Leiden: Brill, 1974–1981). For the title of this section, see Dipesh Chakrabarty, *Provincializing Europe: Postcolonial Thought and Historical Difference* (Princeton, NJ: Princeton University Press, 2000).

[8] Kaplan, *An Alternative Path*; Israel, *Diasporas.*

the way to the late Middle Ages and to Iberia itself. In 1391 and 1392 a wave of riots throughout the kingdoms of Castile and Aragon wreaked havoc on Jewish life.[9] Some families fled to the Italian Peninsula or to the coastal cities of North Africa. Some traveled to the eastern side of the Mediterranean and reached as far as Palestine.[10] Others converted to Catholicism and began to live as New Christians. Still others escaped death and conversion and continued to live as Jews in Castile and Aragon. For over a century between 1391 and the expulsion from Spain in 1492, New Christians in Castile and Aragon lived side by side with their former coreligionists.[11] Through a sustained legal and political effort on behalf of various monarchs that was reinforced by the Catholic Church, these New Christians remained separate from the surrounding Catholic society as well as distinct from the Jews among whom they had once lived. In the middle of the fifteenth century, a series of laws known as *estatutos de limpieza de sangre* (Spa. statutes of purity of blood) institutionalized the distinction between Old and New Christians and sought to prevent the latter from entering various privileged sectors of Spanish society.[12] In 1478 the Catholic Church introduced the Holy Office, or Inquisition, into Spain and began to prosecute New Christians for Judaizing heresy. The Inquisition constituted a legal entity that had jurisdiction over crimes of heresy.[13] If Jews were allowed to live as a protected minority and lay beyond the remit of the Holy Office, New Christians who had lapsed into Judaism or into Jewish practices fell well within its orbit.[14]

[9] For Aragon, see Benjamin R. Gampel, *Anti-Jewish Riots in the Crown of Aragon and the Royal Response, 1391–1392* (New York: Cambridge University Press, 2016).

[10] Joseph Hacker, "The Connections of Spanish Jewry with Eretz Israel between 1391 and 1492" (Hebrew), *Shalem* 1 (1974): 105–156.

[11] Yitzhak Baer, *A History of the Jews in Christian Spain* (Philadelphia: JPS, 1966); Julio Caro Baroja, *Los Judíos en la España moderna y contemporánea* (Madrid: Ediciones Arión, 1962); and the literature cited below.

[12] Albert Sicroff, *Les Controverses de "pureté de sang" en Espagne du XVe au XVIIe siècle* (Paris: Didier, 1960); Yosef Hayim Yerushalmi, "Assimilation and Racial Anti-Semitism: The Iberian and the German Models," in *The Faith of Fallen Jews: Yosef Hayim Yerushalmi and the Writing of Jewish History*, ed. David N. Myers and Alexander Kaye (Hanover, NH: Brandeis University Press, 2014), 176–209; María Elena Martínez, *Genealogical Fictions: Limpieza de sangre, Religion, and Gender in Colonial Mexico* (Stanford, CA: Stanford University Press, 2008), chap. 1.

[13] *Jews and Conversos: Studies in Society and the Inquisition*, ed. Yosef Kaplan (Jerusalem: Magnes Press, 1985); Norman Roth, *Conversos, Inquisition and the Expulsion of the Jews from Spain* (Madison: University of Wisconsin Press, 1995); Francisco Bethencourt, *The Inquisition: A Global History, 1478–1834* (Cambridge: Cambridge University Press, 2009); Henry Kamen, *The Spanish Inquisition: A Historical Revision* 4th ed. (New Haven, CT: Yale University Press, 2014).

[14] Benzion Netanayahu, *The Marranos of Spain: From the Late XIVth to the Early XVIth Century*

With the marriage of Ferdinand of Aragon and Isabella of Castile in 1469, the two largest monarchies in Iberia merged to form Spain.[15] Together the Catholic Monarchs, as they were later titled by Pope Alexander VI, completed the Reconquista. They also realized the dream of a Spain without Jews. In 1492, months after they had conquered Granada, the last Moorish kingdom on Iberian soil, they decided to expel the Jews. Ferdinand and Isabella offered the Jews of their kingdom a stark choice: conversion to Catholicism or expulsion.[16] Many Jews converted to Catholicism and joined the large population of New Christians already living in Spain; many others went into exile. Just as they had a century earlier, Jews left Spain for North Africa and the Italian Peninsula. They also migrated in large numbers to the Ottoman Empire. Many chose to flee to the neighboring kingdom of Portugal. Five years later the entire Jewish population of Portugal, including both the recent immigrants from Spain and the Jews who had been living in Portugal prior to 1492, was forcibly converted to Catholicism.[17] With the expulsion of the Jews from the Kingdom of Navarre in 1498, Iberia was theoretically free of Jews.[18]

Except what was true in theory was hardly true in practice. The forced conversion in Portugal in 1497 differed qualitatively from the mass conversions in Castile and Aragon at the end of the fourteenth century. Whereas in Castile and Aragon there had been an interim period when a group of New Christians lived side by side with professing Jews, all Jews in Portugal converted to Catholicism and became New Christians.[19] This mass forced conversion led to a deep sense of group cohesion among the Portuguese New Christians, who referred

according to Contemporary Hebrew Sources (New York: American Academy of Jewish Research, 1966); Gerson D. Cohen, "Review of B. Netanyahu's The Marranos of Spain," Jewish Social Studies 29 (1967): 178–184; Haim Beinart, Conversos on Trial: The Inquisition in Ciudad Real (Jerusalem: Magnes Press, 1981); The Sephardi Legacy, ed. Haim Beinart (Jerusalem: Magnes Press, 1992); James S. Amelang, Historias paralelas: judeoconversos y moriscos en la España moderna (Madrid: Edicones Akal, 2011).

[15] J. H. Elliott, Imperial Spain, 1469–1716 (London: Penguin, 2002).

[16] Haim Beinart, The Expulsion of the Jews from Spain (Oxford: Littman Library, 2002); Henry Kamen, "The Mediterranean and the Expulsion of Spanish Jews in 1492," P&P 119 (1988): 30–55; Dor Gerush Sefarad, ed. Yom Tov Assis and Yosef Kaplan (Jerusalem: Zalman Shazar Center, 1999).

[17] João Lúcio d'Azevedo, História dos Christãos-Novos portugueses (Lisbon: Livraria clássica editora de A. M. Teixeira, 1921).

[18] Benjamin R. Gampel, The Last Jews on Iberian Soil: Navarrese Jewry 1479/1498 (Berkeley: University of California Press, 1989).

[19] Yerushalmi, Isaac Cardoso; Gérard Nahon, "Les Marranes espagnols et portugais et les communautés juives issues du marranisme dans l'historiographie récente," REJ 136 (1977): 297–367.

to themselves, and were referred to by others, as *homens da nação* (Por. Men of the Nation) or simply as *a nação* (Por. the Nation).[20] As New Christians, the former Jews of Portugal were now subject to the jurisdiction of the Holy Office. As a group of wealthy merchants, they succeeded in convincing the Portuguese crown to delay the introduction of the Holy Office in Portugal until 1536, thirty-nine years after the forced conversion of 1497. Once introduced, the Inquisition was no less zealous in pursuing perceived or actual relapses into Judaizing heresy in Portugal than it had been in Spain.[21] From 1536 until 1580 and beyond, the Portuguese Inquisition prosecuted Judaizing heresy in Portugal itself and in its colonies in the New and Old Worlds.

In 1580 Philip II unified the Spanish and Portuguese crowns. The Portuguese Inquisition remained a juridical entity separate from the Spanish Inquisition. By the late sixteenth century, the Spanish Inquisition had largely ceased to prosecute Judaizing heresy and had begun to focus on heresies other than Judaism, such as the various forms of Protestantism that had made inroads in Spain. Portuguese New Christians began to flood into the major urban centers of Spain, where they lived relatively free of the Inquisition. The influx of Portuguese New Christians into Spain in the late sixteenth century was so pronounced that the term *homens de negócios* (Spa. Men of Affairs) became the rough equivalent of "Judaizer" in Spanish society.[22] Jews and Judaism were suddenly so great a problem in Spanish life that in the seventeenth century the Holy Office in Spain began to prosecute Judaizing heresy with renewed vigor.[23]

Roughly a decade before Portugal became part of the Spanish Habsburg Empire, a revolt began against Spanish rule in the Netherlands. This revolt, which would last until 1648, would subsequently be termed the Eighty Years' War and would lead to the formation of the Dutch Republic.[24] In 1579 the seven northern provinces of the Nether-

---

[20] Miriam Bodian, "'Men of the Nation': The Shaping of Converso Identity in Early Modern Europe," *P&P* 143 (1994): 48–76; David L. Graizbord, "Religion and Ethnicity among 'Men of the Nation': Toward a Realistic Interpretation," *Jewish Social Studies* 15 (2008): 32–65.

[21] Alexandre Herculano, *History of the Origen and Establishment of the Inquisition in Portugal,* with a prolegomenon by Yosef Hayim Yerushalmi (New York: Ktav Publishing House, 1972).

[22] Yerushlami, *Isaac Cardoso,* Ch. 1.

[23] Yosef Kaplan, *Zwischen 'Neuchristen' und 'Neuen Juden': Die verschlungenen Wege von Kryptojuden und westlichen Sefarden in der Frühen Neuzeit* (Trier: Kliomedia, 2014).

[24] Jonathan I. Israel, *The Dutch Republic: Its Rise, Greatness, and Fall 1477–1806* (Oxford: Clarendon Press, 1995).

lands signed the Treaty of Utrecht as a means to guarantee their mutual defense against the Spanish Habsburgs. The treaty also ensured that no one in the Netherlands could be persecuted for religious convictions. Jews and the Portuguese New Christians were probably quite far from the minds of the Dutch burghers when they signed a treaty meant to ensure the practice of Calvinism beyond the jurisdiction of imperial Spain.[25] Almost concurrently Antwerp, which had been the central node for trade between the Netherlands and Portugal, closed its port in 1585. A number of other cities began to compete for the control of trade between Iberia and the Low Countries. Between 1585 and 1610 Portuguese New Christians settled in Middelburg, Hamburg, London, and Rouen. In these cities they established small centers of Jewish life and continued to trade with the members of their families who remained in Iberia. Many Portuguese New Christians began their lives in Portugal, lived for a considerable portion of their youth and early adulthood in Spain, and then migrated to northern Europe as adults.[26] In the cities of northern Europe, they could escape from the clutches of the Holy Office and pursue new economic opportunities.[27] The Portuguese Jews of the Sephardic Diaspora in western Europe went from being New Christians in the Iberian Peninsula to becoming New Jews in northern Europe.

Of all the cities in northern Europe in which Portuguese New Christians settled as New Jews, it was in Amsterdam that they became the most prosperous.[28] It took them many decades to transform the city of Amsterdam into the Dutch Jerusalem.[29] The first Jewish service was held in Amsterdam in 1597. Over the next two decades the Portuguese in Amsterdam established three separate Jewish congregations: Bet Jaacob (Heb. House of Jacob) in 1602, Neve Shalom (Heb. Dwelling

---

[25] *Calvinism and Religious Toleration in the Dutch Golden Age*, ed. R. Po-chia Hsia and Henk van Nierop (New York: Cambridge University Press, 2002).

[26] Kaplan, *Orobio de Castro*.

[27] Daniel M. Swetschinski, "Kinship and Commerce: The Foundations of Portuguese Jewish Life in Seventeenth-Century Holland," *SR* 15 (1981): 52–74.

[28] Miriam Bodian, *Hebrews of the Portuguese Nation: Conversos and Community in Early Modern Amsterdam* (Bloomington: Indiana University Press, 1997); Yosef Kaplan, *Les Nouveaux-Juifs d'Amsterdam* (Paris: Chandeigne, 1999); Daniel Swetschinski, *Reluctant Cosmopolitans: The Portuguese Jews of Seventeenth-Century Amsterdam* (London: Littman Library, 2000).

[29] Salo W. Baron, *A Social and Religious History of the Jews* 2nd ed. (New York: Columbia University Press, 1973), 15:3–73; Yosef Kaplan, "The Jews in the Republic until about 1750: Religious, Cultural, and Social Life," in *The History of the Jews in the Netherlands* ed. J.C.H. Blom et al. (Oxford: Littman Library, 2002), 116–163.

of Peace) in 1608, and Bet Israel (Heb. House of Israel) in 1618. Each of these congregations had its own clergy and its own rules of governance. By the 1630s there were roughly one thousand Portuguese Jews as well as a few dozen Ashkenazi Jews from Germanic lands living in Amsterdam.[30] In 1638 the three congregations agreed to merge under unified leadership and called the new congregation Talmud Torah.[31] As a group of New Jews, the Portuguese of Amsterdam were relatively ignorant of Judaism and the Hebrew language. In order to acquaint themselves with the Judaism of their ancestors they hired a series of rabbis from elsewhere to serve their needs.

As befitted a group of extremely successful merchants, the Portuguese Jews of Amsterdam kept detailed records. The resolution books of the united Talmud Torah, referred to as *Livros de escamot*, contain a wealth of information about the governance, finances, and personnel of the congregation.[32] The Portuguese Jews of Amsterdam founded a series of welfare institutions and confraternities, many of which kept separate and equally detailed records. These records appear in Portuguese, although Spanish, Dutch, and occasionally even Hebrew surface in the pages of their account books. The language of daily life in Amsterdam appears to have been Portuguese, while Spanish was reserved for both belletristic writing and philosophical and theological polemics. The Jews of early modern Amsterdam, and by extension Hamburg and London, are often referred to as Sephardic.[33] And justifiably so. They were quite proud of their Hispano-Jewish heritage and wasted little time in informing other Jews about their pride in their lineage. By and large, however, they were Portuguese Sephardim. Many had lived in Spain for a considerable period of time, some had been born there, and some still had considerable family ties to New Christians in

[30] Hurbert P. H. Nusteling, "The Jews in the Republic of the United Provinces: Origin, Numbers, and Dispersion," in *Dutch Jewry: Its History and Secular Culture (1500–2000)*, ed. Jonathan Israel and Reinier Salverda (Leiden: Brill, 2002), 43–62.

[31] Arnold Wiznitzer, "The Merger Agreement and Regulations of Congregation Talmud Torah of Amsterdam (1638–1639)," *Historia Judaica* 20 (1958): 109–132.

[32] Levie Bernfeld, *Poverty and Welfare*, 8–12.

[33] On Hamburg, see Hermann Kellenbenz, *Sephardim an der unteren Elbe: ihre wirtschaftliche und politische Bedeutung vom Ende des 16. bis zum begin des 18. Jahrhunderts* (Wiesbaden: Franz Steiner Verlag, 1958); *Die Sefarden in Hamburg: zur Geschichte einer Minderheit*, ed. Michael Studemund-Halévy (Hamburg: Buske, 1994–1997); on London, see Yosef Kaplan, "The Jewish Profile of the Spanish-Portuguese Community of London during the Seventeenth Century," in *An Alternative Path*, 155–167.

Spain. They were largely the Portuguese in Spain, and this Portuguese character expressed itself in kinship, in commerce, and in language.

Jacob Sasportas arrived in this congregation of New Jews in the middle of the seventeenth century.[34] He differed from the Portuguese Jews in Amsterdam in three related ways: his lineage, his learning, and his past. Sasportas arrived in Amsterdam as a refugee from North Africa, either from Oran itself or from Tlemcen, a town farther inland to the south. Yet it would be extremely shortsighted to see his point of origin simply as Oran. Much as one can understand the Portuguese Jews of the early modern Sephardic Diaspora only by returning to the late Middle Ages, one can understand Sasportas only by returning to the same time and place: Iberia in 1391. The Sasportas family hailed from Aragon, and went into exile in North Africa during the riots of 1391 and 1392. A lineage replete with rabbis and translators, the Sasportas family along with the Cansinos were the two clans that dominated Jewish life in Oran throughout the sixteenth and seventeenth centuries.[35] The rabbinic heritage of late medieval Aragon functioned for Sasportas as his cultural patrimony. For decades he would never tire of reminding his correspondents that he was an eleventh-generation descendant of Moses ben Nahman, or Nahmanides (1194–1270).

This lineage was not only a point of pride for Sasportas; it also served him as an intellectual resource. Many of the Portuguese New Christians arrived in Amsterdam or in Venice and Verona with the best education one could obtain in early modern Spain. Some, like Isaac Cardoso and Orobio de Castro, had studied at the finest universities in Iberia and wrote Spanish verse and Latin treatises with ease. Others, like Benjamin Mussaphia and Isaac Nahar, studied at university in Padua or in Leiden and wrote medical treatises and polemical literature.[36] Still others, such as Miguel de Barrios, were poets of extraordinary

[34] Matt Goldish, "Rabbi Jacob Sasportas: Defender of Torah Authority in an Age of Change" (MA thesis, Hebrew University of Jerusalem, 1991); Elie Moyal, *Rabbi Yaakov Sasportas: meholel ha-pulmus neged ha-tenuah ha-shabtait u-ma-avakav le-ma-an shilton ha-halakah* (Jerusalem: Rav Kook Institute, 1992).

[35] Jean-Frédéric Schaub, *Les juifs du roi d'Espagne: Oran 1509–1669* (Paris: Hachette, 1999), chap. 2.

[36] On Mussaphia, see David B. Ruderman, "The Impact of Science on Jewish Culture and Society in Venice (with Special Reference to Jewish Graduates of Padua's Medical School)," in *Essential Papers on Jewish Culture in Renaissance and Baroque Italy*, ed. David B. Ruderman (New York: New York University Press, 1992), 519–553; on Nahar, see Yosef Kaplan, "Sephardi Students at the University of Leiden," in *An Alternative Path*, 196–210.

refinement and historians of exceptional reach.[37] In short, the library that these men carried with them, either literally or figuratively, was that of a well-educated Spanish intellectual. Sasportas brought his immense learning with him when he arrived in Amsterdam at midcentury. In it the presence of his ancestor Nahmanides, biblical exegete, poet, and Talmudist, loomed large.[38] It also included the *Zohar*, the great compendium of medieval Jewish mysticism that Sasportas considered a work of antiquity.[39] At its summit stood the writings of Moses Maimonides (1136–1204).[40] Sasportas did not distinguish between Maimonides the legal Talmudist who had codified Jewish law in the *Mishneh Torah* and Maimonides the philosopher who had written the *Guide of the Perplexed*. He did not separate law from philosophy or philosophy and law from mysticism. Nahmanides, the *Zohar*, and Maimonides, both his *Mishneh Torah* and his *Guide of the Perplexed*, constituted the intellectual contours of Sasportas's mental world.

This world was entirely rabbinic and needs to be distinguished from the mental worlds of both the lay elites and his rabbinic colleagues in the Sephardic Diaspora. The lay elites had sprung from the world of European learning and wrote as European intellectuals. Thus Abraham Pereyra drew upon Catholic theology composed in Spain in order to instruct the Portuguese Jews of Amsterdam in the basic requirements of repentance.[41] In his philosophical theology, Isaac Cardoso engaged with the problems of Aristotelianism that had been central to the curriculum he had studied in Spain.[42] It was not only the lay oligarchs who

---

[37] Kenneth R. Scholberg, "Miguel de Barrios and the Amsterdam Sephardic Community," *JQR* 53 (1962): 120–159; Wilhelmina C. Pieterse, *Daniel Levi de Barrios als geschiedschrijver van de Portugees-Israelietische gemeente te Amsterdam in zijn "Triumpho del govierno popular"* (Amsterdam: Scheltema and Holkema, 1968).

[38] Haviva Pedaya, *Ha-Ramban: hit-alut, zeman mahzori ve-tekst kadosh* (Tel Aviv: Am Oved, 2003); Moshe Halbertal, *Al derekh ha-emet: ha-Ramban vi-yetsiratah shel masoret* (Jerusalem: Shalom Hartman Institute, 2006); Nina Caputo, *Nahmanides in Medieval Catalonia: History, Community, and Messianism* (Notre Dame, IN: University of Notre Dame Press, 2007).

[39] Daniel Abrams, *Kabbalistic Manuscripts and Textual Theory: Methodologies of Textual Scholarship and Editorial Practice in the Study of Jewish Mysticism* (Jerusalem: Magnes Press, 2010); Boaz Huss, *The Zohar: Reception and Impact* (Oxford: Littman Library, 2016).

[40] Herbert A. Davidson, *Moses Maimonides: The Man and His Works* (New York: Oxford University Press, 2005); Moshe Halbertal, *Maimonides: Life and Thought* (Princeton, NJ: Princeton University Press, 2014).

[41] Henry Méchoulan, *Hispanidad y judaismo en tiempos de Espinoza: estudio y edición de La Certeza del Camino de Abraham Pereyra, Amsterdam, 1666* (Salamanca: Ediciones Universidad de Salamanca, 1987).

[42] Yerushalmi, *Isaac Cardoso*, chap. 6.

had drunk deeply from the wells of European learning. Sasportas's colleagues in the rabbinate, men such as Menasseh ben Israel, Saul Levi Morteira, and Isaac Aboab da Fonseca, had a familiarity with European intellectual life that was both extensive and deep.[43] Menasseh ben Israel made every effort to demonstrate that he was up to date with the latest developments of European scholarship.[44] Sasportas betrayed no such inclination. Not once in his extant writings did he indulge in a parade of erudition or a barrage of citations from contemporary Latin and vernacular scholarship. His mental world was rabbinic through and through.

If his lineage and his library differed measurably from those of the Portuguese elites among whom he lived, his own immediate past was of a fundamentally different order. Sasportas came from elsewhere and was not taken in by the myths that Portuguese Jews told each other about themselves. Simply put, he had never lived as a Catholic. The entire experience of conversion, even if it amounted to conversion to the faith of one's ancestors, and even if, as historians have demonstrated, New Christians in Iberia preserved many aspects of Jewish life, entailed confusion and change.[45] For men, it was also marked by the ritual of circumcision.[46] Sasportas had no experiential understanding of this process. This inability to comprehend was not only about a lack of empathy, a quality that Sasportas rarely expressed in writing. This discrepancy between Sasportas's own past and that of his colleagues related

[43] On Menasseh ben Israel, see Cecil Roth, *A Life of Menasseh ben Israel: Rabbi, Printer, and Diplomat* (Philadelphia: JPS, 1945); *Menasseh ben Israel and His World*, ed. Yosef Kaplan, Henry Méchoulan, Richard H. Popkin (Leiden: Brill, 1989); J. H. Coppenhagen, *Menasseh ben Israel: A Bibliography* (Jerusalem: Misgav Yerushalayim, 1990); A. K. Offenberg, *Menasseh ben Israel 1604–1657: A Biographical Sketch* (Amsterdam: Menasseh ben Israel Instituut, 2015). On Morteira, see Saul Levi Mortera, *Tratado de verdade de lei de Moisés*, ed. H. P. Salomon (Coimbra: Coimbra University Press, 1988); Marc Saperstein, *Exile in Amsterdam: Saul Levi Morteira's Sermons to a Congregation of "New Jews"* (Cincinnati, OH: Hebrew Union College Press, 2005). On Isaac Aboab da Fonseca, see Anne Oravetz Albert, "The Rabbi and the Rebels: A Pamphlet on the *Herem* by Rabbi Isaac Aboab da Fonseca," *JQR* 104 (2014): 171–191.

[44] Sina Rauschenbach, *Judentum für Christen: Vermittlung und Selbstbehauptung Menasseh ben Israels in den gelehrten Debatten des 17. Jahrhunderts* (Berlin: De Gruyter, 2012).

[45] I. S. Révah, "Les Marranes," *REJ* 118 (1959–1960): 29–77; Yerushalmi, *Isaac Cardoso*, chap. 1; David L. Graizbord, *Souls in Dispute: Converso Identities in Iberia and the Jewish Diaspora, 1580–1700* (Philadelphia: University of Pennsylvania Press, 2004); Nathan Wachtel, *Entre Moïse et Jésus: Etudes Marranes (xve–xxie siècle)* (Paris: CNRS Editions, 2013).

[46] Yosef Kaplan, "Attitudes toward Circumcision among Early Modern Western Sephardim" (Hebrew), in *Rishonim ve-Aharonim: Mehkarim be-toldot yisrael Mugashim le-Avraham Grossman*, ed. Joseph Hacker, B. Z. Kedar, and Yosef Kaplan (Jerusalem: Zalman Shazar Center, 2010), 353–389.

to the most burning intellectual problem of that time and place: the relationship between Judaism and Christianity. This subject dominated
the worlds of the learned elites among whom Sasportas lived for the
second half of his life. Saul Levi Morteira, Menasseh ben Israel, Orobio
de Castro, and Isaac Nahar all wrote some form of Jewish apologia
against Christianity, either in Latin or in the vernacular. They tried to
convince their congregants, their Protestant neighbors, and themselves
that they should continue to cling to the faith of their Jewish ancestors. They sought justification for an arduous process of conversion
that they or members of their immediate family had undertaken as
adults. Sasportas had little, if any, interest in this problem.[47] The importance of this basic difference was not constant over the five decades
that Sasportas lived among the Portuguese Jews in Europe. At a moment of crisis, as occurred with Sabbatianism, it would take on profound significance. Only with the advent of Sabbetai Zevi as the Messiah did Sasportas show any interest in Christianity. This interest was
strictly for the purposes of an analogy between Sabbetai Zevi and his
followers with Jesus and his early disciples. Sasportas demonstrated no
curiosity about contemporary Christianity in any of its various forms,
and sought to use the story of Jesus and his disciples only as a means
to understand the formation of a social movement around Sabbetai
Zevi. For Sasportas, the specter of Christianity was a polemical stick
with which to beat other Jews.

Furthermore, Sasportas was a Talmudist, someone who spent his
time studying Jewish law and issuing legal decisions. In all the European cities in which he lived, there was not a single Talmudist of any
comparable standing. Repeatedly, his colleagues would turn to him for
his expertise on legal issues that they could not resolve themselves,
such as the validity of a bill of divorce, a financial dispute between two
parties, or a ruling on ritual purity. To his colleagues and to the wealthy
Men of the Nation, the law was something narrow and technical. Just
as they had hired a preacher to deliver sermons, a *mohel* to perform
circumcisions, and a cantor to lead the prayers in the synagogue, they
had hired a rabbi to issue a ruling. When viewed through the perspective provided by Sasportas, the Sephardic Jews of the European Dias-

---

[47] For one known exception, see Goldish, "Hakham Jacob Sasportas and the Former
Conversos."

pora emerge as a group of wealthy merchants who had little interest in the law as anything other than a technical issue.

RABBIS AND THE RABBINATE IN THE SEPHARDIC DIASPORA

The merger of the three Portuguese congregations in 1638–1639 in Amsterdam led, like many mergers, to a significant duplication of skills and services. No longer were there three congregations with four rabbis among them; suddenly a single congregation had all four. Instead of rendering three of the rabbinic clergy redundant and placing one of them in charge, the lay oligarchs devised a strategy for them to share the functions of a rabbi. Morteira, who had previously served at Bet Jaacob, was appointed to preach from the pulpit for three weeks in succession, paid an annual salary of 600 florins, and allocated 100 baskets of turf for fuel to heat his home. David Pardo, formerly of Bet Israel, was named administrator of the cemetery, appointed to an honorary function in the synagogue, and paid an annual salary of 550 florins with the same allotment of turf. Menasseh ben Israel, who had served at Neve Shalom, was appointed to preach on the fourth week and paid an annual salary of 150 florins. Isaac Aboab da Fonseca, who had served alongside Morteira at Bet Jaacob, was appointed to teach Talmud in the academy and paid an annual salary of 450 florins.[48] This hierarchy of salary and function probably reflects both the priority of Bet Jaacob as a congregation and Morteira's seniority in terms of age and years of service. The arrangement also reflects a basic fact about early modern Jewish life in Amsterdam and elsewhere in the northern Sephardic Diaspora: the rabbi was a paid employee of lay oligarchs.

Some of these rabbis had come to Amsterdam from elsewhere. Saul Levi Morteira came from an Ashkenazi family in Venice to serve the Portuguese Jews.[49] He had arrived at a sufficiently young age that he could be married off into one of the Portuguese families. He acclimated

---

[48] Wiznitzer, "The Merger Agreement and Regulations of Congregation Talmud Torah of Amsterdam (1638–1639)," 117–118.

[49] Yosef Kaplan, "R. Saul Levi Morteira and His Treatise 'Arguments against the Christian Religion'" (Hebrew), in *Dutch Jewish History* 1, ed. Joseph Michman (Jerusalem: Magnes Press, 1975), 9–31.

sufficiently well to compose polemical literature and preach sermons in Portuguese. In short, he had become a Sephardi of a particular, that is to say, Portuguese, kind. David Pardo was the son of Joseph Pardo, the first rabbi of Amsterdam who had served in Bet Jaacob. Like Morteira, Joseph Pardo had been an outsider. He had come to Amsterdam from another great center of early modern Sephardic life: Salonica. Menasseh ben Israel and Isaac Aboab da Fonseca, who were roughly a decade younger than Morteira, had followed itineraries extremely similar to those of the congregants they served. Both were born as Catholics in Iberia, had moved to Amsterdam while still young, and had reconverted to the Judaism of their ancestors. They were homegrown local talent who had become rabbis rather than merchants. Or, in Menasseh's case, a rabbi as well as a bookseller.

It was into this world that Sasportas arrived as a refugee at some point around the year 1650. The Portuguese Jews gave him shelter and even paid to ransom his family from captivity several years after his arrival. They referred to him as *haham*, the Hebrew word they used for a scholar or a sage. In nearly every seventeenth-century document on which his name appears, whether composed by a Dutch notary, a Portuguese Jewish scribe, or a rabbinic colleague, Sasportas appears as *haham*. While they may have accorded him the title *haham* and even appear to have treated him with respect, the Portuguese Jews of Amsterdam did not offer Sasportas a position as a paid member of the rabbinate. Unlike Isaac Uziel, who came from Fez to serve as the rabbi of Neve Shalom earlier in the century or Hezekiah da Silva who came from Jerusalem and was offered a position later in the century, Sasportas was and remained unemployed as a rabbi for many years. Much of his wandering between 1650 and 1665, which would take him back to Africa to the Republic of Saleh on the Atlantic coast, and from Saleh to London via Amsterdam, and from London to Hamburg, was part of his attempt to secure a paid position as a rabbi or earn a living in another area of life.

Had Sabbetai Zevi not declared himself the Messiah and been welcomed as such by the overwhelming majority of Jews in 1665, Sasportas would hardly be worthy of historical consideration. He would have been another unemployed and disgruntled rabbi, a learned exile who failed to receive his due and lived an embittered life far from the North Africa of his youth: a loser who eked out a meager living on the margins of the learned world. In short, someone who was not much different from any number of well-educated Jews who wandered around Europe in the early modern period, moving from place to place, occasionally appearing in print, and frequently receiving charity from the wealthy.[50]

The advent of Sabbetai Zevi as the Messiah occurred in the late spring of 1665 in Palestine. Roughly two to three months later, news of the Messiah began to circulate in Europe.[51] What began as a trickle soon turned into a torrent of information early in 1666. The news and the reports were often contradictory, frequently convoluted, and almost always dramatic. Thousands of Jews had joined Sabbetai Zevi and declared him King of the Jews. His prophet Nathan of Gaza had exhorted Jews throughout the Ottoman Empire to repent, and they were listening to him. The Messiah and his prophet were about to embark upon a military campaign with the aid of the Ottoman sultan and would soon establish a Jewish Kingdom in Palestine. When reports began to arrive in Hamburg about Sabbetai Zevi as the Messiah, Sasportas was living there among the Portuguese Jews. He had recently fled the plague in London, and, in his departure, he had abandoned his position as a paid rabbi of the newly founded congregation in London.[52] The Portuguese Jews in Hamburg already had a rabbi, named Moses Israel, and there were several other rabbis who lived in the vicinity, such as Aaron Cohen de Lara. While in Hamburg, Sasportas lived hand to mouth, receiving charity from the Portuguese Jews in Amsterdam. Just as Sasportas had arrived in Amsterdam at midcentury as a refugee, he showed up in Hamburg some fifteen years later similarly impoverished and in flight.

[50] On migration of Jews in early modern Europe, see Jonathan I. Israel, *European Jewry in the Age of Mercantilism 1550–1750* (London: Littman Library, 1998), chap.1; David B. Ruderman, *Early Modern Jewry: A New Cultural History* (Princeton, NJ: Princeton University Press, 2010), chap. 1. For a case study of an itinerant rabbi, see Elchanan Reiner, "An Itinerant Preacher Publishes His Books: An Untold Chapter in the Cultural History of European Jewry in the Seventeenth Century}" (Hebrew), in *Hut shel hen: Shai le-Chava Turniansky*, ed. Israel Bartal et al. (Jerusalem: Zalman Shazar Center, 2013), 1:123–156.

[51] Jetteke van Wijk "The Rise and Fall of Shabbatai Zevi as Reflected in Contemporary Press Reports," *SR* 33 (1999): 7–27; Brandon Marriott, *Transnational Networks and Cross-Religious Exchange in the Seventeenth-Century Mediterranean and Atlantic Worlds: Sabbatai Sevi and the Lost Tribes of Israel* (Burlington, VT: Ashgate, 2015), chap. 4.

[52] Isaiah Tishby, "New Information on the 'Converso' Community in London according to the Letters of Sasportas from 1664/1665" (Hebrew), in *Galut ahar golah: mehkarim be-toledot am yisrael mugashim le-Professor Haim Beinart li-melot lo shivim shana*, ed. Aharon Mirsky, Avraham Grossman, and Yosef Kaplan (Jerusalem: Ben Zvi Institute, 1988), 470–496.

In these circumstances, Sasportas greeted news of the redemption with moderate enthusiasm tempered by some skepticism. In order to make sense of events that were unfolding in the Ottoman Empire and beginning to have a dramatic effect on the people with whom he was living in Hamburg, Sasportas paid careful attention.[53] He also began to write letters to his rabbinic colleagues. In his letters and in the responses he received, he tried to separate fact from fiction and assess the veracity of Sabbetai Zevi's claims as the Messiah. For the better part of a year, roughly from the fall of 1665 until the summer of 1666, Sasportas continued to observe and take notes. The crisis did not become a crisis in a single day; it became one only over the course of several months. Eventually, when confirmed reports of repeated violations of the law by the Messiah and his followers reached him, Sasportas decided that Sabbetai Zevi was not the Messiah that he and his followers had claimed. In particular, the transformation of public fast days such as the seventeenth of Tammuz and the ninth of Av into holidays appears to have been decisive for Sasportas. These fasts, which occur in the summer months within a period of three weeks, mark the destruction of the Temple and serve as symbols of Jewish life in exile. Jews observe the fasts with public displays of sorrow, abstention from food and drink, and recitation of the biblical book of Lamentations along with other Hebrew dirges. To signify the advent of Sabbetai Zevi as the Messiah, his followers turned these days into public holidays that they celebrated with song and dance, food and wine. In some cities, believers in Sabbetai Zevi went so far as to compel all Jews to join in their celebration. This transformation of a fast day usually observed through collective mourning into a holiday to celebrate a new Messiah served as a litmus test for adherence to the new movement.[54] One could not have it both ways. Either Sabbetai Zevi was the Messiah and these fast days were holidays, or he was not and these fast days marked the continued plight of life in exile. What may seem to be arcane or trivial was hardly so for a seventeenth-century Talmudist. To fast or not to fast was emblematic of a much larger issue. Had the Messiah arrived in the

---

[53] Avraham Elqayam, *Ha-masa le-ketz ha-yamin: besorat he-ge-ulah ha-shabtait la-meshorer Moshe ben Gideon Abudiente* (Los Angeles: Cherub Press, 2014); Michael Studemund-Halévy, "What Happened in Izmir Was Soon the Talk of Hamburg: Sabbatai Sevi in Contemporary German Press Reports," *El Prezente* 10 (2016): 155–172.

[54] For a twelfth-century parallel, see Bernard Lewis, *The Assassins: A Radical Sect in Islam* (New York: Octagon Books, 1980), 72–73.

form of Sabbetai Zevi and redeemed Jewish life in exile, or had things stayed much the same? In letters written throughout the summer of 1666, Sasportas tried to convince his colleagues that they were mistaken. He had little success in doing so.

Events, though, took a turn of their own accord. In September 1666, the Ottoman sultan summoned Sabbetai Zevi to appear at his palace in Edirne. The celebrations had attracted too much attention. The Messiah and his followers had become a public nuisance; the crowds of penitent Jews were a threat to order. The sultan and his advisers offered Sabbetai Zevi a choice: conversion to Islam or death. Sabbetai Zevi chose conversion over martyrdom.[55] Once he had converted, the movement that had coalesced around him over the previous year collapsed almost as quickly as it had formed. The overwhelming majority of Jews, most of whom had been believers, soon returned to their lives as they had lived them before.[56] Fast days were once again observed as fast days. The ritual innovations introduced by Sabbetai Zevi and his followers quietly disappeared. Jewish life in exile continued much as it had before.

For another few years, Sasportas continued to correspond with colleagues and to take notes about Sabbetai Zevi as the Messiah and the movement around him. In 1669 he sorted through his mail, collected his notes, and edited them into *Zizath novel zvi*. Written entirely in rabbinic Hebrew, the book recounts a history of Sabbetai Zevi and the messianic movement as it occurred in real time. The letters record Sasportas changing his mind, arguing with his colleagues, and looking on in horror. The fact of his writing, at such length and with such eloquence, points to a moment of rupture. For Sasportas, Sabbetai Zevi and the messianic movement constituted a crisis.[57]

This book studies the nature of the Sabbatian crisis and the character of Sasportas's response. It posits that Sabbetai Zevi and the messianic movement around him severely tested Sasportas's deeply held

[55] Jane Hathaway, "The Grand Vizier and the False Messiah: The Sabbatai Sevi Controversy and the Ottoman Reform in Egypt," *Journal of the American Oriental Society* 117 (1997): 665–671.

[56] On those who remained believers, see Paweł Maciejko, *The Mixed Multitude: Jacob Frank and the Frankist Movement, 1755–1816* (Philadelphia: University of Pennsylvania Press, 2011); Marc David Baer, *The Dönme: Jewish Converts, Muslim Revolutionaries, and Secular Turks* (Stanford, CA: Stanford University Press, 2010); Yehuda Liebes, *Le-tzvi u-le-gaon: mi-shabtai zvi el ha-gaon mi-vilna* (Tel Aviv: Idra, 2017).

[57] On crisis, see Randolph Starn, "Historians and 'Crisis,'" *P&P* 52 (1971): 3–22; Reinhart Koselleck, "Crisis," *JHI* 67 (2006): 357–400.

convictions about the nature of the rabbinate and the character of rabbinic law. In letters to his colleagues and in his own journal entries, Sasportas described the messianic activism of Sabbetai Zevi and his followers as an attack on the established social order, an order that was
undergirded by collective and individual adherence to rabbinic law. Instead of leading their followers and inculcating within them a healthy
skepticism that would have translated into an attitude of wait-and-see,
the Jewish leaders, both the rabbis and the wealthy Jews who employed
them, had joined in the untutored enthusiasm of the masses. In his letters Sasportas repeatedly expressed his dismay with his rabbinic colleagues at their lack of opposition to Sabbetai Zevi. Most of his own letters that he included in *Zizath novel zvi* had been written to rabbis or
learned lay leaders he knew personally in the European Sephardic Diaspora. Isaac Aboab da Fonseca, Aaron Zarfati, and Isaac Nahar in Amsterdam and Raphael Supino in Livorno bore the brunt of Sasportas's
vituperative erudition. He chastised them for not having the courage
of his convictions. Sasportas had an image of the rabbinate that was
partially the product of his own past in the North Africa of his youth
and partially the result of an idealized past based on his lineage. This
image invested all authority in the rabbi as the interpreter of sacred
texts, and, just as important, as the person who decided which texts
were sacred and which were not. Sasportas viewed the rabbinate as an
aristocratic institution whose members had always governed Jewish
life and always would. He saw the rabbi as the summit of a social hierarchy rather than a petty employee of rich and ignorant businessmen.

In *Zizath novel zvi* Sasportas was hell-bent on protecting an institution from which he had been excluded for much of his adult life: the
rabbinate. His lack of official status grated on him and caused him last-
ing resentment. For the nearly half a century that he lived in Europe,
he was obsessed with the respect he felt was his due; and he would remain so obsessed long after Sabbetai Zevi had become old news.[58] Sasportas believed in the authority of the rabbinate and in the hierarchy
of that authority. The Men of the Nation may have amassed incredible
wealth, they may also have established a yeshiva to train rabbis, and
they may have patronized the printing of scholarship, yet they treated

[58] Isaiah Tishby, "Letters by Rabbi Jacob Sasportas against the Parnassim of Livorno from 1681"
(Hebrew), *Kovez al yad* 4 (1946): 143–160.

their rabbis as employees. To Sasportas, this patron-client arrangement between the *maamad* and the *haham* traduced the nature of the rabbinate. The rabbi issued the law; he did not receive orders. For Sasportas, a rabbi was not a functionary who simply answered a series of technical questions. The law was not a narrow domain of life confined to dietary laws, Sabbath observance, and ritual purity. The law, or more precisely *halakha*, was a way of being in the world. In his description of the lay oligarchs of the Sephardic Diaspora in western Europe, Jonathan Israel remarked that they were "simultaneously agents and victims of empire."[59] So too was Sasportas both a victim and an agent of the rabbinate: a victim in his seemingly never-ending quest for the respect and recognition he considered his due; an agent in the articulation of an ideal of the rabbinate that had few, if any, precedents.

In this sense, Sabbetai Zevi was the making of Jacob Sasportas. Sabbetai Zevi and the movement that coalesced around him provided Sasportas the chance to articulate a worldview that he would never have had otherwise. Without the occasion provided by the crisis of the 1660s, Sasportas would never have embarked on the greatest writing episode of his long life. Sasportas can thus serve as a primary example of the early modern Jewish ambivalence about the new. Like many people living in an age of crisis, Sasportas tried desperately to create a sense of tradition. Repeatedly throughout his account of Sabbatian messianism, he stressed the continuity between his own position about the Messiah, and the law, and that of the Jewish tradition as he defined it. In his own acutely self-conscious characterization, he articulated no more and no less than the Maimonidean reserve about the messianic age. Sasportas and his stance on the messianic frenzy he experienced firsthand thus present a valuable test case with which to confront a question posed by J. H. Elliott in 1969: "How far can historians accustomed to look for *innovation* among revolutionaries, enter into the minds of men who themselves were obsessed by *renovation*—by the desire to return to old customs and privileges, and to an old order of society?"[60] As Elliott himself remarked later in that same essay, "the deliberate attempt to return to old ways may lead men, in spite of themselves,

---

[59] Israel, introduction to *Diasporas*, 1.
[60] "Revolution and Continuity in Early Modern Europe," *P&P* 42 (1969): 44. Italics in the original.

into startlingly new departures."[61] Sasportas's rejection of Sabbatianism and his composition of *Zizath novel zvi* themselves constituted such a startlingly new departure, and one that would have a long and circuitous afterlife in the modern rabbinate. Few rabbinic works prior to *Zizath novel zvi* combine the careful transcription, sorting, and disposal of contemporary documents with such a strong first-person authorial voice. Few rabbis prior to Sasportas made as extensive an effort to transcribe, recount, and criticize the events of their own time in a single coherent narrative.

Sasportas was not a systematic thinker, nor did he set out to compose a work that would espouse his worldview. The nature of his extant writing provides powerful evidence of this. In terms of genre, Sasportas wrote letters and rabbinic responsa, or briefs in response to legal questions. He often wrote commentary on the letters he transcribed and edited. The epistolary corpus of his writing reflects the fact that it was written in an emergency. Its exegetical character reflects a rabbinic cast of mind, one that was far more likely to respond through reactive commentary than through generic innovation. In relatively few of these letters did Sasportas set forth a credo or a systematic exposition of his beliefs. Thus, on the most fundamental issue that he dealt with in his book, the Messiah, Sasportas did not outline a new position; nor did he attempt to deny the existence of Jewish belief in the Messiah. Rather, he sought to distinguish genuine redemption as described in the Bible, as interpreted by the rabbis of antiquity and the Middle Ages, from the purported redemption that the believers in Sabbetai Zevi claimed to have experienced. In a certain sense, Sasportas made an argument against lived religion as it was believed, experienced, and practiced by thousands of Jews in the year 1666.

Sasportas was willing to rest his case on a negative.[62] His writing demonstrates many of the habits of mind of a destructive thinker, someone who was able to perceive what was false and who sought to alert his readers to the absurdity of a widely sanctioned opinion. If a negative philosopher requires "courage, verbal acuteness, command over the forms of argumentation, and a popular style,"[63] Sasportas had

---

[61] Ibid., 55.

[62] David Bromwich, *The Intellectual Life of Edmund Burke: From the Sublime and Beautiful to American Independence* (Cambridge, MA: Belknap Press of Harvard University Press, 2014), 400.

[63] J. S. Mill, "On Bentham," in *Mill on Bentham and Coleridge*, ed. F. R. Leavis (London: Chatto and Windus, 1950), 42–43.

all of these qualities in abundance. All but one: a popular style. He lacked a popular style because he had no interest in being popular. Sasportas wrote an appallingly difficult Hebrew that was matched only by the difficulty of his handwriting. The density and allusiveness of his prose can at times seem almost willfully perverse, as if he were trying to win his argument simply through one-upsmanship and a parade of his Talmudic erudition rather than through logic and argumentation. To a certain extent, this appearance may well have been the truth. Sasportas thought that the resources within rabbinic literature had all the necessary arguments to defeat a Messiah who had yet to fulfill the criteria established by Maimonides, even and especially a Messiah who was acclaimed by nearly all Jews as God's anointed. Sasportas would not have recognized a distinction between his own rabbinic erudition and the use of logic. For him, the two were inextricably linked.

Zizath novel zvi often takes the form of a legal brief against Sabbetai Zevi prepared by Sasportas to prosecute a particular case. In this sense, the negative character of Sasportas's thought may relate to a negative quality of the book's form. Sasportas circulated copies of his letters, and some evidence suggests that he also circulated part or all of *Zizath novel zvi* in manuscript. He wrote his letters that constitute the majority of the work with the full expectation that they would be read by more than one person. He never printed the book, and this was hardly for lack of means or opportunity. In the last third of his life, between the denouement of the Sabbatian movement as an active force in Jewish public life in the 1660s and his own death in 1698, Sasportas would become a wealthy man. For much of that time he lived in Amsterdam, the most important center of Hebrew printing in the second half of the seventeenth century.[64]

Sasportas himself had extensive ties to the world of print both before and after Sabbetai Zevi declared himself the Messiah. The fact that *Zizath novel zvi* did not appear in print in his lifetime demands consideration, if not explanation. After all, the Sabbatian movement itself owed its success in no small measure to the power of the printed word, as Sasportas himself was all too well aware and as he bemoaned bitterly in *Zizath novel zvi*. Why did he confine his criticism to manuscript? A

---

[64]Jean Baumgarten, *Le peuple des livres: les ouvrages populaires dans la société ashkénaze, XVIe–XVIIIe siècle* (Paris: Albin Michel, 2010); Shlomo Berger, *Producing Redemption in Amsterdam: Early Modern Yiddish Books in Paratextual Perspective* (Leiden: Brill, 2013).

manuscript may have meaning only as a manuscript, in the sense that it is meant for a limited, well-defined, and exclusive group of readers, in the age of print. That Jews from Salonica to Saleh were prepared to believe in Sabbetai Zevi did not surprise Sasportas in the least. They were living in exile, the circumstances of their lives were often miserable, and Sabbetai Zevi offered them something that was incredibly rare in a period of bewildering uncertainty: hope. That the learned elites had failed them in their task—to lead: this Sasportas found appalling. He wrote a series of letters that he later collected into a book as an indictment of his own time. Once the emergency had passed, however, there was no need to publicize his criticism. If one emergency had passed and the masses were no longer violating the law in public, there were other problems that required his attention. Sasportas may well have been correct—Sabbetai Zevi was not the Messiah; the rabbinate, however, was still an idea and an institution that required his defense and his care.

The appearance of a text in print often had unintended consequences. When news of Sabbetai Zevi first arrived in Europe by way of printed broadsides that announced the advent of the Jewish Messiah in the Ottoman Empire, Portuguese Jews in Hamburg and Amsterdam had joyfully celebrated the appearance of a famous Jew in print. Even the gentiles were talking about the Jews, they exclaimed with jubilation. This very same fact filled Sasportas with fear. Sasportas worried that the Jews in Amsterdam and Hamburg were making fools of themselves in public. Publicity was not something Jews living in exile should seek. If Sasportas once harbored hopes of printing *Zizath novel zvi*, the controversial character of its contents may have held him back. Alternatively, he may never have wanted the book to appear in print because of the popular character of the medium. From Elizabethan England to Golden Age Spain, intellectuals in the early modern period often cultivated an aristocratic contempt for print as a vulgar medium.[65] There is simply not enough evidence to assess why the book remained in manuscript for nearly thirty years between the time Sasportas edited it in 1669 and his death in 1698. When the book finally did appear in print, it did so in severely truncated form as an appendix

---

[65]For England, see J. W. Saunders, "The Stigma of Print: A Note on the Social Bases of Tudor Poetry," *Essays in Criticism* 1 (1951): 139–164; H. R. Woudhuysen, *Sir Philip Sidney and the Circulation of Manuscripts 1558–1640* (New York: Clarendon Press, 1996). For Spain see Fernando Bouza, *Corre manuscrito: una historia cultural del Siglo de Oro* (Madrid: Marcial Pons, 2001).

to his posthumously printed responsa, *Ohel ya-akov*, in 1737. Nearly every copy of *Ohel ya-akov* has all or part of this appendix torn out.[66] Almost forty years after the death of its author and seventy-five years after the events it described, *Zizath novel zvi* was still explosive.

SASPORTAS AND MODERN SCHOLARSHIP

This book tries to read Sasportas on his own terms, through his own writing, both his polemic against Sabbatianism, *Zizath novel zvi*, and his rabbinic responsa, *Ohel ya-akov*. In addition, it seeks to expand the documentary corpus relating to Sasportas by examining his position—whether rabbinic, economic, or familial—in the different places that he lived. In some periods and in certain places, archival holdings are particularly rich and allow a historian to reconstruct Sasportas's life in extremely vivid detail; in others, especially for his time in Oran and Tlemcen, a historian must face the facts and recognize that little evidence survives. I have sought to integrate this evidence with a study of Sasportas's own writings to present a portrait of this seventeenth-century rabbi. Sasportas did not conform to the series of oppositions that undergird the intellectual edifice of modern scholarship: he was both a halakhist and a kabbalist, a conservative and a radical, a critic of the rabbinate and the instantiation of its ideals. He was an author obsessed with his own status who simultaneously had complete contempt for contemporary conventions of publication. He was the product of the diaspora, through and through. Unlike so many other Sephardic rabbinic luminaries of the early modern period, Sasportas remained, and flourished, in exile for the entirety of his long life. What follows is a conventional book about an unconventional man.

It would be the height of scholarly naïveté to think that it would be possible simply to read Sasportas on his own terms. To read Sasportas is to engage with his writing itself; it is also to engage with his readers, notably Jacob Emden (1698–1776), Gershom Scholem (1897–1982), and Joel Teitelbaum (1887–1979). Most copies of the truncated edition of *Zizath novel zvi* that appeared in print in 1737 were destroyed. Jacob Emden, a rabbi who lived in nearby Altona, did not know of its

---

[66] Sasportas, *Ohel ya-akov*. The entire book including the appendix is available for download at Hebrewbooks.org and also exists in a photo-offset edition printed at Bnei Brak in 1986.

existence until he discovered it by chance in 1751. In that year Emden was exiled from his hometown when he alleged that Jonathan Eibeschütz, the rabbi of the Ashkenazi Jews of Altona-Hamburg-Wandsbek, had written amulets that contained encoded references to Sabbetai Zevi as the Messiah.[67] Emden's allegations tore the Ashkenazi Jews of Altona-Hamburg-Wandsbek apart, and he later embarked on an extensive campaign to discredit Eibeschütz: the Emden-Eibeschütz controversy, or simply, as later writers referred to it, the controversy.[68] Emden understood Sasportas and felt an elective affinity with him. In this context Emden reedited and reprinted the abbreviated text of *Zizath novel zvi*.[69] More than anyone else, Emden fashioned Sasportas in his own image: an immensely learned rabbi, the scion of an illustrious rabbinic family, who had been unjustly excluded from social power. As Emden reedited Sasportas, he presented an author who had embarked on a campaign to uproot the heresy in his midst.

This admiration may have caused Emden to overlook a fundamental difference between his plight and that of Sasportas. Emden had a printing press in his basement and took his campaign against Eibeschütz public.[70] Emden leveled the charge of heresy against Eibeschütz and his supporters. In 1665–1666, in the period prior to the news of Sabbetai Zevi's conversion, Sasportas's correspondents, men such as Isaac Aboab da Fonseca and Isaac Nahar, leveled the charge of heresy at Sasportas. At the height of the messianic enthusiasm, not to believe in Sabbetai Zevi was to risk such a charge. Rather than a heresy hunter, Sasportas was a dissident. After the Messiah's conversion, things changed dramatically. As the careers of Moses Hagiz and Jacob Emden show in detail, to believe in Sabbetai Zevi in the eighteenth century was to risk being labeled a heretic.[71] Being a Sabbatian in 1705 or 1755 was different from being a Sabbatian in 1665 and 1666. In 1665 and 1666

[67] Sid Z. Leiman and Simon Schwarzfuchs, "New Evidence on the Emden-Eibeschuetz Controversy: The Amulets from Metz," *REJ* 165 (2006): 229–249.

[68] Shmuel Ettinger, "The Emden-Eibeschütz Controversy in the Light of Jewish Historiography" (Hebrew), *Kabbalah* 9 (2003): 329–392.

[69] Sasportas, *Kitzur*, ed. Emden.

[70] Shnayer Z. Leiman, "Rabbi Ezekiel Landau's '*Iggeret shelomim*'" (Hebrew), in *Lo yasur shevet mi-yehuda: hanhaga, rabanut, ve-kehila be-toledot yisrael mehkarim mugashim le-Professor Simon Schwarzfuchs*, ed. Joseph R. Hacker and Yaron Harel (Jerusalem: Bialik Institute, 2011), 317–331.

[71] Jacob J. Schacter, "Rabbi Jacob Emden: Life and Major Works" (PhD diss., Harvard University, 1988); Carlebach, *Pursuit of Heresy*.

nearly all Jews were Sabbatians. In the eighteenth century, this was hardly so. The world Sasportas experienced in 1665 and 1666 was not the same as those inhabited by Hagiz and Emden.

Emden was able to forge an image of Sasportas as a heresy hunter from only a truncated version of *Zizath novel zvi*. Over the course of the next century and a half, Sasportas in his abbreviated form would serve as a polemical resource in a number of rabbinic controversies. In the late nineteenth and the early twentieth centuries references to a considerably longer manuscript of Sasportas's book appeared in print. Both Abraham Epstein in Paris and Arthur Zacharias Schwarz in Vienna referred to the book, and Schwarz went so far as to announce a new edition of *Zizath novel zvi*.[72] Epstein died before he could realize his ambition, while geopolitics thwarted Schwarz's plans. With the Nazi occupation of Austria in 1938, Schwarz fled Vienna for Jerusalem. He died there the following year, and his widow entrusted the publication of the new edition of *Zizath novel zvi* to Gershom Scholem.

Scholem had recently published a long article on Sabbatian theology after the conversion of Sabbetai Zevi and was working on a history of Sabbetai Zevi and the movement that had coalesced around him prior to his conversion.[73] Scholem recognized the importance of Sasportas, and of publishing a new and complete edition of his chronicle. He entrusted the task to one of his students, a scholar named Isaiah Tishby (1907–1992). It would be another fifteen years before Tishby's edition finally appeared in 1954, and a further three before Scholem's history of Sabbetai Zevi appeared in two volumes in 1957.[74] Scholem's treatment of Sasportas represents a case study in the intellectual history of ambivalence. Scholem thought about Sabbetai Zevi through, with, and against Sasportas. He understood the importance of Sasportas as a historical source and as an eyewitness to the events that he himself was attempting to narrate. He poured substantial resources—both intellectual and material—into the creation of Tishby's edition. He also condemned Sasportas as a historical actor and pronounced a series of astonishingly harsh judgments on him as a person. Scholem's

---

[72] Abraham Epstein, "Une lettre d'Abraham ha-Yakhini a Nathan Gazati," *REJ* 26 (1893): 209–219, esp. 218; A. Z. Schwarz, *Die Hebräischen Handschriften in Österreich (Ausserhalb der Nationalbibliothek in Wien)* (Leipzig: Verlag Karl W. Hiersemann, 1931), MS 142, p. 92.

[73] "Mitzvah ha-ba-ah ba-averah: le-havanat ha-shabtaut." *Keneset* 2 (1937): 347–392.

[74] On Tishby's edition, see Sasportas, *ZNZ*; Gershom Scholem, *Shabbetai Sevi ve-ha-tenuah ha-shabetait bi-yeme hayav* (Tel Aviv: Am Oved, 1957).

portrait of Sasportas constitutes a "masterpiece of clinical accuracy and sanctimonious malice."[75]

There are a number of ways to deal with the looming presence of Gershom Scholem in the study of Sabbatianism. One way is to become an epigone. While occasionally one can cross a t or dot an i, one works entirely within his paradigm. In this framework, Sabbatianism constituted a revolt against the law and was characterized by acute antinomian activity. Sabbatianism was the cause of a genuine crisis within modern Jewish history rather than the result of a socioeconomic crisis that had engulfed Europe and the Mediterranean in the middle decades of the seventeenth century. The sources of the movement were entirely immanent within Judaism in general and Kabbalah in particular. Another way is to become a slayer of the father, for a young scholar to make his or her reputation by trampling on that of an older one. Scholem was thus wrong in his portrait of Sabbatianism and misunderstood both its causes and its effects. Rather than a history of a man and a movement, he had written a novel with heroes and villains. Both methods are tried and true ways of coping with Scholem's scholarship. Both have their advantages and disadvantages. To some extent, the phase of the epigones coexisted with the later decades of Scholem's life, while the phase of oedipal attacks began in the decades after his death. Even this chronology oversimplifies. Upon its appearance in print in Hebrew, *Sabbatai Sevi* elicited some of the harshest criticism Scholem ever received in his long career. A third way, one that is facilitated by the nearly four decades that have elapsed since Scholem's death, is to make Scholem part of the story.

In writing this study of Sasportas, I engage Scholem on two separate planes. In the first seven chapters, and primarily in chapters 2 through 5 and in chapter 7, I have treated Scholem as a scholar of Sabbatianism. His writing has guided and accompanied this study of Sasportas's opposition to Sabbatianism in the 1660s as well as Emden's reception and edition of Sasportas in the 1750s. In the final chapter, I have treated Scholem as a historical actor and sought to reconstruct the making of Tishby's edition under Scholem's guidance. In doing so, I ask what Scholem found so unsettling about Sasportas and why he pro-

---

[75] As Erwin Panofksy described an account of Hugo van der Goes by Gaspar Ofhuys. *Early Netherlandish Painting: Its Origins and Character* (Cambridge, MA: Harvard University Press, 1966), 1:331.

nounced judgment on his person. What emerges is that several of Scholem's central insights into Sabbatianism, such as the phenomenological parallel between early Christianity and Sabbatianism or Scholem's emphasis on the pious faithful people of Israel, had their origins in *Zizath novel zvi*. Sasportas was the living representative of Maimonides and Jewish law in the story of Sabbetai Zevi that Scholem chose to tell. As such, he was the target of Scholem's considerable intellectual ire.

This book suggests that Sasportas and his writing were a crucial juncture in the making of the modern rabbinate. The habit of mind that rejects novelty as such, that responds with erudite aggression to anything new, that seeks to return to an idealized past that never was: all of these qualities find expression in Sasportas's writing and in his image. Sasportas or his book played a role in a series of modern rabbinic controversies—Emden and Eibeschütz, Hasidim and Mitnagdim, Reform and Orthodox, Zionism and anti-Zionism. In some, such as Emden and Eibeschütz or Zionism and anti-Zionism, his role and his book's role were more significant than in others, such as Hasidim and Mitnagdim or Reform and Orthodox. Almost always his readers held him up as a paragon of traditionalism as such, as an ideologue of opposition to all change.

This book consists of eight chapters. Chapter 1, "Exile," plots the life of Sasportas prior to Sabbatianism. It places Sasportas in a series of different contexts: a member of a leading Sephardic family in Spanish Oran, a corrector in the printing house of Menasseh ben Israel in Amsterdam, and a minister to the fledgling congregation of Portuguese Jews in London. In each of these contexts, Sasportas emerges as "a man against," challenging truisms and opposing received opinions, even as he sought patronage from wealthy Jews whom he scorned.

The following four chapters, a study of Sasportas's opposition to Sabbatian messianism as it expressed itself in *Zizath novel zvi*, constitute the core of the book. Chapter 2, "Authority," situates the polemic over Sabbatianism as a problem of authority. It casts Sasportas, a man who saw authority as manifested in the written word, versus the Sabbatians, particularly Nathan of Gaza, enthusiasts who claimed authority as rooted in personal experience. The Sabbatians could cite scripture as well as Sasportas. The chapter concludes by examining the debate over messianic authority as it transformed into one of text versus text. Chapter 3, "Crowds," plots the doubt of an individual versus the certainty of the crowd. It posits that Sasportas's aversion to Sabbetai Zevi as the Messiah was as much a response to the force of perceived social chaos as it was an attack on the truth-value of Sabbetai Zevi's claims. Chapter 4, "Prophecy" discusses Sabbatian messianism as an epistemological problem. How does one know whether or not someone is the Messiah? In the middle of the seventeenth century, prophecy was one way of obtaining such knowledge. This chapter examines Sasportas's response to the Sabbatian renewal of prophecy as well as to other modes of knowing, such as dreams and astrology. Chapter 5, "Christianity," studies *Zizath novel zvi* within the context of Jewish responses to Christianity. Unlike the overwhelming majority of Sephardim in northwestern Europe, Sasportas had little to say about Christianity for much of his life. This changed dramatically in 1665–1666 when he made a pointed analogy between the followers of Sabbetai Zevi and the early followers of Jesus.

Chapter 6, "Aftermath," surveys the last three decades of Sasportas's life, when he moved between Hamburg, Amsterdam, Livorno, and Amsterdam again. During this period, Sasportas continued to enter the fray of rabbinic controversy and rarely mentioned Sabbetai Zevi or Jewish messianism. This chapter posits that for Sasportas, the problem posed by Sabbetai Zevi was actually symptomatic of a much larger issue: the rabbinate itself.

When Sasportas died in 1698, he thought he had written a history of the past. *Zizath novel zvi* recounted an episode of extraordinary turmoil, a crisis when nearly anything seemed possible, that had ended. As a result, his book remained sequestered among his papers. He did not realize that in *Zizath novel zvi* he had actually written the history of the future. The final two chapters study Sasportas through his greatest readers. Chapter 7, "Zealot," focuses on Jacob Emden, who crafted Sasportas in his own image as a heresy hunter in the middle of the eighteenth century. Chapter 8, "Zion," moves forward two centuries and focuses on Gershom Scholem and Joel Teitelbaum as readers of Sasportas. Both Scholem and Teitelbaum considered the middle of the twentieth century as a period of crisis, and each, in his own way, turned to *Zizath novel zvi* as part of a larger response to that crisis.

ONE

EXILE

Exile is strangely compelling to think about but terrible to experience. It is the unbearable rift forced between a human being and a native place, between the self and its true home: its essential sadness can never be surmounted.

—Edward W. Said

Figure 1. Frontispiece to *Toledot ya-akov* (Amsterdam: Menasseh ben Israel, 1652). Sasportas's first foray into print as an independent author. His index to the Palestinian Talmud appeared as an appendix with a separate title page. Private collection.

ORAN AND TLEMCEN CA. 1610—CA. 1651

When Jacob Sasportas was born there, around the year 1610, the town of Oran (modern-day Wahran in Algeria) had been under Spanish Habsburg rule for just over a century. A *presidio*, Oran was both a trading post for the interior of Africa and a defensive fort across the sea. A toehold on the southern coast of the Mediterranean, Oran was also a possible staging point for future imperial ambitions. The town had a population of several thousand, the overwhelming majority of whom were Spanish Catholics, a few hundred of whom were Muslims, and a few hundred of whom were Jews.[1] These Jews, the "Jews of the king of Spain" in the felicitous phrase of Jean-Frédéric Schaub, were the last remaining Jews under Spanish sovereignty. Two rival families dominated Jewish life in Oran from the year 1509, when the Spanish established their presence in the city, until the year 1669, when the Spanish summarily expelled them from Oran and sent them into exile to Livorno, Genoa, and elsewhere. The Cansino and the Sasportas families vied with one another for the post of imperial translator, a position that came with privileges, such as protection and remuneration, as well as responsibilities, such as serving as brokers between the Spanish crown and local powers farther inland. For more than a century and a

[1] On early modern Oran, see Beatriz Alonso Acero, *Orán-Mazalquivir, 1589–1639: una sociedad española en la frontera de Berbería* (Madrid: Consejo Superior de Investigaciones Científicas, 2000); on its Jews, see Schaub, *Les juifs du roi d'Espagne*, 16–17. Epigraph from Edward W. Said, *Reflections on Exile and Other Essays* (Cambridge: Harvard University Press, 2000), 173.

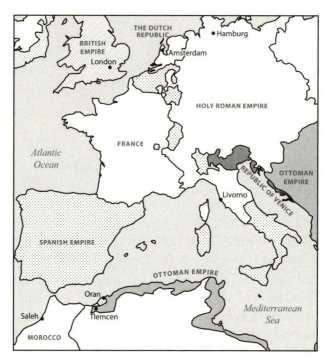

Map 1. The world of Jacob Sasportas

half, men in the Cansino and Sasportas families served as ambassadors, interpreters, slave-traders, and soldiers for the king of Spain. In the middle decades of the seventeenth century, the Spanish court even granted permission to several members of the Sasportas family to reside on the Iberian Peninsula.

Jacob Sasportas, spelled variously as Sasportas, Saportas, Saporta, and Caporta in contemporary documents, was a common name among the Jews of Oran.[2] Rabbi Jacob Sasportas, who would die in 1698 in Amsterdam, was born either in the year 1610, according to a sermon preached upon his death by his friend Daniel Levi de Barrios, or around 1614 or 1615, according to a rabbinic responsum composed by Sasportas in Hamburg in 1669.[3] Jacob the son of Aaron Sasportas was born

---

[2] See Schaub, *Les juifs du roi d'Espagne*, 62, and chap. 2; *The Jews in Genoa*, ed. Rossana Urbani and Guido Nathan Zazzu (Leiden: Brill, 1999), 1:354; Levie Bernfeld, *Poverty and Welfare*, 290n179.

[3] "Mas hay dolor que en año 88 de su Vida," Daniel Levi de Barrios, *Monte Hermoso de la Ley Divina: Sermon Exemplar* (Amsterdam, 1698), 9. כי אמנם אנכי בן נ״ד שנים Sasportas, *Ohel ya-akov*, #24, 34a. Sasportas indicates that he was fifty-four years old at the time of writing this respon-

into a family of rabbis who had fled from the Crown of Aragon to the coast of North Africa in the wake of riots against the Jews in 1391 and 1392.[4] At least two distinguished rabbis were among his ancestors, Moses ben Nahman, or Nahmanides (1194–1270), and Joseph Sasportas (ca. 1400). Exegete, mystic, and poet, Nahmanides was an eleventh-generation ancestor of Jacob Sasportas. Joseph ben Abraham Sasportas wrote a collection of rabbinic responsa in North Africa in the fifteenth century.[5] Unlike Nahmanides, who lived nearly his entire life in the Crown of Aragon, Joseph Sasportas flourished in Tlemcen, a city to the south and west of Oran with a sizable Jewish population. How much of this rabbinic legacy reached Aaron Sasportas, Jacob's father, remains unknown. Apart from mentioning his name, Jacob Sasportas does not discuss his father in his surviving writings. What can be deduced with some degree of certainty is that Jacob Sasportas took his familial inheritance as a scion of a distinguished rabbinic family with great seriousness and even greater pride.

It was not simply filial piety that linked Jacob Sasportas to his ancestors. Like Joseph ben Abraham Sasportas, Jacob Sasportas was a rabbinic jurist whose primary means of literary composition was the rabbinic responsum, a question posed by either a layperson or a colleague followed by an answer that provided a detailed legal opinion. Like Joseph ben Abraham Sasportas, Jacob Sasportas served as a jurist for the Jewish court of Tlemcen and issued opinions to communities in the surrounding area. Like Nahmanides, Sasportas had a penchant for mysticism and composed occasional poetry. Like Nahmanides—whose activity in two major controversies, one internal to Jewish life over the place of Maimonides, and the other a public disputation about Christianity, defined a substantial part of his intellectual legacy—Jacob Sasportas was defined by his positions in a series

---

sum, which is signed with a date of January 1669 on 35a. This would make his birth year either 1614 or 1615. The eighteenth-century historian David Franco Mendes variously describes Sasportas as aged eighty-eight upon his death, which would put the year of his birth in 1610, and aged thirty-three upon his arrival in Amsterdam in 1651, which would put the year of his birth in 1618. See Franco Mendes, *Memorias*, 27 and 58. On the limits of Franco Mendes as a source for the dates of Sasportas's life, see Goldish, "Hakham Jacob Sasportas and the Former Conversos," 151n4.

[4] On a possible ancestor named Salomó Saporta, see Gampel, *Anti-Jewish Riots in the Crown of Aragon*, 118.

[5] Noah Aminoah, *R. Yosef Sasportas ve-sefer teshuvotav* (Tel Aviv: Tel Aviv University Press, 1994).

of controversies. Sasportas never mentioned Joseph ben Abraham Sasportas but never tired of reminding his correspondents that he was a descendant of Nahmanides. Nahmanides and Jacob Sasportas had a similar cast of mind: aristocratic, Talmudic, mystical, Maimonidean, and, perhaps most crucially, reactive.

Who were Sasportas's teachers? Where did he study as a boy and as a young man? To these questions and to many others about the first four decades of Sasportas's life, the historical record remains obstinately silent. From sources composed many decades later, a few basic facts can be ascertained and substantiated with some degree of certainty. In all likelihood Sasportas had a thorough rabbinic education. Judging from the style of the Hebrew prose he composed in adulthood, Sasportas had command of the Bible and the Babylonian Talmud while still young. This would also coincide with his own account and with that of De Barrios that he served as a rabbinic judge while in his teens and the head of a rabbinic court while in his twenties. Not a single document in his own hand survives from Sasportas's time in Oran and Tlemcen. When he arrived in Europe, Sasportas entered the historical record fully formed. But it would be a great mistake to conclude that because the historical record is silent, his time in North Africa was insignificant. If anything, the opposite appears to be the case. Sasportas's response to the different centers in the western Sephardic Diaspora—Amsterdam, Hamburg, London, and Livorno—was conditioned by the fact that he experienced them as an outsider. Much of this was a rhetorical posture. Sasportas repeatedly placed himself on the margins of the places in which he lived, even as the Jews in these cities provided him and his family with material support. But his marginality was not only rhetorical; or perhaps the rhetoric itself bears close scrutiny. What few accounts remain indicate that Sasportas was perceived by others, particularly other Jews, as an outsider as well. Occasionally, this led to comity and a meeting of the minds. No one doubted Sasportas's substantial learning, and many drew upon it for instruction in the academies and for guidance in the law. More often, though, this posture of the outsider led to conflict, and these conflicts frequently left a long paper trail, a paper trail that offers a perspective, however partial, on the Sephardic Diaspora in western Europe in the seventeenth century.

AMSTERDAM CA. 1651 TO CA. 1655–1658

The first and most basic fact that distinguished Sasportas from the Portuguese Jews of western Europe was his having had no personal or familial experience of conversion. The overwhelming majority of the Portuguese Jews of Amsterdam and Hamburg had either lived as Catholics themselves or were descendants of Catholic parents or grandparents. When Sasportas arrived in Amsterdam at some point around the middle of the seventeenth century, he entered a nation (Por. *naçao*) that defined itself as new.[6] The Portuguese Jews of Amsterdam had undergone a major transition, a conversion from living as New Christians to living as New Jews, in the precise formulation of Yosef Kaplan.[7] The very fact that these "Men of the Nation," as they referred to themselves, had lived as Christians had had an enormous impact upon their intellectual and cultural life. Their mental worlds had been shaped by Christianity in general and Catholicism in particular. As a consequence, they invested extraordinary intellectual effort in distinguishing themselves as Jews from their former coreligionists. Sasportas's future colleagues in the rabbinate, men such as Menasseh ben Israel and Isaac Aboab da Fonseca, were deeply enmeshed in the perennial theological polemic between Judaism and Christianity. These men had lived as Catholics and sought to justify the experience of conversion back to the faith of their ancestors on theological grounds. The obsession with Christianity was so pervasive that even men who were not rabbis, such as Isaac Orobio de Castro, or who were rabbis who had not actually lived as Catholics but had been born in Amsterdam or Venice, such as Moses Raphael D'Aguilar and Saul Levi Morteira, wrote sustained treatises polemicizing against Christianity.

Sasportas did not undergo a process of conversion. The reasons for his departure from North Africa and the precise timing of his arrival in Amsterdam remain unclear. In an account of his father's life published as an introduction to the printing of *Ohel ya-akov* nearly forty years after Sasportas's death, Abraham Sasportas alludes to troubles

---

[6] On the terms "nation" and "men of the nation," which were used by the Portuguese Jews themselves, see Yerushalmi, *Isaac Cardoso*, 12–21; Bodian, " 'Men of the Nation,' " 48–76.

[7] *Mi-notsrim hadashim li-yehudim hadashim* (Jerusalem: Zalman Shazar Center, 2003).

between Sasportas and the local political authorities in Tlemcen.[8] After a certain period in prison, Jacob Sasportas escaped from Tlemcen and arrived in Amsterdam. Why Sasportas ended up in prison and how he managed to escape, Abraham Sasportas did not disclose. Given that the account appeared in print roughly ninety years after the events that it described, and that no corroborating evidence has been identified, one cannot assess its veracity. It would be equally foolish to minimize the stress of forced migration and separation from his family that Sasportas experienced in his late thirties or early forties. Traces of these dislocations continued to appear in his writings for the rest of his life. Exile and captivity, however, were not the same thing as conversion from Catholicism to Judaism. This basic difference in experience between Sasportas and the Men of the Nation would have significant repercussions in the decades to come.

By 1651 Sasportas was living in Amsterdam; his name surfaces in several Hebrew books printed there. Sasportas appears to have arrived in Amsterdam alone, as the *Livro dos Acordos de Naçao e Ascamot* (The book of ordinances of the Nation) of the Portuguese Jews in Amsterdam records a payment of 150 fl. to ransom his wife and children from captivity in March 1653.[9] This brief mention of Sasportas and his family in the *Livro dos Acordos* offers an important perspective on his relative insignificance to the Portuguese Jewish Nation in Amsterdam. The basic structure of Portuguese Jewish life in Amsterdam differed from Jewish life in the cities in which Sasportas had previously lived in several crucial ways. The Portuguese Jewish Nation in Amsterdam governed itself through a board called a *maamad*, an administrative body composed of six *parnassim*, and one *gabai*, or treasurer.[10] The *maamad* coordinated the collection of taxes, the organization of social welfare, and the education of youth. In short, the *maamad* saw itself as possessing supreme authority over the Men of the Nation. The members of the *maamad* came from the highest strata of Portuguese society, and this ensured that the Jews of early modern Amsterdam were

---

[8] Abraham Sasportas, introduction to Sasportas, *Ohel ya-akov*, 3b.

[9] SAA entry no. 334, no. 19, p. 342. On the nature of this source, see Yosef Kaplan, "The Social Functions of the *Herem*," in Kaplan, *An Alternative Path*, 110. On the ransom of the Sasportas family, see the note by Fuks and Fuks-Mansfeld to Franco Mendes, *Memorias*, 160n122.

[10] Levie Bernfeld, *Poverty and Welfare*, 79.

governed by a lay oligarchy. Sasportas addressed his petition to the *maamad* for funds to redeem his family from captivity. The *maamad* not only had power of the purse; they had power over the rabbis and other religious functionaries who served the Portuguese Jews, such as ritual slaughterers, circumcisors, teachers, and cantors. All of these men, and they were all men, were hired and fired by the *maamad*.

Little is known about Sasportas's time in North Africa, but if one judges from his own descriptions as a rabbinic jurist in Oran and Tlemcen and from the description provided by his son, Sasportas served as a judge for the Jews of Oran and Tlemcen and those who lived nearby. As the *haham* of the Jews of Oran and Tlemcen, Sasportas had the ultimate authority. It is difficult to know how much of Sasportas's own description of his time in North Africa is a projection of an idealized past on what was actually a much more contentious and fraught period in his life. Nonetheless, it seems reasonable to extrapolate from the experience of Sasportas, and that of a series of other North African rabbis who traveled to or resided in Amsterdam in the seventeenth and eighteenth centuries, to sketch a fundamental distinction between the Men of the Nation in northern Europe and the Jews of North Africa. In cities like Oran, Tlemcen, Fez, and even places somewhat farther afield such as Cairo and Jerusalem, the Jews treated the *haham* with respect and accorded him extraordinary authority. In Amsterdam and in other cities such as Hamburg and London, the lay oligarchs treated the *haham* as simply another religious functionary. Men of the Nation reserved their respect for wealthy oligarchs and consigned authority to these men, who were not exemplars of rabbinic learning. This division between wealth and knowledge, with a concurrent consequence of the professionalization of the rabbinate, did not occur in a single moment in a single place. It was a process that occurred gradually, in fits and starts, over the course of several centuries. Sasportas's experience of the difference between his social position as a *haham* in North Africa and a *haham* in the Sephardic Diaspora in western Europe offers one instance of this process. In this respect, Sasportas was simply one in a long line of *hahamim* from North Africa—beginning with Isaac Uziel in the early seventeenth century, continuing with Hezekiah da Silva, all the way through Moses Hagiz and Hayim Joseph David Azulai in the eighteenth century—who came into conflict with the wealthy lay oligarchs who administered Jewish life for the Men of the Nation.[11] For men such as Uziel, Sasportas, Da Silva, Hagiz, and Azulai there had long been an alliance, often unstated but always perceived, between wealth and learning. As *hahamim* they were used to telling the Jews with whom they lived what to do. To the wealthy lay oligarchs who had built the Jewish institutions that served the Men of the Nation, the rabbi was simply another religious employee who took orders and collected a salary.

When Sasportas arrived in Amsterdam around the middle of the century, there was no shortage of *hahamim*. The Portuguese Jews of Amsterdam already employed Saul Levi Morteira, Menasseh ben Israel, Isaac Aboab da Fonseca, and David Pardo. The situation that Sasportas encountered was similar to that of many other refugee scholars in the centuries before and since. He may have been eminently qualified by his learning, his lineage, and his charisma to serve as the *haham* of the Portuguese Nation in Amsterdam, but there was simply no opening for him. The very absence of Sasportas from the record books of the Portuguese Jews, in contrast to the repeated mention of Morteira and Menasseh ben Israel, and in further contrast to his continued mention in the record books during the last two decades of the seventeenth century, appears to indicate that he played a relatively marginal role in the lives of the Portuguese Jews in Amsterdam during the 1650s.

If he did not serve as a *haham* in an official and therefore salaried capacity, what did Sasportas do for the better part of a decade in Amsterdam? Sasportas's presence in Amsterdam is documented from 1651. For the first two years, he worked in the Hebrew book industry, and in the latter part of his stay he appears to have taught in the yeshiva. His presence in the Hebrew print shops constituted a new type of encounter with the written word. When Sasportas reached Amsterdam, he arrived in a city that was markedly different from any of the places where he had lived previously. In the middle of the seventeenth century, Amsterdam had a population of roughly 150,000 and constituted one of the largest cities in Europe. The number of Jews in the city, somewhere between two and three thousand, was far greater than the number of Jews in Oran or Tlemcen. The size and centrality of Amsterdam meant that the city could support at least two different types of institutions that

[11] Carlebach, *Pursuit of Heresy*, 3–7.

do not appear to have existed in early modern Oran and Tlemcen: Hebrew printing houses and the Ets Haim library.[12] In addition, the Ets Haim Yeshiva, a place in which Sasportas would spend a considerable amount of time at later points in his life, was probably larger and better endowed than the Talmudic academies that may have existed in Oran and Tlemcen.

Historians of Jewish life in early modern North Africa have yet to reconstruct the literary culture of its learned elites. Yet the absence of such a study should not lead one to the conclusion that no such culture existed. One way to assess the rigor and intensity of learned life in Jewish North Africa in this period is through the history of Hebrew printing in Venice and Amsterdam. A number of figures, such as Jacob ben Hayim ben Adoniahu in the sixteenth century and Jacob Sasportas in the seventeenth, arrived in Europe from North Africa with extraordinarily vast rabbinic knowledge. Rather than serve as preachers or teachers, these men found employment as a new social type: the corrector to Hebrew books produced in print.[13] Jacob ben Hayim ben Adoniahu served as the principal intellectual and editorial force behind the making of the second edition of the rabbinic Bible at the Hebrew printing house of Daniel Bomberg. He arrived in Venice from North Africa with near total control of the corpus of rabbinic literature and used this knowledge to create a new kind of anthology: the Rabbinic Bible.[14]

---

[12] While the term "library" may well be anachronistic, Ets Haim as a yeshiva had an extraordinarily large collection of books that was repeatedly replenished through the seventeenth century. This collection of books would have been at Sasportas's disposal during the time he lived in Amsterdam. On the books in Ets Haim, see the repeated entries in SAA, entry no. 334, no. 19, and no. 20. For the eighteenth century, see David Sclar, "Books in the Ets Haim Yeshivah: Acquisition, Publishing and a Community of Scholarship in Eighteenth-Century Amsterdam," *Jewish History* 30 (2016): 207–232. On the term "library" in early modern European intellectual life, see Roger Chartier, *The Order of Books: Readers, Authors, and Libraries in Europe between the Fourteenth and Eighteenth Centuries* (Stanford, CA: Stanford University Press, 1994), chap. 3.

[13] Amnon Raz-Krakotzkin, *The Censor, the Editor, and the Text: The Catholic Church and the Shaping of the Jewish Canon in the Sixteenth Century* (Philadelphia: University of Pennsylvania Press, 2007); Anthony Grafton, *The Culture of Correction in Renaissance Europe* (London: The British Library, 2011).

[14] On Jacob ben Hayim ben Adoniah, see Jordan S. Penkower, "Jacob ben Hayyim and the Rise of the Biblia Hebraica" (PhD diss., Hebrew University of Jerusalem, 1982); on the Rabbinic Bible, see David S. Stern, "The Rabbinic Bible in Its Sixteenth-Century Context," in *The Hebrew Book in Early Modern Italy*, ed. Joseph R. Hacker and Adam Shear (Philadelphia: University of Pennsylvania Press, 2011), 76–108. Penkower's dissertation as cited by Stern, 78n8; David Stern, *The Jewish Bible: A Material History* (Seattle: University of Washington Press, 2017), chaps. 3 and 4.

It seems reasonable to assume that Sasportas had used and studied printed books in both Oran and Tlemcen. A city or town need not have a printing press for its inhabitants to use printed books. With his arrival in Amsterdam, Sasportas moved from being a consumer of printed books, no matter how active and aggressive a reader, to a producer of them. Sasportas's activities as an editor were nowhere near as significant as those of Jacob ben Hayim ben Adoniahu; nor did he own his own print shop as did his new colleague Menasseh ben Israel. Indeed, as shall be apparent throughout this study, very little of Sasportas's own writing actually appeared in print in the course of his lifetime. The reasons for this remain unclear, although they seem to involve some combination of the lack of means to finance the printing of his own writing, an aristocratic contempt for the vulgarity of print as a medium, and a reticence to allow his polemical writings to circulate in the public domain as a printed book.

When Sasportas arrived in Amsterdam around the year 1651, he was a refugee. He did not have the luxury of studying in well-protected solitude. He needed to earn a living, and one avenue open to him was to serve as a corrector at the Hebrew press of his colleague Menasseh ben Israel.[15] In the period Sasportas worked there, in 1651 and 1652, Menasseh ben Israel's second son, Samuel, had taken over day-to-day operations of the press.[16] Sasportas began work there on *Nishmat hayim.* Menasseh ben Israel had used his press to print his own work for years; *Nishmat hayim* represents a departure from his earlier work. Much of his previous writing had appeared in print in the vernacular, addressed to the immediate audience of Portuguese Jews in Amsterdam or the learned Protestant clerics with whom Menasseh ben Israel was in frequent contact.[17] *Nishmat hayim,* by contrast, appeared in Hebrew; treated a sensitive subject in contemporary theology, the transmigration of souls; and addressed a circle of learned elites who could follow the relatively complex theological arguments employed in the work.[18]

[15] Roth, *A Life of Menasseh ben Israel: Rabbi, Printer, and Diplomat; Menasseh ben Israel and His World,* ed. Kaplan, Méchoulan, and Popkin ;Coppenhagen, *Menasseh ben Israel: A Bibliography;* Offenberg, *Menasseh ben Israel 1604–1657: A Biographical Sketch.*

[16] Fuks-M., *Typography,* 1:109. On the market for Menasseh ben Israel's books beyond Amsterdam, see Jonathan Israel, "Menasseh ben Israel and the Dutch Sephardi Colonization Movement of the Mid-17th Century," in Israel, *Diasporas,* 389n7.

[17] Rauschenbach, *Judentum für Christen: Vermittlung und Selbstbehauptung Menasseh Israels in den gelehrten Debatten des 17. Jahrhunderts.*

[18] J. H. Chajes, *Between Worlds: Dybbuks, Exorcists, and Early Modern Judaism* (Philadelphia: University of Pennsylvania Press, 2003), chap. 5.

Figure 2. Salomon Italia, portrait of Menasseh ben Israel. This portrait depicted Sasportas's colleague and employer Menasseh ben Israel. Rijksmuseum, Amsterdam.

Sasportas served as a *magiah* to the production of *Nishmat hayim*. The precise equivalent of the word *magiah* in the world of the early modern Hebrew print shop remains elusive. "Corrector" probably serves as the best translation, as Sasportas corrected the page proofs of the text before the book was sent to press. The corrector was a new social type who had emerged from the margins, both literal and figurative, of the print shop in early modern Europe.[19] Correctors were often immensely learned polyglots who just as often nourished ambitions of authorship themselves. If they were printing a text written by a living author, correctors often worked alongside authors, a process that turned the print shop into a new space of intellectual collaboration.[20]

---

[19] Grafton, *The Culture of Correction in Renaissance Europe.*

[20] Pamela O. Long, *Artisan/Practitioners and the Rise of the New Sciences, 1400–1600* (Corvallis: Oregon State University Press, 2011).

Like many other forms of collaboration, the relationship between author and corrector was often fraught. Thus, in the corrector's apology that served as a preface to his errata list, Sasportas described this tension:

> The task is onerous, the workers lazy, and the author presses day in and day out: have you finished the task? [21]

As an author, and as the primary force behind the press, even as daily operations were in the hands of his son, Menasseh ben Israel played a crucial role in turning his manuscript into a printed book. Sasportas attributed the proliferation of errors in the printed book to the constant back-and-forth among author, corrector, and printer:

> And since, as soon as the book was published, the rabbi himself came up with several new insights and prepared another edition. [22]

Sasportas may refer here to the simultaneous appearance of *Nishmat hayim* with a Latin title page, a descriptive table of contents, and a dedication to Emperor Ferdinand III.[23]

Following a relatively extensive errata list, two folios with two columns per page, *Nishmat hayim* concluded with an autobiographical apologia accompanied by a commendatory poem composed by Sasportas. This one-page composition is, to my knowledge, Sasportas's earliest writing to survive. The opening phrase contains an elaborate citation to a medieval work of ethics entitled *Behinat olam* by Yedaiah Bedersi, an author to whom Sasportas would repeatedly return in his future controversies.[24] Sasportas alluded to a dramatic change in his personal circumstances, a fall from the greatest heights to the lowest depths, without actually providing any detail about those circumstances. He continued to describe his life prior to his arrival in Europe:

---

[21] המלאכה מרובה הפועלים עצלים והרב המחבר דוחק כלו מעשיכם דבר יום ביומו

Menasseh ben Israel, *Nishmat hayim* (Amsterdam: Menasseh ben Israel, 1651), 174b.

[22] ויען הרב תכף להדפסו נתעורר על קצת חידושים ועשה לו מהדורא בתרא

Ibid., 174b.

[23] On the Latin edition with the dedication to the German emperor, see Fuks-M., *Typography*, 1:133–134, entry 190. For examples of authors interfering in the printing of their books in the same place, the Dutch Republic, but slightly later in the seventeenth century, see Anne Goldgar, *Impolite Learning: Conduct and Community in the Republic of Letters, 1680–1750* (New Haven, CT: Yale University Press, 1995).

[24] The opening phrase, צעיר הזבובים קצוץ הכנפים, שקוע בכלא מעוך ככלוב, appears in Yedaiah Bedersi, *Behinat olam* (Ferrara, 1552), 57b.

Wherefore the wind of a tempest lifted me by a lock of my head (Ez. 8:13) from the land of my birth and threw me into one of the valleys of the city of Tlemcen. I was unwittingly exiled from Arabian provinces, and I passed to the other end of the sea. I came upon the famous city of Amsterdam, may the Lord protect it, and I lifted up my eyes, gazed and observed the Jewish inhabitants of this city and their extraordinary splendor. [25]

From this passage, it appears that Sasportas's sojourn in Tlemcen was brief, and that the majority of his life spent in North Africa prior to his abrupt departure had been in Oran, a place that he refers to with reverence "as the land of my birth." One must guard against accepting Sasportas's romanticized depiction of his time in Oran as an empirical description, as refugee intellectuals in exile often referred to their homeland with outpourings of affection. Nonetheless, this short passage seems to be in tension with an account composed considerably later by Abraham Sasportas that suggests Sasportas had lived in Tlemcen for a substantial period of time and served as the chief justice of a rabbinic court there.[26] The current sources available do not offer a clear indication of when and where Sasportas spent his time in North Africa in the first several decades of his life. Nonetheless, most accounts agree that when Sasportas went into exile, he departed from Tlemcen rather than from Oran. The distinction is not simply one of geography but also one of politics. In the late 1640s or early 1650s, whenever it was during this period that Sasportas arrived in Amsterdam, Oran was still under Iberian sovereignty, whereas Tlemcen was not. Sasportas seems to have gotten into some trouble with the local rulers in Tlemcen rather than the Spanish authorities who ruled Oran. Had he been sent into exile by the Spanish, he might have had a considerably harder time entering Spain later in the 1650s, a trip that he appears to have taken in 1658.

[25] אי לזאת כאשר רוח סערתו נשאתני בציצת ראשי מארץ מולדתי ותשליכני באחת הגאיות לעיר תלמסאן ומרוב הרפתקי דעדו עלי גליתי מבלי דעת גלילות ערב ועברתי מעברה מעבר לים ובאתי לעיר המהוללה עיר אמש״טירדם יע״א ונשאתי עיני ואביטה אבחינה בעם ה׳ יושביה ובעליונתם המופלא.

Menasseh ben Israel, *Nishmat hayim*, 176b.

[26] Abraham Sasportas, introduction to Sasportas, *Ohel ya-akov*, 3b, where Abraham states that Jacob Sasportas was twenty-four years old when he became the head of the rabbinic court in Tlemcen. Sasportas may have served as the head of the rabbinic court in Tlemcen while resident in Oran. In his eulogy for Sasportas, De Barrios states, "el Preceptor Rabinico y Politico de muchas Sinagogas Africanas." See De Barrios, *Monte Hermoso de la Ley Divina*, 9.

Amsterdam made a deep impression upon Sasportas. The extraordinary size of the city and the vast wealth of the Portuguese Jews who lived there were profoundly unfamiliar. The Jews of Oran among whom Sasportas had lived may have been wealthy court Jews of the Spanish king, but the wealth of the Cansino and Sasportas families in Oran was easily dwarfed by the wealth of the Men of the Nation. Oran was and would remain a garrison town for the entirety of the seventeenth century. When Sasportas arrived in Amsterdam, the Eighty Years' War had just drawn to a close, and the city was one of the wealthiest, if not the wealthiest, in Europe. Faced with this overwhelming urban landscape and confronted by Jews whose wealth distinguished them from the Sephardic Jews he had known, Sasportas took refuge in the world of books.

> I stood upon my watch, stationed myself upon a lookout, and in my looking, I looked to him who looketh toward Damascus (S. of S. 7:5), who draws and gives to drink from the rivers of wisdom, the wisdom of nature, the wisdom of theology, a mover of mountains.... Menasseh ben Israel, may God preserve him, who brought me into his treasure house, which was perfumed with the scent of Torah, and showed me the many books he had written. For he excelled at promoting that which is beneficial and rejecting that which is harmful. [27]

Two things emerge from Sasportas's report of his encounter in Menasseh ben Israel's print shop. The first has to do with the subject matter discussed, and the second with the quantity of books. Sasportas specified that Menasseh ben Israel drew upon the wisdom of nature and the wisdom of theology. From even the most cursory reading of Sasportas's short apologia and from the very fact that he was able to serve as a corrector in a Hebrew print shop, one can deduce that Sasportas had a thorough rabbinic education. Nearly every sentence he wrote alludes to a passage in biblical or rabbinic literature or both. His expressed admiration for Menasseh ben Israel's breadth of learning indicates that his parameters of knowledge prior to his arrival in Amsterdam were narrower than his employer's. Sasportas wrote about Me-

---

[27] ועל משמרתי אעמודה אתיצבה על מצפה ובצפייתי צפיתי לצופה פני דמש״ק דולה ומשקה מנהרי החכמה חכמת הטבע וחכמ׳ האלהות עוקר הרים . . . מנשה בן ישראל נר״ו ובבית נכאותו הביאני הראני דכולהו בריחה של תורה, ובספריו הרבה שחיבר והגביר חיילים בהקרבת המועיל והרחקת הנזק.

Menasseh ben Israel, *Nishmat hayim*, 176b

nasseh ben Israel's mastery of different bodies of knowledge in an admiring tone. Furthermore, when Sasportas entered Menasseh ben Israel's treasure house, a term that may refer either to his print shop or to his library or to both, he entered a place that was simultaneously foreign and familiar. In either his late thirties or his early forties when he arrived in Amsterdam, Sasportas had spent most of his life immersed in the study of rabbinic literature. When he entered the treasure house, he saw Hebrew books of rabbinic literature—nearly the entirety of his intellectual world—constitute a part of a larger book collection. The overwhelming majority of Menasseh ben Israel's own books had been written in the vernacular or in Latin. Sasportas seems to have known Spanish, as many of the notarial documents that survive from his time in Amsterdam were written in Spanish; those that were composed in Dutch specify that they were read aloud to Sasportas in Spanish translation.[28] There is, however, no indication that Sasportas knew Latin. Sasportas found himself in a room that encompassed books of different branches of knowledge in the same physical space. To this stranger in a strange world, this collection of Jewish books was extremely familiar. Sasportas described his intoxicated response in somatic terms: he could smell the scent of Torah.[29]

Menasseh ben Israel did very different things with books from what Sasportas did. For starters, he printed them. Books served a polemical purpose for Menasseh ben Israel that Sasportas saw fit to remark upon.

In his philosophizing he broke the iniquitous jaws of our enemies who rise up against us.[30]

Sasportas appears to refer to the perennial conflict between Judaism and Christianity, and to have considered Menasseh ben Israel's writings in general and *Nishmat hayim* in particular to be a defense of Judaism against Christian theological polemics. The tone with which Sasportas wrote about both Menasseh ben Israel and his books expressed considerable admiration and even wonder at the intellectual abilities

---

[28] See chapter 6 below.

[29] On Judaica collections in Amsterdam in the early seventeenth century, see Leo Fuks, "Jewish Libraries in Amsterdam in 1640," in *Aspects of Jewish Life in the Netherlands: A Selection from the Writings of Leo Fuks*, ed. Renate G. Fuks-Mansfeld (Assen: Van Gorcum, 1995), 38–57.

[30] בהתפלספותו שבר מתלעות עול נגד אויבינו הקמים עלינו.
Menasseh ben Israel, *Nishmat hayim*, 176b.

of his colleague. This may simply have been the fawning praise of an employee for his employer. Immediately thereafter, Sasportas inserted a poem about Menasseh ben Israel's book that attempted to entice a potential reader to open and peruse its contents. Finally, Sasportas signed the apologia, as follows:

> These are the words of a young and happy [man], like words of the sages who break the stone with a hammer. [31]

For all of the genuine difficulties posed by his dislocation, Sasportas described himself as happy in the final line of his editorial note to *Nishmat hayim.*

Menasseh ben Israel and the press operated by his son Samuel continued to serve Sasportas as a refuge into the following year. In 1652 Menasseh ben Israel reissued *Toledot aharon,* an index of biblical citations in the Babylonian Talmud compiled in the sixteenth century by Aaron of Pesaro that had been printed twice before.[32] This third printing included a substantial appendix entitled *Toledot ya-akov,* an index to biblical citations in the Palestinian Talmud that Sasportas had compiled. The work marked Sasportas's first and, to a certain extent, his most significant foray into print as an independent author. The substantial appendix included a relatively short introduction composed by Sasportas where he repeated many of the same sentiments and even used some of the same phrases as in his editorial note to *Nishmat hayim.*

> Thus sayeth he who has been exiled and banished. [33]

Sasportas began his introduction and recounted in highly compressed and profoundly allusive language the litany of sorrows he had experienced. He indicated that he saw himself as having been at extraordinary risk and described his imprisonment in North Africa. Nevertheless, in spite of his genuine and repeated travails, he assured his reader that he had continued to devote himself to the study of God's word.

---

[31]. כה דברי הצעיר השמח כדברי חכמים המפוצצי׳ סלע בפטיש.
Ibid., 176b.

[32] Fuks-M., *Typography,* 1:134, entry 191.

[33]. אמר הגולה ונדח.

Jacob Sasportas, *Toledot ya-akov,* printed as an appendix to Aaron of Pesaro, *Toledot aharon* (Amsterdam: Menasseh ben Israel, 1652), 2a. Hereafter, *Toledot ya-akov.*

But none of this was sufficient to annul my acceptance of the yoke of heaven in reading and receiving like those earnest ones who rise with the sun [for prayers.][34]

Sasportas seems to allude to the rabbinic topos that knowledge was acquired only through suffering; he framed his exile and wandering as a trial that he was able to overcome only through constant devotion to the study of God's word.[35]

His description of his presence in Amsterdam contains some of the same exuberance as his editorial note to *Nishmat hayim*, while also betraying a hint of distress that had been absent in his autobiographical fragment printed the previous year.

> Moreover, when I arrived in the great city of scholars and writers, the city of Amsterdam, may the Lord protect it, I was a stranger in the land and a guest for the night. But my feet have held fast to their steps (Job 23:11), and I established myself daily in two *yeshivot*, over and above the time I dedicated myself to study in my own house.[36]

Sasportas had found refuge in two of the yeshivot or Talmudic academies in Amsterdam. One of these may well have been Ets Haim, the central school for the children of the Portuguese Jews whose upper-level classes included instruction in Talmud. Sasportas would have a long and occasionally stormy relationship with Ets Haim over the course of the next several decades. The term *yeshiva* and its possible Spanish equivalent *academia* may have referred to other types of institutions apart from Ets Haim. The Portuguese Jews established numerous confraternal societies that often included daily or weekly study.[37] Sasportas may have been referring to one or more of these academies or societies, which he may have joined shortly after his arrival in Amsterdam. Whatever familiarity and comfort Sasportas derived from the presence of books and other Jews who produced them,

---

[34] וכל זה איננו שוה לי לבטל ממני עול מלכות שמים בקריאה ובקבלה כותיקים עם נץ החמה.
Toledot ya-akov, 2a.

[35] On this topos, see the sixth chapter of Mishnah Avot.

[36] ואף גם זאת בהיותי היום בעיר גדול' של חכמי' ושל סופרי' עיר אמשטירדם יע״א כגר בארץ וכאורח נטה ללון
באשורי אחזה רגלי בקבע קבוע בשתי ישיבו' דבר יום ביומו זולת קביעותי הנהוג לעצמי בקרב ביתי.
Toledot ya-akov, 2b.

[37] Swetschinski, *Reluctant Cosmopolitans*, 210–211.

he saw himself as an exile and as a temporary resident in Amsterdam. The city was a city of scholars and writers, but it was not his home.

Sasportas described the role that Menasseh ben Israel had played in the genesis of his own composition.

> Therefore when the Lord awakened the spirit of the sage of Torah and philosopher of theology, the chief, the minister, the leader in Israel, our master and teacher, Menasseh ben Israel, may the Lord preserve him, prompting him to reprint *Toledot aharon*, an index of passages from the Torah, the Prophets, and the Writings contained in the Babylonian Talmud, and in the *Zohar, Akeda[t yitzhak]* and the *Ikkarim*, and he wanted to embellish that earlier edition, it occurred to me to fill in that which had been missing, so that, thanks to this, "a chip from that log would come to me" [BT Sanhedrin 7b], appearing under the name of Israel, [that is, my] name, Jacob [Isa. 44:5].[38]

Sasportas described Menasseh ben Israel as a sage and a philosopher, terms that appeared to indicate an intellectual respect and perhaps even a mutual affection between the two scholars. Whatever bookish camaraderie may have developed between the two men, both recognized that the market for copies of *Toledot aharon* was already saturated by the two editions in circulation. No matter how impressive Menasseh ben Israel's typeface or the quality of books produced at his press, both he and Sasportas understood that a reprinting of *Toledot aharon* would have to offer a possible purchaser something new.

Here Sasportas made his presence in the print shop felt. By mutual agreement, Sasportas composed a supplementary index to the Palestinian Talmud that appeared as its own work with a completely new title page. *Toledot aharon* was a new kind of reference work, a book whose very existence was predicated upon an emerging culture of Hebrew print in the sixteenth century. The method employed by Aaron of Pesaro depended upon a relatively stable text of the Babylonian Talmud, whose pagination was more or less the same across the different editions that had appeared in print in the sixteenth century.[39] Thus

---

[38] לכן ובכן בהעיר ה' את רוחו בהחכם התורני ופלוסוף האלהי שר וגדול בישראל כמוה״רר מנשה בן ישראל נר״ו להדפיס ספר תולדות אהרן מפתח תורה נביאים וכתובים הנמצאי' בתלמוד בבלי ובמדרש הזוהר עם ספר העקידה והעיקרים ורצה להוסיף נפך על הדפוס הישן ההוא וכי היכי דלימטי לי שיבא במכשור' בזכו' עלה בלבי להשלים מה שחסר ממנו ובשם ישראל יכונה ויקרא בשם יעקב.

Toledot ya-akov, 2b–3a.

[39] Marvin J. Heller, *Printing the Talmud: A History of the Earliest Printed Editions of the Talmud*

Aaron of Pesaro listed verses from the Bible in sequential order. Beneath each verse he listed the places that the verse had appeared in the Babylonian Talmud, providing first the tractate and then the pagination. The first edition of *Toledot aharon*, which had appeared in Freiburg in 1583, included references only to the Babylonian Talmud. The second edition, which had appeared in Venice less than a decade later in 1591, added references to three other works: the *Zohar*, *Akedat yitzhak* by Isaac Arama, and *Sefer ha-ikkarim* by Joseph Albo. These references, which were incorporated into the previous list, did not point the reader to pagination, as the printed editions of these three works did not adhere to a uniform pagination; rather, they indicated chapter headings within each work.

Sasportas introduced a significant change between the second and third editions of Aaron of Pesaro's work. Rather than incorporate references to the Palestinian Talmud within the previously existing text, as the author or compiler of the second edition had done with the *Zohar*, Arama, and Albo, Sasportas composed an entirely new book devoted exclusively to the Palestinian Talmud. He justified the existence of his compilation on three grounds. The first was simply one of scope. The Mishnah contains six orders, each of which is subdivided into different tractates. The first order of the Mishnah, entitled *Zeraim*, deals largely with the laws of agriculture. With the exception of the first tractate, *Berakoth*, the Babylonian Talmud does not treat any other tractates in this order. Sasportas explained that the biblical verses dealing with these laws were left undiscussed and hence unexplained in the Babylonian Talmud but had been treated extensively in the Palestinian Talmud. A reader who wanted to understand the rabbinic discussion of these verses could now turn to Sasportas's index to identify where these passages appeared in the Palestinian Talmud. The second advantage had to do with difficulty. The Babylonian Talmud contained many difficult passages, Sasportas explained, and a reader could now use his index to identify a passage in the Palestinian Talmud that would help him explain the difficulty. The third advantage had to do with audience. *Toledot aharon* and *Toledot ya-akov* addressed themselves to Jewish preachers. The turn of the seventeenth century

(Brooklyn, NY: Im Hasefer, 1992); Yaakov S. Spiegel, *Amudim be-toledot ha-sefer ha-ivri: ketivah ve-ha-taka* (Ramat Gan: Bar-Ilan University Press, 2005).

was a golden age of Jewish preaching. In cities with relatively large Jewish populations such as Venice, Amsterdam, and Prague, preachers delivered sermons on nearly every Sabbath, sometimes in more than one synagogue and sometimes more than once a Sabbath.[40] These preachers frequently turned to the printing press in these same cities, an industry in which many of them often found employment, to publish their sermons. In turn, printers began to furnish preachers with all kinds of different reference works that they could use in the preparation and composition of their sermons. *Toledot aharon* and *Toledot ya-akov* both addressed themselves to preachers. The former sought to make the Babylonian Talmud a more accessible work upon which preachers could draw as they discussed passages from the Bible in their sermons; in the latter, Sasportas sought to expand the literary corpus of works upon which preachers might draw to compose their sermons. The Talmud they preached about in the synagogue would refer not only to the Babylonian Talmud but would include the Palestinian Talmud as well.

As an author and as a pressman, Sasportas had to distinguish his work not only from the previous editions of *Toledot aharon* but also from other works that offered commentary on and interpretation of the Palestinian Talmud. The most obvious predecessor was Samuel Yafe Ashkenazi's *Yefe mareh*, printed in Venice in 1567. Ashkenazi had composed a substantive commentary, and his book included the text of the Palestinian Talmud set in the center of the page with his own commentary arranged around it. Sasportas distinguished his own book from Ashkenazi's by claiming that Ashkenazi had dealt only with the narrative portions of the Palestinian Talmud. His book lacked an index, rendering it virtually useless for a reader who wanted to dip into the book to examine a single biblical passage. He envisioned readers of his index using it in tandem with *Yefe mareh*.[41] Finally, Sasportas specified that he had arranged his index according to the edition of the Palestinian Talmud printed in Krakow in 1609.

Immediately before Sasportas's signature to the introduction, he included this entreaty:

[40] For an overview, see Marc Saperstein, *Jewish Preaching, 1200–1800: An Anthology* (New Haven, CT: Yale University Press, 1989); for a series of case studies, see *Preachers of the Italian Ghetto*, ed. David B. Ruderman (Berkeley: University of California Press, 1992).

[41] For a later reference to *Yefe mareh* in a letter to Raphael Supino, see Sasportas, *ZNZ*, 93.

May the Lord render us worthy to make many books without end
(Ecc. 12:12).[42]

Less than a year after he had begun working in the shop of Menasseh
ben Israel, Sasportas had already acclimated to the conventions of Hebrew printing. He was able to set his own work within a competitive
market, distinguish the features of his own index that would make it
appeal to a potential customer, and take account of the publishing landscape. In short, he had learned how to sell his own work. The closing
sentence does not seem to be simply a pious gesture; rather, it reveals
an ambition that would occasionally surface in his other writings. It
remains unclear as to whether this ambition was editorial, in which
case Sasportas would serve as the midwife to the writings of others
that would appear in print, or authorial, in which case Sasportas would
print his own compositions. The line between author and editor in the
seventeenth century was by no means hard-and-fast: as one follows
Sasportas through the annals of Hebrew printing over the course of
the next half a century, he will appear repeatedly at the margins, as an
editor and as an approbator, rather than at the center, as an author. For
all of the dexterity as a bookman Sasportas demonstrated in the introduction to *Toledot ya-akov*, the final line of the introduction reveals that
he was still very much in exile in Amsterdam:

> Jacob Sasportas, a pure Sephardi, son of my master and father, Aaron
> Sasportas, may the Lord preserve and protect him, resident of Oran, may
> the Lord preserve it.[43]

Apart from his name, next to nothing is known about Jacob Sasportas's father, Aaron Sasportas. In 1652 when *Toledot ya-akov* appeared
in print, he was still very much alive, as the acronym following his
name indicated a wish for his long life. Furthermore, well over a year
into his stay in Amsterdam, when he had already found work teaching
in the yeshiva and editing books in a print shop, Sasportas continued
to think of himself as a resident of Oran rather than Amsterdam.

When Sasportas prepared his index to the Palestinian Talmud remains unclear. From the remark he made about Menasseh ben Israel's

---

[42] השם יזכנו לעשות ספרים הרבה אין קץ
Toledot ya-akov, 2b.
[43] יעקב ששפורטרש סט בב״אא אהרון ששפוטרש נר״ו מתושבי אוראן יע״א
Ibid., 2b.

desire to add an incentive to potential purchasers of *Toledot aharon*, and from his praise of Amsterdam as a city of books and scholars, it appears that he prepared it in Amsterdam as a supplement to a book that was on its way to press. Sasportas was apparently acquainted with the Palestinian Talmud as a book prior to his arrival in Amsterdam. It seems unlikely that he would have been able to compose a reference work as thorough and as detailed as *Toledot ya-akov* had he encountered the Palestinian Talmud for the first time only upon his arrival in Europe. Alternatively, this may be another instance in the long tradition within the early modern Sephardic rabbinate of a scholar shepherding a book written far from a center of Hebrew printing through the process of printing. Only a year later, in 1653, Sasportas served as the editor of *Sefer heikhal ha-kodesh* at the printing press of Imanoel Benveniste.[44] Sasportas edited this kabbalistic commentary on the liturgy that had been composed a century earlier in North Africa by Moses b. Maimon Elbaz and included annotations by Aaron Sabuni of Saleh. Sasportas had evidently arrived in Amsterdam with Elbaz's book in manuscript and saw it through to print. Many Sephardic rabbinic luminaries throughout the Mediterranean—such as Joseph Karo, Moses Alshekh, and Solomon Lebeit Halevi—had composed their books in one place, such as Salonika or Safed, and had them printed in another, notably Venice. Men such as Isaac Gershon and Hayim Alshekh often served as intermediaries between Safed and Salonika and the Hebrew presses in Venice, importing manuscripts, editing them, and overseeing their appearance into print. Sasportas played a similar role with Elbaz's book, and possibly with his own *Toledot ya-akov*, although in his case the place of printing was Amsterdam rather than Venice. By the middle of the seventeenth century Amsterdam had eclipsed Venice as the center of Hebrew printing.[45]

As a book *Toledot ya-akov* appears to be part of an ongoing process of the Babylonification of the Palestinian Talmud, a process that had begun in Daniel Bomberg's printing shop in Venice over a century earlier with the first appearance of the Palestinian Talmud in print in 1523.[46] The Venice edition had quickly become scarce, although with the appearance of Ashkenazi's *Yefe mareh* in 1567 substantial portions

---

[44] Fuks-M., *Typography*, 1:177, entry 234.

[45] Baumgarten, *Le peuple des iivres*.

[46] See Jacob Sussmann, introduction to *Talmud Yerushalmi* (Jerusalem: Academy of Hebrew Language, 2001).

reappeared in print. The second printing of the Palestinian Talmud in Krakow in 1609 indicated a growing demand for the book and conformed to a pattern within the publication history of other Hebrew books in the early modern period. A first edition would appear at a major center of print in Italy, often Venice, in the sixteenth century, and a second edition or sometimes a simple reprint of the first would appear later in the sixteenth century or in the seventeenth century somewhere north of the Alps, whether in Krakow, Amsterdam, or Prague. His index participated in the commodification of the Palestinian Talmud as a physical book and the domestication of the Palestinian Talmud as a rabbinic work: it could now serve both a learned audience seeking to understand a difficult passage in the Babylonian Talmud and a preacher seeking to impress his audience with a reference to a hitherto obscure rabbinic book. The appearance of *Toledot yaakov* in the same volume as *Toledot aharon* participated in a larger and longer shift in the organization of knowledge that had been ongoing for the previous century and a half. In the High and late Middle Ages, Jewish scholars lamented their inability to obtain a copy of the Palestinian Talmud.[47] With its appearance in print twice in less than a century, the Palestinian Talmud began to enter and thus transform the canon of rabbinic literature. Sasportas's index was a small part of this larger process.

Toledot aharon was the last Hebrew book to appear at Menasseh ben Israel's press for a substantial period of time. In fact, the press printed only one other Hebrew book, *Mekor hayim*, which appeared in 1655, before it folded. Some of the pressmen made their way to a rival Hebrew press in Amsterdam owned and operated by Imanoel Benveniste. This press had printed a set of the Babylonian Talmud in the 1640s and issued a substantial number of books in rabbinic literature. It was thus an obvious place for Sasportas to serve as an impresario of print. In this instance, Sasportas did not work as a corrector. He seems to have functioned as the early modern equivalent of an acquisitions editor for two books, *Heikhal ha-kodesh* by Moses b. Maimon Elbaz and an untitled commentary on Ecclesiastes and the Psalms by Moses de Mercado.[48]

---

[47] Ibid., 10.

[48] Fuks-M., *Typography*, 1:177–178, entries 234 and 236. See Goldgar, *Impolite Learning*, for numerous parallels in the republic of letters.

Moses b. Maimon Elbaz was a kabbalist who flourished in Morocco until his death in 1598.[49] In addition to *Heikhal ha-kodesh*, he composed a kabbalistic commentary on the Passover Haggadah entitled *Perhei shoshan*. Sasportas had arranged for the printing of *Heikhal ha-kodesh* by enlisting the financial support of the members of a yeshiva.

> We wanted to arrange for its [*Heikhal ha-kodesh*] printing as it was in our possession, yet since we had no money and lacked the funds to finance its printing, we depended upon the members of the yeshiva in whose shade we sit, which is called by a new name, which the mouth of the Lord shall name (Isa. 62:2), the light of life. [50]

Sasportas referred to Or ha-haim, a yeshiva that has left scant documentation in the abundant literature by and about the Portuguese Jews of seventeenth-century Amsterdam. The verse from Isaiah that emphasizes the name's newness and included the Hebrew word for life, *hayim*, may be an allusion to the central yeshiva in Amsterdam, Ets Haim.

Elbaz's *Heikhal ha-kodesh* consisted of a kabbalistic commentary on the daily liturgy. Sasportas composed and appended a substantial introduction to the book. Repeatedly throughout his life, Sasportas's name appeared in print alongside two words: *haham* and *mekubal*. Law and mysticism were not mutually exclusive categories in the seventeenth century, and these two titles, *haham*, scholar, and *mekubal*, mystic, offer some indication of this. Nonetheless, the overwhelming majority of Sasportas's writing fell within the realm of the law. As a *posek*, or rabbinic jurist, Sasportas may well have been one of the most important, if not the most important, in the western Sephardic Diaspora during the seventeenth century. Nonetheless, he saw himself and was seen by others as a kabbalist. The introduction he composed to *Heikhal ha-kodesh* and the accompanying poems are the most sustained writings he composed on Kabbalah that survive. In this introduction, Sasportas demonstrated a thorough familiarity with the basic literature of Kabbalah and cited authors as different from one another as Azriel of Gerona, Menahem Recanati, and Meir ibn Gabbai. Most of the intro-

---

[49] Dan Manor, "R. Moses bar Maimon (Elbaz): Kabbalistic Exegesis and Sources" (Hebrew), *Kabbalah* 7 (2002): 199–223.

[50] רצינו להתעסק בהדפסתו בהיותו נמצא ברשותנו ויען כי הכסף אזל מכלינו ולא מצאה ידינו די הספקת הדפוס
נתלינו בבעלי הישיבה אשר אנו מסתופפי' בצלה אשר קורא לה שם חדש פי ה' יקבנו אור החיים

Jacob Sasportas, introduction to Moses b. Maimon Elbaz, *Heikhal ha-kodesh* (Amsterdam: Benveniste, 1653), 5b. Sasportas's introduction is paginated separately from the rest of the book.

duction he devoted to the vexed and somewhat exhausted question of the relationship between the kabbalistic sefirot and the Godhead. Sasportas drew repeatedly on Moses Cordovero's *Pardes rimonim* to argue that the existence of the ten sefirot did not necessitate a plurality or multiplicity within God. In this sense, Sasportas followed a long line of kabbalists who viewed the sefirot as a mystical articulation of Maimonides's doctrine of the divine attributes. Although he did not quote Maimonides by name in this context, Sasportas cited Cordovero, a kabbalist who openly acknowledged his dependence on Maimonides. All of this infuriated Gershom Scholem, who dismissively remarked of Sasportas's introduction to *Heikhal ha-kodesh*:

> The kabbalah ... fulfilled a double function in the history of the Jewish religion: a conservative function by interpreting traditional forms, and a revolutionary function by releasing the springs of utterly new ideas. Sasportas represented the conservative aspect.[51]

Sasportas sought to defend Kabbalah from the perennial charge of polytheism, and it was in this context that he drew upon Cordovero and his doctrine of the sefirot. He went so far as to cite a standard medieval criticism by Isaac bar Sheshet, a rabbi in medieval Aragon who had written scores of responsa similar in style and in format to those that Sasportas would write over the course of his career. Bar Sheshet had rebuked kabbalists for being even worse than Christians: Christians had at least believed in the Trinity but kabbalists had gone so far as to believe in the Decad. Bar Sheshet's aphorism had become a standard rebuke of kabbalists by the middle of the seventeenth century, so standard that Sasportas felt compelled to raise it unsolicited in order to attempt a rebuttal.

If Cordovero and *Pardes rimonim* represented one aspect of Sasportas's kabbalistic intellectual world, the *Zohar* represented another. From his repeated references to the words of Rabbi Simeon bar Yohai, one can deduce that Sasportas had no interest in taking a historical approach to the question of the *Zohar*'s authorship, an issue that had concerned a growing number of scholars, Jewish, Catholic, and Protestant, in the sixteenth and seventeenth centuries.[52] Sasportas may not have

---

[51] Scholem, *Sabbatai Sevi*, 570–571.
[52] Huss, *The Zohar*, chap. 7.

bothered to ask the burning contemporary questions about the *Zohar*, but he was not a fool. In one of the final comments to his introduction, he demonstrated with piercing clarity that he understood both the merits and the limitations of the book he was about to send into print:

> Although he did not innovate, any more than what could be garnered from the writings of the kabbalists prior to the dissemination of the books by Moses Cordovero, of blessed memory, and Isaac Luria, of blessed memory, nevertheless, he deserves praise for his hard work, which has produced a prayer book that amplifies the words of Simeon bar Yohai whenever he spoke about prayer.[53]

In short, Elbaz had written a synthetic treatment of the kabbalistic literature on prayer, and his anthology had given added emphasis to the discussions of prayer scattered throughout the *Zohar*. Sasportas made the revealing comment that when Elbaz had composed his liturgical commentary in Morocco, in the last quarter of the sixteenth century, writings by Cordovero and Luria were relatively unknown to him. Just over half of a century later, Sasportas referred to Luria and Cordovero as if they were household names.

The following year, one of the star students of the Ets Haim Yeshiva, named Moses de Mercado, died at the age of twenty. Even at a time when the death of children and young adults occurred with extraordinary frequency, that of Moses de Mercado came as a shock to the Portuguese Jewish elites.[54] His death occasioned a series of funeral sermons that appeared in print, and the posthumous publication of his commentary on Ecclesiastes and Psalms. Sasportas played a substantive role in both of these publications, and these printed books, in turn, offer a number of insights into his life in Amsterdam. Both Saul Levi Morteira, the presiding rabbinic authority in Amsterdam, and Sasportas, who appears to have been one of Mercado's teachers, delivered eulogies. A variety of sources indicate that Sasportas delivered many sermons over the course of his long life, but few survive. His eulogy for Moses de Mercado survives owing to the intervention of a rich

---

[53] הגם שלא חידש אלא מה שלקט מספרי המקובלים קודם שנתפשטו ספרי מהרמ״ק ז״ל וספרי האר״י ז״ל בין כה
וכה אפריין נמטיה ביגעותו רבה כי בסידורו זה עשה אזנים לדברי הרשב״י בכל מקום שדבר בתפילה.
Sasportas, introduction to Elbaz, *Heikhal ha-kodesh*, 5a.

[54] On the ubiquity of early death in early modern Amsterdam, see Derek Phillips, *Well-Being in Amsterdam's Golden Age* (Amsterdam: Pallas Publications, 2008), chap. 3.

uncle: Jacob de Mercado.[55] Imanoel Benveniste's press printed both eulogies, Morteira's in Portuguese and Sasportas's in Hebrew, in a pamphlet that survives in a single copy in the Bodleian Library.[56]

Although a relatively brief composition, Sasportas's eulogy provides a wealth of detail about his life in Amsterdam, even as it says very little about the deceased. Sasportas wrote that he recognized Moses de Mercado's sterling character from the moment he had arrived in Amsterdam. Although he had been in the city for a number of years by the time he delivered the eulogy, Sasportas continued to perceive Amsterdam as a foreign place. He expressed profound ambivalence about the medium of print and the very fact that he allowed his eulogy to appear as a pamphlet:

> Although I have vowed and maintained my vow to guard myself from putting into print anything I have written in my notebooks until the Lord on High resolves to assist me, and may the Lord assist me in completing them and printing them in their entirety. [57]

One can catch a glimpse of Sasportas as an author who nurtured considerable ambitions for his own writing. Beyond the relatively banal apologia about appearing in print, Sasportas indicated that he had voluminous notebooks he hoped would one day appear in print. But he offered his readers, or his listeners, absolutely no indication of their contents.

In the final lines of the eulogy, however, he mentioned his writings again:

> Behold it is written in other notebooks, to which I have given the name *Ohel ya-akov* (Heb. The tent of Jacob), that are devoted to the adjudication of the law and contain questions and answers that have been posed

[55] Evidence for a merchant named Jacob de Mercado who dealt in diamonds and tobacco survives from 1693. See Levie Bernfeld, *Poverty and Welfare*, 447n28. It is unclear whether this is the same Jacob de Mercado who financed the publication of these books in memory of his nephew forty years earlier.

[56] As identified in Fuks-M., *Typography* 1:176, entry 232, who state that though the place-name and printer do not appear on the title page, the typography indicates that the pamphlet was printed by Benveniste. Oxford, Bodleian Library, Shelfmark Opp. 4o 1102. For an English translation of the Hebrew text of Morteira's eulogy, which survives in manuscript in Hebrew in parallel to the Portuguese text that appeared in print, see Saperstein, *Exile in Amsterdam*, 536–543.

[57] ולולי שנשבעתי ואקיימה לשמור פתחי פי מהעלות על ספר חוקה שום ענין מקונדרסי עד שתחפץ ימין עליון לסעדני ותעזר האלהי לעזרני להשלימם ולהדפיסם בשלמו.

Jacob Sasportas, untitled and unpaginated eulogy for Moses de Mercado, fifth leaf, verso.

Figure 3. Frontispiece to *Eleh divre ya-akov Sasportas* (Amsterdam: Benveniste, 1652). Sasportas appears as both a *hakham*, a sage, and a *mekubal*, a kabbalist. This piece of printed ephemera appears to survive in a single copy. Reproduced by permission of the Bodleian Libraries, University of Oxford.

to me since I served as a judge in the congregation of Tlemcen, as well as during the period of my peripatetic wandering all the way up until the current time, may the Lord God assist me to complete it and print it.[58]

As early as 1653, nearly eighty-five years before it would actually appear in print, Sasportas planned to print a collection of his rabbinic responsa under the title *Ohel ya-akov*, a name that he, rather than his son Abraham or his posthumous editor David Meldola, had given to the book. Sasportas offered a crucial insight into his working habits at the conclusion of his eulogy. Like many other intellectuals in early modern Europe, Sasportas kept notebooks, or something similar to note-

---

[58] הלא היא כתובה בקונדריסי' אחרים אשר יחדתי להם שם אהל יעקב המיוחד לדינין תשובות השאלות המתחדשות
מיום היותי על מדין במלאכת הדיינות בקהל תלמסאן ובימי הנדות והטלטול ועד היום ועד בכלל ה' אלהים יעזר לי
להשלימו ולהדפיסו.

Ibid., fourth leaf, recto.

books, an attempt to render the Hebrew word *kundres* in English. In these notebooks, Sasportas recorded the legal queries that had been posed to him, as well as his own responses. He preserved these queries from the time that he served as a judge in Tlemcen and hoped that they would one day appear in print under the title *Ohel ya-akov*. The book that eventually appeared under that title contains dozens of responsa written by Sasportas from every period in his life after his initial arrival in Europe at midcentury, including a number of responsa written while he was in Saleh in the late 1650s and early 1660s. The book does not, however, include responsa from his period in Tlemcen or Oran. The manuscript used by the printers in the eighteenth century as the basis for *Ohel ya-akov* resurfaced in the 1980s and is currently housed at the library of Yeshiva University. This manuscript does not contain responsa from his time in Tlemcen or Oran. It appears that Sasportas continued to write rabbinic responsa over the course of his entire life and kept a series of notebooks in which he recorded his answers. By chance, two of these notebooks have survived, the printer's copy of *Ohel ya-akov* and the initial drafts of his letters included in *Zizath novel zvi* that served as the basis for Tishby's edition. It would be a mistake, however, to conclude that these notebooks represent the entirety of Sasportas's literary output. They seem to represent a portion of it, but how large a portion is not at all clear. In a passing aside within *Zizath novel zvi*, Sasportas mentioned a commentary on the Mishnah that he had worked on for many years and hoped to print. To the best of my knowledge, this commentary, which would probably also have been in a notebook similar to those that included the responsa in *Ohel ya-akov*, has not survived.

In his eulogy Sasportas confronted the basic question that must have been gnawing at many in his audience: How could someone so young with so much potential have died in the prime of his life? As he would do throughout his writings, Sasportas went to the bookshelf. This time he sought to grapple with the perennial question of theodicy. None of the answers that Sasportas offered to his audience provided a theological or philosophical innovation. In this sense, his sermon functions much as does, in his own description, Elbaz's *Heikhal ha-kodesh*, a synthetic summary of available explanations. Nonetheless, two of the sources upon which he drew for his sermon provide an indication of his reading habits. They foreshadow the type of argument that he would repeatedly employ in later controversies. Sasportas turned first to Maimonides in *The Guide of the Perplexed* and, in particular, to his discussion of divine providence in the third section. Sasportas drew upon the commentary composed by Shem Tov ibn Falaquera in the thirteenth century that had appeared in print alongside *The Guide of the Perplexed* in the sixteenth century. Immediately thereafter Sasportas turned to the *Zohar*, a work he attributed without hesitation to Simeon Bar Yohai, and stressed its discussion of human suffering as a means to cope with the problem of grief. This juxtaposition of the *Zohar* with *The Guide of the Perplexed* releases two insights about Sasportas. The first has to do with his reading of Maimonides, and the second with the relationship between Kabbalah and philosophy in the seventeenth century. Sasportas's invocation of *The Guide of the Perplexed* and Falaquera's commentary underscores a critical point about his relationship to Maimonides. Sasportas did not distinguish between Maimonides as the author of *The Guide of the Perplexed* and Maimonides as the author of the *Code of Law*. Both books constituted crucial repositories of knowledge and tradition. As a legal jurist, Sasportas drew upon the *Code of Law* to determine the correct ruling in particular cases; as a preacher seeking to comfort a group of mourners, he turned to the section on providence in *The Guide of the Perplexed*. Furthermore, Sasportas's embrace of Maimonides did not necessitate his opposition to Kabbalah or the *Zohar*, nor did he seek to turn Maimonides into a kabbalist as dozens of others had done in prior centuries. Sasportas was a kabbalist and a jurist, a *haham* and a *mekubal*, as he repeatedly appeared in the paratextual materials to printed books in the seventeenth century. His eclectic reading did not condemn certain sections of the medieval Jewish bookshelf. At this point in his intellectual life, Sasportas does not appear to have been extraordinarily vexed by the problem of the new. He does not seem to have felt any burden to innovate either philosophically, legally, or mystically.

In the same year and at the same press, Sasportas oversaw the printing of Moses de Mercado's commentary on the Psalms and Ecclesiastes in a single volume. With this book, Sasportas returned to the role he had played for Menasseh ben Israel's *Nishmat hayim*, corrector. Like the eulogies, this volume was financed by Jacob de Mercado, the author's uncle, as a memorial to his departed nephew. As with the eulogies, both Morteira and Sasportas composed texts in his memory, in this case, introductory statements that described the scholarly character of the author and his commentary. The volume also included poems in memory of Mercado composed by Isaac Nahar and Selomoh de Olivera, figures who would continue to appear in Sasportas's life for decades to come. In his editorial note, Sasportas emphasized that he sought to print Mercado's work with as little editorial intervention as possible:

> When these notebooks were discovered after his death as a first draft composed in his own hand, we attempted to publish them upon clean and pure white paper without any additions or subtractions or commentary, only the words as they were.[59]

The extent to which Sasportas actually interfered as an editor remains a fundamentally open question. In his eulogy Morteira indicated that Mercado's commentary on Ecclesiastes remained incomplete at the time of his death, and Sasportas may well have written the commentary on the concluding chapters.[60] Sasportas, however, sought to represent himself in this context simply as a conduit to the writings of another and minimized his role as an editor. In his signature, Sasportas continued to describe himself as an exile:

> Thus sayeth... the exiled and the banished who toils in the labor of Torah. [61]

His signature indicates that as of 1653 his father, Aaron, was still alive and serving as a rabbi in Oran. To the best of my knowledge, this is the only reference in all of Sasportas's extant writings to his father serving as a rabbi in an official capacity in Oran. Sasportas uses the term מרביץ תורה (Heb. One who dispenses Torah), which was a technical term in the early modern Sephardic rabbinate.[62] If Aaron Sasportas had indeed served as a rabbi in Oran, this may help explain why Jacob

---

[59] אשר לזאת בהגלות נגלות אחרי מותו קונדריסיו אלה בכתיבת ידו מהדורא קמא, השתדלנו להוציאם על נייר לבן טהור בלי תוספת ומגרעת בשום פירוש או ענין כי אם הדברים אשר הם.

Jacob Sasportas, introduction to Moses de Mercado, *Perush sefer kohelet ve-tehilim* (Amsterdam: Benveniste, 1653), 5b. On this book, see Fuks-M., *Typography* 1:178, entry 236.

[60] Saperstein, *Exile in Amsterdam*, 542n30.

[61] נאמר הגולה ונדח . . . ומתעמל בעמלה של תורה.

Sasportas, introduction to Mercado, *Perush sefer kohelet ve-tehilim*, 5b.

[62] Meir Benayahu, *Marbits Torah: samkhuyotav, tafkidav, ve-helko be-mosdot ha-kehilah bi-Sefarad, be-Turkiyah uve-artsot ha-mizrah* (Jerusalem: Rav Kook Institute, 1953).

Sasportas had gone to serve as a judge in Tlemcen. His father's position in Oran obviated the need for him to serve there as well. At this point, however, knowledge of both father and son prior to the 1650s is simply too scarce to draw any firm conclusions.

In 1653 Sasportas composed a long responsum addressed to Saul Levi Morteira. Responsum number 17 within *Ohel ya-akov* covers four folio pages and constitutes an independent essay in and of itself.[63] The subject was the rabbinic ruling in the case of false witnesses. The book of Deuteronomy states, "And behold, if the witness be a false witness and hath testified falsely against his brother then shall ye do unto him, as he had thought to have done unto his brother" (Deut. 19:18–19). In the biblical ruling, false witnesses would be incriminated, and punished, precisely as they had hoped to incriminate the person they had falsely accused. The Babylonian Talmud interpreted the biblical passage as a reference to the testimony of false witnesses and not to what was actually carried out on the basis of their testimony.[64] In other words, if witnesses had given false testimony and had been proven false before punishment had been meted out, the false witnesses would receive that punishment; however, if the punishment had already been meted out, the witnesses would not be punished. The rabbinic ruling defies both logic and a basic sense of fairness. As a result, a number of medieval commentators sought to restrict its impact or to explain it away. Maimonides ruled that this applied only when the punishment in question was the death sentence, in which case the false witnesses would not be put to death.[65] Thus, if the witnesses were proven to be false prior to the death of the person about whom they had testified, the witnesses would be put to death; however, if they were proven false after the person about whom they testified had been put to death, the witnesses would not be put to death.

Morteira objected to this ruling and argued that if the false witnesses should not be put to death under the rubric of the laws of testimony as interpreted by the rabbis both in the Talmud and later on, they should be put to death under the rubric of the laws against murder. Sasportas took objection to Morteira's argument. He began his essay with an extended discussion about the importance of tradition and cited a pleth-

---

[63] Sasportas, *Ohel ya-akov*, #17, 22a–26a.
[64] BT Makot, 5b.
[65] Maimonides, Laws of Testimony, 20:2.

ora of sources to support his own position, including Maimonides's introduction to the *Code of Law* and Joseph Karo's commentary on Maimonides. In citing these sources, Sasportas established his complete control over the rabbinic tradition in whose name he spoke, and simultaneously raised the stakes of the argument. Morteira and Sasportas were not simply having a dispute about the laws pertaining to false witnesses, an issue that was not new and of only theoretical interest to two rabbis in seventeenth-century Amsterdam who could not administer capital punishment. They were now having an argument about the nature of the rabbinic tradition and their respective stances toward it. Repeatedly, Sasportas questioned Morteira's ability to make the argument he had attempted to make:

> How has your honor had the temerity to argue against everyone? [66]

> By-the-by I will not cease asking how your honor has come up with his ruling and upon what he is able to base his ruling? [67]

Sasportas twice attributed Morteira's ruling to apologetics. Morteira understood the lack of fairness in the rabbinic ruling and sought to work around it as a means to respond to Christians polemicizing against the absurdity of the ruling:

> On the issue of false witnesses, the Christians criticized our sages, of blessed memory, and our tradition. [68]

To Sasportas, such an apologia was completely beside the point when it came to determining the law.

In his attack on Morteira, Sasportas began to articulate an intellectual position that would characterize many of his later arguments in a range of controversies:

> By the by we shall not budge from our tradition, even if all the winds were to come and blow, they would not budge us from what has been passed down to us from our teachers. And even if matters of tradition do not need to conform to logic in order to be explained, we accept them

---

[66] ואיך מעכ״ת מלאו לבו לחלוק נגד כולם?
Sasportas, *Ohel ya-akov*, #17, 22b.

[67] ובין כה וכה לא אחדל מלדרוש מהיכן הוציא כ״ת הדין ההוא ועל מה יש לו לסמוך.
Ibid.

[68] קראו נוצרים בקורא תגר נגד חכמינו ז״ל ונגד קבלתינו בדין העדים זוממין.
Ibid.

nonetheless. This is the difference between belief on account of logic and belief on account of tradition.[69]

Morteira, Sasportas conceded, had a point. The rabbinic rulings on false witnesses did not make a lot of sense. If one were to apply reason strictly to this ruling, it would defy logic to let the witnesses off in a case where the person against whom they had testified falsely had been put to death. But strict logic was not the only source of knowledge available either to Sasportas or to Morteira. Both men saw themselves as bearers of the rabbinic tradition. Morteira was willing to dispense with certain parts of this tradition when logic and Christian polemics demanded; Sasportas, however, would have none of it. Against Morteira's ruling he hurled a plethora of sources that he cited chapter and verse, a technique he would often use in his later polemics. He appealed to tradition itself. In the articulation of his argument against Morteira, Sasportas began to gesture toward an intellectual posture that can be characterized not unjustly as conservative. It was not quite an argument against novelty as such, nor was Sasportas being difficult simply for the sake of being difficult. Both of those positions would come in due time. There was something more at stake for Sasportas in this seemingly arcane dispute over false witnesses.

Why did Sasportas write what amounted to a declaration of war against the principal *haham* of the place in which he was living as a temporary refugee? There was no doubt about the rabbinic hierarchy: only the year before in the printed pamphlet containing their respective eulogies for Moses de Mercado, Morteira had appeared as "el primero." Why would a guest attack his host who also happened to be some fifteen years his senior? In the final paragraph of his essay, Sasportas explained why he felt the need to argue with such ferocity about such an elementary issue:

> Indeed, it is true, all of these things are idle nonsense and wearisome to any sage who concedes the truth and follows the plain sense of the Oral Torah and does not become too sophisticated so as not to become stupefied, but it seemed worth it to me to suffer the shame of being de-

---

[69] ובין כה וכה מקבלתינו לא נזוז ואפילו כל הרוחות באות ונושבות אינם מזיזות אותנו ממה שנמסר לנו מפי רבותינו ואף אם דברי קבלה אינם נכנסי׳ תחת החקירה לתת טעם לה כי קבלה נקבל, וזה ההבדל יש בין האמונה מפאת החקירה ולאמונה מפאת הקבלה.

Ibid., #17, 23a.

nounced as a simpleton because of the great evil that would come to pass if I were to refrain from issuing instruction against the error that I have seen many people make in the wake of yours. Because you have publicized your opinions in print, and in order that this error not repeat itself among the masses, I have instructed you in the proper path.[70]

Morteira had publicized his errant views in print, and this, Sasportas claimed, demanded a response.

Prior to 1653 Morteira had published one book, a collection of fifty sermons that had appeared at the Benveniste press in 1645 under the title *Givat shaul*. In sermon 45, Morteira had made the argument about false witnesses that Sasportas attributed to him: in the event that the person against whom they falsely testified had been put to death, the false witness should be tried under the rubric of the law of murder.[71] I have been unable to find Morteira attributing his argument to the cause of Christian polemics as Sasportas insisted. Nonetheless, the legal argument, if not the social cause, had indeed appeared in print as Sasportas claimed. Sasportas had evidently read *Givat shaul* shortly after his arrival in Amsterdam. Although the book may have appeared in print eight years earlier, Sasportas encountered it as new when he arrived in the city. In this delayed reading, one catches a glimpse of the nonsimultaneity of print. What had been new in Amsterdam in 1645 was still new to a refugee scholar in 1653. People in Amsterdam were still talking about Morteira's printed sermons. This chatter among the elites about Morteira's position on false witnesses compelled Sasportas to respond to a sermon, a genre of rabbinic literature that had no legal consequences and usually did not invite response. Print was an ideologically neutral medium. Sasportas recognized its power to spread information and mold opinion, but it could be used equally for good or for ill. In the very same period that he worked intensively at the Hebrew presses in Amsterdam and expressed his ardent wish to appear as a printed author himself, he also wrote a blistering letter to his

---

[70] והן אמת כי כל הדברים הללו הם להג הרבה ויגיעת בשר לכל חכם המודה על האמת והולך בעקבות פשט תורה שבע״פ ואינו מתחכם יותר כדי שלא להשתומם אבל נראה לי לסבול חרפת איני לקרותי קטיל קני באגמ׳ בעד הרע הגדול המגיע אם אחדל מלהורות הטעו׳ שראיתי רבים נוטים אחרי טעותיך והדפסת דעתך זה בדפוס וללא תהיה הטעות הזו הולכת ומוספת בהמון הורייתיך הדרך הישרה

Ibid., #17, 26a.

[71] Saul Levi Morteira, *Givat shaul* (Amsterdam: Benveniste, 1645), sermon 45, 76b–78a. Discussion of false witnesses on 77a–77b.

colleague condemning his use of print to peddle what he considered false legal opinions.

Morteira evidently did not take kindly to being lectured by a younger man who was a relative newcomer to the city in which he served as *haham*. His response to Sasportas's letter does not survive, or has yet to be found. More likely he responded in the most devastating way that one intellectual can reprimand another: silence. In this case, the absence of evidence may actually indicate an absence. Without casting aside all due scholarly caution, I surmise that a second letter written by Sasportas to Morteira the following year indicates that Morteira was well practiced in the art of refusing to respond in writing to Sasportas.

At some point in 1654, Jacob de Mercado, the wealthy merchant who had financed the printing of his recently deceased nephew's biblical commentary, conveyed a legal question posed by David Israel Meldola in Livorno to Sasportas in Amsterdam. The case concerned the inheritance of a piece of property, and Sasportas ultimately decided in favor of the family who had been living on the property for the previous four years and who had undertaken considerable renovations, such as the construction of new buildings and the digging of wells. Their continued residence, he ruled, amounted to a right of possession.

There the matter would have ended and would have provided a vivid illustration of Sasportas's reach as a legal authority in his early forties. Even as he lived in Amsterdam without an official position, he still commanded the respect of his colleagues in Livorno, who appealed to him for his legal expertise. But the issue continued to preoccupy Sasportas, as one can determine from the very next responsum in *Ohel ya-akov* which begins:

> Concerning the previous issue, as I was told by a student that Rabbi Saul Levi Morteira contested my ruling.[72]

Later on in the same responsum, Sasportas named the emissary as Moses Raphael D'Aguilar, a rabbi who was considerably younger than both Sasportas and Morteira, and who would continue to play a minor role in Sasportas's life for years to come. Sasportas spent nearly half of the responsum taking issue with the form with which Morteira had

---

[72] על ענין הנז' לבעבור הוגד לי ע״י תלמיד א' שכמהו״רר שאול לבית לוי מורטירה פקפק בפסק ההוא.
Sasportas, *Ohel ya-akov*, #10, 11a.

criticized him. Sasportas described himself as a *haham* who was worthy of respect, not only at the level of his person but especially at the level of his office. As a *haham* he represented the law, the Torah, and Morteira should have given him his due even if he disagreed with him. Once again, the problem was not a simple disagreement between Sasportas and Morteira over a legal issue, although both in the case of false witnesses and in the case of inheritance Sasportas maintained to the end that he was in the right. The problem pertained to the social ramifications of rabbinic knowledge. In the first case, Morteira had made an argument that had been rational but had violated tradition, and he had promulgated his argument in print. In the second case, Sasportas had issued a ruling on a query that had been posed to him by a colleague in Livorno. His ruling had evidently circulated in writing among the rabbis in Amsterdam, something one can readily imagine in a city with only a few thousand Jews and a handful of rabbis, many of whom studied and taught at the Ets Haim Yeshiva. Morteira had slandered Sasportas, and this he could not abide. In justification of his scathing response to the comments he had heard repeated in Morteira's name, Sasportas wrote:

> I shall not worry if it is a denigration of my honor [to respond] for it would be a greater denigration to me if I were silent, and I allowed you to offer the ignoramuses an opportunity to turn toward your opinion in an instance when they should listen and follow the truth from whoever utters it. For I do not require that great scholars [would listen to what I say], as they will themselves understand the clarity of the truth and judge between us. [73]

Morteira had gone public and had made a mockery of Sasportas's ruling in front of the "ignoramuses," perhaps a reference to students in the yeshiva or the wealthy oligarchs who governed the Men of the Nation. Sasportas could not sit in silence while his reputation was destroyed. The law was on his side. He challenged Morteira to present his opinion next to his own and to let the people decide. What followed was a pyrotechnical display of erudition designed to overwhelm any

---

[73] ולא אחוש אם הוא זלזול בכבודי כי יותר זלזול הוא לי אם אשתוק ואניח כ״ת נותן מקום לדלת עם להטות לדבריו כ״ת במקום שהיה להם לשמוע אחר האמת ממי שאמרו. כי לת״ח אין אני צריך כי הם מעצמם ירדו לסוף דעת האמת הברור ויוכיחו בין שנינו

Ibid., #10, 11b.

countercriticism, a technique Sasportas would hone to almost perverse effect in the decades to come. It is not clear whether Morteira responded. His extant written work divides cleanly into two categories: sermons, only a fraction of which have appeared in print, and polemics against Christianity. Morteira was a *haham*, but it is not possible to assess from his surviving writings whether he was a Talmudist in Sasportas's mold.

SALEH CA. 1655–1658—1664

Documentation for the next few years in Sasportas's life is relatively scarce. His second fight with Morteira occurred in 1654, the same year that Isaac Aboab da Fonseca returned from Recife and took his place among the salaried clergy. Sasportas appears to have stayed in Amsterdam for another few years before he left Europe and returned to North Africa. As of September 1658, Sasportas can firmly be placed in Saleh. Why would Sasportas have left a bustling metropolitan center, with a Hebrew press and a flourishing yeshiva, for Saleh? Sasportas's connections with the Jews of Saleh appear to have predated his time in Amsterdam. In his eulogy for Moses de Mercado, Sasportas had discussed the book of Ecclesiastes. Toward the end of the eulogy he wrote:

> In a homily I preached in the town of Saleh when I heard about the complete sage, the pietist, the humble, the holy, my beloved soulmate, R. Isaac Sasportas, of blessed memory, who died in the prime of his life, I expounded at too great length upon the verse in Ecclesiastes "if the clouds be full of rain" (11:3).[74]

Prior to 1653, when his eulogy for Moses de Mercado appeared in print, Sasportas had visited or resided in Saleh and delivered a eulogy for a colleague named Isaac Sasportas who, like Moses de Mercado, had died at a young age.

Unlike Oran, a *presidio* of the Spanish Empire with a large population of Catholics and smaller populations of Jews and Muslims, Saleh

---

[74] ובדרוש שדרשתי במתא סאל״י לשמעות פקידת החכם השלם החסיד וענו קדוש יאמר לו אהובי ידיד נפשי כה״ר יצחק ששפורטש ז״ל שמת בקצרות שנים הארכתי יותר מדאי בפי׳ פסוקי קהלת 'אם ימלאו העבים גשם' וכו'. Sasportas, eulogy for Moses de Mercado, third leaf, verso.

in the mid-seventeenth century was an independent republic of sorts.[75] Between 1624 and 1666, Saleh had a population of around ten thousand people, the majority of whom were Muslim. The Muslim population was deeply divided between Moriscos, who had been expelled from Spain in 1609 and settled in Saleh, and the native population. In the middle of the 1620s, the sister towns of Rabat and Saleh had rebelled against the Saadian dynasty that governed Morocco. For a period of forty years, including all of the time that Sasportas lived there, Saleh operated as an independent republic that derived its revenue from the extremely profitable business of piracy. The governing council of Saleh enjoyed a productive relationship with the Dutch Republic, whose calculus was relatively simple: the corsair republic required recognition and good trade relations, especially a continuous flow of arms, and Saleh's council, in turn, offered the Dutch protection for their ships sailing off the Atlantic coast of North Africa. This relationship was hardly stable over the course of four decades, as it waxed and waned depending upon the larger context of Dutch-Spanish relations. Continuous political instability in North Africa itself ensured that the Dutch found it "impossible to maintain a coherent relationship with Morocco, or any part of Morocco, at state level."[76]

By the middle of the 1620s a small group of Portuguese Jews had gathered in Saleh; they serviced the pirate republic's burgeoning commerce with the Dutch Republic. Over the next several years, these Portuguese Jews served as the primary arms dealers between the Dutch Republic and pirates. The pirates needed the Jews of Amsterdam to supply them with arms and to handle the resale in northern Europe of high-value merchandise.[77] As a result of this commercial relationship a number of Portuguese Jewish families sent a representative to reside in Saleh and conduct their affairs in person. In a notarial deed in Amsterdam dated 23 September 1658, David de Mercado, described as a businessman in Amsterdam, granted power of attorney to David de Vries, consul in Saleh, to receive property from Jacob Sasportas, resident in Saleh who owed property to David de Mercado.[78] David de

---

[75] Jonathan Israel, "Piracy, Trade and Religion: The Jewish Role in the Rise of the Muslim Corsair Republic of Saleh (1624–1666)," in Israel, *Diasporas*.

[76] Ibid., 309.

[77] Ibid., 301.

[78] SAA entry no. 5075, no. 2205, Not. A. Lock, 23 September 1658, fol. 466.

Mercado may well have been a relative of Jacob de Mercado, who had financed the printing of Sasportas's eulogy for Moses de Mercado. In the 1650s, Sasportas had extensive dealings with the Mercado family, and it seems reasonable to assume that in addition to financing the publication of his eulogy and conveying the substance of a legal responsum from Livorno, members of the Mercado family would have loaned him money in advance of a long journey to Saleh. Yet the notarial deed only establishes Sasportas's presence in Saleh. It does not explain why he was there or what he was actually doing there. Sasportas may have served as an agent for the Mercado family in Saleh just as Eleazar Ribeiro had served the Curiel family a few decades earlier, or Benjamin Cohen had served his own family for several decades.[79] The suggestion is not as absurd as it may seem at first blush. Sasportas may have been a *haham* and a kabbalist, but he also needed to earn a living. His relations with the other *hahamim* in Amsterdam were at best fraught. He hailed from a family that had extensive experience serving as diplomats, and he himself had probably visited Saleh at some point in the past. It seems plausible that the Mercado family would have sent him there as a representative.

For the next six to seven years Sasportas resided in Saleh, apart from a short visit to Spain, a subject to which I shall return presently. Whatever his dealings with the Mercado family while in Saleh, Sasportas continued to serve as a *haham*. Just as had occurred in Amsterdam, when Jews from elsewhere in the Sephardic Diaspora turned to Sasportas for his expertise, Jews from elsewhere in Morocco looked to him for legal guidance. *Ohel ya-akov* contains a handful of responsa Sasportas composed while in Saleh. Unfortunately these legal writings cannot be supplemented with records kept by the state in the form of notarial archives, or by the local Jews in the form of tax receipts and salary payments. Nonetheless, the responsa offer some insights into the conditions of Sasportas's life while he was in Saleh. Sasportas signed one of the responsa that he composed in Saleh "the exiled and the banished," the same phrase that he used in the signature he appended to some of his editorial notes in the books he had edited in Amsterdam. [80] Rather than an empty cliché, the phrase appears to indicate that Sasportas continued to see himself as out of place while living in

---

[79] Israel, "Piracy, Trade and Religion," 293.
[80] Sasportas, *Ohel ya-akov*, #11, 14b.

Saleh. Sasportas had positive things to say about his time in Oran and in Tlemcen only in retrospect.

In a series of responsa that appear to date from the year 1662, Sasportas wrote to a rabbinic court in Fez about a marriage case.[81] In Jewish law marriage involves a two-step process, with the rites of betrothal followed separately by the rites of marriage. In the case at hand, Sasportas had ruled that the court should compel through the use of force a man who had performed the rites of betrothal but was refusing to perform the rites of marriage. The court in Fez consisted of three members: Emmanuel Siriro, Saadiah Danan, and Isaac ben Vidal Tzarfati.[82] The rabbis in Fez had not taken kindly to Sasportas's ruling and wrote a blistering response, extensive portions of which Sasportas included in his second responsum on the subject in *Ohel ya-akov*.[83] At issue between Sasportas and his colleagues in Fez was the problem of jurisdiction, a problem that would repeatedly resurface throughout Sasportas's life. Sasportas may have been a great Talmudist, but he was living in Saleh and not in Fez. It was not at all clear whether he had the authority to intervene in a legal dispute that was taking place in another city. The extant evidence does not indicate how the case was resolved; however, it does indicate that Sasportas was prepared to go to great lengths to defend his own honor. The jurists in Fez had rebuked Sasportas for infringing upon their jurisdiction and issuing a contrary ruling. Sasportas responded that he had frequently done so in the past when asked by other judges to issue a ruling, but he had never been accused of infringement upon another court's jurisdiction.

> You have further said, "by morning and we saw the hardships that had befallen us" (Ex. 18:8), through your rebuke. With your rage and your writing you have come to rule over us in our own house! Thus far your own words. But these words reveal the main point of your complaint, which is that the crown of the law is worn by someone other than your-

---

[81] Tishby dates the responsa to 1660 (see Sasportas, *ZNZ*, 136n9); however, the manuscript of *Ohel ya-akov*, which surfaced at auction after Tishby completed his edition, appears to give the date of 1662. See YU MS 1251, vol. 2 5b. The dating remains tentative, as the long-standing problem of Sasportas's handwriting is compounded in this instance by faded ink.

[82] Haim Bentov, "The Siriro Family" (Hebrew), in *Fez ve-arim aherot be-Morocco*, ed. Moshe Bar-Asher, Moshe Amar, and Shimon Sharvit (Ramat Gan: Bar-Ilan University Press, 2013), 338–339. Isaac ben Vidal Tzarfati should not be confused with a rabbi of the same name who died in 1620. See Bentov, 338n4.

[83] For a reconstruction of their response, see Haim Bentov, introduction (Hebrew) to Isaac ben Vidal Tzarfati, *Toledot Yitzhak* (Jerusalem: Sephardic Community in Beit ha-Kerem, 1996).

selves, and this you cannot bear. And that is why you claim that I have come to rule over you in your own house. But the Lord knows that my intention has been to submit myself to those who study the law, not to rule over them. My letter was thus meant to exalt the Torah and to glorify it, just as I have done in my dealings with other sages and rabbis, who accepted my rulings as balm to the soul even when they ran counter to their own rulings, never judging me harshly as if I had come to rule over them in their own house. And I hardly need to add that even the Ashkenazi sages who sit in judgment today, and who were distant from me throughout my stay in Amsterdam, would tell you as much. Learn from them how to chastise me![84]

The letter from the court in Fez had left Sasportas fulminating with rage. He resented his colleagues who had portrayed his contrary ruling as a quest for power and an infringement upon their territory. He saw his ruling as a simple quest for the truth of the Torah. Sasportas portrayed his colleagues in Fez as having breached the bounds of rabbinic decorum. In many other instances, he had overturned the rulings of other courts, but his decisions had never been dismissed as a quest for power, not even by the Ashkenazim in Amsterdam.

At a number of points in his second letter to Fez, Sasportas revealed crucial aspects about his life in Saleh.

I did not refrain from showing [your letter] to several members of our yeshiva, Ayelet Ahavim, so that they would serve as my witness. [85]

And slightly later on:

When your letter arrived, we were studying the first chapter of [tractate] Sanhedrin in our yeshiva.[86]

---

[84] עוד נאמר ויהי בבקר וירא את התלאה אשר מצאתנו בתוכחת כ״ת יבא עלינו בכעסו ובקולמוסו לרדותינו בתוך ביתנו עכ״ד גיליתם עיקר תלונותכם בתיבות הללו כי כל עיקרה הראות בכתר ההיא שיש יושב על כסא דין זולתכם מה שהוא נמנע ולכן אמרתם לרדותינו בתוך ביתנו אל אלדים הוא ידע כי כונתי להשתעבד ללומדי דת ודין לא לרדותם ולהגדיל תורה ולהאדיר היה כתבי על האופן ההוא כאשר נסיתי עם חכמים ורבנים זולתכם והיו דברי להם למשיב נפשם ואף שהיו כנגד הוראותם ומעולם לא דנו אותי לכף חובה לומר לרדותינו בתוך ביתנו ואין אני צריך לומר היושבים היום על כסא דין ופסקי חכמי אשכנז הרחוקים ממני כל עוד היותי באמשטרדם יגידו נא לכם ומהם תקחו מוסר השבט כנגדי.

Sasportas, *Ohel ya-akov*, #3, 5b.

[85] אך לקצת בני ישיבתנו איי״לת אהבי״ם לא חדלתי מלהראותה בעבור תהיה לי לעדה

Ibid., #3, 5a.

[86] בבוא כתיבכם בישיבתנו היינו קורים פ״ק דסנהדרין.

Ibid., #3, 6a.

Evidently the very small Jewish population of Saleh supported a yeshiva called Ayelet Ahavim where Sasportas taught Talmud. Saleh was
also a destination for rabbinic emissaries from Palestine who traveled
to raise funds for charity.

> In fact, when I showed the severity of your words to the emissaries
> from Palestine, may the land be rebuilt and restored, they tore their
> clothing.[87]

The emissaries visiting Saleh were so appalled by the language used by
the rabbis of Fez that they tore their clothing as a sign of mourning.
These emissaries, who remained anonymous in this letter, were probably Solomon Navarro and Elisha Ashkenazi.[88] A few years later Elisha Ashkenazi's son, Nathan of Gaza, would contribute to a considerably greater crisis of rabbinic authority in Sasportas's life than the one
his father watched as a bystander in Saleh.

Saleh was on the circuit of emissaries from Palestine, and Sasportas
was thus able to meet other colleagues during his time there. Nonetheless, he still thought of himself as living at the edge of the known
world. One indication of its relative remoteness appears in an undated
responsum signed from Saleh. The responsum pertained to an inheritance case. A colleague of Sasportas named David b. Solomon had recently died, leaving behind a widow with a seven-year-old son and a
five-year-old daughter. David b. Solomon, however, had been previously married. A son from this prior marriage, who had not attended
his father at his death, arrived shortly thereafter to make an inheritance claim. When he discovered that his father had very few assets,
he took possession of his father's books as his inheritance. When his
father's widow took the son to court, Sasportas's colleagues turned
to him for legal counsel. Sasportas initially sought to rebuff the question entirely:

> When I sat as a judge in the city of Tlemcen, may God preserve and pro-
> tect it, which was sovereign over all of the surrounding areas, there was
> no question that from time to time you could turn to me for instruction
> about an issue, for there was no great distance between us. But now,

---

[87] ובאמת שלוחי א״י תו״בב שנמצאו כאן בהראותי אותם חוזק דבריכם קרעו בגדיהם.
Ibid., #3, 6b.
[88] As discovered by Tishby see Sasportas, ZNZ, 136n9.

when the distance is great, even though our minds are quite close, why do you have to trouble yourself about such a case?[89]

Tlemcen, where Sasportas had once served, was considerably closer to Tafilat, the source of the question, than Saleh, if not in actual miles then in the legal jurisdiction of a seventeenth-century rabbi. Sasportas had a form of sovereignty at the time that he served in Tlemcen that he claims to have lacked in Saleh. Sasportas's apologia was largely rhetorical as he proceeded to answer the question at hand in great detail. His rhetoric reveals that he considered his rabbinic position in Saleh a considerable step down from his previous one in Tlemcen.

Sasportas's answer offers a number of glimpses into the conditions of his reading and writing. The legal issue pertained to the possession of books, and Sasportas sought to assess whether the books had been jointly possessed by David b. Solomon and his wife. The issue was not quite as obvious as it might have seemed, and Sasportas posed the following question as a means to answer it:

> But if the aforementioned books were in a place designated especially for the *haham*, of blessed memory, where he would study and meditate upon God's Torah, and the aforementioned widow had no use for that place, which is called a *studio* in our foreign language, then we do not rule that the books are in the possession of the widow.[90]

Scholars, Sasportas seemed to say, studied in solitude. The rooms for their solitary contemplation had a designated name in a foreign language: the studio. If the rabbi used his books in isolation and separated them from his domestic life, then his widow could not claim that they belonged to her rather than her stepson.

Sasportas's own working conditions in Saleh were far from ideal when he composed his response to the query. Thus he recalled seeing a phrase in a source that he could no longer find:

---

[89] כי בהיותי יושב על מדין דינא דמתא תלמסאן יע״א אשר כל גלילותיכם מתנהג׳ על פיה אין מהתימה שכ״ת
לפעמי׳ ישאל מפי דבר להורות היאך נתנהג בענין ההוא וליכא מרחק רב בינותינו אבל לעת כזאת שהמרחק רב אף
שהלבבות קרובות ובמלתא דתליא בדינא למה לך לצער עצמך בכולי האי.
Sasportas, *Ohel ya-akov*, #11, 12b.

[90] אבל אם הספרים הנז׳ הם במקום מיוחד לחכם ז״ל ששם תמיד הוא מעיין והוגה בתורת ה׳ ואין לה לאלמנה הנז׳
תשמיש כלל במקום ההוא הנקרא בכאן בלשון לע״ז איסטודיו לא אמרינן דברשות האלמנה קיימי הספרים הנז׳
Ibid., #11, 13a.

I have already found this in a manuscript of responsa by R. Solomon ibn
Adret but I cannot recall the passage. [91]

Saleh was not Amsterdam. Sasportas lacked both the treasures of Menasseh ben Israel's private collection and the vast library in the semi-
public collection of Ets Haim. He recalled having seen a reference but
could not pin it down and had to make do with an admission of his
own inaccuracy.

SPAIN 1659

While he resided in Saleh, Sasportas may have traveled to Spain.
Sources for this possible trip are late and contradictory and must be
used with considerable caution. Before turning to them, however, it is
worth examining the limits and possibilities of Jewish life in Spain in
the middle of the seventeenth century, over 150 years after the expulsion of the Jews. Historians have discovered several types of Jews who
lived in Spain. Conversos, or descendants of conversos who had reverted to the Judaism of their ancestors in one of the many centers of
the Sephardic Diaspora, occasionally returned to Spain.[92] Knowledge
of these men and women emerges both from the archival records of
the Jewish settlements in which they lived after leaving the Iberian
Peninsula as well as from the archives of the Holy Office in Spain itself. In one instance, a figure named Cristóbal Méndez, Yosef Kaplan
has demonstrated how careful historians must be in reconstructing the
life of an individual Jew in the seventeenth century.[93] Cristóbal Méndez appears in a number of different places, as a Jew in Amsterdam, a

[91] כי כבר מצאתי בכתיבת יד שו״ת להרשב״א בשאולות הכתובות בכ״י ולא זכרתי סימנו.

Ibid., #11, 14a.

[92] Yosef Kaplan, "The Travels of Portuguese Jews from Amsterdam to the 'Lands of Idolatry'
(1644–1724)," in *Jews and Conversos: Studies in Society and the Inquisition*, ed. Yosef Kaplan (Jerusalem: Magnes Press, 1985), 197–224; Natalia Muchnik, "Des intrus en pays d'inquisition: présence
et activités des juifs dans l'Espagne du xvii sièscle," *REJ* 164 (2005): 119–156. Muchnik refers to
Jacob Saportas in seventeenth-century Spain; see 126, 145–146, 149. Given that this Jacob Saportas was in Madrid in 1642, rather than in 1659, it seems to be a different person with the same
name rather than the rabbi who later opposed Sabbetai Zevi.

[93] "Between Cristóbal Méndez and Abraham Franco de Silveyra: The Odyssey of a Converso
in the Seventeenth Century" (Hebrew), in *Asupah le-Yosef: Kovetz mehkarim shai le-Yosef Hacker*,
ed. Yaron Ben-Naeh et al. (Jerusalem: Zalman Shazar Center, 2014), 406–440.

repentant Catholic in Madrid, and again as a Jew in Amsterdam. As a former Catholic, Cristóbal Méndez and other Jews like him were subject to the jurisdiction of the Holy Office. Kaplan has demonstrated how much these files have to reveal about the conditions of Jewish life in places as far away from the inquisitorial courtroom as Venice or Amsterdam.

Sasportas was not born and raised as a Catholic and would not have been subject to the jurisdiction of the Holy Office if he indeed traveled to Spain. In addition to conversos and former conversos, historians have discovered another category of Jews who visited and, in some cases, even lived for substantial periods of time in early modern Spain.[94] These men, and they were usually men, obtained authorization to travel and reside in Spain and constituted a category referred to as "judíos de permiso."[95] They were usually either businessmen or diplomats or both. If Sasportas traveled to Spain from Saleh, he would have traveled as a "judío de permiso." Sasportas was a man who wrote about himself repeatedly throughout the second half of his life. Virtually every text he wrote contains some autobiographical reflections, many of which refer to his travels.[96] To the best of my knowledge, he does not discuss his visit to Spain at any point in his extant writings. These possible silences in the historical record reinforce the need for caution when turning to the two early modern sources that point to Sasportas's presence in Spain. The first appeared in a book printed in Sasportas's lifetime by his friend Daniel Levi de Barrios. A Spanish poet and chronicler who knew Sasportas quite well in his later years when they both lived in Amsterdam, De Barrios composed a book entitled *Triumpho del govierno popular*, printed in Amsterdam in 1683. At the time Sasportas had recently returned to Amsterdam from Livorno, and would have been in a position to speak with De Barrios prior to the publication of his book. De Barrios discussed Sasportas on a number of occasions, and in

---

[94] Yosef Hayim Yerushalmi, "Professing Jews in Post-Expulsion Spain and Portugal," in *Salo Wittmayer Baron Jubilee Volume*, ed. Saul Lieberman (Jerusalem: American Academy of Jewish Research, 1974), 2:1023–1058.

[95] Mercedes García-Arenal and Gerard Wiegers, *A Man of Three Worlds: Samuel Pallache, a Moroccan Jew in Catholic and Protestant Europe* (Baltimore: Johns Hopkins University Press, 2003), 13, as cited by Kaplan, ""Between Cristóbal Méndez and Abraham Franco de Silveyra," 406n2.

[96] Thus he recalls seeing the Tower of London in his glosses to Nathan of Gaza's prophecy adduced in Sasportas, *ZNZ*, 10, and he mentions his stopover in Marseilles on his way from Livorno to Amsterdam; see Tishby, "Letters by Rabbi Jacob Sasportas," 148.

one instance traced his lineage to Maimonides rather than Nahman-ides.[97] In his discussion of the Jews of Spanish Oran, De Barrios included a single sentence about Sasportas's visit to Spain:

> In the year 1659 Jacob Sasportas, chief rabbi of the Jews of the king of Tlemcen, undertook a diplomatic mission on behalf of Santon Ben-buquer, who was besieged in the fortress of Saleh by the Arabs of the city, to request help from the queen regent of Spain, who sent him to the Duke of Medinaceli who at the time was living in Puerto de Santa Maria.[98]

A number of points in De Barrios's account can be corroborated with some qualification. By 1659 it had been roughly a decade since Sasportas had been the rabbi of Tlemcen, but he continued to refer to his time as a rabbinic jurist there throughout his life, and De Barrios may well have taken his cue from his subject. There was chronic instability throughout the entire duration of the corsair republic of Saleh. Three constituent populations vied for power: the Moriscos expelled from Spain who had settled there after 1609, the local population, and the Moroccan sultan. Relations between the Moriscos and the local Arab population were often quite tense. H. Z. Hirschberg identified the figure referred to by De Barrios as Santon Benbuquer with Marabout Ben Bakr, a leader who was allied with the Moriscos.[99] Whether or not this identification is correct, it is within the realm of possibility that the local population had besieged one of the leaders allied with the Moriscos in the Castillo, or Kasbah, in Saleh as control over the Kasbah changed hands repeatedly during this period.[100] Sasportas was in Saleh at the time, and the Jewish merchants who resided in Saleh repeatedly served as diplomats between the European powers and the corsair republic. As De Barrios recounts the episode, Santon Benbuquer sent Sasportas to the Spanish court to obtain relief from the siege.

---

[97] Goldish, "Hakham Jacob Sasportas and the Former Conversos," 150n1.

[98] "Jacob Saportas Cabeça Rabinica de los Judios del Reyno de Tremecen, passó en el Año de 1659. por Embiado del Santon Benbuquer que estava cercado en el Castillo de Salé por los de la Ciudad y los Arabes apedir Socorro a la Reyna Regente de España, que se lo concedio por via del Duque de Madina Celi, que entonces vivia en el Puerto de Sancta Maria." Daniel Levi de Barrios, *Triumpho del govierno popular* (Amsterdam, 1683), "Historia Universal Iudayca," 15.

[99] *A History of the Jews of North Africa* (Leiden: Brill, 1981), 2:67.

[100] Israel, "Piracy, Trade and Religion."

De Barrios wrote that the queen regent sent Sasportas to the Duke of Medinaceli to deal with this request. This seems to reflect the political situation at the time De Barrios published his book in 1683 rather than the time of Sasportas's ostensible visit to Spain in 1659. Simply put, in 1659 Phillip IV was still in power, and his second wife, Marianna of Austria, did not begin to rule as regent until his death in 1665.[101] Nonetheless, it would have made perfect sense for the Spanish court to have sent Sasportas to the Duke of Medinaceli. In 1659 Phillip IV had other priorities apart from the persistent low-level conflict on the Atlantic coast of North Africa. He desperately wanted to end the decades-long conflict with France and was negotiating the Treaty of the Pyrenees, which was signed that November. The Duke of Medinaceli was a powerful figure at the Spanish court whose influence "was of great importance for the defense of the Andalusian coast and the southern frontier with Portugal."[102] Finally, De Barrios indicated that Sasportas was sent to him at his residence in Puerta Santa Maria on the southern coast of Spain outside of Cadiz. As he reports it, Sasportas's mission was a great success.

Another mention of Sasportas's mission to Spain appeared in the summary of his life composed by his son Abraham as one of the introductions to the posthumous publication of *Ohel ya-akov*. As in the case of De Barrios, Abraham Sasportas needed only a single sentence:

He settled here [in Amsterdam] for some time, about a decade, until the land of his youth became considerably calmer. There he returned to the height of his glory, for the king of Marrakech sent for him, and dispatched him with respect and glory on a mission to the king of Spain, may he be exalted. About this, he [Jacob Sasportas] gave thanks for his lot, for the Lord restored the captivity of Jacob (Ez. 39:25). [103]

---

[101] De Barrios made a passing reference Sasportas's mission to Spain in his eulogy that appeared in print fifteen years after his chronicle. In this brief mention, he refers to the king of Spain, "al Rey Hispano," rather than the queen regent. I am unable to resolve this discrepancy. See Daniel Levi de Barrios, *Monte Hermoso de la Ley Divina*, 1 (Arabic numeral pagination rather than Roman numeral pagination).

[102] Alistair Malcolm, *Royal Favouritism and the Governing Elite of the Spanish Monarchy, 1640–1665* (Oxford: Oxford University Press, 2017), 160.

[103] וישב פה ימים או עשור עד אשר נחה שקטה הארץ מקום גדולתו וחזר לאיתנו מקום נטיעתו כי מלך מרואיקוס
שלח לקרא אותו לשלחו בשליחותו אל מלך ספרד יר"ה בכבוד ובגדולה ועל זה נתן הודאה על חלקו כי שב ה' את שבות
יעקב.

Abraham Sasportas, introduction to Sasportas, *Ohel ya-akov*, 3b.

Nearly four decades after his father's death, Abraham Sasportas described his diplomatic errand as having been undertaken on behalf of the king of Marrakech to the king of Spain. From the narrative context in which it appears, one can deduce that the mission occurred at some point between Sasportas's first stay in Amsterdam in the early 1650s and his residence a decade later in London, the next episode in his father's life to which Abraham turned. In short, Abraham Sasportas and De Barrios agree that Jacob Sasportas entered Spain from Saleh. They differ as to his employer, the Marabout who was allied with Moriscos in Saleh, as implied by De Barrios, or the king of Marrakech, as implied by Abraham. Who was the king of Marrakech? The answer to this question depends largely upon the date of Sasportas's mission, a date about which Abraham remained obstinately silent. In short, the Saadian dynasty that had governed Morocco and against which the corsair republic had rebelled in the 1620s was collapsing in the late 1650s, and a new dynasty begun by Sultan Mawlay Al-Rashid was in the process of consolidating power. De Barrios and Abraham Sasportas both mention Sasportas's mission to Spain as a point of pride. De Barrios explicitly described it as a success, and Abraham cast the episode as his father's return to glory in his native land. These ostensible triumphs should be treated with considerable skepticism. At the level of diplomacy, Saleh remained unstable until the collapse of the corsair republic in 1666. Sasportas's own time in Saleh did not last all that much longer.[104]

LONDON 1664–1665

Sasportas left Saleh in a hurry. The increasing political instability in the region as well as a famine compelled his flight. When he arrived in the Dutch Republic, two of his colleagues in the rabbinate had since died: his former employer Menasseh ben Israel in 1657 and his former rival Saul Levi Morteira in 1659. The lay oligarchs in Amsterdam had appointed Isaac Aboab da Fonseca as *haham*, a position he would occupy until his death in 1693. Still there was no room for Sasportas. There were, however, other possibilities for employment in the rabbinate in the western Sephardic Diaspora. At this juncture, Sasportas may

---

[104] Sasportas, *ZNZ*, 136.

have received an invitation to serve as *haham* in Livorno. Evidence for
this possibility survives only in accounts written by Sasportas and post-
dates the period by several years.[105] Whether or not wealthy merchants
from Livorno actually implored Sasportas while he was in Amsterdam
in 1664 to serve the Men of the Nation in their hometown, Sasportas
would not move there until well over a decade later in 1678. By that
point, Sabbetai Zevi would be old news. Instead, in 1664 Sasportas traveled with his family to London, where a group of Portuguese conversos had openly reverted to Judaism.[106] The resettlement of the Jews in
England was bound up with the Portuguese Jews in Amsterdam from
its inception. Menasseh ben Israel had embarked on a mission, less than
a decade earlier, to persuade Oliver Cromwell to allow Jews to reside
in England.[107] Cromwell may well have demurred at granting the official recognition Menasseh ben Israel had sought, but by the early 1660s
Restoration London was home to a growing number of Jews. In 1664
they constituted a small but significant group, and they appealed to
their coreligionists in Amsterdam for help in finding a rabbi and ritual
slaughterer. In answer to this call, Sasportas set out to serve as the first
haham of the Spanish and Portuguese Jews in London.

Sasportas's time in London would prove to be relatively brief, just
over a year between March 1664 and August 1665 when he fled owing
to the plague.[108] Very little survives either of London itself, which was
consumed by the Great Fire a year later, or of Sasportas's writing from
this period. The few letters that do remain indicate that he wasted little time in entering into a contentious dispute with the lay oligarchs.[109]
He continued to serve as a rabbinic jurist while he was in London and

---

[105] For the account from 1668, see Sasportas, *ZNZ*, 57–58, and Tishby's note on 58n1; for the
account from 1671, see Sasportas, *Ohel ya-akov*, #41, 45a, as cited by Tishby in the aforementioned
note.

[106] On the readmission of the Jews to England, see David S. Katz and Yosef Kaplan, *Gerush ve-
shivah: yehude Angliyah be-hilufe ha-zemanim* (Jerusalem: Zalman Shazar Center, 1993); David S.
Katz, *The Jews in the History of England, 1485–1850* (New York: Clarendon Press, 1994), chap. 3;
Todd M. Endelman, *The Jews of Britain, 1656–2000* (Berkeley: University of California Press, 2002),
chap. 1.

[107] Ismar Schorsch, "From Messianism to Realpolitik: Menasseh ben Israel and the Readmission of the Jews to England," *Proceedings of the American Academy of Jewish Research* 45 (1978):
187–208; Andrew Crome, "English National Identity and the Readmission of the Jews, 1650–1656,"
Journal of Ecclesiastical History 66 (2015): 280–301.

[108] Lionel D. Barnett, *El libro de los acuerdos, being the records and accompts of the Spanish and
Portuguese synagogue of London from 1663 to 1681* (Oxford: Oxford University Press, 1931), 19, 30.

[109] Tishby, "New Information on the 'Converso' Community in London."

answered questions from Amsterdam and Saleh. In a letter to his former student in Amsterdam Isaac Nahar, he indicates that he and his family had experienced a considerable amount of distress shortly after their arrival in London:

> But grief turned to joy since my little son Abraham, may the Lord protect him, a baby who was so ill that the doctors had despaired and thought he was at death's door... has improved dramatically, and is now convalescing.[110]

Sasportas had arrived in London with his son Samuel, who was old enough to serve as the ritual slaughterer, and his son Abraham, who at the time was a baby and quite sick. Both sons would play critical roles in Sasportas's later life. Samuel would predecease his father, but his estate would add considerably to his father's wealth; Abraham would live well into the eighteenth century, and it was only through his efforts that his father's writings would appear in print.

Nahar had turned to his former teacher with a question about the legal status of a Torah scroll that contained sections of parchment of different lengths. Sasportas ruled that the Torah scrolls in Amsterdam were fit for use and recounted the following anecdote along the way:

> I remember a similar circumstance that occurred in one of the congregations of Rabbi Ephraim Nakawa, of blessed memory, and I examined their Torah scrolls and I found that three pages of the parchment were not even, some were longer than others, and there were open spaces on the top and on the bottom. At the time I had doubts very similar to yours. But we found a professional scribe named Aaron ibn Simin, and when we examined the scrolls we could not find any reason to render them invalid. When I asked the members of the congregation about these scrolls, they responded that when the city had been beseiged, the Jews had fled to a citadel and had taken all of the scrolls from the synagogues for safekeeping. But they had removed the staves and separated the parchment so that they would no longer be holy and would be easier to carry. As a result, they mixed up the pieces of parchment. When there

---

[110] ותוגה לשמח' נהפכ' מהיו' בני הקטן אברה' ה"י תינוק מוטל בעריסה באשתא צמירתא עד שנתיאשו בעלי רפוא' ממנו כעומד למיתה . . . והנו הי' עומד לרפואה.

Sasportas, *Ohel ya-akov*, #5, 7a. On Nahar, see Carsten L. Wilke, "*Midrashim from Bordeaux*: A Theological Controversy inside the Portuguese Jewish Diaspora at the Time of Spinoza's Excommunication," *European Journal of Jewish Studies* 6 (2012): 207–247, and below.

was peace in the city, they went back and reassembled the scrolls one by one, and they attached the pieces of parchment to one another and even though they were not equal in their shape, they were equal in their writing. [111]

Sasportas's letter to Nahar from London expressed all the warmth of a teacher writing to a former student who had become his colleague. The dismembered Torah scrolls in the unnamed town in North Africa had left a vivid impression on Sasportas. He was keenly aware of the fragility of Jewish life, given the political instability that troubled so much of the seventeenth century. Both his relationship with Nahar and his fear of instability would accompany his response to the upheaval that began a year later when news of the Messiah Sabbetai Zevi began to arrive in Europe.

Repeatedly Sasportas ascribed his flight from London to the arrival of the plague.[112] The Great Plague of 1665 had a devastating impact on Restoration London.[113] Sasportas fled the city in August, roughly four months after the plague had begun to spread uncontrollably the previous April and at the height of the epidemic. By September of 1665, the death rate had reached eight thousand per week. Much like his departure from Saleh less than two years earlier, Sasportas's departure from London occurred in extreme haste. His family did not remain together, as his eldest son, Samuel, traveled to Barbados while Sasportas himself traveled to Hamburg.[114] The choice of his destination might not have been much of a choice at all. Although he continued to remain in close

---

[111] ומה שאני זוכר בזה הוא מעשה רב שבא לידי בכעין זה בקהל א' של הרב אפרים נקאוה ז"ל ובדקתי בספריה
ומצאתי ג' מהם שאין הדפים שוין בשיטין וקצתם עודפים על קצתם שנראה כמקום פנוי למטה או למעלה וחששתי כעין
חשש כ"ת ונמצא שם סופר א' שמו ה"ר אהרון ז' שימין בקי בספרי' ודקדקנו ולא מצאנו שום מקו' לפסול ושאלתי לבני
הק"ק על טיבן של ספרים ההם והגידו לי שכאשר הוקפה העיר כרכום ברחו היהודים למבצר ולקחו כל ספרי בתי
כנסיות עמהם להיותם לפלטה והסירו והסירו עמודיהם והפרידו היריעות ללא השאירם בקדושתם ולהיותם נוח לשאת אשר
מזה נתערבו כל הספרים וכל היריעות וכאשר היה שלום בעיר חזרו לחבר כל הספרים כל ספר בפני עצמו וקצתם
לקחו מיריעות קצתם ואע"פ שאינם שווים בדמותם היו שוים בכתיבתן.

Sasportas, *Ohel ya-akov*, #5, 7a. Nahar and Sasportas also exchanged letters about a ruling concerning clay utensils. See *Ohel ya-akov* ##7–8, 8a–8b. The exchange concerning the Torah scrolls is signed from London; the signature to the exchange about clay utensils does not contain a location. For the probability that it too was sent from London, see Tishby, "New Information on the 'Converso' Community in London," 473n18.

[112] Sasportas, *ZNZ*, 58, 167; Sasportas, *Ohel ya-akov*, #16, 21b.

[113] A. Lloyd Moote and Dorothy C. Moote, *The Great Plague: The Story of London's Most Deadly Year* (Baltimore: Johns Hopkins University Press, 2004).

[114] On Samuel Sasportas's flight to Barbados, see Wilfred S. Samuel, "The Jews of London and the Great Plague (1665)," *Miscellanies of the Jewish Historical Society of England* 3 (1937): 12.

touch with his colleagues in Amsterdam, he left London in the summer of 1665 in the midst of the Second Anglo-Dutch War, and travel to Amsterdam from London may not have been possible. In the fall of 1665 Sasportas found himself in the Free Imperial City of Hamburg, where he lived on charity sent to him by the Portuguese Jews of Amsterdam. It was thus by a series of accidents that Sasportas arrived in Hamburg, and these accidents conditioned his ability to respond to the most central crisis of seventeenth-century Judaism: the acceptance of Sabbetai Zevi as the Messiah. Had Sasportas accompanied his son Samuel to Barbados, he might not have heard about Sabbetai Zevi at all; had Sasportas fled London for Amsterdam rather than for Hamburg, he would never have written the many letters to the rabbinate in Amsterdam that form so much of *Zizath novel zvi*.

TWO

AUTHORITY

One does not defeat a Messiah with common-sense arguments.
—Czeslaw Milosz

Figure 4. Menasseh ben Israel, *Nishmat hayim* (Amsterdam: Menasseh Ben Israel, 1651), title page. This book, which was edited and corrected by Sasportas upon his arrival in Amsterdam, contained a discussion of *Sefer hasidim*. A work of medieval Ashkenazi pietism, *Sefer hasidim* was seemingly quite far from Sasportas's intellectual world, but it became a crucial source for his argument against Sabbatianism. © The British Library Board. Sefer Nishmat hayim/1933.d.14.

Rabbis have had a vexed relationship with the Messiah and messianic movements since antiquity. Gerson D. Cohen distinguished between the messianic postures of Ashkenazi Jews, whose predominant cultural influence was Franco-Germany in the Middle Ages and Poland-Lithuania in the early modern period, and that of Sephardic Jews, whose predominant cultural influence was Babylonia and the Iberian Peninsula in the Middle Ages and the Ottoman Empire and western Europe in the early modern period. Cohen characterized Ashkenazi Jews as quietist, passive, and given to heroic acts of martyrdom, in contrast to Sephardic Jews, who were politically activist, intellectually dynamic, and revolutionary.[1] In response to Cohen's framework, Elisheva Carlebach has written, "The grand role in Jewish messianism of Sephardic rabbinic conservatism, from the *Geonim* [of Babylonia] to Maimonides through Jacob Sasportas simply did not enter into Cohen's neat typology."[2] The list of Sephardic conservative thinkers identified by Carlebach runs from Maimonides and Nahmanides in medieval Iberia and Egypt, through Isaac Abravanel and Solomon Lebeit Halevi in

[1] Gerson D. Cohen, "Messianic Postures of Ashkenazim and Sephardim," in *Studies in the Variety of Rabbinic Cultures* (Philadelphia: JPS, 1991), 271–297. Epigraph from Czeslaw Milosz, *The Captive Mind* (New York: Penguin Classics, 2001), 42.

[2] Elisheva Carlebach, "The Sabbatian Posture of German Jewry," in *Ha-halom ve-shivro*, ed. Rachel Elior (Jerusalem: Hebrew University, 2001), 2:6. See also eadem, "Between History and Hope: Jewish Messianism in Ashkenaz and Sepharad," *Third Annual Lecture of the Victor J. Selmanowitz Chair of Jewish History* (New York: Touro College, 1998). On this debate, see David Berger, "Sephardic and Ashkenazic Messianism in the Middle Ages: An Assessment of the Historiographical Controversy" (Hebrew), in *Rishonim ve-Ahronim: mehkarim be-toledot yisrael mugashim le-Avraham Grossman*, ed. Joseph Hacker, B. Z. Kedar, and Yosef Kaplan (Jerusalem: Zalman Shazar Center, 2010), 11–28.

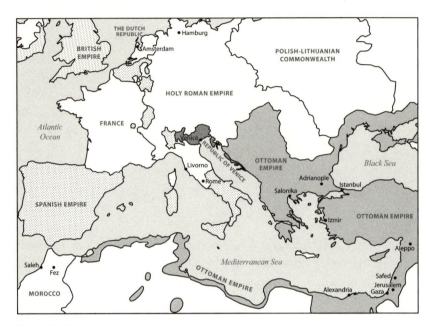

Map 2. Sabbatian messianism, 1665–1666

the Ottoman Empire after the expulsion, up through Moses Hagiz and
Hakham Zvi Ashkenazi in the western Sephardic Diaspora in the aftermath of Sabbetai Zevi.[3]

TEXT VERSUS EXPERIENCE

The contours of Sephardic rabbinic conservatism involve a complex
mix of philosophical rationalism, emphasis on the law, and, with the
death of Maimonides in 1204, a pronounced struggle over the proper
interpretation of his discussion of the messianic age in his code of
law, the *Mishneh Torah*, and his "Epistle to Yemen."[4] Scholars agree that

[3] On Maimonides and Nahmanides, see below. On Solomon Beit ha-Levi, see Leon Wieseltier,
"A Passion for Waiting: Liberal Notes on Messianism and the Jews," in *For Daniel Bell*, ed. Leon
Wieseltier and Mark Lilla (n.p., 2005), 141–142; for mention of Sasportas, see 133. On Hagiz, see
Carlebach, *Pursuit of Heresy*. On Hakham Zvi Ashkenazi, who was not Sephardic but ministered
to a Sephardic congregation for a time, see Jacob J. Schacter, "Motivations for Radical Anti-
Sabbatianism: The Case of Hakham Zevi Ashkenazi," in *Ha-halom ve-shivro*, 2:31–51. For mention
of Sasportas, see 34–35n5.

[4] See Joel L. Kraemer, "On Maimonides' Messianic Postures," in *Studies in Medieval Jewish History and Literature*, ed. Isadore Twersky (Cambridge, MA: Harvard University Press, 1984), 2:109–

Jacob Sasportas constituted an important link in this chain, but have yet to explain how these elements were adumbrated in the pages of *Zizath novel zvi.* Sasportas upheld a series of texts as sources of authority to counter the immediate religious experience of the Sabbatians. He repeatedly emphasized an imperative to doubt and beseeched the recipients of his letters to question the certainty of their messianic sensibility. Behind both the authority of these written works and his demand for skepticism was the law as the fundamental point of departure for thinking about the Messiah. This stress on the law, which Sasportas held himself up as uniquely capable of interpreting, and from which he excluded almost everything but the written word as a possible source, went hand in hand with a deep-seated fear of the crowd. His appeal to legal expertise and pietist sensibility evolved in reaction to the expressions of mass enthusiasm and the public celebration of the Messiah's arrival. In his invocation of the authority of the written word and in his denunciation of the Jewish crowd, Sasportas articulated a distinction between the lettered and the unlettered that had a long afterlife in the early modern period.

Sasportas developed this position—the imperative to doubt popular sentiment, the authority of the written word, the denigration of experience as a source of religious truth, and his fear of the crowd—only in response to the Sabbatian theology articulated by Nathan of Gaza and other Sabbatian prophets. In a series of letters by Nathan of Gaza before the apostasy of Sabbetai Zevi and by a number of other figures, such as Abraham Miguel Cardozo, subsequent to the Messiah's conversion to Islam, Sabbatian prophets espoused a new conception of time. With the revelation of the Messiah in the form of Sabbetai Zevi, the redemption had begun. What exactly this redemption meant was the subject of fierce internecine dispute among the Sabbatians, particularly in the period after Sabbetai Zevi's conversion. For some believers, this new sense of time was reflected in their approach to the calendar.[5] Their letters bore the date of the first or the second year since the arrival of the Messiah; they addressed one another as if they were

---

142. David Berger, "Some Ironic Consequences of Maimonides' Rationalist Approach to the Messianic Age" (Hebrew), *Maimonidean Studies* 2 (1991): 1–8, reprinted and translated in his *Cultures in Collision and Conversation: Essays in the Intellectual History of the Jews* (Boston: Academic Studies Press, 2011), 278–288; for mention of Sasportas, see 282–284; Israel J. Yuval, "Moses *Redivivus*: Maimonides as the Messiah's Helper" (Hebrew), *Zion* 72 (2007): 161–188.

[5] Scholem, *Sabbatai Sevi*, 262, 528, and passim.

living in a new era. For figures such as Raphael Supino, a preacher and printer in Livorno who corresponded with Sasportas, this new sense of time did not impinge upon observance of the law. Supino and many believers like him continued to observe the commandments as they had done before the arrival of the Messiah. For others, however, this new sense of time was accompanied by a radical reevaluation and restructuring of the legal norms that governed Jewish observance. This reordering took a number of forms and developed gradually over the course of the roughly sixteen months between Nathan of Gaza's declaration of Sabbetai Zevi as the Messiah and the latter's conversion to Islam. It took on even more radical forms in the immediate aftermath of the conversion, but the fundamental point of the enterprise was the same.

In the period of redemption, the law lost much of its former social power. Sabbatians jettisoned significant legal norms as a result of their experience of redemption. For the masses of Jews swept up by the charismatic authority of the leaders of their movement, the Sabbatian prophet replaced the Talmudist as the source of authority. These prophets embraced a form of antinomianism that involved the reinterpretation of a celebrated rabbinic saying, "A transgression committed for its own sake is greater than a commandment not committed for its own sake," which they construed as "The abrogation of the law is its fulfillment."[6] In light of the experience of redemption, days of mourning for the destruction of the Temple in Jerusalem, traditionally observed with ascetic restraint and fasting, became days of joy celebrated with food, drink, and general merriment. Sabbetai Zevi reintroduced the ritual slaughter of animals on Passover, a practice abolished with the invention of rabbinic Judaism in the wake of the Temple's destruction in the first century CE. Sabbatians did not confine their innovations to the abrogation of the law; they introduced new liturgies into the daily service and transformed obscure rituals, such as the fourth meal at the conclusion of the Sabbath, into prolonged celebrations of their Messiah.[7] At the same time, they engaged in a series of provocative sexual

---

[6] BT Nazir, 23b. See Gershom Scholem, "Redemption through Sin," in *The Messianic Idea in Judaism and Other Essays on Jewish Spirituality* (New York: Schocken Books, 1971), 110; Maoz Kahana, "Sabbetai Zevi—the Halakhic Man" (Hebrew), *Zion* 81 (2016): 391–433.

[7] See Gershom Scholem, "Tradition and New Creation in the Ritual of the Kabbalists," in *On the Kabbalah and Its Symbolism* (New York: Schocken Books, 1965), 145–146.

practices, including the suspension of Jewish laws governing conjugal relations and the demand for sexual abstinence. This was the ultimate form of antinomianism, as it threatened the primary unit of all social discipline: the family.[8]

If Sabbatian prophets and their followers drew on their ecstatic physical experience of redemption as the source of legitimacy for their suspension of the law and their introduction of new rituals, Sasportas turned to the bookshelf in order to reinstitute textual discipline. Against the authenticity of their revelations, Sasportas upheld written norms as the sole source of authority. Trained in a tradition that placed emphasis on erudition at the expense of local custom or individual experience, Sasportas took pride in his mastery over the entirety of Jewish law from the Mishnah and the Talmud of antiquity through the codes and commentaries of the Middle Ages up through the most recent responsa. His saturation in rabbinic literature was so thorough that when a Sephardic merchant who lived in Frankfurt, David de Mercado, claimed to have derived the ability of the Sabbatians to establish their own laws from a passage in the Mishnah—the compendium of Jewish law attributed to Judah the Prince at the close of the second century— Sasportas retorted:

> This Mishnaic passage that you quote does not exist; rather it is imagined and its location is entirely unknown. In my opinion, you yourself have not even seen it but you have heard about it from others who made it up and should be punished by something more than simply being shamed and disgraced in front of the sages. How is it that I have been diligently studying the Mishnah since my youth, and that to this day I continue to be occupied with and to interpret it in order to compose a fitting and pleasing work, in clear and concise language, should God grant me life, and yet I have never come across this Mishnaic passage of yours?[9]

[8] Allegations of sexual improprieties surfaced in the period of peak Sabbatian enthusiasm between 1665 and 1666; however, it turned into a leitmotiv in the anti-Sabbatian literature of the eighteenth century. See Rapoport-Albert, *Women and the Messianic Heresy*; Maciejko, *The Mixed Multitude*.

[9] משנתך זאת המפורשת אצלך אינה משנה אלא בדותא היא ולא נודע מקומה איו. ולפי דעתי גם אתה לא ראית אותה כי אם שמעת מפי אחרים ובדו אותה מלבם וראויים הם לעונש זולת חרפתם ובשתם לפני חכמים. איך בהיותי שוקד על דלתות המשנה מנעורי ועד היום אני מתעסק בה ובפירושה לעשות חיבור נאה ומתקבל בלשון צח וקצר אם יגזור ה' בחיים לא באה לידי המשנה הזאת המפורשת לך?

Sasportas, *ZNZ*, 229. On Mercado, see Scholem, *Sabbatai Sevi*, 784

In a dazzling display of learning, Sasportas had earlier raised two possible texts in the Mishnah and dismissed them as potential sources for Mercado's claim before accusing him of inventing the passage out of whole cloth. Sasportas manifested here what Amnon Raz-Krakotzkin has called a "new mishnaic consciousness" that was a unique feature of the early modern period.[10]

Sasportas drew most frequently on medieval rabbinic literature, rather than the Mishnah and the Talmud of antiquity. At the center of his antimessianism stood the *Mishneh Torah*, the legal code of Moses Maimonides. Sasportas repeatedly drew upon the fourteen books of Maimonides's code, especially his treatment of the messianic age in the Laws of Kings at the conclusion of the code's final volume, the *Book of Judges*. His dispute with the Sabbatians, however, was not merely about this celebrated discussion of the Messiah in Maimonides's writing. Throughout *Zizath novel zvi*, Sasportas reverted to passages scattered all over the code, including those concerning the Laws of Evidence, the Laws of Repentance, and the Laws of Prayer. And even as he accused Mercado of inventing new sources, he appears to have quoted Maimonides from memory and on one occasion remembered a passage in the law code that did not actually exist.[11]

At the very beginning of the outbreak of Sabbatian enthusiasm, Sasportas wrote an open letter to the rabbinate of Amsterdam in general and to its leader, Isaac Aboab da Fonseca, in particular.[12] In this letter, he outlined the reasons for his skepticism and drew upon Maimonides's code.

> When I received the first letters, I had doubted; with the recent arrival of the second letters that increase your belief and practically establish the matter as something definite that will occur shortly, I have come as one who questions... and I agree with the words of Maimonides at the

---

[10] "Persecution and the Art of Printing: Hebrew Books in Italy in the 1550s," in *Jewish Culture in Early Modern Europe: Essays in Honor of David B. Ruderman*, ed. Richard I. Cohen et al. (Cincinnati, OH: HUC Press; Pittsburgh, PA: University of Pittsburgh Press, 2014), 102. On the Mishnah in the Sephardic Diaspora, see Yosef Kaplan, "Jews and Judaism in the Hartlib Circle," *SR* 38–39 (2006): 197–200.

[11] Sasportas, *ZNZ*, 144n4.

[12] On the rabbinate in Amsterdam and Sabbatianism, see Yosef Kaplan, "The Attitude of the Sephardi Leadership in Amsterdam to the Sabbatian Movement, 1665–1671," in *An Alternative Path*, 211–233, discussion of Sasportas on 211, of Sasportas and Isaac Aboab da Fonseca on 220–221.

conclusion of his Laws of Kings, who wrote, "but no one is in a position to know the details of this and similar things until they have come to pass… no one should ever occupy himself with the legendary themes or spend much time on Midrashic statements bearing on this and like subjects. He should not deem them of prime importance… one should wait (for his coming) and accept in principle this article of faith." Here end his words. For this [belief in Sabbetai Zevi], I shall not impinge my faith, heaven forfend, or cast doubt upon it; on the contrary, I uphold it [my faith] in my questioning to ascertain the truth, and it appears to me that my doubt is more appropriate than certainty.[13]

A few lines later, Sasportas rejected the claims of the believers who declared him to be a sinner for not having believed in Sabbetai Zevi and Nathan of Gaza. He again pointed to Maimonides's code as the source of his doubt:

Even though I have not believed in this man [Sabbetai Zevi] as the King Messiah, I have not sinned as long as I have not seen his claims established according to the [standard] in Maimonides at the conclusion of the Laws of Kings: "If there arise a king from the House of David who meditates on the Torah, occupies himself with the commandments, as did his ancestor David, observes the precepts prescribed in the written and oral law, prevails upon Israel to walk in the way of the Torah and to repair its breaches, and fights the battles of the Lord, it may be assumed that he is the Messiah. If he does these things and succeeds, rebuilds the sanctuary on its site, and gathers the dispersed of Israel, he beyond all doubt is the Messiah." Here end his words.[14]

To his colleagues in the Amsterdam rabbinate, Sasportas insisted that "skepticism is not a mark of disbelief in the coming of the Messiah, but

[13] ואם בעד כתבים הראשונים הייתי כמספק עכשיו בכתבים שניים המגדילים יתר אמונתכם וכמעט שמחזיקים העניין לודאי קרוב באתי כשוואל . . . ואסכים לדברי הרמב"ם ז"ל בסוף הלכות מלכים שכתב: וכל אלו הדברים וכיוצא בהן לא ידע אדם איך יהיו עד שיהיו וכו' ולעולם לא יתעסק אדם בדברי אגדות ולא יאריך במדרשים האמורות בעניינים אלו וכיוצא בהן ולא ישימם עיקר וכו' אלא יחכה ויאמין בכלל הדבר וכו' ע"כ. ולא בעבור זאת אפגע באמונתי ח"ו או אטיל ספק בה, אדרבא אני מקיים אותה בשאלתי לדעת האמת, ונראה לי שיותר טוב ספקי מודאי.

Sasportas, ZNZ, 18. The ellipses in the quotation from Maimonides are those of Sasportas. For the source of the citation, see Maimonides, *Book of Judges*, Laws of Kings, 12:2.

[14] ואעפ"י שאם לא הייתי מאמין בזה האיש למלך המשיח לא הייתי חוטא כל עוד שלא ראיתי חזקתו כדברי הרמב"ם ז"ל בסוף הלכות מלכים וז"ל: ואם יעמוד מלך מבית דוד הוגה בתורה ועוסק במצוות כדוד אביו כפי תורה שבכתב ושבעפ"ה ויכוף כל ישראל לילך בה ולחזק בדקה וילחם מלחמות ה' הרי זה בחזקת שהוא משיח ואם עשה והצליח ובנה מקדש במקומו וקבץ נדחי ישראל הרי זה משיח בודאי עכ"ל.

Sasportas, ZNZ, 18–19. Maimonides, *Book of Judges*, Laws of Kings, 11:4.

rather the foremost duty of the learned," in the articulation of Amos Funkenstein.[15] One may push Funkenstein's formulation even further. Skepticism regarding the Messiah was not only incumbent upon the learned; it was a legal obligation. Repeatedly throughout *Zizath novel zvi*, Sasportas clung to his doubt in the face of Sabbatian certainty. The Sabbatians pointed to experience, revelation, and prophecy as evidence of the Messiah. Sasportas countered with an authoritative law code that in his reading provided a clear series of necessary stipulations as the prerequisites for the proclamation of the Messiah. Following Maimonides, Sasportas subjected the doctrine of the Messiah to the demands of skepticism and to the rigors of the law.

Another letter to the rabbinate in Amsterdam written by Sasportas about six months later provides some indication of how central Maimonides was to his demand for skepticism:

> Have you ever seen a single book that compels us to believe in anyone who says of himself, "I am the Messiah," or of whom people say, "This is the King of Glory" (Ps. 24), before he has performed the deeds of the Messiah according to the formulation of Maimonides in the Laws of Kings; even if he provides several other signs and wonders, are these sufficient to establish him as the Messiah? ... The Messiah's deeds are dependent upon him fighting the war of the Lord, the construction of the Temple, and the gathering of exile. For if this were not the case, anyone who wanted to take the name Messiah, would simply come and take it, as long as his piety served as proof. And there would be as many Messiahs as there were pietists.[16]

Like a good Maimonidean, Sasportas saw a legal imperative to believe in the Messiah; but none whatsoever to believe in Sabbetai Zevi. For Sasportas, following in the footsteps of Maimonides, the messianic age would involve no dramatic change in the observance of the law. In fact, the antinomianism of the Sabbatians was proof positive that the Mes-

---

[15] "Maimonides: Political Theory and Realistic Messianism," in *Perceptions of Jewish History* (Berkeley: University of California Press, 1993), 135; for mention of Sasportas, see n11.

[16] האם ראיתם בשום ספר שמחייב להאמין למשיח מי שאומר על עצמו משיחא אנא או אומרים עליו שזה מלך הכבוד קודם עשותו מעשה משיח כדברי הרמב"ם בהל' מלכים, ואעפ"י שיתן כמה אותות ומופתים אחרים האם כדאים להחזיקו למשיח . . . אבל משיח במעשיו הדבר תלוי ללחום מלחמת ה' ולבנות מקדש ולקבץ גלות, שאם לא כן כל הרוצה ליטול שם משיח יבא ויטול אם חסידותו מוכחת עליו וכפי החסידים ירבו המשיחים. ZNZ, 102.

siah had not yet arrived. What was more, once Maimonides's code had been abandoned, the way to messianic anarchy was open to all. If the Sabbatians could subvert the power of the written word according to the conduct of their Messiah and their prophet, what was there to stop any Jew who behaved in a particularly pious manner from claiming to be the Messiah?

If the code of Maimonides was the primary point of departure for Sasportas's response to Sabbatianism, he drew on a number of other works by Maimonides to buttress his arguments. He engaged in a protracted dispute with the Sabbatians and their moderate supporters, such as Isaac Aboab da Fonseca, as to whether the "Epistle to Yemen" justified their belief or his skepticism. He obliquely referred to *The Guide of the Perplexed* in his definition of belief and explicitly invoked it as a means to limit the scope of prophecy and to exclude Nathan of Gaza and other Sabbatians entirely from that category.[17] In his reading, *The Guide of the Perplexed* offered a stinging rebuttal of all the would-be prophets who claimed direct communication with the divine rather than authorization to engage in prophetic speculation. He drew on *The Book of Commandments* in a protracted legal dispute about the recitation of the priestly blessing in the public synagogue service of the Jews of Amsterdam.[18] From this array of sources, Sasportas conjured up a Maimonides who was sober, rational, and definitive. The law more than any other aspect of Judaism was both the point of departure and the telos for all thinking about the Messiah. Sasportas's Maimonides had counseled patience to the Jews of Yemen and sought to attenuate their false expectations of the advent of the Messiah in the middle of the twelfth century.[19] In his legal code, Maimonides had formulated a set of criteria that all but ensured that the laws of Judaism would continue to be authoritative in the messianic age. To return to Funkenstein's

---

[17] For the oblique references, see *ZNZ*, 51, 82, 342; for the explicit citation, where Sasportas referred to *The Guide of the Perplexed* as "his [Maimonides's] book," see *ZNZ*, 364.

[18] *ZNZ*, 217.

[19] For the text see Moses Maimonides, *Epistle to Yemen*, ed. Abraham S. Halkin (New York: American Academy of Jewish Research, 1952). On this work, see Mordechai Akiva Friedman, *Harambam, ha-mashiah be-teman ve-ha-shemad* (Jerusalem: Ben Zvi Institute, 2002). Prior to Sabbetai Zevi, the "Epistle to Yemen" had appeared in print on two occasions, the first as part of Joseph Solomon Delmedigo, *Ta-alumot hokhmah* (Hanau, 1629–1631), and the second as an appendix to Maimonides, *Sefer ha-mitzvot* (Amsterdam: Joseph Attias, 1660). On the latter, see Fuks-M., *Typography*, entry 379, 2:309–310.

Figures 5 and 6. Maimonides, *Code of Law* (Venice: Giustiniani, 1550), title page. Bibliotheca Rosenthaliana, Special Collections of the University of Amsterdam. Maimonides, *Guide of the Perplexed* (Venice: Bragadin, 1551), title page. Image provided by

reading of Maimonides once again: "The Messiah will not change an iota of the law. An antinomian attitude is the clearest indication of an impostor."[20]

But the Sabbatians were no more willing than Sasportas to give up on the authority of Maimonides. Isaac Nahar, a rabbi and doctor in Amsterdam who was swept up in the enthusiasm to such a degree that he made his way to Livorno on an intended pilgrimage to greet the new Messiah, invoked Maimonides's law code itself in an attempt to convince Sasportas to keep quiet:

> I do not know why you, my Lord, have not remained silent. Why have you publicized your opinion among the masses who walk innocently and uphold their faith... For in all of the places where we have heard these rumors, people are returning to God with all their heart, and to

[20] Funkenstein, "Maimonides: Political Theory and Realistic Messianism," 136.

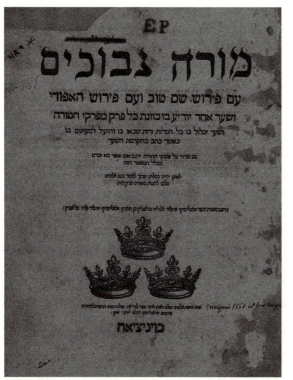

the Jewish Theological Seminary. Sasportas did not separate Maimonides the philosopher from Maimonides who codified the law. Both *The Guide of the Perplexed* and *Code of Law* were integral sources for his messianic reserve.

me, this is one of the signs of redemption as Maimonides wrote in the Laws of Repentance.[21]

Sasportas was all for repentance, as he made clear in his response, but these seizures of penitential behavior were not indicative of the redemption or the correct interpretation of Maimonides. In a letter written to a believer, no less a Sabbatian authority than Nathan of Gaza invoked the very passage in Maimonides's Laws of Kings that Sasportas had cited in his rebuke of the Amsterdam rabbinate:

For although nothing of the kind is indicated in the plain sense of Scripture, yet we have seen that the sayings of the ancient rabbis on these

---

[21] ואתה האדון לא ידעתי למה לא שמר הדברים בלבו ולמה פרסם הדברים בפני המון העם ההולכים בתמים ומחזיקים באמונתם . . . כן בעינו ראינו במקום זה וכן בכל המקומות ששמענו שמעם לשמע שמועות אלו כלם שבים אל ה' בכל לבם, והוא אצלי א' מסימני הגאולה כמו שכתב רמב"ם בהלכות תשובה.

Sasportas, *ZNZ*, 25.

[eschatological] matters are obscure and utterly inexplicable, and we have the testimony of the great luminary Maimonides [who declared] that the rabbinic dicta would become intelligible only after the event.[22]

What Sasportas had read as an authorization of his doubt and an imperative for skepticism, Nathan of Gaza embraced as the basis for the esoteric nature of his prophecies. For Sabbatians of all stripes, from an enthusiast such as Isaac Nahar to the very leaders of the movement such as Nathan of Gaza, Maimonides had authorized their belief in Sabbetai Zevi as the fulfillment of their messianic hopes. In a certain sense, much of the dispute concerning the messianic claims of Sabbetai Zevi depended upon how one read Maimonides.[23]

SASPORTAS AND THE MEDIEVAL JEWISH BOOKSHELF

Sasportas went to great lengths to convince his readers in the western Sephardic Diaspora that they had misconstrued Maimonides. He also sought to construct an antimessianic tradition out of a number of medieval sources. As he had written to the Amsterdam rabbinate, "Have you ever seen a single book that compels us to believe in anyone who says of himself, 'I am the Messiah'?" Sasportas seemed to prefer any book to the experiential evidence of the Sabbatians. In a long letter to Raphael Supino in Livorno that marked the first sustained articulation of his opposition to Sabbetai Zevi, Sasportas drew upon a passage in *Sefer hasidim*, a work composed by the German pietists of the Rhineland and attributed to Judah the Pious (d. 1217). He advised Supino to

---

[22] ואף כי לא מצאנו רמז בפשטי התורה דבר זה כבר ראינו דברי חז"ל בענינים אלה כמה תמוהים ולא יכולנו להשיג סוף דעתם בשום דבר מדבריהם, כמו שהעיד ג"כ על דבר זה המאור הגדול הרמב"ם ז"ל, ולא יובנו דבריהם כי אם בשעת מעשה בע"ה.

Ibid., 260. As translated by Werblowsky in Scholem, *Sabbatai Sevi*, 741. For further discussion of this passage, see Berger, "Some Ironic Consequences of Maimonides' Rationalist Approach to the Messianic Age," 284.

[23] For repeated discussion of Maimonides in a letter justifying the conversion of Sabbetai Zevi, see "The Letter of the Shield of Abraham from the Land of the West, Written Apparently by Abraham Miguel Cardoso" (Hebrew), in Scholem, *Mekhere shabtat*, 146–181. The author of the letter invokes Maimonides's commentary on the Mishnah (149) as well as his "Epistle to Yemen" (155). In his appendix to Scholem's article, 179–181, Yehuda Liebes concludes that the author of this letter was Abraham Perez. Abraham Miguel Cardozo discusses Maimonides at considerable length in a letter written in 1669. See "The Letter from Abraham Miguel Cardozo to the Judges of Izmir" (Hebrew), in Scholem, *Mekharim*, 298–331.

turn to passage 206, which espoused a messianic pacifism at odds with the active campaigning of the Sabbatians and their allies:

> If you see a man prophesizing about the Messiah, know that he is engaged in witchcraft, evil spirits, or the Ineffable Name. And since Angels are disturbed by this, they will tell him about the Messiah so that he could be exposed to the world as [a fraud] for disturbing the angels. In the end, it shall be shame and embarrassment to the entire world that he has disturbed the angels. Or the demons will come and instruct him in calculations and secrets that will redound to his shame and to the shame of those who believe in his words.[24]

It would be hard to imagine a medieval Jewish book further from Maimonides's code than *Sefer hasidim*. Where Maimonides sought to compose a code that would represent the Oral Torah in its entirety, *Sefer hasidim* sought to codify the will of the creator in a way that would define for the pietist precisely how to submit to the divine yoke.[25] If Maimonides's code argued that the advent of the messianic age would involve no change in the law, *Sefer hasidim* argued that the pietist was in need of constant guidance that the traditional corpus of Jewish law could not provide; the messianic state of perfection was a moral imperative that was, perforce, unobtainable. Maimonides produced a nor-

---

[24] אם תראה שמתנבא אדם על משיח דע כי היו עוסקים במעשה כשפים או במעשה שדים או במעשה המפורש ובשביל שהם מטריחים את המלאכים אומרים לו על משיח כדי שיתגלה לעולם על שהטריחו את המלאכים. ולבסוף יהיה לבושה ולחרפה לכל העולם על שהטריחו המלאכים. או השדים באים ולומדים לו חשבונות וסודות לבושתו ולבושת המאמינים בדבריו.

Sefer hasidim (Bologna, 1538), par. 206, 30b. Sasportas, *ZNZ*, 81, 94. A slightly different version of this passage appears in the Parma edition. See *Sefer hasidim*, ed. Jehuda Wistinetzki, with an introduction and index by Jacob Freimann (Frankfurt: M. A. Wahrmann, 1924), par. 212, 76–77. I have given the text as it appears in the edition printed in Bologna, where it appears as paragraph 206, the paragraph number that Sasportas quoted. On the textual history, see Haym Soloveitchik, "Piety, Pietism and German Pietism: 'Sefer Hasidim I' and the Influence of Hasidei Ashkenaz," *JQR* 92 (2002): 455–493; Ivan G. Marcus, *Sefer Hasidim and the Ashkenazic Book in Medieval Europe* (Philadelphia: University of Pennsylvania Press, 2018). See also the *Sefer hasidim* database available at https://etc.princeton.edu/sefer_hasidim/. Sasportas was apparently unaware of *Sefer hasidim* (ed. Wistinetzki), par. 1543, p. 378. For discussion of this passage, see Ephraim Kanarfogel, "Medieval Rabbinic Conceptions of the Messianic Age: The View of the Tosafists," in *Me'ah She'arim: Studies in Medieval Jewish Spiritual Life in Memory of Isadore Twersky*, ed. Ezra Fleischer et al. (Jerusalem: Magnes Press, 2001), 156n17.

[25] On the code, see Moshe Halbertal, "What Is the *Mishneh Torah*? On Codification and Its Ambivalence," in *Maimonides after 800 Years: Essays on Maimonides and His Influence*, ed. Jay M. Harris (Cambridge, MA: Harvard University Press, 2007), 81–111. On the will of the creator as a central issue in *Sefer hasidim*, see Haym Soloveitchik, "Three Themes in the *Sefer Hasidim*," *AJS Review* 1 (1976): 311–325.

mative legal guide for a lay readership; the German pietists wrote a work that taught the aspiring pietist how to transcend the law.

Sasportas mentioned this particular passage of *Sefer hasidim* on no fewer than five occasions in *Zizath novel zvi*.[26] Any source, no matter how far from his own intellectual universe, was preferable to the experiential claims made by the Sabbatians about the arrival of redemption. He would choose messianic pacifism in any guise, even that of the supernatural, as long as it appeared in a written work that he could uphold as authoritative. Furthermore, it is conceivable that Sasportas identified a conservative tendency in the world of the pietists that was the antithesis of Sabbatian enthusiasm. As Haym Soloveitchik has shown, the pietists were fighting a rearguard action against the rise of the dialectical method of Talmud study that came of age in twelfth-century France, which prized intellectual speculation at the expense of legal or moral adjudication.[27] The German pietist had to contend with a revolution in intellectual Jewish life that redefined the study of the Talmud, and he responded with a novel form of piety that went far beyond the bounds of the law. Sasportas faced a very different type of revolution in Jewish life, a mass messianic movement, and he responded with a novel form of criticism that far exceeded the norms of rabbinic writing.

For all of the differences between *Sefer hasidim* and the writings of Maimonides, Sasportas may have been attuned to affinities between these sources that have eluded modern scholarship. Both the pietists of *Sefer hasidim* and Maimonides were unabashed elitists. Both emphasized the importance of the written word. Their elitism may have had different sources: Maimonides valued a certain type of philosophical contemplation completely foreign to the supernatural world of the German pietists. He put the spiritual use of reason at the center of his universe rather than the will of the creator. The pietists, by contrast, ide-

---

[26] Sasportas, *ZNZ*, 81, 94 (letter to Supino), 113 (letter to the Venetian rabbinate), 115 (letter to the Viennese rabbinate), 298 (response to Cardozo). His emphasis on this passage may have served as a precedent for Moses Hagiz, who scolded Moses Hayim Luzzatto while invoking this very passage. Hagiz advised Luzzatto to study this passage, and the preceding one, as a form of therapy for his messianic pretensions. See the letter from Hagiz to Luzzatto and from Isaiah Bassan (Luzzatto's teacher) to his student, both in *R. Moshe Hayim Luzzatto u-venei doro*, ed. Simon Ginzburg (Tel Aviv: Dvir, 1937), 1:79; and see the letter from Isaiah Bassan to Luzzatto that repeats the same passage in *Sefer hasidim*, 1:86. Both letters as cited and discussed in Carlebach, *Pursuit of Heresy*, 326–327n45; on Hagiz's silence about Sasportas, see ibid.,150, and Maciejko, *The Mixed Multitude*, 46.

[27] Soloveitchik, "Three Themes in the *Sefer Hasidim*," 352.

alized the model of a spiritual superman and emphasized the rigors of physical discipline and penance. But both the pietist in *Sefer hasidim* and Maimonides set themselves apart from their respective environments, which they saw as morally corrupt and rendered degenerate by wrongheaded popular opinion. Sasportas too cultivated the posture of the critic and set himself apart from his addressees, whom he held to have betrayed the Sephardic learned ideal in the name of which he now spoke.

If Maimonides and *Sefer hasidim* anchored Sasportas's antimessianism in the Jewish textual tradition, he turned to a third source to justify his skepticism of Sabbatian prophecy: a legal responsum of the Iberian jurist Solomon ibn Adret (d. 1310). As Matt Goldish has shown, the possibility of reviving prophecy underlay many of the claims to authority made by the Sabbatians.[28] Nathan of Gaza and his fellow prophets invoked divine revelation as proof of their authority and sought to transform the charisma of learning that had long served to cement the alliance between the rabbinate and the lay oligarchy in Jewish life. In a retort that paralleled his appeal to Maimonides in terms of his unbelief in the Messiah, Sasportas turned to a medieval legal discussion of prophecy to justify his unbelief in the Messiah's prophet. Writing to Joseph Halevi in Livorno, a preacher to the Livornese Portuguese Jews who was one of the few allies Sasportas had in his opposition, he pointedly invoked Ibn Adret:

> Whoever heard of such a thing, that while matters were still unclear we should set aside the words of Torah and tradition and hasten on hearing the one who says, "Thus sayeth the Lord," to sentence me to death for not believing in him [a belief] which God has not commanded. Nathan who prophesies does not realize that by refusing to offer a sign and a proof he absolves those who are weak in their faith while making himself liable in the event that his prophecy is not fulfilled. And if he declares that time will prove him right, and when his words are fulfilled it shall be known that he is a prophet—I too will concede this. But you must concede to me that he has not yet attained the status of a prophet. How good and how pleasing are the words of Rabbi Solomon ibn Adret, responsum 548 about that prophet from Avila.[29]

[28] Goldish, *The Sabbatean Prophets.*

[29] מי שמע כזאת שבעד שבריהם תלויים ברפיון נניח דברי תורה וקבלה ונחוש לדברי האומר כה אמר ה' לחייבני מיתה על העדר אמונתי בו וה' לא צוה. ולא ידע נתן המתנבא שבמנעו אות ומופת פטר את חלושי אמונתו וחייב את

Sasportas continued to cite Ibn Adret as justification for his skepticism of Nathan's claims to prophecy and directed his addressee to examine the passage himself. In the responsum, Ibn Adret had skeptically addressed claims about a possible prophet in Avila. He informed his reader that while prophecy was a theoretical possibility, it could issue only from someone who was particularly pious and living in Palestine. Ibn Adret was doubtful that the particular man in question was the prophet that he claimed to be: "But this shocked me, that a man who was neither a sage nor knowledgeable about books nor a servant to the sages should be who they said he was."[30] Like Sasportas several hundred years later, Ibn Adret upheld knowledge of written texts as a requirement for the attainment of a certain rank within the religious hierarchy, in this case a prophet rather than the Messiah. Elsewhere in his writings Sasportas turned to Ibn Adret as a legal precedent in his rulings.[31] What is more, Sasportas felt an almost filial connection to him, as Ibn Adret had been a student of his ancestor Nahmanides. At one point in the midst of a vituperative exchange with Isaac Nahar, Sasportas pointedly invoked the protective merit of Nahmanides and Ibn Adret in the same breath.[32]

Solomon ibn Adret can hardly be construed as a late medieval Maimonidean or as a German pietist. He belonged to a tradition of Sephardic jurisprudence that was adamantly opposed to the philosophical rationalism of *The Guide of the Perplexed* as well as to the exegetical supernaturalism of *Sefer hasidim*. On a number of occasions in the second controversy surrounding the writings of Maimonides that dominated Jewish intellectual life in Provence and Catalonia at the turn of

---

עצמו אם לא תתקיים נבואתו. ואם יאמר אומר שזמנו מוכיח עליו ובוא דברו יודע כי נביא הוא, גם אני אודהו אבל יודה לי מיהת דעדיין לא עליו שם נביא. והנה מה טוב ומה נעים דברי הרשב״א על אותו דברי נביא די אבילה.

Sasportas, *ZNZ*, 145–146. On Levi, see Scholem, *Sabbatai Sevi*, 486. .

[30] Solomon ibn Adret, *She-elot u-teshuvot* (Venice: Giustiniani, 1545–1546), no. 548, 89b–90a. Citation on 90a, col. 1. For other invocations of this responsum by Sasportas, see his letter to Aaron Zarfati of Amsterdam, *ZNZ*, 31–33, and his letter to Isaac Aboab da Fonseca, *ZNZ*, 46. For Samuel Aboab's, see Meir Benayahu, "News from Italy and Holland on the Beginning of Sabbatianism" (Hebrew), *Erez yisrael* 4 (1956): 198. On Ibn Adret's responsa in the early modern period, see Simcha Emanuel, "Manuscripts of the Responsa by Ibn Adret in the Writings of Scholars between the Fifteenth and Nineteenth Centuries" (Hebrew), *Jewish Studies, an Internet Journal* 13 (2015): 1–46. On Ibn Adret and the prophet of Avila, see Yoel Marciano, "The Messianic Movement in Ávila in 1295" (MA thesis, Bar-Ilan University, 2001).

[31] Sasportas, *Ohel ya-akov*, #11, 14b; #12, 14b, where Sasportas sides with Ibn Adret and Jacob ben Asher against Nahmanides on a question about marriage law.

[32] Sasportas, *ZNZ*, 51.

the thirteenth century, Ibn Adret had scathing things to say about *The Guide of the Perplexed*.[33] He appears to have been completely unaware of *Sefer hasidim*, as recent scholarship has suggested that the work made few if any inroads into the Iberian Peninsula in the late Middle Ages.[34]

In addressing the Sabbatians and their supporters, Sasportas thus constructed a textual antimessianic tradition out of sources that sat awkwardly next to one another on his imagined or actual bookshelf. Nonetheless, he used them to draw out a number of points that he sought to impress upon his correspondents. First, he turned to the stipulations for the Messiah's arrival in Maimonides's code to caution his readers about their certainty. Second, he drew upon both Maimonides and the German pietists to ask his readers to imagine the anarchy and disorder that would arise from a proliferation of Messiahs. Finally, he drew upon Maimonides and Ibn Adret to define prophecy in such a way that would pointedly exclude Nathan of Gaza and his colleagues from that category. Important as each of these individual claims was, the total impact of Sasportas's argument amounted to a demand for provisional skepticism in the face of experiential certainty. Authority manifested itself in a text, whether it was a law code, a pietist manual, or a responsum, and in those who were invested with the power of interpreting those texts. Experience, feeling, spirituality, should not enter into consideration when messianic claims were assessed.

TEXT VERSUS TEXT

It would severely limit the extent and scope of the disputes over Sabbatianism were one to reduce the conflict entirely to one of the written word as opposed to the experience of revelation. Sabbatian prophets and pamphleteers proved equally adept at invoking the authority

[33] On Ibn Adret and Maimonides, see David Berger, "Judaism and General Culture in Medieval and Early Modern Times," in his *Cultures in Collision: Essays in the Intellectual History of the Jews* (Boston Academic Studies Press, 2011), 70–78 and the literature cited there. On his criticism of Maimonides's code, see Michael A. Shmidman, "Rashba as Halakhic Critic of Maimonides," in *Turim: Studies in Jewish History and Literature Presented to Dr. Bernard Lander*, ed. Michael A. Shmidman (New York: Touro College Press, 2007), 257–273.

[34] For the possibility, see Israel M. Ta-Shma, "German Pietism in Sepharad: Rabbi Jonah Gerondi, the Man and His Work" (Hebrew), in *Keneset mehkarim iyunim be-sifrut ha-rabanit be-yeme ha-benayim: Sepharad* (Jerusalem: Bialik Institute, 2004), 2:109–148. For a rebuttal, see Soloveitchik, "Piety, Pietism, and German Pietism," 473–479.

of texts. Maimonides played a central role in the prophecy of Nathan of Gaza; as even the most avid Sabbatian knew, however, Maimonides's law code was hardly the ideal source upon which to build a robust messianic theology. The passages on the Messiah were too brief and too ambiguous to serve as the basis for a theory of an antinomian Messiah. Nathan of Gaza and other Sabbatian prophets understood that Maimonides's authority was such that he could not be circumvented; but he was not the easiest route to a Sabbatian theology. Over and above Maimonides's law code and its passages concerning the Messiah, the Sabbatians employed two strategies to invoke the authority of the written word. First, they turned to a work entitled *The Book of Zerubbabel* as a prophetic description of the events they had witnessed. Second, they discovered hitherto unknown prophecies that predicted the advent of Sabbetai Zevi. Behind both strategies was the same intellectual impulse: an appeal to ancient texts, or those that purported to be ancient, as a justification for the conduct of their Messiah.

Sabbatians repeatedly invoked *The Book of Zerubbabel,* an early medieval Hebrew apocalypse in which God reveals secrets to the Persian governor Zerubbabel mentioned in the biblical prophecies of Haggai, Zechariah, and Ezekiel.[35] Echoing a rabbinic tradition that appeared in the Babylonian Talmud, *The Book of Zerubbabel* develops the notion of two Messiahs, the Messiah son of Joseph and the Messiah son of Judah.[36] At the end of days, the Messiah son of Joseph would gather all of Israel in Jerusalem and offer sacrifices to the Lord. Armilos the son of Satan would come to rule the world and kill the Messiah son of Jo-

---

[35] For editions of the Hebrew text, see Solomon Wertheimer, *Batei midrashot* (Jerusalem: Rav Kook Institute, 1954); Israël Lévi, *Le Ravissement du Messie à sa naissance et autres essais,* ed. Evelyne Patlagean (Paris: Peeters, 1994), 173–227. A reprint of "L'Apocalypse de Zorobabel et le roi de Perse Siroès," *REJ* 68 (1914): 129–60; 69 (1919) 108–121; 71 (1920): 57–65; Yehudah Even-Shmuel, *Midreshe geulah* (Tel Aviv: Bialik Institute, 1943), 53–88, 351–370, 379–389. For an annotated English translation, see Martha Himmelfarb, "Sefer Zerubbabel," in *Rabbinic Fantasies: Imaginative Narratives from Classical Hebrew Literature,* ed. David Stern and Mark J. Mirsky (New Haven, CT: Yale University Press, 1990), 67–90. On the book, see Martha Himmelfarb, *Jewish Messiahs in a Christian Empire: A History of the Book of Zerubbabel* (Cambridge, MA: Harvard University Press, 2017).

[36] For the passage in the Talmud, see BT Sukkah 52a. For discussion of whether *The Book of Zerubbabel* was dependent upon the Talmud for this tradition or both derived it from a third source, see Martha Himmelfarb, "*Sefer Zerubbabel* and Popular Religion," in *A Teacher for All Generations: Essays in Honor of James C. VanderKam,* ed. Eric F. Mason et al. (Leiden: Brill, 2012), 2:621–634. On the Messiah son of Joseph, see Himmelfarb, *Jewish Messiahs in a Christian Empire,* chap. 5; Israel Knohl, *Be-ikvot ha-mashiah* (Tel Aviv: Schocken, 2000), 68–80.

seph.[37] The Messiah son of Judah would then announce his arrival, only to be mocked by the remaining sages of Israel. Nevertheless, the Messiah son of Judah would vanquish Armilos, raise the dead including the Messiah son of Joseph, and usher in the redemption. *The Book of Zerubbabel* survives in a number of different versions, many of which differ significantly from one another, and circulated among medieval Hebrew poets who cited it in their liturgical poetry.[38] Beginning with Israël Lévi in the early twentieth century, scholars have dated the work to the early seventh century prior to the Islamic conquest.[39] For our purposes, however, the crucial point has to do with how the Sabbatians related to it: they treated it as an ancient rabbinic text that formed part of the canon of rabbinic literature from antiquity. They had ample grounds for doing so, as the first and only early modern edition of the work had appeared as part of a collection of rabbinic midrashim printed in Constantinople in 1519 entitled *Likutim shonim.*[40]

One of the first instances in which a Sabbatian appealed to the authority of *The Book of Zerubbabel* appeared in a letter written by Hosea Nantawa from Alexandria to Livorno in the summer of 1666 prior to the conversion of the Messiah to Islam.[41] A fervent believer and skilled writer, Nantawa sought to justify the imprisonment of Sabbetai Zevi in Gallipoli to the faithful across the Mediterranean.[42] At the end of an elaborate justification for the antinomian behavior of Sabbetai Zevi and his followers, Nantawa appealed to *The Book of Zerubbabel,* which he referred to as a prophecy rather than a book:

[37] On the spelling of Armilos versus Armilus, see Himmelfarb, "Sefer Zerubbabel," 81n3. On the identification of this figure, see David Berger, "Three Typological Themes in Early Jewish Messianism: Messiah Son of Joseph, Rabbinic Calculations, and the Figure of Armilus," in *Cultures in Collision,* 253–277.

[38] For a number of the variants, see Even-Shmuel, *Midreshe geulah.* For some of the challenges posed by Even-Shmuel's edition, see Himmelfarb, "Sefer Zerubbabel," 82n15. For citations of the work in liturgical poetry, see Lévi, *Le Ravissement du Messie à sa naissance et autres essais,* 215–226; for its impact in the Middle Ages, see Joseph Dan, *Ha-sippur ha-ivri bi-yemei ha-beinayim* (Jerusalem: Keter, 1974), 43–46.

[39] For an attempt to place it a century earlier, see Hillel I. Newman, "Dating *Sefer Zerubavel*: Dehistoricizing and Rehistoricizing a Jewish Apocalypse of Late Antiquity," *Admantius* 19 (2013): 324–336.

[40] On the scarcity of this edition, see Even Shmuel, *Midreshe geulah,* 67n71.

[41] Scholem, *Sabbatai Sevi,* 490.

[42] For the impact of the news of the Messiah's imprisonment on some of the Jewish elites in Amsterdam, see Carsten L. Wilke, "Le 'Messie mystique' et la Bourse d'Amsterdam, le 3 mai 1666," *Sefarad* 67 (2007): 191–211.

What shall I say? Indeed, you should know about this. For surely the entire episode of his imprisonment is written down in the prophecy of Zerubbabel, which we have with us here. It states that the eminences and sages of Israel shall deny the Messiah, subject him to shame, and strike him down. He shall be taken prisoner, as anyone can see who looks there.[43]

For Nantawa, this ancient text offered a prophetic and authoritative account of contemporary events. Both the imprisonment of Sabbetai Zevi and his rejection by the rabbinate had a written precedent available to anyone who was able to read.

Sasportas, of course, would have none of this. In response to Nantawa's letter, he exclaimed:

And concerning your proof about this—that from the moment he [Sabbetai Zevi] went to Izmir enveloped in the sin that preceded him to the point that he was placed in his prison—the prophecy of Zerubbabel about which you said that it referred to him is nowhere to be found and does not exist, all the more so such an explanation to it.[44]

When confronted by an ostensibly authoritative and ancient text, Sasportas reverted to a powerful and nearly irrefutable strategy: he denied its existence and implied that it was a forgery. Such a strategy could work, however, only if Sasportas understood himself and was understood by others to be a master of the textual tradition that he claimed to represent.

In an earlier comment to Joseph Halevi in Livorno, Sasportas had dismissed Nantawa's proof from *The Book of Zerubbabel* but added a telling aside:

He who strays from the path of reason [Nantawa] further said: that this approach was written in the prophecy of Zerubbabel, which, according to him, states that the sages and scholars of Israel shall deny the King Messiah, and despise him, that he shall be imprisoned, etc. He responded with a lie. One cannot find this in any book. There is a passage like this

[43] מה אומר ובכן תדעו על ענין זה, הלא ענין זה של התפיסה היא כתובה בנבואת זרובבל, הלא היא אצלנו, שאומרת שגדולי וחכמי ישראל יכפרו במלך המשיח ויבזו אותו ויכו אותו ויהיה תפוס בתפיסה כאשר יראה הרואה שם. Sasportas, *ZNZ*, 157.

[44] והראיה על זה כי מעת לכתו לאיזמיר וחטאתו מלפפתו והולכת לפניו עד שהושם בבית הסוהר דיליה, כי נבואת זרובבל שאמרת שמדברת עליו אינה בעולם ולא נמצאת ומכ"ש פירושה. Ibid., 182.

in the *Zohar*, but it does not concern someone who has not yet performed the deeds of the Messiah and the given signs that offer proof.[45]

Over and above his response to Nantawa, where he denied the very existence of *The Book of Zerubbabel*, here he denied that the theory of the
fallen Messiah could be substantiated by any written text. In order to
buttress his argument, Sasportas mentioned a possible passage in the
Zohar only to dismiss it as irrelevant to Sabbetai Zevi as a Messiah who
had yet to substantiate his messianic pretensions. Sasportas's reaction
to the invocation of *The Book of Zerubbabel* was to deny its existence.
This was patently false, as Gershom Scholem gleefully exclaimed in
1942: "The words of Rabbi Jacob Sasportas are incorrect!"[46] *The Book of
Zerubbabel* had appeared in print nearly a century and a half before
Sabbetai Zevi and had been cited by liturgical poets a millennium earlier. The Sabbatians were almost certainly not the only Jews in the seventeenth century who attributed the work to rabbinic antiquity. Sasportas's error, however, may have been an honest one. He may have
been unaware of the book's existence or of its citation in the liturgical
hymns. In any event, his strategy was quite clear: to repudiate its existence entirely. A text that does not exist cannot be authoritative.

Sasportas need not have responded this way. A Yiddish chronicle of
Sabbatianism by Leyb ben Ozer, *Bashraybung fun shabsai tsvi* (Yid. The
story of Sabbetai Zevi), offers a valuable counterpoint to his denial.[47]
Written by the sexton of the Ashkenazi congregation in Amsterdam in
1718, *Bashraybung fun shabsai tsvi* recounts a series of conversations
and stories that the author had heard about the Sabbatian movement.[48]
Sasportas and Leyb ben Ozer both discussed a somewhat shadowy

---

[45] ועוד אמר הנוטה מדרך השכל כי תפיסה זאת כתובה בנבואת זרובבל הלא היא אצלו האומרת שגדולי וחכמי
ישראל יכפרו במלך המשיח ויבזזו אותו ויהיה תפוס וכו', ושקר ענה ולא נמצאה זה בשום ספר ובזוהר איתא בר"מ
מענין זה אבל לא על מי שעדיין לא עשה מעשה משיח ולא סימנים הנראים ומוכיחים עליו.
Ibid., 154.

[46] "New Sabbatian Documents from the book *To-ei Ruah*" (Hebrew), in *Mehkere shabtaut*, 43.

[47] Leyb ben Ozer, *Sippur ma-asei shabbtai sevi: Bashraybung fun shabsai tsvi*, trans. Zalman Shazar, ed. Shlomo Zucker and Rivka Plesser (Jerusalem: Zalman Shazar Center, 1978). On this edition, see the review by Chava Turniansky, *KS* 54 (1979): 161–167. For a French translation, see *La
beauté du diable: Portrait de Sabbataï Zevi*, ed. and trans. Nathan Weinstock (Paris: Honoré Champion, 2011); for an analysis, see Irit Shapira-Meir, "Historiography and Autobiography in Leyb
ben Ozer's 'Bashraybung fun Shabsai Tsvi'" (Hebrew) (MA thesis, Hebrew University of Jerusalem, 2014).

[48] Paul Ira Radensky, "Leyb ben Ozer's *Bashraybung fun Shabsai Tsvi*: An Ashkenazic Appropriation of Sabbatianism," *JQR* 88 (1997): 43–56.

figure named Nehemiah Hacohen, an Ashkenazi prophet who, as far as scholars have been able to ascertain, left no written works.[49] The two accounts agree that Nehemiah traveled from Poland on behalf of his coreligionists to the Ottoman Empire in the summer of 1666 with the express intention of interviewing Sabbetai Zevi and ascertaining whether he was the Messiah. Both agree that he spent three days in interviews with Sabbetai Zevi before departing in haste. Although he referred to Nehemiah on a number of occasions and repeatedly mentioned his series of conversations with Sabbetai Zevi, Sasportas gave little indication as to their content.[50] Much of this may be the result of Sasportas's prejudice against him: at various points, he referred to him as a madman and a false prophet.[51]

By contrast, Leyb ben Ozer, described him as an erudite man and a kabbalist unlike any other in all of Poland.[52] Unlike Sasportas, who appears to have learned of Nehemiah from the reports of others, Leyb ben Ozer had met the Polish prophet and had hosted him for fourteen weeks in Amsterdam in 1690.[53] He recounted the contents of Nehemiah's conversations with Sabbetai Zevi in relative detail:

On the second day, he [Nehemiah] returned to Sabbetai Zevi and began to engage with him in the dialectical study of kabbalistic books. He said to him: How can you say that you are the Messiah son of David, the redeemer of Israel? According to all our kabbalistic books, you cannot be the Messiah son of David, because they stipulate that the Messiah son of Joseph must precede him and wage war with Gog and Magog. In the first war, the Messiah son of Ephraim shall win; but in the second, he shall fight with them again and the Messiah son of Ephraim shall be slaughtered at the gates of Jerusalem.[54]

[49] Scholem, *Sabbatai Sevi*, 658–668; idem, "The Sabbatian Movement in Poland" (Hebrew), in *Mehkarim*, 74–76; for a challenge to Scholem's reconstruction of Nehemiah and Sabbetai Zevi, see Isaiah Sonne, "Sabbatian Issues in the Notebook of R. Abraham Rovigo" (Hebrew), *Sefunot* 3–4 (1960): 62–67.

[50] Sasportas, *ZNZ*, 77, 172, 174, 345.

[51] Sasportas, *ZNZ*, 174: "He had never been a prophet, but in Poland he was crazy and spoke utter madness."

[52] On Nehemiah's sojourn with Leyb ben Ozer in Amsterdam, see L. Fuks, "Sabatianisme in Amsterdam in het Begin van de 18 Eeuw. Enkele Beschouwingen over Reb Leib Oizers en zijn Werk," *SR* 14 (1980): 24. For skepticism about Nehemiah's capabilities as a kabbalist, see Scholem, *Sabbatai Sevi*, 658.

[53] Leyb ben Ozer, *Sippur ma-asei shabbtai sevi*, 165. Sasportas was in Amsterdam at the time and could have met either or both of them; however, I have found no trace of any such meeting.

[54] דען אנדרן טאג ווידר קומן בייא ש"צ אונ' מיט אים בגונן מפלפל צו זיין אויש ספרי הקבלה אונ' צו אים גזאגט:

Leyb ben Ozer continued to recount the destruction of the Jews in the wake of the Messiah son of Ephraim's death and the redemption that would come only with the arrival of the Messiah son of David. In his account, Leyb ben Ozer referred alternatively to the Messiah son of Joseph and to the Messiah son of Ephraim without discriminating between them.[55] Nehemiah's crucial point as filtered through Leyb ben Ozer was quite clear: according to kabbalistic books the redemption would necessarily entail the coming of two Messiahs, not one. Sabbetai Zevi and his followers were not sticking to the script, and, therefore, he was not the genuine Messiah. Sabbetai Zevi attempted to rebut Nehemiah's queries by claiming that one of his students had been Messiah son of Ephraim and had been killed, but Nehemiah remained unconvinced.

Leyb ben Ozer did not mention the titles of any of the kabbalistic books discussed by Sabbetai Zevi and Nehemiah.[56] Furthermore, the report of the conversation did not contain any mention of the sages mocking the Messiah son of David or of his subsequent imprisonment. Nevertheless, Scholem's assertion that Nehemiah was referring to *The Book of Zerubbabel* appears quite reasonable.[57] If Nehemiah was indeed referring to the work in his conversation with Sabbetai Zevi, he came to a conclusion about it that was very different from Sasportas's. The Sephardic rabbi rejected the invocation of *The Book of Zerubbabel* as an authoritative text; the Polish prophet accepted its authority but argued that the events it described did not correspond to the events he was witnessing. Leyb ben Ozer leaves little doubt as to the centrality of the written word in the exchanges between Sabbetai Zevi and Nehemiah:

וויא זאגשטו דז דוא בישט משיח בן דוד דר גואל פון ישראל? פאלגנש אל אונזר ספרי הקבלה קאנשטו קיין משיח בן דוד זיין דען לפי דבריהם מוז משיח בן יוסף ערשטן קומן אונ' מלחמה האלטן מיט גוג ומגוג אונ' דיא ערשטי מלחמה וער משיח בן אפירו גוווינן אונ' צום צווייטן מול ווערט ער ווידר מלחמה מיט זיא הלטן זא ווערט משיח בן אפרים נהרג ווערן אין די פפורטן פון ירושלים.

Ibid., 96–97.

[55] In addition to Berger and Himmelfarb cited above, see Joseph Heinemann, "The Messiah of Ephraim and the Premature Exodus of the Tribe of Ephraim," *Harvard Theological Review* 68 (1975): 1–15.

[56] In the third account of the exchange between Nehemiah Hacohen and Sabbetai Zevi, Barukh of Arezzo described Sabbetai Zevi as sitting with tractate Hullin of the Babylonian Talmud and the *Zohar*. See Barukh of Arezzo, "Memorial to the Children of Israel" (Hebrew), in *Inyene shabetai tsevi*, ed. Aron Freimann (Berlin: Mekize Nirdamim, 1912), 53. An English translation appears in David J. Halperin, *Sabbatai Zevi: Testimonies to a Fallen Messiah* (Oxford: Littman Library, 2007), 48.

[57] Scholem, *Sabbatai Sevi*, 661. Scholem also includes *Otot mashiah*, a text not mentioned by Sasportas or his correspondents.

Thus the two of them disputed fiercely with one another and their dialectical dispute continued for three days and three nights, and they slept
very little those three nights. They did nothing except take out kabbalistic books, one after the other, each man against the other.[58]

For three days Sabbetai Zevi and Nehemiah disputed the correct interpretation of a particular text, but neither one doubted that authority
lay with the written word. In fact, their disputes took place in the presence of and concerning the contents of books.

In all three accounts of Nehemiah Hacohen's visit to Gallipoli, his
abrupt departure precipitated the interrogation of Sabbetai Zevi by the
Ottoman sultan and the Messiah's conversion to Islam. In order to escape the throng of believers surrounding the prison, Nehemiah hast-
ily converted to Islam, informed upon Sabbetai Zevi to the Ottoman
authorities, and returned to Poland where he reverted to Judaism. Nehemiah's visit may have triggered a moment of crisis within the Sabbatian movement, but the repeated invocations of *The Book of Zerubbabel* did not disappear. Quite the opposite: Nathan of Gaza appealed
to the work to justify the Messiah's subsequent conversion to Islam.
This conversion posed a profound problem for Nathan's career as a
prophet.[59] The empirical fact of the Messiah as a Muslim appeared to
contradict all of his earlier prophecies, but Nathan of Gaza worked hard
to ensure that the contradiction was only apparent. One of his primary
strategies was to seek textual precedents that spoke of a Messiah's conversion. Nathan of Gaza amassed a mélange of texts, including some
that referred to a Messiah's conversion to Islam, such as the diary of
the sixteenth-century Sephardic rabbi Joseph Taitazack, and others that
referred to a Messiah's conversion without specifying a religion. Nathan of Gaza then proceeded to apply these texts to Sabbetai Zevi.
Among these passages he wrote:

> Furthermore it is found in the prophecy of Zerubbabel, which said ex-
> plicitly that they shall call the King Messiah an apostate, and so too the
> books of Rabbi Judah Loew of Prague, the teacher of Yomtob Lipmann

[58] זא דז דיזי צווייא גר שטארק קיגן אננדר ווארן אונ' איר פלפול אונ' טושיף האט גדייארט דרייא טאג אונ' דרייא
נאכט דז זיא אין דיא זעלביגי דרייא נאכט גר ווינג גשלאפן האבן אונ' אנדרשט ניקש גטאן אז אין ספר קבלה פור אונ'
זך אנדרי דר נאך אפור גנומן

Leyb ben Ozer, *Sippur ma-asei shabbtai sevi*, 98.

[59] Chaim Wirszubski, "The Sabbatian Ideology of the Messiah's Conversion" (Hebrew), in *Ben
ha-shitin* (Jerusalem: Magnes Press, 1990), 126; the article first appeared in *Zion* 3 (1938): 220.

Figure 7. Sabbetai Zevi, in Thomas Coenen, *Ydele verwachtinge de Joden getoont in den person van Sabethai Zevi* (Amsterdam, 1669). This image of Sabbetai Zevi, which appeared in an account published in Amsterdam in 1669, shows the Jewish Messiah pointing to a book. The written word was no less important to Sabbetai Zevi and his followers than it was to Sasportas. The National Library of Israel.

Heller, dealt extensively with the issue of the King Messiah who shall be bound and tied to the Ishmaelite nation.[60]

60 ועוד שנמצא בנבואת זרובבל שאומר' בפ' שלמלך המשיח יקראו משומד. וכן בספרי מהר"י לווא רבו של תוספת
י"ט נושא ונותן הרבה בספריו ענין מה"מ שיהיה אדוק וקשור באומת ישמעאל.
Ibid., 138–139. Scholem republished the text as "Nathan of Gaza's Letter on Sabbetai Zevi and His Conversion" (Hebrew), *Kovez al Yad* 14 (1966): 419–456. The article was reprinted in Scholem, *Mehkarim*. Quotation on 245. Quotation as it appears in Scholem.

As Chaim Wirszubski noted, none of the extant versions of *The Book of Zerubbabel* contain a discussion of an apostate Messiah. This may not have mattered to Nathan of Gaza. With this textual hodgepodge—the diary of a Spanish exile living in the Ottoman Empire (Taitazack), the theological treatises of a sixteenth-century Ashkenazi rabbi in Prague (Judah Loew), and a medieval apocalypse that had no apparent author (*The Book of Zerubbabel*)—Nathan hoped to fix upon any text as a source of authority. In this instance, unlike Hosea Nantawa's earlier invocation, the issue was not so much the antiquity of *The Book of Zerubbabel* as the mere fact of its existence.

Sasportas was apparently unaware of this fragment of Nathan of Gaza's writing, but one can easily imagine his response to it. *The Book of Zerubbabel* made one further and significant appearance in *Zizath Novel Zvi*. In 1669, several years after Sabbetai Zevi's conversion, Sasportas corresponded with Jacob ibn Sa-adun of Saleh.[61] Ibn Sa-adun defended the Jews of Saleh who persisted in their belief in Sabbetai Zevi, and cited Nantawa's correspondence with the Jews of Livorno as proof:

> Furthermore, a third letter arrived and offered decisive evidence. It is a strong pillar that is certainly reliable, for it was found among the archives of the sage, Rabbi Saul Siriro of Fez, may he rest in paradise. It is the prophecy of Zerubbabel, who testified that he used to speak with Metatron, the ministering angel, just as someone would speak with his fellow man. The text of this prophecy was exactly the same, word for word, letter for letter as the others. Two identical versions of the prophecy arrived, one from the land of Israel and one from Egypt. Apparently the sage [Nantawa], to whom your student [Joseph Halevi] responded, had also sent you a version of it since you [Sasportas] appended a note to it saying that the prophecy of Zerubbabel, which he [Nantawa] claimed spoke about him [Sabbetai Zevi], did not exist, all the more so with such an explanation. This shows that he [Nantawa] had sent you [Sasportas] a copy of it. The principles of the prophecy and the things which Metatron the ministering angel told Zerubbabel as a sign: the man who became known throughout the world and who would subsequently be slandered as an apostate, accused of all the abominations hated by God, that man is the true redeemer. But because of the sins of the rab-

---

[61] On *The Book of Zerubbabel* in North Africa, see Elie Moyal, *Ha-tenuah ha-shabtait be-Morocco: toldoteha u-mekoroteha* (Tel Aviv: Am Oved, 1984), 219–223 and passim.

bis and the scholars who slandered him, he shall remain imprisoned for eight years in order to atone for their sins.[62]

Ibn Sa-adun claimed to have discovered a copy of the prophecy of Zerubbabel in the archives of a rabbi from Fez that made a prediction similar to that made in the letter sent by Nantawa to Livorno. In his rendering, the prophecy of Zerubbabel foretold not only that the Messiah would be subject to the mockery of the sages; he would also be imprisoned for a period of eight years. This held out the possibility that Sabbetai Zevi, who was still very much alive in 1669, was indeed the Messiah. Ibn Sa-adun thus returned to *The Book of Zerubbabel*, which had been held authoritative both prior to the Messiah's conversion, by Hosea Nantawa, and subsequent to his conversion, by Nathan of Gaza, as a source of still further hope for another five years.

Sasportas held his ground and insisted that *The Book of Zerubbabel* was a falsification. He then proceeded to identify inconsistencies between its supposed prediction of an eight-year imprisonment and one of Nathan of Gaza's subsequent prophecies identifying the year 1670 as the year of redemption:

> Look at the false prophecy of Zerubbabel, how it contradicts the words of Nathan: for he [Nathan] claimed that the year 1670 would be the year of redemption while the other testimony [*The Book Zerubbabel* cited by Ibn Sa-adun] claimed that it would come after years of imprisonment. Both of them contradict each other and are completely false. For in the beginning, Nathan said nothing about his conversion or his imprisonment, and the prophecy of Zerubbabel said nothing about his conversion or his imprisonment for so many years. Unless you are referring to the imprisonment of his soul, and in the end "that soul shall be utterly cut off: his iniquity shall be upon him"[63] (Num: 15:31).

[62] ועוד כי בא הכתב השלישית והכרייעה לכף זכות והיא עמוד חזק שראוי לסמוך עליה שנמצאת בבית גנזיו של החכם השלם כמה"ר שאול סירירו נ"ע בפי"ס, והיא נבואת זרובבל שהעיד שהיה מדבר עם מטטרון שר הפנים כאשר ידבר איש לרעהו, ונוסח הנבואה הזאת ג"כ כמו שמצאנו כתוב בה אות באות ותיבה בתיבה ככה באו שני נוסחת הנבואה ההיא א' מארץ ישראל ונסח אחר ממצרים, ונראה שגם החכם אשר השיב לו תלמידך גם הוא שלח לכם נסחה שהרי השיב על זה בהגהה ואמר כי נבואת זרובבל שאמרת שמדברת עליו אינה בעולם ולא נמצאת ומכ"ש פירושה, נמצא ששלח לכם נסחה. וכללות נבואתו ודבריו שנתן לו סימן מטטרון ש"ה לזרובבל, כי האיש אשר יצא שמעו בכל העולם ואחר כך יוציאו עליו דבה שנשתמד ויוציאו עליו כל תועבות אשר שנא ה' הוא הוא הגואל האמיתי, ובעון החכמים והרבנים שהוציאו עליו דבה רעה ישאר שמנה שנים מצוצמות במאסר לכפר על עונם.
Sasportas, *ZNZ*, 333.
[63] וראה נבואת זרובבל השקרייית איך הכחישה דברי נת"ן כי הוא אמר שנת תת"ל והאחרת אומרת לאחר שמונה

In this instance, Sasportas appeared to have anticipated Scholem's re-mark that not all references to *The Book of Zerubbabel* in the Sabbatian literature referred to the same text.[64] Ibn Sa-adun may indeed have pos-sessed a prophecy that Sabbetai Zevi would be released from prison after eight years, and attached it to the tradition of the scorned Mes-siah associated with *The Book of Zerubbabel*. If this had occurred, Sas-portas dismissed Ibn Sa-adun's invocation of *The Book of Zerubbabel* as inconsistent with the Sabbatians' own evidence.

Sasportas, however, was not finished. Ibn Sa-adun had impugned the name of a North African rabbinic luminary, Saul Siriro, and he could not let this pass unnoticed:

> Heaven forfend that I should believe that it was found in the archive of
> the judge, our holy rabbi, Saul Siriro, of blessed memory; rather, one of
> your friends who subscribes to this faith of yours invented it and attrib-
> uted it to the great figure after his death.[65]

Saul Siriro had served as a rabbi and judge in Fez for over half a cen-tury until his death in 1654.[66] His nephew and successor, Emmanuel Siriro, had consulted Sasportas on a question concerning Jewish mar-riage law some five years after his uncle's death when Sasportas was resident in Saleh. Siriro and his colleague had asked Sasportas about a Jewish man who had pursued a woman to the point that he had be-trothed her but did not want to marry her. Sasportas responded that the court should compel the man to marry her, lest the daughters of Is-rael be turned into concubines. To judge from the remaining half of the correspondence that appeared in Sasportas's responsa, the exchange had been sharp. At one point Sasportas exploded, "You are not a bath and I am not Aphrodite," alluding to a passage in the Mishnah (Avodah Zarah 3:4) about a pagan philosopher and Rabban Gamliel in Aphro-dite's bath.[67] For all the vitriol between Sasportas and Emmanuel Siriro,

---

שנים למאסרו, ושניהם מוכחשים ומוזמים כי נת״ן בתחילה לא דיבר כלום מהמרתו ולא ממאסרו ולא נבואת זרובבל
דיברה כלום מהמרתו וגם לא היה במאסר כל כך שנים, אם לא שנאמר על מאסר הנפש ולסוף הכרת תכרת עונה בה.
Ibid., 357.

[64] "New Sabbatian Documents from the book *To-ei Ruah*," 47.

[65] וחלילה לי להאמין כי נמצאת בבית גנזיו של האב״ד כמהו״ר שאול סירירו ז״ל כי אם אחד מחביריך בעלי אמונתך
זו בדאה והמציאה ותלאה באילן גדול אחרי מותו.
Sasportas, *ZNZ*, 357.

[66] Bentov, "The Siriro Family," 337–338.

[67] Sasportas, *Ohel ya-akov*, #3, 5b. On the passage in the Mishnah, see Seth Schwartz, *Imperi-*

however, they were fighting over a matter of Jewish law. Ibn Sa-adun had invoked the memory of Saul Siriro as an accessory to Sabbatian messianism, something Sasportas contemptuously referred to as "this faith of yours."

"This faith" of the Sabbatians was built upon a different corpus of texts from the Oral and Written Torah upheld as authoritative by Sasportas. The disputes over *The Book of Zerubbabel* point to the importance of an early medieval Hebrew book in the period before and after the conversion of Sabbetai Zevi to Islam. They are of far greater interest, however, for what they indicate about the role of textual authority in this episode of early modern messianism. Three different attitudes toward *The Book of Zerubbabel* appear in the Sabbatian controversies: those of the Sabbatians, Nehemiah Hacohen as recounted by Leyb ben Ozer, and Sasportas. To the Sabbatians, *The Book of Zerubbabel* was an authoritative text. It contained a relatively detailed picture of the advent of the Messiah as represented by Sabbetai Zevi. In addition, the book derived its authority for some of the Sabbatians from its antiquity. None of the Sabbatians offer a full-fledged theory of its authorship, but both Hosea Nantawa and Jacob ibn Sa-adun implied the work was ancient. Nathan of Gaza made no such claim, and he mentioned it in the same breath as two sixteenth-century works. He did not appear to be troubled by or interested in the work's age. For all of them, though, *The Book of Zerubbabel* served to authorize Sabbetai Zevi as the Messiah.

Nehemiah Hacohen agreed with the Sabbatians on one crucial point: the authority of *The Book of Zerubbabel*. In his interrogation of Sabbetai Zevi, Nehemiah confronted him with the doctrine of the two Messiahs as it appeared in "our kabbalistic books." Nehemiah did not mention their antiquity, but this seems a reasonable inference from the way in which he referred to them. If Nehemiah agreed with the Sabbatians about the authority of these kabbalistic books, he parted company with them concerning their interpretation, which he rejected. Their dispute focused on the correct exegesis of what they both agreed was an authoritative text. Nehemiah found the lack of a previous Messiah son of

alism and Jewish Society, 200 B.C.E. to 640 C.E. (Princeton, NJ: Princeton University Press, 2001), chap. 5; Azzan Yadin, "Rabban Gamliel, Aphrodite's Bath, and the Question of Pagan Monotheism," *JQR* 96 (2006): 149–179.

Joseph particularly damning; the Sabbatians found the story of a scorned Messiah particularly useful.

If the divide between Nehemiah and the Sabbatians focused on exegesis, the distinction between their position and that of Sasportas was epistemological. Sasportas was completely underwhelmed by the dispute over the correct interpretation of *The Book of Zerubbabel*; he claimed that the work was not an authoritative source and was the product of the Sabbatian imagination. Sasportas was wrong on the last account, as the Sabbatians had clearly not invented the book out of whole cloth. His error offers a crucial window into one of the tensions that undergirded the totality of the Sabbatian controversies. Sasportas and Nathan of Gaza argued over many things: the nature of prophecy, the doctrine of the Messiah, the validity of the law, to name only a few. Their argument over *The Book of Zerubbabel* points to a conflict between two competing bodies of knowledge. For Sasportas, the corpus of rabbinic literature was authoritative. This corpus, which can roughly be identified with the Sephardic legacy he held so dear, was wide and variegated. It included the Mishnah and the Talmud, both Babylonian and Palestinian, Maimonides and the *Zohar*, Nahmanides and Solomon ibn Adret.[68] It even went so far as to include *Sefer hasidim*, a work of medieval German piety seemingly quite far from the learned Sephardic elite. But this corpus was not so porous as to include a book he had never heard of that posited a messianic doctrine that contradicted his own reading of the Talmud and Maimonides. The Sabbatians, by contrast, had opened up the corpus of the Oral Torah and treated *The Book of Zerubbabel* as if it were just as authoritative as Talmud and Maimonides. They were more than happy to draw upon *The Book of Zerubbabel*, and were perfectly capable of explaining or explaining away any passage from Maimonides invoked by Sasportas or any other critic.

Medieval rabbinic literature served as the point of departure for Sasportas's reasoning. In his sobering antimessianism he reacted with caustic erudition to the anarchic enthusiasm of Sabbetai Zevi and his followers. At one point he rebuked the Sabbatians for using "the joy of

---

[68] Sasportas repeatedly pointed to a messianically charged passage about a bird's nest in the *Zohar* that he wanted the Sabbatians, whether it be Nathan of Gaza or his colleagues in the Sephardic Diaspora, to interpret to his satisfaction. For his challenges, see Sasportas, *ZNZ*, 48, 66, 69; on this passage as a significant text in the *Zohar* in the context of the Messiah, see Yehuda Liebes, "The Students of the Gra, Sabbatianism, and the Jewish Point" (Hebrew), in *Le-tzvi u-le-gaon: mi-shabtai zvi el ha-gaon mi-vilna* (Tel Aviv: Idra, 2017), 130n37.

redemption" as the ill-founded basis for verifying their prophecies.[69] Happiness, Sasportas seemed to say, was not a normative Jewish value. The law, as represented in the writing of prior rabbinic scholars, rather than the ecstatic experience of contemporary prophets and their followers, was the standard by which events should be assessed. Sasportas had a manual, the law code of Maimonides and the totality of medieval rabbinic literature, and the experience of the Sabbatians did not correspond to the written description of the messianic age within these texts. *Zizath novel zvi* constituted an elaborate justification for his reading of these sources and his response to contemporary events. Sasportas's confidence in the textual traditions of rabbinic literature equipped him with a certain suspicion toward experience. This hostility toward untutored sensibility emerged in his pronounced fear of the Jewish crowds that gathered to celebrate the news of the Messiah.

THE NEWS IN THE SYNAGOGUE

News of redemption spread throughout the Jewish world by way of the mail. Jews who lived in closer proximity to the Messiah in the Ottoman Empire sent letters to their coreligionists throughout Europe and North Africa. The network of Sephardic merchants that was such a central conduit for early modern commerce was quickly transformed into a messianic news corps. When letters from the Ottoman Empire or one of the intermediary ports of call, such as Livorno, arrived in Amsterdam or Hamburg, they were declaimed in public before a crowd eagerly awaiting news of redemption. In her memoirs Glickl bas Judah-Leib recalled the arrival of news in Hamburg:

> The joy each time the letters were received is impossible to describe. Most of the letters that arrived were sent to the Sephardim; each time, they took them to their synagogue and read them aloud. Ashkenazim, young and old, also went along to their synagogue. Portuguese youth dressed up in their finest clothing.[70]

[69] Sasportas, *ZNZ*, 350.

[70] דיא שמחה וואז ג׳וועזין ווען מאן כתבי׳ האט ג׳יקראגין דאז איזט ניט זו בישרייבן. דיא מיינשטי כתבי׳ דיא קומן זיין, האבין דיא ספרדיי׳ ביקומן, זוא זענין זיא אלי צייט מיט אין איר בית הכנסת גנגין אונ׳ לשם גילייאט. זענין טייטשי, יונג אונ׳ אלט, אך אין איר בית הכנסת גנגין. אונ׳ דער פורטיגיזין יונגי גיזעלין האבין זיך אלי מאלט אין איר בעשטי קליידיר אן גיטאן.

Upon hearing news of the Messiah, Glickl's own father-in-law sold his possessions and packed up in preparation for his emigration to Palestine.

Glickl expressed considerable empathy for those who believed in the news of the redemption, but regretted the loss of property, foodstuffs, and, on an entirely different scale, hope caused by the eventual demise of the Sabbatian movement. Sasportas, who witnessed similar scenes of jubilation in Hamburg, perhaps even the very same ones, drew a rather different and less empathetic conclusion:

> All these prophecies entered the ears of the masses without any examination or investigation, and even some of the learned men among them accepted it as well, without casting any doubt on the rumors, even if they were things exceedingly difficult for the intellect to accept. They said whoever casts doubt on this is a heretic and has no portion with the God of Israel.[71]

Here and elsewhere in *Zizath novel zvi* Sasportas objected to the gullibility of the crowds, their willingness to accept the reports of redemption without thorough and careful consideration of what was actually contained in them. They failed to subject the news either to the critical rigors of their own intellects or, more importantly, to the sources of their tradition. Even worse, this enthusiasm of the crowd was infectious. Time and again, Sasportas lamented that the rabbinic elite, or those with knowledge of tradition, were caught up in the same enthusiasm. In this instance, the learned men of the Portuguese Nation in Hamburg went so far as to declare as heretics anyone who doubted the veracity of the Messiah. To Sasportas, the denial of doubt led to a confusion of categories on the part of the believers: they redefined those who upheld Mosaic law as heretics.

Glickl, *Zikhronos 1691–1719*, ed. and trans. Chava Turniansky (Jerusalem: Zalman Shazar Center and Ben-Zion Dinur Center, 2006), 152–155, as cited by Tishby in Sasportas, *ZNZ*, 17n3 with reference to *Die Memorien der Glückel von Hameln (1645–1719)*, ed. David Kaufmann (Frankfurt, 1896). See Elisheva Carlebach, "Die messianische Haltung der deutschen Juden im Spiegel von Glikls 'Zikhroynes,'" in *Die Hamburger Kauffrau Glikl: jüdische Existenz in der Frühen Neuzeit*, ed. Monika Richarz (Hamburg: Christians, 2001), 238–253; eadem, "The Sabbatian Posture of German Jewry," 26–27.

[71] וכל אלו הדברים נכנסו באזני ההמון בלתי חקירה ודרישה, וקצת מבעלי תורה עמם מחזיקים ידיהם בלתי מטילים ספק בענין אף אם הם דברים רחוקים מהשכל, לפי שהיו אומרים כל המספק בזה הוא כופר ואין לו חלק באלק"י ישראל. Sasportas, *ZNZ*, 17.

The public celebration of the Messiah's arrival in the synagogue and on the street, however, had consequences far beyond the Ashkenazic and Sephardic Jews in places such as Hamburg and Amsterdam. The crowd not only swept up the rabbinic elite in their enthusiasm; it made a mockery of the Jews in the eyes of the gentiles:

> The entire city of Amsterdam shook with fright, and they were terrified of the Lord. They increased their celebration with great joy in the markets and the streets. They danced joyously in the synagogue and carried the Torah scrolls out of the synagogue adorned with beautiful jewels without paying any attention to the jealousy and the hatred of the nations. To the contrary, they called out in public and announced it to everyone, and whoever heard about it, thought it was ridiculous.[72]

Sasportas continued to describe a similar although even more jubilant response in Hamburg upon the arrival of the news from Amsterdam. The gentiles, or this "jealousy and hatred of the nations," played an important role in Sasportas's criticism of the Sabbatians. Sasportas's sole concern with the gentiles, whom he elsewhere referred to as "our enemies," was what they would think about the public display of Jewish enthusiasm. Shame and embarrassment mark his discussion of the Jews in the eyes of foreign observers. He saw the public display of joy and celebration of the new Messiah as an invitation for the gentiles to mock Jewish gullibility and as a possible threat to Jewish safety, lest the declaration of a new Jewish king engender charges of rebellion against the Jews.

The anxiety about the effect of Jewish crowds upon gentile opinion stands out in terms of Sasportas's own intellectual trajectory within the early modern Sephardic Diaspora. Sasportas was deeply concerned about the effects of Sabbatian enthusiasm on the gentile perception of the Jews; he thought his contemporaries were making fools of themselves in public. At best, they would simply be the object of scorn and derision; at worst, they would generate anger and resentment that might jeopardize their all too tenuous position within host societies throughout western Europe and beyond. Sasportas betrayed no con-

[72] ותהום כל עיר אמסטרדאם ותהי לחרדת אלקי"ם, הגדילו השמחה בתופים ובמחולות בשוקים וברחובות ובבית הכנסת ריקוד ומחול וספרי תורה כולם מוציאים חוץ להיכל בתכשיטין נאים בלתי שים על לב הסכנה של קנאת ושנאת האומות. ואדרבא היו מכריזים בפומבי ומגלים לאומות כל הנשמע ולשחוק היינו בעיניהם.
Ibid.

cern for the knowledge or the methods produced and used in the contemporary European republic of letters. Not once throughout *Zizath novel zvi* did he indulge in that parade of erudition so central to the image of the *haham kolel*, an attempt by his Jewish contemporaries to translate the notion of the universal man into a rabbinic idiom.[73] As his discussion of Maimonides, *Sefer hasidim*, and Solomon ibn Adret indicated, Sasportas was quite confident that the Jewish tradition itself had the intellectual resources with which to handle the challenges of a messianic movement. If only his contemporaries could read Maimonides and other sources with the proper care and attention they deserved, then Sabbetai Zevi and Nathan of Gaza would be relegated to their proper place in the hierarchy of Jewish life, those very margins that Sasportas chafed at occupying.

In this lack of concern for alien wisdom, both the content of European learning and the methods of historical criticism, and his nearly obsessive focus on the impact of Jewish crowds upon the image of the Jew in the eyes of the gentiles, Sasportas stood in marked contrast to other rabbinic intellectuals in his own milieu, such as Menasseh ben Israel, Isaac Aboab da Fonseca, and Joseph Solomon Delmedigo. Sasportas knew the former two quite well and cited the third at one point in *Zizath novel zvi*. To varying degrees, all these figures engaged with the world of European learning around them. Menasseh ben Israel composed works in the vernacular as well as in Latin and devoted one of his most important books, *Conciliador*, to the reconciliation of discrepancies in the Hebrew scriptures, a burning question in the European republic of letters. Isaac Aboab da Fonseca translated Abraham Cohen de Herrera's kabbalistic treatise *El Puerto del Cielo* from Spanish into Hebrew and amassed an impressive library of which Judaica was only a small fraction.[74] In his wanderings throughout Europe and the Ottoman Empire, Joseph Solomon Delmedigo sought to translate Kabbalah into the terms of Neoplatonism and expressed sustained interest in the new science of the seventeenth century.[75] By contrast, Sas-

---

[73] Ruderman, *Early Modern Jewry*, 120, 200.

[74] See Yosef Kaplan, "The Libraries of Three Sephardi Rabbis in Early Modern Western Europe" (Hebrew), in *Sifriyot ve-osfe sefarim*, ed. Moshe Sluhovsky and Yosef Kaplan (Jerusalem: Zalman Shazar Center, 2006), 225–260.

[75] For Sasportas on Delmedigo, see *ZNZ*, 147. On Delmedigo, see David B. Ruderman, *Jewish Thought and Scientific Discovery in Early Modern Europe* (New Haven, CT: Yale University Press, 1995), chap. 4.

portas did not adduce a single non-Jewish source throughout the pages of *Zizath novel zvi*. He had neither desire nor claim to be current with the latest developments in European learning. Rather than the image of the heresy hunter favored by prior scholars of Sabbatianism, Matt Goldish has suggested that the more accurate analogue for Sasportas was the contemporary critic of enthusiasm, intellectuals such as Henry More and Meric Casaubon studied by Michael Heyd.[76] Like Sasportas's, a considerable part of their criticism was what Heyd called theological criticism. Yet even this analogue has limits: if More and Casaubon turned to Seneca via Justus Lipsius and the newly issued editions of the church fathers, Sasportas drew upon Maimonides seemingly without any cognizance of them or their sources.

Sasportas differentiated himself from a number of distinct but sometimes overlapping groups. He rejected the Sabbatians and the Sabbatian prophets; he stood apart from his educated colleagues in the Sephardic Diaspora; and he distanced himself from his would-be constituents, the lay members of the Portuguese Jewish Nation that he contemptuously referred to as the crowd (Heb. *hamon*) and the masses (Heb. *hedyotot*). In *Zizath novel zvi* he sought to invent a normative Jewish textual tradition that would regulate both the lives of laypeople and the intellectual habits of the elite. The Jewish laity he found guilty of indiscriminate enthusiasm. They seized every piece of news as cause for celebration and made fools of themselves before gentile witnesses who were at best indifferent to their joy and at worst extremely suspicious of such public gatherings by a questionably useful minority population. The elites, those rabbis who by his account should have served as allies in his campaign to defer the Messiah, had forgotten their training. Instead of studying Maimonides and *Sefer hasidim* and Solomon ibn Adret, they had drunk deeply from the wells of European learning. In a period of peace and security, Sasportas would not have had any problem with such wide reading and diverse interests, as one can discern from his enduring friendship with the Spanish poet Miguel Levi de Barrios. But the middle years of the 1660s were not normal times. The intellectual promiscuity of his colleagues had left them woefully unprepared to counter the claims of redemption with skepticism and

---

[76] Goldish, *The Sabbatean Prophets*, 149. Michael Heyd, *"Be Sober and Reasonable": The Critique of Enthusiasm in the Seventeenth and Early Eighteenth Centuries* (Leiden: Brill, 1995).

doubt, which Sasportas saw as the principal obligation of a Jewish intellectual in the service of the Jewish textual tradition and the law. Instead of turning to the sources, they had abandoned their learning and joined the crowd. The behavior of his colleagues was a particularly damning symptom of the decline in the authority of the rabbinate, the expanding power of ignorant but often wealthy laypeople, and the decreasing emphasis on a core set of Jewish texts that Sasportas deemed authoritative.

Sasportas's embattled and competitive relationship with the Sephardic intellectual elite points to a central paradox of *Zizath novel zvi*. In his criticism, Sasportas was relentlessly elitist and relentlessly egalitarian at one and the same time. The level of training required for a reader to understand his letters all but assumed a thorough and grueling rabbinic education. His message, however, was fundamentally antiplutocratic. Every Jew, rabbi or lay, elite or common, had an obligation to turn to the sources of the medieval past and draw upon them in the affirmation of doubt, because textual mastery was the summum bonum of Judaism. All Jews were equally subordinate to the hegemony of the text. The sources, for all of their disparity, would allow his colleagues and his constituents to combat the gullibility of the masses, to face down the testimony of experience with the authority of the written word.

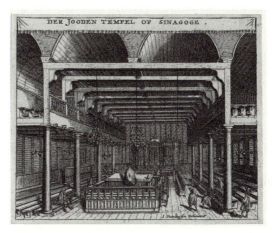

THREE

~

CROWDS

The common people are nothing but a synagogue of pretentious ignoramuses who, the less they understand of things, the more they discuss them.

—Baltasar Gracián

Figure 8. Jan Veenhuysen, *Der Jooden tempel of Sinagoge* (The Jewish Temple or Synagogue) around 1662, from *Beschryving der Stat Amsterdam* by Tobias van Domsealer (1665). The Portuguese Jewish Synagogue in Amsterdam depicted roughly three years before the advent of Sabbetai Zevi as the Messiah. Rijksmuseum, Amsterdam.

THE ARRIVAL OF THE MESSIAH OCCURRED IN PUBLIC. The abrogation of Jewish law through communal celebration on scheduled fast days, the expression of mass enthusiasm through song and dance in the synagogue, and the dissolution of social hierarchies through the subversion of traditional authorities all contributed to making Sabbatian messianism into a public phenomenon in Jewish history. In *Zizath novel zvi* Sasportas juxtaposed the religious experience of an individual with the religious experience of the many. His constant and contemptuous invocation of the Jewish crowd might suggest that thousands of Jews in Hamburg and Amsterdam, the two most frequently discussed cities, had become Sabbatian believers. Drawing on Sasportas's own narrative of Sabbetai Raphael, a Sabbatian prophet who arrived in the northern Sephardic Diaspora after the Messiah's conversion, this chapter begins with the proposition that the crowd invoked in *Zizath novel zvi* was primarily discursive rather than descriptive. When Sasportas reverted to the notion of "the crowd," his criticism had very little relation to actual numbers and much more to do with social chaos. The chapter then moves backward in time to examine Sasportas on the confusion generated by the public expression of joy and the reversal of social hierarchies at the height of the messianic movement two years earlier. Finally, it turns to the attempt to silence dissent and the polemic over doubt that marked Sasportas's struggle with his colleagues in the rabbinate and lay leadership in Amsterdam and Hamburg.

THE CROWD AND THE ASHKENAZIM

On a number of occasions in the first section of *Zizath novel zvi*, Sasportas identified the crowd with the Ashkenazim resident in the western Sephardic Diaspora. From the outset, Sasportas saw Ashkenazim as particularly susceptible to the propaganda of the Sabbatian prophets. Nathan of Gaza had originally predicted that the Ottoman sultan would crown Sabbetai Zevi and then embark on a joint conquest. This military expedition would be bloodless with the exception of the lands of Ashkenaz, where many gentiles would perish. In a marginal gloss to this prophecy, which he had reproduced in the text of *Zizath novel zvi*, Sasportas took Nathan of Gaza to task for pandering to the Ashkenazim:

> Why is Ashkenaz different from all other [lands]? If this is because of the thousands from Israel who were slaughtered in Ashkenaz and Poland, why does he not recall the many expulsions and persecutions in Aragon, Castile and Portugal... Rather, it seems his entire intention was to draw and entice the people of Ashkenaz and Poland to follow his lying words.[1]

Sasportas's reference to the slaughter of Jews in Ashkenaz and Poland probably alluded to the Chmielnicki rebellion of 1648–1649 that targeted Jewish communities as agents of Polish noble power on the eastern frontier of the Polish-Lithuanian Commonwealth.[2] Invoking the expulsions from the Iberian Peninsula, Sasportas seemed to say that Ashkenazim were indeed more vulnerable to deception. Sephardic Jews had also experienced persecution, but Nathan of Gaza did not target

---

[1] ומה נשתנו אשכנז, אם בעד הרוגי ישראל אלפי אלפים מבני פולין ואשכנז, למה לא יביא בזכרונו כמה גירושין ושמדות שבאראגון, וקשטיליא ופורטוגאל?... ונראה שכל כונתו היתה למשוך ולגנוב לב קהלות אשכנז ופולין להמשיכם אחרי דבריו השקריים.

Sasportas, *ZNZ*, 10; see also Joseph Halevi's reference on 248; on Nathan of Gaza and Ashkenaz, see David J. Halperin, "The Son of the Messiah: Ishmael Zevi, and the Sabbatian Aqedah," *HUCA* 67 (1996): 196n177. Epigraph as cited by Américo Castro, *The Structure of Spanish History* (Princeton, NJ: Princeton University Press, 1954), 27.

[2] As observed by Tishby in Sasportas, *ZNZ*, 10n6. On these massacres, see "The Chmielnitzky Massacres, 1648–1649: Jewish, Polish, and Ukrainian Perspectives," ed. Kenneth Stow and Adam Teller, *Jewish History* 17 (2003); on their literary afterlife, *Stories of Khmelnytsky: Competing Legacies of the 1648 Ukrainian Cossack Uprising*, ed. Amelia M. Glaser (Stanford, CA: Stanford University Press, 2015).

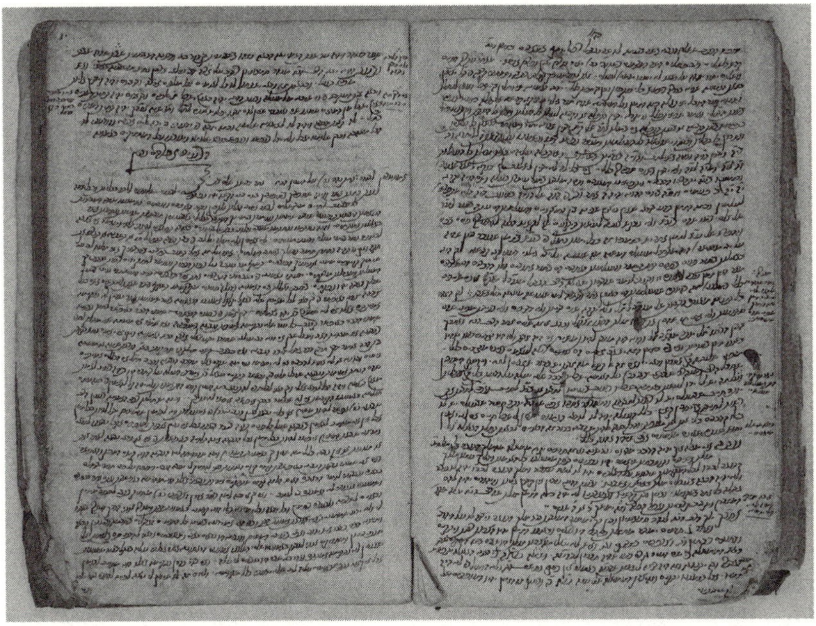

Figure 9. Jacob Sasportas, *Zizath novel zvi*, Yeshiva University, MS 1251. Sasportas annotated his copy of a prophecy by Nathan of Gaza with his own acerbic comments. The Mendel Gottesman Library, Yeshiva University, MS 1251.

them with his propaganda. Nathan of Gaza had tailored his prophecy to those Jews who he thought would have been most susceptible to his prophecies. Sasportas may have been contemptuous of this shameless appeal to the gullibility of recent victims, but he disputed neither its veracity nor its efficacy. Rather, he seems to have interpreted these tactics as pure deception and projected his own contempt for Ashkenazim onto Nathan of Gaza.

A single comment on the final page of the first section of *Zizath novel zvi* bears this out. The first section of the work recounts the history of the Sabbatian movement from the early reports of the Messiah in Europe in late 1665 up until news of his conversion was confirmed in the Sephardic Diaspora, roughly a year later in December of 1666.[3] Over the remainder of the book, which constitutes approximately two-thirds of the chronicle, Sasportas stiffened his tone considerably. His own doubts had now been decisively resolved. Where earlier Sabbetai

[3]On the timing of the news see Wilke, "Le 'Messie mystique' et la Bourse d'Amsterdam," 194–195.

Zevi appeared as an errant or misguided rabbi, in the latter sections his name usually preceded an abbreviation that indicated an imprecation. In one of the final paragraphs of the first section, immediately following an account of Sabbetai Zevi's conversion, Sasportas wrote:

> Some of the Ashkenazim who were more devoted refused to believe and would not hear a negative word spoken against him [Sabbetai Zevi], much less that he had converted. Therefore, they said he had ascended to heaven, and only his material form had appeared as an apostate and other such nonsense about which it is forbidden to waste paper.[4]

The Ashkenazim were so convinced of the Messiah's existence as Sabbetai Zevi that they simply would not accept the reports that he had converted to Islam. Sasportas's depiction of the Ashkenazim as more fervent in their belief in Sabbetai Zevi contains an implicit comparison to the Sephardim in Hamburg and Amsterdam. As Sasportas indicated elsewhere, and as has been corroborated by a number of other accounts, the confirmation of Sabbetai Zevi's conversion put a definitive end to the acute messianic expectations of the Sephardic elites, both rabbinic authorities and wealthy lay leadership.[5] At this stage, however, Sasportas had yet to associate either group with his criticism of the crowd.

Nine months later, when Sabbetai Raphael showed up in the western Sephardic Diaspora in September 1667, things had changed. Although he arrived well after news of the Messiah's conversion had been confirmed, this Sabbatian prophet possessed something that these Jews had hitherto lacked: a personal connection to the Messiah. According to his own report given to Sasportas in Hamburg, Sabbetai Raphael had made his way as a young man from Moravia to Istanbul, where he had convinced the local authorities to support his travel to the Holy Land.[6] In Palestine he hoped to study with Sabbetai Zevi. Upon arrival in the

---

[4] וקצת מהאשכנזים שהיו יותר אדוקים היו ממאנים להאמין ולא לשמוע דבר רע כנגדו ומכל שכן שהמיר דת, ולכן
אומרים שהוא עלה לשמים וצורתו נדמית להם כאיש מומר ודברים אחרים של הבאי שאסור לאבד בהם הנייר.
Sasportas, *ZNZ*, 175.

[5] Kaplan, "The Attitude of the Sephardi Leadership"; Wilke, "Le 'Messie mystique' et la Bourse d'Amsterdam."

[6] In 1662 he was in Venice where he printed a kabbalistic pamphlet of magical formulas. See Sabbetai Raphael, *Sefer ta-alumot u-mekorot ha-hokhmah* (Venice, 1662). Copy in the Scholem Library, R 2725.

Holy Land he joined the group of students who had gathered around the future Messiah and became a member of his circle. He had actually been present on the night of Shavuot when Nathan of Gaza had received his prophecy about Sabbetai Zevi as the Messiah. Shortly thereafter, he had traveled with an unnamed member of the circle from Palestine to spread the gospel to other Jews in the Ottoman Empire. Sabbetai Raphael was thus an eyewitness to the extraordinary events about which the Jews of Amsterdam and Hamburg had heard so much. Thus Sasportas described his entry to Amsterdam:

> He arrived from Frankfurt in Amsterdam and the entire city was in turmoil, especially the masses of believers, most of whom were Ashkenazim who joyfully received him. But the Sephardim sent three scholars to interrogate him and found him to be like a latrine.[7]

The Talmudic phrase "like a latrine" referred to something that was obviously disgusting.[8] The very quality Sasportas had hitherto associated with crowds of Sephardim in Hamburg and Amsterdam was now the exclusive province of the Ashkenazim: enthusiasm. The Sephardim, by contrast, had apparently wised up. Like Sasportas himself prior to the Messiah's conversion, they now interrogated the source of news with considerable skepticism. Their very dismissal of Sabbetai Raphael demonstrated the same learning that had earlier served to characterize the Sephardic philosophical tradition of which Sasportas himself claimed ownership.

Were there any doubt about the comparative foolishness of the Ashkenazim, their response to Sabbetai Raphael in Amsterdam confirmed all of Sasportas's prejudices about the ignorance of the crowd:

> He went to the Ashkenazi synagogue where he gave a sermon. But they did not understand what he said because he quoted passages from the *Zohar* that he himself did not understand. But the masses attributed it all to the esoteric method and to prophecy.[9]

---

[7] ובא מפראנקפורט לאמשטרדאם ותהום כל העיר ובפרט המון המאמינים ורובם אשכנזים שקיבלוהו בשמחה, והספרדים שלחו ג' ת"ח לבדקו ומצאוהו עביט של מי רגלים.

Sasportas, *ZNZ*, 271.

[8] BT Berakhot 25b.

[9] והלך לו לבה"כ של אשכנזים ושם דרש ולא הבינו מה שהיה דורש לפי שהיה אומר לשונות מהזוהר שהוא עצמו לא היה מבינם וההמון היו מיחסים הכל לדרך סוד ונבואה

Sasportas, *ZNZ*, 271.

Like fools who attribute profundity to that which they cannot understand, the Ashkenazi crowd was emotionally overwhelmed by Sabbetai Raphael's sermon. Like many Sabbatians, Sabbetai Raphael drew upon a book as the source of his wisdom. In his case, it was the *Zohar*, rather than Maimonides or Judah Loew of Prague. Sasportas, however, did not take kindly to a Sabbatian prophet using the *Zohar* as the source of his ostensible wisdom. Sasportas was no more willing to share the authoritativeness of the *Zohar* than he was that of Maimonides or *Sefer hasidim*.[10]

Sabbetai Raphael appears to have been quite adept at exploiting the already-extant interethnic tensions between Ashkenazim and Sephardim, first in Amsterdam and later in Hamburg. Upon his arrival in Amsterdam, he drew upon the doctrine of two Messiahs, the Messiah ben Ephraim and the Messiah ben David, to excite the hopes of the remaining believers. He informed them that Sabbetai Zevi was the Messiah ben Ephraim, the messianic figure who would serve as a forerunner and was destined to perish, but that the Messiah ben David, the one who would usher in the actual redemption, would be revealed shortly. He led them to understand that he considered himself the likely Messiah ben David. This contradicted nearly the entirety of Nathan of Gaza's prophecy, which had either passed over the doctrine of the two Messiahs in silence or insisted that the Messiah ben Ephraim, often referred to as the Messiah ben Joseph, had already perished before the revelation of Sabbetai Zevi. In either case, Nathan of Gaza left no doubt that Sabbetai Zevi himself was the Messiah ben David. None of these fine-grained distinctions in messianic eschatology mattered to the Ashkenazi crowd:

> The Ashkenazim, that is to say, the majority of the masses, were seduced by his statement. Although the great and discerning among them thought he was a liar, given that he said Sabbetai Zevi (who Nathan [of Gaza] considered the Messiah ben David) was the Messiah ben Ephraim.[11]

The gullible masses were now entirely Ashkenazim, but not all of the Ashkenazim were gullible masses. Sasportas was careful to note that

---

[10] See chapter 2 above.

[11] והאשכנזים נפתו למאמרו היינו רוב ההמון, כי אמנם הגדולים והחריפים שבהם חשבוהו לדובר שקרים בהיות
שאמר על שבתא"י צב"י (המוחזק להם למשיח בן דוד על פי נתן) שהוא משיח בן אפרים.
Sasportas, *ZNZ*, 273.

the learned among them were quite capable of seeing through Sabbetai Raphael's messianic inconsistencies.

The Sephardic oligarchy in Amsterdam had had quite enough. Within a relatively short amount of time, they did to him what they had done to so many other undesirables throughout the seventeenth century: they sent him away.[12] Only a short while later he showed up in Altona, a suburb of Hamburg with a settlement of Ashkenazi Jews.[13] This left Sasportas completely incensed with his colleagues in Amsterdam who had been content to export a public nuisance to another place. As he saw fit to remind the Amsterdam rabbinate in a blistering letter written shortly thereafter, they should have printed and circulated a ban (Heb. *herem*) against Sabbetai Raphael so as to ensure he did not harass other Jewish populations in the vicinity. At the time, however, Sasportas had a pressing problem on his hands in the form of a Sabbatian prophet in his own backyard. What had been a matter of interethnic Jewish tension in Amsterdam quickly became one in Hamburg.

As he had done so skillfully in Amsterdam, Sabbetai Raphael played upon the hopes of the Ashkenazim:

> When he saw the impoverished crowd of Ashkenazim following him, he told them about his prophet [Nathan of Gaza] and his Messiah [Sabbetai Zevi] and how he had been one of the chosen ones and that he had heard the heavenly voice in the yeshiva in Gaza calling out in the name of the Messiah and prophet, and they were entranced by him and followed him like animals.[14]

Sabbetai Raphael offered the poor Ashkenazi masses a touch of the real. He had been in Gaza at the moment of revelation. In order to forestall

[12] Yosef Kaplan, "The Self-Definition of the Sephardi Jews of Western Europe and Their Relation to the Alien and the Stranger," in *An Alternative Path*, 51–77; on Dutch Sephardim and Ashkenazim, see Yosef Kaplan, "Relations between Spanish and Portuguese Jews and Ashkenazim in Seventeenth-Century Amsterdam" (Hebrew), in *Temurot ba-historyah ha-yehudit ha-hadasha: kovetz maamrim shai li-Shmuel Ettinger*, ed. Shmuel Almog (Jerusalem: Historical Society of Israel and Zalman Shazar Center, 1988), 389–412; Bodian, "'Men of the Nation.'"

[13] Jaap Meijer, "Sabetai Rephael in Hamburg: Korte bidrage tot de geschiedenis van de Joodse wereld na Sabetai Tswi," in *Weerklank op het werk van Jan Romeim: Liber Amicorum* (Amsterdam: Wereldbibliotheek, 1953), 103–108.

[14] אחר כך כשמצא דלת העם מהמון האשכנזים נגררים אחריו, והגיד להם עניני נביאו ומשיחו ושהוא מן הקרואים לעדה עדת מרעים ושהוא שמע את הקול בבת קול הנשמעת בישיבה בעז"ה המכרזת וקוראה בשם למשיח ונביא, נפתו אחריו ונמשכו כבהמה.

Sasportas, *ZNZ*, 278.

any possible skepticism, he showed them a series of documents signed by the rabbinate of Istanbul, which he claimed endorsed his account. Sasportas bitterly noted that these signed documents dated from well before the declaration of Sabbetai Zevi as the Messiah, but that no one in the crowd had bothered to interrogate them with sufficient skepticism. Sabbetai Raphael had arrived in Altona-Hamburg shortly after the Jewish holidays in the fall of 1667. By the time Passover arrived in the spring of 1668, he was still causing trouble. Unlike his stay in Amsterdam, which was relatively short-lived, his time in Hamburg lasted for almost half a year. The extensive rabbinic efforts to have him removed or expelled ended in absolute failure, as he had enlisted the protection of the secular authorities by having temporarily cured the gout of a rich and powerful patron. Ultimately the very fortuitous circumstances that had enabled his rapid ascent also led to his equally rapid demise. The rich man's gout, although it had been briefly relieved, refused to go away. Sabbetai Raphael was out of luck and fled Hamburg for Poland.

Sasportas's account of Sabbetai Raphael in Amsterdam and Hamburg points to the socially circumscribed nature of rabbinic authority at this particular juncture. It reflects the futility of rabbinic opposition in the face of popular enthusiasm, especially when the latter was allied with secular power. Sasportas's narrative of his prolonged run-in with Sabbetai Raphael raises two further issues: the size of a crowd and the nature of Sephardic and Ashkenazic relations that determined, at least to a certain extent, the future of Sabbatianism after the conversion. When Sasportas repeatedly bemoaned the crowds of Ashkenazim who had refused to accept the confirmation of Sabbetai Zevi's conversion or who had flocked to hear Sabbetai Raphael's sermons, he gave very little indication as to how large a crowd he was actually describing. When reading *Zizath novel zvi*, however, one might come away with the impression that thousands of people were flocking to hear Sabbetai Raphael preach in the Ashkenazi synagogue in Amsterdam or parading with him down the street where the Sephardim lived in Hamburg. Anyone who believed became one with the crowd. In fact, numbers mattered considerably less than the nature of the response to Sabbatianism. Amsterdam, one of the largest cities in Europe, had a population between 150,000 and 200,000 at midcentury, of which there were roughly 2,500 Sephardim and a few hundred Ashkenazim.[15] Historians of seventeenth-century Hamburg estimate the total population of the city at 75,000 at midcentury and the population of Altona, a small suburb, at 2,500.[16] Of these, there were roughly six hundred Sephardi Jews who lived in Hamburg when the population was at its peak between 1652 and 1681, and between two and three hundred Ashkenazi Jews in neighboring Altona. Between 1649 and 1697 the Ashkenazi Jews had officially been expelled from Hamburg, although there is evidence that this was honored in the breach.[17]

These numbers offer a crucial perspective on Sasportas's perception of a crowd throughout *Zizath novel zvi*. Sephardim in Hamburg actually outnumbered the Ashkenazim in Altona at a ratio of 4:1 or 4:1.5. If any group of Jews constituted the crowd in Amsterdam and Hamburg, it was the Sephardim. In both cities the Sephardim were the dominant ethnicity not only in terms of numbers but also in terms of wealth. The Sephardi ascendance further expressed itself in terms of real estate. Although they did not own the magnificent mansions they called home, the wealthy Sephardim of Hamburg lived in the center of the city in opulent houses they leased from Christians.[18] By contrast, the Ashkenazim lived farther out and were allowed to enter Hamburg only during the day. What is more, the Sephardic leadership expressed a pronounced condescension toward their Ashkenazi coreligionists. In 1670 only a short while after Sabbetai Raphael departed Hamburg for Poland, the Sephardic *maamad* investigated a report about a Jew who had visited a new pastor in Hamburg. When they were unable to identify the culprit, they concluded,

[15] On the population of Amsterdam, see Israel, *The Dutch Republic*, 620–622; on the number of Sephardim, see idem, "Sephardic Immigration into the Dutch Republic, 1595–1672," *SR* 23 (1989): 45–53; on the number of Ashkenazim, see Yosef Kaplan, "Amsterdam and the Ashkenazi Migration in the Seventeenth Century," in *An Alternative Path*, 78–107; Nusteling, "The Jews in the Republic of the United Provinces," 43–62, esp. 53n23 and table 1a.

[16] Joachim Whaley, *Religious Toleration and Social Change in Hamburg: 1529–1819* (Cambridge: Cambridge University Press, 1985), chap. 3; Yosef Kaplan, "The Place of the *Herem* in the Sephardi Community of Hamburg," in *An Alternative Path*, 169, hereafter cited as Kaplan, "*Herem* in Hamburg"; Stefan Rohrbacher, "Die Drei Gemeinden Altona, Hamburg, Wandsbek zur Zeit der Glikl," *Aschkenas* 8 (1998): 105–124; Michael Studemund-Halévy, "*Senhores* versus *criados da Nação*: Portugueses, asquenasíes y tudescos en el Hamburgo del siglo xvii," *Sefarad* 60 (2000): 349–368.

[17] Felix Sprang, " 'I was told they were all Iewes': Mentalities and Realities of Segregation, Sephardi and Ashkenazi Jews in Early Modern Hamburg and Altona," in *Frühneutzeitliche Ghettos in Europa im Vergleich*, ed. Fritz Backhaus et al. (Berlin: Trafo, 2012), 400.

[18] Jonathan I. Israel, "The Sephardi Diaspora and the Struggle for Portuguese Independence from Spain (1640–1668)," in *Diasporas*, 336–337.

It may very well be that the elders of the Ashkenazim were the ones who did this [i.e., sent the man]; for although they belong to our nation, and the Torah is one, this [unity] does not extend to matters of conduct [Por. *governo*].[19]

Sasportas was hardly alone in imputing unsavory or unappealing aspects of Jewish life in Hamburg to the Ashkenazim as a matter of course. What Sasportas described as a crowd of Ashkenazim during Sabbetai Raphael's stay probably did not total much more than two or three dozen young men. But this only begs the question: If the crowd was actually so small, why was Sasportas so anxious about it? Perhaps the problem Sasportas confronted when he saw a couple of dozen Ashkenazim dancing joyously in Hamburg was not so much a matter of numbers as one of social chaos. More than anything else Sabbatian enthusiasm led to a loss of control. The terms *hamon* and *hamon-am* used by Sasportas throughout *Zizath novel zvi* do not indicate a numerical mass of people. If common sense dictates that they be rendered into English as "the crowd" or as "the people," the context of Sasportas's writing in the northern Sephardic Diaspora might also warrant "rabble" as an equally legitimate translation.[20]

THE WORLD TURNED UPSIDE DOWN

If the story of Sabbetai Raphael in Amsterdam and Hamburg appears in *Zizath novel zvi* as a farce, the reports about Sabbetai Zevi in the same cities two years earlier recount a tragedy. Sasportas described Sabbetai Raphael as a nagging nuisance, but by the time he had arrived in the northwest of Europe in the fall of 1667, the outburst of messianic enthusiasm had fizzled out. In turning to Sasportas's account of the crowd or the rabble in the period of peak messianic expectation, between the fall of 1665 and late 1666, I examine his depiction of the confusion generated by the public expression of joy and the reversal of accepted social hierarchies.

---

[19] As cited and discussed in Bodian, "'Men of the Nation,'" 73–74.

[20] As Werblowsky translated the term as used by Scholem, *Sabbatai Sevi*, 12. For the Hebrew word *hamon* see Scholem, *Shabbetai Sevi ve-ha-tenuah ha-shabetait bi-yeme hayav*, 10.

In a letter to Sasportas written in December of 1665, Aaron Zarfati described the enthusiasm for the Messiah that had gripped the Jews of Amsterdam:

> If you could see with your own eyes, you would certainly say this is the Lord's doing (Ps. 118:23). All day and all night, they fill the synagogue as if it were a day of atonement to the Lord; ten thousand florins were pledged on the holy Sabbath; several benches were added to our yeshiva on that very day (BT Berakhot 28b). Furthermore, you would see a world turned upside down (BT Bava Batra 10b). All of the houses where they play dice and cards have been closed at their own behest, without an order from the heads of the holy nation.[21]

Like his addressee, Zarfati was a rabbi from North Africa, in his case Morocco, who had come to Amsterdam and served as a preacher alongside Isaac Aboab da Fonseca.[22] Elsewhere in this letter he mentioned that he had recently given a sermon exhorting the congregation to repent. Himself a believer, Zarfati addressed Sasportas as he would have addressed a colleague, and urged him to retract an earlier letter he had written in condemnation of the believers in Amsterdam. He even went so far as to suggest that Sasportas burn his correspondence as if it were leavened bread on Passover. If people discovered Sasportas's initial skepticism, it would cause him considerable embarrassment in the imminent messianic age.

Zarfati noted two crucial elements that would come to characterize Sabbatianism: the relative size of the group and the spontaneous character of its activity. On the Day of Atonement, the synagogue usually filled to capacity. Jews who might not otherwise attend made certain to do so on this occasion. The enthusiasm for the new Messiah had turned an otherwise insignificant winter day into a time of fervent devotion. If the synagogue was packed, the house of study, the yeshiva, had also swelled in numbers. So many people had taken upon themselves the

---

[21] ואם היית רואה בעיניך בודאי היית אומר מאת ה' היתה זאת, כי כל היום וכל הלילה כלם בבית הכנסת כיום כפורים לה', ועשרת אלפים פרחי כסף התנדבו ביום שבת קדש וכמה ספסלים הוסיפו בישיבתנו כמו בו ביום. ועוד היית רואה עולם הפוך, כי כל בתי משחקים בקוביא ובאגרות הם מעצמם בטלוה בלי הסכמת ראשי עם קדש. Sasportas, *ZNZ*, 29. On this passage, see Scholem, *Sabbatai Sevi*, 522–524.

[22] See Meyer Kayserling, *Sephardim: Romanische Poesien der Juden in Spanien: Ein Beitrag zur Literatur und Geschichte der Spanisch-Portugiesischen Juden* (Leipzig, 1859), cited after the reprint (Hildesheim: Georg Olms Verlag, 1972), 212, as cited by Tishby in Sasportas, *ZNZ*, 24n2.

urge to contemplate God's word that several benches had to be added to the hall.

Zarfati took care to distinguish between the messianic responses of the synagogue and the study house, although both were substantial. He separated the synagogue, a space where all Jews convened for worship, from the study house, an academy where the learned elites studied Talmud in seclusion. The synagogue was theoretically open to all Jewish men; the study house was reserved for the elite, who studied in splendid isolation. In fact, the Portuguese Sephardim of Amsterdam referred to a number of institutions as "yeshivas," including the study circles associated with confraternities that met as adult discussion groups in private homes.[23] But here, it seems reasonable to assume that Zarfati was referring to Ets Haim, the central academy that had been founded in 1639 and was devoted to full-time study.[24] Ets Haim was a particularly exclusive institution. Only five years earlier, its leadership had declared it would not admit Jews of Italian, German, or Polish descent.[25] Excitement about the Messiah seems to have cut across all sectors of the Jewish life in such a dramatic fashion that the synagogue and the study house were alike transformed. Following the explosion of messianic excitement, both witnessed a dramatic increase in their respective constituencies. If there were any doubt that enthusiasm had affected every group within Jewish society, Zarfati mentioned a third social institution that had experienced a sudden change: the gambling houses. He noted that these dens of iniquity had closed of their own accord without any pressure from the lay or religious leadership. This was an astonishing development within Sephardic life in northern Europe. Only a year earlier, the Portuguese Jews of Amsterdam had organized a unique and macabre kind of lottery: the winner correctly guessed the number of deaths in the city in a given week.[26] A decade

[23] Thus Crown of the Law (Heb. *Keter torah*) met daily to study the Bible and had been founded by Saul Levi Morteira; Light of the Torah (Heb. *Torah or*) met daily for half an hour to study Maimonides. See Scholberg, "Miguel de Barrios and the Amsterdam Sephardic Community"; Swetschinski, *Reluctant Cosmopolitans*, 211.

[24] M. C. Paraira and J. S. Da Silva Rosa, *Gedenkschrift uitgegeven ter gelegenheid van het 300-jarig bestaan der onderwijsinrichtingen Talmud Tora en Ets Haïm* (Amsterdam: Roeloffzen-Hübner, 1916).

[25] Levie Bernfeld, *Poverty and Welfare*, 18–19.

[26] See Yosef Kaplan, "*Gente Política*: The Portuguese Jews of Amsterdam vis-à-vis Dutch Society," in *Dutch Jews as Perceived by Themselves and by Others*, ed. Chaya Brasz and Yosef Kaplan (Leiden: Brill, 2001), 38.

earlier the *maamad* in Hamburg had prohibited gambling on fast days such as the ninth of Av and Yom Kippur, the day that Zarfati now used as his frame of reference.[27] According to Zarfati, messianic enthusiasm acted as a social solvent. Prior distinctions between groups of Jews were disappearing, and a new kind of collective consciousness had begun to emerge. This unexpected sense of mutual reinforcement among the synagogue, the study house, and the gambling dens may even have contributed to Zarfati's own developing faith.

Sasportas had little patience with Zarfati's exuberance. In his rejoinder he included extensive citations from Zarfati's original letter "lest your joy about the prophet and the Messiah has confused you, and you do not know what your own hand has written." What was more, Zarfati had addressed Sasportas as a colleague, and had even dared to patronize him by offering him advice. This Sasportas could not bear:

> What is this love and fraternity between me and you? One finds this only among equals and colleagues, and here it is only relative.[28]

We are not of equal rank, Sasportas insisted, and do not presume to offer me counsel as to how I should conduct myself. Within the first few months of the messianic enthusiasm, one of the central problems posed by collective frenzy was beginning to manifest itself. Excitement for the Messiah seemed to undermine social distinctions even within the rabbinic elite. When it came to the expression of joy about the imminent redemption, all Jews appeared to have stood on equal footing. At least to Zarfati. On the face of it, Zarfati and Sasportas had much in common. Both served the new Jews in Amsterdam and Hamburg as Sephardic rabbis from abroad. Both came from North Africa, Sasportas from the Mediterranean coast of Oran and Zarfati from the Atlantic coast of Morocco. Neither one had risen to the top position in the places in which he lived; however, they both continued to perform rabbinic

---

[27] Kaplan, "*Herem* in Hamburg," 180–182. Gambling was rife throughout the western Sephardic Diaspora; see idem, "The Social Functions of the *Herem*," in *An Alternative Path*, 117n33; idem, "Deviance and Excommunication in the Eighteenth Century," in *An Alternative Path*, 148; idem, "The Jewish Profile of the Spanish-Portuguese Community of London during the Seventeenth Century," in *An Alternative Path*, 164. For bets placed on the London stock exchange as to whether or not Sabbatai Zevi was the Messiah, see Van Wijk, "The Rise and Fall of Sabbatai Zevi as Reflected in Contemporary Press Reports," 25.

[28] מה אהבה ואחוה ביני ובינך ולא תמצא כי אם בשוים ובדומים ולא תמצא כי אם יחסית.
Sasportas, *ZNZ*, 32. For other instances of this phrase, see *ZNZ*, 36; *Ohel ya-akov*, #28, 39b.

functions such as preaching sermons, issuing responsa, and writing approbations. In spite of these commonalities, they reacted to the same phenomenon in opposite fashions. Zarfati became a believer, in no small measure, it seems, because everyone around him believed, while Sasportas became a committed and increasingly embittered unbeliever in nearly the same circumstances a few hundred miles away.

Letters from his colleagues in Amsterdam continued to reach Sasportas in Hamburg. A substantial number came from Isaac Nahar, whose training as a physician and in rabbinics placed him at the juncture of the learned and lay elites. A native of Hamburg, Nahar had made his way to Amsterdam and joined the fellowship Crown of Torah (Heb. *Keter torah*), which met to study Bible under the direction of Saul Levi Morteira in the 1640s and 1650s.[29] In 1652 at the age of nineteen, he had studied with Sasportas in the yeshiva in Amsterdam.[30] Three years later he received his medical degree from the University of Leiden.[31] Over the years he had addressed a series of legal queries to Sasportas, who was more than two decades older. Some of their correspondence survives in *Ohel ya-akov*. The tone of their exchanges was collegial, if occasionally sharp, but Sasportas felt sufficiently close to Nahar to recount a number of anecdotes about his own experiences in North Africa in his answers. Only a few years prior to his letters to Sasportas in London, Nahar had been asked by the Amsterdam *maamad* to evaluate whether the poetry of Miguel de Barrios could appear in print. A former captain in the Spanish army, De Barrios had arrived in Amsterdam in late 1662 or early 1663 and asked the *maamad* for permission to print his Spanish poems. Nahar's response betrayed a cast of mind similar to his former teacher's:

> He invokes gentile deities and attributes divinity to them (albeit for poetic reasons). I am of the opinion that one should not tolerate to be said in jest things which, if said in truth, are so criminal.[32]

[29] Kaplan, *Orobio de Castro*, 112; Wilke, "*Midrashim from Bordeaux.*"

[30] *Ohel ya-akov*, #41, 45a. In a responsum dated to 1670, Sasportas wrote to Nahar: "And you, who have genuine knowledge, for it is now eighteen years since you studied with me in the yeshiva." See also Benayahu, "News from Italy and Holland on the Beginning of Sabbatianism," 202n38.

[31] Kaplan, "Sephardi Students at the University of Leiden," 203. A copy of his thesis, "De Pleuritide," is in the Special Collections of the library at the University of Glasgow, shelf mark Sp. Coll 82 b.4.

[32] Israel S. Revah, "Les Écrivains Manuel de Pina et Miguel de Barrios et la censure de la com-

The *maamad* concluded that de Barrios could print his work only if he undertook the revisions called for by Nahar and submitted the revised version to Nahar and Isaac Aboab da Fonseca for examination.[33] Furthermore, Nahar polemicized against Christianity in tone and in substance that would have made his former teacher proud. He had scathing things to say about Jesus, whom he dismissed as "a deceiver and sorcerer."[34] In the decade after he had studied in the yeshiva and obtained his medical degree, Nahar had joined the intellectual elite of the Portuguese Sephardim in Amsterdam. At the advent of Sabbetai Zevi, he had served the *maamad* as a censor, worked as a physician, and written polemical treatises against Christianity.

Like Zarfati, Nahar was close to Sasportas, both personally and intellectually. Their difference of opinion over Sabbatian messianism thus cut both of them to the quick. When Nahar wrote Sasportas after the revelation of Sabbetai Zevi, he exhorted him to subdue his skepticism. As Zarfati had done only a short while earlier, he advised Sasportas to repent lest he regret an opportunity to join in the messianic movement. Sasportas responded:

> The happiness is so great that it has confused clear thinking. You consider my merits to be deficiencies. You tell me, to my face, that I should use regret as the opening to repentance. Not even from my most distinguished teacher have I heard such a thing.[35]

Momentary ecstasy led only to mental confusion. It distorted clear thinking and allowed otherwise reasonable people to elevate themselves far above their natural and social station. Nahar was a perfect case in point. In Sasportas's mind he had transformed from a deferential and

---

munauté judéo-portugaise d'Amsterdam," *Tesoro de los Judíos Sefardies* 8 (1965), lxxxi, as cited and translated by Swetschinski, *Reluctant Cosmopolitans*, 244.

[33] De Barrios settled in Brussels and had his poems published there as *Flor de Apolo* in 1665. On his later Sabbatianism and connection with Sasportas, see *ZNZ*, 364; Scholberg, "Miguel de Barrios and the Amsterdam Sephardic Community," 152–153; for a study of his life, see Pieterse, *Daniel Levi de Barrios*; for his political thought, see Miriam Bodian, "Biblical Hebrews and the Rhetoric of Republicanism: Seventeenth-Century Portuguese Jews on the Jewish Community," *AJS Review* 22 (1997): 209–221.

[34] As cited by Kaplan, *Orobio de Castro*, 254. For his other polemical treatises against Christianity, see 340, 342, 343; Wilke, "*Midrashim from Bordeaux*."

[35] וכל כך היא השמחה שבלבלה הדעת הצלולה לחשוב הזכיות לזדונות ולומר לי בפני כי צריך לעשות מההרטה פתח לתשובה, אפילו מרבי המובהק לא שמעתי זה.

Sasportas, *ZNZ*, 50.

talented disciple to an arrogant and patronizing upstart all in the course of a few months.

Sasportas's correspondents either ignored his monitory letters or did their best to match his polemical eloquence in their own. As the frenzy in Amsterdam deepened, Sasportas could count on fewer allies in his campaign against Sabbatianism. Samuel Aboab, a rabbi in Venice who took a similar if not quite as militant position on the messianic movement, wrote to Sasportas with the following report:

> Come and see how far the strength of our brethren has reached in their recklessness to exhume those lying down; they gather up the bones of the dead from their graves as we have heard from the city of Amsterdam.[36]

The Jews of Amsterdam had gone so far as to overturn yet another institution of social control: the cemetery. Burial of the dead served as a means to reinforce social hierarchies among the living. The cemetery functioned as a permanent instantiation of divisions between rich and poor, learned and ignorant. Acts of Loving Kindness (Heb. *Gemilut hassadim*), one of the many confraternities maintained by the Sephardim of Amsterdam, appointed a watchman to guard the burial places in the cemetery against vandalism and defilement.[37] With the arrival of the Messiah, the Jews of Amsterdam sought to demolish distinctions among the dead as well as the living. They dug up graves so as to transport the dead to the inevitable kingdom that Sabbetai Zevi would establish in Palestine. In short order, they fully expected the revival of the dead.[38] The synagogue and the study house, the casinos and the cemetery: in the course of less than half a year, enthusiasm for the Messiah had left its imprint on the central public institutions of Sasportas's once and future home in Amsterdam.

Social chaos, however, was not limited to the Portuguese Jews of the Dutch Republic. It was happening right before Sasportas's own eyes in

---

[36] בואו וראו עד היכן הגיעה כחם של אחינו בפחזותם לחטוטי שכבי ולהניע עצמות המתים מקבריהם כנשמע מעיר אמסטרדאם.

Ibid., 59. On Aboab, see Scholem, *Sabbatai Sevi*, 497–99; Meir Benayahu, *Dor ehad ba-aretz: Igrot R. Shmuel Aboab ve-R. Moshe Zakut be-inyene eretz yisrael* (Jerusalem: Yad ha-Rav Nisim, 1988).

[37] Scholberg, "Miguel de Barrios and the Amsterdam Sephardic Community," 134–135.

[38] In Sasportas's Hamburg Sabbatian enthusiasm left its trace on a number of epitaphs. See Marian Sárraga and Ramón F. Sárraga, "The Poet Moses Gideon Abudiente and His Family in Amsterdam and Hamburg: Echoes of 1666 Sabbatian Polemics in Hamburg Epitaphs," *SR* 35 (2001): 214–240.

Hamburg. Sasportas repeatedly recounted the public declamation of letters about Sabbetai Zevi in the city. Early in the spring of 1666 he described the following scene:

> These letters were read in public in the Sephardic synagogue and the entire congregation here in Hamburg erupted in song and dance along with musical accompaniment... the chaos increased to such a degree that they all wanted to dance, and they completely confused the order. The rabbi of the city, R. Moses Israel, had to get up on the podium and call for order, and he suggested that only twelve young men chosen by lots should be allowed to dance. But they paid him no heed because they all wanted to join in and participate in the happiness that had been commanded. The *parnasim* of the congregation forced their way over the heads of the people.[39]

Song, dance, and music. What Sasportas found so terrifying in this scene was the loss of control. The eruption of enthusiasm led directly to the violation of order. When the rabbi of the city attempted to organize the dancing and impose some semblance of control, he was ignored.[40] The reconstituted fellowship of believers pointedly disregarded the rabbinic attempts to orchestrate their joy. Order in the synagogue had been a constant problem that nagged at the authorities throughout the western Sephardic Diaspora. Reports of boisterous chatter, comings and goings, and even an occasional fistfight persist in the accounts of visitors to the Sephardic synagogues, as well as in record books.[41] In the Sephardic synagogue in London at some point between December 1664 and June 1665, the very period when Sasportas served as rabbi, the Holy Office received testimony "that one of the Francia brothers, being in Synagogue dressed in the vestments of his church

---

[39] והכתבים הללו נקראו בפומבי בב"ה הי"ג ותהום כל הקהילה בכאן האמבורגו במחול וריקוד וכל אחד בכלי זמר . . . וגדל כה ההמיה בריקוד עד שכלם היו רוצים לרקוד ובילבלו סדר ריקודים, והוצרך הרב מאריה דאתרא כה"ר משה ישראל לעמוד בבימה ולדרוש ברבים על הריקוד שיהיה בתיקון וכסדר ושלא ירקדו כי אם י"ב בחורים העולים בגורל, ולא שמעו לאזהרתו שכולם חפצים להתעסק במצות הרקוד ושמחה ופרנסי הקהל היו הם בתחילה מפסיעים על ראשי עם.

Sasportas, *ZNZ*, 61.

[40] On the use of lots to determine order, see Kaplan, "*Herem* in Hamburg," 185.

[41] For a fistfight in eighteenth-century Amsterdam, see Kaplan, "Deviance and Excommunication in the Eighteenth Century," 147n11; for unruly behavior in seventeenth-century London, see Kaplan, "The Jewish Profile of the Spanish-Portuguese Community of London during the Seventeenth Century," 165; for a shouting match between a Jesuit and a Sephardic preacher in seventeenth-century Amsterdam, see Israel, "The Sephardi Diaspora and the Struggle for Portuguese Independence from Spain (1640–1668)," 339.

said: 'Gentlemen, all this is suited either to very great fools or very wise men,' saying which he took off the vestment, threw down the book, and went out."[42] The lay leadership in London and Amsterdam had been scrupulous in demanding courteous and orderly behavior so as to present an ideal of dignified social and religious life.[43] What was true for the Sephardim in Amsterdam and London was no less the case in Hamburg.[44] The arrival of the Messiah threatened the normalizing social rules of Jewish civility.

Sasportas returned repeatedly to the social implications of collective joy. Several months after the initial outbreak, when news of Sabbetai Zevi's annulment of the fast on the ninth of Av arrived in Hamburg, he deplored the fact that a traditional day of mourning had been turned into a holiday with food and drink. Lamentation for the destruction of the Temple had given way to rejoicing at the arrival of the Messiah. What was more, the joy described in letters arriving from the Sephardic communities in the Ottoman Empire was contagious: "When I heard the letter read out in public, it brought glad tidings to all those who listened among the believers."[45] Public expression of collective joy posed a basic problem to the existing social order: it generated confusion and bred chaos. Sasportas seemed to stress that it was not a normative Jewish value, nor was it the correct emotional response to the constant flow of news from and about Sabbetai Zevi.

Instead of exultation, Jews should have responded either with fear or with lamentation. From the very outset, Sasportas took issue with unrestrained joy as the wrong emotional response to the possibility of messianic revelation: "Rather than rejoicing, there should be trembling and great fear," he wrote to his colleagues in Amsterdam when news of Nathan of Gaza's prophecy first arrived.[46] A few months later, in a letter to his colleagues in Venice, he contrasted the ecstasy of the Sab-

---

[42]Lucien Wolf, *Jews in the Canary Islands: being a calendar of Jewish cases extracted from the records of the Canariote Inquisition in the collection of the Marquess of Bute* (Toronto: University of Toronto Press, 2001), 205. As cited after the first edition (London, 1926) by Tishby, "New Information on the 'Converso' Community in London," 482.

[43]Yosef Kaplan, "Order and Discipline in the Portuguese Synagogue of Amsterdam," in *Jewish Studies and the European Academic World*, ed. Albert van der Heide and Irene E. Zwiep (Paris: Peeters, 2005), 1–14.

[44]Kaplan, "*Herem* in Hamburg," 168.

[45]Sasportas, *ZNZ*, 131.

[46]Ibid., 20. See Ps. 2:11.

batian believer with the anguish of the learned skeptic: "This one laughs lightheartedly for the time being, while the other one sheds tears for generations."[47] Joy was blinding and ephemeral. The correct response to the violation of the law, to the renewal of prophecy under suspicious auspices, to the marginalization of the rabbinate, in short, to the Jewish world turned upside down as described by Aaron Zarfati, should not have been laughter or lightheartedness. It should have been anguish and tears.

At various points in *Zizath novel zvi*, Sasportas reverted to the necessity for tears. Thus in describing the reaction to the public recitation of a letter in Hamburg, he wrote: "And I impoverished among the thousands... I cried doubly, and I said out loud: Rise up and mourn for the Torah, for its glory has been desecrated, its crown has fallen, from the day when your children have exchanged it for a new Torah that is not the heritage of the congregation of Jacob."[48] Sasportas's lament echoed one of the dirges recited in the synagogue on the ninth of Av.[49] The abstract entity of the Torah, the law itself, which had been desecrated and exchanged for a new Torah of Sabbatianism, caused Sasportas to cry out in the synagogue. In his outburst he invoked a long poetic tradition that personified the Torah and addressed it in personal terms.[50] Sasportas understood Sabbatian enthusiasm as an assault on Jewish law, the crown of Torah.

The people, in short, were tone-deaf to history and the law. Where they should have cried, they laughed. Instead of focusing on the implications of their own conclusions for the law, they were caught up in the moment. The immediate experience of happiness went hand in hand with delusional optimism. The constant flow of joyful tidings led the Jewish crowd to expect even more good news. This patently false expectation distorted their capacity to interpret the reports of the Messiah's activities from the Ottoman Empire when they did arrive. One of Aaron Zarfati's sons had taken a skeptical view of the new Messiah.[51]

[47] Sasportas, *ZNZ*, 112.

[48] Ibid., 131.

[49] Ibid., 131n2.

[50] Menahem Schmelzer, "Poems in Praise of Books by David ben Joseph ibn Yahya" (Hebrew), in *Asupah le-Yosef: kovetz mehkarim shai le-Yosef Hacker*, ed. Yaron Ben-Naeh et al. (Jerusalem: Zalman Shazar Center, 2014), 325.

[51] Sasportas signed the letter with a verse that indicated the year 1667; see Sasportas, *ZNZ*, 259. Because two paragraphs of the letter conclude with the name David, Tishby posited that the ad-

For taking such a stance, he earned Sasportas's praise as well as an explanation of his rationale. In a letter written well after the Messiah's conversion, Sasportas positioned himself as a corrector rather than a prophet. From his reading of the biblical passage he invoked in his correspondence, one can deduce that he saw himself as someone who had been unwillingly pressed into the reproof of collective folly. He wrote to Zarfati fils, "And as for the masses, who are like 'six-score thousand of Nineveh' (Jonah 4:11), their desire and longing is to see the imagined and limited good in their eyes, just like the passing good that leads them to follow the false idols they have purchased for themselves."[52] Invoking God's rebuke of the prophet in the final verse of the book of Jonah, Sasportas compared the contemporary Jewish crowd to the people of Nineveh who Jonah thought did not deserve the opportunity to repent. The Sabbatians were like the gentiles of Nineveh who did not know any better and simply clung to their false idols. The prophet Jonah had only begrudgingly fulfilled his mission and exhorted them to repent. To reprove Jonah, God held back from inflicting his punishment upon the city of Nineveh. Appalled that such foolish people should escape unscathed, Jonah had begged God for his own death. After giving Jonah a gourd for shade, God took it away from him. He asked him, just as you had pity on the gourd, "should not I pity Nineveh that great city wherein are more than six-score thousand persons that cannot discern between their right hand and their left hand?" (Jonah 4:11). Although he did not cite the conclusion of the verse, Sasportas implicitly invoked it. Like the residents of Nineveh, the Jewish crowd was too blind to discern between right and left. Sasportas understood Sabbatianism as a failure of judgment rather than a failure of obedience. Sasportas did not quote the words of the prophet Jonah, a figure identified in a number of rabbinic traditions as the future Messiah ben Joseph, but rather God's final and unanswered rebuke of the prophet.[53] Unlike the biblical prophets who railed against a persistent failure to

---

dressee was Aaron Zarfati's son David Zarfati de Pina. See Sasportas, *ZNZ*, 257n2. If this was indeed the case, he was aged ten or eleven when he received Sasportas's letter. David de Pina obtained his medical degree from Leiden at the age of twenty-one in 1678. See Kaplan, "Sephardi Students at the University of Leiden," 204–205.

[52] Sasportas, *ZNZ*, 258.

[53] Yehuda Liebes, "Jonah ben Amitai as Messiah ben Joseph" (Hebrew), in *Mehkarim ba-kabalah, be-filosofiyah yehudit uve-sifrut ha-musar vehehagut mugashim le-Yishayahu Tishby*, ed. Joseph Dan and Joseph Hacker (Jerusalem: Magnes Press, 1986), 269–311.

obey, Sasportas criticized a mistake in understanding. Sabbatianism was a problem of perception. God had to teach Jonah, like the city of Nineveh itself, how to see. Sasportas was trying to give the crowd a lesson in discernment.

A FAILURE OF THE INTELLECTUALS

In his condescension toward the people, Sasportas took a pitying view of their ignorance. He had few illusions about the modern Nineveh and its Jews. As a stranger to the northern Sephardic Diaspora, which he had taken upon himself to reprove, Sasportas transformed his radical marginality into an intellectual privilege. What he found so threatening about the enthusiastic frenzy was the disorder and disarrangement of the Jewish social hierarchy. Much of his criticism of the supposed crowd actually involved an indictment of the wealthy lay leaders and his rabbinic colleagues who had acquiesced in the revolt of the masses. That the masses of Jews who believed in Sabbetai Zevi were foolish and, in this sense, more like gentiles than Jews, Sasportas seems to have taken for granted. He almost certainly would have agreed with the later judgment of Robert Alter: "Against those who imagine the Jews as great rationalists, the Essenes, like the 17th century Sabbatean messianists and the contemporary believers in the messianic status of the late Lubavitcher Rebbe, vividly demonstrate that Jews can be as crazy as anybody else."[54] For Sasportas, what separated Jews from non-Jews was an epistemological rather than a genealogical or even moral gap. Gentiles, like the people of Nineveh, did not know any better. But that his ostensibly learned colleagues and their wealthy patrons had abdicated their responsibility to lead, this Sasportas found most appalling. These leaders were the people charged with bearing and transmitting the law to the Jews.

In his aforementioned description of the joyous celebration in Hamburg, Sasportas continued, "the masses overcame their leaders and there was no one to respond to them."[55] What was already a problem in Hamburg was similarly manifest in Venice, as Samuel Aboab reported:

[54] "Where's Esther?" *London Review of Books* 35.17, 12 September 2013, 29–30.
[55] Sasportas, *ZNZ*, 47.

By the by the leaders held their tongues because they were afraid lest the people abandon their work, their holy work, and so it seems that the great ones listen to the small ones.[56]

The term "holy work" referred to the penitential seizures that had gripped the Jews of Venice, along with so many other believers.[57] Acts of public penitence rendered the rabbinic establishment reluctant to challenge the sincerity of popular enthusiasm generated by messianic experience. Rabbis were afraid to speak out against the people for fear of deflating their desire for moral perfection. Atonement for sin was a good thing, and an activity very much valued by the rabbis.[58] One is hard-pressed to find a collection of sermons printed during this great age of preaching where a rabbinic homilist did not issue a call to his congregation to repent and return to the ways of God. Public outbursts of contrition were inextricably bound up with the belief in the new Messiah. They were thus part and parcel of the social disarray that accompanied the spread of messianic enthusiasm. This social reversal seems to have occurred in a number of stages. First the leaders kept silent; next they began to follow the people. The abdication of responsibility was thus doubly reinforced: the rabbis were not only quiet; they became members of the crowd in their own right. It was one thing to praise the contrite mood of the people, but the rabbis themselves had been seduced by the spectacle of mass repentance, which, in turn, had become a sign of the Messiah's arrival. News of Sabbetai Zevi seemed able to achieve what myriad calls for repentance could not. This demonstrated the kernel of good that reposed in the general evil of false prophecy. The phenomenology of religious experience produced by Sabbatian enthusiasm served to verify the prophecies of Nathan of Gaza.

What had happened at the level of society was also happening in the realm of ideas. Just as the rabbinic establishment had been margin-

---

[56] בין דא לדא שרים עצרו במלין כי חששו לעצמם מחטאת אם ירפו ידי העם ממלאכתם מלאכת עבודת הקדש, ובכן נראים הגדולים נשמעים לקטנים.

Ibid., 59.

[57] Isaiah Tishby, "The Penitential Rituals of Nathan of Gaza" (Hebrew), in *Netive emunah u-minut* (Jerusalem: Magnes Press, 1994), 30–51.

[58] Jacob Elbaum, *Teshuvat ha-lev ve-kabalat yisurim: iyunim be-shitot ha-teshuvah shel hakhme Ashkenaz u-Polin, 1348–1648* (Jerusalem: Magnes Press, 1992); in early modern Safed, see Lawrence Fine, "Penitential Practices in a Kabbalistic Mode," in *Seeking the Favor of God*, ed. Mark J. Boda et al. (Atlanta, GA: Society of Biblical Literature, 2008), 3:127–148.

alized by the people or had rendered itself irrelevant, the texts and ideas they were supposed to uphold had been brushed aside. Sasportas emphasized this in a long letter to Raphael Supino of Livorno:

> The foolish people who were listening [to Sabbetai Zevi] considered his speech to them as if it were the voice of God, without discerning whether the stipulations of Isaiah had been fulfilled... they easily believed the most recent [prophecies] and contradicted the first prophecies. They made that which is central peripheral and that which is peripheral central. There was no one zealous for the honor of heaven and for his true prophets who could say to them: the prophets who spoke before you, the spirit of God was with them, "but ye are forgers of lies" (Job 13:4).[59]

People listening to Sabbetai Zevi in Izmir lacked rational discernment. They accepted his claims to kingship, and, by extension, Nathan of Gaza's to prophecy, without subjecting them to the rigors of the textual tradition. They ignored that the Sabbatians contradicted the messianic prophecies outlined in the book of Isaiah. Just as the rabbis had been ignored, their ideas had likewise been abandoned. Throughout this long letter to Supino, Sasportas peppered his response with references to the book of Job, and in particular to God's rebuke from the whirlwind in the thirty-ninth chapter. Few biblical books provided Sasportas with as rich a lexicon of rebuke as Job while simultaneously allowing him to display his learning without taking up the mantle of the prophet. The Sabbatians had appropriated prophecy as a category with extraordinary success. Sasportas's language was saturated with allusions, implicit and explicit, to biblical and rabbinic literature. The voice from the whirlwind in Job and the final verse of Jonah provided him with a biblical language of admonition that was not prophetic. Sasportas invoked God as the judge rather than the prophet. A prophet's knowledge, which was dependent upon his own experience, was always certain and could not be tested by any outside standard. Judgment, in contrast to prophecy, was the product of a textual tradition mediated by legal reasoning.

---

[59] . . . ודלת העם השומעים היו דבריו אליהם כקול אלקי״ם מדבר בלתי הבחין בתנאי ישעיה אם כולם נתקיימו בו
ודעתם קלה להאמין האחרונים ולהכחיש נבואת הראשונים ועשו מן העיקר טפל ומן הטפל עיקר, ואין איש מאנשי
הקנאה על כבוד שמים ונביאיו האמיתיים המיטפל אליהם ואומר: הנביאים אשר היו לפניכם רוח ה׳ דיבר בם ואולם
אתם טופלי שקר.

Sasportas, *ZNZ*, 85.

In a letter written shortly thereafter, Isaac Aboab da Fonseca appealed to Sasportas to soften his attack on the crowd.

> But you know this people. It is terrible for whoever contradicts them in their belief, their crafted belief in the matter of our Messiah, to such an extent that all day in the markets and the streets they dispute and fight with those who scorn them... Who could judge this burdensome people?[60]

He informed Sasportas that the people were so insistent in their belief that they fought with whoever dared to contradict them. He threw up his hands in despair and asked rhetorically who could possibly manage to rise above the general chaos. Aboab spoke from the perspective of someone who was beholden to a specific group of people. Leaving aside the question of his own belief in Sabbetai Zevi, about which there is no scholarly consensus, Aboab wrote to Sasportas as a leader who was unable and also unwilling to oppose his own constituents.[61] He thought a position as strident as Sasportas's was untenable. Sasportas, by contrast, used his marginality within the rabbinic hierarchy to uphold an extremely unpopular stance. Having fled or been forced out of rabbinic positions in Oran, Tlemcen, Saleh, and London, Sasportas did not have the official recognition he considered his due. But he was unwilling to abandon his obligations to the tradition in whose name he spoke. He willingly responded to Aboab's rhetorical question. In point of fact, he would judge "this burdensome people," and what was more, he was prepared to oppose his colleagues.

It would be a mistake to reduce Sasportas's opposition to his contemporaries to biographical circumstances. While his social position undoubtedly informed and played a role in his unwillingness to condone popular enthusiasm, an indictment of the contemporary rabbinate pulsed throughout his account. In a letter to a colleague in Vienna, he rejected the penitential seizures and outlined the state to which the rabbinate had fallen:

> For the sake of repentance, which is incumbent upon us at all times, we should not consider someone the Messiah who has not been

[60] הלא ידע כת"ר מעלתו את העם הזה כי ברע הוא על כל אשר יתריס נגדם על אמונתם אמונה אומן בדבר משיחנו, עד אשר תמיד כל היום בשוקים וברחובות מתוכחים ומריבים אלו עם אלו מלעיגים בוזים ... ומי יוכל לשפוט את העם הכבד הזה

Ibid., 106.

[61] Kaplan, "The Attitude of the Sephardi Leadership."

proven... And in the meantime, the sages who embark on numerous inquiries, interpretations, and investigations have been treated with contempt, while the authority of the laity takes precedence over [their] superior authority.[62]

Repentance was an abiding legal obligation; it was not subject to occasional moods. Recent episodes of collective atonement did not offer any indication one way or another as to whether Sabbetai Zevi was the Messiah. Sasportas proceeded to deliver a scathing indictment of his colleagues. As they sat on the sidelines endlessly weighing each and every obscure issue, they had effectively abdicated their responsibility of decision making. The powerful laypeople had replaced the rabbis as the arbiters of religious truth.

The rabbis were beginning to mimic the crowd in their responses to reports about the Messiah. Almost a year after news first arrived in Europe, Sasportas expressed his frustration in a candid letter to his fellow opponent of Sabbatianism Joseph Halevi in Livorno:

> Today it is nearly an entire year since the letter from the prophet of Gaza arrived. I wrote to the sages in Amsterdam, including R. Isaac Nahar who arrived in your camp on his way to greet his prophet and his Messiah, both of whom they consider as such. I saw them leaning toward the opinion of the masses. They believed the letters written by laypeople or by those only somewhat knowledgeable who were called by the title "Sage." I wrote to them repeatedly but no one paid any attention. To the contrary, they hold up the lowly people and warn about their new faith without considering whether or not it agrees with the traditions of the rabbis, of blessed memory.[63]

Sasportas's previous complaint about the Jewish crowd was now true of the rabbinic establishment in no less a city than Amsterdam. The crowd had seized on incoming letters as confirmation of their newfound belief in the Messiah. But the rabbis had not bothered to examine who

---

[62] ובעבור התשובה המחוייבת עלינו בכל זמן לא נחזיק למשיח למי שלא הוחזק . . . ובין כה וכה נתבזו החכמים המרבים בחקירות ודרישות ובדיקות להשגת האמת ועדיף כהן של ההדיוטות מכח גבוה.
Sasportas, *ZNZ*, 119–120.

[63] והיום כמו שנה תמימה בעת בוא מכתב נביא עזה כתבתי לחכמי אמשטרדאם ובכללם ה״ר יצחק נהר אשר בא למחניכם ללכת להקביל פני נביאו ומשיחו המוחזקים אצלם, וראיתים נוטים לדעת ההמון והאמינו מכתב ההדיוטות או יודע ספר הנקרא בשם חכם, וחזרתי כמה פעמים לכתוב ולית מאן דמשגח אדרבא מחזיקים בידי דלת העם ומזהירים על אמונתם החדשה בלתי השקיף אם תסכים עם קבלת רז״ל או לא.
Ibid., 148.

was actually writing these letters. Sasportas mentioned two different types of writers who were sending the eagerly awaited good news: laypeople and "those only somewhat knowledgeable who were called by the title 'Sage.'" It hardly comes as a surprise that Sasportas would put little stock in the writings of laypeople. The second group, however, was more nebulous, and possibly of even greater concern. The Hebrew phrase *yode-a sefer*, rendered above as "somewhat knowledgeable," may be better translated as "literate." Sasportas switched into the passive voice and described these somewhat knowledgeable people as those "who were called by the title 'Sage.'" Someone had bestowed upon these men the title of sage, *haham*, but they clearly did not deserve the appellation. This group, men who were merely literate in rabbinic texts but hardly outstanding scholars, had been caught up in the frenzy. It was their letters, written with sufficient skill so as to be vaguely plausible, that his colleagues in the Amsterdam rabbinate had failed to submit to learned scrutiny. Given that these men possessed enough learning to mimic rabbinic style, it was all the more critical that their claims be tested against the rigors of rabbinic erudition.

Sabbatian leadership had also appropriated the very category of the sage, or *haham*. In *Zizath novel zvi*, Sasportas included an edition of a Sabbatian prophecy entitled "The Vision of Abraham" (Heb. *Mar-eh avraham*). He incorrectly attributed the letter to the Sabbatian preacher Abraham Heikhani rather than to its actual author, Nathan of Gaza.[64] Sasportas's error is instructive. After including a transcription in his chronicle, he added the following gloss:

> It is unknown what went on in the mind of that aforementioned sage about whose wisdom everyone testified and who was the greatest preacher in Constantinople. All the masses in Constantinople followed him, and the sages had no ability to punish him.[65]

Sasportas spent much of his intellectual energy refuting Sabbatian claims to prophecy. The "Vision of Abraham" included a description of the birth of Sabbetai Zevi and a prediction of his messianic mission.

[64] Ibid., 160n4. Scholem edited this letter on at least two occasions. See *Be-ikvot mashiah* (Jerusalem: Tarshish, 1944), 53–58; "Sabbatian Documents on R. Nathan of Gaza from the Writings of Mahallallel Halleleyuah of Ancona," in *Mehkere shabtaut*, 68–69.

[65] ולא נודע מה עלה בדעתו של הח' הנ"ל שכולם מעידים עליו ועל חכמתו ודרשן עצום אשר אין כמוהו בקוסטנטינא. ועל זה היו נגררים אחריו כל המון העם שבקוסטנטינא ולא היה יכולת ביד החכמים להענישו. Sasportas, *ZNZ*, 160.

The publication of this letter would have afforded him a perfect opportunity to resist the Sabbatian appropriation of this biblical model of spiritual leadership. In his discussion of the man he assumed was the author of this letter, Abraham Heikhani, Sasportas contested the Sabbatian appropriation of another type of figure, that of the Talmudic sage. Heikhani was such a successful demagogue that he had seduced the entirety of the Jewish crowd in Istanbul. Earlier the crowd had accepted Nathan of Gaza's prophecy as the word of God; but in this case, they had testified to the depth of Heikhani's wisdom. What Sasportas had described in Amsterdam was evidently occurring in the Ottoman Empire as well. The actual sages had abdicated their responsibility and joined in with the crowds of Jewish people who had been seduced by a charismatic preacher. This withdrawal of the sages had created a vacuum that people like Nathan of Gaza and Abraham Heikhani were all too ready to fill. Nathan of Gaza repeatedly referred to himself as a prophet and drew upon the rich discussion of prophecy in the Bible to bolster his credentials. Heikhani, by contrast, had convinced the Jewish crowd of his learning. Wisdom, a traditional endowment of the Jewish sages, was now the possession of the Sabbatians. The result, as Sasportas stressed with palpable frustration, was that the actual sages in the Ottoman Empire lacked both the resolve and the ability to punish Heikhani.

SILENCING DOUBT

Things were no better in northern Europe. The rabbinic leadership of Amsterdam, which included Isaac Aboab da Fonseca, Moses Raphael D'Aguilar, and Aaron Zarfati, were reluctant to express any challenge in public. The wealthy layman Abraham Pereyra was so taken up by the enthusiasm that he prepared himself for a journey to the Holy Land. But Sasportas's skepticism nagged at them, and they sought to silence him. In one of his early letters to Sasportas, Nahar chided, "As for you, dear sir, I do not know why you have not kept things to yourself and why you have publicized [your doubts] before the masses who walk innocently and uphold their faith."[66] Nahar chastised his former teacher

---

[66] Ibid., 25.

for breaking ranks with the rabbinate, who leaned heavily toward accepting the veracity of Sabbetai Zevi and Nathan of Gaza's claims. The purported reason given by Nahar was the very thing Sasportas was so afraid of himself: confusion and chaos. Nahar accused Sasportas of public dissent and therefore of sowing disorder. Behind Nahar's rebuke lay an implicit claim that his former teacher would have found appalling: Judaism was socially, not textually, constituted. If the people were repenting, they should be applauded, and, better yet, the rabbinate should join them. This was not the occasion on which to express doubt.

With the passage of time, attempts to silence Sasportas continued and spread from the rabbinate to the wealthy laity. The Jews of Amsterdam had heard reports in which Sasportas challenged the authenticity of Nathan of Gaza's prophecy and called on his colleagues to suspend their judgment until they had received independent verification from well-known sages in Jerusalem. In a narrative passage, Sasportas summarized the contents of various letters he had received but had chosen not to include in his chronicle:

> And the wealthy layman Abraham Pereyra, who was the leader of the believers, wrote me an open rebuke about this. He asked me not to say such things or to contradict the prophecy of their prophet Nathan [of Gaza], as one should not do this about a prophet of God. For if a great sage who is learned in Torah and fearful of sin [expressed doubt], what would the lowly people say, for they have neither Torah nor the commandments, and this will cause them to fail and to sin. And other wealthy laypeople wrote similarly.[67]

Sasportas was clearly making himself a public nuisance, or, as he described himself on another occasion, "a lacerating thorn," in the side of the Sabbatians.[68] Pereyra even went so far as to claim that Sasportas's doubts might lead the people into sin. Although he lived several hundred miles away, in Hamburg, Sasportas was well known to the Jews of Amsterdam. They thought of him as a sage. Like Nahar before him,

---

[67] והגביר כה"ר אברהם פירירה שהיה ראש המאמינים כתב לי תוכחת מגולה על זה ומבקש ממני שלא אדבר כדברים האלה ולא הדומה להם להכחיש נבואת נתן נביאם ונביא ה' ושכן לא יעשה, שאם איש חכם וגדול בתורה ובירא את חטא יאמר זה מה יאמרו דלת העם שאין בידם תורה ומצוות ותהיה סיבה להכשיל את הרבים ולהחטיאם, וכן כתבו לי גבירים אחרים.

Ibid., 48–49.
[68] Ibid., 132.

Figure 10. Oil portrait of Jacob Sasportas attributed to Isaac Luttichuys, ca. 1670. This painting depicts Jacob Sasportas holding a Bible open to Ezekiel 28. In a letter he had written to his colleagues in Amsterdam, Sasportas called himself a painful thorn, קוץ מכאיב, a Hebrew phrase that appears only once in the Bible, in Ezekiel 28. Photo © The Israel Museum, Jerusalem by Elie Posner.

Pereyra worried what would happen to the common people if they perceived an open rift in the rabbinic leadership.

Abraham Israel Pereyra (d. 1699) was a prominent figure among the Amsterdam Sephardim. Born a Catholic in Madrid, he made his way to Amsterdam via Venice and reverted to Judaism in the later 1640s.[69] Around the time Sasportas first arrived in Amsterdam, he was already playing a leading role in Portuguese Jewish life. A decade later his philanthropy took on an additional dimension as he established a yeshiva

[69] Israel, "Menasseh Ben Israel and the Dutch Sephardi Colonization Movement," 393.

in Hebron.[70] Under the epistolary influence of Meir b. Hiyya Rofe, a rabbi in Hebron, he became a fervent believer in Sabbetai Zevi.[71] In the spring of 1666, shortly after he had written to Sasportas, he set out along with Isaac Nahar to greet the Messiah in Palestine. Like Nahar, he did not get much farther than Italy, stopping in Venice before returning to Amsterdam.

Pereyra was not only a rich man; he was an author of several moralistic tracts in Spanish including *La Certeza del Camino* (1666) and *Espejo de la vanidad del mundo* (1671).[72] Although he could not detect any Sabbatian beliefs in *La Certeza del Camino*, Scholem suggested that its publication in 1666 "cannot have been accidental, and it was probably meant to encourage the Sabbatian revival among the marranos."[73] Yosef Kaplan and Henry Méchoulan have decisively rejected this interpretation and demonstrated that the work has no connection to Sabbatianism.[74] What is more, from their studies of Pereyra one can deduce several intriguing parallels with Sasportas. Like Sasportas, Pereyra returned repeatedly to the book of Job in his moralistic exhortations.[75] Furthermore, in his strict emphasis on personal rather than collective salvation, Pereyra betrayed an almost "inquisitorial intransigence" toward the moral failings of former conversos.[76] In a responsum written from London only a short time before the outbreak of Sabbatian messianism, Sasportas had also taken an extremely hard line against the former conversos to whom he was ministering.[77] Sasportas and Pereyra wrote independently of one another in different intellectual traditions. Sasportas was a rabbinic jurist through and through for whom Jewish law was paramount; Pereyra was a former converso whose writing was saturated with the Catholic thought of Luis de Granada and other sixteenth-century Spanish theologians.[78] Nevertheless, both Sasportas

[70] Abraham Yaari, "The Pereyra Yeshivot in Jerusalem and Hebron" (Hebrew), in *Yerushalayim: mehkere erez yisrael*, ed. M. Benayahu et al. (Jerusalem, 1953), 185–202.

[71] Kaplan, *Orobio de Castro*, 220–222.

[72] Méchoulan, *Hispanidad y judaismo en tiempos de Espinoza*. On Sasportas see 53n35.

[73] Scholem, *Sabbatai Sevi*, 530.

[74] Kaplan, *Orobio de Castro*, 221. Henry Méchoulan, "La Pensée d'Abraham Pereyra dans *La Certeza del Camino*," in *Dutch Jewish History* 2, ed. Joseph Michman (Jerusalem: Magnes Press, 1989), 82.

[75] Méchoulan, "La Pensée d'Abraham Pereyra dans *La Certeza del Camino*," 84.

[76] Henry Méchoulan, "Abraham Pereyra, juge des marranes et censeur des ses coreligionnaires à Amsterdam au temps de Spinoza," *REJ* 138 (1979): 397.

[77] Goldish, "Hakham Jacob Sasportas and the Former Conversos."

[78] Méchoulan, *Hispanidad y judaismo en tiempos de Espinoza*, 69. Isaac Orobio de Castro called

and Pereyra took a similar stance on the moral and intellectual imperatives of returning conversos. It hardly comes as a surprise that modern scholars have applied the adjective "inquisitorial" to Pereyra and the noun "inquisitor" to Sasportas.[79] Although Pereyra and Sasportas came from different worlds—the former a converso merchant from the imperial capital steeped in Catholic thought, and the latter a Sephardic rabbi from a *presidio* at the edge of the Iberian Empire—both expressed a deep suspicion of lay piety. Pereyra may not have mastered the rabbinic tradition himself, but he funded and continued to support an elitist institution in Hebron devoted to the study of Talmud by a highly selective group of learned rabbis.[80] With their epistolary encouragement, Pereyra had become an avid believer. From Pereyra's perspective, rabbis worked for him. Sasportas should have taken the same position on Sabbetai Zevi as the rabbis he employed, either literally in Hebron or figuratively in Amsterdam. But Sasportas refused to do as he was told. It had clearly begun to sting that someone who was theoretically so close to Pereyra's own ideals of learning, and had such a similar habit of mind, should have dared to express serious doubt. His letter to Sasportas may have been written in Spanish, which may account for Sasportas's failure to include it in *Zizath novel zvi*.[81] Zarfati, Nahar, and Aboab da Fonseca among the rabbinate had all written to Sasportas individually and collectively. One of Nahar's letters included greetings and concern about Sasportas's unbelief from his colleagues Zarfati and D'Aguilar, and Sasportas's responses were often written to the Amsterdam rabbinate as a whole.[82] Among the wealthy laity, Pereyra had now weighed in as well. He had not taken kindly to the interventions of someone who had once been held in such esteem by the Amsterdam Sephardim, and had told Sasportas to keep his mouth shut.

Luis de Granada an "outrageous idolater." Kaplan, *Orobio de Castro*, 237n23. On Pereyra's debts to Luis de Granada, see Kaplan, *Orobio de Castro*, 310.

[79] For the former, see above; for the latter, see Scholem, *Sabbatai Sevi*, 566–567.

[80] According to its bylaws, the Pereyra yeshiva was an institution that funded the full-time study of a small group of men called a *hesger*. See Yaari, "The Pereyra Yeshivot in Jerusalem and Hebron," 187. On the selective nature of the *hesger*, see Elchanan Reiner, "Wealth, Social Status, and Talmud Torah: The *Kloyz* in Jewish Society in Eastern Europe in the Seventeenth and Eighteenth Centuries" (Hebrew), *Zion* 58 (1993): 290–294. On Pereyra's knowledge of Hebrew, see Méchoulan, "La Pensée d'Abraham Pereyra dans *La Certeza del Camino*," 69.

[81] On Pereyra's preference for Spanish, see Swetschinski, *Reluctant Cosmopolitans*, 278–279.

[82] For the former, see Sasportas, *ZNZ*, 24–26; for the latter, see 100–105 and passim.

There is some evidence that Sasportas got the memo, at least for a time. In the aforementioned letter to Samuel Aboab in Venice, Sasportas quoted his exchange with Nahar and described how he had also been told by the lay leadership in Hamburg to remain silent.

> Therefore I said I shall guard my mouth with a barrier until "righteousness shall look down from heaven" (Ps. 85:12), and he shall give truth to Jacob. And would that I were caught lying about this issue.[83]

Sasportas went on to express his grave doubts to Samuel Aboab in the remainder of the letter but was willing to cease from his open criticism for a time. At this point he had already received news of Sabbetai Zevi's annulment of the fast on the tenth of Tevet. This flagrant violation of the law left Sasportas appalled and relatively certain of his own position. He invoked the psalmist's call for truth and righteousness and left little doubt that he thought both were on his side. What he wanted from his colleagues, however, was a careful and thorough discussion of the evidence at their disposal. Instead, the lay leadership in Hamburg, his rabbinic colleagues in Amsterdam, and one of the wealthiest Jews in Amsterdam had all instructed him to keep quiet.

As the enthusiasm continued to gain momentum, the efforts to stifle opposition continued apace. Sasportas had clearly not remained silent for very long. News of Sabbetai Zevi's annulment of the fast on the ninth of Av several months later led to the inevitable celebrations. As he witnessed another outbreak of public jubilation in the Hamburg synagogue, Sasportas called out that the people should rise up and mourn for the new Torah. His interruption of the celebration was not appreciated: "Many of the believers surrounded me in the Sephardic synagogue and they were examining my words, saying that I claimed this Messiah wants to create a new Torah like Jesus of Nazareth, and they wanted to harm me."[84] Sasportas had made precisely this claim on a number of occasions. The believers rejected his comparison of Sabbatianism to early Christianity as an impious utterance bordering on sacrilege.

It remains unclear what type of harm, if any, the believers intended to inflict upon Sasportas. The chaos in the synagogue, however, only

---

[83] על כן אמרתי אשמרה לפי מחסום עד שמשמים צדק נשקף ויתן אמת ליעקב, ומי יתן והייתי נתפס כבדאי בענין זה.

Ibid., 66.

[84] Ibid., 131. See Scholem, *Sabbatai Sevi*, 579–580.

increased, and open disagreement proved a very foolish strategy. One of the ritual innovations the Sabbatians had introduced into the synagogue service consisted of a blessing for the Messiah recited when the Torah scroll was declaimed in public. The believers in Hamburg were so fervent that they recited this blessing upon the declamation of the Torah on Mondays and Thursdays in addition to the Sabbath and holidays. Sasportas recounted the grief that came to his rabbinic colleague in Hamburg David Cohen de Lara, who had imprudently tried to protest the recitation of this blessing.[85]

> In the synagogue there was an old sage, a priest, who had served and led this congregation for many years and instructed many students. Since he was not a believer, he uttered abuses and curses when he heard their blessing. He did not want to hear a blessing with the name of the aforementioned Messiah, and he would leave the sanctuary when it began. One time, he went to leave but found the doors deliberately locked. Yet even this was not sufficient. They decided to recite it prior to the opening of the ark, so that no one, meaning especially the aforementioned sage, would be able to leave. When he heard the beginning of the blessing, he tried to leave, but they grabbed him against his will so he would be forced to hear it. As a result, there was extraordinary confusion in the synagogue. Although they opposed his skepticism, his students expressed concern for his honor. But they objected to his actions because they were sick like the believers.[86]

In his account of this incident Sasportas blurred the line between the public intimidation of dissent and his own sense of personal grievance. He emphasized the divide between the learned skeptics and the crowd. Although he did not mention the rabbi's name, he singled out two facts about him: his relative age and his role as a teacher. Cohen de Lara was an older man who had served the congregation for many years and had

---

[85] On Cohen de Lara, see Peter T. van Rooden and Jan Wim Wesselius, "Two Early Cases of Publication by Subscription in Holland and Germany: Jacob Abendana's *Mikhlal Yophi* (1661) and David Cohen de Lara's *Keter Kehunna* (1668)," *Quarendo* 16 (1986): 110–130.

[86] והיה נמצא בב"ה חכם אחד זקן וכהן ששימש ונהג הקהלה הזאת שנים הרבה והעמיד תלמידים, ויען שלא היה מאנשי אמונתם ומחרף ומגדף בעת שמעו ולא היה רוצה לשמוע ברכתו של שם המשיח הנקוב והיה יוצא בתחילת הברכה חוץ לב"ה, ופעם אחד רצה לצאת ומצא הדלת סגור בכונה רעה. ולא הספיק להם זה עד שקבעו הברכה קודם פתיחת הארון כדי שלא יצא אחד מהקהל וכונתם בעבור הח' הכהן הנ"ל, וכאשר שמע תחילת הברכה רצה לצאת ותפשו בו בעל כרחו לשמוע מה שאינו רוצה. והיה בעבור זה בלבול רב בב"ה לפי שתלמידיו אעפ"י שלא היו כמוהו באמונתו חסו על כבודו, ואף אם לא ישרו מעשיו בעיניהם לפי שגם הם חולו כבעלי האמונה.

Sasportas, *ZNZ*, 132.

accumulated many students. At the time he wrote this, Sasportas was in his midfifties and had taught in a number of different places including Amsterdam. Much—if not all—of the crowd in the Hamburg synagogue that had intimidated Sasportas and that had scuffled over Cohen de Lara were younger men. Nathan of Gaza was in his early twenties at the peak of the Sabbatian movement, and the Messiah himself was only around forty. The crowd of believers, and the two most important figures in the movement, were relatively young; skeptics like Sasportas and Cohen de Lara were considerably older. As Gershon David Hundert has observed in a different context, "turning head over heels is not something people advanced in years tend to do."[87] The dispute over Sabbatianism pitted exuberant young men against teachers and other figures of authority. But this was not all. What was so striking to Sasportas was the effect of these younger men on some of the older and wealthier members. If one shifts from Hamburg to Amsterdam, Isaac Aboab da Fonseca, who was five years older than Sasportas, refused to challenge the certainty of the Sabbatians lest they cease their penitential practices. Abraham Pereyra, who was closer in age to Sasportas than to the young men in the Amsterdam synagogue and wealthy enough to resist the entreaties of impudent upstarts, had pointedly asked Sasportas to keep quiet.

THE TRUTH VALUE OF DOUBT

Doubt, for Sasportas, had validity independent of any report about the Messiah. It was a legal category that any jurist had to consider before issuing a ruling. It was also a philosophical precondition for belief or faith. Sasportas impressed upon his correspondents that they had an imperative to subject any claim about the Messiah to radical skepticism. Early on in the sequence of reports, Sasportas tried to convince his colleagues in Amsterdam:

> It seems to me that my doubts are better than certainty. Because if all of the principles and details about the coming of the redeemer prophesied by the man of God are not fulfilled after some time, then the difference

---

[87] *Jews in Poland-Lithuania in the Eighteenth Century: A Genealogy of Modernity* (Berkeley: University of California Press, 2004), 181.

will be destruction. All of the masses, and some of the leaders as well, have accepted as truth that he is the King Messiah and have called out in the camp of the Hebrews (1 Sam. 4:6) that one cannot challenge what has been heard and that the voice of one who doubts shall not roar in his wake (Job 37:4). After they have seen that his truth has not been fulfilled, they shall say there is no Messiah in Israel, for he has already been consumed in the days of the prophecy of Gaza. And this, if they do not contradict the Torah and prophecy altogether.[88]

The very idea of the Messiah hinged upon the relationship between doubt and certainty. If the crowd and its leaders were to experience the bitter disappointment of unfulfilled expectations, they were likely to despair of the Messiah and even of the Torah itself. The costs of disillusionment were so high, Sasportas reasoned, that a still greater degree of skepticism was required. Invoking a celebrated statement in the Talmud, "There is no Messiah in Israel for he has already been consumed in the days of Hezekiah," Sasportas applied it to one possible outcome of Sabbatian beliefs.[89] If Sabbetai Zevi did not fulfill his messianic promise, his followers would deny the Messiah in Judaism altogether by claiming he had already been consumed. The initial impulse to doubt thus came from an attempt by Sasportas to protect the truth-value of the messianic idea from the dangerous certitude of the Sabbatians. Sasportas tried to impress upon his colleagues that his recourse to messianic doubt did not contradict an abiding belief in the possibility of the Messiah. As he wrote to Aaron Zarfati:

> What is important to emphasize is that I allowed for the possibility. This is the very essence of the true faith: on each and every day the Messiah might actually come. It is possible that it is this aforementioned rabbi [Sabbetai Zevi], even though to me this is a very distant possibility and almost certainly not the case.[90]

---

[88] ונראה לי שיותר טוב ספקי מודאי. כי לאחר ימים אם לא יתקיימו כל הכללים והפרטים בביאת הגואל המתנבא עליו איש האלקי"ם נפקא מינא חורבא, שכל המון העם וקצת מראשיהם אשר נתאמת אצלם כי הוא מלך המשיח והעבירו קול במחנה העברים שאין לגרוע ממה שנשמע ולא אחריו ישאג קול המטיל ספק, ואחר כך בראותם שלא נתקיימה אמיתתו יאמרו שאין משיח לישראל שכבר אכלוהו בימי נבואת עזה. וזה אם לא יכחישו דברי התורה והנבואה מעיקרם. Sasportas, ZNZ, 18.

[89]BT Sanhedrin, 99a, as cited by Tishby, Sasportas, ZNZ 18n2.

[90] אבל מה ששייך לומר הוא כי דברי היו באפשרות והוא עצם האמונה האמיתית שבכל יום ויום אפשר להיות ולבוא משיח, ואיפשר שהוא הרב הנ"ל ואף אם הוא אצלי אפשר רחוק וקרוב לנמנע. Sasportas, ZNZ, 36.

Sasportas used the skeptical imperative in order to drive a wedge between the Jewish doctrine of the Messiah and the person of Sabbetai Zevi.

Sasportas took care to impress upon his correspondents the compatibility of doubt with sincere repentance on the part of the deluded believers who claimed to have experienced the messianic advent. As he wrote to Isaac Aboab da Fonseca, "It seems to me that considering it as a possibility, saying this might be the Messiah and a prophet, would lead to an even greater repentance than considering this as something definite in the near future."[91] The insistence upon certainty led to an extraordinary risk Sasportas refused to take. If Sabbetai Zevi did not in fact turn out to be the Messiah, then the disappointment could lead to collective despair and possibly even conversion. Sasportas's point, however, went beyond the specific circumstances of Sabbetai Zevi. The possibility—as opposed to the certainty—of the Messiah's arrival better served the final ends of repentance. Skepticism offered a better path to the truth, and to true faith, than did certainty. In order to achieve sufficient abjection before God, or genuine repentance, the penitent had to suspend certainty in belief. The absolute believers in Sabbetai Zevi challenged the transcendence of God with their very certainty. They thought they had experienced his revelation directly in the person of the Messiah. In this way, they behaved exactly like the early Christians who had a personal God in the form of Jesus.

In another letter to the Amsterdam rabbinate, Sasportas made it piercingly clear how the leaders should go about exhorting their congregation to repent:

> It is better to warn people to repent, while raising the possibility of doubt, saying, "Turn, O backsliding children" (Jer. 3:14), perhaps there may be proximate hope… If in your consideration, this doubt of mine causes them to turn away, then it is an indirect effect and not the actual cause. One is not liable in the laws of man and my judgment will be in the hands of heaven.[92]

[91] Ibid., 47.

[92] ויותר טוב להזהיר על התשובה בלשון ספק ולומר שובו בנים שובבים אולי יש תקוה קרובה . . . ואם לפי סברתכם
ספקי זה גורם החזרה לאחור הנה הוא גרמא בנזקים לא בגוף המעשה ופטור מדיני אדם ודיני בידי שמים.
Ibid., 103.

Sasportas sought to counter the opposition to his validation of and emphasis on doubt. If the people were so fickle that elimination of certainty caused them to renege upon their repentance, then he was prepared to deal with the consequences. He invoked a principle from the Talmud to explain his position.[93] In a number of instances the Talmud had ruled that one who caused damage by indirect effect was not held liable. As far as Sasportas was concerned, if the people stopped their penitential rites because the exhortation to repent was stated as a possibility rather than as a certainty, then he could not be held liable. Their decision to cease repentance because of his validation of doubt was analogous to an indirect effect of damage. Sasportas's invocation of this legal principle was clearly rhetorical, but it also demonstrated a larger thematic behind his reasoning. He argued and formulated his opinions like a jurist. Doubt was a crucial category for him and one that had to be respected rather than silenced. The people could not hold the rabbis responsible, as they surely would, if messianic expectations, encouraged by the rabbis themselves, were disappointed. Skepticism and doubt had an intrinsic moral and legal worth. Sasportas seems to have set greater store by the truth-value of doubt than by the dubious social value of keeping people in the fold by encouraging their self-assured repentance. The ultimate responsibility for repentance rested with the penitent. If it were contingent upon the definitive arrival of the Messiah or the validity of a prophet's visions, then it was not genuine repentance.

Sasportas connected the validity of doubt to the relationship between faith and belief. As he wrote to Supino, "How can faith that contains doubt be settled in the understanding of the believer and be accepted by the intellect of the thinking person?"[94] Drawing implicitly upon the discussion of belief in Maimonides's *Guide of the Perplexed*, Sasportas silently invoked the opening of chapter 50 of the first section:

> Know, thou who studiest this my Treatise, that belief is not the notion that is uttered, but the notion that is represented in the soul when it has been averred of it that it is in fact just as it has been represented. If you

---

[93] BT Bava Kamma, 55b, as cited by Tishby, 103n6.
[94] Sasportas, *ZNZ*, 82.

belong to those who are satisfied with expressing in speech the opinions that are correct or that you deem to be correct, without represent-
ing them to yourself and believing them and still less without seeking
certain knowledge regarding them, you take a very easy road. In accor-
dance with this you will find many stupid people holding to beliefs to
which, in their representation, they do not attach any meaning whatever. If however, you belong to those whose aspirations are directed toward ascending to that high rank which is the rank of speculation, and
to gaining certain knowledge with regard to God's being One by virtue of a true Oneness, so that no composition whatever is to be found
in Him, and no possibility of division in any way whatever—then you
must know that He, may He be exalted, has in no way and in no mode
any essential attribute, and that just as it is impossible that He should
be a body, it is also impossible that He should possess an essential
attribute.[95]

Maimonides went on to introduce and expand upon the doctrine of the
negative attributes of God for the next several chapters. As part of his
larger critique of religious language, Maimonides argued that one can
only negate the association of certain attributes with God, but no positive attributes can be associated with him. The negative attributes are
categorical negatives; that is, one may infer no positive attributes from
them. "Categorical negation maintains that the category of absence or
presence, as we know it, does not apply to God; the same is true of
unity and multiplicity," as Moshe Halbertal has described it.[96]

In *Zizath novel zvi*, Sasportas did not cite Maimonides's *Guide* with
anywhere near the same frequency as he invoked either his *Code of
Law* or his "Epistle to Yemen." Nevertheless, there can be little doubt
that Tishby correctly identified Sasportas's implicit invocation of this
passage in the *Guide*. In addition to the textual similarities between the
two passages, Sasportas cited Maimonides's doctrine of negative attributes in chapters 56 and 57 from the first section of the *Guide* in the
context of a legal responsum whose first half dealt with a problem of

---

[95] Moses Maimonides, *The Guide of the Perplexed*, I, 50, trans. Shlomo Pines (Chicago: University of Chicago Press, 1963), 111. Hereafter Maimonides, *Guide*, with Roman numeral to indicate
the section and Arabic numeral to indicate the chapter within the section. Tishby identified the
passage in Maimonides in Sasportas, *ZNZ*, 82n4.

[96] Halbertal, *Maimonides*, 299.

dietary laws and whose second half dealt with theology. The responsum dates from Sasportas's stay in Hamburg and was written roughly three years after his letter to Supino but in the period when he was editing *Zizath novel zvi*.[97] In the opening of this section in the *Guide*, Maimonides distinguished between two types of readers. The first, those who take the "very easy road," express their faith in speech. The second, those who seek to ascend to the higher ranks of philosophical speculation, attain belief through contemplation. The quest for certainty in belief under optimum conditions was difficult. But under the circumstances in which the Sabbatians presented their certainty, belief was not simply difficult to obtain; it was impossible. Belief was the result of solitude and contemplation rather than observation and enthusiasm.

In the third section of the *Guide*, Maimonides dealt with the purpose of the commandments. In these chapters he gave a twofold explanation for the law: to ensure the welfare of the people and to provide for the welfare of the soul.

> As for the welfare of the soul, it consists in the multitude's acquiring correct opinions corresponding to their respective capacity. Therefore some of them [namely, the opinions] are set forth explicitly and some of them are set forth in parables. For it is not within the nature of the common multitude that its capacity should suffice for apprehending that subject matter as it is. As for the welfare of the body, it comes about by the improvement of their ways of living one with another. This is achieved through two things. One of them is the abolition of their wrongdoing each other. This is tantamount to every individual among the people not being permitted to act according to his will and up to the limits of his power, but being forced to that which is useful to the whole. The second thing consists in the acquisition by every human individual of the moral qualities that are useful for life in society so that the affairs of the city may be ordered. Know that as between these two aims, one is indubitably greater in nobility, namely the welfare of the soul—I mean the procuring of correct opinions—while the second aim—I mean the welfare of the body—is prior in nature and time.[98]

---

[97] *Ohel ya-akov*, #29, 39b. In the numbering within *Ohel ya-akov* there are two responsa with the number 29. The invocation of Maimonides is in the first of the two.

[98] Maimonides, *Guide*, III, 27.

Sasportas did not cite this particular section of the *Guide* in *Zizath novel zvi*. Nevertheless, the distinction between the philosopher and the multitude that Maimonides articulated in the section Sasportas invoked about the negative attributes pertained to the purpose of the law. The multitude needed the law to ensure the health of the body politic. Without the law, social chaos would ensue. The philosopher needed the law to ensure the health of the soul. But he could not cultivate the correct opinions and ensure the welfare of his soul without social order. The welfare of the body politic was thus a precondition for the welfare of the soul.

The world Maimonides described in philosophical abstraction, with its acute distinction between the multitude who needed the law for the health of the body politic and the philosopher who needed the law to engage in philosophical contemplation, confronted Sasportas with terrifying immediacy. The Hebrew word Sasportas used to refer to "the crowd" or "the rabble," *hamon*, may have come from Maimonides's *Guide*. In his medieval Hebrew translation of the Judeo-Arabic original, Samuel ibn Tibbon used the word *hamon* to refer to the multitude. The word appears throughout the *Guide* and often in opposition to the elite reader to whom Maimonides had addressed his treatise. Thus in his definition of the Hebrew word *Adam*, the name of the first man, Maimonides wrote, "It is also a term designating the multitude, I mean the generality as distinguished from the elite."[99] The multitude were those who took the easy path toward belief. They adopted certainty with alacrity. The elite philosopher struggled to attain belief and had a difficult path in his efforts of philosophical speculation.

Ibn Tibbon's translation had twice appeared in print in the sixteenth century.[100] Sasportas may not have needed to use the medieval Hebrew translation, as he had a firm knowledge of Arabic and possessed a manuscript with Maimonides's responsa written in Judeo-Arabic.[101] The available evidence does not offer a definitive resolution as to whether

[99] See ibid., I, 14. For other instances of the word *hamon*, see I, 35, I, 47, III, 12, III, 27.

[100] Venice, 1551, and Sabbioneta, 1553. See Jacob I. Dienstag, "Maimonides' *Guide for the Perplexed*: A Bibliography of Editions and Translations," in *Occident and Orient: A Tribute to the Memory of Alexander Scheiber*, ed. Robert Dán (Budapest: Akadémiai Kiadó; Leiden: Brill, 1988), 95–128.

[101] Copenhagen, Kongelige Bibliothek, Cod. Sim. Jud.-Arab. 1. As cited in Benjamin Richler, *Guide to Hebrew Manuscript Collections* (Jerusalem: Israel Academy of Sciences and Humanities, 2014), 196.

Sasportas derived the word *hamon* from Ibn Tibbon's translation of the *Guide* or deployed the word on his own. The concept of "the crowd" or "the multitude," however, appears to have emerged from his reading of Maimonides. The multitude for Maimonides had very little to do with numbers. Rather, he set it in opposition to the elite. Throughout the *Guide*, Maimonides identified the elite with the intended reader of his treatise, the perplexed student of philosophy who wanted to engage in philosophical speculation. Sasportas did not distinguish between the Maimonides of the *Guide* and the Maimonides of the *Code*. He upheld the *Guide* as the highest exemplar of philosophical skepticism and the *Code* as the most important source of the law.

Sabbatianism posed an acute philosophical problem to Sasportas. The certainty with which the Sabbatian believers propagated their new-found faith, the confidence and imperiousness with which they attempted to silence dissent, and their contempt for doubt as a condition for belief, all of these threatened the welfare of the body politic. Belief, or the acquisition of the correct opinions, could be cultivated and acquired only if the welfare of the body politic and the welfare of the soul had been adequately regulated. In the conditions of Sabbatian enthusiasm, this was far from the case. The enthusiasm of the multitude threatened the welfare of the body politic and by extension rendered the welfare of the soul unattainable. These intellectual and social demands forced Sasportas to draw upon the single most important resource he had in order to confer intellectual legitimacy upon his argument for the conditionality of messianic belief: Maimonides.

The position Sasportas advocated was a lonely one. He was acutely conscious that his imperative to doubt, on legal, social, and philosophical grounds, put him in a distinct minority. As opposed to the collective need for instant certainty, he upheld the individual quest for discernment. Throughout *Zizath novel zvi* and throughout his long career in the Sephardic Diaspora, Sasportas consciously cultivated the posture of an articulate outsider. He saw himself as a figure of authority, the product of his lineage and his learning, who was quite capable of seeing the problems in Jewish society. Sasportas repeatedly rebuked the crowd and his colleagues, learned and lay, for their gullibility. On occasion, however, he let slip that a number of people actually agreed with him. The terminology he used to describe those few kindred spirits fits in with his interest in Maimonides, both as a Talmudist who employed legal reasoning and as a philosopher who validated the category of doubt as a precondition for belief. Describing his colleagues in Hamburg whose patience with him had begun to wear thin, Sasportas indicated that

> they wrote an indictment of me to Amsterdam, and I was like a piercing thorn in their eyes. I disappointed their hopes to the point of sorrow. My scent was rank in the eyes of the masses, but not in the eyes of those with an intellect.[102]

Sasportas separated those with an intellect, *ba-alei sekhel* in Hebrew, from the masses. The phrase appears in the *Code*, where Maimonides used it to describe the Sages (Heb. *hahamim*).[103] *Sekhel* indicated the quality of discernment that the Jewish rabble lacked; *hokhmah*, the Talmudic knowledge that characterized the *haham* who was endowed with legal expertise. Sasportas demanded both philosophical discernment and legal knowledge from his correspondents.

---

[102] וכתבו שטנה עלי לאמשטרדם והייתי בעיניהם כקוץ מכאיב ומדאיב תקותם למפח נפש וריחי מובאש בעיני ההמון אבל לא בעיני בעלי שכל.

Sasportas, *ZNZ*, 131–132.

[103] Maimonides, Law of Oaths, 5:22. As cited and discussed in Bernard Septimus, "What Did Maimonides Mean by *Madda*?" in *Me'ah She'arim: Studies in Medieval Jewish Spiritual Life in Memory of Isadore Twersky*, ed. Ezra Fleischer et al. (Jerusalem: Magnes Press, 2001), 90.

FOUR

PROPHECY

"Sabbatai Zevi," I cried, "you false Messiah! Is this the world of deception in which you are living?"

He looked at me with so much genuine sorrow that I realized at once there could be no question of deception. I became confused.

"And are not the true Messiahs also false?" he asked, smiling sadly.

—Jacob Glatstein

Figure 11. Nathan of Gaza in Thomas Coenen, *Ydele verwachtinge de Joden getoont in den person van Sabethai Zevi* (Amsterdam, 1669). Nathan of Gaza, the primary Sabbatian intellectual, was in his early twenties during the peak period of messianic enthusiasm. The National Library of Israel.

PROPHECY PLAYED A DECISIVE ROLE in the success of Sabbatianism. Adherents to the new movement emphasized the renewal of revelation both in the period of its rapid spread prior to Sabbetai Zevi's conversion as well as in the years that followed. Beginning with the leading Sabbatian propagandist, Nathan of Gaza, and continuing well into the eighteenth century, Sabbatians spoke and wrote about their activities as prophecy. Repeatedly they invoked their own capacity to communicate with the divine as a source for their own authority. Prophecy often served as the legitimating grounds for their suspension of legal norms and invention of new rituals.[1] The public nature of Sabbatian prophecy—Nathan of Gaza received revelation in the presence of his colleagues on Shavuot in 1665 rather than in isolation—propelled the spread of Sabbatian messianism. Sabbatian prophecy had a significant impact on established social hierarchies. Nathan of Gaza may have come from the same section of society as Sasportas, the learned elite, but those affected by his message included many who did not. Women and children, social groups who did not constitute this clerical stratum within Jewish society, suddenly spoke as prophets who had received revelation. Their behavior as prophets and prophetesses violated time-honored social boundaries within established hierarchies.[2]

Sabbatians did not invent prophecy as a religious phenomenon, nor did they constitute the first Jewish prophets. The Sabbatians drew upon a rich storehouse of biblical and rabbinic literature about prophecy to

[1] Goldish, *The Sabbatean Prophets*, 7. Epigraph from Jacob Glatstein, *The Glatstein Chronicles* (New Haven, CT: Yale University Press, 2010), 290.

[2] Rapoport-Albert, *Women and the Messianic Heresy*.

buttress their claims to revelation. These contentions of traditional sanction, which they combined with an elaborate textual apparatus, constituted a formidable challenge to Sasportas. He used a variety of strategies to combat what he described as the illegitimate renewal of revelation. No phrase better captures Sasportas's stance than the Talmudic dictum "A sage is better than a prophet."[3] Sasportas cited this aphorism in a letter of rebuke he had written to the rabbinate in Izmir.[4] Using this phrase as a point of departure, this chapter examines Sasportas's attitude toward these competing models of spiritual authority.

The sage and the prophet had long vied with one another in the history of Judaism. At times, such as the dispute between Solomon ibn Adret and Abraham Abulafia in the late thirteenth century, the prophet stood in direct opposition to the sage; at others, as in the philosophical writings of Maimonides, composed nearly a century earlier, the ideal of prophecy competed with the value of wisdom in the same figure.[5] Place often played as decisive a role as time. In medieval Ashkenaz sages often uttered prophecy. The rabbinic elite did not campaign against prophets as Solomon ibn Adret had in medieval Iberia. In cases such as Nehemiah ben Solomon sages were actually prophets themselves.[6] Portions of this medieval heritage, particularly Maimonides's and Solomon ibn Adret's positions on prophecy, had a direct bearing on the debate between Sabbatians and their opponents. Sabbatian

[3]BT Bava Bathra, 12a. Boaz Huss, " 'A Sage Is Better than a Prophet': R. Simeon bar Yohai and Moses in the *Zohar*" (Hebrew), *Kabbalah* 4 (1999): 103–139; Alon Goshen-Gottstein, " 'The Sage Is Superior to the Prophet': The Conception of the Torah through the Prism of the History of Exegesis" (Hebrew), in *Study and Knowledge in Jewish Thought*, ed. Howard Kreisel (Beer Sheva: Ben Gurion University Press, 2006), 37–77; Elliot R. Wolfson, " 'Sage Is Preferable to Prophet': Revisioning Midrashic Imagination," in *Scriptural Exegesis: The Shapes of Culture and the Religious Imagination; Essays in Honour of Michael Fishbane*, ed. Deborah A. Green and Laura S. Lieber (Oxford: Oxford University Press, 2009), 186–210.

[4]Sasportas, *ZNZ*, 166; see also Sasportas, *Ohel ya-akov*, #3, 5b.

[5]On the former, see Moshe Idel, "Rabbi Solomon ibn Adret and Abraham Abulafia: History of a Submerged Controversy about Kabbalah" (Hebrew), in *Atarah le-hayim: Mehkarim ba-sifrut ha-talmudit veha-rabanit-li-khevod Profesor Hayim Zalman Dimitrovksi*, ed. Daniel Boyarin et al. (Jerusalem: Magnes Press, 2000) , 235–51; on the latter, see Abraham Joshua Heschel, *Prophetic Inspiration after the Prophets: Maimonides and Other Medieval Authorities*, ed. Morris M. Faierstein (Hoboken, NJ: Ktav, 1996); Howard Kreisel, *Prophecy: The History of an Idea in Medieval Jewish Philosophy* (Dordrecht: Kluwer Academic Publishers, 2001), chap. 3.

[6]See Moshe Idel, "R. Nehemiah ben Shlomo the Prophet on the Star of David and the Name Taftatfia: From Jewish Magic to Practical and Theoretical Kabbalah" (Hebrew), in *Ta-shma: mehkarim be-madae ha-yahadut le-zikhro shel yisrael M. Ta-Shma*, ed. Avraham (Rami) Reiner et al. (Alon Shvut: Tevunot, 2011), 1:1–76.

prophecy, however, took place on an altogether different scale from the known instances of Jewish prophecy in the Middle Ages. The medieval Jewish prophets prior to the outbreak of Sabbatianism had almost always acted as individuals. They frequently attracted followers and occasionally even crowds, but figures such as Abraham Abulafia and Nehemiah ben Solomon prophesied alone. A number of conversas in Iberia in the late fifteenth century such as Inés of Herrera and Mari Gómez of Chillón, offer the most striking early modern precedent of collective prophecy by Jews or their descendants.[7] With Sabbatianism, however, prophecy occurred on an even larger scale. Men, women, and children prophesied together and in public.

The Sabbatian embrace of prophecy forced Sasportas to respond. His understanding and criticism of prophecy emerged in exchange with the claims made by Nathan of Gaza and other Sabbatians. The first section of this chapter examines Sasportas's criticism of Sabbatian prophecy and his attitude toward the prophet as a figure of authority. It traces his basic argument—that the Sabbatians failed to fulfill the requirements of prophecy as laid out in rabbinic literature—through a number of his letters. The second section turns to Sasportas's conception of the sage. Throughout his account, the sage certainly appeared to be preferable to the prophet; however, Sasportas's attitude toward the sage was hardly one of uncritical acceptance. He was capable of pointed ambivalence when it came to the intellectual legacy of particular individuals from antiquity. By examining his attitude toward two Talmudic figures, Elisha ben Abuyah and Akiba ben Joseph, this chapter situates the critical reserve with which Sasportas embraced the ideal of the sage. Not all Jewish sages were equally worthy of his admiration, and not everything a recognized sage had uttered in the past should be accepted at face value. Only after having been subjected to the scrutiny of tradition, as Sasportas understood it, could the ideas of a particular sage acquire normative force. Prophecy and learning were the two central means through which Sabbatians claimed spiritual authority for their messianic movement. They were not the only ones. This chapter

---

[7] Haim Beinart, "The Conversos of Halia and the Movement of the Prophetess Inés of Herrera" (Hebrew), *Zion* 53 (1988): 13–52; on Mari Gómez of Chillón, see idem, "Conversos of Chillón and Siruela and the Prophecies of Mari Gómez and Inés, daughter of Juan Esteban" (Hebrew), *Zion* 48 (1983): 241–272; as cited and contrasted with Sabbatianism in Rapoport-Albert, *Women and the Messianic Heresy*, 72–73.

concludes with a discussion of Sabbatian astrological claims and Sasportas's use of his own dreams.

Each of these three sections traces an aspect of Sasportas's confrontation with a basic question in his response to Sabbatianism: How does one know when the Messiah has arrived? Prophecy, astrology, and dreams all represented competing ways of obtaining knowledge in the middle of the seventeenth century. Without Sabbatianism Sasportas might well have never articulated his objection to the renewal of prophecy or his indictment of Elisha ben Abuyah and Akiba ben Joseph. Sabbatianism provided Sasportas with an ideal polemical circumstance to circumscribe the prophetic mode of knowing within Judaism. Sasportas argued from within the tradition, and the prophet was a category and a figure indigenous to Judaism. For all of Sasportas's profound skepticism about the Sabbatian revival of prophecy, he refused to condemn the category outright. Throughout *Zizath novel zvi*, he registered ambivalence about the prophet. He acknowledged the potential authority of a prophet while simultaneously seeking to circumscribe it so as not to encompass anything that a Sabbatian had said or done. Just as he had continued to insist on his belief in the messianic idea but rejected Sabbetai Zevi as its fulfillment, he continued to hold open the possibility of prophecy while denying the legitimacy of Nathan of Gaza.

PROPHECY

Prophecy was central to Nathan of Gaza's self-understanding between his public revelation in 1665 and his death in 1680.[8] Two well-known facts about Nathan of Gaza's career as a prophet provide an important backdrop to Sasportas's response. Although scholars continue to debate the precise date of Sabbetai Zevi's private revelation as the Messiah, they largely agree that his first public revelation occurred in the spring of 1665. This critical moment depended upon Nathan of Gaza's prophecies uttered in the presence of other rabbis. From this point forward, Nathan took on the role of prophet and spokesman for the new

---

[8]Goldish, *The Sabbatean Prophets*, chap. 3; Avraham Elqayam, "'To Know the Messiah': The Dialectics of Sexual Discourse in the Messianic Thought of Nathan of Gaza" (Hebrew), *Tarbiz* 65 (1996): 637–670.

movement.[9] Prophecy accompanied Sabbatianism for the next sixteen months. Following Sabbetai Zevi's conversion, a rabbinic court in Venice interrogated Nathan of Gaza in the spring of 1668.[10] It compelled him to recant his belief in Sabbetai Zevi as the Messiah. From the text of his recantation, a copy of which Sasportas included in *Zizath novel zvi*, one can sense the centrality with which the court dealt with prophecy. The rabbinic jurists compelled Nathan to declare:

> Upon the instruction of the rabbis and eminences of Venice: Although I have said I saw the chariot as Ezekiel the prophet had seen it, and had [received] prophecy saying that Sabbetai Zevi is the Messiah, I am mistaken and have no proof. I admit to their statement, and I said that what I prophesied about Sabbetai Zevi has no substance. Nathan Benjamin.[11]

By compelling Nathan of Gaza to recant his prophecy as a means of abjuring his belief in Sabbetai Zevi, the rabbinic court implied an equivalency between his prophecy and his messianism. In the Sabbatian world, the prophet went hand in hand with the Messiah. Public discussion of prophecy marked both the beginning of the movement and one of the initial rabbinic attempts to mark its formal conclusion. At the annunciation of the Messiah, the prophet Nathan, rather than Sabbetai Zevi, played the central role. When the Messiah subsequently converted to Islam and a rabbinic court attempted to bring Nathan of Gaza back into the fold of Judaism, the rabbis forced him to forswear his role as a prophet.

Sasportas's rebuttal of Sabbatian prophecy constitutes a central leitmotif of *Zizath novel zvi*. His approach contained several intertwined arguments. First, he systematically rejected Nathan of Gaza's claims to legitimate prophecy. Second, he attempted to separate both the doctrine of the Jewish Messiah and the obligation of repentance from the phenomenon of prophecy. The disjunction of prophecy from the messianic idea served a crucial function in Sasportas's polemic. Even if one were to accept Nathan of Gaza's claim of revelation, Sasportas seemed

---

[9]Scholem, *Sabbatai Sevi*, 216–220.

[10]Ibid., 764–770.

[11]מאחרי אשר הורו רבני וגאוני ויניציאה, שאעפ"י שאמרתי שראיתי המרכבה כמו שראה יחזקאל הנביא והיתה הנבואה לומר כי שבתאי צבי הוא המשיח מוטעה אני ואין באותה ראיה ממש, הודיתי לדבריהם ואמרתי כי מה שהתנבאתי על שבתי צבי אין בו ממש. נתן בנימין.

Sasportas, *ZNZ*, 267; Scholem, *Sabbatai Sevi*, 766–767.

to say, this should have no impact upon the messianic idea in Judaism or the public phenomenon of mass repentance.

Sasportas first sought to delegitimize Nathan of Gaza as a prophet. At an early stage in the movement, the conflict between the sage and the prophet erupted with particular force. Nathan of Gaza had received his revelation in Gaza. As word spread, the scholars of Hebron, especially those associated with the yeshiva supported by Abraham Pereyra, greeted the news of Nathan's prophecy with jubilation. The reaction of scholars in Jerusalem, particularly that of Jacob Hagiz, was more subdued. They expressed skepticism and concern rather than joy and exaltation. Reports of their incipient opposition reached the major centers of the western Sephardic Diaspora, and Sasportas seized upon them to challenge his colleagues in the Amsterdam rabbinate. He first expressed concern for his Jerusalem colleagues. If Nathan of Gaza were indeed a prophet, they had committed a grave sin: "With their lack of belief in prophecy, they have rendered themselves liable to death by heavenly decree, as it is stated, 'I Myself will call him to account' "[12] (Deut. 18:19). Sasportas cited the conclusion of a verse from Deuteronomy that treated those who refused to believe in God's prophets. The rabbis of antiquity had stipulated death by heavenly decree for particular transgressions. Failure to believe in a genuine prophet was one such transgression. The ambiguous tone of Sasportas's stated concern for his colleagues in Jerusalem can be construed either as earnest worry or as a sarcastic quip. At this early stage in the circulation of rumors, Sasportas was still open to the possibility of Sabbetai Zevi as the Messiah. Only as he learned about the persistent violation of the law did he come to express his vituperative opposition.

Nonetheless, his skepticism about Nathan of Gaza's claims to prophecy emerges in the continuation of the letter to the Amsterdam rabbinate. If the rabbis in Jerusalem were indeed liable, why was Nathan of Gaza sitting idly by?

> One must also really wonder about the prophet [Nathan of Gaza]. Why has he not prophesied against them by word of God, saying, "Because you have not believed in me" (Num. 20:12), while appointing a catastrophe that would visit them or shouting out to God like Moses his teacher,

[12]Sasportas, *ZNZ*, 20.

"If these men die [as all men do]... it was not the Lord who sent me" (Num. 16:29). Or like Elijah, "If I am a man of God, let fire come down from heaven..." (2 King 1:10, 12) because God does not like those who violate his Torah.[13]

Sasportas adduced three biblical examples—God, Moses, and Elijah—of punishment for those who doubted divine authority. He took his first example from God's chastisement of Moses and Aaron at the well in the desert. God had commanded Moses to speak to the rock in order to draw water. Instead, Moses had struck it. As punishment, God prevented Moses from entering the land he had promised to the people of Israel. Sasportas took his other examples from celebrated rebellions against God's prophets: Korah's revolt against Moses, and King Ahaziah's messengers' contempt for Elijah. In these latter two examples, Moses and Elijah had confronted and condemned those who doubted their authority. By analogy, Sasportas implied, if Nathan of Gaza actually possessed the word of God as he claimed, he had failed to condemn those very people, the sages of Jerusalem, who had doubted his mission. Sasportas seemed to say that Nathan of Gaza could not have it both ways. Either he was a genuine prophet and had to punish those who doubted the authority invested in him by God, or he was a charlatan who should keep quiet. His refusal to respond decisively to those who doubted him, as Moses and Elijah had done, was proof positive that he was not actually the prophet he claimed to be.

Furthermore, Sasportas argued, there was something inconsistent about the form of Nathan's prophecy. In an early letter to Aaron Zarfati, Sasportas dissected one of Nathan's first prophecies he had included in *Zizath novel zvi*. The prophecy appeared as a letter to Raphael Joseph, a resident of Cairo who occupied a position of prominence among the Jews of Egypt.[14] Zarfati had described the letter to Sasportas as the words "of our prophet" Nathan of Gaza who had come to fulfill the biblical prophecies about the Messiah.[15] Sasportas retorted:

---

[13] גם על הנביא יפלא הפלא ופלא למה לא נתנבא עליהם לרעה בדבר ה' לאמר יען אשר לא האמנתם בי וכו', ומיעד עליהם פורענות, או לצעוק לבו אל ה' כמשה רבו אם כמות כל האדם וכו' לא ה' שלחני, וכאליהו אם איש אלקי"ם אנכי תרד אש וכו', כי לא חפץ ה' באלה העוברים על תורתו.

Ibid.

[14] Scholem, *Sabbatai Sevi*, 129, 177–179.

[15] Sasportas, *ZNZ*, 26.

Heaven forbid that I should believe that this letter was produced by a true prophet, either in terms of its substance or its style. In all the days of your study, have you ever seen a single one of our true prophets who speaks this way, in the form of a notice to an individual in the language of the common folk, and who doesn't announce his statement with "thus sayeth the Lord," or one of the types of prophecy such as "a pronouncement," "a vision," or "a sermon," etc.[16]

Prophecy adhered to a series of accepted conventions. Time and again the Bible introduced the words of a prophet with the formula "thus sayeth the Lord." Alternatively certain key words served to indicate a prophetic account, such as a "vision" as in the opening of Isaiah or Obadiah, or the "pronouncement" as in the opening of Habakuk, or "the proclamation" as in Ezekiel 21:2. Nathan's letter to Raphael Joseph did not adhere to the accepted conventions of prophecy as laid out in the Hebrew scriptures, and, as a consequence, Sasportas deemed it unworthy of being accepted as authentic prophecy.

As time wore on and as rumors of an initial group of believers turned into a full-fledged movement whose leaders called for the suspension of the law, Sasportas reversed the very same argument he had initially made against Nathan. When Nathan did use the prophetic formulation "thus sayeth the Lord" and combined it with an injunction to violate the law, Sasportas turned around and deemed him a false prophet. At the behest of the Sabbatian prophets, a number of believers in Amsterdam and elsewhere in the Sephardic Diaspora had suspended the laws of ritual purity that applied to men with a priestly lineage. Sasportas was quick to express disapproval of these decisions and even confirmed the priestly lineage of the cantor in Hamburg by mentioning other members of his family he had met in Fez. The impact of these decisions hardened Sasportas's initial doubts, and he was unimpressed by a letter Nathan of Gaza had written to his supporters in Amsterdam. In the letter, a copy of which reached Sasportas in Hamburg, Nathan declared, "Thus sayeth the Lord, behold your Savior has come and his name is

---

[16] חלילה לי להאמין שהכתב ההוא נאמר מפי נביא אמת הן כפי העניין הן כפי הלשון, האם ראית כל ימי לימודיך בשום נביא מנביאנו אמיתיים שמדבר כך בלשון הודעה ליחיד בלשון הדיוט, ולא יכריז בכה אמר ה' או אחד מלשונות הנבואה משא או חזיון או הטפה וגו'

Ibid., 37.

Sabbetai Zevi."[17] In a narrative passage immediately following, Sasportas commented:

> How angry have I become about the loss of this man's [Nathan's] soul, after seeing him explain his [Sabbetai Zevi's] name as the Messiah and utter a prophecy with "thus sayeth the Lord."[18]

The use of the formula "thus sayeth the Lord" was a necessary but hardly sufficient requirement for genuine prophecy. If Nathan's initial pronouncement was too casual and lacked the correct form, his later one may have taken the correct form—he employed the phrase "thus sayeth the Lord"—but it violated the basic tenets of the law.

Nathan of Gaza's use of a prophetic formula and his insistence on declaring Sabbetai Zevi the Messiah proved decisive in resolving Sasportas's initial doubts:

> For up until that time I used to say that maybe he only spoke in general terms about the redemption being close at hand, and he had done so by means of a prophetic dream, or the holy spirit, or a heavenly voice through his piety and holiness, as Isaac Luria, of blessed memory, had done.[19]

Sasportas was aware that within the Jewish tradition itself there were different ways of knowing and obtaining knowledge. In this instance he raised three possible avenues beyond the written word: a prophetic dream, a holy spirit, and a heavenly voice. All of these had ample precedent within biblical and rabbinic literature. The specific instance Sasportas chose reveals that he did not think these means of obtaining knowledge had necessarily become impossible with the passage of time. Isaac Luria had lived less than a century earlier, and Sasportas implied that his piety and holiness had enabled him to obtain knowledge by means of a dream or heavenly voice. These modes of obtaining knowledge were not equivalent. Sasportas implied a clear hierarchy between knowledge obtained through a dream, a holy spirit, or

---

[17] Ibid., 138.

[18] מה מאד הטיב חרה לי על אבדן נפשו של האיש ההוא לאחר ראותי שפירש את השם למשיח ונתנבא בכה אמר ה'. Ibid., 139.

[19] כי עד אותו זמן הייתי אומר שמא לא אמר כי אם על דרך כלל גאולה קרובה לבוא והיה זה על ידי חלום נבואיי או רוח הקדש או נשתמש בבת קול מצד חסידותו וקדושתו וכמו שזכה האר"י ז"ל Ibid.

a heavenly voice and knowledge garnered through prophecy. By using the formula "thus sayeth the Lord," Nathan of Gaza claimed a higher and considerably less mediated knowledge of and from God. If one invoked a dream or a heavenly voice, Sasportas implied, one did not lay claim to the same level of divine sanction and consequent certainty of knowledge.

Sasportas used this distinction as the basis for his declaration of Nathan of Gaza as a false prophet.

> But now that he [Nathan of Gaza] has written thus [his prophetic letter to Amsterdam] by way of R. Shalom ben Joseph who is well known to us, and his signature has been authenticated, I have judged him to be a false prophet entirely.[20]

As he wrote shortly thereafter to Joseph Halevi, Sasportas saw the combination of a prophetic formula with the instruction to violate the law as a definitive indication that Nathan of Gaza was not a prophet as he had claimed.

> Whoever heard of such a thing: while matters are still unclear should we put aside words of Torah and tradition and hasten to listen to someone who says "thus sayeth the Lord?" Who renders me liable to death for my lack of belief in him, something which God has not commanded? Does the prophesizing Nathan not realize that by refusing to give a sign and a proof he has absolved those who are unsure of him, and has rendered himself liable if his prophecy is not fulfilled? If someone were to say, "Time will tell," and "When his words are fulfilled it shall be known that he is a prophet," I will concede. But then concede to me that he still does not have the status of a prophet.[21]

About the tone of this passage there can be little doubt. Sasportas was writing to his colleague in Livorno who shared his skepticism. Nathan had claimed the mantle of prophecy, a mode of knowledge that was in

---

[20] אבל עכשו שכתב על כן על ידי כה"ר שלום בן יוסף הנודע וניכר אצלנו ונתקיימה חתימתו באשרתא והנפק אז דנתיו לנביא השקר לגמרי

Ibid.

[21] מי שמע כזאת שבעד דברים תלויים ברפיון נניח דברי תורה וקבלה ונחוש לדברי האומר כה אמר ה' לחייבני מיתה על העדר אמונתי בו וה' לא צוה, ולא ידע נתן המתנבא שבמנעו אות ומופת פטר את חלושי אמונתו וחייב את עצמו אם לא תתקיים נבואתו. ואם יאמר אומר שזמנו מוכיח עליו ובבוא דבריו יודע כי נביא הוא, גם אני אודהו אבל יודה לי מיהת דעדיין לא חל עליו שם נביא.

Ibid., 145–146.

an altogether separate category from a dream or a heavenly voice. Sasportas did not spell out the differences between these two means of obtaining knowledge, but judging from his statement, one can reconstruct his position. Prophecy entailed a prediction about the future with God's sanction. In order to justify this divine sanction, the prophet had to offer "a sign and a proof." Once these had been fulfilled, they would serve as proof of the prophet's election. By refusing to offer a sign and a proof to his prophecy of Sabbetai Zevi as the Messiah, Nathan of Gaza had forfeited the right to be called a prophet.

After Sabbetai Zevi's conversion to Islam, Sasportas had no doubt about Nathan's status as a false prophet. As he emphasized in a letter to one of the believers in Alexandria named Hosea Nantawa, Nathan had issued a prophecy about Sabbetai Zevi as the Messiah. The prophecy had failed to materialize in the time Nathan had allotted. Therefore, Nathan was not a prophet and Sabbetai Zevi was not the Messiah. In his letter to Nantawa, Sasportas drew upon a biblical precedent and its rabbinic interpretation for determining a false prophet. In the twenty-eighth chapter of Jeremiah, Hananiah son of Azur issued a prophecy about the imminent return of the exiles from Babylonia and the destruction of the king of Babylon. Jeremiah responded to this prophecy with a wish for its fulfillment but a note of caution. Given that Hananiah had uttered a prophecy of good fortune, he could be deemed a true prophet only after his message had been fulfilled. When Jeremiah subsequently received word from God that the king of Babylon would continue his reign, he accused Hananiah of prophesying falsely and predicted his death. The chapter concludes with Hananiah's death. The Palestinian Talmud contains an extensive discussion of this episode. Joshua ben Levi, a Palestinian sage of the early third century, described Hananiah as "a true prophet who had had an intermission" when his gift of prophecy was in abeyance.[22]

In his letter to Nantawa, Sasportas alluded to this passage in the Palestinian Talmud:

> By the by we have learned that before he spoke with [the formula] "thus sayeth [the Lord]," Nathan may well have been considered a prophet by his believers, but after he spoke "thus sayeth [the Lord]," his deceit became clear to them. The reason is that the soul of Hananiah son of Azur

[22]PT Sanhedrin 11:5; Jastrow, s.v. *kiboset.*

transmigrated into him, because even he had been a prophet before his deceit.[23]

After the Messiah's conversion, Sasportas's position hardened considerably. Where earlier he had allowed for the possibility of Nathan's prophecy, now he allowed for it only among Nathan's followers. In both scenarios, Nathan's use of a prophetic formula, "thus sayeth the Lord," combined with his sanction of the violation of the law indicated his lack of probity. Sasportas's explanation for Nathan's prophecy combined his vast erudition with the kabbalistic doctrine of the transmigration of souls. He alluded to the rabbinic discussion of Hananiah as a true prophet whose prophetic gift had deserted him. Sasportas did not proceed to make an analogy between Hananiah and Nathan; instead, he made a kabbalistic argument. Hananiah's soul had transmigrated into Nathan and led to his false prophecy. The transmigration of souls was a critical doctrine in early modern Kabbalah, from the kabbalists of sixteenth-century Safed to Menasseh ben Israel's *Nishmat hayim*, a work Sasportas had edited fourteen years earlier. Sasportas's invocation of the transmigration of souls illustrates a critical point about his polemic with the Sabbatians. They were not involved in a dispute over the validity of Kabbalah, with the Sabbatians using it to buttress their movement and Sasportas denying its legitimacy. Their argument was one within Kabbalah itself, with both sides claiming the mantle of tradition.

The same cannot be said, however, about prophecy. For all of the typological thinking broached in this passage, Sasportas did not make the second half of the analogy either. He did not tell Nantawa that just as Nathan is like Hananiah, I am like Jeremiah. Just as Nathan and Hananiah prophesied something positive and required verification in order for it to be considered genuine prophecy, so too Jeremiah and I have prophesied doom and destruction and therefore can be considered prophets without verification. Sasportas repeatedly refrained from characterizing himself as a prophet, and this instance is no exception. The sage who was the embodiment of learning served as his model. It seems hardly accidental that his use of a kabbalistic doctrine came

---

[23] ובין כך ובין כך למדנו דנת"ן קודם שדיבר בכה אמר איפשר שהיה בחזקת נביא אצל מאמיניו, אבל לאחר שדיבר בכה אמר נתברר להם שקרותו והטעם לפי שנתגלגלה בו נשמת חנניה בן עזור דאף הוא נביא היה קודם שקרותו. Sasportas, *ZNZ*, 183.

wrapped in an allusion to the most difficult of rabbinic texts, the Palestinian Talmud.[24] Sasportas argued against the Sabbatians from the perspective of someone who accepted prophecy as a possible means of obtaining knowledge, and who believed that the transmigration of souls could have a decisive impact upon the course of events. Both prophecy and the transmigration of souls adhered to accepted conventions, and both were fundamentally subordinate to the law.

Kabbalah, both as a set of concepts such as the transmigration of souls and as a library of texts such as the *Zohar*, served a vital function in Sasportas's polemical arsenal. He drew upon Kabbalah in order to split the fusion of messianism and prophecy that characterized Sabbatianism. At an early stage of the movement, Sasportas rebuked Aaron Zarfati: "For I have spoken the truth. The arrival of the Messiah does not require a prophet. But after his arrival, there is no question, for it is written, 'I will pour out my spirit upon all flesh' "[25] (Joel 3:1). Nathan had declared himself a prophet of the Messiah's arrival; Sasportas insisted that he had it backward. The arrival of the Messiah was a precondition for the phenomenon of mass prophecy, which according to the biblical book of Joel would follow rather than precede or accompany the Messiah. Among the variety of sources Sasportas used to rebut Zarfati's argument about prophets announcing the arrival of the Messiah was a passage he attributed to Simeon bar Yohai.[26] Sasportas contended that the corpus of rabbinic literature, in which he included the *Zohar*, did not stipulate the prophet as a herald of the Messiah. The single exception was Elijah. Some sources indicated that he would announce the arrival of the Messiah. Nathan of Gaza was not Elijah.

Sasportas expounded the distinction between messianism and prophecy in an early letter to Isaac Nahar, well before reports of Sabbatian antinomianism reached Europe.

> But the chance of this being correct is not equal in both cases, for belief in [Sabbetai Zevi] as the Messiah is possible without the prophecy of Nathan the prophet, for if this rabbi [Sabbati Zevi] is worthy with his name and with his deeds, it is not impossible that he is the Messiah. For

---

[24] For this passage in his index of the Palestinian Talmud, see *Toledot ya-akov*, 23b.

[25] Sasportas, *ZNZ*, 39.

[26] Ibid., 40. And see Tishby's n4.

it is a doctrine of the law that each and every day and at every instance and at every moment, the master we are seeking may come.[27]

With a revealing double negative, Sasportas allowed for the possibility that Sabbetai Zevi, a man he dignified at this point with the title of rabbi, was actually the Messiah. This remained his position until the following summer of 1666 when reports about the violation of fast days reached him. The public abrogation of the law convinced Sasportas once and for all that Sabbetai Zevi was not the Messiah. Sasportas upheld his doubt in contrast to the certainty of the Sabbatians as the proper demonstration of his faith in God. Simultaneously and concurrent with his doubt, he articulated another crucial element of his faith in the law. This position was very much in line with the Sephardic rabbinic reticence toward active messianism that Sasportas had argued throughout *Zizath novel zvi*. The Messiah could come at any moment but almost certainly would not. Validation of his arrival was dependent upon his actions and his conduct, which in the case of Sabbetai Zevi would soon prove to be contrary to the law Sasportas upheld as paramount.

This was not the case with prophecy. Prophecy may have been partially dependent upon the conduct of the prophet, but it adhered to a set of norms. Sasportas articulated a number of these rules for prophecy at various points in his polemic. He did not derive these norms from his own unmediated reading of the Hebrew Bible; rather, he interpreted the phenomenon of biblical prophecy primarily through the screen of rabbinic writing. In Sasportas's view, the rabbis of antiquity had all but foreclosed the possibility of prophecy. In this sense, his view of the ancient sages was quite similar to that of the twentieth-century scholar Ephraim E. Urbach, who argued that as a result of rabbinic teachings "there is evidence to suggest that it [prophecy] was stopped; it did not stop."[28] On various occasions within *Zizath novel zvi*, Sasportas had recourse to at least three different claims about the inadequacies of Sabbatian prophecy. First, prophecy required a sign and a

---

[27] ואך אין האפשרות הזה צודק בשניהם בשוה, יען שבאמונת המשיח איפשר שזה הוא בלא נבואת נתן הנביא שאם זה הרב ראוי לכך בשמו ובמעשי"ו אינו נמנע שיהיה משיח, כי אמונת הדת היא שבכל יום ויום ובכל שעה ורגע בוא יבוא האדון אשר אנו מבקשים.

Ibid., 41.

[28] "The Religious Meaning of the Law" (Hebrew), in *Al Yahadut ve-hinukh* (Jerusalem: School of Education of the Hebrew University, 1966), 128; as cited by Yaacov Sussmann, "The Scholarly Oeuvre of Professor Ephraim Elimelech Urbach" (Hebrew), in *Ephraim Elimelech Urbach: Bio-bibliyografit Mehkarit*, Supplement to *Madae yahadut*, ed. David Assaf (Jerusalem: World Union of Jewish Studies, 1993), 64n110.

proof. Second, the Sabbatians all prophesied in the same style. Third, the Sabbatians served as witnesses to each other's message.

Prophets verified the authenticity of their message with a sign and a proof. In the book of Deuteronomy the discussion of a false prophet revolves around a figure who has actually provided an authentic sign and proof yet whose message contradicted the law. In such a case, the Deuteronomist exhorts the people of Israel, "thou shalt not hearken unto the words of that prophet" (Deut. 13:3). From this and other passages in the Bible, the rabbis of antiquity and their successors in the Middle Ages derived a theory of prophecy that stipulated a sign and a proof as a precondition for the verification of a prophet's message. The Sabbatians and their opponents were keenly attuned to this requirement. The rabbis of Hebron, Jerusalem, and elsewhere beseeched Nathan to provide a sign and proof to authenticate his message. Nathan alternatively claimed to have provided one, deferred the request, or ignored it altogether. To Sasportas, Nathan's failure proved he was not an actual prophet. In a letter to Joseph Halevi written before he learned of Sabbetai Zevi's conversion, Sasportas turned to two medieval sources as the basis for his position on the sign and proof as the prerequisites for prophecy: the code of Maimonides and the responsa of Solomon ibn Adret.

Sasportas invoked Maimonides and his law code both to emphasize and to circumscribe the necessity of a sign and a proof for the rabbinic doctrine of prophecy:

> One must truly wonder about the prophet, in that he has refused to give a sign and proof for its requirement [by the Torah] has escaped neither him nor those who ask him. For even if he is upheld in his wisdom and his piety, scripture decrees that he give a sign and proof and that nothing else matters. It is sufficient that the Torah made him credible with a sign and a proof; however, if he could have done this, it would have only been by means of magic or incantation, and something would have been amiss, as Maimonides, of blessed memory, wrote in the laws of the foundations of the Torah.[29]

[29] על הנביא יפלא הפלא ופלא במה שנמנע לתת אות ומופת כי לא נעלם ממנו חיובה עליו ועל המבקשים, דאף אם מוחזק בחכמה ובחסידות גזרת הכתוב לתת אות ומופת והבו דלא לוסיף עלה ודי במה שהאמינה אותה תורה באות ומופת ואף אם היה יכול לעשותו בלט ובכישוף כי הם דברים בגו, כמו שכתב רמב"ם ז"ל בהל' יסודי התורה.

Sasportas, ZNZ, 142. As Tishby observed in n2, Sasportas paraphrases rather than quotes Maimonides, "Laws of the Foundation of the Torah," Book of Knowledge, 3:1–3.

Sasportas turned to Maimonides to serve seemingly contradictory purposes. In the third chapter of the laws of the foundation of the Torah, which appears in the first book of his code, Maimonides both upholds the scriptural requirement for a sign and proof as a means to authenticate prophecy and emphasizes that the sign and proof are somewhat beside the point in terms of obedience to the law. Using the example of Moses, Maimonides argues that the belief in Moses as a prophet did not depend upon the plethora of signs he performed. Divine revelation at Sinai was the fundamental source of belief. For the prophets who succeeded Moses, a sign was a necessary component of their prophecy, but it was hardly sufficient. If one were to gain acceptance as a prophet, his or her prophetic message had to conform to Mosaic law. According to Sasportas, Nathan should be doubly condemned. His message contradicted the law of Moses, and he refused to provide a sign and a proof. There is a sense in which Sasportas used Maimonides on prophecy in order to register his skepticism of prophecy as such. By making the requirements for prophecy so difficult to attain and by rendering prophecy itself so peripheral to the ultimate goal of obedience to the law, Sasportas strove to delegitimize Sabbatian prophecy on Nathan's terms—the experience of prophecy—as well as on his own: the paramount importance of the law.

Sasportas turned immediately to a later interpreter of Maimonides, Yedaiah Bedersi, to bolster his position about the imperative of a sign and proof for the verification of prophecy. A philosopher and poet who lived in Provence at the turn of the fourteenth century, Bedersi wrote an extensive reply to the series of bans imposed on the public study and teaching of philosophy by Solomon ibn Adret.[30] Bedersi's reply, known as "The Letter of Apology," had appeared in print as part of Ibn Adret's responsa, a volume well known to Sasportas and to which he had recourse elsewhere in this very letter to Halevi.[31] Sasportas drew on Bedersi to explain the necessity of a sign and proof. As quoted by Sasportas, Bedersi distinguished sequentially between two different

---

[30] On his response to Ibn Adret, see A. S. Halkin, "Yedaiah Bedershi's Apology," in *Jewish Medieval and Renaissance Studies*, ed. Alexander Altmann (Cambridge, MA: Harvard University Press, 1967), 165–184; on his career as a poet, see Susan L. Einbinder, *No Place of Rest: Jewish Literature, Expulsion and the Memory of Medieval France* (Philadelphia: University of Pennsylvania Press, 2009), chap. 2.

[31] For Sasportas's earlier citations of Ibn Adret, see chapter 2; for the letter of apology, see Ibn Adret, *She-elot u-teshuvot*, no. 418, 67a–75a.

signs offered by a prophet. At the outset of his mission, a prophet had to offer his believers a first sign in order to establish himself. It was incumbent upon the believers, not the prophet, to request this sign in order to prevent simply anyone from taking up the mantle of prophecy. The second sign, by contrast, occurred after the prophet had already established himself. It was incumbent upon the prophet to offer this one in order to publicize God's power. Nathan of Gaza, Sasportas was quick to deduce from Bedersi's letter, had failed on both counts. To the immediate circle of believers who upheld Sabbetai Zevi as the Messiah, Nathan had deferred or sidestepped requests for a sign and proof. This was the equivalent of the first sign, the sign that would establish him as a prophet, mentioned by Bedersi. To those who doubted his mission, Nathan had an obligation to offer a sign and proof of his divine mission. This sign, the second one described by Bedersi, was incumbent upon the prophet to produce of his own accord without any prompting. Nathan, however, had done nothing of the sort.

Sasportas had little patience for the Sabbatian counterclaim that Nathan would duly provide a sign and proof:

> Does the prophesying Nathan not know that by withholding a sign and proof he has exempted those weak in faith and rendered himself liable if his prophecy is not fulfilled? ... How pleasing are the words of Rabbi Solomon ibn Adret in responsum number 548.[32]

To buttress his claim that a sign and proof were necessary but not sufficient criteria for prophecy, Sasportas turned to Bedersi's disputant, Solomon ibn Adret, only a few paragraphs after having adduced Bedersi himself. In this responsum, one written independent of his debate with Bedersi and which Sasportas invoked throughout his account, Ibn Adret had denied the possibility of prophecy that had been reported to him about a prophetess in Avila. Bedersi and Ibn Adret may have held opposing views during the second Maimonidean controversy that dominated Jewish life on both sides of the Pyrenees at the turn of the fourteenth century. They may have taken contrary positions on the allegorical readings of the Bible. They may have written in different genres.

---

[32] ... ולא ידע נתן המתנבא שבמנעו אות ומופת פטר את חלושי אמונתו וחייב את עצמו אם לא תתקיים נבואתו
... והנה מה טוב ומה נעים דברי הרשב"א בס' תקמ"ח
Sasportas, *ZNZ*, 146; for other instances of his invocation of this responsum, see Sasportas, *ZNZ*, 31, 46, 94, 113, 115.

Bedersi has survived primarily as a poet and Ibn Adret largely as a jurist. To Sasportas, however, these disputes and differences were relatively minor when it came to the question of Sabbatian sectarianism, in which prophecy played a critical role. Sasportas glossed over the distinctions between Bedersi and Ibn Adret, much as he had elided those individuating *Sefer hasidim*, Maimonides, and Ibn Adret. His citations, however, were not haphazard. Just as he had earlier marshaled an array of seemingly contradictory sources to make an argument for the authority of the written word in the making of tradition, in this instance he adduced the two opposing sides of the second Maimonidean controversy in order to limit the potential of prophecy. For all of the intensity of their dispute about the place of philosophy in the Jewish curriculum, Ibn Adret and Bedersi recognized the potential power of prophetic knowledge. Drawing upon the rabbinic interpretation of the Bible, each in his own way had used the doctrine of the sign and proof to control the prophet as a competing source of authority. As a polemicist who used any and every source at his disposal, Sasportas turned to both of them to rebut Nathan's claims.

Nathan's failure to provide a sign and proof may have been the most damning flaw in his prophecy, but it was not the only one. In a later letter to Nantawa, Sasportas accused the Sabbatian prophets of prophesying in the same style and implied that this violated rabbinic norms. His claim derived from a passage in the Babylonian Talmud. In tractate Sanhedrin, the Mishnah had given several definitions of a false prophet, including "he who prophesies what he has not heard." In the succeeding Talmudic discussion, the rabbis adduce Zedekiah son of Chenaanah as an example. In the first book of Kings, Zedekiah prophesied falsely to Jehoshaphat, king of Judah (1 Kings 22:11). In this context, Rabbi Johanan cited an enigmatic statement attributed to Rabbi Isaac: "A single style may be shared by several prophets, but no two prophets prophesize in an identical style."[33] The English translation fails to capture the epigrammatic ambiguity of Rabbi Isaac's dictum, which repeats two words—*ehad* (Heb. single, identical) and *signon* (style)—in two seemingly different contexts. In the remainder of his statement, which quotes the same biblical phrase, "arrogant heart" (Heb. *zedon*

---

[33]. סיגנון אחד עולה לכמה נביאים ואין שני נביאים מתנבאין בסיגנון אחד.
BT Sanhedrin 89a, as cited by Tishby in Sasportas, *ZNZ*, 182n 4.

libkha), that appears in Jeremiah (49:16) and Obadiah (1:3), Rabbi Isaac grapples with the issue of whether two prophets can prophesize in the same style. In his allusion to this passage, Sasportas flattened the ambiguity of R. Isaac's aphorism, which seems to allow for the possibility that prophets prophesize in a similar fashion, and marshaled the Talmudic dictum against the Sabbatian phenomenon of collective prophecy:

> As if in your court you have received from them [the prophets] a sign and proof as scripture decrees. In order to fulfill this, you have exaggerated [the capacity] of boys and girls, old men and old women, who struck by a seizure speak with a wicked spirit that terrifies them, and they all do so in one style, but this indicates their falsehood, for no two prophets have the same style, all the more so an entire group of them.[34]

Unlike his invocation of Maimonides, Bedersi, and Ibn Adret, where Sasportas had cited chapter and verse and informed his correspondent about the precise source of his quotations, this argument about prophecy and style only obliquely alluded to the Talmudic passage in Sanhedrin. As it passed from a statement attributed to a specific rabbi who sought to explain a particular exegetical phenomenon into a hackneyed phrase that seemed to attain the level of principle, Rabbi Isaac's aphorism lost its ambiguity and became something Sasportas could adduce as if it were obvious to all. Having been transformed into a cliché, Rabbi Isaac's statement could thus serve as the basis for Sasportas's argument that the phenomenon of mass prophecy was an oxymoron.

Mass prophecy had a further consequence in terms of the verification of Sabbatian messianism. In his discussion of Abraham Miguel Cardoso and his correspondence with his older brother Isaac, Sasportas wrote:

> But since his brother who lives in Verona scorned and mocked him and sent him a derisive letter, he [Abraham Miguel] was forced to respond and to uphold Nathan's prophecy along with his own. Behold, they are

---

[34] כאילו בבית דינך נתקבל מהם אות ומופת כגזרת הכתוב, ולקיום זה הוגזמת בילדים ובילדות זקנים וזקנות הנכפים ומדברים ברוח רעה המבעתתם וכלם בסגנון אחד, וזה מורה על שקרותם דאין סיגנון אחד עולה לשני נביאים כל שכן לכמה וכמה.

Sasportas, *ZNZ*, 182.

like merchants suspected of collusion: Nathan authenticates his prophets, and they authenticate him.[35]

As he had done previously, Sasportas tacitly reverted to the language of the Talmud in order to make his point. Drawing on a discussion in the second chapter of Ketubot concerning the rules of evidence and testimony, Sasportas alluded to the case of two food merchants who entered a city and offered testimony about each other's goods. The Talmud records a dispute as to whether they are believed or suspected of collusion.[36] Mass prophecy posed a basic problem in terms of its verification: it was circular. Without the external evidence provided by an authentic sign and proof, Sabbatian prophets simply testified to the authenticity of each other's message. Sasportas, or for that matter any other skeptic, had no recourse beyond the charmed circle of those who were in the know. In this instance, Sasportas was either unaware of or uninterested in the later rivalry that would emerge between Nathan of Gaza and Abraham Miguel Cardoso. His basic point, however, applied to Sabbatian prophecy well before Cardoso emerged on the scene in the years after the Messiah's conversion. Without external validation, the Sabbatian prophets simply repeated each other's messages as if they were in an echo chamber. Sasportas harped on the imperative to produce proof precisely because it made prophecy so difficult. For all of the effort he invested in separating the figure of the Messiah from the phenomenon of prophecy, his argument about prophecy bore a striking resemblance to his argument about the Messiah. He seemed to hold out both as hypothetical possibilities independent of one another; but both were only hypothetical possibilities. Neither would ever be realized.

THE SAGE

Sasportas acknowledged the potential and actual authority of the prophet even as he sought to neutralize him. Throughout his polemical writings he studiously avoided adopting the posture of a prophet.

---

[35] ויען שאחיו הדר בבירונא היה מצחק ומהתל בו ושלח לו כתבים של ליצנות וע״כ הוצרך להשיב לו ולקיים נבואת

נתן בנבואתו הרי הם כחמרין גומלין זה לזה נתן מעיד על נביאיו ונביאיו מעידין עליו

Ibid., 289. On Isaac and Abraham Cardoso, see Yerushalmi, *Isaac Cardoso*, chap. 7.

[36] BT Ketubot, 24a, as identified by Tishby, Sasportas, *ZNZ*, 289n4.

Job rather than Jeremiah served him with the biblical arsenal he sought in order to perform his erudition and put the Sabbatians in their place. By contrast, he willingly took up the mantle of the sage throughout *Zizath novel zvi*. At the level of genre, the work constituted a collection of his rabbinic responsa and overlapped extensively with his own posthumously printed collection *Ohel ya-akov*. Sasportas upheld his mastery of rabbinic literature, both ancient and medieval, as the source of his own intellectual and religious authority. The figure of the sage, while certainly greater than the prophet, was not without his drawbacks. In reconstructing Sasportas's attitude toward the sage, one must distinguish between the sage as the model of authority in the abstract sense and the teachings attributed to specific sages. Sasportas may have considered the sage as the arbiter of the law and the source of authority, but he was not shy about criticizing the teachings of particular sages no matter how ancient. Furthermore, he was not particularly restrained in rejecting the legacy of an individual sage even if he had occupied a central place in the rabbinic tradition.

In an exchange with David de Mercado, Sasportas rebuked his correspondent about the figure of Elisha ben Abuyah, known as "Other" (Heb. *aher*) in rabbinic literature and as an archetypal heretic in medieval Judaism.[37] Mercado's original letter does not survive, yet Sasportas's response contains sufficient detail that can serve as the basis for its partial reconstruction—if not its precise style, then at the very least its overall content. Mercado and Sasportas engaged in a sustained polemic over the recitation of the priestly blessing in the synagogue service. The priestly blessing was an ancient part of the Jewish liturgy that had fallen into partial abeyance in many but not all synagogues.[38] Reasons for its nonrecitation varied with time and place, and periodically throughout Jewish history various rabbinic luminaries made a concerted effort to revive its recitation.[39] As part of their messianic frenzy

---

[37] In rabbinic literature, see Yehuda Liebes, *Heto shel Elisha* (Jerusalem: Akademon, 1990); Jeffrey L. Rubenstein, *Talmudic Stories: Narrative Art, Composition and Culture* (Baltimore: Johns Hopkins University Press, 1999), chap. 3; Alon Goshen-Gottstein, *The Sinner and the Amnesiac: The Rabbinic Invention of Elisha ben Abuya and Eleazar ben Arach* (Stanford, CA: Stanford University Press, 2000). In medieval Judaism, see below.

[38] Yitzhak (Eric) Zimmer, "The Times of the Priestly Blessing" (Hebrew), in *Olam ke-minhago noheg: perakim be-toldot ha-minhagim, hilkhotehem ve-gilgulehem* (Jerusalem: Zalman Shazar Center, 1996), 132–151; discussion of Sasportas and Sabbatianism on 140–142.

[39] See ibid.; Haym Soloveitchik, "*Minhag Ashkenaz ha-Kadmon*: An Assessment," in *Collected Essays* (Oxford: Littman Library, 2014), 2:60n88.

the Jews of Amsterdam had begun to recite the priestly blessing every Sabbath rather than only on holidays. After Sabbetai Zevi converted to Islam and the leadership recanted its belief, Sasportas had advised the Jews of Amsterdam to return to their prior custom and recite the blessing only on holidays. In contrast, Mercado argued that they should continue to recite it every Sabbath as they had begun to do with Sabbatianism. Although they had since recanted, the Jews of Amsterdam had adopted a praiseworthy practice. In support of his argument, Mercado pointed to the figure of Elisha ben Abuyah in the Talmud. The very presence of teachings attributed to Elisha ben Abuyah and his considerable impact upon his student Rabbi Meir demonstrated that not everything associated with someone who was deemed a heretic should be rejected. Mercado cited a Talmudic passage about Rabbi Meir's attitude toward his teacher: "He found a pomegranate, ate the inside, and cast off the shell."[40] The Talmud had compared Elisha ben Abuyah with the shell but his teachings with the fruit inside. By analogy, Mercado equated the Sabbatian impetus for the weekly recitation of the priestly blessing with the shell, while the practice itself was like the fruit inside. The fruit within the shell, whether it was Elisha ben Abuyah's teaching or a practice reinstituted under Sabbatian influence, should be preserved. Furthermore, the Talmud had not seen fit to erase Elisha ben Abuyah's teachings. His very existence, according to Mercado, seemed to offer evidence that one could derive meaningful lessons from wicked people.

Sasportas would have none of this and denied the very basis for Mercado's analogy.

> In terms of the words of Elisha ben Abuyah, which were not erased, I have not found them with the exception of the statement: "He who studies Torah as a child [To what can he be compared? To ink written on fresh paper]."[41] But this has no relation to the law or to the words of Torah. Even if this is [the same] Elisha referred to as Other in the Palestinian Talmud, that has no bearing upon the fulfillment or nullifica-

---

[40]BT Hagigah 15b. For use of this aphorism to justify the reading of Sabbatian literature in the eighteenth century, see Maoz Kahana, "The Allure of Forbidden Knowledge: The Temptation of Sabbatean Literature for Mainstream Rabbis in the Frankist Moment, 1756–1761," *JQR* 102 (2012): 608, 613, 616.

[41]Avot 4:20. Translation of the Mishnah as given in Goshen-Gottsein, *The Sinner and the Amnesiac*, 40.

tion [of the law], for these are words of wisdom in terms of education, and they do not make any difference. Just as the masters of natural science have no bearing on the faith of the Torah, for better or worse, to turn [the study of science] into a principle of faith. Rather, it remains like a handmaiden to its mistress. There is even someone who argues that this is not actually Elisha referred to as Other in the Palestinian Talmud. In any event, it is not for us to decide. Whatever the case may be, this statement of his has no bearing upon the fulfillment or nullification of a commandment, an ordinance, or a custom, for better or worse, so why should it be erased? In the Talmud, there are many people who transmit traditions, and the sages repeat wisdom even in the name of gentile sages.[42]

What was at stake for Sasportas was the autonomy and the primacy of the law. Sasportas had no problem conceding to Mercado that the Talmud ascribed and preserved statements of Elisha ben Abuyah, or even that it recognized him as a sage. What he refused to grant, however, was the legal impact of these statements. He compared the epistemic relationship between Elisha's aphorism and the law to that between the natural sciences and faith. Just as the natural sciences would never actually serve as the basis for faith in the Torah and would always remain in a secondary, and consequently subordinate, position in terms of the fundamentals of faith, so too Elisha's statement about education would remain subordinate to juridical decision making. It would have absolutely no bearing upon a commandment, a custom, or an ordinance. The one statement that Sasportas attributed to Elisha had no more authority than the statements attributed to gentile sages in the Talmud.

Sasportas carefully noted three distinct but related areas upon which Elisha ben Abuyah's statements had no impact: a commandment, an ordinance, and a custom. In this particular letter, Sasportas did not extrapolate an overall rubric under which to group these three catego-

---

[42] ומדברי אלישע ן' אבויה שלא נמחקו, אני לא מצאתי דברי אלישע בן אבויה כתובים כי אם הלומד תורה לילד וזה אין בו דבר נוגע להלכה או ד"ת, ואף אם הוא אלישע אחר כדברי הירושלמי אין כאן בזה דבר לקיים או לבטל, מילי דחכמה בהנהגת הלימוד הם ולא מעלין ומורידין מידי דהוה כבעלי חכמת הטבע במילי דלא נגעו באמונת התורה להרע או להטיב לעשות ממנה עיקר אלא כשפחה לפני גברתה. ויש מי שסובר דאינו אלישע אחר כמו שסובר הירושלמי ואין לנו להכריע, ויהי מה שיהיה דבריו אלה אין בהם כלום לענין קיום מצוה או ביטולה או תקנה או מנהג לא טוב ולא רע ולמה ימחק, ובגמרא יש הרבה מוסרים ודברי חכמה אמרו חכמים מפי גויים.

Sasportas, *ZNZ*, 232.

ries. Nevertheless, his position in this letter and in *Zizath novel zvi* as a completed work hinged upon the law, or *halakha*. Implicit in his rebuke of Mercado, Sasportas gestured toward a reflection on the law as a category and the Talmud as a written work. That the Talmud served as the primary basis for the law according to Sasportas there can be little doubt. He held himself up as the arbiter of the law and buttressed his authority with the citation of the Talmud, both Babylonian and Palestinian, and their commentaries. He was keenly aware that not everything in the Talmud had a bearing upon the law. In terms of Sasportas's approach to Elisha ben Abuyah, this had a direct effect upon his neutralization of him as a sage. Sasportas seems to have accepted that Elisha ben Abuyah was a sage, but attempted to circumscribe his wisdom within the domain of good counsel.

This represents an extremely selective reading of the evidence about Elisha ben Abuyah preserved in rabbinic literature available to Sasportas. Thus, in one particular story preserved in the Talmud, Elisha ben Abuyah appears riding on a horse on the Sabbath while instructing Rabbi Meir in the Torah as he accompanied him on foot. At a certain point, Elisha instructs Rabbi Meir to turn back, as he had already walked the distance permissible to travel on foot on the Sabbath.[43] If Elisha ben Abuyah does not serve as the source of a legal ruling in this story, he certainly appears as someone who is knowledgeable about the law and in a position to offer instruction to Rabbi Meir. In another Talmudic passage, Elisha actually does serve as the source of the law. In the third chapter of Moed Katan, which treats the laws of mourning, the Talmud records: "There was the case of the father of R. Zadok who died at Ginzak and he was not informed for three years. He [thereupon] came and asked Elisha ben Abuyah and the elders who were with him and they told him to observe seven [days] and thirty [days]."[44] Jewish law stipulates a seven-day period of mourning immediately after the death of a relative during which a range of activities are prohibited and a number of obligations are incumbent upon the mourner.

---

[43] BT Hagigah, 15a. A parallel version of this story appears in PT Hagigah, 2:1. For Elisha's relationship with Rabbi Meir, see Liebes, *Heto shel Elisha*, chap. 4; Goshen-Gottstein, *The Sinner and the Amnesiac*, chap. 5; for discussion of the parallel in the PT, see chap. 6.

[44] BT Moed Katan, 20a; as translated in Goshen-Gottstein, *The Sinner and the Amnesiac*, 43; Liebes, *Heto shel Elisha*, 12.

This period of mourning extends, with slightly fewer restrictions and obligations, until the end of the first thirty days. Upon hearing of his father's death that had occurred three years earlier, R. Zadok appealed to Elisha ben Abuyah and other rabbinic colleagues for a legal ruling. Elisha ben Abuyah ruled that the laws of mourning applied and directed R. Zadok to observe a period of seven days followed by thirty days. In the story in Hagigah, Elisha ben Abuyah demonstrated a detailed knowledge of the law even as he violated it himself; in the story in Moed Katan, he actually appeared as a legal authority. Given Sasportas's knowledge of the Talmud, it seems unlikely that he was unaware of these passages. Rather, Sasportas had little interest in a historical reconstruction of Elisha ben Abuyah as a Talmudic sage. Nor was he interested in dissecting the multiple stories and legends that had circulated around him as a heretic. He sought to preserve the sanctity of the law and his own authority to interpret it. In order to do so, he defined Elisha ben Abuyah as a sage who had had no impact upon the law. He pointedly ignored instances in which he appeared as a legal authority, as it was profoundly inconvenient to the integrity of his argument.

It stands to reason that Sasportas would use Elisha ben Abuyah as a stick with which to beat the Sabbatians. Had Mercado not mentioned him first in his correspondence, Sasportas might even have discussed him of his own accord. Elisha ben Abuyah served as the archetypal Jewish heretic. For Maimonides, the primary source for Sasportas's messianic reserve, Elisha ben Abuyah served as just such a paradigm, and he transferred many attributes ascribed to arrogant freethinkers in medieval Islamic theology to his description of Elisha.[45] In this respect, Sasportas could have made even greater use of Elisha ben Abuyah as a rabbinic topos for contemporary wayward Jews. Had he taken up where Maimonides had left off, he would have applied the attributes of the Sabbatians—contempt for the law, subversion of authority, appeal to the masses—to Elisha ben Abuyah. In this instance, as in many others in *Zizath novel zvi*, Sasportas adopted a fundamentally reactive stance. Mercado had raised Elisha ben Abuyah in a legal context, which, in turn, compelled Sasportas to circumscribe Elisha ben

[45] Sarah Stroumsa, *Maimonides in His World: Portrait of a Mediterranean Thinker* (Princeton, NJ: Princeton University Press, 2009), 42–46.

Abuyah to the role of a sage who had appeared in the Talmud in an extralegal context.

If Sasportas sought to neutralize Elisha ben Abuyah as a possible source for Sabbatian authority, he also had to grapple with another rabbinic sage who was frequently paired with him: Akiba ben Joseph. In a Talmudic story, Elisha ben Abuyah and Akiba ben Joseph had appeared as two out of a group of four sages who had entered a garden [Heb. *pardes*]. Each of these sages met a different fate: Ben Azzai perished; Ben Zoma gazed and was smitten; Elisha "cut the shoots," an enigmatic phrase taken by some to indicate his heresy; and only Akiba emerged whole.[46] Unlike Elisha ben Abuyah, a scholar the rabbinic tradition had treated with some ambivalence, Akiba featured as one of the critical links in the chain of rabbinic transmission.[47] What was more, Akiba figured in rabbinic literature as the ideal of a legal scholar. One measure of his centrality can be taken from a rebuke leveled at him in a number of Talmudic passages. On occasion Akiba offered an exegetical interpretation of a biblical verse that his colleagues deemed somewhat far-fetched. In one such instance Rabbi Eleazar ben Azariah leveled the following quip: "Akiba, what do you have to do with Haggadah, lead your words to *Nega-im* and *Ohlot*," referring to two subfields of Jewish law that dealt with ritual purity.[48] *Nega-im*, or lesions in one's body or property, and *Ohlot*, tents, the term used to discuss the laws of corpse impurity, were areas of the law associated with the most difficult elements of legal decision making.[49] While Elisha had surfaced in a number of suggestive passages and on one occasion as the source of a legal ruling, Akiba appeared throughout rabbinic literature both as one who formulated aphorisms and as a sage whose hermeneutics was central to the process of legal decision making. Sasportas could not

---

[46] BT Hagigah 15a–b; PT Hagigah 2:1. On "cut the shoots," see Goshen-Gottstein, *The Sinner and the Amnesiac*, 85–86.

[47] Louis Finkelstein, *Akiba: Scholar, Saint, and Martyr* (New York: Atheneum, 1970) [1936]; Judah Goldin, "Towards a Profile of the Tanna, Aqiba ben Joseph," in *Studies in Midrash and Related Literature*, ed. Barry L. Eichler and Jeffrey H. Tigay (Philadelphia: JPS, 1988), 299–323; Azzan Yadin-Israel, *Scripture and Tradition: Rabbi Akiva and the Triumph of Midrash* (Philadelphia: University of Pennsylvania Press, 2015).

[48] BT Hagigah, 14a; BT Sanhedrin 38b.

[49] On these areas of the law as Talmudic metonymies for the rabbinic study-culture itself, see Mira Balberg and Moulie Vidas, "Impure Scholasticism: The Study of Purity Laws and Rabbinic Self-Criticism in the Babylonian Talmud," *Prooftexts* 32 (2012): 320–321.

simply dismiss Akiba with a wave of the hand and continue to cast himself as the embodiment of the rabbinic tradition.

Dismiss Akiba is precisely what Sasportas did. Far more than Elisha ben Abuyah, who merited only an occasional mention in Sasportas's polemic, Akiba appeared throughout. Sasportas referred to him perhaps more than any other sage from antiquity. Law and hermeneutics may have been the telltale signs of Akiba's presence in rabbinic literature, but at least one rabbinic tradition recorded his support for Bar Kokhba as the Messiah in the Jewish revolt against the Roman emperor Hadrian in the fourth decade of the second century. The Palestinian Talmud recounts, "When R. Akiba beheld Bar Kozeba/Kozba, he exclaimed: 'this one is the King Messiah.' "[50] Akiba may in fact never have made this statement, and an editor or redactor of the Palestinian Talmud may have attributed it to him only centuries after his death.[51] Furthermore, "the name of Akiba appears nowhere in the Bar Kochba documents," such as the coins, letters, and papyri that ancient historians have used to reconstruct this period.[52] For the purposes of understanding Sasportas and his response to Sabbatianism, however, one should bear in mind that Sasportas did not approach rabbinic literature with the assumptions of a modern Talmudist. Nor did he approach the Jewish revolt against Rome from the perspective of an ancient historian. He did not attempt to distinguish between the different literary strata of rabbinic literature and treated both the Palestinian and Babylonian Talmud as the products of antiquity. More important than their temporal dating, however, was their authority. For Sasportas, the Talmud was the authoritative source. If it recorded Akiba as a supporter of Bar Kokhba, then he had no reason to doubt its authenticity.[53]

---

[50] PT Ta-anit, 4:8. On the various forms of his name Simeon bar Kosiba, Bar Kokhba see William Horbury, *Jewish War under Trajan and Hadrian* (Cambridge: Cambridge University Press, 2014), 1.

[51] Peter Schäfer, "Bar Kokhba and the Rabbis," in *The Bar Kokhba War Reconsidered: New Perspectives on the Second Jewish Revolt against Rome*, ed. Peter Schäfer (Tübingen: Mohr Siebeck, 2003), 2–3; Matthew V. Novenson, "Why Does R. Akiba Acclaim Bar Kokhba as Messiah?" *Journal for the Study of Judaism* 40 (2009): 551–572.

[52] G. W. Bowersock, "A Roman Perspective on the Bar Kochba War," in *Approaches to Ancient Judaism*, vol. 2, ed. William Scott Green (Missoula, MT: Scholars Press, 1980), 132; Peter Schäfer, *Der Bar Kokhba-Aufstand: Studien zum zweiten jüdischen Krieg gegen Rome* (Tübingen: Mohr, 1981).

[53] Richard G. Marks, *The Image of Bar Kokhba in Traditional Jewish Literature: False Messiah and National Hero* (University Park: Pennsylvania State University Press, 1994); on Bar Kokhba and Sabbatianism, see 194–199.

Bar Kokhba first appeared in *Zizath novel zvi* in a letter written by Aaron Zarfati that sought to convince Sasportas to recant his skepticism. The Sabbatians were well aware of the rabbinic traditions about Bar Kokhba as the Messiah and sought to distinguish clearly between contemporary events and rabbinic precedent. At the conclusion of his letter to Sasportas, Zarfati sought to preempt any analogy between Bar Kokhba and Sabbetai Zevi: "You should know that our prophet and our king are not like Bar Kozeba, heaven forbid, who certainly did not receive the spirit of the Lord, and the rabbis killed him."[54] Zarfati alluded to a Talmudic passage in tractate Sanhedrin that discussed whether the opening verses of the eleventh chapter of Isaiah, a biblical text often read in a messianic context, referred to Bar Kokhba.[55] The Talmud concluded decisively that Bar Kokhba was not the figure Isaiah had described as having received the spirit of the Lord. In positing the rabbis of antiquity as the principal causes for Bar Kokhba's death, Zarfati alluded to another passage in rabbinic literature that assigned his death to the rabbis themselves rather than to the Roman legions. After Bar Kokhba had failed to fulfill his messianic promise, the rabbis interpreted the Aramaic form of his name, Koziba, through the Hebrew and Aramaic root *kzb*, "to lie," as "liar."[56] At stake for Zarfati was the applicability of the analogy between both Nathan of Gaza and Sabbetai Zevi, "our prophet and our king," and Bar Kokhba as he appeared in rabbinic literature. The possible danger of the analogy between Sabbetai Zevi and Bar Kokhba was thus present in the mind of at least one Sabbatian supporter as soon as the movement began to take shape.

Sasportas responded contemptuously to Zarfati:

I know that our true king and prophet is not like Bar Koziba, but he smells and judges by the spirit of the Lord, not as you understand the matter.[57] Yet even schoolchildren know the conditions of the Messiah, "He shall not judge by what his eyes behold" (Isaiah 11:3), and I do not know what you[r interpretation] has innovated. If you seek to claim with your testimony that these conditions have been fulfilled, then let

[54] Sasportas, *ZNZ*, 29.

[55] BT Sanhedrin, 93b, as cited by Tishby, Sasportas, *ZNZ*, 29n6.

[56] *Midrash Ekha Rabba*, ed. Salomon Buber (Vilna, 1899), 101–103; on this passage see Schäfer, "Bar Kokhba and the Rabbis," 6–7; Horbury, *Jewish War under Trajan and Hadrian*, 1n2.

[57] See Isaiah 11:3 and BT Sanhedrin 93a, where Bar Koziba fails to meet the messianic condition of being able "to smell [the truth] and judge."

us hear it from your own lips in a court of law rather than judge by what the eyes behold, and then you will make a greater impression on us than the words of Isaiah.[58]

At this relatively early stage in the messianic frenzy, Sasportas did not turn to the figure of Akiba and reports of rabbinic support for Bar Kokhba. He concentrated on the applicability of the analogy. He agreed with Zarfati's initial impulse to separate the actual Messiah from the rabbinic accounts of Bar Kokhba but differed as to whether or not Sabbetai Zevi was this Messiah. For Sasportas, the analogy between Bar Kokhba and Sabbetai Zevi was all too apt. Like his argument about Nathan of Gaza as a prophet, he argued that Zarfati's support for Sabbetai Zevi would have genuine consequences. If Zarfati actually believed in Sabbetai Zevi as the Messiah, he should cease writing letters and offer his testimony in a court of law. Sasportas sought to distinguish between an exegetical flight of fancy and a declaration of Sabbetai Zevi as the Messiah. In his response to Zarfati, he attempted to impress upon him a basic fact that had apparently eluded him and other supporters of Sabbetai Zevi. The insistence that Sabbetai Zevi was "our king" and the Messiah had normative force. The most significant realm in which this would play out was the law. Thus Sasportas urged Zarfati to adopt the courage of his messianic convictions and offer his statement as testimony in a rabbinic court rather than simply citing passages from the Bible in support of a theoretical position. Zarfati made no such declaration, but he did not have any reason to do so. In the early stages of the movement, he numbered among the overwhelming majority of the Amsterdam Sephardim who accepted Sabbetai Zevi as the Messiah on faith and on hearsay.

The specter of Bar Kokhba as a failed Messiah continued to haunt the correspondence of the Sabbatians and Sasportas. As Sabbatianism gained momentum, both sides turned to this earlier instance of messianism for instruction. In his extended letter to Supino, Sasportas himself drew on the analogy and pointedly invoked the figure of Akiba. Several months into the movement, Nathan of Gaza had yet to provide

---

[58] וידעתי כי מלכנו ונביאנו האמיתי אינו כבר כוזיבא אלא מריח ודאין ברוח ה' ולא כאשר אתה מבין. ותנאי המשיח תינוקות של בית רבן ידעום לא למראה עיניו ישפוט ולא ידעתי מה חידשת, אם הוא לקיימם בעדותיך תתקבל בב"ד מפיך שלא על פי הראיה ותעשה בנו רושם יותר מישעיה.

Sasportas, *ZNZ*, 33.

a sign and a proof as validation of his prophecy, and Sabbetai Zevi had yet to perform the miraculous accomplishments, political and military, associated with a Messiah. At the conclusion of his long letter to Supino, Sasportas asked a series of rhetorical questions intended to shake his correspondent out of his messianic stupor. The letter to Supino survives in two recensions, one in Sasportas's notebooks and another in the edited version of *Zizath novel zvi* that was available to A. Z. Schwarz. Supino's prior letter to Sasportas had sought to match the rhetorical exuberance and clever wordplay that characterized Sasportas's writing. Every paragraph of Supino's letter concluded with the Hebrew word *emet*, truth, in an attempt to convince Sasportas that Sabbetai Zevi was the true Messiah. Never one to shrink from intellectual combat, Sasportas responded to Supino in kind, and he concluded every paragraph of his response with the Hebrew word *sheker*, falsehood. But lest Supino think that he and Sasportas were intellectual equals, Sasportas responded with a letter that was four times the length of Supino's, and that displayed a technical feat of erudition far exceeding anything with which Supino had confronted Sasportas. Throughout the entirety of the letter Sasportas threaded citations to the thirty-eighth and thirty-ninth chapters of Job. This selection from the Bible was not happenstance. In these chapters, God rebuked Job for daring to challenge his authority and his supremacy. Similarly, Sasportas rebuked Supino for daring to challenge his skepticism. This biblical model was decidedly not prophetic. In this context Sasportas asked Supino, at the conclusion of the letter,

> Does he shake kingdoms with fierceness and rage (Job 39:24), does he swallow and consume the land (Job 39:24) to such a degree that all who see him shall mistake him just as R. Akiba erred in saying, "This is the King Messiah?"[59]

Throughout this penultimate paragraph in the letter to Supino, Sasportas heaped up a series of rhetorical questions about the parallel between Bar Kokhba and Sabbetai Zevi. Sasportas was unabashed in his criticism of Akiba and his messianic gullibility. Only a few lines later, he approvingly quoted R. Johanan ben Torta's rebuke of Akiba recorded

---

[59] אם ברע"ש ורוג"ז מרעיד ממלכות מרגיז ומגמא ארץ אשר כל רואיו יטעו בו כטעות ר' עקיבא באמרו דא הוא מלכא משיחא.

Ibid., 99.

in the Midrash on Lamentations: "Leaves shall grow on your cheeks and the Messiah will still not have arrived."[60] When Akiba declared Bar Kokhba the Messiah, he had ceased acting like a sage and began to act as if he were a prophet. Sasportas carefully harnessed a rabbinic tradition that rebuked Akiba in the service of his own polemic. In this instance it was Johanan ben Torta, not Akiba, who had spoken like a sage.

In a certain sense, Sasportas agreed with the Sabbatians that Bar Kokhba and Sabbetai Zevi were not analogous to one another. The Sabbatians saw this as cause for celebration: Bar Kokhba had been a false messiah, but Sabbetai Zevi was genuinely God's anointed. Sasportas derived a different conclusion from the same analogy. For all of the criticism to which Akiba was subjected to in *Zizath novel zvi*, Sasportas could at least understand the basis for his error. Bar Kokhba had waged a military campaign against the Romans and, for a short time, had managed to "shake a kingdom with fierceness and rage." It was only after Bar Kokhba's defeat that Akiba's colleagues subjected him to such scathing criticism. There had been, Sasportas seemed to concede, a genuine possibility that Bar Kokhba might fulfill the promise of the Messiah as a political leader. Behind this concession to Bar Kokhba as a potential Messiah seems to hover a distinction in messianic theology that remains somewhat inchoate and unarticulated but can be deciphered nonetheless. Bar Kokhba the Messiah had a function that was entirely political and of this world. Bar Kokhba had fought wars, his supporters had minted coins, and together they had challenged the enemy of the Jews. In this sense, before his defeat Bar Kokhba had conformed to some of the basic characteristics of the Messiah as outlined by Maimonides in the Laws of Kings. Indeed, Maimonides had mentioned Bar Kokhba and Akiba's mistaken support for him in a critical passage of his discussions of the laws of the Messiah.[61] These passages in Maimonides had repeatedly served Sasportas as his point of departure in his rebuke of the Sabbatians. By contrast, Sabbetai Zevi was a Messiah who had achieved absolutely nothing in terms of politics. He waged no wars, established no sovereignty, and acquired no temporal power. For Sasportas, his chief accomplishment consisted in the public violation of the law.

---

[60] Ibid.; citation in *Midrash Ekha Rabba*, ed. Buber, 101.
[61] Maimonides, Laws of Kings, 11:3; Marks, *The Image of Bar Kokhba*, 81–95.

In a letter to the Amsterdam rabbinate written immediately following his letter to Supino, Sasportas hewed closely to the Maimonidean
position on Bar Kokhba and Akiba:

> But I do not know what deed has been done that would cause me and
> my colleagues to bestow upon him [Sabbetai Zevi] the name Messiah.
> For Rabbi Akiba only mistook Ben Koziba when he saw his deeds in his
> battles against the enemies of God, his strength and his heroism, the
> number of his supporters, and because of this he erred and said he is the
> Messiah.[62]

As if to underscore the validity of his own skepticsm, Sasportas cited
yet again Johanan ben Torta's rebuke of Akiba, adding a critical gloss.
Referring to Johanan ben Torta, he wrote, "But he was not considered
a denier or a skeptic in faith because of this." Just as the rabbis of antiquity had accorded Johanan ben Torta's skepticism its proper due and
had concluded their account of Akiba's support for Bar Kokhba with
his stunning rebuke, Sasportas implied that the Sabbatians should accord him and his skepticism about Sabbetai Zevi the same due.

Sasportas continued to emphasize the difference in character between Akiba's error and that of the Sabbatians. In a letter to the rabbinate in Vienna shortly after the flurry of exchanges with Supino and
his rabbinic colleagues in Amsterdam, Sasportas raised the issue of the
sages and their support for a messianic figure. Sasportas stressed the
distinction between a prophet, who required a sign and a proof, and a
Messiah, who had to perform certain deeds. Writing about a Messiah,
Sasportas emphasized:

> For even though he does not require a sign and a proof, he still must
> perform the deeds of a Messiah, as Maimonides specifies at the conclu-
> sion of the Laws of Kings, for if he does not, anyone who wants to take
> the name, shall come and say, "I am the Messiah." If they had seen a sin-
> gle deed like the deeds of Ben Koziba, after whom Rabbi Judah the Prince
> and Rabbi Akiba had strayed... then the sages of Izmir would have erred,
> and applied to him [Bar Koziba] the verse "A star went forth" (Num.

---

[62] ואני לא ידעתי מה מעשה נעשה הגורם לי ולחברי להחליט עליו שם משיח ואפילו בטעות, שר' עקיבא לא טעה
בבן כוזיבא אלא בשביל שראה מעשיו במלחמותיו נגד אויבי ה' כחו וגברותו וריבוי אוכלוסיו ומזה טעה לומר דא הוא
מלכא משיחא.
Sasportas, *ZNZ*, 103.

24:17), quite literally. But how much more are they mistaken now [in the case of Sabbetai Zevi], when not only have they not seen this or anything like it, but, on the contrary, they have witnessed strange acts that no proper Jew is permitted to peform, especially not someone who is held to be or considered a possible candidate for the role of King Messiah. [63]

At least Akiba, and according to another tradition Judah the Prince, had a string of military victories upon which to hang their errant messianic convictions concerning Bar Kokhba. This was hardly the case with the sages of Izmir and Sabbetai Zevi. What Sasportas found so galling in the conduct of his colleagues was their collective failure to examine Sabbetai Zevi's conduct for what it actually was. Of all the bombastic prophecies by Nathan of Gaza that had accompanied the annunciation of Sabbetai Zevi as the Messiah, not a single one of them had come to fruition. Sabbetai Zevi had yet to wage war with or against the Ottoman sultan; he had yet to recover the ten lost tribes; and he had yet to establish a kingdom of Jews in Palestine. Instead, he had committed a series of strange deeds, which, while they may have garnered him a considerable amount of publicity, offered no indication that he was behaving like the Messiah as outlined by Maimonides. Thus the sages of Izmir and, by implication, all of the other rabbinic supporters of Sabbetai Zevi were not even like Akiba, a sage whom the rabbinic tradition had felt no compunction in ridiculing for his misplaced messianic convictions. In a certain sense, Sasportas was noting ruefully the cyclical drama that seemed to attend a Messiah in Jewish history. If Bar Kokhba represented something of a military tragedy, Sabbetai Zevi was playing out before his own eyes as a halakhic farce.

ASTROLOGY

One of the most frequently adduced texts used to prove the messianism of both Bar Kokhba in the second century and Sabbetai Zevi in the

---

[63] דאע"גב דאינו צריך לאות ומופת מעשי משיח מיהת בעי וכדברי הרמב"ם בסוף הל' מלכים, דאם לא כן כל הרוצה ליטול את השם יבא ויטול ויאמר משיחא אנא. ואלו היו רואים שום מעשה כבן כוזיבא דטעו אחריו ר' ור' עקיבא . . . היו גם חכמי איזמיר טועים וקורים עליו דרך כוכב כמשמעו, ומכ"ש שלא די שלא ראו זה וכדומה אלא אדרבא ראו דברים זרים שלא ניתנו ליעשות לאיש כשר שבישראל וכ"ש למי שהוא מוחזק או בספק למלך המשיח
Ibid., 117.

seventeenth came from Balaam's prophecy in the book of Numbers. Balak king of Moab had hired Balaam as a prophet to curse the Israelites who were threatening to overrun his kingdom. Much to Balak's chagrin, when Balaam set out to do his bidding, he found he could only utter prophecies of their ascendance. One of these prophecies included the verse "There shall come a star out of Jacob and a scepter shall rise out of Israel and shall smite the corners of Moab" (Num. 24:17). The Hebrew word for star, *kokhav*, echoes Bar Kokhba's name, and rabbinic exegetes drew on this verse as a biblical prediction of Bar Kokhba's messianic status. After Bar Kokhba's defeat, the rabbis reread the verse. Instead of interpreting *kokhav* as a reference to a star, they read the word as *kazab*, or lie. Thus the verse became a prediction of Bar Kokhba's failure: "There shall come a lie out of Jacob."[64] The link between the Messiah and the heavens remained, and this verse continued to serve as a point of departure for exegetes who sought to connect the figure of the Messiah with astrology through the means of biblical prophecy.

With Sabbetai Zevi, this verse was one of a number of sources that his supporters adduced to bolster his messianic claims. It served as one of several astrological aspects of the messianic propaganda they circulated. The Hebrew word *Sabbetai* referred both to the Messiah and to the planet Saturn. As a planetary deity, Saturn had long been associated with melancholy.[65] Beginning in antiquity and continuing throughout the Middle Ages, pagan and Christian thinkers also associated Saturn with the Jews. Saturn ruled over Saturday, the Jewish day of rest. Avarice, blindness, and miserliness, all pejorative stereotypes of Jews, were related to Saturn. In the late Middle Ages and early modern period, Saturn himself began to assume some ostensibly Jewish characteristics. In a number of images, Saturn appears as a devourer of children, a motif scholars have linked to accusations of blood libel against the Jews. In others, Saturn appears with an image of the scorpion, which, although not one of the prime zodiacal signs of Saturn, was associated with the Jewish betrayal of Christ.[66] Beginning with Abraham

[64] Horbury, *Jewish War under Hadrian and Trajan*, 1.

[65] Raymond Klibansky, Erwin Panofsky, and Fritz Saxl, *Saturn and Melancholy: Studies in the History of Natural Philosophy, Religion, and Art* (New York: Basic Books, 1964); Rudolf and Margot Wittkower, *Born under Saturn: The Character and Conduct of Artists* (New York: Random House, 1963).

[66] Eric Zafran, "Saturn and the Jews," *Journal of the Warburg and Courtauld Institutes* 42 (1979): 16–27.

ibn Ezra in the twelfth century and continuing with a number of kabbalists in succeeding centuries, Jews began to take on this affiliation
with Saturn and describe themselves as Saturnine.[67] Some ascribed the
troubles suffered by Jews to Saturn's dominance, while others focused
on the connection between Saturn and the Sabbath. Thus in their propaganda the Sabbatians drew upon a fairly well-established discourse
about Saturn in Jewish astrological and kabbalistic literature prior to
the advent of Sabbetai Zevi. Over and above these Saturnine characteristics of the Jews, Sabbetai Zevi's name and his melancholic behavior further strengthened the astrological connection between the Messiah and the planet.

In his lengthy letter to Supino, Sasportas responded implicitly to a
number of claims Sabbatians had made about the relationship between
Saturn and Sabbetai Zevi.

> But it was not enough to establish him as the Messiah through the sages
> of the gentiles and their astrologers, as you said that they saw the light
> of the planet Saturn shine and radiate, and that this was a sign of salva-
> tion. "Knowest thou the ordinances of heaven?" (Job 38:33). For you have
> ignored the words of the true prophet who states: "Let now the astrol-
> ogers, the star-gazers, the monthly prognosticators stand up, and save
> thee from these things that come upon thee" (Isa. 47:13). And tradition
> teaches, [the verse states] "from these things," and not "from all
> things." . . . But if we have come to conduct ourselves according to their
> calculation, we would establish that when Saturn [Heb. Sabbetai] coin-
> cides with the sign of Scorpio, there shall be a new law, just as it was
> when Israel worshipped the [golden] calf or when they bowed down to
> the statue of Nebuchadnezzar. "Would you impose his authority on
> earth?" (Job 38:33) because of their words?[68]

Sasportas attributed to Supino a series of arguments that drew on astrology as a proof for Sabbatianism. Supino's original formulation does

---

[67] Moshe Idel, *Saturn's Jews: On the Witches' Sabbat and Sabbateanism* (London: Continuum, 2011).

[68] ולא סגי בקיום משיחותו על ידי חכמת האומות ותוכניהם כאשר שראו אור שבתא"י מאיר ומזהיר
וסימן הוא לישועה. הידעת חקות שמים ולא השגחת לדברי נביא אמת האומר נא ויושיעוך הוברי שמים החוזים
בכוכבים מודיעים לחדשים מאשר יבואו עליך, ובאה הקבלה על מאשר ולא כל אשר . . . ואלו באנו להתנהג כפי חשבונם
היינו מקיימים שבזמן היות שבתא"י מתיחד במזל עקרב יהיה חידוש דת, וכאשר היה זה בזמן עשיית העגל ובזמן
השתחוייתם לצלמו של נבוכדנצר. האם בעד דבריהם תשים משטרו בארץ?
Sasportas, *ZNZ*, 93–94. See Idel, *Saturn's Jews*, 74.

Figures 12 and 13. Johannes
Wierix, *Saturnus*, 1609. Rijksmuseum, Amsterdam. Harmen

not survive, and Sasportas's rebuttal renders it somewhat difficult to reconstruct in all of its specificity.

Nonetheless, one can discern a number of claims. First, astrologers had pointed to the light or radiance of Saturn as proof of redemption. This claim about Saturnine redemption appears to be somewhat non-specific, and Sasportas countered with a citation from Isaiah and its rabbinic gloss that essentially advised against trusting astrologers.[69] His rebuttal, however, did not end there. He proceeded to mention one of the central astrological theories about Saturn referred to as the great conjunction.[70] According to a range of astrological teachings, the conjunction of Saturn with Jupiter in Scorpio would lead to the emergence

[69] The gloss " 'from these things' and not 'from all things' " appears in *Genesis Rabbah* 85:2 as identified by Tishby in n8.

[70] Idel, *Saturn's Jews*, 53; on astrological conjunctions, see Margaret Aston, "The Fiery Trigon Conjunction: An Elizabethan Astrological Prediction," *Isis* 61 (1970): 159–187.

Jansz Muller after Maarten van Heemskerck, *Melancholisch temperament*, 1566. Rijksmuseum, Amsterdam. These prints depict Saturn consuming his children, a motif that Sasportas alluded to as he criticized Sabbetai Zevi, a Messiah associated with Saturn.

of a new religion or a new law. *Hiddush [ha-]dat*, the Hebrew phrase used by Sasportas, can refer to the emergence of either a new law or a new religion. Drawing on a medieval Jewish astronomical treatise, Sasportas pointed to two other instances of this conjunction as generative of a new law: the story of the Golden Calf, recounted in Exodus 32, and the statue that Nebuchadnezzar, king of Babylon, had erected to himself in Daniel 3.[71] Sasportas seemed to take the astrological claims of the Sabbatians quite seriously. He effectively told Supino that if one were to use astrology as the basis for the belief in Sabbetai Zevi as the

[71] Abraham bar Hiyya, *Megilat ha-megaleh*, ed. A. Poznanski (Berlin, 1924), 139–140; as cited by Tishby in n10.

Messiah, this would lead to the formation of a new law or a new religion. If the biblical examples adduced by Abraham bar Hiyya in his treatise *Megilat ha-megaleh* and cited by Sasportas were to serve as precedent, things would end very badly. Sasportas concluded the paragraph with another allusion to the thirty-eighth chapter of Job implying that Supino should ignore astrologers altogether.

Sasportas referred to another astrological claim at the conclusion of his letter:

> In truth, his eye led him astray at the start of his dispute with R. Escafa, "From thence he seeketh the prey" (Job 39:29) with deadly poison, and "his eyes behold from far off" (Job 39:29) the vision of the chariot, "he gazed and was smitten," and in the end, "his young ones," who hatch too early, "gulp blood" (Job 39:30), the planet that signifies blood slaughter, and devours its own children, like the planet Saturn, according to the teachings of the astrologers, and even devours itself. "Because where the slain are, there he" (Job 39:30) stands, like one of the corpses, in the place for those condemned to death whose sins cannot be expiated and are imprisoned, this is the punishment of a charlatan, a wicked man who perpetrates lies.[72]

In a passage dense with allusions, Sasportas criticized Sabbetai Zevi as having been destined for ill from the very beginning. He wove references to the final two verses of the thirty-ninth chapter of Job, the crescendo of God's response from the whirlwind. Sasportas substituted the eagle discussed at the conclusion of God's rebuke of Job with Sabbetai Zevi himself. He also referred to Sabbetai Zevi's relationship with his former teacher Joseph Escafa. Elsewhere in his polemic, Sasportas had reported that Escafa had disavowed his former student out of fear that he would create a new faith.[73]

Sasportas also obliquely referred to the Talmudic story about four scholars who had entered the orchard. The Talmud records that "Ben Zoma gazed and was smitten."[74] In his description of Sabbetai Zevi, Sas-

[72] והאמת כי עינו הטעתו בתחילת המחלוקת בימי הרב איסקאפא ומש"ם חפ"ר אוכ"ל בסם הממית ומרחו"ק במעשה המרכבה עיניו יביט"ו והציץ ונפגע, ולבסוף אפרוחיו הפורחים קודם זמנם יעלע"ו ד"ם כוכב המורה דם והרגה הורג את בניו כככוכב שבתא"י בדברי התוכנים ואף אם עצמו, כי ובאשר חללים שם הוא עומד כאחד הנבלים מקום אשר הרוגי מלכות שלא ניתן עונם לכפרה אסורים שם וזה ענשו של בדאי רשע עושה פעולת שקר. Sasportas, *ZNZ*, 100.

[73] Ibid., 4; see Idel, *Saturn's Jews*, 74; on Escafa, see below.

[74] BT Hagigah 14b.

portas recounted that when he was looking at the chariot, he had "gazed and was smitten," using the identical phrase the Talmud had applied to Ben Zoma. He implied that Sabbetai Zevi had engaged in the study of esoteric subjects but could not cope with them and was smitten like Ben Zoma. Sasportas did not define what it meant to be smitten. He proceeded to refer both to Job and to an astrological teaching. Like the eagle at the conclusion of Job 39, Sabbetai Zevi was destined to have his progeny "gulp blood." Sasportas added another reference to Job and predicted that Sabbetai Zevi would behave like the planet Saturn, who, according to astrologers, would consume his own children.[75] But Sabbetai Zevi would even outdo the planet with whom he shared a name. He would consume himself. The paragraph and the letter conclude with an application of the second half of the final verse of Job 39—"where the slain are, there is he"—to Sabbetai Zevi's imprisonment in Gallipoli. In contrast to his earlier reference to Saturn, which quite clearly appeared in response to a claim made either by Supino or by one of his fellow Sabbatians, this astrological invocation of Saturn may not have had an immediate referent. Unlike his general posture throughout the work, Sasportas's tone in this passage comes close to that of a prophet.

Sasportas's attitude toward astrology remains ambiguous. In these passages, as well as a number of others in *Zizath novel zvi*, he offered a well-informed response to Sabbatian astrological propaganda.[76] In the second passage, not only did he respond to a claim made by his disputant, Supino, but he appears to have referred to the astrological tradition of Saturn as a devourer of his own children without provocation. Sasportas may have thought about astrology much as he thought about Kabbalah: a valid technology and method that the Sabbatians had misappropriated. If this were the case, Sasportas's response to Supino was an argument not against the validity of astrology but about the correct method of its interpretation. Jewish scholars from antiquity through the early modern period had practiced astrology.[77] Sasportas cited one

[75] Zafran, "Saturn and the Jews."

[76] See Sasportas, ZNZ, 165, 298; on the latter, see Idel, *Saturn's Jews*, 78n141. For Sasportas's correspondent Ber Perlhefter on Sabbetai Zevi and astrology, see Avraham Elqayam, "The Rebirth of the Messiah: New Revelations about R. Isaachar Beer Perlhefter" (Hebrew), *Kabbalah* 1 (1996): 109–111.

[77] Reimund Leicht, "Toward a History of Hebrew Astrological Literature: A Bibliographical

of them, Abraham bar Hiyya, earlier in this letter without attribution.[78] Intellectuals throughout early modern Europe practiced astrology to accomplish a range of tasks. They used it to offer political counsel to rulers of state, diagnose medical ailments, and predict the end of the world.[79]

Alternatively, Sasportas may have been making an argument of an entirely different order. His citations from both Isaiah and Job may indicate a rejection of astrology as such. His knowledge about astrology need not imply his support for it: to study something did not mean to approve of it. One further factor has to do with Maimonides's negative attitude toward astrology.[80] Given Sasportas's overarching Maimonideanism throughout his polemic, it stands to reason that his position on astrology would be in line with that of Maimonides, although he adduced neither Maimonides's letter on astrology nor any of the passages in Maimonides's *Guide* or *Code of Law* critical of astrology.[81] The available evidence may simply not allow for a definitive reconstruction of Sasportas's position on astrology. One can assess Sasportas's attitude toward Kabbalah with relative certainty. By contrast, Sasportas's extant writings do not contain anywhere near the same engagement with astrology.

DREAMS

Sasportas's knowledge of astrology appears to have derived from writers within the medieval Jewish astrological tradition and from exchanges with the Sabbatians. It appears to have been largely derivative rather than generative. Sasportas showed awareness of astrology as a

Survey," in *Science in Medieval Jewish Cultures*, ed. Gad Freudenthal (Cambridge: Cambridge University Press, 2011), 255–291.

[78] Shlomo Sela, "Abraham bar Hiyya's Astrological Work and Thought," *Jewish Studies Quarterly* 13 (2006): 128–158.

[79] Anthony Grafton, *Cardano's Cosmos: The Worlds and Works of a Renaissance Astrologer* (Cambridge, MA: Harvard University Press, 1999).

[80] Stroumsa, *Maimonides in His World*, 141; Halbertal, *Maimonides*, 221.

[81] For Maimonides's letter on astrology, see Alexander Marx, "The Correspondence between the Rabbis of Southern France and Maimonides about Astrology," *HUCA* 3 (1926): 311–358. For doubts on Maimonides's authorship, see Davidson, *Moses Maimonides*, 494–501. Given that it was ascribed to Maimonides in the 1517 Constantinople edition of his letters, most early modern authors, including Sasportas, would probably not have questioned its authenticity. See Marx, 340. For passages on astrology in the *Guide*, see part III; for the Code, see Laws of Idolatry, 11:8.

potential and actual resource for Sabbatian propaganda; his ambivalence was pronounced, even fierce, but he does not appear to have practiced astrology himself. He did, however, engage the medium of dreams to confirm his own knowledge about the Sabbatian movement. Sasportas recounted the following experience in a freestanding entry in *Zizath novel zvi*:

> But I, the humblest of my clan (Jud. 6:15), when these letters arrived, which indicated that he [Sabbetai Zevi] set out for Constantinople, after the proper preparation and the appropriate procedure [for summoning a dream], I made an inquiry by way of a dream. In my dream, I encountered: "They were driven forth from among men" (Job 30:5), "Men shall clap their hands at him" (Job 27:23), "They cried after them as after a thief" (Job 30:5). Then I knew that the end of these men who had sinned and led others astray, the Messiah and the Prophet, would be to be driven forth from Israel, from the portion of God, and their only resolution would be death or conversion. This was on the twenty-second day of Tevet, when the rumor had already arrived that he Sabbetai Zevi would go to Constantinople, and on the same day occurred the dream question and response. On the day immediately following, I revealed what had occurred to a few people, but when a number of the believers heard, I became a laughingstock to them. But I said to them: If only your prophecy came true and not mine and my friends', if only your prophet were correct as those laypeople who do not believe and rely upon the truth and the words of the sages, of blessed memory, are correct. When the time comes we shall know who the true prophet is.[82]

This passage seems to undo many of the distinctions that had governed and would continue to govern Sasportas's polemic. He employed a technology, a dream, that had a long history as a determinant of the law in rabbinic Judaism.[83] When faced with a seemingly incontrovertible

---

[82] ואני הדל באלפי כאשר באו הכתבים ששם פעמיו לדרך לקוסטנטינא אחר ההכנה הראויה וההזמנה הנאותה נשאלתי בחלום ואקרו לי בחלמי מן גן יגורשו וגו' יספוק עלמו כפימו יריעו עלימו כגנב. ואז ידעתי כי אחרית האנשים החטאים המטעים משיח ונביא להתגרש מתוך ישראל מנחלת ה' ואין להם תקנה כי אם במתה ובהמרה. והיה אז ביום כ"ב לטבת שכבר באה השמועה שבאותו יום ילך לקוסטנטינא ובאותו יום היתה השאלה והתשובה, ותכף למחר גליתי הדברים לקצת ונשמעו הדברים למאמינים והיה כמצחק בעיניהם, והייתי אומר להם: ומי יתן שתתקיים נבואתכם ולא שלי ושל חברי, ומי יתן שיהיה נביאכם צודק כמו שצודקים ההדיוטות הבלתי מאמינים הסומכים על האמת ועל דברי קבלת רז"ל, ובבוא הדבר ידע מי הוא הנביא האמיתי.

Sasportas, *ZNZ*, 79; see Goldish, *The Sabbatean Prophets*, 149–151.

[83] Ephraim Kanarfogel, "Dreams as a Determinant of Jewish Law and Practice in Northern Eu-

problem, rabbinic authorities would occasionally resort to a dream as a medium to solve the legal issue. As Sasportas made clear, this method required preparation, which he had duly carried out. The dream technique had a number of variations. In some instances, the person who had the dream would receive a revelation from the prophet Elijah or from a heavenly angel or even God himself; in others, such as the one recounted by Sasportas, the dreamer would be shown one or more biblical verses that would point him in the direction of a solution to his legal problem. For Sasportas, all of these verses came from the book of Job and indicated that the subjects of his question, Sabbetai Zevi and Nathan of Gaza, would end up shunned by society.

In his report of the dream, Sasportas recounted that it served as a decisive moment when he realized that the nascent movement would end with either the death or the conversion of its principal authority. He then indicated that he had shared his experience with a number of people. The boundary between believers and unbelievers at this point was apparently anything but stable in Sephardic Hamburg. Word quickly traveled, and the believers in Hamburg who had heard about Sasportas's nighttime activities soon began to mock him. In response, Sasportas seems to have embraced the role of the prophet while simultaneously pouring scorn on the category itself. He used the word *hedyotot*, which translates roughly as "laypeople" and which elsewhere in his polemic serves to mark the rabble, to refer to those nonbelievers who were content to follow the teachings of the sages and had refused to accept the veracity of Sabbatian prophecy. And he referred to his own deliberate and measured skepticism as a prophecy. His final assertion—when the time comes we'll see who the true prophet is—seems to be dripping with irony at the expense of the very category of prophecy itself.

A SAGE IS BETTER THAN A PROPHET

Over the course of *Zizath novel zvi*, one can sense a gradual hardening of Sasportas's position on prophecy. In a sense, this is simply reflective

---

rope during the High Middle Ages," in *Studies in Medieval Jewish Intellectual and Social History: Festschrift in Honor of Robert Chazan*, ed. David Engel et al. (Leiden: Brill, 2012), 111–143.

of his position on Sabbatianism more generally, a position that moved from subdued excitement through mild skepticism to absolute denunciation over a period of about a year. In order to understand Sasportas's position on prophecy specifically and Sabbatianism more generally, however, it is critical not to ignore or to explain away his early confusion. If one returns to the Talmudic dictum with which Sasportas rebuked the sages of Izmir, "A sage is better than a prophet," one can grasp the difficulty prophecy posed as a constitutive factor in Sabbatian messianism. Sasportas deployed a Talmudic statement that offered a relative assessment of the prophet and the sage; he did not dismiss prophets and prophecy altogether and uphold the sage as the only arbiter of tradition. As someone who used his own dreams as a means of determining his position on a matter of critical importance, who wrote within the generative tradition of Kabbalah, and who recognized the category of transcendence, Sasportas had no intention to deny either the possible validity or the potential authority of subjective experience. For all of the centrality that the book of Job played in his polemic and in the letter to Supino, he fought his battle with the Sabbatians on the grounds of prophetic utterance. This need not imply that Sasportas claimed to be a prophet; rather, this indicates that his dispute with the Sabbatians depended largely upon the interpretation of the texts of biblical prophecy, and not as a rejection of prophecy as such. Like the rabbis of antiquity, upon whom he modeled himself, Sasportas claimed interpretive authority, the relative authority of the sage, over the authority of the prophet.

For Sasportas, this authority of the sage depended upon a number of factors. Interpretive skill and the mantle of tradition served as two critical components authorizing the dicta of a given sage. At various other points in his writing, Sasportas also appealed to erudition, lineage, and reason. In his discussion of the written word, Sasportas pointed to his own erudition as constitutive of his own wisdom. He seemed to miss no occasion to remind his various correspondents of his own distinguished ancestry, which he traced back all the way to the medieval giant of Catalonia Moses ben Nahman. His appeal to reason, an inherent feature of his Maimonideanism and a critical aspect of his argument against the enthusiastic frenzy of the synagogue, remains one of the most elusive aspects of his argument. He frequently employed the word *sekhel*, a term in medieval Hebrew philosophy that referred to the intellect. He clearly had little patience with the more manifestly theatrical aspects of Sabbatianism, such as the public antinomianism and the reversal of social hierarchies. Yet he did not revert to the absolute authority of reason. Prior to Sabbetai Zevi's conversion, he formulated his skepticism in such a way as to still allow for the possibility of Sabbetai Zevi as the Messiah. Throughout the polemic, he frequently emphasized the possibility of prophecy, and he went out of his way to articulate and rehearse the various conditions for its possibility. The refusal to revert to the absolute authority of reason goes some way toward explaining the difficulty that Sabbatianism posed for Sasportas. Only the absolute authority of reason would render Sabbetai Zevi entirely wrong; but Sasportas had the authority of a sage, not that of pure reason. The position of the sage would always leave open the possibility of doubt.

FIVE

~

CHRISTIANITY

There to stumble into an orgy held by a Messiah no one has quite
recognized yet, and to know, as your eyes meet, that you are his
John the Baptist, his Nathan of Gaza, that it is you who must convince him of his Godhead, proclaim him to others, love him both
profanely and in the Name of what he is…

—Thomas Pynchon

Figure 14. Frontispiece to *Nahalat shiva* (Amsterdam, 1667). The frontispiece to this book indicates the year of its publication through the use of the Hebrew phrase "the year in which the Messiah son of David arrived." The book was printed in Amsterdam, with an approbation composed by Sasportas in Hamburg. Bibliotheca Rosenthaliana, Special Collections of the University of Amsterdam.

FOR THE SEPHARDIM OF NORTHWESTERN EUROPE, Christianity posed a social and theological problem. In the urban centers where Sasportas spent the majority of his adult life, they were engaged "in a dramatic process of disentanglement from the Christian world—theologically, linguistically, socially, and culturally."[1] This process occurred over decades and drew on opposing social forces. The members of the Amsterdam *maamad* had a keen sense of the precariousness of their settlement in the Dutch Republic. In 1616, at a relatively early stage in their settlement, they banned all religious polemics. This ordinance was renewed when the three congregations united in 1639 under a decree that explicitly "forbade controversies with Gentiles on matters of religion."[2] The lay leadership in Amsterdam made every effort to avoid interreligious polemic and any other type of theological controversy that might reflect poorly on the fledgling Jewish settlement. While this process has been most carefully documented for Amsterdam, there is no reason to assume that the leadership in London, Livorno, or Hamburg adopted a different stance. The Sephardim in London and Livorno modeled themselves explicitly on their colleagues in Amsterdam, and whatever rivalry had existed between Hamburg and Amsterdam at the turn of the seventeenth century disappeared with the ascendance of

---

[1] Miriam Bodian, "The Portuguese Jews of Amsterdam and the Status of Christians," in *New Perspectives on Jewish-Christian Relations in Honor of David Berger*, ed. Elisheva Carlebach and Jacob J. Schacter (Leiden: Brill, 2012), 334. The epigraph appears in Thomas Pynchon, *Gravity's Rainbow* (New York: Penguin Books, 2006), 14.

[2] Kaplan, *"Gente Política,"* 32.

the Dutch Sephardim in demographic and material terms by the middle of the century.[3]

Concurrent with this elaborate and continuous effort to keep theological controversy out of the public domain, the Dutch Sephardim produced some of the most extraordinary polemical literature against Christianity in the long history of the Jewish-Christian debate. Saul Levi Morteira, Isaac Orobio de Castro, Moses Raphael D'Aguilar, and Isaac Nahar, rabbis or doctors or both, each wrote critical treatments of Christianity in the middle decades of the seventeenth century.[4] Two salient features characterize this literature and help to place it in the context of Sasportas's engagement with Sabbatianism and Christianity. First, these writers circulated their polemical writings about Christianity in manuscript rather than in print. Second, they composed their treatises in the vernacular rather than in Hebrew. The writings of Isaac Orobio de Castro, for the most part in Spanish, and Saul Levi Morteira, for the most part in Portuguese, circulated fairly extensively in manuscript.[5] This suggests a degree of internal censorship. The rabbis and doctors who constituted the intellectual elite among the Dutch Sephardim directed their polemical writings both at Jews who had recently reverted to Judaism from Iberian Catholicism and conversos who were considering such a move. In addition, some of them polemicized against intellectuals affiliated with different forms of Protestantism. Thus Isaac Orobio de Castro had a remarkably civil debate in Latin with the Dutch Remonstrant Phillip van Limborch. His response appeared in print on this occasion, but only at the initiative of his Christian interlocutor.[6]

Nearly all of these men were well known to Sasportas.[7] Unlike them, some of whom were born in Iberia or were descendants of recent Iberian émigrés, Sasportas came from a family that had left Aragon after

[3] Jonathan I. Israel, "Venice, Salonika, and the Founding of the Sephardi Diaspora in the North (1574–1621)," in Israel, *Diasporas*.

[4] On the latter three, see Kaplan, *Orobio de Castro*, chap. 9; on Morteira see Saperstein, *Exile in Amsterdam*, chap. 8.

[5] For a census of Isaac Orobio de Castro's manuscript writings on Christianity, see Kaplan, *Orobio de Castro*, appendix E; on Morteira, see Kaplan, "R. Saul Levi Morteira and His Treatise," 9–31. Hereafter, Kaplan, "Morteira."

[6] Kaplan, *Orobio de Castro*, 273–285. For Morteira's engagement with the Socinians, see Benjamin Fisher, "Opening the Eyes of the *Novos Reformados*: Rabbi Saul Levi Morteira, Radical Christianity, and the Jewish Reclamation of Jesus, 1620–1660," *SR* 44 (2012): 117–148.

[7] Although he did not appear in *Zizath novel zvi*, Orobio de Castro was probably known to Sasportas. Kaplan, *Orobio de Castro*, 209–211.

the 1391 riots and settled in North Africa.[8] This difference in family history provides a critical perspective on their respective worlds. The very proximity of the Dutch Sephardim to Iberian Catholicism helps to account for the vehemence of their rejection of it.[9] By contrast, Sasportas had not been formed and molded in the Catholic world of Portugal or Spain, or even that of multiconfessional Venice. He hailed from Oran, an outpost of the Iberian Empire that gave the Jews in the town a considerable degree of social and confessional independence.[10] That said, the relative autonomy of Jewish life in Oran did not translate into complete separation from Spanish Catholicism or entirely peaceful relations between Catholics and Jews. Only a few years after Jacob Sasportas left Oran, Don Felipe de Moscoso, the son of the *xeque* of the *judería* named Yaho Çaportas and a member of the extended Sasportas family, converted to Catholicism. Moscoso lived in Madrid for a number of years, where he continued to trade with the Jews of Oran, before eventually settling in Alicante. On the eve of Good Friday in 1663, the Jews of Oran mounted a sacrilegious procession in the *judería*, which precipitated a full-scale riot by the local Catholics.[11] Thus the place in which Sasportas had lived in for the first part of his life was hardly isolated from Christianity. Prior to his arrival in Amsterdam he had lived among Catholics in Oran and would have been entirely familiar with the patterns and norms of Catholicism. But he had lived among Catholics rather than as a Catholic.

This distinction had important consequences for Sasportas's intellectual preoccupations. Prior to the Sabbatian movement, Sasportas had not produced an original book-length text of any kind. Like the rabbinic jurists of North Africa who had preceded him, and like the print professionals with whom he had worked in Amsterdam in the 1650s, he wrote within established genres. In all of this occasional and episodic writing composed over the course of several decades, Sasportas rarely broached the subject of Christianity. One of the few occasions on which he did proves instructive for evaluating his attitudes toward popular piety in general, and toward Sabbatianism in particular.

---

[8] De Castro was born in Portugal; see Kaplan, *Orobio de Castro*, 1; D'Aguilar was born either in Portugal or in Amsterdam; see Kaplan, *Orobio de Castro*, 110–111; Morteira was born in Venice; see Kaplan, "Morteira," 10; on Nahar, see above.

[9] Kaplan, "An Alternative Path to Modernity," 23.

[10] Schaub, *Les juifs du roi d'Espagne*.

[11] Israel, "The Jews of Spanish North Africa," 174–177.

In a responsum written in 1655, Sasportas prescribed a series of penitential rituals for conversos who returned to Judaism. These exercises were based on the writings of Elijah de Vidas, a sixteenth-century kabbalist from Safed. Sasportas was not being purposefully obscure in turning to ethical literature written half a world away; rather, he was prescribing a work that was accessible in the vernacular. Although he did not mention it, a Portuguese translation of De Vidas's Hebrew treatise on penitence had appeared in Amsterdam two decades earlier.[12] Sasportas's ruling "was typical of the treatment of conversos in rabbinic literature."[13] In his responsum, he referred to Christianity as idolatry and took care to cite the opinion of Abraham ben David of Posquières, a medieval Talmudist referred to by the acronym Rabad.[14]

> He who believes in that man from Edom is called a sectarian, as Rabad, of blessed memory, wrote.[15]

Although Sasportas cited Rabad's opinion without reference to a particular passage, the wording suggests that he was paraphrasing a gloss on Maimonides "Laws of Repentance."[16] Rabad had written:

> He who has turned to the law of the gentiles, he has accepted Jesus. He is a heretic.

Rabad's gloss was frequently censored, and the passage often appeared without a specific reference to Jesus:

> For he has accepted their gods, and he is a heretic.[17]

---

[12] *Ohel ya-akov*, #3, 2a–3a. Elijah de Vidas, *Tratado del temor divino* (Amsterdam, 1633). On the translation, see Yosef Hayim Yerushalmi, "The Re-education of Marranos in the Seventeenth Century," in *The Faith of Fallen Jews: Yosef Hayim Yerushalmi and the Writing of Jewish History*, ed. David N. Myers and Alexander Kaye (Hanover, NH: Brandeis University Press, 2014), 118.

[13] Goldish, "Hakham Jacob Sasportas and the Former Conversos," 156.

[14] For Rabad on Christianity, see Jeremy Cohen, "Rationales for Conjugal Sex in RaBaD's *Ba'alei ha-nefesh*," *Jewish History* 6 (1992): 65–78.

[15] הגם כי המאמין באיש ההוא של אדום נקרא מין כאשר כתב הרא"בד ז"ל
Ohel ya-akov, #3, 2a.

[16] Sasportas knew Rabad principally as a glossator of Maimonides, which "was a sixteenth-century creation." See Haym Soloveitchik, "Rabad of Posquières: A Programmatic Essay," in *Studies in the History of Jewish Society in the Middle Ages and in the Modern Period Presented to Jacob Katz on His Seventy-Fifth Birthday*, ed. E. Ektes and Y. Salmon (Jerusalem: Magnes Press, 1980), 19.

[17] For the uncensored: ומי שחזר לדתי הגויים הנה הוא מודה בישו והרי הוא מין
For the censored version: הנה הוא מודה באלהיהם והרי הוא מין
Maimonides "Laws of Repentance," in *The Book of Knowledge*, 3:9. A Spanish translation of

In Sasportas's formulation "the man from Edom" seems to refer to Jesus. Whether or not he had access to the uncensored version of Rabad's gloss, which explicitly designated a believer in Jesus as a heretic, Sasportas invoked the standard medieval rabbinic typology for Christianity and by extension Jesus: Edom.[18] Sasportas thought of Christianity strictly within a legal context and adopted a response entirely dependent on precedent, explicitly invoking a medieval authority in his treatment of returning conversos.

One finds further evidence of his lack of concern with Christian theology and belief when he arrived in London as a rabbi to the new group of Portuguese Jews in 1664. Of all Jewish rituals that these new Jews had to practice, circumcision often proved the most difficult for adult men seeking to to revert to Judaism.[19] As the nominal religious head of the new Jews in London, Sasportas waited patiently for six months in hopeful expectation that all the men in London would accept the necessity of circumcision.[20] When he saw that uncircumcised men continued to attend synagogue, Sasportas shamed them publicly and made every effort to prevent their participation in the life of the synagogue. This problem would have afforded as good as an opportunity as any for Sasportas to polemicize against Christianity. As he reported the sequence of events in a series of letters to Josiah Pardo, his rabbinic colleague in Rotterdam, Sasportas focused exclusively on the importance of the Marranos' "entrance into the tradition of the covenant."[21] He did not engage with Christianity or make any acerbic remarks about the gentiles. He wrote about circumcision as if it were a self-evident obligation incumbent upon all Jewish men; clearly, he did not regard uncircumcised conversos as "sectarians" or "heretics" beyond the pale of Jewish society. In this sense, comparison with his contemporary Isaac Cardoso offers an instructive parallel. In his apologia for Judaism *Las excelencias de los Hebreos*, which was printed in Amsterdam in 1679, Cardoso included "one of the most glowing panegyrics of circumcision

---

Maimonides's "Laws of Repentance" had appeared in Amsterdam in 1613. See Yerushalmi, *Isaac Cardoso*, 256n112.

[18] Israel Jacob Yuval, *Two Nations in Your Womb: Perceptions of Jews and Christians in Late Antiquity and the Middle Ages*, trans. Barbara Harshav and Jonathan Chipman (Berkeley: University of California Press, 2006), chap. 1.

[19] Kaplan, "Attitudes toward Circumcision."

[20] Tishby, "New Information on the 'Converso' Community in London," 479.

[21] Ibid.

to be found in Jewish literature."[22] What is more, Cardoso pressed the rite of circumcision into the service of anti-Christian polemic and used it as part of his rejection of Christian history. In his telling, the circumcision of Abraham and the binding of Isaac took the place of the crucifixion of Jesus.[23] Sasportas may not have found Cardoso's later discussion of Christianity and circumcision at all objectionable, but he did not discuss circumcision in an explicitly theological context. Following the medieval halakhic literature that he saw as the core of the Jewish tradition, he focused on it largely as a legal and social obligation. Cardoso, who had been raised as a Catholic in the Iberian Peninsula, confronted Christianity as a part of his own past. He wrote of circumcision, a rite that had served to separate him from that past, with all of the polemical vigor of a converso returning to Judaism. Cardoso defended Judaism within a theological context. For a converso trained in the rigors of Catholic doctrine, the genre of an apologia for Judaism afforded him the occasion to focus on Jewish theology. Hence he framed the violation of Jewish law as ideological and as heretical. Sasportas, by contrast, did not think in these generic terms. For him, the problem of circumcision was a social one. He designated those who refused the rite as violators, separatists, or sinners. He understood ideological differences as the product, and not the cause, of fundamentally social distinctions. Sasportas does not seem to have been particularly concerned with Christianity as an idea.

Sasportas's attitude changed in the course of his confrontation with Sabbatianism. The law continued to serve as Sasportas's principal framework, but he now added several new terms, including repeated references to the literary sources that had been at the center of the Jewish and Christian debate for over a millennium. Furthermore, what had once been of marginal concern, Christianity, now became a leitmotiv in his treatment of Sabbatianism. Sabbetai Zevi and the Sabbatian movement forced Sasportas to confront Christianity. The emergence of a contemporary Jewish heresy—for no actual social distinctions divided "believers" from "unbelievers" in the early stages of the movement—propelled him to reimagine Christianity, which he now described as a heretical or ideological offshoot of ancient Judaism. Or, more precisely, the appearance of Sabbetai Zevi as the Messiah and Nathan of Gaza as his prophet forced Sasportas to invoke ancient Chris-

[22] Yerushalmi, *Isaac Cardoso*, 378.
[23] Ibid., 409.

tianity as a polemical tool in his debate with the supporters of Sabbetai Zevi. He saw how religious ideas could function as a social force. They were not simply doctrinal errors. Belief suddenly began to compete with the law. Sasportas's turn to Christianity was not at all directed at learned Protestant readers in contemporary Hamburg or Amsterdam. Rather, it was an attempt to convince his fellow Jews that the figure they had embraced as the Messiah was closer to Jesus than to the redeemer envisioned in the final chapters of Maimonides's *Code*. Religious belief threatened the inviolate status of the law and, therefore, undermined the social authority of the one who determined the law: the rabbi.

This novel argument developed over a number of stages. In the early phases of the movement, Sasportas sought to establish a basic framework for comparison between Sabbatianism and Christianity. He invoked several biblical passages that had occasioned charged exchanges in medieval Jewish-Christian polemic. With the conversion of Sabbetai Zevi to Islam, Sasportas focused on a particular thread that had been present in his earlier discussions but had remained relatively underdeveloped. In the second section of *Zizath novel zvi*, which covers the period immediately following Sabbetai Zevi's conversion, he argued with extraordinary force that Sabbatianism constituted a new faith (Heb. *emunah hadasha*). Finally, at various points in the latter parts of his work, Sasportas raised the specter of Sabbatianism as a potential cause for Jewish conversion to Christianity. The Sabbatians themselves, including Nathan of Gaza himself, were hardly oblivious of Christianity. Occasional comments by Sabbatian prophets about Jesus and Christianity did much to ignite Sasportas's polemical ire and to confirm his anxieties. These statements, as well as their reverberations in the writings of Sabbetai Zevi's supporters closer to Hamburg, appear to have played a critical role in turning Sasportas's attention to Jesus and Christianity. While Sasportas's engagement with Christianity began as a reaction to the Sabbatians, it soon took on an independent polemical task in his attempt to found a new Jewish heresiology.

SABBATIANISM AND CHRISTIANITY

By the middle of the seventeenth century, Jews and Christians had been engaged in polemic for centuries. These exchanges had generated a voluminous literature, some of it exegetical and homiletic, and some of it political and philosophic. No less a figure than Sasportas's own ancestor Nahmanides had participated in a celebrated disputation with Friar Pablo Christiani at Barcelona in 1263.[24] In spite of his repeated references to his forebear, Sasportas did not discuss this debate or Nahmanides's response. Arguments from silence are not arguments; Sasportas's refusal to summon up Nahmanides's disputation requires some comment. The Hebrew account of the Barcelona disputation did not appear in print until Johann Christoph Wagenseil included it in his compendium of Jewish polemical literature about Christianity, *Tela ignea Satanae*.[25] Furthermore, Sasportas had shown little awareness of the extensive interest of Protestant intellectuals in Jewish learning that developed in Amsterdam throughout the seventeenth century, and would therefore have been unlikely to encounter Wagenseil's anthology.[26] Nevertheless, Sasportas knew Wagenseil's Hebrew tutor Ber Perlhefter and corresponded with him on a number of occasions.[27]

Sasportas had been in contact with Perlhefter both before and after his collaboration with Wagenseil. Immediately prior to the appearance of *Tela ignea Satanae* in 1681, he had written him a cordial letter from Livorno. Perlhefter included it in one of his works that appeared while Sasportas was still alive in 1686. Thus Sasportas could have known of Nahmanides's account. Given that he revised *Zizath novel zvi* in the 1670s, and given the filial piety he expressed toward Nahmanides, the absence of references to the Barcelona disputation is striking. Sasportas's own arguments about the authority of the written word and the

[24] Robert Chazan, *Barcelona and Beyond: The Disputation of 1263 and Its Aftermath* (Berkeley: University of California Press, 1992); David Berger, "The Barcelona Disputation," in *Persecution, Polemic, and Dialogue: Essays in Jewish-Christian Relations* (Boston: Academic Studies Press, 2010), 199–208.

[25] Johann Christoph Wagenseil, *Tela ignea Satanae: hoc est arcani & horribiles Judaeorum adversus Christum* (Altdorf, 1681). Nahmanides's Hebrew account did not appear as part of a compilation printed by Jews until over a decade after Sasportas's death. See *Milhemet hovah* (Constantinople, 1710).

[26] For the earlier half of the seventeenth century, see Aaron L. Katchen, *Christian Hebraists and Dutch Rabbis: Seventeenth Century Apologetics and the Study of Maimonides' Mishneh Torah* (Cambridge, MA: Harvard University Press, 1984); for the latter half, see Theodor Dunkelgrün, " 'Like a Blind Man Judging Colors': Joseph Athias and Johannes Leusden Defend Their 1667 Hebrew Bible," *SR* 44 (2012): 79–115.

[27] Nathaniel Riemer, "Zwischen christlichen Hebraisten und Sabbatianern—der Lebensweg von R. Beer und Bila Perlhefter," *Aschkenas* 14 (2004): 163–201.

force of social enthusiasm drew heavily on medieval rabbinic literature. Indeed, much of his argument involved his upholding the writing
of medieval rabbis as a rebuke to the experience of Sabbatian messianists. The Barcelona disputation would have fit within this kind of argument. Its absence is emblematic of a larger lacuna in his polemic: his
account passes over nearly the entire medieval Sephardic literature on
Christianity—from Nahmanides to Hasdai Crescas to Profiat Duran—
without comment.

There may be something more than the vagaries of early modern
printing at work in this asymmetry. Unlike his Sephardic predecessors,
including most obviously Nahmanides, Sasportas had very little interest in Christianity on its own terms. He sought to make a basic analogy between Sabbatianism and Christianity in order to address a Jewish social problem. This is not to imply that Sephardic polemicists
against Christianity designed their arguments solely for Christian consumption. This was far from the case, as many of them were written in
Hebrew and explicitly addressed to Jews. But for the purposes of Sasportas's analogy, he did not need the intellectual imprimatur of Hasdai Crescas or Profiat Duran, or even that of his distinguished ancestor Nahmanides. He was responding to behavior and arguments that
were not merely intellectual but seemed to implicate the original
Jewish-Christian split directly. In his construction of events, the Sabbatians and their supporters provided evidence of this original schism
in abundance.

Sasportas deployed a number of texts in his accusation that the Sabbatians behaved like Christians. On certain occasions he ironically alluded to the Gospels, and on others he invoked descriptions of Jesus in
the Talmud. More than any other text, however, the Suffering Servant
section in the book of Isaiah stood at the center of his polemic. The
meaning of Isaiah 53 and the final three verses of 52 had long been contested by Jews and Christians.[28] For the purposes of Sasportas's polemic, the crucial question involved the character of the "servant" described by the biblical prophet. Did Isaiah's prophecy refer to a
collective representation of the Jewish people who suffered for the ben-
efit of the world, as Jews had maintained throughout the Middle Ages,

---

[28] *The Fifty-Third Chapter of Isaiah according to the Jewish Interpreters*, trans. Samuel R. Driver
and Adolf Neubauer (Oxford: James Parker, 1876). Cited after the reprint (New York: Hermon
Press, 1969).

or did it refer to an actual Messiah who took the guilt of humanity onto his own person?

Sasportas did not turn to Isaiah 53 immediately following the Sabbatian outbreak. In the opening weeks and months of the enthusiastic frenzy, references to Christianity in general and to these biblical passages in particular seldom appeared, but neither the subject nor the text was ever entirely absent from his discussion. In one of his early letters to the Amsterdam rabbinate, he included a sarcastic aside that mentioned the passage:

> And how much have my insides rejoiced in seeing the prophecy of the fifty-third chapter of Isaiah partially fulfilled according to the interpretation of the Christians. I have confidence in the kindness of God that it shall all be fulfilled through him.[29]

"The interpretation of the Christians" understood these passages as a reference to the Messiah. Sasportas sarcastically contrasted his own joy with the rejoicing of the Sabbatians at the arrival of the Messiah. At this early stage, he still hoped that Sabbetai Zevi might turn into a Suffering Servant like Jesus of Nazareth. Just as the combined force of Jewish and imperial discipline had crucified Jesus, a similar conjuncture of rabbinic and imperial forces would punish and ostracize Sabbetai Zevi.

Sasportas began to focus more and more on Christianity as reports of Sabbetai Zevi's incarceration in Gallipoli in the summer of 1666 reached northern Europe. Prior to his imprisonment, Sabbetai Zevi and his followers had carried out their messianic activities relatively undisturbed. They could still be absorbed into the framework of an internal Jewish dispute and were still subject to rabbinic discipline. With his captivity in Gallipoli, the nascent movement faced a series of crises that required an explanation to the faithful. In a letter to the rabbinate in Vienna written prior to his knowledge of the conversion but when he had already learned Sabbetai Zevi was in Gallipoli, Sasportas described a nation split in two.

> Meanwhile our Torah became like two sets of scripture and the people were divided in two. Half of them washed their hands of this belief of

29 ומה מאד תעלוזנה כליותי בראותי כי נבואת נ"ג של ישעיה נתקימה במקצתה כפירוש הנוצרים בטחתי בחסד אל שכלה תתקיים בנפש"ו.

Sasportas, ZNZ, 21.

theirs on hearing that the aforementioned rabbi is confined in a prison for those condemned to death by the crown, and he has not freed himself, let alone those who are caught up by their hope for [salvation through] him. But had this been before he had been revealed as the Messiah, we could have said, it is because of "but he was wounded because of our sins"[30] (Isaiah 53:4).

Sasportas described an early stage in the movement's fracture. Sabbetai Zevi was still a Jew, and Sasportas himself referred to him as "the aforementioned rabbi." His incarceration, however, had left his believers divided between the zealously faithful and the newly skeptical. Sabbetai Zevi's inability to extricate himself from prison rendered him completely powerless in the eyes of his supporters. The Messiah as promised by Maimonides was supposed to be a figure of extraordinary strength and someone who waged the wars of the Lord. Sabbetai Zevi, it turned out, lacked military power. In this context, Sasportas made a revealing comment about Isaiah 53. Had the Sabbatians not already declared that Sabbetai Zevi was the Messiah, the words of the biblical prophet could have served as a source of comfort. "But he was wounded because of our sins," a phrase used by Isaiah to describe the Suffering Servant, could have been applied to Sabbetai Zevi as part of the Jewish people. Once his followers had declared Sabbetai Zevi to be the Messiah, however, they could no longer turn to Isaiah 53 as a source of comfort in their distress. If they insisted upon invoking the Suffering Servant as a prooftext for Sabbetai Zevi, his followers would be reading the Bible as Christians did. They would thus vest the "suffering" in a single person rather than in the collective of the Jewish people. The exegetical strategies of the Sabbatians marked them as sectarians because they cleaved the Torah into two competing truths.

In characterizing Sabbatian prophecy as the rival interpretation of Isaiah 53, Sasportas actually anticipated the exegetical strategy of the Sabbatians in response to the unexpected travails of the new Messiah. Prior to Sabbetai Zevi's conversion to Islam, Nathan of Gaza had mentioned Jesus in an ambiguous context. In his "Treatise on the Dragons,"

---

[30] ובין כה וכה נעשית תורתנו כשתי תורות ויחלק העם לשנים, החצי רפו ידיהם מאמונתם זאת בשמעם כי הרב הנ"ל חבוש בבית האסורים מקום שניתן להרוגי מלכות ולא התיר את עצמו ומכל שכן להתיר אסירי תקותו. ואלו היה זה קודם שנגלה למשיח היינו אומרים משום והוא מחולל מפשעינו.

Ibid., 115.

a work Sasportas does not seem to have known, he referred to Jesus as the husk of impurity that surrounded the Messiah:

> And finally, he [Sabbetai Zevi] will restore [to holiness] his shell which is Jesus the Nazarene.[31]

In the course of his wanderings in the weeks following Sabbetai Zevi's conversion to Islam, Nathan of Gaza addressed a public letter to Sabbetai Zevi's two brothers in Smyrna. He grappled with the Messiah's conversion and sought to use the prophecies in Isaiah as a rationale:

> About him, scripture says, "Indeed, my servant shall prosper" (52:13), which refers to the King Messiah, "he was despised, shunned by men" (53:3), "he was maltreated, yet he was submissive, he did not open his mouth" (53:7), "And his grave was set among the wicked" (Isa. 53:9), "And was numbered among the sinners" (53:12). This refers to the fact that many people consider him a sinner, and, as a result, he bore the sin of many.[32]

Nathan of Gaza assembled a pastiche of no fewer than five quotations from whole or partial verses in the Suffering Servant passage to translate Sabbetai Zevi's conversion into distinctly Christological terms. He explicitly connected the Messiah's suffering to the violation of the law. "Many people," which may refer to the growing disillusionment among the faithful, now considered the converted Messiah a transgressor. The direct consequence in Nathan of Gaza's mind was to turn Sabbetai Zevi into a messianic figure who bore the sins of the people upon himself. If there were any doubt that Nathan of Gaza was playing Paul to Sabbetai Zevi's Jesus, the continuation of the letter points to the advent of Sabbetai Zevi as a reason to suspend the law altogether, not merely to engage in the symbolic violation of particular rituals as Sabbetai Zevi had done when he declared himself the Messiah. Nathan of Gaza went

---

[31] שהוא קליפתו שהוא יש"ו הנוצרי שעתיד הוא לתקנו.

Nathan of Gaza, "Treatise on the Dragons" (Hebrew), in *Be-ikvot mashiah*, ed. Scholem, 43; I have slightly modified the translation in Scholem, *Sabbatai Sevi*, 285; on this passage, see Ada Rapoport-Albert, "On the Position of Women in Sabbatianism" (Hebrew), in *Ha-halom ve-shivro*, ed. Rachel Elior (Jerusalem: Magnes Press, 2001), 296n745, 319.

[32] ועליו אמר הכתוב הנה ישכיל עבדי האמורה על מלך המשיח נבזה וחדל אישים נגש הוא נענה ולא יפתח פיו ויתן את רשעים קברו ואת פושעים נמנה. והוא ענין זה שעל ידי כן רבים חשבוהו פושע ועל ידי כן חטא רבים נשא.

Sasportas, *ZNZ*, 200–201. On this letter, see Scholem, *Sabbatai Sevi*, 720–721. For Jesus in another letter by Nathan of Gaza, see Scholem, "Works on Sabbetai Zevi, the Majority from the Writings of Nathan of Gaza in MS Adler 494" (Hebrew), in Scholem, *Mehkere shabtaut*, 20.

one step further than the Pauline epistles, which argued for the abrogation of the law for gentile converts to faith in the salvific power of the Passion. He now argued for the abrogation of the law for Jews and provided an elaborate theological justification for sin that would come to play a central role in Sabbatian theology.

> For this issue is like the prostration upon one's face [in the daily liturgy], when one projects one's soul into the husk to draw out the sparks of holiness that have fallen because of sin, which is alluded to in the verse "while men still had authority over men to treat them unjustly"[33] (Ecc. 8:9).

Nathan of Gaza drew upon the kabbalistic theology of the *Zohar* and Isaac Luria to provide a transvaluation of sin and to justify Sabbetai Zevi's conversion to Islam. The apostasy represented the Messiah's descent into the husk of evil to redeem the fallen sparks of holiness.

Sasportas disposed of Nathan of Gaza's explanation of Sabbetai Zevi's apostasy by spelling out its connection to Christianity:

> Let someone look at the words of this denier with the fine eye of Jewishness... for he [Nathan of Gaza] reveals aspects of prophecy that are contrary to truth and falsifies its meaning. For this interpretation is actually the opinion of the Christians who explain it [Isaiah 53] as a reference to Jesus of Nazareth. [Nathan of Gaza] has seized upon their way, the way of the sectarians, and he will not rest in his wickedness until he called him [Sabbetai Zevi] God like those who believe in Jesus.[34]

In Sasportas's mind Nathan of Gaza's invocation of the Suffering Servant as a reference to Sabbetai Zevi amounted to a Christian reading of the Bible. He proceeded to go one step further, however. Nathan of Gaza not only read the Bible like a Christian, rather than with the precise eye of Jewish interpretation; he referred to Sabbetai Zevi as if he were a god. Just as the followers of Jesus had declared him a god after

---

[33] כי עניננו זה הוא כענין נפילת אפים שמוסר אדם נפשו אל הקליפה לברר משם ניצוצות קדושה שנפלו על ידי החטא בסוד עת אשר שלט האדם באדם לרע לו.
Sasportas, *ZNZ*, 201.
[34] יראה הרואה בעין יפה של יהדות בדברי הכופר הזה . . . והרי זה מגלה פנים בנבואה שלא כפי האמת ועושה אותה פלסתר, והיא ממש דעת הנוצרים המפרשים אותה על יש"ו הנוצרי ואחז דרכם דרך מינות ולא זז מרשעו עד שקראו ה' כמו מאמיני יש"ו.
Ibid.

his crucifixion, the followers of Sabbetai Zevi had declared him a god after his conversion to Islam.

The term Sasportas used in this instance reveals the critical role Christianity played in his polemic. Sasportas designated Nathan of Gaza as following "the way of sectarianism." Elsewhere he referred to Sabbatianism as *apikorsut*, a word that appears in rabbinic literature from antiquity and suggests irreverence for authority.[35] The word bears a phonetic coincidence with Epicureanism, and suggests skepticism or licentiousness when it appears in the Talmud.[36] Sasportas referred to Nathan of Gaza as "adopting the way of sectarianism," when he accused him of behaving like a Christian. Sasportas used the terms "the way of sectarianism" and "skepticism" to make an analogy between Sabbatianism and early Christianity. Both terms imply a specific attitude toward the law, a rejection of reward and punishment, and the divine sanction for the violation of the law. In Sasportas's understanding, when the Sabbatians rejected the law and embraced God's grace, they behaved and thought as if they were Christians rather than Jews. In a discussion of Sasportas, Paweł Maciejko distinguished his use of *apikorsut* from the term *minut*: "It is significant that Sasportas called Sabbatianism 'irreligion' (*apikorsut*) and not 'heresy' (*minut*)."[37] Sasportas, however, did refer on a number of occasions to Nathan of Gaza as following the "way of sectarianism" (Heb. *derekh minut*). Given that Sasportas used both terms—*apikorsut* and *minut*—in the context of Sabbatianism and Christianity, it seems that the terms should be aligned with one another rather than sharply distinguished. In Sasportas's epistemology of sectarianism, *apikorsut* and *minut* referred to violations of social norms.

What Nathan of Gaza had written to Sabbetai Zevi's brothers in Smyrna immediately after the conversion soon became a model for the treatment of Isaiah 53 by other spokesmen for Sabbatianism. In the years following Sabbetai Zevi's conversion, the movement that had co-

---

[35] Hans-Jürgen Becker, "'Epikureer' im Talmud Yerushalmi," in *The Talmud Yerushalmi and Graeco-Roman Culture*, ed. Peter Schäfer (Tübingen: Mohr Siebeck, 1998), 1:397–421; Jenny R. Labendz, "'Know What to Answer the Epicurean': A Diachronic Study of the *'Apiqoros* in Rabbinic Literature," *HUCA* 74 (2003): 175–214; Moulie Vidas, *Tradition and the Formation of the Talmud* (Princeton, NJ: Princeton University Press, 2014), 132–134.

[36] Marcus Jastrow, *A Dictionary of the Targumim, the Talmud Babli and Yerushalmi, and the Midrashic Literature* (New York: Judaica Press, 1992), 104.

[37] *The Mixed Multitude*, 43.

alesced around him splintered into a number of smaller cells that competed for loyalty among the remaining faithful. Although he continued to work as a prophet and a publicist for Sabbetai Zevi until his own death in 1680, Nathan of Gaza was no longer the only figure who looked to Sabbetai Zevi to legitimate his own prophecies. Abraham Miguel Cardoso, the younger brother of Isaac, emerged as an important and peripatetic prophet in the years following Sabbetai Zevi's conversion. A former converso from Spain and nearly two decades older than Nathan of Gaza, Cardoso moved between Livorno, Tripoli, Tunis, Izmir, and Constantinople before dying in Egypt at the hands of his nephew in 1706.[38] Prior to the outbreak of Sabbatianism, he served as a physician to a number of rulers in Tripoli, where he lived between 1663 and 1672. In a series of letters written in 1668 in Hebrew and in Spanish, Cardoso initially accepted Nathan of Gaza as the Messiah's prophet. By June of 1669, however, he began to compete with him for the mantle of Sabbatian leadership. In the preface to a letter to the rabbinic judges in Izmir, he assured them, "Still more convincingly do you show that there is no substance in Nathan Benjamin [Nathan of Gaza]. Time and again was he put to the test: in Your Worships' presence, in Adrianople, in Venice. It was discovered each time that there was no truth to his dreams or his speeches."[39]

Both Hebrew letters, the first from April 1668 and the second from June 1669, demonstrate the centrality of Isaiah 53 in Cardoso's messianic eschatology. "The text which he never fails quoting is Isa. 53," noted Carlo Bernheimer.[40] The addressee of the first Hebrew letter remains somewhat unclear. Cardoso wrote the letter from Tunis, and somehow an anti-Sabbatian named Abraham de Souza in Amsterdam obtained a copy. De Souza forwarded it to Sasportas in Hamburg and requested his comments; Sasportas included the letter along with his

---

[38] For a biography, see *Abraham Miguel Cardozo: Selected Writings*, ed. and trans. David J. Halperin (Mahwah, NJ: Paulist Press, 2001), 5–106; hereafter, Halperin, *Selected Writings*. On the orthography of his last name, see Nissim Yosha's review of Halperin, *Selected Writings*, in *JQR* 94 (2004): 410.

[39] Translation in Halperin, *Selected Writings*, 131; for the Hebrew, see Scholem, "The Letter of Abraham Miguel Cardoso to the Judges of Izmir," 303, where Scholem dates it to June 1669. On the competition between the two prophets, see Nissim Yosha, "Time and Space: A Theological Philosophical Controversy between Miguel Cardoso and Nathan of Gaza" (Hebrew), *JSJT* 12 (1996): 259–284.

[40] "Some New Contributions to Abraham Cardoso's Biography," *JQR* 18 (1927): 106n20.

refutation in *Zizath novel zvi*.[41] Sasportas thought that the addressee of the letter was Abraham's brother Isaac, and most scholars have followed him in this assumption.[42] David J. Halperin, however, noted that Isaac Cardoso may not have been able to read the extremely difficult Hebrew of the letter. He argued that the letter assumed an addressee who shared Abraham Cardoso's belief in Sabbetai Zevi as the Messiah; Isaac Cardoso did not.[43] Be that as it may, Sasportas worked under the assumption that the addressee of the letter he edited and refuted was, indeed, Abraham Cardoso's brother Isaac.

Cardoso began to develop his notion of the suffering Messiah, an idea that he expanded upon in a letter to the judges in Izmir written the following year.[44]

> The principle that emerges: the King Messiah in the future shall be higher than the ministering angels and the most scorned and cursed of all people. But these two opposing poles cannot occur at the same time. Rather, at first he shall be lowly, and the Jews shall think of him as a very wicked man. He shall accept torture and all that shall be decreed against him for the sins of Israel, for upon this condition he has come into the world and for this he was created. After that he shall ascend to the highest level, to the point that all the greatness spoken about him by the prophets and the rabbis of blessed memory shall be fulfilled.[45]

Cardoso envisioned the redemption as occurring in two stages: first the Messiah would arrive and receive the scorn of all Jews. At this point, he would bear the sins of Israel as described by the prophet Isaiah. Only after having been subjected to degradation would he ascend to the heights of glorious kingship described elsewhere by the biblical prophets and ancient rabbis.

[41]For the letter, see Sasportas, *ZNZ*, 289–297; for its dating, 308n2; on De Souza, see Yerushalmi, *Isaac Cardoso*, 315.

[42]See Tishby's annotations in *ZNZ*; Scholem, "New Information on Abraham Cardoso" (Hebrew), in *Mehkere shabtaut*, 396; Yerushalmi, *Isaac Cardoso*, 315.

[43]On Isaac's knowledge of rabbinics, see Yerushalmi, *Isaac Cardoso*, 365; for Halperin's argument, see Halperin, *Selected Writings*, 324n63 and 325n77.

[44]Sasportas appears to have been unaware of the letter to the judges in Izmir, although a copy made its way to Hamburg. See Yerushalmi, *Isaac Cardoso*, 321n41.

[45]כלל העולה שמלך המשיח עתיד להיות עליון ממלאכי השרת ושסוי ומחורף מכל האדם ושני הפכים אלו לא יוכלו להיות בזמן אחד, אלא שבראשונה יהיה שפל וחשוב בעיני היהודים כרשע מתועב ויקבל היסורין וכל מה שנגזר עליו בעד עונות ישראל כי על זה התנאי בא לעולם ולזה נברא, ואחר כך יעלה מעלה ומדרגה עד שיקיים עליו כל הגדולה שאמרו עליו הנביאים וחז"ל.

Sasportas, *ZNZ*, 292. See Yerushalmi, *Isaac Cardoso*, 318.

Cardoso left no room to doubt the role played by Isaiah 53 in his eschatological schema:

> Everything that Isaiah the prophet said in chapter 53 must be fulfilled by our Messiah, for so our sages have received and explained to us.[46]

Isaiah 53 explicitly dealt with the suffering of the future Messiah rather than with the collective suffering of the Jewish people. What was more, Cardoso insisted that the rabbis of antiquity had maintained a similar interpretation of this passage. In his application of Isaiah 53 to the suffering of Sabbetai Zevi in prison and as a convert to Islam, Cardoso obviously thought he was simply carrying on an ancient rabbinic interpretive tradition. To that end, he adduced chapter and verse from the Midrash, the *Zohar*, and various other classical Jewish sources he claimed supported his reading.[47] He explicitly rejected the standard medieval Jewish interpretation of Isaiah 53 as a polemical response to Christianity and as a perversion of the text's meaning. Referring to the signs of the Messiah he had discussed earlier in terms of his suffering followed by his ascendance, he wrote:

> So you shall find in Isaiah chapters 49 and 53 and Psalm 89 about which it was said, and so among the sages of the Talmud and the sages of the *Zohar*, from whose waters we drink. But the recent commentators you may have encountered, who offered another interpretation, have done so [only] in order to rescue themselves from the questions posed to them by the uncircumcised ones who use these texts to prove that the bastard [i.e., Jesus] was the Messiah. But we pay no attention to their words, for our strong pillars are the prophets, the *tannaim*, and the *amoraim*.[48]

[46] כי כל מה שאמר ישעיה הנביא ס' נ"ג צריך שיתקיים במשיחנו כי כך קיבלו חכמים וביררו לנו בבירור.
Sasportas, *ZNZ*, 293.

[47] See Halperin, *Selected Writings*, 347n12. On the Messiah in rabbinic literature, see Ephraim E. Urbach, *Hazal: Pirke emunot ve-deot* (Jerusalem: Magnes Press, 1969), chap. 17; Judah Goldin, "Of Midrash and the Messianic Theme," in *Studies in Midrash and Related Literature*, ed. Barry L. Eichler and Jeffrey H. Tigay (Philadelphia: JPS, 1988), 359–379; Michael Fishbane, "Midrash and Messianism: Some Theologies of Suffering and Salvation," in *Toward the Millenium: Messianic Expectations from the Bible to Waco*, ed. Peter Schäfer and Mark Cohen (Leiden: Brill, 1998), 57–71; Peter Schäfer, *The Jewish Jesus: How Judaism and Christianity Shaped Each Other* (Princeton, NJ: Princeton University Press, 2012), chaps. 8–9.

[48] וכן תמצא בישעיה סי' מ"ט וס' נג ובמזמור פ"ט שעליו נאמר וכך העתיקו לנו חכמי הגמרא וחכמי הזוהר כי מימיהם אנו שותים. וזה שתמצא במפרשים אחרונים בענין אחר עשו להנצל מן הקושיות שהערלים עושים להכריח מן הכתובים שהממזר היה משיח, אבל אנחנו אין אנו משגיחים על דבריהם כי העמודים החזקים שלנו הם הנביאים והתנאים והאמוראים.
Sasportas, *ZNZ*, 292–293.

In Cardoso's reading, the rabbis of antiquity interpreted Isaiah 53 correctly as a reference to the Messiah, while the medieval rabbis and his own contemporaries, challenged by Christianity, refused to accept its manifest significance. He considered his own reading as a return to the rabbis of antiquity, and, over and above this, as resolutely anti-Christian.

In this letter and in the later letter to the judges of Izmir, which repeats and elaborates on this biblical passage, Cardoso did not specify which of the more recent Jewish authorities he had in mind.[49] Nonetheless, in a Spanish letter to his brother-in-law Abraham Baruch Henríquez, who lived in Amsterdam and who had remained a firm believer after the conversion, Cardoso listed a number of medieval Jewish authorities who had refused to read Isaiah 53 within its appropriate messianic context. The letter to Henríquez was written from Tripoli in October 1668, in the period between the two Hebrew letters, and reflects the same preoccupation with later Jewish commentators on Isaiah 53. On this occasion, Cardoso named the authorities he had in mind:

> And the later commentators, such as Don Isaac Abravanel... Ibn Ezra, Rashi, Saadia Gaon in order to flee from Idumean arguments, some explain it [Isaiah 53] as referring to the Jewish people, others as Josiah or Jeremiah, or any righteous man, or as the Messiah son of Ephraim.[50]

Like Sasportas in his own responsa from the prior decade, Cardoso drew on the medieval Jewish typology equating Edom, or "Idumean" in his formulation, with Christianity. In Cardoso's mind, any reading of Isaiah 53 outside of a messianic context implied a reaction to Christian polemic. With the invocation of "later authorities" in these letters, Cardoso sought to dissociate his discussion of Sabbetai Zevi from the medieval Jewish-Christian debate.

The effect on Sasportas, however, was quite the opposite. His response did not take the form of a letter addressed to Cardoso. Nearly two years after the Messiah's conversion, Sasportas may not have considered it worth his while to engage Cardoso directly. His ideas, however, he deemed worthy of harsh rebuttal. This took the form of an extensive letter to his initial source, Abraham de Souza.

---

[49] Scholem, "The Letter of Abraham Miguel Cardoso to the Judges of Izmir," 305–308.
[50] As cited and translated in Yerushalmi, *Isaac Cardoso*, 336.

Who would not rebuke him [Cardoso] with grievous curses for having rendered the Torah fraudulent and for having said that the Messiah needed to convert, heaven forbid, and become a forced convert in order to fulfill "but he was wounded because of our sins" (Isa. 53:5), "And he was numbered among the sinners" (Isa. 53:12). This is precisely the spirit of heresy of the Christians who interpret the entire passage in reference to Jesus of Nazareth.[51]

Sasportas vehemently rejected Cardoso's claim that he was interpreting Isaiah 53 in line with the rabbis of antiquity. Any attempt to read the verses in the context of the Messiah was perforce a Christian reading. In this sense, his response to Abraham Cardoso in the midst of Sabbatian polemic was quite similar to those of Isaac Cardoso and Isaac Orobio de Castro in the context of the Jewish-Christian debate. Both of these apologists for Judaism "realized instinctively that to concede a suffering Messiah is already to grant the overwhelming portion of the Christian messianic claim."[52] Sasportas, however, went one step further than his contemporaries, of whose work he was apparently unaware.

In his response, Sasportas used a phrase similar to the one he had used in discussing Nathan of Gaza's letter to Sabbetai Zevi's brothers. There he had described Nathan of Gaza's similarity to Christianity as the "way of sectarianism," while here he described Cardoso's as "the spirit of sectarianism." For all of the differences that would later emerge between Nathan of Gaza and Abraham Cardoso, Sasportas thought of the two of them as linked. In discussing Nathan of Gaza's letter, he explicitly directed his reader to his later discussion: "Concerning all of his [Nathan of Gaza's] words in particular, look at the response I wrote to the writing of the quack Cardoso in Tripoli."[53] Sasportas had little patience with the chaos generated by messianic enthusiasm or with the Sabbatian embrace of prophecy as a form of knowledge, yet in his criticism of these aspects he did not refer specifically to the social implications of "sectarianism." When the leaders of the movement began

---

[51] ומי לא יקללהו קללות נמרצות על עשותו התורה פלסתר ואומר שהמשיח צריך להמיר דתו ח"ו ולהיותו אנוס כדי שיתקיים והוא מחולל מפשעינו ועם פושעים נמנה, והרי זה ממש יש בו רוח מינות כנוצרים המפרשים אותה הפרשה על יש"ו הנוצרי.

Sasportas, *ZNZ*, 298.

[52] Yerushalmi, *Isaac Cardoso*, 339; Kaplan, *Orobio de Castro*, chap. 9 and 439.

[53] Sasportas, *ZNZ*, 263.

to read the Bible as if they were Christians, Sasportas responded with a phrase that came very close to designating them as separatists or social revolutionaries, and not merely religious enthusiasts or deluded "fanatics."

In his subsequent treatment of Cardoso Sasportas extended his analogy between Christianity and Sabbatianism. He posited that Sabbatianism in general and Cardoso in particular were actually worse than the Jewish inventors of Christianity. In his responsa and letters dealing with former conversos, Sasportas showed keen insight into the hardship former conversos had to endure in their return to Judaism. When the occasion demanded it, he could be unstinting in his praise of their perseverance. In the context of Sabbatianism, however, the converso past that had been overcome by a repentant Jew could easily turn into a confessional liability. In his discussion of Cardoso's letter, Sasportas explicitly invoked this past and connected it to his Christian reading of Isaiah 53.[54]

> In my opinion, this man, who had been of converso lineage in Portugal and knew that the Christians had interpreted it [Isaiah 53] as a reference to their Messiah, applied [the Christian exegesis] to this Messiah of his, the apostate... He is so zealous in his faith, thinking that through it he will obtain the salvation of his soul just like the faith of the Christians in Jesus as an absolute god [who similarly provides salvation]. Therefore, this simpleton and denier thought that he [Sabbetai Zevi], in being like him [Jesus], was similarly [a god]. But he [Cardoso] did not know that he [Sabbetai Zevi] was a wicked man rather than a god.[55]

Sasportas seems to have assumed that Abraham had been born in Portugal like his elder brother Isaac, rather than in the Castilian town of Medina del Rioseco.[56] Just as the Christians had turned the Messiah

---

[54] Goldish, "Hakham Jacob Sasportas and the Former Conversos," 159.

[55] ולפי דעתי שהאיש הזה כמו שהיה בפורטגאל מזרע האנוסים והיה יודע שהנוצרים המליצוה על משיחם העתיקה הוא על משיחו זה המומר . . . וכל כך הוא אדוק באמונתו זאת כסבור שבה ישיג תשועת נפשו כמו שהיא אמונת הנוצרים ביש״ו בתתם לו אלקו״ת גמורה, ולכן חשב זה הפתי הכופר שזה ג״כ בהיותו משיח לפי סברתו כמוהו ולא ידע כי הוא אדם בליעל ולא אל.

Sasportas, ZNZ, 301–302. In a later letter apparently unknown to Sasportas, Cardoso made use of the same fact to make the opposite argument. See Scholem, "New Information on Abraham Cardoso," 416.

[56] Bernheimer, "New Contributions," 106–107; Yerushalmi, *Isaac Cardoso*, 68–70; on conversos

into a divinity upon whom their salvation depended, Cardoso had turned Sabbetai Zevi into a god and the source of his personal hopes for salvation. Sasportas connected this interpretation to Cardoso's unregenerate converso past. He referred to Cardoso in Hebrew as one of the *anusim*, which dignified him with the status of a forced convert. Cardoso's concern with the question of salvation and his claim that Sabbetai Zevi was himself divine stemmed directly from his upbringing among Christians. Sasportas was apparently unaware of Cardoso's numerous other writings on Sabbatianism, and he appears to have fundamentally misread his theology. Cardoso, in fact, vigorously disputed the attempt by Nathan of Gaza to deify Sabbetai Zevi both before and after the alleged Messiah's death in 1676.[57]

Cardoso's interpretation of Isaiah 53 continued to disturb Sasportas even after he had forwarded his refutation to De Souza. Reports reached Hamburg that the Jews of Saleh and Marrakech had celebrated the ninth of Av in the summer of 1668 as a holiday in the spirit of Sabbatianism rather than as a fast day in mourning for the Temple as mandated by rabbinic law. Although Sasportas had spent only a few years on the Atlantic coast of North Africa, he felt a kinship with and responsibility for these Jews that was quite similar to the proprietary feelings he had toward those of Oran and Tlemcen. To that end, he wrote an extended letter to his colleagues in Saleh and Marrakech that condemned the suspension of the fast. In the context of this letter, he invoked Cardoso. He pointed to his residence in Tripoli on the Mediterranean coast of North Africa, implying that his proximity may have further increased the local appeal of his ideas. Moreover, in an explicit reference to Cardoso, Sasportas argued that Sabbetai Zevi was actually worse than Jesus:

> The [Christian] nations' interpretation of Isaiah 53 is more applicable to their Messiah than to this apostate [Sabbetai Zevi]. The clear truth is

in Medina del Rioseco, see Nathan Wachtel, *The Faith of Remembrance: Marrano Labyrinths*, trans. Nikki Halpern (Philadelphia: University of Pennsylvania Press, 2013), 77.

[57] Nissim Yosha, "The Philosophical Background of Sabbatian Theology: Guidelines toward an Understanding of Abraham Michael Cardoso's Theory of the Divine" (Hebrew), in *Galut ahar golah: Mehkarim be toldot am yisrael mugashim le-Profesor Haim Beinart li-melot lo shivim shanah*, ed. Aharon Mirsky, Avraham Grossman, and Yosef Kaplan (Jerusalem: Ben Zvi Institute, 1988), 541–572; Elliot R. Wolfson, "Constructions of the Shekinah in the Messianic Theosophy of Abraham Cardoso," *Kabbalah* 3 (1998): 11–143.

that he [Sabbetai Zevi] bears much greater guilt than Jesus. The latter did not deny the Torah and the received tradition. The phrase "I am the Messiah" never passed his lips, and he never did anything against the tradition. Rather, his friends—and they were few in number—assisted him, while those who besmirched our law were the ones who said in his name things that he had not commanded. They were the ones who testified to his birth, his death and resurrection, and they were the ones who called him father, son, and holy-spirit. But this one [Sabbetai Zevi] denied the Torah and the tradition as is well known from his actions.[58]

Early modern Jewish intellectuals such as Leon Modena, Saul Levi Morteira, and later on Jacob Emden distinguished variously between Jesus and his later followers.[59] Some treated him as an errant Jew, others as a religious reformer whose message had been distorted. Morteira, and perhaps Modena as well, wrote about Jesus for recent conversos who had returned to Judaism. Sasportas, too, emphatically distinguished Jesus the law-abiding Jew from later Christians who broke the law in his name and deified him. But Sasportas praised Jesus only in order to denigrate the messianic pretensions of Sabbetai Zevi and to establish the supremacy of the law and the rabbinic tradition. If Sabbetai Zevi actually came off worse than Jesus, where did that leave Sabbatianism? Sasportas did not formulate a direct response, but his work leaves little doubt that the new movement was sectarian rather than merely misguided. In order to explain the implications of this interpretive move, one must trace Sasportas's usage of two phrases: "a new faith" and "a new Torah."[60]

[58] והמלצת האומות נבואת ישעיה נ"ג יותר מתקבלת על משיחם מעל זה המומר. והאמת הברור כי זה הרבה אשמה יותר מאש"ם ששי, ביען שהוא לא כפר בתורה ובקבלה, ולא יצא מפיו דבר לומר משיחא אנא וגם לא עשה מעשה נגד הקבלה, אך חבריו ואם מעטים הם היו בעוזריו ועוכרי דתנו הם המדברים על פיו מה שלא צוה, הם המעידים על לידתו הם המעידים על מיתתו ותחיתו, הם שקראו לו א"ב ב"ן ורו"ח. ואולם זה כפר בתורה ובקבלה כנודע ממעשיו.
Sasportas, *ZNZ*, 315.

[59] On Modena, see David Berger, "On the Uses of History in Medieval Jewish Polemic against Christianity: The Quest for the Historical Jesus," in *Persecution, Polemic, and Dialogue: Essays in Jewish-Christian Relations* (Boston: Academic Studies Press, 2010), 156–157; Talya Fishman, "Changing Early Modern Jewish Discourse about Christianity: The Efforts of Rabbi Leon Modena," in *The Lion Shall Roar*, ed. David Malkiel (Jerusalem: Magnes Press, 2003), 159–194; on Morteira, see above; for Emden, see below.

[60] Scholem, *Sabbatai Sevi*, 489, 717–718; Tishby, introduction (Hebrew) to Sasportas, *ZNZ*, 29–34 (Hebrew pagination); Goldish, *The Sabbatean Prophets*, 142–146; Maciejko, *The Mixed Multitude*, 41–47.

SABBATIANISM AS A NEW RELIGION

Sabbatianism constituted a fundamental break with Judaism, but Sasportas only gradually came to see Sabbatianism as a new faith. In his view its novelty represented a threat to the already-fragile normative structure of authority in Jewish settlements. The antinomianism preached and practiced by the Sabbatians—the transformation of traditional fast days into public holidays, the ritual sacrifice of animals beyond the bounds of the long-destroyed Temple in Jerusalem, the utterance of the divine name, the suspension of the Sabbath on Saturday, and the declaration of other days in the week as the Sabbath—and its accompanying messianic theology appeared to him as the basis of a new confession. When examining Sasportas's use of the terms "new faith" and "new Torah," one must keep an important qualification in mind. His recognition of Sabbatianism as a new faith did not come about immediately. Rather, it was the product of his thinking, reflecting, and writing about the events as they were reported in Hamburg over the course of approximately fifteen months. Only after considerable reflection did Sasportas label Sabbatianism a new confession. Sasportas recognized that religious ideas could generate new social formations. This may relate to his tacit understanding of Protestantism not as a revolt against the Catholic Church but as a new confession.

Sasportas signaled the importance of the Sabbatian *novum* in the short preface to *Zizath novel zvi* composed in 1669. At two critical junctures, he used the Hebrew word for novelty. The second paragraph of the book opens with a retrospective declaration:

> When these letters filled with deceit and vanity first began to arrive, I said to myself: I worry lest this wicked man of Sabbetai, may his memory be erased, wants to create a new Torah, as indeed his actions proved in the end.[61]

Toward the end of the preface, Sasportas attributed a statement to the recently deceased Joseph Escafa, a rabbi who had taught Sabbetai Zevi

---

[61] ומתחילה בבוא כתבים המכתבים עמל ואון אמרתי אני בלבי חוששני שמא זה הרשע של שבתאי יש"ו רצונו לעשות תורה חדשה כאשר הוכיח סוף מעשיו.
Sasportas, *ZNZ*, 1.

in his youth but who had not lived to see the full-fledged movement that emerged in 1665: "Whoever gets to him [Sabbetai Zevi] first shall attain merit, for in the future he shall cause many to sin and create a new faith."[62] If the sentiment was Escafa's, the precise formulation was probably Sasportas's. In the brief retrospective preface that framed his entire chronicle, Sasportas used two terms that he associated negatively with Sabbetai Zevi: "a new Torah" and "a new faith."

Beginning in the summer of 1666, shortly before Sabbetai Zevi's conversion, Sasportas began to fixate on the novelty of Sabbatianism. After he had learned of the suspended fast days and the repeated public violation of the law, Sasportas wrote to the rabbinate of Izmir and called them to account. He concludes with a revealing passage about the relationship between novelty and writing:

> Wherefore, when I saw the spread of this new faith that uprooted the edifices of the rabbis and paid no attention to them, and all the people hung themselves upon the trees of the great sages of Izmir and Constantinople, I said: This is not a time to be silent,[63] O Jacob, as they come to establish a new Torah. I shall pay no heed to anyone's anger, for his anger is not eternal, and if he, a rabbi, should get angry and Jacob should remain silent, O Torah, what shall become of you?[64]

Sasportas used the two terms—"a new Torah" and "a new faith"—almost interchangeably and described the threat of the new as the impetus for his own decision to speak out and champion the old law. In a phrase that echoed the biblical Mordecai's appeal to Esther on behalf of their coreligionists, Sasportas declared that he would not remain silent. He continued to ask a rhetorical question that appeared in the Babylonian Talmud attributed to Simeon bar Yohai. When confronted by a biblical verse that implied man should tend the fields in order to supply his daily needs, Simeon bar Yohai responded, "O Torah, what shall become of you?"[65] In invoking the same phrase, Sasportas fol-

---

[62]Ibid., 4. It is unclear whether this means to kill him or to silence him. On Escafa, see Jacob Barnai, "Rabbi Joseph Escafa and the Rabbinate in Izmir" (Hebrew), *Sefunot* 18 (1985): 53–81.

[63]After Es. 4:14.

[64]אי לזאת בראותי התפשטות האמונה החדשה העוקרת העוקרת בניני רז"ל בלתי השקיף לדבריהם ז"ל וכלם נתלים באילני רברבי חכמי איזמיר וקוסטנטינא אמרתי לא עת להחריש יעקב עד בואם להקים תורה חדשה, ולא אחוש לכעסו של כועס דאין כעסו כעס עולם ואם הרב כועס ויעקב שותק תורה מה תהא עליה.

Sasportas, *ZNZ*, 166.

[65]BT Berakhot, 35b.

lowed a medieval tradition that had turned Simeon bar Yohai's complaint about the mundane tasks of life that distract from the study of Torah into a clarion call for a response to crisis. Sasportas desperately tried to impress upon the rabbinate of Izmir the urgency of the situation. In order to do so, he invoked the novelty of the Sabbatians and their activities. Their newness was cause in and of itself to speak out against them.

At this stage, however, Sasportas had yet to connect the notion that Sabbatianism was a new faith with his analogy to ancient Christianity. What had been an occasional theme in the first half of the work emerged as a primary one in the second. Sasportas would eventually come to the conclusion that Nathan of Gaza and other Sabbatians had intended to create a new faith from the very moment that Sabbetai Zevi had been declared the Messiah:

> He [Nathan of Gaza] revealed himself: his intention from the beginning was only to lead Israel astray after these new gods and make a new Torah for them.[66]

This comment, which appears in a narrative portion of the text, finds an echo a few pages later when Sasportas learned that many Jews in Izmir planned not to fast on the ninth of Av the year following Sabbetai Zevi's conversion:

> This was even worse than the first, for it indicated that wickedness of the hearts of the masses, who chose new gods for themselves, and that they only wanted to make a new Torah for themselves and nothing else.[67]

In this instance, Nathan of Gaza was joined by the masses of Sabbatians in his intention to create a new Torah. Both passages appear in narrative portions rather than embedded within letters. These passages often appear in the first-person voice and form the connective tissue between the different letters that tell the history of the Sabbatian movement. Such passages were critical in the composition of *Zizath novel*

[66] וגילה דעתו כי כונתו מתחילה לא היתה כי אם להניא את ישראל אחרי הבעלים ולעשות להם תורה חדשה. Sasportas, *ZNZ*, 205.

[67] וזו קשה מן הראשונה המורה על רוע לב ההמון שבחרו להם אלקי"ם חדשים ולעשות תורה חדשה היה רצונם ולא לדבר אחר. Ibid., 207.

zvi. They provided introduction, commentary, and analysis of the letters that constitute the majority of the work. At the point of putting the work together, Sasportas hardened in his conviction that Sabbatianism was a new faith and sought to replace the Torah with a new one. What he had mentioned as a possible outcome in a number of letters in the first part had become a virtual certainty in the second. It had also become retroactively the express intention of the Sabbatians.

The formation of a new faith and a new Torah threatened the very core of Sasportas's worldview; the same could not be said if Sabbatianism was to be characterized as a mass delusion or an error. As he remarked in another passage without a direct addressee, "I worry lest this new faith shall stand against the words of the rabbis, of blessed memory."[68] The structure of Judaism, which in Sasportas's view was entirely coterminous with the received teachings of the rabbis, was at risk. In a letter to David Zarfati, whose father, Aaron, had been a believer in Amsterdam, Sasportas praised the steadfastness of the son and sought to underscore the severity of the threat: "You have done well in refusing to follow the foolishness with false and incorrect teachings against the Oral Torah, and [in refusing] to take up a new Torah that is not like the Jewish law."[69] This letter, written well after Sabbetai Zevi's conversion to Islam, made a crucial point that had been latent in Sasportas's earlier use of the term "new faith" but had remained unarticulated: Sabbatianism was a new religion that was unlike Judaism. In his description of the activities of the Sabbatian prophet Sabbetai Raphael, Sasportas attempted to draw the lines as clearly as possible: "If it had not been the Lord who was on our side (Ps. 124:1–2), they [the Sabbatians] would have led us astray from the ways of His Torah, and they would have brought us into their new Torah and covenant and 'would have caused us to fall into deep pits that we would not rise up again' (Ps. 140:11), heaven forfend."[70]

With the conversion of the Messiah to Islam, Sasportas repeatedly compared the followers of Sabbetai Zevi with the early followers of Jesus. For the purposes of his comparison, Sasportas turned entirely to early Christianity. This understanding of early Christianity seems to reflect a tacit conception of Protestantism as the formation of a new

[68] Ibid., 168.
[69] Ibid., 257.
[70] Ibid., 280.

confession. Sasportas pointedly ignored the specific mention of other religions in the contemporary world. Sabbetai Zevi's new religion, Islam, was, likewise, incidental to his polemic. Throughout *Zizath novel zvi* and throughout his responsa, Sasportas had little to say about Islam, ancient or modern, and seemed content to ignore it. This may have been a direct response to the development of Sabbatianism itself. In spite of its being the Messiah's new religion, Islam had had relatively little impact upon Sabbatian doctrine in the period between 1666 and 1680. By contrast, the Christian notions of a suffering Messiah and the necessity of faith served as axial nodes in Sabbatian theology in the immediate aftermath of Sabbetai Zevi's conversion.[71]

In *Zizath novel zvi* Sasportas provided an almost anthropological explanation of confessional formation within Judaism that can be read as a diagnosis of the confessional crisis in contemporary Europe.[72] Sasportas does not explicitly mention this process of confessionalization as a direct analogue, but throughout his long life he was an acute observer of contemporary religious difference. If one follows Sasportas in the places where he lived, one catches glimpses of a discerning observer who was attuned to the differences between eastern and western Sephardim, Ashkenazim and Sephardim, and Jews in the North and Jews in the South. Furthermore, in a responsum written nearly a quarter of a century after the peak of Sabbatian enthusiasm, Sasportas reflected on the difference between the Protestant North and the Catholic South. Sometime around the year 1690, Sasportas wrote to Isaac da Costa of Peyrehorade, one of the satellite settlements of former conversos in the orbit of Bayonne.[73] The legal issue concerned how to compel Jews to observe the Sabbath. In the final sentences of his opinion, Sasportas described the difference between

[71] Halperin, "The Son of the Messiah," 213. For possible Shiite influences, see Gershom Scholem, "The Crypto-Jewish Sect of the Dönmeh (Sabbatians) in Turkey," in *The Messianic Idea in Judaism and Other Essays on Jewish Spirituality* (New York: Schocken Books, 1971), 142–166, as cited by Halperin.

[72] Thomas A. Brady Jr., "Confessionalization: The Career of a Concept," in *Confessionalization in Europe, 1555–1700: Essays in Honor and Memory of Bodo Nischan*, ed. John M. Headley et al. (Aldershot, UK: Ashgate, 2004), 1–20; Benjamin J. Kaplan, *Divided by Faith: Religious Conflict and the Practice of Toleration in Early Modern Europe* (Cambridge, MA: Belknap Press of Harvard University Press, 2007); Daniel Jütte, "Interfaith Encounters between Jews and Christians in the Early Modern Period and Beyond: Toward a Framework," *AHR* 118 (2013): 393.

[73] Gérard Nahon, *Les "Nations" Juives Portugaises du Sud-Oest de la France (1684–1791): Documents* (Paris: Fundãço Calouste Gulbenkian Centro Cultural Portugês, 1981), 271–281.

Amsterdam, the city in which he wrote, and Peyrehorade, the town that he addressed:

> Let the left hand always push away while the right hand draws closer. Because in that place [Peyrehorade] the people who rule over it are our genuine enemies; unlike in this place [Amsterdam] with its rulers, where everyone is equal and judged on the same equal scale.[74]

The confessional divide of Christian Europe did not map onto the confessional crisis generated by Sabbatianism in a precise one-to-one formulation. In Sasportas's depiction, Sabbetai Zevi and Nathan of Gaza did not serve as some form of Jewish Protestants or as Jewish Jesuits. Nor did Sasportas himself serve as a direct analogue to Martin Luther or Ignatius of Loyola. In his thinking, he demonstrated filiations both with Luther, who demanded that the clergy assert itself against the populace, and with Catholic reformers, who spoke in the name of a tradition they upheld as unchanging. Rather, the fact that Sasportas lived in an age, the middle of the seventeenth century, and a series of places, the urban centers of northern Europe, deeply enmeshed in a long crisis of confessionalization made him attuned to a basic question to which he might otherwise have been relatively oblivious. In his analysis of Sabbatianism, Sasportas looked at how a religion came into being and how a confession formed.

In Sasportas's understanding, early Christianity introduced a new faith with a new Torah that was categorically different from Judaism; so too, Sabbatianism was a new faith with a new Torah and therefore categorically different from Judaism. In a narrative passage that responded to Nathan of Gaza's letter to Sabbetai Zevi's brothers, Sasportas made the analogy in a pointed formulation: "He [Nathan of Gaza] knew that people were seduced by him, and he wanted to create a new faith greater than the faith of Jesus the Nazarene."[75] Sasportas's concern about the newness of Sabbatianism and its analogous relationship to early Christianity fell largely on deaf ears.[76] Partisans of the movement saw Sabbatianism as the fulfillment of the messianic

---

[74] ולעולם תהא שמאל דוחה וימין מקרבת כי המקום ההוא והאנשים המושלים בו הם אויבנו בעצם לא כמקום הזה ומושליו שכולם שוים ונתקלים בפלס שוה.

Ohel ya-akov, #63, 69b.

[75] Sasportas, *ZNZ*, 202.

[76] Maciejko, *The Mixed Multitude*, 46.

promise held out in scripture and in rabbinic literature, while other skeptics dismissed the Messiah as a misguided or an errant Jew. Joseph Halevi was the significant exception.[77] In a letter to Sasportas, Halevi echoed the words of his correspondent nearly verbatim:

> It seems to me that this is the beginning of Epicureanism in Israel and the foundation of a new Torah and a new faith as that which arose in the days of that man [Jesus].[78]

Like Sasportas, Halevi used the word "Epicureanism" in the context of Christianity. It implied the Christian belief in Divine Grace, with its attendant rejection of reward and punishment, enabled by the redemptive death of Jesus. For Sasportas and Halevi, the movement that had coalesced around Sabbetai Zevi was a radical departure from Judaism, embodied in the law. Why, Sasportas asked Ibn Sa-adun, "did you want to make a name for yourself in propagating a new faith that stood between the Sadducees and the Christians?"[79] Sabbatianism, like Christianity, was extra-Talmudic and therefore beyond the boundaries of Judaism.

In the period following the Messiah's conversion to Islam, a number of Sabbatians themselves used one of the terms invoked by Sasportas, referring to their teaching as a new Torah. Beginning with Sabbetai Zevi himself, Sabbatians referred to the postconversion movement as having a new scripture or as having bequeathed to the Jewish people a new Torah. In a Ladino letter written shortly after his conversion, Sabbetai Zevi wrote that he intended to "bring to the people, if it were not the people of Ishmael, a New Testament."[80] In this letter "the people" appeared to refer to those among his followers who had remained Jews. The phrase *ketubah hadashah*, rendered as "a New Testament," appeared in Hebrew in the Ladino letter. Sabbetai Zevi's use of the word *ketubah* may have been similar to the Arabic *kitab*, a word that encompasses sacred scripture such as Torah or Quran.[81] Building upon

---

[77] Scholem, *Sabbatai Sevi*, 717–718.

[78] וכמדומה לי שזאת תחילת אפיקורסות בישראל ויסוד לתורה חדשה ואמונה אחרת כמו שאירע בימי אותו האיש. Sasportas, *ZNZ*, 256.

[79] Ibid., 357.

[80] Abraham Amarillo, "Sabbatian Documents from the Collection of Rabbi Saul Amarillo" (Hebrew), *Sefunot* 5 (1961): 266–267.

[81] Yehuda Liebes, "The Attitude of Sabbetai Zevi to His Conversion" (Hebrew), in *Sod ha-emunah ha-shabtait* (Jerusalem: Bialik Institute, 1995), 21n36.

this observation, one can posit that *ketubah* explicitly violates the received character of the law. With his rabbinic cast of mind, Sasportas resisted the idea of a written text. Writing was reserved for the divine, not for the "testament" of an individual such as Sabbetai Zevi.

On at least two occasions, Nathan of Gaza referred to Sabbetai Zevi as giving a new Torah. Nathan of Gaza appended a note to a collection of his works that Scholem tentatively dated to after Sabbetai Zevi's conversion. The note described events that were alleged to have taken place in 1658, several years before Sabbetai Zevi's public revelation as the Messiah but around the time he had been declared the Messiah by his closest followers. Referring to Sabbetai Zevi, Nathan of Gaza wrote:

> To him the Holy One, blessed be He, shall give a new Torah and new commandments to repair the worlds. In 1658 he shall bless that which is forbidden.[82]

If Sabbetai Zevi had used a phrase similar to the terms for "a new scripture," Nathan of Gaza used the very same term as Sasportas: a new Torah. In a passage from *The Book of Creation*, his theological magnum opus, Nathan of Gaza discussed the hidden secret of the manna that descended from heaven to feed the people of Israel in the desert. Drawing on the Babylonian Talmud, Nathan of Gaza wrote, "The secret of the manna swallowed up by the limbs is the secret of the new Torah which he [the Messiah] shall teach us."[83] Nathan of Gaza was almost certainly unaware of *Zizath novel zvi*. Nevertheless, the most important Sabbatian thinker, Nathan of Gaza, and the most important critic of the movement, Sasportas, came to use the very same term independently of one another in the period following Sabbetai Zevi's conversion. Both the prophet and the sage described Sabbatianism as bearing "a new Torah." The common sources in rabbinic literature of the phrase "a new Torah" with its antinomian connotations were readily available to both.

A number of other Sabbatians used the term as well. The phrase "a new Torah" had appeared in a number of rabbinic sources in an explic-

---

[82] ואליו יתן הקב"ה תורה חדשה ומצוות חדשות לתקן כל העולמות בשנת התי"ח יברך מתיר אסורים.

"New Sabbatian Documents from the Book *To-ei Ruah*," in Scholem, *Mehkere shabtat*, 40; "A Commentary to the Psalms from the Circle of Sabbetai Zevi in Adrianople" (Hebrew), in Scholem, *Mehkere shabtaut*, 95.

[83] Liebes, "The Attitude of Sabbetai Zevi to His Conversion," 21n69. As Liebes indicated, the teachings of Jesus had similarly been compared to the manna from heaven. See John 6:49.

itly messianic context, and the Sabbatians sought to mobilize these passages to their full effect after Sabbetai Zevi's conversion. In 1668 a letter entitled "Epistle of the Shield of Abraham from the Maghreb" directly confronted the question of Sabbetai Zevi's apostasy. Liebes has posited one of Nathan of Gaza's students, Abraham Perez, as the most likely author of this letter.[84] Perez invoked the phrase "a new Torah" in a somewhat different fashion from Sabbetai Zevi or his teacher Nathan of Gaza. Perez adduced passages from rabbinic literature with the phrase in order to buttress his support of Sabbetai Zevi after his conversion. He cited a portion of the Midrash in Leviticus Rabbah, as well as an anthology of Midrash entitled *Yalkut shimoni.* With reference to a verse in Isaiah, the Midrash stated:

> The Holy One, blessed be He, sits and expounds a new Torah, which he shall give in the future through the King Messiah.[85]

This contained a description of the messianic age directly applicable to contemporary events. Perez argued that Sabbetai Zevi and his antinomian behavior simply fulfilled the rabbinic promise of the messianic age as outlined in *Yalkut shimoni* on Isaiah. In the Midrash, "the new Torah" referred exclusively to interpretation rather than to a written work. In order to make his case, Perez was forced to undermine the spirit of rabbinic exegesis and the implicit resistance to writing that the Midrash had taken for granted.

Sabbatians continued to refer to the teachings of Sabbetai Zevi as "a new Torah." With Sabbetai Zevi's death in 1676, the movement faced a new series of challenges to account for the death of the alleged Messiah. Around a decade after Perez's letter, Israel Hazzan composed a commentary on the Sabbatian liturgy for the midnight vigil.[86] A ritual associated with the Safed kabbalists, the midnight vigil took on a central place in Sabbatian practice. Sabbetai Zevi himself had rewritten

---

[84] The text appears as "The Letter of the Shield of Abraham from the Land of the West, Written Apparently by Abraham Miguel Cardoso" (Hebrew), in Scholem, *Mehkere shabtaut,* 142–179. Hereafter, "Shield of Abraham." On the authorship of the letter, see the appendix by Liebes, 179–181.

[85] והקב"ה יושב ודורש תורה חדשה שעתיד ליתן ע"י מה"מ.

"Shield of Abraham," 169. For the passage in the Midrash, see *Sefer ha-yalqut: helek sheni* (Livorno, 1650) 79b–80a.

[86] Scholem, "A Commentary to the Psalms," 89–138; on its character as a commentary on the midnight vigil, see Halperin, "The Son of the Messiah." Scholem dated the text to 1678 or 1679, a judgment with which Halperin seems to agree: "It cannot be earlier than 1677, or later than 1680" (152).

and transformed the liturgy of the vigil, and one of his followers had taken up the task to transform the text yet again after his death. Israel Hazzan developed a contrast between the "Torah of grace" and the "Torah of truth" as taught by Sabbetai Zevi in the years between his conversion and his death. Hazzan applied the term "Torah of grace" to Islam—presumably because the conversion mitigated the death sentence imposed on Sabbetai Zevi by the law—and the "Torah of truth" to Judaism, seemingly a reference to the reward and punishment mandated by Jewish law.[87] In his eschatological schema Hazzan predicted that this religious syncretism, by God's grace, would ultimately culminate in the resurrection of Sabbetai Zevi from the dead. Here too Hazzan argued for something strikingly similar to the Christian account of death and resurrection through God's grace. In the period of the final redemption, Sabbetai Zevi would reveal his ultimate teaching, "The secrets of the new Torah, which the Holy One, blessed be He, shall teach to his people Israel, they have all been revealed to *Amirah*."[88] Repeatedly Hazzan described Sabbetai Zevi's final teachings as "a new Torah."[89] The phrase became so widespread in Sabbatian literature that it even appeared in a Sabbatian poem.[90]

Sasportas and the Sabbatians were in complete agreement that they were witnessing something radically new, but differed on how to interpret this fact. For the Sabbatians, beginning with Sabbetai Zevi himself, continuing with his primary prophet, Nathan of Gaza, and extending after the death of the Messiah to an unknown follower named Israel Hazzan, the new Torah of Sabbetai Zevi fulfilled the messianic promise held out by the biblical prophets and discussed by the rabbis in antiquity. The Sabbatians clung to the rabbinic precedent of "a new Torah," which they could stretch with their exegetical imagination to include even the most radical interpretation of the Torah. They did not think of themselves as inventing a new confession and avoided using the term for faith. The Sabbatians sought to turn popular belief into a new

[87] Scholem, "A Commentary to the Psalms," 115; Halperin, "The Son of the Messiah," 181, 185.

[88] Scholem, "A Commentary to the Psalms," 118. *Amirah* served as the standard designation for Sabbetai Zevi. It comprised the initials for the Hebrew phrase *adonenu meshihenu yarum hodo*, "Our Lord and Messiah, may his majesty be exalted." See Halperin, "The Son of the Messiah," 154n38.

[89] Scholem, "A Commentary to the Psalms," 124, 127, 134; Liebes, "The Attitude of Sabbetai Zevi to His Conversion," 20n67.

[90] Moshe Attias and Gershom Scholem, *Shirot ve-tishbahot shel ha-Shabetaim* (Tel Aviv: Dvir, 1947), 128, as cited by Scholem, "A Commentary to the Psalms," 118n90.

doctrine but not into a new religion. To Sasportas, by contrast, the new Torah of Sabbatianism was analogous to Christianity. He did think of the Sabbatians as a new confession, and hence repeatedly used the term "a new faith." This term referred to a creed rather than to an interpretive activity. Sasportas was thus something of a conservative radical: he rejected the religion of the people in the name of an ancient law.

The analogy between Sabbatianism and Christianity had two significant consequences for Sasportas: one in terms of contemporary relations between Jews and gentiles and another in terms of his attitude toward the law. Sasportas feared that contemporary Christians would point to the antinomian practices of the Sabbatians in their attempt to convert Jews to Christianity. Concern about the prospects for mass conversion pulsed throughout *Zizath novel zvi*. In a passing reference to Nathan of Gaza's father, Elisha Ashkenazi, Sasportas contemptuously referred to one of Elisha Askenazi's colleagues who had converted. At a relatively early stage in the Sabbatian movement, Sasportas recounted that a schoolteacher from Amsterdam named Shalom b. Joseph had reported meeting Elisha Ashkenazi in Livorno on his way to Palestine. Sasportas emphasized that his colleague had left Amsterdam for the Holy Land before the public declaration of Sabbetai Zevi as the Messiah. He used this occasion to recount his own acquaintance with Elisha Ashkenazi a few years earlier:

> But I, the humblest of my clan (Jud. 6:15), when I was in Saleh, hosted Elisha. I sent him on his way to Algiers, and I arrived in Amsterdam with my entire household owing to the wars and famines. But he stayed in Algiers and then returned here to Amsterdam and Hamburg, where he lost all the money he had collected as an emissary. This happened because his friend Solomon Navarro, who had been a sage, a kabbalist, and a pietist, fell in love with a gentile woman when he arrived in Reggio, Italy. He married her and converted, may his name and memory be erased.[91]

These events had taken place before the Sabbatian movement had begun, but Sasportas recounted them through the filter of the more re-

---

[91] ואני הדל באלפי בהיותי בעיר סאלי נתאכסן אצלי ושלחתיו לעיר ארגיל ובאתי אני לאמשטרדאם עם כל בני ביתי מחמת המלחמות והרעב. ונתעכב שם בארגיל וחזר לכאן לאמשטרדאם והאמבורגו והפסיד כל הממון השליחות, ביען שחברו שלמה נאבארו שהיה חכם ומקובל וחסיד בבואו לעיר ריג'ו באיטליא שם חשק גויה אחת ונשאה והמיר דתו יש"ו.

Sasportas, *ZNZ*, 136.

cent past. The anecdote about Elisha Ashkenazi demonstrates the circumscribed rabbinic world of the Sephardic Diaspora in the middle of the seventeenth century. Sasportas had served as Elisha Ashkenazi's host during his time in Saleh, and dispatched him, possibly with his recommendation in hand, all the way to Algiers. He used this personal connection to cast aspersions on his character. Elisha Ashkenazi had consorted with a suspicious figure named Solomon Navarro.[92] Although Sasportas designated him as a sage, a kabbalist, and a pietist, which was seemingly the trifecta of Jewish spiritual attainment, Navarro had been attracted to a trinity of an altogether different sort. He followed his lover into Catholicism, and in the process caused Elisha Ashkenazi to squander the money he had raised as an emissary. Once the Sabbatian movement had begun, Sasportas narrated all of this as if the descent of the son followed inevitably from the bad reputation of the father.

In the summer of 1666, before he had heard about the suspension of the fast on the ninth of Av, Sasportas raised the specter of Sabbatian practices leading to a schism: "I said this is not the time to be silent, Jacob, when they have come to erect a new Torah."[93] A few lines later in this letter to the rabbinate in Izmir, he spelled out the potential outcome of this new Torah.

> This is mostly jealousy, rivalry, and hatred, all in the name of hatred for the law. As we have seen, this one calls his colleague a heretic, and his colleague counters with the same. But I worry about conversion from our law or, at the very least, denial of the essential belief in the coming of the Messiah by way of saying there is no [future] Messiah among the Jews, for he has already been delivered [lit. consumed, after BT San. 99a] in the days of the prophecy from Gaza. This would strengthen the belief of the Christians who claim that their Messiah has already come.[94]

Confronted by the possibility of an open schism within the Jewish world, where opposing parties designated each other as heretics, Sasportas went out on a limb and cast out the Sabbatians. According to

---

[92] On Elisha Ashkenazi and Solomon Navarro, see Scholem, *Sabbatai Sevi*, 75–77 and passim.
[93] Sasportas, *ZNZ*, 166.
[94] ורוב קנאה ותחרות ושנאה בשנאת הדת כאשר ראינו זה קורא כופר לחברו וזה אומר אדרבא, וירא אנכי מהמרת דתנו לפחות מכפירה בעיקר ביאת המשיח לומר דאין משיח בישראל שכבר אכלוהו בימי נבואת עזה ותתחזק אמונת הנוצרים לומר שכבר בא משיחם.

Ibid., 166–167.

Sasportas, Sabbetai Zevi placed the entirety of the Jewish messianic idea at risk, and thereby undermined the fundamental confessional distinction between Jews and Christians. Furthermore, the new Torah Sabbetai Zevi had given to his followers provided an opening for the Christian mission to the Jews. If Jewish contemporaries could believe in a Messiah named Sabbetai Zevi, Sasportas reasoned, what was to stop them believing in a Messiah named Jesus? Sasportas was not the only opponent of Sabbatianism who expressed such a fear: Isaac Cardoso adopted a similar stance. But in this respect, Sasportas's fear was particularly prescient and articulated at a particularly early juncture of the movement. Sabbetai Zevi's conversion to Islam appears to have led a number of believing Sabbatians to convert to Christianity. A French gazette entitled *Muse de la Cour* reported in December 1666 that Jesuit missionaries had baptized over a thousand Jews after Sabbetai Zevi's conversion to Islam. Scholem dismissed the report as "an obvious journalistic canard," although Isaiah Sonne cautioned that this dismissal was somewhat cavalier.[95] Nonetheless, both seem to agree that some Sabbatians did convert to Christianity, with the dispute concerning only the number of converts, not whether or not some sort of collective conversion actually occurred.

The analogy between Sabbatianism and Christianity led Sasportas to a second, more substantive conclusion, over and above his fear of the Christian mission to the Jews. By virtue of the fact that Sasportas had defined Sabbatianism as a new faith and beyond the pale of Jewishness, any novelty associated with Sabbatianism that had been accepted by practicing Jews had to be renounced. A call against the Sabbatians was potentially an uncompromising stand against all forms of popular religion. This theoretical position came to a head when the Jews of Amsterdam appealed to Sasportas for his advice about the public recitation of the priestly blessing on the Sabbath. From the perspective of Jewish law, Jews should recite the priestly blessing every Sabbath in normal times. But these were not normal times. Because the Jews of Amsterdam had changed their practice, which had been less than ideal, to the ideal practice under the aegis of their belief in Sabbetai Zevi as the Messiah, they should discontinue it and return to their former ways. Sasportas then elevated this to the level of principle:

[95] Scholem, *Sabbatai Sevi*, 757; Sonne, "Sabbatian Issues," 54.

In their wickedness they are greater than Jeroboam because they seek to uproot our Torah and the words of our sages in order to make a new Torah, which we can now see from the outcome of their deeds that offer proof about their beginnings. On account of this and in order that their memory shall not be recalled to any man, and all the more so before God, any positive thing that was invented by them or on account of them should be nullified, and all of their books are the books of heretics and worthy of being burned.[96]

If the Jews of Amsterdam genuinely wanted to change their custom to the weekly recitation of the priestly blessing, Sasportas advised them to wait for a time, long enough that no one could associate the practice with the Sabbatians, and then reinstitute the practice. The weekly recitation of the priestly blessing, or for that matter anything new that was associated with the Sabbatians, even if it were consistent with Jewish convention, should be nullified on principle. Custom was transformed into ideology. Ideology granted the learned Talmudic elite considerably more authority.

Sabbatianism had constituted a profound rupture in the course of time, and Sasportas wanted to elevate what remained of rabbinic authority. He may have begun to redefine the scope of rabbinic authority precisely through his confrontation with Sabbatianism. In one specific sense, Sasportas and the Sabbatians agreed with one another: the events of 1665–1666 differed decisively from any previous dispute. The Sabbatians concluded from this difference that the law was now suspended and authority vested in charismatic prophets. To Sasportas, this had led to the creation of a new faith and a new Torah that undermined the law. But Sasportas seems to have drawn one further conclusion from this. In the midst of his correspondence with the Jews of Amsterdam about the recitation of the priestly blessing, he wrote:

And nevertheless I am not inclined to invent anything at this time.[97]

This statement appeared within a discussion about the priestly blessing; without too much exegetical strain, it may be taken as emblematic

---

[96] וגדולים הם ברשעתם מירבעם המבקשים לעקור תורתנו ודברי חכמינו כדי לעשות תורה חדשה כנראה מתחילת מעשיהם שסופם הוכיח עליהם. אשר על זה לכדי שלא יעלה על לב אנוש זכרונם וכל שכן טובה לפני ה', כל דבר טוב המתחדש על ידם ובסבתם יהיה מתבטל וכל ספריהם ספרי מיני מינין וראויים לשרפה.
Sasportas, *ZNZ*, 213.

[97] ואפילו הכי אין דעתי לחדש שום דבר כעת הזה.
Ibid., 220.

of Sasportas's overall stance in the years immediately following Sabbetai Zevi's conversion to Islam. Sasportas was not opposed to innovation as such. He was opposed to innovation at this time. All innovation associated with Sabbatianism, no matter how positive, merited opprobrium. If the Sabbatians were analogous to the early followers of Jesus, Sasportas himself may have been analogous to the rabbis of antiquity. According to some scholars, the rabbis of antiquity emerged from a crisis of authority ideologically empowered by their confrontation with Christianity.[98] Similarly, Sasportas emerged from his confrontation with Sabbatianism with considerable polemical resources.

Much of Sasportas's resistance to Sabbatianism hinged upon its claims to novelty. In his statements about the new faith, one can see the formation of a habit of mind that would come to characterize several (but by no means all) rabbinic figures in succeeding centuries. This attitude opposed novelty for its own sake. One need not suggest that Moses Sofer (d. 1839), whose dictum was "Novelty is forbidden by the Torah," read Sasportas on Sabbatianism.[99] Sofer celebrated innovation in Talmudic commentary and in the study of Torah, and thus offers an instructive parallel to Sasportas.[100] The positive evaluation of *hiddush*, a word roughly translated as interpretive innovation, did not correlate or translate into a positive attitude toward innovative social practices. *Hiddush* in the study of the Talmud was not the same thing as *hadash*, the Hebrew word for new, in matters of confession. Quite the opposite. What was true for Sofer in the early nineteenth century was true for Sasportas in the middle of the seventeenth. As his rabbinic responsa indicate, Sasportas valued interpretative Talmudic innovation.[101] His attitude toward the new in religion, however, was another matter entirely. Talmudic *hiddush* underwrote the learned resistance toward *hadash*; the assertion of mastery over the text kept the "multitude" away from religion and protected the integrity of the law.

[98] Schwartz, *Imperialism and Jewish Society*; Hayim Lapin, *Rabbis as Romans: The Rabbinic Movement in Palestine, 100–400 CE* (New York: Oxford University Press, 2012).

[99] On Moses Sofer, see Jacob Katz, "Towards a Biography of the Hatam Sofer," in *Divine Law in Human Hands: Case Studies in Halakhic Flexibility* (Jerusalem: Magnes Press, 1998), 403–443; for Sofer on Sabbatianism, see 418; Maoz Kahana, "The Hatam Sofer: The Authority in His Own Eyes" (Hebrew), *Tarbiz* 76 (2007): 519–556.

[100] Maoz Kahana, "How Did the Hatam Sofer Seek to Trump Spinoza? Text, Hermeneutics and Romanticism in the Writings of R. Moses Sofer" (Hebrew), *Tarbiz* 79 (2011): 557–585, especially 569–575.

[101] Sasportas, *Ohel ya-akov*, #3, 6a.

What then did Sasportas propose as an alternative? Sasportas was not a systematic thinker who laid out his defense of rabbinic Judaism in a well-organized apologia like his contemporaries Isaac Cardoso and Isaac Orobio de Castro. The nature of his written corpus, including his rabbinic responsa and especially *Zizath novel zvi* itself, was reactive in the literal sense of the term. Sasportas wrote in response to legal problems posed by a colleagues or to letters that brought news about the Sabbatian movement. Nevertheless, a number of comments scattered throughout *Zizath novel zvi* offer some indication that his preference was to continue to live within the norms laid out by rabbinic Judaism. In terms of conduct, this meant scrupulous adherence to the law. In terms of messianic aspirations, this meant endless deferral. Or, as he wrote to Raphael Supino in Livorno,

> But intellectuals understand that the word of God shall come to the world at the moment He wants, in the place that He wants, and through the person that He wants, not by means of a vacuous liar.[102]

In short, Sasportas had a passion for waiting.[103]

Sasportas was acutely aware of the new and sought desperately to preserve the old. His near-obsessive focus on novelty as such was itself novel, as was the form in which he expressed it. *Zizath novel zvi* marks a generic innovation in the history of Jewish writing. Beyond Sasportas this had two consequences: one for genre and another for the history of ideas. *Zizath novel zvi* set the template for much (but not all) of rabbinic controversy into the modern period. Collections of letters had been used to record rabbinic disputes, particularly over Maimonides, since the Middle Ages. The editing and preservation of documents, combined with a strong and forceful narrative by and about the editor himself, mark a point of departure in the genre. Jacob Emden in a number of his writings followed this template in his pursuit of alleged Sabbatians in the eighteenth century. The letter and the epistolary collection were a standard vehicle for controversy throughout the Haskalah. For the history of ideas, Sasportas's description of Sabbatian-

---

102 והמשכילים יבינו כי דבר אלקי״נו יקום לעולם בעת שיחפוץ במקום שיחפוץ עלי ידי איש שיחפוץ לא איש הולך רוח ושקר.

Sasportas, *ZNZ*, 88.
103 Wieseltier, "A Passion for Waiting."

ism as a new faith and a new religion would prove central to the intellectual framework developed by the greatest student of Sabbatianism, Scholem. Scholem's attitude toward Sasportas combined all the ecstatic rigors of his critical and historical scholarship with a deep ambivalence about rabbinic Judaism in general and Sasportas in particular.

SIX

❧

AFTERMATH

"When I use a word," Humpty Dumpty said, in rather a scornful tone, "it means just what I choose it to mean—neither more nor less."

"The question is," said Alice, "whether you can make words mean so many different things."

"The question is," said Humpty Dumpty, "who is to be master—that's all."

—Lewis Carroll

Figure 15. Text of agreement with Sasportas signature, Hamburg, 1669. Sasportas's signature appears alongside that of Moses Israel as one of the two rabbis of the Portuguese Nation in Hamburg. Staatsarchiv Hamburg, 522-1 Jüdische Gemeinden, 993, II *Verträge zwischen den deutsch-jüdischen gemeinden in Hamburg und Altona*, 1669, 9 Adar II, 429

SABBETAI ZEVI AND THE MESSIANIC MOVEMENT that coalesced around him afforded Sasportas the opportunity to formulate the fundamental tenets of his worldview. His insistence on textual authority as a means to restore social discipline, his indictment of the Sephardic rabbinic elite for their abandonment of their training and embrace of the crowd, his parallel between the early followers of Jesus and the followers of Sabbetai Zevi, and his grasp that the declaration of a Messiah posed a profound and probably irresolvable epistemological problem appeared in the written form of *Zizath novel zvi* as a response to an emergent social crisis. In this respect, Sabbetai Zevi was much the making of Sasportas. Sabbetai Zevi converted to Islam in the fall of 1666. Over the next century and a half, the movement that had gathered around him remained a vital and often divisive force in Jewish life. *Zizath novel zvi* as a printed book in an abbreviated version played a role in one of the most acrimonious Jewish disputes in the eighteenth century. Jacob Emden transformed Sasportas into his intellectual ancestor in his controversy with Jonathan Eibeschütz, as will emerge in the next chapter. While *Kitzur zizath novel zvi* served as a principal text in one of the great eighteenth-century Sabbatian controversies, Sabbatianism would not remain a crucial issue for Jacob Sasportas in the last third of his life. Sasportas lived for over thirty years after Sabbetai Zevi converted to Islam; with few exceptions, he did not remain preoccupied with Sabbetai Zevi and Sabbatianism.

The relative insignificance Sabbatianism held for Sasportas in the last third of his life releases two insights about his own historical significance. The first has to do with the received image of Sasportas, the second with changes in seventeenth-century Jewish society. Rather than a heresy hunter in the mold of Moses Hagiz or Jacob Emden, Sasportas should be seen as a dissident who objected to the prevailing opinion of his time. Simply put, Sasportas did not pursue real or imagined followers of Sabbetai Zevi in an effort to purge Jewish life of all vestigial traces of Sabbatianism; he confronted other issues that he deemed more pressing. He did not attempt to organize a large coalition of rabbis against people he perceived as heretics, as Hagiz would do in the case of Moses Hayim Luzzatto in the early eighteenth century. Nor did he seek to decipher the writings of his contemporaries for veiled allusions to Sabbetai Zevi in an effort to unmask their clandestine deviance, as Emden would do with amulets written by Eibeschütz. What is more, Sasportas's attitude toward one persistent believer seems to have been quite tolerant. In the case of the Spanish writer Miguel de Barrios, Sasportas took great care to look out for his welfare and that of his family rather than censure him for his persistent belief in Sabbetai Zevi after the Messiah's conversion. When De Barrios had withdrawn from the world and refused to eat as part of his insistence that he had received a vision of Sabbetai Zevi as the Messiah, Sasportas wrote a sentence that could not have been written by Hagiz or by Emden:

> If he [Miguel de Barrios] wants to believe that Sabbetai Zevi is the Messiah, let him believe, but he should not cease striving to provide food for his children.[1]

Once the overwhelming majority of Jews had recanted their belief in Sabbetai Zevi, Sasportas concerned himself with the welfare of his friend rather than with his friend's ideological purity. In the last third of his life, Sasportas was deeply concerned with the problem of rabbinic authority but rarely wrote about Sabbetai Zevi or Sabbatianism; by contrast, for Emden, the problem of rabbinic authority was coterminous with the problem of vestigial Sabbatianism. As a result, Emden fashioned Sasportas into a zealot through his new edition of *Kitzur zizath novel zvi.*

---

[1] ואם רצונו להאמין ששבתאי צבי משיח יאמין אבל לא יחדל מלהשתדל לבקש מחית בניו

Sasportas, ZNZ, 364–365. Epigraph from Lewis Carroll, *Through the Looking Glass*, chap. 6.

Emden was no fool, and there is a certain truth to his depiction of Sasportas as a zealot. Emden was no historian either, and his focus on this aspect of Sasportas elides a basic and unstated point about the place of Sabbetai Zevi and Sabbatianism in Sasportas's world. Without the occasion provided by a mass messianic movement, Sasportas would not have amounted to much more than a bibliographic curiosity. He would have joined the ranks of the peripatetic, learned, and disillusioned Sephardic rabbinate who appear throughout the annals of early modern Hebrew printing. Sabbetai Zevi and the Sabbatian movement provided Sasportas with the conditions of possibility to compose a book that both documented the course of events and articulated a viewpoint. Once articulated, however, many of the tenets Sasportas had expressed in an incisive formulation in response to Sabbetai Zevi reappeared in his other writings and in other writings about him. For Sasportas, the world of rabbinic learning was the point of departure for his thought. He approached Sabbetai Zevi and the question of his messianism from the point of view of rabbinic law. The problem of rabbinic authority, and ancillary issues such as honor, respect, and jurisdiction, surfaced repeatedly in *Zizath novel zvi*. In the last three decades of his life, these problems would persist. The themes of rabbinic authority and jurisdiction run like red threads through Sasportas's writing composed during the remainder of his stay in Hamburg, his second prolonged stay in Amsterdam, his relatively brief tenure in Livorno, and the last eighteen years of his life during his third and final period in Amsterdam.

This chapter follows a rough chronological order. The first section surveys Sasportas's time in Hamburg, where he lived after the Sabbatian controversy had died down, and Amsterdam, where he lived for a second extended interval between 1671 and 1678. The second covers Sasportas's relatively brief residence in Livorno from 1678 to 1680, where he initially experienced a seemingly welcome change of scenery; his stay was truncated, however, by a bitter dispute with the lay oligarchs that resulted in his hasty departure. The third treats Sasportas as a writer of approbations to Hebrew books. It focuses largely but not entirely on his third and final stay in Amsterdam, from 1681 until his death in 1698. The fourth recounts his final years in Amsterdam, where he first served as the head of the Ets Haim Yeshiva and later as chief rabbi of the Portuguese Jews. It concludes with his death and the dispersal of his estate in 1698. The chapter draws on some sources that have long been known to scholars, as well as others that are newly discussed. Throughout one can sense Sasportas plagued by the problems of authority and order. In this respect, Sasportas serves as an eloquent witness to changes in the Sephardic Diaspora at the end of the seventeenth century, a world whose principal urban centers continued to be linked by familial and commercial networks, whose congregations were increasingly affected by prolonged contact with Ashkenazi Jews, and where rabbis fought a persistent battle for authority with a powerful lay leadership.

HAMBURG 1666–1671

Sasportas continued to live in Hamburg for several years after the conversion of Sabbetai Zevi. In the years between 1666 and 1671, when he departed for Amsterdam, he served as judge alongside Moses Israel who was the official rabbi of the Sephardic Jews. The record book of the Sephardic Jews often refers to Sasportas and Moses Israel collectively as *hahamim*, the plural of *haham*.[2] Several responsa that date from Sasportas's period in Hamburg bear their joint signatures. During his residence in Hamburg, the Portuguese Jews of Amsterdam continued to support Sasportas financially.[3] Early on during his stay the local *maamad* sent a measure of wood to the Sasportas home, which may suggest that the Hamburg Sephardim supported him as well.[4] In his capacity as a member of the Sephardic rabbinic court in Hamburg, Sasportas appears to have achieved a certain level of stability and security.

During the years 1667 and 1668, Sasportas participated as a judge in a legal dispute between the Ashkenazi communities of Altona and

---

[2] SAH, Jüdische Gemeinden, 993/I, 371, 375, 403, 435, 436, 453, 457. I am grateful to Hugo Martins for his help in deciphering these records. The protocol books has two sets of numbers; I have followed the pagination in pencil.

[3] SAA, entry no. 334, no. 174, p. 733, 21 Tebet 5426. "A mandej pagar ao H. Sasportas em Hamb." I owe this reference to the kindness of Dr. Tirtsah Levie Bernfeld. On the phenomenon of people who had left Amsterdam receiving poor relief abroad, see Levie Bernfeld, *Poverty and Welfare*, 89.

[4] SAH, Jüdische Gemeinden, 993/I, 305: "Em 26 ditto [Tebet] constando ao maamad padese necessecidade o H. Sasportas se lhe mandou 2 brasadas de lenha serrada e partida posta nesse dia."

Wandsbek, towns that neighbored Hamburg but that fell under the sovereignty of the Danish crown.[5] The evidence for his involvement appears in a series of responsa in *Ohel ya-akov*. Responsa 21 through 24 convey the ambiguity of Sasportas's position in Hamburg after the conversion of Sabbetai Zevi. In texts written within a relatively short period of time, Sasportas appears both as a judge with extraordinary authority and as a cantankerous old man subject to the scorn of a younger colleague.

In 1667 a dispute broke out between the Ashkenazim of Altona and the Ashkenazim of Wandsbek. The Ashkenazim of Altona sought a contribution from the Ashkenazim of Wandsbek to the payments they made to the city of Hamburg. These payments ensured free passage in and out of the city for the conduct of commerce. The Ashkenazim of Wandsbek refused payment and negotiated a separate arrangement with the Hamburg authorities. They claimed that the Altona Jews had not mentioned them in their prior agreements as they had stipulated. The Ashkenazim of Altona responded by placing the Ashkenazim of Wandsbek under a ban, or *herem*. The Ashkenazim of Wandsbek appealed to the Sephardim in Hamburg to intercede on their behalf. The dispute centered on questions of urban jurisdiction and personal authority. Did the Sephardim of Hamburg have jurisdiction over the neighboring Ashkenazi Jews, and did Sasportas have the authority to sit on a rabbinic court in Hamburg? The second question appears somewhat absurd. Knowledge of this case comes from rabbinic responsa written by Sasportas as one of the rabbinic judges, which would apparently indicate that he had rabbinic authority in Hamburg; however, an epilogue to this incident involving one of the Ashkenazi rabbis of Altona indicates that the matter of Sasportas's personal authority was not as simple as it might seem.

The Ashkenazim of Wandsbek appealed to the Sephardim of Hamburg as the neighboring court to assess the validity of the Altona *herem*. The Sephardic court of Hamburg, which consisted of Moses Israel and Sasportas, requested that Ashkenazi representatives of both Altona and Wandsbek appear before them. When the Ashkenazim of Altona refused to appear, Sasportas sent them a series of blistering letters that

[5] On the Ashkenazim of Altona, Hamburg, and Wandsbek, see Rohrbacher, "Die Drei Gemeinden Altona, Hamburg, Wandsbek zur Zeit der Glikl"; Debra Kaplan, "'To Immerse Their Wives': Communal Identity and the 'Kahalishe' Mikveh of Altona," *AJS Review* 36 (2012).

contain generous citations of their earlier letters. In the first letter, Sasportas resorted to a tactic he had employed in the midst of the controversy over Sabbetai Zevi and would use again several decades later. He ventriloquized his opinions in the mouth of a fictitious student. The letter ostensibly written by this anonymous student sounds out some of the central themes that had appeared in *Zizath novel zvi*. The student cited a defense of his teacher's honor as his immediate cause for writing. Furthermore, much as Sasportas had railed against the rabble in his criticism of Sabbatian enthusiasm, the fictive student employed the same terminology. Thus when the Ashkenazim of Altona refused the summons, he referred to Sasportas crying and laughing at their written response:

> When their letter arrived in the name of their court signed by four laypeople of whom not a single one can be described as learned... [6]

The Ashkenazim of Altona had refused the summons of a rabbinic court with a letter signed by four laypeople. To Sasportas this represented an assault on the social hierarchy, at the top of which he placed the learned rabbi, similar to that presented by the messianic enthusiasm of the Jewish rabble a few years earlier. The same word, *hedyotot*, appears throughout *Zizath novel zvi* as a descriptive designation of the ignorant. "Let Israel speak," Sasportas continued in the voice of his student, "whether laypeople who come with the power of force can oppose a court of law that speaks with the power of Torah."[7] In the contest between the learned rabbi and the wealthy laypeople, rabbinic knowledge was clearly losing. Sasportas continued in the voice of his student to instruct the Ashkenazim of Altona that they could not choose the court in which they wished to be tried but had to be judged in the closest neighboring court: that is to say, by the Sephardim in Hamburg.

In the succeeding letters, in which Sasportas dropped the mask of pseudepigraphy, the problem of interethnic tension and the question of lay authority resurfaced. Sasportas described his own position:

---

[6] כי בבא הכתב של הכותב בשם ב״ד וחתום מד׳ הדיוטות, אשר אין גם א׳ בהם גמיר וסביר

Sasportas, *Ohel ya-akov*, #21, 30b.

[7] יאמר נא ישראל בכללו אם יש כח באנשים הדיוטות הבאים בכח הזרוע לעמוד נגד הב״ד המדברים בכחה של תורה.

Ibid.

We wrote to the judges and the lay leadership, summoning them peacefully.[8]

Sasportas addressed his letter both to the judges—that is, the rabbis—and to the lay leadership, referred to here as the *parnassim*; however, he received a response from only one of the groups:

> But the lay leaders withheld the summons from the court and responded of their own accord that they want to be judged only by judges [from] Ashkenaz.[9]

The *parnassim* refused the subpoena from the Hamburg Sephardim and demanded that a court of Ashkenazim arbitrate the case.

Sasportas read this as indicative of a split between the wealthy lay leaders and the rabbinate in Altona. Slightly later he continued:

> But there was no hint, not at the beginning, the middle, or the end, that the hand of the wise elders was the one that produced this incompetent piece of writing. From this it becomes clear that right from the start Rabbi Meir, the rabbi of the town, may the Lord preserve and protect him, had excluded himself from their agreement.[10]

Sasportas pointed to the absence of a signature by the rabbi of Altona, Meir b. Benjamin Wolf Ashkenazi, as evidence that the lay leadership had decided to take matters into their own hands and rejected the council of their own rabbi. Meir Ashkenazi hailed from Poland and had arrived in Altona some time prior to 1667.[11] Sasportas and Ashkenazi had appended approbations to *Nahalat shivah*, a work of Ashkenazi *halakha* written by Samuel b. David Halevi.[12] Although the book appeared

---

[8] וכתבנו להם דק"ק אלטונא לדיינים ופרנסים ולקרות להם לשלום.
Ibid., #22, 32a.

[9] והפרנסים הסתירו האגרת מהב"ד והשיבו מדעת עצמ' וכלל דבריהם שאינם רוצים לידון כי אם בפני דייני אשכנז.
Ibid.

[10] אבל לא נרמז כלל, לא בראשו ולא באמצעו ולא בסופו שיד הזקנים שקנו חכמה היתה הכותבת הכתיבה בלתי
תמה, ומזה אגלאי מלתא למפרע שהרב המובהק אב"ד ומ"ץ כמה"רר מאיר נר"ו הוציא עצמו מכללל הסכמת'.
Ibid.

[11] For a date as early as 1660, see Eduard Duckesz, *Iwoh lemoschaw* (Krakow: Josef Fischer, 1903), 3–5; for an estimate of some time prior to 1667, see Avraham Brik, "Rabbi Meir Ashkenazi and Rabbi Jacob Sasportas, First Rabbis of the Congregation Altona, Wandsbek, Hamburg" (Hebrew), *Moriah* 8 (1978): 72–78.

[12] *Sefer nahalat shivah* (Amsterdam: Uri Phoebus, 1667–1668). As cited in Max Grunwald, *Hamburgs deutsche Juden bis zur Auflösung der drei Gemeinden* (Hamburg: A. Janssen, 1904), 66n1. See Fuks-M., *Typography*, 2:258, entry 310.

in print in Amsterdam, both Sasportas and Meir Ashkenazi indicated in their approbations that the author had come to visit them in Hamburg seeking their authorization of his work. A year later Sasportas continued to heap praise upon Ashkenazi, as he castigated the lay leadership for having insulted him and Moses Israel by refusing to obey their summons.

Much of his letter Sasportas devoted to the form in which the Altona lay leaders had responded to the rabbinic court in Hamburg.

> For it never occurred to us to serve as judges, but we said we have no choice but to enter the fray, however much we do not want to do so, since the group that opposes you was crying out bitterly to us, and, as the neighboring court, we agreed to help them, by way of conciliation and appeasement rather than belligerence. But why have you responded with something that did not occur to us, and stated that it is only fitting for you to present your claim before Ashkenazi judges?[13]

Sasportas and Moses Israel had simply been doing their job. A group of neighboring Jews had asked for their help in a dispute with a common neighbor, and they had respectfully invited both parties to discuss their differences. Their gracious invitation had been met with an incitement to ethnic tension. Sasportas rejected the implicit suggestion by the Altona Ashkenazim that he and his colleagues were unfit to serve as their judges because they were Sephardim.

> Even if this had something to do with the Sephardim, we could remove ourselves and be judged by you, for we are not dealing with either a regular or temporary tax here, and what is more, everyone is equal to us, for we are all the children of one man[14] (Gen. 42:11).

Even if the issue concerned Sephardi litigants, Sasportas would have been perfectly happy for it to be judged and resolved by an Ashkenazi rabbinical court, and concluded his appeal with a plea for Jewish unity. When it suited his purposes, Sasportas was perfectly capable of over-

---

שלא עלה בדעתנו להיות לדיינים כי אמנ' אמרנו כי עלינו מוטל הדבר להכנס בתגר זה שלא מרצוננו יען שהכת[13] שכנגדכם היא צועקת מר לפנינו וכב"ד הסמוך וקרוב אליהם יצאנו לעזרתם דרך פיוס ורצוי ולא דרך מלחמה ולמה תשיבו אלינו דבר שלא בלבבנו ולומר שאין ראוי להציע דבריכם כי אם לפני דייני אשכנזים.

Sasportas, *Ohel ya-akov*, #22, 32b.

והלא אף אם היו הדברים הנוגעים לספרדים יכולים אנו להסתלק ולידון בפניכם דאין כאן מס לא קבוע ולא עראי[14] ועוד דכל אפיא שוין אצלנו וכולנו בני איש א' נחנו.

Ibid.

looking the condescension that characterized his description of the Ashkenazim in Hamburg during the messianic enthusiasm and appealing to the shared genealogy of Ashkenazim and Sephardim as "children of one man."

Over and above the problem of politesse, Sasportas insisted that on legal grounds, he and his colleagues were correct:

> Even if each party were a separate city and a congregation unto itself, nonetheless, in the matter at hand, we are considered a single city and a single congregation.[15]

Sasportas invoked the concept of the majority, Wandsbek and Hamburg as two parties versus Altona as one, and furthermore pointed to the precedence of the Sephardim in Hamburg. This letter bears the joint signature of Sasportas and Moses Israel, although both its tone and the concluding paragraph suggest that Sasportas was the primary author. Both at the level of epistolary etiquette and on the substantive issues of the law, Sasportas seemed to say, the Ashkenazi Jews of Altona should have submitted to the judgment of the Sephardim in Hamburg. The following responsum in *Ohel ya-akov*, labeled as section 23 and again signed jointly by Sasportas and Moses Israel, appears to indicate that the Ashkenazim in Altona backed down. Given that Sasportas's responsa remain the principal source for this incident, it is difficult to know the extent of their success.

On the face of it, these three letters appear to show Sasportas at the height of his powers. His skepticism about Sabbetai Zevi had been more than vindicated by the course of events, and his attempt to shore up the authority of the Sephardic court in Hamburg had been largely successful in preventing a conflict between two neighboring groups of Ashkenazi Jews from erupting into a larger scandal. Nonetheless, the next letter by Sasportas in section 24 of *Ohel ya-akov* provides an important coda to this story. Sasportas addressed the letter to Meir Ashkenazi, the rabbi of Altona he had singled out for praise. In 1668 Meir Ashkenazi had departed from the Ashkenazim of Altona, Hamburg, and Wandsbek on the condition that he could resume his position as rabbi if he did not prolong his absence. He then returned to Poland and

---

[15] ואע"כ אף אם כל א' הוא בעיר אחרת וקהל בפני עצמו אפ"ה בענין זה שאנחנו דנין עליו הרי אנו נחשבים לעיר
א' וק"ק א'

Ibid., #22, 33a.

accepted a position as the rabbi of Chelm, but only a short while later he reappeared and demanded to be reinstated in his former position. The Ashkenazim of Altona accepted him with open arms, but the Ashkenazim of Wandsbek and Hamburg refused, stating that they knew of his appointment in Chelm and had appointed David Tevyle of Posen in the interim. The Ashkenazim in Hamburg appealed to Aaron Samuel Kaidanover, an Ashkenazi rabbi who was then resident in the city, who ruled in favor David Tevyle.[16] Meir Ashkenazi rejected Kaidanover's ruling and demanded to serve as a rabbi for all three groups of Ashkenazi Jews. When those in Wandsbek and Hamburg continued to refuse, he placed them both under *herem*.

In turn, the Ashkenazim of Wandsbek, now joined by those in Hamburg, once again appealed to Sasportas to serve as mediator. Sasportas invited Ashkenazi to present his claims, but Ashkenazi refused his summons. Ashkenazi's written refusal does not survive, but Sasportas's response offers a summary of the case and includes sufficient citations to allow for a partial reconstruction. In short, Ashkenazi refused to submit to Sasportas's judgment because he lacked an official position. Sasportas's bristled at this dismissal and responded to this perceived slight with barely concealed rage:

> Do you not know, have you never heard that if you serve as a judge in the congregation of Altona, you have no reputation anywhere else? Meanwhile, I am fifty-four years old, and I have been granted permission by the Resh Galuta to issue legal rulings... I served as a jurist to six congregations in a great city of sages and scholars, and all of the surrounding areas sought after me, and I was a king in the western province [of North Africa]. [17]

After reminding Meir Ashkenazi of his long career, Sasportas cited the written praise lavished on him by two Ashkenazi rabbis in the more recent past.

---

[16]For Kaidanover's ruling, see Brik, "Rabbi Meir Ashkenazi and Rabbi Jacob Sasportas," 77–78; a separate ruling by Kaidanover appears in Sasportas, *Ohel ya-akov*, #29, 39b–40a. See Duckesz, *Iwoh lemoschaw*, 5. Two responsa in *Ohel ya-akov* appear in succession with the number 29. The one cited here appears second.

הלא ידע מכ״ת אם לא שמע שאם ישב לכסא שופט בק״ק אלטאנה לא יצא מוניטון שלו במקום אחר כי אמנם[17] אנכי בן נ״ד שנים שקליתא מראשי גלותא לומר יורה יורה ידין ידין... ומ״ץ לששה קהלות בעיר גדולה של חכמים ושל סופרים וכל גלילותיה נכספים לי והיית מלך במחוז המערב

Sasportas, *Ohel ya-akov*, #24, 34a.

Meir Ashkenazi eventually abandoned his attempt to serve as rabbi of all three groups of Ashkenazi Jews in Hamburg, Altona, and Wandsbek, and took up the position he had previously been offered in Chelm.[18] Sasportas described his own letter, which appears to have been written after the matter was resolved peacefully in Hamburg but before Ashkenazi's departure, as an attempt at interpersonal communication rather than a legal ruling.

> Do not think that I have instructed thus so as to compel you to accept it, for had this been the case, I would have issued a ruling prior to the incident. It is already known from the beloved R. Moses Israel, may the Lord protect him, that the matter has reached a peaceful conclusion... Yet the principle behind my writing is to inform you that you have wronged me, that you have spoken too freely [about me] in front of others, and that you should rectify your wrongdoing. But I inform you that I have forgiven this slight to my honor, and I will not hold it against you in the future. [19]

Much as he had done throughout his polemic against Sabbatianism, Sasportas expressed an extraordinary sensitivity to any offense against his honor. The Hebrew word *kavod* may be translated as "honor" or as "due." Given the instability of his professional status, Sasportas clung tightly, almost desperately, to his reputation.

Furthermore, Sasportas referred explicitly to his lack of an official position among the Sephardim in Hamburg:

> I may not be an official rabbi of a city in your eyes, and I may not be in the eyes of the rabbi of the court, whose modesty has made me great (Ps. 18:36), as well as in the eyes of others, who know that I shun high office yet it continues to pursue me to this very day. [20]

This letter bears Sasportas's signature and a Hebrew date of the year 5429, which corresponds to the year 1668–1669. After the conversion

---

[18]Duckesz, *Iwoh lemoschaw*, 3–5.

[19]ואל יקחך לבך לצד א' לחשוב שהוראתי זאת היא להכריחך לקבלה שאם כן הייתי אומר הלכה קודם מעשה וכבר נודע מפי האהוב כה"רר משה ישראל נר"ו שכבר תוך שלום וגמר הדבר . . . אבל עיקר כתבי זה הוא להודיעך שחטאת כנגדי ושלחת לשונך יותר מדי בפני אחרים ועליך לתקן את מעוותך ולהודיעך שמחלתי על כבודי ואין אני מקפיד על דבריך מהיום והלאה.

Sasportas, *Ohel ya-akov* #24, 34b.

[20]ברם אנא לאו מריה דאתרא אנא בעיניך אבל לא בעיני הרב האב"ד אשר ענוותו תרבני ולא בעיני אחרי' היודעי' שאני בורח מן השררה אשר עוד היו רודפת אחרי.

Ibid.

of Sabbetai Zevi, when the course of events had validated his skepticism, Sasportas was in a position of some but by no means comprehensive power among the Jews of Hamburg, Altona, and Wandsbek. In two separate episodes, the Ashkenazim who lived in the neighboring towns had appealed to Sasportas to serve as a mediator. In both cases, he appears to have orchestrated the course of events to the resolutions he sought, if one accepts the accounts in his letters, which appear to be corroborated by the circumstantial evidence: the Ashkenazim of Altona seem to have lifted their *herem* against the Ashkenazim in Wandsbek in the first case, and Meir Ashkenazi wrote an apology to Sasportas and departed for Poland in the second.[21] Sasportas's signature appears jointly with that of Moses Israel, who held the official position as rabbi of the Sephardim in Hamburg. Their relations were apparently cordial and even friendly. Sasportas continued to describe himself as someone who lacked an official position. Some of this was clearly a rhetorical pose, as Sasportas, throughout his time in western Europe, played with great skill on the fact that he came from the farthest edges of the Sephardic world. It was not all posturing: Sasportas could not without considerable effort compel the wealthy Ashkenazim of Altona to lift their *herem*, and Meir Ashkenazi, who had once appeared to him to be his close ally, openly flouted his authority and reminded Sasportas without any compunction of his status as an outsider.

A responsum written to another Ashkenazi rabbi in Hamburg from the same year corroborates Sasportas's stature as a rabbinic authority and simultaneously underscores the significance of the issues raised in *Zizath novel zvi*. Sasportas addressed his letter to someone named Samuel Issachar known as Ber. The letter dealt with three issues: the status of kosher meat that had not been properly salted, the unity of God as it appeared in the writings of Maimonides, and the correct interpretation of a passage in the *Zohar*. Here in miniature one can grasp the contours of Sasportas's mental and intellectual world: a technical question of Jewish law about which he advised his correspondent toward a more stringent ruling, a passage in Maimonides's philosophical work that led to a sermon on the stature of the medieval sage, and an exegetical exercise in the most important work of Jewish mysticism.

[21] Ibid., #25, 35a–35b.

Sasportas took umbrage at the untoward familiarity with which Samuel Issachar had written about Maimonides:

> In addition, in the course of challenging him, you said: "I am sorry for you, Maimonides, my brother, for you were attacked from all sides." What love and friendship exists between you and him? Even your teachers, of blessed memory, would never have addressed him in terms of love; rather, they would have used terms of subservience. [22]

In an almost precise echo of the rhetorical posture he had adopted in the Sabbatian controversy, Sasportas focused on the form of address that his correspondent employed when writing about Maimonides. Just as Aaron Zarfati had taken a liberty in expressing his love for Sasportas in the midst of a dispute about Sabbetai Zevi, Samuel Issachar had taken a liberty in writing about his fraternal affiliation with Maimonides in his question to Sasportas.

Sasportas's criticism, however, was not entirely about form. Much as his dispute with Zarfati had hung on a substantive theological issue, whether or not Sabbetai Zevi was the Messiah, his response to Samuel Issachar concerned Maimonides's theory of the divine attributes and its theological ramifications. Samuel Issachar had criticized Maimonides's theory of negative attributes as leading to a conception of multiple gods or to a plurality within God. Sasportas castigated him as having strayed from "our tradition." He urged him to turn to Yedaiah Bedersi's defense of Maimonides in his letter to Solomon ibn Adret, a source that he had invoked in *Zizath novel zvi*. He appealed to Nahmanides as his ancestor and to the writings of Moses Cordovero and Meir ibn Gabbai about the divine attributes of God. All of these writers, Sasportas claimed, had been kabbalists who rejected the multiplicity of God. In positing this line of argument, Sasportas positioned himself within a long line of medieval and early modern kabbalists who interpreted the kabbalistic sefirot as a theological expression of Maimonides's theory of the divine attributes.[23]

---

[22] ג״כ בכלל קרית תגר עליו אמרת צר לי עליך אחי הרמב״ם כי היתה עליך המלחמה פנים ואחור מה אהבה ורֵיעות יש בינך לבינו ואפילו רבותיך ע״ה לא היו קוראים לו בלשון אהבה כי אם בלשון אדנות.

Ibid., #29, 39b. Two successive responsa in *Ohel ya-akov* have the number 29. The one cited here appears first.

[23] Eli Gurfinkel, "Maimonides and Kabbalah: An Annotated Bibliography" (Hebrew), *Daat* 64–66 (2009): 417–485.

Sasportas saw his correspondent as lacking rudimentary knowledge of Maimonides's philosophy and was not afraid to say so:

> If you had any knowledge of the divine attributes, and could distinguish the negative from the positive, you would not dare to criticize Maimonides, and you certainly would not refer to him as a brother. [24]

Even the most cursory reader of Maimonides knew that he had rejected the positive description of God and outlined a theory of negative attributes. Human beings could describe God only in the negative, as any positive description would be an inherent limitation of God. Just as he had done throughout *Zizath novel zvi*, Sasportas pointed his reader to the specific passages in the writings of Maimonides.

> As Maimonides expounded upon this in section 1, chapters 56 and 57 [of the *Guide of the Perplexed*]. [25]

If earlier Sasportas had dwelled upon the *Code of Law* and the "Epistle to Yemen," the two crucial texts in which Maimonides had outlined his resistance to active Messianism, in this responsum he pointed to the *Guide of the Perplexed*. Sasportas saw absolutely no contradiction between his own Maimonideanism and his kabbalism. Thus he continued to instruct his correspondent about the relationship between Mamionides's theory of negative attributes and the kabbalistic doctrine of the sefirot.

> For this is the explanation of the negative attributes, and this is the importance of Kabbalah to demonstrate that the sefirot are the essence of unity and divinity. From now on, hold your tongue from sinning about such matters, for your lack of knowledge will lead you toward heresy.[26]

Sasportas saw no contradiction between the Kabbalah of Nahmanides and the philosophy of Maimonides, both of which constituted critical

---

[24] ואם יהיה למעכ״ת שום ידיעה בתארים הבאים על דרך החיוב ולהבדילם מהבאים על דרך שלילה לא הי׳ פוצה פה נגד הרמב״ם ואף לא היה קורא לו אח.
Sasportas, *Ohel ya-akov*, #29, 39b.

[25] וכמו שהאריך בזה הרמב״ם בח״א פ׳ נ״ו ונ״ז וזולתו.
Ibid.

[26] וזהו פירוש התוארים ע״ש השלילה וזהו עיקר הקבלה להראות שהספירות הם עצם האחדות והאלדות. ומעכשיו שמור פיך מחטוא בדברים הללו כי חסרות הידיעה בהם תבא לקצץ בנטיעות.
Ibid.

elements of "our tradition." Given that his correspondent did not seem to understand either one, Sasportas counseled silence.

Who was this man referred to simply as Samuel Issachar known as Ber? Isaiah Sonne identified a letter written by Sasportas that appeared in a small pamphlet printed in Prague entitled *Sefer ma-aseh hoshen u-ketoret*.[27] Sasportas addressed his recipient in flattering terms and asked for a copy of the author's commentary on particular passages in the *Zohar*. In his introductory paragraph before he adduced Sasportas's letter, the author, named Issachar Ber Perlhefter, referred to the period when he had served as an Ashkenazi jurist in Hamburg while Sasportas had served as a Sephardic jurist in the same city. Sasportas, he now informed his reader, was on the coast of Italy and serving as a judge to the Jews in Livorno. By the time this pamphlet appeared in 1686, Sasportas had already left Livorno. A native of Prague, Perlhefter married a learned woman named Bella. The couple and their children moved around and at various points lived in Hamburg, Altdorf, and Modena before returning to Prague.[28] Ber or Berl Perlhefter also served as the Hebrew tutor to Johann Christoph Wagenseil for a period in the mid-1670s. Perlhefter and his wife Bella jointly composed a Yiddish encyclopedia known as *Be-er sheva* that survives in a number of different manuscript recensions.[29] Isaiah Tishby identified the author of the diary of a *maggid*, or a celestial mentor, in the circle of Abraham Rovigo in Modena as the very same Berl Perlhefter who had printed Sasportas's letter in 1686. In the same article, Tishby identified Sasportas's correspondent from 1669 referred to as Samuel Issachar known as Ber as Berl Perlhefter.[30] The discoveries by Sonne and Tishby offer a crucial insight into Sasportas in the decades after Sabbetai Zevi's conversion. In all likelihood, Sasportas was unaware of Perlhefter's Sabbatian leanings, as Tishby posited.[31] The more crucial point, however, has to do with the fact that Sasportas was not interested in parsing Perlhefter's writings, or those of anyone else for that matter, for allusions to

[27] See *Ma-ase hoshen u-ketoret* (Prague, 1686), 1b; Isaiah Sonne, "On the History of Sabbatianism in Italy" (Hebrew), in *Sefer ha-yovel le-Alexander Marx* (New York, 1943), 95–101.

[28] Riemer, "Zwischen christlichen Hebraisten und Sabbatianern."

[29] Nathaniel Riemer and Sigrid Senkbei, eds., *'Beer Sheva' by Beer and Bella Perlhefter: An Edition of a Seventeenth Century Yiddish Encyclopedia* (Wiesbaden: Harrassowitz, 2011).

[30] Isaiah Tishby, "The First Sabbatian *Magid* in R. Abraham Rovigo's House of Study" (Hebrew), in *Netive emunah u-minut* (Jerusalem: Magnes Press, 1994), 86n32.

[31] Ibid., 98.

Sabbatianism. He had enough problems with Perlhefter's approach to Maimonides. Sabbetai Zevi and the messianic movement he initiated may have been the greatest and most widespread assault on Sasportas's worldview. By 1669, however, it had largely run its course. Sabbatianism was only one arena of a much larger battle that Sasportas saw himself as waging. He remained committed to protecting the legacies of Maimonides and Kabbalah, crucial sources for his defense of rabbinic Judaism as articulated in *Zizath novel zvi*, from any and all attacks that he perceived. Once these attacks had been met, however, he was quite willing—in fact, even eager—to study Perlhefter's writings.[32]

The one reference to Sabbetai Zevi I have been able to find in Sasportas's writings after *Zizath novel zvi* occurs in passing and conforms to the general insignificance of the subject but the persistence of the themes that he had sounded out in his polemic. While Sasportas lived in Hamburg, he received a letter from Amsterdam written by Moses D'Aguilar and Jacob Benveniste that requested his legal opinion on the status of a woman who had borne her master two children and sought to compel her master to marry her. The legal issue centered on her status as either a concubine, in which case she was required to wait before marrying her master, or a prostitute, in which case she could marry her master immediately. Sasportas ruled that she did not have the status of a concubine and thus did not have to wait.[33]

There the matter would have ended had Sasportas not received a follow-up from his old friend Isaac Nahar in Livorno. Sasportas's responsa include only his two letters to Nahar, but from both of them one can deduce that Nahar had first resisted Sasportas's ruling and then protested even more vigorously. In his first response to Nahar, Sasportas adopted an extremely polite and even flattering tone. He wrote to Nahar that had he known the query had been sent by such a scholar, he would have answered briefly and not gone on at such length. Furthermore,

> the aforementioned scholar [Aguilar] wrote that the question had come from a distant land but I do not consider your residence a distant land, as transport comes every week, and, in fact, I think you are quite close.[34]

[32] Ibid., 93n76.

[33] Sasportas, *Ohel ya-akov*, #32, 43a–43b. The letter is dated to the year 1669–1670.

[34] אך אמר החכם הנ״ל שבאה השאלה מארץ מרחקים ואין מחניכם אצלי עיר מרחקים ביען שהרצים מצוים מכל שבוע ואצלי תחשב קרובה.

Here, in passing, Sasportas indicated the relative size of his world: he was living in Hamburg, the question had been sent to him by his colleagues in Amsterdam, and his answer had been forwarded on to Livorno. These three cities were within the known boundaries of his world, even though at the time he wrote the letter, he had not yet traveled to Livorno. Sasportas politely informed Nahar that he maintained his position.

Nahar insisted on standing his ground. He responded to Sasportas's first letter with one that must have been much sharper. Although Nahar's letter does not survive, Sasportas's long response was so blistering as to be worthy of some of his rhetoric in *Zizath novel zvi*. Sasportas reminded Nahar that he had been asked repeatedly by the Sephardim in Livorno to serve as their rabbi but had refused. He questioned how Nahar had even dared argue with him, a rabbi who had served in an official position before Nahar had even begun studying Mishnah. In the midst of this scathing counterattack, Sasportas included the following sentence:

> In addition, about your belief in the Messiah and the prophet, which was the entire reason for your going there [to Livorno], you wrote harshly to me, as if you were going to teach me the right way, until I had to let loose my tongue against you, saying you should live with this belief of yours, but then I saw your apology written on your way to the Holy Land, and I was no longer resentful of you. [35]

Sasportas brought up Nahar's belief in Sabbetai Zevi and Nathan of Gaza only in passing and only in the third letter that he had written about this case. What is more, the context for Sasportas's statement was entirely personal and relational, that is, how it had affected his relationship with his former pupil.

One further confirmation of Sasportas's status in Hamburg appears in an agreement between the Ashkenazim and Sephardim in Hamburg in 1669. Ashkenazim had resided in Hamburg since early in the seven-

---

Ibid., #40, 43b–44a. The prior responsum is numbered #32, which included the original question sent by Benveniste and Aguilar to Sasportas. *Ohel ya-akov* does not contain responsa numbered #33 through #39.

[35] וגם על אמונת משיח ונביא שהיתה סיבה להליכתך לשם כפי הנראה כתבת לי קשות כמלמדני דרך ישרה עד שהוצרכתי לשלוח רסן לשוני נגדך ולומר לך חיה באמונתך זאת, וכאשר ראיתי כתב פיוסך בעת שומך לדרך ארץ הקדש פעמיך נתפייסתי ולא נשאר בלבי עליך.

Ibid., #41, 45a.

teenth century. While they were officially expelled from the city in 1649 and readmitted only in 1697, some continued to reside in Hamburg. These Ashkenazim were very much at the mercy of the Sephardim, as their 1669 agreement amply demonstrates.[36] In this agreement, they effectively ceded all power, from the use of the *herem* to the hiring of ritual slaughterers, to the Sephardim. One copy of this agreement, which was recorded in Hebrew, bears three sets of signatures. The first belong to the *parnassim* of the Sephardim and the third to a group of Ashkenazim who do not bear designated titles. The second group, which contains the signatures of the *bet din*, or court, of the Sephardim consists of two signatures: Moses Israel and Jacob Sasportas. The text of the agreement corroborates a number of details contained in Sasportas's own writings. First and foremost, the *parnassim* exercised power among the Sephardim. Their signatures appear first, and the document repeatedly invokes their authority. Second, the Sephardim of Hamburg took considerable pride in the precedence of their settlement within Hamburg itself. The 1669 agreement leaves no doubt as to their priority. Finally, all of the sources examined thus far—Sasportas's own writings, the register of the Sephardim in Hamburg, and the text of this agreement—seem to point in the same direction: Sasportas sat on the rabbinic court with his colleague Moses Israel, received some support from the local Sephardim, and had earned their respect, if not quite adulation. He did not, however, serve as the principal rabbi. In his history of the rabbinate in Altona-Hamburg-Wandsbek, Eduard Duckesz concluded, "Rabbi Jacob Sasportas was not the chief rabbi of the court in Hamburg, but everyone listened to him."[37] As a legal authority, or a *posek*, in the western Sephardic Diaspora in the second half of the seventeenth century, Sasportas appears to have had few rivals. His colleagues, both at home and somewhat farther afield, turned to him for his opinion. This, however, did not translate into actual control or sovereign power. His rabbinic colleagues respected his learning, and the lay leadership in Hamburg understood that they could not ignore him completely, but neither group gave him what he deemed was sufficient

---

[36]SAH, Jüdische Gemeinden, 993, II, *Verträge zwischen den deutsch-jüdischen gemeinden in Hamburg und Altona* 1669, 9 Adar II, 429. There is no pagination in the files. The agreement, written in Hebrew, covers three pages, which, if numbered sequentially from the start of the file, are pages 7, 8, and 9. Sasportas's signature appears on page 8 alongside that of Moses Israel.

[37]Duckesz, *Iwoh lemoschaw*, 4.

due. The lay leadership appears to have viewed Sasportas an accomplished technician. Just as they required a ritual slaughterer to perform his task correctly so that they could eat kosher meat, or a *mohel* to circumcise baby boys on the eighth day so that they could enter the covenant of Abraham, they needed a rabbi who could interpret the law correctly. Sasportas, however, did not view the law as a technical matter that required problem solving. At issue in nearly all of Sasportas's disputes was the centrality of the law in Jewish life.

AMSTERDAM 1671–1678

At some point in 1671 or 1672 Sasportas left Hamburg and traveled to Amsterdam, where he resided until 1678. The record book of the Portuguese Sephardim in Hamburg mentions preparations for his departure on the second of Iyar 5431, which corresponds to 12 April 1671.[38] Given the stature he had attained in Hamburg, Sasportas's decision to uproot himself and his family again requires some explanation. The existing documentation does not point to a definitive cause, like the famine that precipitated his departure from Saleh in 1664 or the plague in London in 1665. Be that as it may, a pair of pamphlets printed in Amsterdam in 1672 offers a set of clues and also yields new biographical information. The pamphlets pertain to a dispute between Sasportas and Benjamin Mussaphia about the behavior of Mussaphia's daughter Leah on her deathbed. In a pamphlet printed in Amsterdam in 1672, Benjamin Mussaphia argued that his daughter's conduct on her deathbed was of no legal consequence and that her estate should revert to him as her primary heir.[39] The final page of the pamphlet includes two texts. The first contains a summons by Isaac Aboab da Fonseca to one of the agents who represented the orphaned children of Leah's husband. Leah's husband had predeceased her by a week, and his children, named Moses and Jacob ibn Zur, stood to receive a gift from Leah's estate issued to them on her deathbed.[40] Aboab's summons, which bears a date

[38] SAH, Jüdische Gemeinden, 993/I, 491.

[39] Benjamin Mussaphia, *Shtem esreh she-elot* (Amsterdam: Uri Phoebus, 1672). National Library of Israel, Shelfmark, R 8=75A, 265. On Mussaphia, see Wilke, "*Midrashim from Bordeaux.*"

[40] For the death of Leah's husband a week earlier, see the text by Mussaphia reproduced with Sasportas's adversarial marginalia in Jacob Sasportas, *Va-yakem edut be-ya-akov* (Amstedam: Uri Phoebus, 1672), 14a. A substantial portion of *Va-yakem edut be-ya-akov* was subsequently re-

of the tenth of Ab 5431 or 17 July 1671, ordered the agent to appear before a rabbinic court either in Amsterdam or in Venice.

Beneath Aboab's summons and the final text in this short pamphlet is a copy of a text that had originally been written in Spanish but survives only in Hebrew translation. This seven-line text bears a signature by Moses Israel, and is dated to Hamburg on the twenty-ninth of Shevat 5471 or 9 February 1671—that is to say, roughly five months before the summons of Isaac Aboab from Amsterdam.

> In such a way that after all of the details that she desired were written down, R. Jacob Sasportas was summoned, and when she was asked by the two of us, we found her of sound mind, and we read out the entire document to her, word for word, and she said after each and every thing, this is my will.[41]

From this short text, it appears that Leah, the daughter of Benjamin Mussaphia, had died in Hamburg in the late winter of 1671. On her deathbed, Moses Israel and Jacob Sasportas had read out to her a revised list of things she wished to do with her property. They had served as the witnesses and judged her of sound mind. Mussaphia's short printed pamphlet sought to invalidate Leah's wishes with a relatively straightforward argument. Her wishes had no legal standing because the two witnesses, Moses Israel and Sasportas, stood to gain by receiving gifts from her estate that were promised to them.

Mussaphia's pamphlet had appeared in print, and Sasportas responded in kind. In 1672 at the same press in Amsterdam, Uri Phoebus printed a somewhat longer pamphlet by Sasportas, *Va-yakem edut be-ya-akov ve-torah shem be-yisrael*. The title of the pamphlet, a verse of Psalms (78:5) rendered as "for he established a testimony in Jacob, and appointed a law in Israel," articulated the argument Sasportas sought to make. His testimony was valid, Leah's last wishes had the validity of a legal document, and her property should be disbursed accordingly. In the pamphlet, Sasportas not only insisted on the validity of his tes-

---

printed with Sasportas's responsa in the eighteenth century. See Sasportas, *Ohel ya-akov*, #42, 43, 44, 48b–51b. On relations between the Abensur or ibn Zur and Mussaphia families, see Kellenbenz, *Sephardim an der unteren Elbe*, 398.

[41] באופן שאחרי שנכתבו כל הפרטים שרצתה שיעלו בכתב נקרא החכם כמ״ר יעקב ששפורטש ובהיותה נשאלת משנינו כפי הנראה לנו לדעת אם היתה דעתה שלמה מצאנוה בשכל ראוי ובדעת שלמה וקראנו לפניה הכתוב מלה במלה והיא היתה אומרת על כל דבר זה רצוני וחופצת אני שכן יתקיים.

Mussaphia, *Shtem esreh she-elot*, 3b.

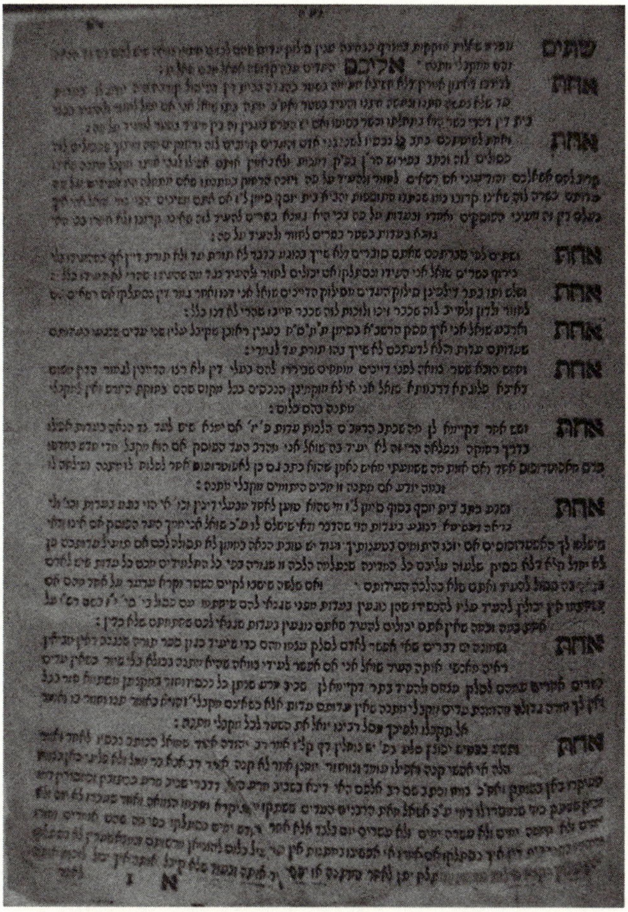

Figure 16. Mussaphia, *Shtem esreh she-elot* (Amsterdam: Uri Phoebus, 1672), cover page. Benjamin Mussaphia, a rival of Sasportas, published a pamphlet in Amsterdam about Sasportas's conduct at the deathbed of Mussaphia's daughter in Hamburg. The National Library of Israel.

timony; he also sought the corroboration and support of his colleagues. Many of them obliged, and rabbis from Altona, Frankfurt, Hamburg, Hildesheim, Halberstadt, and Amsterdam wrote approbations in support of the decision that Sasportas included in the pamphlet.[42] As he had in *Zizath novel zvi*, and as Hagiz and Emden would do in the eighteenth century, Sasportas was perfectly capable of galvanizing his colleagues to support a particular cause. In addition to Sasportas's ruling and the approbations of his colleagues, *Va-yakem edut be-ya-akov* included a lengthy justification by Sasportas for his own testimony, as well as an opinion by Mussaphia with Sasportas's adversarial margi-

---

[42]Sasportas, *Va-yakem edut be-ya-akov*, 2a–4a, 13b.

nalia.[43] Sasportas signed his justification for his own testimony from Amsterdam and acknowledged that he was one of the witnesses to Leah's last wishes. The legal question at stake was whether her last wishes had the status of a will, as Sasportas argued, or whether they did not because Sasportas was not a valid witness, as Mussaphia argued. The contest pitted Mussaphia's claim against Sasportas's integrity as a witness.

The pamphlet yields a number of other biographical details about Sasportas. Sasportas apparently paid for the printing of his own accord, as at one point in the pamphlet he complains about the time and money he wasted on its printing.[44] Bibliographers remain uncertain as to whether Mussaphia's pamphlet or Sasportas's pamphlet appeared first.[45] Sasportas may have felt compelled to put his opinion in print as a response to Mussaphia, or he may have taken the initiative himself. In either case, he appears to have traveled to Amsterdam to oversee his pamphlet into print. Finally, *Va-yakem edut be-ya-akov* makes passing reference to a trip that Sasportas had taken to London to visit his son.

> Since I am here in London, as a guest for the night, where I have come to see my beloved son, may the Lord protect him, and may I return in peace, I have not gone on at such great length, except with a prayer to God that He shall restore our glory and the glory of the Torah and those who study it for its own sake, and He should light up the eyes of those who study it, these are the words of the slave, he who is bound to his work, Jacob Sasportas. [46]

Sasportas traveled to London for a short period at some point in 1671 or 1672 to visit his son. The son in question was probably Samuel, who had originally accompanied him to London in 1665 when he went to serve as the rabbi of the new Portuguese congregation. Sasportas's prayer for his peaceful return may not have been simply rhetorical. The

---

[43] Ibid., 4b–13a for Sasportas's justification, and 14a–20a for Mussaphia's opinion with Sasportas's adversarial marginalia. Mussaphia's opinion reproduced by Sasportas differs from the text in *Shtem-esreh she-elot.*

[44] Sasportas, *Va-yakem edut be-ya-akov,* 6b.

[45] See the handwritten note possibly by Israel Mehlman in the copy of *Shtem esreh she-elot* in the National Library of Israel referred to above.

[46] ובעבור שאני בכאן בלונדון כאורח נטה ללון שבאתי לראות שלום בני חמודי יצ״ו ואחזור לשלום לא הארכתי
יותר כי אם בתפלה לאל שיתבע עלבוננו ועלבון התורה ולומדיה ויאיר עיני הלומדים בה לשמה כה דברי עבד נרצע
לעבודתו הצעיר ישפ״ה ע״כ

Sasportas, *Va-yakem edut be-ya-akov,* 5a.

period between April 1672 and early 1674 marked the Third Anglo-Dutch War, and Sasportas may have tried to travel in the midst of the conflict.

Sasportas's run-ins with Mussaphia did not stop with his daughter's will. A year after the printing of *Va-yakem edut be-ya-akov*, Sasportas wrote a letter to his colleague Joshua da Silva in London. From the introductory paragraphs to the letter, one can deduce that Da Silva had taken offense over a disagreement he had had with Sasportas. In the course of a letter that covered a number of legal issues, such as carrying on the Sabbath and levirate marriage, Sasportas adopted a conciliatory tone and sought to establish his deep respect for his colleague. In doing so, he referred twice to Benjamin Mussaphia and his conduct in the house of study. He recounted a conversation he had had with Isaac Aboab da Fonseca and Moses Raphael D'Aguilar.

> Afterward, I was told that in the house of study, Benjamin Mussaphia was present, and he confused everything and filled the house of study with shards and scraps as was his wont, and with passages from the Mishnah that lacked a plain interpretation and had been corrupted with faulty texts with which he misled them with words such that anyone who listens to them will burst out laughing. [47]

Mussaphia, according to Sasportas, could not make heads or tails out of the most basic rabbinic texts such as the Mishnah.

> And a man whose knowledge of legal literature is so limited and who is filled with nonsense riding on the wings of the wind, and does not consider the legal literature, will people not consider the words and lies of this man to be squabbles and drivel? [48]

Once again, one encounters Sasportas charging his opponent with boorish ignorance. Sasportas fashioned himself as someone who had command over the entirety of legal literature, from the Mishnah through

---

[47] ולאחר מכאן הוגד לי כי בבית המדרש נמצא שם הרופא כמהור״ר בנימין מוספיא ובילבל את הכל ומילא בית המדרש בקיעים ורסיסים כאשר זה דרכו ובמשניות חסרי פשט וגירסאו׳ משובשות הטה את לבבם בדברים אשר כל שומעים ימלא שחוק פיו.

Sasportas, *Ohel ya-akov*, #66, 71b.

[48] ולאיש אשר קצרה ידיעתו בספרי הפוסקים וכלו מלא קטטות ורוכב על כנפי רוח ולא יחשוב הפוסקים לכלום מי יחוש לדבריו ומהתליו כהוכא ואטלולא.

Ibid.

the writings of more recent Talmudists; he described Mussaphia, by contrast, as unable to read a passage in the Mishnah.

In the continuation of the letter, Sasportas turned to the issue of levirate marriage.

> Just as with the issue [the childless widow awaiting a levirate marriage] he sought to aggravate, and he came before a group of scholars with a copy of the Palestinian Talmud in his hand, as if he were girded with a new interpretation. But he revealed his ignorance of the plain meaning and the explanation of the term, and sought to prove that the levirate must be forced to release her [from such a marriage], until I showed him to his face that this had nothing to do with the Palestinian Talmud, which accorded exactly with the ruling in the Mishnah that the levirate must first release the childless widow from the levirate marriage. [49]

In this case, however, Sasportas sought to prove not only Mussaphia's lack of literacy in rabbinic literature, but also his pretension. Mussaphia had come before a group of scholars hoping to perform his erudition through his interpretation of a passage in the Palestinian Talmud. Instead, he made himself look like a fool.

Benjamin Mussaphia was many things—a doctor, a businessman, a textual critic, and a commentator—but an ignoramus was not one of them. Born slightly earlier than Sasportas somewhere in the Iberian Peninsula, he had followed a similar itinerary with some meaningful differences. In 1625 he earned a degree in medicine at the University of Padua, where he numbered among a group of Jewish medical students.[50] In the succeeding decades he resided in Amsterdam, where he published a number of books, including medical works in Latin and biblical scholarship in Hebrew.[51] In addition, he edited the most important medieval Hebrew dictionary, Nathan ben Jehiel's *Arukh*, in 1655.[52] Like Sasportas, Mussaphia shuttled back and forth between Amster-

---

[49] וכמו שג״כ בענין השומרת יבם רצה לקנטר ובא לו לוועד של חכמים וירושלמי בידו כאילו חגור חדשה וגילה חסרון ידיעתו אפילו בפשט ובפירוש המלה ורצה להוכיח דכופין ליבם לחלוץ עד שטיפחתי לו על פניו לומר דאין כאן מקום לירושלמי כלל דהוא אזיל לשיטתיה כמשנה שניה דמצות חליצה קודמת.

Ibid.

[50] Ruderman, "The Impact of Science on Jewish Culture and Society in Venice," 519n4.

[51] Kellenbenz, *Sephardim an der unteren Elbe*, 331–338; Levi Bernfeld, *Poverty and Welfare*, 168, 468; Wilke, "*Midrashim from Bordeaux*."

[52] Marvin J. Heller, "Benjamin ben Immanuel Mussafia: A Study in Contrasts," *Gutenberg Jahrbuch* 89 (2014): 208–218.

dam and Hamburg. In the early and mid-1660s, he resided in Hamburg before he returned to Amsterdam, where he died in 1675. Mussaphia was thus a rival whom Sasportas had known for many years in different settings.

One other crucial factor about Mussaphia requires consideration both in its own right and for the insights it offers into Sasportas's polemics and competition with him in the 1670s. Repeatedly in *Zizath novel zvi*, Sasportas indicated that Mussaphia numbered among the most devoted adherents to Sabbetai Zevi in Amsterdam.[53] Again and again he referred to Mussaphia as one of the leaders of the Sabbatians in Amsterdam. By 1667, most of the Sephardic elite in Amsterdam—men like Isaac Aboab da Fonseca, Abraham Pereyra, and Benjamin Mussaphia—had recanted their belief in Sabbetai Zevi as the Messiah. With the Messiah's conversion, they had recognized that the jig was up. Only a few years later, Sasportas sparred with Mussaphia over a series of issues: his daughter's inheritance, his conduct in the house of study, and his interpretation of a passage in the Palestinian Talmud. Sasportas had no compunction about besmirching Mussaphia's reputation to a colleague abroad or criticizing him openly and sharply in print. In none of these writings did Sasportas cast aspersions on Mussaphia's Sabbatian past. This silence beggars explanation. Unlike his letters to Perlhefter, where one can plausibly argue that Sasportas had no clue about his correspondent's Sabbatian tendencies, the letters to and about Mussaphia describe someone Sasportas had known to have been a believer.

Perhaps Sasportas did not mention Mussaphia's Sabbatian past because many of those to whom he was writing had a Sabbatian past as well. One cannot gainsay a judicious use of tact on Sasportas's part. For all of the biliousness that has justifiably been attributed to him, he was not one to insult someone if doing so undercut his own purposes. Over and above the simple possibility of tact, there seems to be another equally likely explanation for Sasportas's silence. Sabbetai Zevi was old news in the early 1670s. Sasportas had fought that battle, and events had borne out his skepticism. The rabbinate, however, was still a work in progress, and Sasportas would continue to fight for what he deemed its proper and correct recognition among the Sephardic elite.

[53] Sasportas, *ZNZ*, 126, described Mussaphia as "the leader of the believers."

LIVORNO 1678–1681

Sasportas remained in Amsterdam during his second residence for roughly seven years. In his letter to Nahar, he had reminded his former student that the Jews in Livorno had repeatedly begged him to come and serve as a rabbi. In 1678, when he was in his late sixties, Sasportas finally accepted the invitation. Sasportas seems to have been accorded considerable respect in his new hometown.[54] He renewed his friendship with Raphael Supino, a former Sabbatian who looked to Sasportas for counsel and advice. In 1679 his wife, Rachel Sasportas née Toledano, gave birth to a baby girl named Buenaventura, Portuguese for Mazal Tov or good fortune.[55] In the years Sasportas spent in Livorno, approximately eighty marriages took place among the Sephardic Jews. Sasportas served as a witness to roughly a quarter of them.[56] *Ohel ya-akov* contains a cluster of responsa written by Sasportas during his time in Livorno. In one instance, Sasportas's colleagues in Amsterdam turned to him for counsel about a paternity suit. The case pitted an unmarried woman who attributed her son's paternity to a particularly wealthy man. Sasportas did not refer to the man by name and simply called him Reuben, the equivalent of John Doe in rabbinic literature. Reuben denied paternity to his dying day. When the son was old enough to ascend to the Torah, he referred to himself as the son of Reuben. This led Reuben's other children to exclaim that he had besmirched their deceased father's reputation. Sasportas ruled that the unmarried woman was to be believed that her son was a Jew but not that the particular Reuben was his father:

[54] On seventeenth-century Livorno, see Francesca Trivellato, *The Familiarity of Strangers: The Sephardic Diaspora, Livorno, and Cross-Cultural Trade in the Early Modern Period* (New Haven, CT: Yale University Press, 2009).

[55] Livorno, Archivio della Comunità Ebraica, Repertorio delle nascite dal'anno 1668 a 1810, 114b, 1679: "Saporta Buenaventura de H: Jacob." Registro dei nati dal 1668–1740, 26b: "aos H. Jacob e Rachel Saportas lhe nasceu uma filha que chamaram Buenaventura a dia 8 Sebat."

[56] Livorno, Archivio della Comunità Ebraica, Registro de Ketubot D, 1672–1679. Sasportas's signature appears on the ketubot included on the following pages: 55b, 56a, 56b, 57a, 63b, 63a (duplicate pagination), 63b (duplicate pagination), 65a, 67b, 68a, 73a, 74a, 75a, 76a, 76b, 79a, 88b. This represents 17 out of 79 ketubot included in the register. In addition, his signature appears twice in Registro de Ketubot, 1678–1686, 2b, 3b. The signature of Sasportas's son Moses appears on the ketubah included on 10a.

For we do not live according to the testimony of an unmarried woman, for if we were to do so, all the prostitutes who became pregnant would attribute their children to the elders of the land, and it is sufficient that she is believed to allow her son to enter the congregation. [57]

Sasportas had left Amsterdam, but his colleagues still relied upon him for his legal expertise in matters of Jewish law. Just as he had done a few years earlier in his pamphlet against Benjamin Mussaphia, Sasportas garnered the support of his colleagues in Livorno and elsewhere for this decision.[58]

In a letter written from Amsterdam around 1680, Isaac Saruco appealed to Sasportas for his ruling in a case about inheritance law and the precedence of a wife to collect her *ketubah* from her husband's estate prior to his other debts being paid. Saruco also mentioned that Isaac Aboab da Fonseca was aging, and that anarchy had taken hold among the Portuguese Jews in Amsterdam.[59] Sasportas responded to Saruco's question with extraordinary politesse. This may have been an attempt by Sasportas to arrange for his own return to Amsterdam, which occurred in the summer of 1680. The immediate cause for his departure was a job opening as head of Ets Haim, a position that Isaac Aboab da Fonseca had held while serving as chief rabbi of the Portuguese Jews.

Sasportas's journey took him from Livorno to Marseilles and on to Amsterdam. While in Marseilles he dispatched a letter to one of his former hosts in Livorno that set off an epistolary controversy. The point of contention between Sasportas and the *parnassim* in Livorno turned upon a question of jurisdiction. Since the Duke of Tuscany had invited members of the Portuguese nation, or conversos, to settle in Livorno in 1591, the newly formed Jewish settlement had practiced a form of autonomy. Most legal matters between Jewish litigants were tried before the *parnassim*; however, within this framework, if two litigants agreed to try their case before a rabbinic court in a matter involving

---

[57] שלא עפ"י הפנויה אנו חיים שאם כן כל הזונות שתתעברנה תאמרנה שהם מעוברות מגדולי הארץ ודיה שתהא נאמנת להכשירו לבוא בקהל.

Sasportas, *Ohel ya-akov* #49, 55a. For another copy of this responsum, see Amsterdam, Bibliotheca Rosenthaliana, HS Ros. 281. Fuks-M., *Ros.*, 55, MS #110.

[58] For their approbations in *Ohel ya-akov*, see #50, #51, #52, 56a–57b.

[59] Ibid., #53, 58a. As cited in Tishby, "Letters by Rabbi Jacob Sasportas," 148n1.

commerce, they were free to do so. At some point in 1679 or 1680, the *parnassim* in Livorno decided that all legal cases, even financial cases where the litigants had agreed to appear before a rabbinic court, should be judged only by the *parnassim*.[60] Upon arrival in Marseilles, Sasportas sent a letter to Gabriel Ariasz, one of the *parnassim* in Livorno who had been among his chief supporters. Sasportas complained bitterly about the poor treatment he had received at the hands of the Portuguese Jews in Livorno. He claimed that his family had lacked sufficient financial support. They had not shown him the proper deference and respect, certainly not compared to the other places in which he had served. Sasportas claimed that his financial situation was so dire that once he was no longer able to earn money from the sale of books he had printed in Amsterdam, he needed to look for other sources of income.[61] He claimed that the recent decision taken by the *parnassim* in Livorno severely constrained the authority of the rabbinate and amounted to a scandal. He informed Ariasz that upon arrival in Amsterdam he planned to print a pamphlet.[62] In this pamphlet, he would reveal the embarrassment the Livorno *parnassim* had caused to the Torah and announce his own *herem* in order to annul their decision. When Ariasz circulated Sasportas's letter to the other *parnassim* in Livorno, they turned to the Amsterdam *maamad* to mediate. Sasportas did not print the pamphlet, and the Livorno *parnassim* changed the wording of their bylaws to allow rabbis to serve as judges of financial cases. In this way, they avoided a public conflict that could have erupted in the press and pitted the Livorno *parnassim* against the head of Ets Haim in Amsterdam.

The conflict may have been stifled but the sources discovered by Tishby and Toaff reveal a number of facts about Sasportas's time in Livorno. In his letter written to Isaac Nahar from Amsterdam several years earlier, Sasportas described the Jews in Livorno as having repeatedly pressed him into their service. From their own defense, written in response to Sasportas's allegations and preserved in the communal record book in Livorno, things looked rather different. In the view of the leaders of the Portuguese Jews in Livorno, Sasportas had sought shel-

[60] Alfredo S. Toaff, "The Controversy between R. Sasportas and the Jewish Community in Leghorn (1681)" (Hebrew), *Sefunot* 9 (1964): 172–175.

[61] Ibid., 180.

[62] Ibid.; Tishby, "Letters by Rabbi Jacob Sasportas," 148.

ter in Livorno in order to take advantage of the climate and in the hope of finding a cure for an ailment that afflicted his eyes.[63] Although his reputation as a firebrand had preceded him, the Livorno *maamad* had accepted Sasportas on the strength of the letters of recommendation that had accompanied his arrival. They specified that he had been asked to teach a number of students and stipulated the generosity with which they had supported him and his family during the course of his stay. They pointedly remarked that he had not been hired to serve as the sole rabbi of Livorno. Finally, they openly accused him of a lack of gratitude for the hospitality that he had been shown in Livorno.

Sasportas had waited until he was well out of Livorno and in Marseilles to write to Ariasz. His letter included a threat to turn to the press in order to shame the Jews in Livorno into compliance with his vision. In a draft of a letter that he planned to send to other rabbinic scholars discovered among his papers and published by Tishby, Sasportas articulated what had left him so appalled by the Jews in Livorno:

> That their first statutes are no good is regrettable, but now, they have acted even more rebelliously, by abrogating the covenant, breaking all bonds and casting off the yoke of the Torah from their holy congregation, and are calling out in public in the synagogue that from now on, anyone who seeks a judgment according to the Torah shall cry out and receive no answer.[64]

According to Sasportas, the system of governance in Livorno was terrible to begin with, as it granted far too much power to the *parnassim* and practically none to the rabbis. On the eve of his departure, the *parnassim* had gone a step further and sought to erode what little authority the rabbinate had by eliminating their jurisdiction over financial matters. A fight about honor and respect was also a struggle over power. From Sasportas's perspective, he was the embodiment of the law as a *haham*. His opinion, the product of his training, his lineage, and his erudition, should have been accepted as the correct interpretation of the Torah. From the perspective of the *parnassim*, Sasportas

---

[63] Toaff, "The Controversy," 176–177.

[64] ועל החקים הראשונים אשר לא טובים אנו מצטערים, והן עתה הוסיפו סרה להפר ברית ולנתק מוסרות לפרוק עול התורה מעל קהלם הקדוש ולהכריז בפומבי בבית הכנסת לומר רם כי מהיום והלאה כל התובע דין תורה בתחלה יהיה צועק ואינו נענה

Tishby, "Letters by Rabbi Jacob Sasportas," 150.

was an impoverished rabbi with poor eyesight upon whom they had showered money and gifts. They controlled the finances, they negotiated the Jews' relationship with the Tuscan authorities, and they hired and fired the religious functionaries.

AMSTERDAM 1680–1698

On his way to Amsterdam, Sasportas stopped for a short period in The Hague, where he established an *eruv*, a legal boundary that allowed Jews to carry in public on the Sabbath.[65] Sasportas arrived in Amsterdam in the fall of 1680. The initial impetus for his return was a job opening in Ets Haim, but one cannot gainsay the presence of the Hebrew press in Amsterdam as an additional factor.

In a letter to his rabbinic colleagues in Livorno, Sasportas described his arrival in Amsterdam:

> On the first Sunday upon my arrival, the *parnassim* came to my home and escorted me [to the synagogue] and Haham Aboab was among them. They seated me upon the throne of glory and all of the chattering classes stood standing on their feet.[66]

Sasportas seemed to have arrived. The *parnassim*, Haham Aboab, and the leaders of the Portuguese Jews in Amsterdam had all paid him his due.

> On the Sabbath, whose weekly reading was the first pericope of Genesis, I delivered a great sermon, and the entire congregation was very happy. And one of the *parnassim*, who was honored as the *hatan bereshit*, Isaac da Pinto, asked me to print it, and I will do so. And when it has appeared in print, I will send you a copy.[67]

Sasportas seems to have received the recognition that he had been craving for so many years. The arrival ceremony and the sermon had

[65] Goldish, "Hakham Jacob Sasportas and the Former Conversos," 154.

[66] ביום הראשון לבואי באו הפרנסים לביתי וליוווני והחכם אבוהב עמהם. והושיבוני בכסא כבוד וכל חשובי העיר עומדים על רגליהם.

Toaff, "The Controversy," 182.

[67] ביום שבת בראשית דרשתי דרשה גדולה ושמחו כל הקהל מאד. ובקשו הא' הפרנסים והחתן בראשית שהיה הא' יצחק דה פינטו שאדפיס אותה וכן אעשה, וכאשר תסתיים ההדפסה אשלחנה לכב'.

Ibid.

Figure 17. Aernout Nagh-
tegael, portrait of Isaac
Aboab da Fonseca, 1688.
Isaac Aboab da Fonseca, the
chief rabbi of the Portuguese
Jews of Amsterdam until his
death in 1693, retired from
his position as the head of
Ets Haim Yeshiva in 1680.
Rijksmuseum, Amsterdam.

taken place in the synagogue, known as the Esnoga, which had been
opened with great fanfare only five years earlier.[68] On that occasion, a
number of prominent rabbis and scholars delivered sermons, which
had later appeared in print in a special edition to mark the occasion.
Sasportas, who had been in Amsterdam in 1675 and had delivered a
sermon a week later, did not see his sermon printed in the special edition.[69] Five years later, Isaac da Pinto urged Sasportas to print a copy
of his recently delivered sermon. In a particularly wicked gesture, Sasportas informed his colleagues in Livorno that he would send them a
copy as soon as it appeared. To the best of my knowledge, the sermon
Sasportas delivered in the fall of 1680 never appeared in print.

[68] Leo and Rena Fuks, "The Inauguration of the Portuguese Synagogue of Amsterdam, Netherlands, in 1675," *Arquivos do Centro Cultural Portugês* 14 (1979): 489–507
[69] Franco Mendes, *Memorias*, 79.

Figure 18. Emanuel de Witte, interior of the Portuguese Synagogue in Amsterdam, 1680. A view of Portuguese Synagogue painted in the year that Sasportas returned to Amsterdam from his sojourn in Livorno. Rijksmuseum, Amsterdam.

DAVID LIDA

Upon his return to Amsterdam, it did not take long for Sasportas to re-enter the fray of rabbinic combat. This time the controversy revolved around a rabbi from Poland named David Lida.[70] Lida had arrived in Amsterdam from Mainz at around the same time that Sasportas had returned in 1680. An extremely learned man who had his enemies, Lida had followed a trajectory similar to those of many of the learned elites in Poland-Lithuania in the second half of the seventeenth century.[71] He had moved repeatedly, serving as a rabbi and printing his books in the years he moved from east to west and back east. The Ashkenazi Jews among whom he was invited to serve in Amsterdam were riven by fac-

[70] Adolf A. Eisner, *Toledot ha-gaon rabbi David Lida* (Breslau, 1938).
[71] Reiner, "An Itinerant Preacher Publishes His Books."

tion. A congregation of largely German Jews had existed in Amsterdam since 1635. In the wake of the Thirty Years' War and the rebellion in the Polish-Lithuanian Commonwealth of 1648 and 1649, Polish Jewish refugees had flooded into Amsterdam. In 1660 the Polish Jews had established their own congregation, which lasted until 1673, when the Amsterdam authorities ordered them to rejoin the German Jews and form a single Ashkenazi congregation.

In the second half of the seventeenth century, Amsterdam had become an increasingly important center for the printing and publication of books by Ashkenazim, both in Hebrew and in Yiddish. Almost immediately upon his arrival in Amsterdam, Lida took advantage of the availability of a Hebrew printing press and issued a commentary on the biblical book of Ruth entitled *Migdal David*.[72] As rabbi of the Ashkenazi Jews, he also issued approbations to books that appeared in Amsterdam. In at least three instances, his approbation appeared alongside that of the rabbis of the Portuguese Jews, Isaac Aboab da Fonseca and Sasportas.[73] During this period, another Ashkenazi scholar, named Nissan b. Judah Leib, lived in Amsterdam, where he was overseeing the printing of a book by his father-in-law, Benjamin Zeev Wolf.[74] At some point after the appearance of *Migdal David*, Nissan b. Judah Leib and a number of other members of the Ashkenazi congregation in Amsterdam accused David Lida of plagiarism. They alleged that his commentary on Ruth had actually been the work of another scholar, named Hayyim Cohen of Aleppo. Lida was also accused of including allusions to Sabbetai Zevi in his sermons. Allegations and accusations quickly flew on both sides, and Lida's position as rabbi immediately became polarizing. Lida, who was aware of his own unpopularity, turned to the Council of Four Lands, a supracommunal organization of Polish and Lithuanian Jewry, for support.[75]

[72] David Lida, *Migdal David* (Amsterdam: Uri Phoebus Halevi, 1680).

[73] *Olat tamid* (Amsterdam, 1681); *Marat ha-zedek* (Amsterdam: Uri Phoebus Halevi, 1682); *Zivhei tuviah* (Amsterdam, 1683).

[74] *Nahalat Binyamin* (Amsterdam: Uri Phoebus Halevi, 1682).

[75] On the Council of Four Lands, see Adam Teller, "Rabbis without a Function? The Polish Rabbinate and the Council of Four Lands in the 16th–18th Centuries," in *Jewish Religious Leadership: Image and Reality*, ed. Jack Wertheimer (New York: Jewish Theological Seminary, 2004), 1:371–400, discussion of Lida on 392; on its authority beyond Poland, see Moshe Rosman, "Authority of the Council of Four Lands beyond Poland" (Hebrew), *Bar-Ilan* 24–25 (1989): 11–30, discussion of Lida on 20–23.

The Council of Four Lands quickly came to Lida's defense. In September 1681, on the day after Yom Kippur, Uri Phoebus Halevi printed a broadsheet written by the Council of Four Lands with a vociferous *herem* condemning the Ashkenazi Jews in Amsterdam who had unjustly slandered David Lida.[76] Lida's opponents among the Ashkenazi Jews, in turn, appealed to the Sephardic rabbis in Amsterdam, and it was at this juncture that Sasportas played a crucial, perhaps decisive role. *Ohel ya-akov* includes a series of letters signed by a *bet din* of the Sephardic Jews in Amsterdam. The court consisted of Isaac Aboab da Fonseca, Selomoh de Olivera, and Sasportas.[77] Some of the letters bear only Sasportas's signature, others those of Sasportas and Olivera, and still others all three. When the letters bear all three, Sasportas's name appears second, after Isaac Aboab da Fonseca, the chief rabbi, but before Olivera. The letters survive in Sasportas's handwriting, and Tishby posited that Sasportas was the prime mover of the three rabbis on the Sephardic *bet din*.[78] The Sephardic rabbis sought to keep the peace, and tried, rather unsuccessfully at first, to placate their colleagues in Poland. They patiently but firmly explained that the demand for a *herem* against David Lida's opponents put them in a difficult position.

> If this issue had remained amongst the elders and leaders of the congregation, the fear would not be so great, because they would have hidden it from the masses out of concern for their honor and for ours, and the result would not be destruction; however, "there went out a champion of the camp named Goliath" (I Samuel 17:4) and with wicked intentions he had revealed and printed it, to the point that it is being sold for a pittance to Jews and gentiles, and it has even been translated into their language, and this is the cause of shame and anger, and has awakened hatred and jealousy among the nations. [79]

[76] L. Fuks, "De Amstderamse Opperabbijn David Lida en de Vierlandensynode (1680–1684)," *SR* 6 (1972): 175–176.

[77] Sasportas, *Ohel ya-akov*, #75, #76, 80a–82b. The text of the responsa contains two passages marked #75, the first of which contains two letters.

[78] Tishby, introduction to Sasportas, *ZNZ*, 18.

[79] ואם היתה מגעת ליד הבעלים פרנסי הק״ק לא היתה החרדה כל כך כי הם מעיני ההמון יעלימוה בעבור כבודם וכבודנו ולא נפיק מינה חורבא, אך יצא יצא איש הבינים גלית שמו ולכונה רעה גילה אותה והדפיסה עד שהיה נמכרת בפחות משוה פרוטה לישראלי׳ ולערלים והועתקה והועתקה בלשונם וכדי בזיון וקצף לעורר שנאה וקנאה עלינו בין האומות.

Sasportas, *Ohel ya-akov*, #76, 81a.

Figure 19. Broadside, David Lida. This printed broadside signed by the rabbinic lumi-naries of Poland attempted to defend David Lida from the attacks against him by Ashkenazi Jews resident in Amsterdam. Reproduced by permission of the Bodleian Libraries, University of Oxford.

The Sephardic rabbinic court, and Sasportas among them, objected to the way that Lida and his allies had conducted their fight. Had it re-mained circumscribed within the Ashkenazi elites, there would have been little cause for concern. Lida had gone public, and he had printed his complaints for all to see. This may refer to a pamphlet Lida printed about the controversy that survives in a number of copies and was pub-lished in its entirety by Aron Freimann.[80] It may, however, refer to an-other broadsheet that has not survived. The point, for the Sephardic rabbinic court, was that Lida and his allies had publicized an internal Jewish dispute. At least some type of printed text had appeared in "their language," which the members of the court do not specify but may refer to Dutch or Spanish. This cheap printed ephemera was making a mock-ery of the Jews in front of the gentiles.

[80]David Lida, *Be-er eshek* (Amsterdam: Uri Phoebus Halevi, 1680). Aron Freimann, "R. David Lida and His Justification in *Be-er eshek*" (Hebrew), in *Sefer ha-yovel shai li-khevod Nahum Soko-lov* (Warsaw: Shuldberg, 1904), 455–480.

Sasportas and his colleagues insisted that the demand by the Council of the Four Lands to issue a ban against Lida's opponents betrayed a misunderstanding of the local Dutch context:

> And specifically, the members of the secular authorities do not want [us to employ] the ban and excommunication, and in the past, following some discussions among the leaders of our congregation, they decreed that we should not ban or excommunicate anyone because this only increases the likelihood of its settlement.[81]

The Sephardic *bet din* continued to explain cogently but firmly to their colleagues in Poland that they had intervened in a case about whose details they were misinformed and about whose context they did not understand.

Members of the Council of Four Lands were unimpressed by their Sephardic colleagues and responded with an even stronger ban against Lida's opponents that appeared as a printed broadsheet in March 1683.[82] Lida was out of luck. His supporters were far away in Poland, and his adversaries among the Ashkenazi Jews were insistent that he leave. After stepping down temporarily and returning for a short period, Lida left his position as rabbi of the Ashkenazi Jews in 1684. The Council of Four Lands had proved powerless to help David Lida. In the spring of 1684, a group of rabbis in Krotoshin wrote to the Ashkenazi congregation in Amsterdam, rescinding their previous bans and directing them to seek the guidance of the Sephardic rabbinic court in reaching a settlement. A few months later, a group of rabbis in Posen wrote to the Sephardic rabbinic court and asked them to establish peace in the Ashkenazi congregation.[83]

The letters written by the Sephardic rabbinic court to the Council of Four Lands, whether written entirely by Sasportas or with his input, sound out a number of familiar themes from his other writings. Sas-

---

[81] ובפרט בין אנשי השררה אשר בחרם ונידוי לא יחפוצו ובימים שעברו מהדורי מילי בין יחידי קהילתנו גזרו עלינו לשלא נדות והחרים לשום בר נש כי בזה יתרבה ישובה.

Sasportas, *Ohel ya-akov*, #76, 81a.

[82] Fuks, "De Amstderamse Opperabbijn David Lida en de Vierlandensynode (1680–1684)," 177–178.

[83] L. Fuks, "Nieuwe Gegevens over de Amsterdamse Opperabbijn David Lida en de Vierlandensynode," *SR* 10 (1976): 189–194; Leib Fuks, "Disharmony between the 'Council of Four Lands,' and the Ashkenazi Kehilla of Amsterdam during the Rabbinate of R. David Lida (1680–1684)" (Hebrew), *Michael* 6 (1980): 170–176. Between 1684 and 1687 Lida continued to live in Amsterdam. In 1687 he received 250 fl. from the Ashkenazi Jews and returned to Poland, where he died in 1696.

portas distinguished between the elites and the rest of the people and expressed deep concern about Jews discussing their differences in public. The printed broadsheet, just as it had a decade and a half earlier during the peak of Sabbatian messianic enthusiasm, had the potential to expose Jewish life to public shame before the secular authorities. The Sephardic rabbinic court in Amsterdam insisted that they had intervened in a dispute among Ashkenazi Jews only after they had been asked to do so, just as Sasportas and Moses Israel had similarly insisted in Hamburg in 1669. Finally, the issue of *kavod*, honor or due, repeatedly resurfaced in the letters of the Sephardic *bet din*.

APPROBATIONS TO HEBREW BOOKS

In the years between the conversion of Sabbetai Zevi and his return to Amsterdam from Livorno, Sasportas occasionally composed approbations to Hebrew books. In 1667 he had issued from Hamburg an approbation to *Nahalat shiva* that appeared in Amsterdam. A set of glosses by Samuel b. David Halevi of Mesritz to *Even ha-ezer*, the book appeared with a frontispiece that indicated the year of its printing with a Hebrew phrase: "The Messiah son of David arrives." As he explained in his approbation, Sasportas had examined the manuscript of *Nahalat shiva* while the author had passed through Hamburg on his way to Amsterdam. He may not have seen the frontispiece until well after the fact of its publication and the Messiah's conversion, if at all. Sasportas's approbation to *Nahalat shiva* reveals a number of details about him. The first has to do with nomenclature. The heading of the approbation referred to Sasportas as החכם השלם המקובל האלהי (Heb. the complete sage and divine kabbalist).[84] Sasportas, as he perceived himself and as he was perceived by others, was both a *haham*, a learned scholar of the Talmud, and a kabbalist. The two categories, far from being mutually exclusive, reinforced one another in the second half of the seventeenth century. The second has to do with Sasportas's attitude toward the genre of the approbation. Most of Sasportas's text, which takes up roughly two-thirds of a single page, constituted a denunciation of the genre and an expression of his contempt for writing. Most authors who

[84] *Sefer nahalat shivah*, 1a.

write books, Sasportas declared, plagiarize the work of others. Most approbations, he confessed, constituted worthless praise. In the second half, he allowed that in this one instance he saw fit to make an exception and issue an approbation.

This posture would change during the last eighteen years of his life when Sasportas resided in Amsterdam and issued over twenty approbations to Hebrew books, all but one of which were printed in Amsterdam. What was an approbation and what, if anything, can this scattered corpus of texts indicate about Sasportas's in the last two decades of his life? The increasing number of approbations he issued in his final period in Amsterdam and the frequency with which his name appeared alongside those of other rabbis, such as Isaac Aboab da Fonseca and Moses D'Aguilar, appear to be part of his official duties among the Portuguese Jews of Amsterdam, first as head of Ets Haim and eventually as chief rabbi.

The approbation as a genre was a direct consequence of the culture of Hebrew print and served a number of different functions in the early modern period.[85] The first concerns an attempt to prevent the unauthorized reproduction of a book by another printer. While it may be anachronistic to define this as copyright, a concept that did not actually exist before the eighteenth century, rabbinic authorities including Sasportas warned enterprising bookmen against reissuing a given book for a period ranging from five to fifteen years.[86] In this sense, rabbinic approbations may be analogous to the privileges issued by either the state or the church to printers for a set period of time.[87] Approbations also appear to have functioned as an early modern blurb or public letter of recommendation. The proliferation of celebrated rabbinic authorities in a book's prefatory material would serve (at least theoretically) as an enticement to a potential buyer. Whether the author of an approbation received compensation, in cash or in kind, remains unclear. By the time Sasportas began issuing approbations, the genre had existed for nearly two centuries.[88] Its efficacy as a means to prevent unauthor-

[85] Meir Benayahu, *Haskamah u-reshut bi-defuse Venetzyah* (Jerusalem: Ben Zvi Institute, 1971); Nahum Rakover, *Zekhut ha-yotsrim ba-mekorot ha-yehudiyim* (Jerusalem: Moreshet ha-mishpat be-yisrael, 1991).

[86] Mark Rose, *Authors and Owners: The Invention of Copyright* (Cambridge, MA: Harvard University Press, 1993).

[87] Elizabeth Armstrong, *Before Copyright: The French Book-Privilege System, 1498–1526* (Cambridge: Cambridge University Press, 1990).

[88] Rakover dates the first approbation to *Sefer ha-Agur* printed in Naples in 1490.

ized reproduction and as an inducement to purchase was much in doubt. A culture of worthless praise had induced a period of hyperinflation, as authors of approbations became ever more exaggerated in their assessments, and printers garnered an increasing number of approbations for each book that issued from their presses. This would precipitate a backlash in the eighteenth century, as some rabbis refrained from issuing them altogether or issued them only sparingly.[89] But in the late seventeenth century, the genre was flourishing, and Sasportas participated in it during his final period in Amsterdam.

When viewed in the aggregate, Sasportas's approbations manifest a number of features. First, and perhaps most importantly, they were relatively few in number. Over and above the fact that he had issued only a handful before he had reached his seventies, Sasportas gave approbations to only a quarter of the eighty books printed in Amsterdam between 1681 and 1698. By way of comparison, David Oppenheim, perhaps the most prominent rabbi in central Europe at the turn of the eighteenth century, issued over eighty approbations between 1678 and 1722.[90] During the first half of the eighteenth century, Jonathan Eibeschütz issued approbations to twenty-one books, a number roughly equivalent to Sasportas's output. A second factor pertains to the physical proximity between Sasportas and the books to which he issued approbations. Many rabbis who issued approbations did so from afar. Thus a book printed in Amsterdam might have an approbation from a rabbi in Frankfurt or Prague or Hamburg. At times, the rabbi would mention specifically that he had read the book in manuscript before it appeared in print; at others, he would simply praise the author or the subject in such generic terms as to leave one in doubt as to whether he had read it at all. Two of the books to which Sasportas issued approbations appeared in print in places where he was not resident at the time. *Nahalat shiva* appeared in Amsterdam while he was living in Hamburg, and the Babylonian Talmud was printed in Frankfurt an der Oder in 1697 while he was living in Amsterdam.[91] Apart from these two, the other books to which Sasportas appended approbations appeared in Amsterdam while he was resident there. A third issue relates

[89] Carlebach, *Pursuit of Heresy*, 267–270.

[90] Michael Laurence Miller, "Rabbi David Oppenheim on Trial: Turks, Titles, and Tribute in Counter-Reformation Prague," *JQR* 106 (2016): 64.

[91] *Massechet Berachoth* (Michael Gottschalk: Frankfurt an der Order, 1697), 1b.

to a continuity in genre between the types of books Sasportas edited and corrected in the 1650s and those to which he gave his imprimatur several decades later. The books that Sasportas edited were reference works, anthologies, and abridgments; those to which he issued approbations were of similar ilk. One can also note a remarkable shift between the two periods. As an editor, Sasportas dealt almost exclusively with works written by Sephardim; as a rabbi who issued approbations, Sasportas dealt with many books written by and intended for Ashkenazi Jews, including a Yiddish translation of the Bible, an index to *Shnei luhot ha-berit* by the Ashkenazi kabbalist Isaiah Horowitz, and a volume of Talmudic commentary by the Polish luminary Solomon Luria. Amsterdam had long been a center of Yiddish book production. Solomon ibn Verga's *Shevet yehudah* had appeared in Yiddish in Amsterdam for a second time even before Sasportas's arrival in midcentury. Nevertheless, as the century drew to a close, Yiddish and Hebrew books by and for Ashkenazi Jews began to appear with increasingly frequency. This bibliographic shift reflects a change in the overall demographic balance of the Jewish population of Amsterdam, as well as the growing wealth of the Ashkenazi Jews. Much as Venice had served as a hub for Sephardic printing in the sixteenth century, Amsterdam began to play a similar role for the Ashkenazi world, east and west, in the second half of the seventeenth century. This also reflects a shift in Sasportas's activities as a *posek*, or legal authority. His responsa from his first period in Amsterdam and his time in Saleh address Sephardic Jews. Books written by Ashkenazi Jews may appear, but actual Ashkenazi Jews and their questions do not. By the end of his time in Hamburg in the late 1660s, Ashkenazi Jews take on an increasingly prominent role in Sasportas's legal writing.

ETS HAIM YESHIVA

For more than a decade after his return to Amsterdam in the fall of 1680, Sasportas taught at Ets Haim.[92] Early in the seventeenth century, Portuguese Jews set up a primary school for boys called Talmud To-

---

[92] Paraira and da Silva Rosa, *Gedenkschrift uitgegeven ter gelegenheid van het 300-jarig Bestaan der Onderwijsinrichtingen Talmud Tora en Ets Haim.*

rah.[93] At the age of thirteen boys who wanted to continue their studies, or, more likely, whose parents wanted them to continue their studies, could apply to Ets Haim.[94] During the period 1659–1750, 800 Portuguese Jews belonged to Ets Haim.[95] By the end of the seventeenth century, when Sasportas served as *rosh yeshiva* (head of the academy), there were roughly 209 students divided among seven classes according to age and level with an average of 30 students per class. It was not the only institution in early modern Amsterdam called a yeshiva, a Hebrew word roughly translated as academy, but it was by far the largest and most important. It had its own library, its own building, and its own staff. Many of its alumni went on to serve as rabbis in other Jewish communities, such as Moses Zacuto in Mantua, Isaac Nahar in Verona, and Josiah Pardo in Curaçao and Jamaica.[96] Its elitist admissions policy was a direct reflection of the Jews it served. In the 1650s, the yeshiva dismissed several students, retaining only those who were well-mannered and studious.[97] In 1660, the yeshiva announced that it would no longer admit *italianos, tudescos,* or *polacos,* referring to Jews from Italy, Germanic lands, or Poland-Lithuania.[98]

Sasportas had taught in Ets Haim during his first extended stay in Amsterdam in the 1650s, when he had taught Isaac Nahar. During that period, he had served as one of several teachers but had not been designated head of the academy. In the period between 1680 and 1693, his status changed as he assumed the position and title vacated by the retirement of Isaac Aboab da Fonseca. The 1680s, then, seemed to mark his arrival and his acquisition of the recognition he had long craved. The yeshiva was flourishing, if one were to judge by the number of its students and the placement of its alumni. These facts all mask a basic

[93] Julia R. Lieberman, "Academias literarias y de estudios religiosos en Amsterdam en el siglo XVII," in *Los judaizantes en Europa y la litteratura castellana del Siglo de Oro,* ed. Fernando Díaz Esteban (Madrid: Letrúmero, 1994), 247–260; Gérard Nahon, "Les institutions éducatives au XVIIe siècle: trois paradigmes—Palestine, Amsterdam, Maroc," in *Le Monde Sépharade,* ed. Shmuel Trigano (Paris: Seuil, 2006), 2:302–318.

[94] Levie Bernfeld, *Poverty and Welfare,* 98.

[95] Ibid., 126n474.

[96] Ibid., 98n175.

[97] Ibid., 92.

[98] Ibid., 18. On the elitist character of the admissions policy of Ets Haim well into the eighteenth century, see Gerard Nahon, "R. Rafael b. Eleazar Meldola in Bayonne, 1728–1741" (Hebrew), in *Lo yasur shevet mi-yehuda: hanhaga, rabanut, ve-kehila be-toledot yisrael mehkarim mugashim le-Professor Simon Schwarzfuchs,* ed. Joseph R. Hacker and Yaron Harel (Jerusalem: Bialik Institute, 2011), 279–280.

although somewhat more intangible fact. Beginning in the 1670s and continuing through the next several decades, young Portuguese Jewish men had less and less interest in studying Jewish sources.[99]

A responsum in *Ohel ya-akov* reflects a yeshiva roiling with tension and barely contained conflict.[100] It contains no date, but its placement within the collection and internal evidence suggest it was composed between Sasportas's return from Livorno in 1680 and the death of Isaac Aboab da Fonseca in 1693. In one passage, the names Isaac Uziel and Saul Levi Morteira appear followed by the phrase "of blessed memory," while Aboab's name does not appear with the same honorific. Furthermore, the putative author of the responsum, Moseh Sasportas, referred to his father, Jacob, as an old man at the time of his writing. Without too much exegetical strain but without suggesting a definitive time, I date it between 1680 and 1693.

Moseh Sasportas recounts a rebellion of students against his father, who had served as their teacher. Unlike other responsa in *Ohel ya-akov*, which name an addressee and attempt to resolve a specific legal problem, this one reads as if it were a lengthy report of an incident rather than a letter written to a given individual. The tone shifts throughout, as at times the author appears to address the rebellious students, at others his father, and at still others no one in particular. In terms of the legal issue, the most recurring legal problem appears to be one of issuing instruction in the presence of one's teacher. This takes on two manifestations: the first and the ostensible cause for the writing of the responsum has to do with the students' flouting the authority of Jacob Sasportas; the second has to do with Moseh Sasportas's ability to write such a responsum in the presence of his father. Responsum 61 in *Ohel ya-akov*, which immediately follows, actually serves as a coda to this one, in which Jacob Sasportas applauded Moseh's efforts on his father's behalf.

The description of the student rebellion against Sasportas in Ets Haim bears a number of striking parallels to Sasportas's account of Sabbatianism. The two central issues broached in the responsum, the authority of the rabbi and the honor of his position, were leitmotifs of

[99] Yosef Kaplan, "Secularising the Portuguese Jews: Integration and Orthodoxy in Early Modern Judaism," *Simon Dubnow Institute Yearbook* 6 (2007): 99–110, as cited by Levie Bernfeld, *Poverty and Welfare*, 129n510.

[100] Sasportas, *Ohel ya-akov*, #60, 65a–68a.

Zizath novel zvi. What was happening in Ets Haim in the late seventeenth century was being narrated in terms strikingly similar to those in which Sasportas described Sabbatianism, and much of the language used in this responsum echoes various passages in *Zizath novel zvi.* Thus Moseh Sasportas lamented the reversal of social hierarchies:

> The order has been reversed, and those on top are now on the bottom, and those on the bottom are now on the top. [101]

Just as the reversal of traditional social hierarchies in the period of Sabbatian enthusiasm had led Sasportas to embark on an epistolary campaign, the unbecoming impudence of the students in Ets Haim had compelled Moseh Sasportas to defend his father.

Much of the discussion in the responsum revolved around a Talmudic passage about Rabbi Judah the Prince and Rabbi Hiya, and respect for rabbinic authority. In discussing the story, Moseh Sasportas concluded,

> Whoever considers this rationally will see even at the most superficial level, what punishment is meted out to those who behave arrogantly in the presence of their rabbi.[102]

In *Zizath novel zvi,* Sasportas had responded in a very similar style to one of Nathan of Gaza's letters, alluding to

> anyone who looks with the fine eye of Jewishness at the words of this denier.[103]

In another passage toward the end of the responsum, Moseh Sasportas dwelled at length on the affront to his father's honor.

> As if it were not enough what they had done in the study house, with their instruction, denigration, and seizure of authority in the presence of the rabbi, but even in the synagogue, in public, they sought to denigrate his honor. When he rose to the lectern and was summoned to the Torah, the members of the study house usually stood in his honor as

---

[101]. והן עתה נהפך הסדר ועליונים למטה ותחתונים למעלה.
Ibid., #60, 65b.
[102]. יראה הרואה בעין שכלו משטחיות הדברים באיזה עונש נידונים אותם אשר בפני הרב מתיהרים.
Ibid., #60, 66a.
[103]. יראה הרואה בעין יפה של יהדות בדברי הכופר הזה.
Sasportas, *ZNZ,* 201.

long as he was reading from the Torah scroll, even if by law they were not required to do so apart from the times that he passed right in front of them until he reached his own seat. In any case, from the time this congregation was founded, the time of Rabbi Isaac Uziel and Rabbi Saul Levi of the house of Morteira, of blessed memory, [up to] and [including] Rabbi Isaac Aboab, the students have always humbled themselves before their teacher and showed him their respect so long as he stood at the lectern. This was the appropriate way for them to behave, and it honored them, too. They all used to do this for my father as well. But this time, some of them refused, considering themselves superior to their colleagues and no longer subjected to the authority of a rabbi who, according to them, is not their rabbi. And so they remained seated while others stood.[104]

The rebellion against Sasportas was partial rather than total. That is to say, not all of the students openly flouted his authority. Some continued to stand out of respect for their teacher, while others sat in defiance. The student revolt appears to have focused on instruction and a sentiment that they no longer needed Sasportas as a teacher. If this incident did indeed take place in the 1680s or 1690s, it hardly comes as a surprise that a group of students, not always the most staid stratum within society, bristled at the instruction of an irascible old man.

Moseh Sasportas drew a very clear distinction between the study house, the *bet midrash*, and the synagogue, the *bet kenesset*. There can be little doubt that Ets Haim was an elitist institution meant to provide in-depth training for a number of outstanding students. One of the remarkable facts about the Portuguese Jews of Amsterdam was their ability to found and maintain a yeshiva that could produce its own rabbinic elite. To a certain extent, what happened in the study house stayed in the study house. The synagogue, however, was an altogether different story. Almost by its very nature it was a public institution. Gentiles came to gawk in the synagogue; deals were made in its court-

ולא די מה שעשו בבית המדרש בהוראותם ולזלזולם ונטילת שררה לפני הרב אלא בבה״כ בפומבי נתכוונו לזלזל[104] בכבודו כי כאשר עלה לבימה לס״ת היו רגילים כל בני המדרש לעמוד לכבודו כל עוד שהוא קורא בס״ת ואף אם מדינא אינם צריכים כי אם מידי עברו עד שישב במקומו מכל מקום מעת הוסדה הקהלה הזאת מזמן כמוה״רר יצחק עוזיאל וכמוה״רר שאול הלוי לבית מורטירא ע״ה וכמוה״רר יצחק אבוהב נהגו ענוה יתרה התלמידים לחלוק כבוד לרב וכל עוד היותו שם בביימה וזה דרך מוסר וכבוד להם ג״כ. וגם לא״א נר״ו היו עושים כן כולם אך בפעם הזאת קצתם אשר נראה להם שיותר שאת יש להם על חבריהם וכבר הם אינם כפופים לרב לפי שאינו רבם לפי דעתם ישבו במקומם וחבריהם עומדים.

Sasportas, *Ohel ya-akov*, #60, 67b.

yard; Jewish life manifested itself as a collective in the synagogue. Even though Ets Haim of the 1680s and 1690s was in the same physical complex as the Esnoga, the one was a private, elitist place of instruction, the other a raucous, boisterous display of power and wealth. Thus when the yeshiva students took the liberty of breaking publicly with established convention and sitting while their teacher was called to the Torah, this was an affront of an altogether different order from their contempt for Sasportas's instruction in the classrooms and corridors of the study house. It was a public humiliation of a kind that neither Sasportas nor his family could suffer in silence.

This very distinction between the synagogue and the study house appeared within *Zizath novel zvi*. Responsum 60 thus reads somewhat like one of Sasportas's own letters. In terms of its language, many of the very same phrases used in *Zizath novel zvi* reappear in this responsum; the density of allusions that characterized Sasportas's own writing, the acerbic criticism, the penchant and almost relish for intellectual combat—all hold true for the depiction of the rebellious students. Equally significant is the overlap in terms of content. Fear of social chaos and concern for rabbinic honor dominated Sasportas's account of Sabbatianism.

Jacob, rather than Moseh, may have been the actual author of this account. Sasportas had ventriloquized himself in at least two other instances: in a letter to his colleagues in North Africa who continued to celebrate the ninth of Av as a holiday after the conversion of Sabbetai Zevi, and in a letter to the Ashkenazim of Altona. In those cases, Sasportas spoke to colleagues slightly farther away from his actual residence in the voice of an anonymous student; in this instance, he spoke to his own constituents in the voice of his son. That Sasportas had adopted a similar practice on a number of occasions several decades earlier would not be sufficient grounds to conclude that he, rather than his son, wrote this letter. In this case, the material evidence offers additional data. *Ohel ya-akov* survives in a single manuscript that has all the telltale signs of having been used in the printer's shop for the one and only printing in 1737. Many of the texts have the marks of a corrector; paragraph breaks correlate between the manuscript and printed edition; when the printed text includes a note that the responsum ends abruptly, the text in the manuscript ends abruptly as well. In his preface to *Ohel ya-akov*, Abraham Sasportas indicated that the manuscript used by the editor, David Meldola, had been written in Sasportas's own hand. Many of the scholars who read Sasportas's handwriting after his death mentioned the difficulty of his script. Responsum 60 survives in the same semicursive hand as the rest of the manuscript and as other known samples of Sasportas's handwriting. Furthermore, there is continuity between responsum 60 and responsum 61, which Jacob Sasportas acknowledged having written. One may object that Moseh may have had awful handwriting like his father, but no manuscripts in Moseh's hand are known, and Sasportas's one son whose Hebrew manuscripts survive, Isaac, wrote in a perfectly legible hand.

What difference does it make whether Jacob or Moseh wrote responsum 60? Sasportas was an old man at the time of his fight with the students in Ets Haim. He may have written his response to their rebellion in the voice of his son because he considered it unbecoming for someone his age to defend himself in public. The offense by the students was so great, particularly once it had spilled over into the synagogue, that some form of response was necessary. Who better to defend the honor of a maligned rabbinic luminary than that luminary's son?

CHIEF RABBI AND DEATH

In April 1693 Isaac Aboab da Fonseca died. Shortly thereafter the *parnassim* in Amsterdam appointed Sasportas chief rabbi. At long last, it seemed, Sasportas had arrived. He had replaced the colleague in whose shadow he had worked intermittently for the previous four decades. The two rabbis appear to have had a functional working relationship. Their signatures appear together on many documents, from approbations to printed books to legal responsa. At the peak of Sabbatian enthusiasm, when Sasportas resided in Hamburg and Aboab da Fonseca in Amsterdam, they had exchanged sharp letters about how to interpret the news of the Messiah's arrival. The public absence of Sasportas at the inauguration of the Esnoga in 1675, when all of Aboab da Fonseca's students delivered celebratory sermons that later appeared in print, seems to indicate that their relationship remained correct rather than warm.

When Aboab da Fonseca died, Sasportas would have seemed a natural and even obvious choice to replace him. He knew the Portuguese Jews for several decades; he had earned their respect as a legal authority, if not their affection as a pastor. But he was old. He was not the only choice, nor does he appear to have been the first choice of the lay oligarchs. One need not look further than Sasportas's own irascibility to find reasons for the *parnassim* to have passed over him. In this instance, some evidence suggests that they actively sought another candidate with the assumption that he would inherit the position when Aboab da Fonseca died. The single source for this information was composed in 1778, well over eighty-five years after the incident allegedly occurred.

In 1778 Hayim Joseph David Azulai recorded an incident in his travel diary, a manuscript with which he traveled and which later appeared in print under the title *Sefer Ma-agal Tov*.

R. David Meldola came to The Hague for his daughter's wedding and called upon me. He spoke incessantly about R. [Solomon] Salem. He said that when [Hezekiah da Silva, the author of] the *Peri hadash* was in Amsterdam, R. Isaac Aboab was quite old. The congregation asked him [Hezekiah da Silva] to serve as a rabbi while the aged rabbi continued in his position. When Aboab died, it would all be his. He responded that he did not want to receive any gifts, and therefore the congregation would have to ensure that he was well paid. Furthermore, he did not want to be subservient to the *maamad* in matters of Jewish law. They accepted his second stipulation that concerning matters of Jewish law the *maamad* would not be able to oppose him. In terms of his first, they offered to double his salary but nothing more. He responded that he would accept nothing less than 1,000 ducats. The members of the *maamad* consulted with one another before finally agreeing to pay him the 1,000 ducats that he had demanded. They told him happily, but he said that he would have to think it over. On Sunday, he went to the *maamad* and said that he thought it was impossible. They began to argue with him. Finally, he acquiesced and said: Tomorrow I will notify all the distinguished members of the congregation that they will have me [as their rabbi]. On Monday, I will pay a visit. On Saturday, I will deliver a sermon. On Sunday, I will go and declare that my reign has begun. And I will tell the members of the congregation that they have been quite lax in their observance and that they should repent from their wicked ways. In the beginning, I will tell the first *parnas* who resides with two gentile women that he is under suspicion and that he should banish them from his house. Then, I will tell the second *parnas*, such and such, and

so on and so forth, for I want to save my soul, but they are sunk deep
in the mire (Ps. 69:3) of publicly known sins. This is what I asked to do:
I want to be able to issue the law, to purge and purify the congregation
from all of its sin. I shall rebuke them for their iniquity, and I shall curse
them and order their destruction. I think you will then join up against
me, and the conspiracy will be strong[enough] to expel me from the land
(2 Sam. 15:12). But who knows what the day will bring. Perhaps you
have it in your hearts to purge the impurity from the land to fulfill the
words of the rabbis correctly. If [this turns out to be] so, then God will
renew a steadfast spirit in me (Ps. 51:12). I will have fulfilled an important commandment while at the same time I will be able to study Torah
as I wish, quietly and calmly. Other congregations will learn from you
and do as you have done, so the merit of many now depends on you.
But I can see that you only want me to serve as a figurehead, and not
for the sake of heaven. You want to pursue whatever your heart desires
without any resistance. Therefore, even though you have pledged 1,000
ducats per annum, you have not really understood my request. I want
to be able to decide the law without any resistance. When the *parnassim* heard these holy words, they said to the rabbi, [the author of the]
Peri hadash, of blessed memory, you are correct. In truth, you cannot
serve as the rabbi of our congregation. He departed peacefully. Here
ends the story as told me at length by the aforementioned R. David
Meldola.[105]

[105] ור״ד מילדולא בא להשיא בתו פה האייא ובא לבקרני ופיו מילא לדבר על ה׳ שלם. וסיפר כי כאשר היה הפר״ח
באמשט׳ היה הרב יצחק אבוהב זקן מופלא וביקשו הקהל ממנו להיות רב והרב הזקן יהיה בכבודו וכשיפטר ישאר הכל
לו. והוא אמר שרצונו שלא יתנו לו שום מתנה ולכן צריך שיתנו מהק״ק בשופע. וגם שאינו רוצה להיות תחת אנשי
המעמד בדבר הנוגע לדין ואמרו שמקבלים שבדבר הנוגע לדין תורה המעמד לא יוכלו לבא נגדו ולענין הפרס יוסיפו
לו אך שיהיה כפל העניין ותו לא והוא אסר שאין פחות מאלף טוקטוני והיו אנשי המעמד נושאים ונותנים וסוף דבר
הסכימו לתת לו האלף טוקאטוני הכל כמו ששאל ויגידו לו בשמחה והוא השיב שעדיין הוא יחשוב. וביום ה׳ הלך למעמד
וא״ל שחשב שלא אפשר ליה והתחילו לחלוק עמו. והשיב א״כ מחר אשלח לכל היחידים להודיעם שקבלוני ויום ב׳
אלך לבקר ושבת אדרוש ויום א׳ אלך לו׳ להם שכבר התחילה מלכותי ואני אומר ליחיד הק״ק שאינם נזהרים בכמה
דברים וישובו מדרכם הרעה ובתחילה אני או׳ לפרנס הראשון שיש לו שתי גויות בבית והוא חשוד עליהם שיוצאים
ואומר לפרנס ב׳ כך וכך לכלם שאני רוצה להציל נפשי והם מוטבעים במצולות טיט היון מעבירות מפורסמות והוא
הדבר אשר שאלתי שאוכל לעשות דין תורה לזקק ולטהר הקהל מכל עון ואת פושעים אוכיחם ואקללם ואמר השמד.
ואני סובר שאז תתחברו כנגדי ויהי הקשר אמיץ לגרשני מן הארץ ומי יודע מה יולד יום ואם יש את לבבכם לבער הטומאה
מהארץ ותהיו מקיימים כל דברי חז״ל על נכון אז רוח נכון חדש״ש בקרבי לזכות למצוה רבה זו וגם אוכל לעסוק בתורה
כרצוני בישוב והשקט בטח ומזה יראו וכן יעשו בכמה קהילות קדושות וזכות הרבים תלוי בכם אך אני רואה שאתם
אינכם חפצים בי כי אם להיות לכם שם ולא לשם שמים ואתם רוצים ללכת בשרירות לבבכם מבלי מוחה כלל ולכן אף
שאתם התנדבתם אלף טוקטני לשנה מ״מ בענין שאלתי שאוכל לדון דין תורה ולית דימ₪וא בידי בזה אני רואה שלא
ירדתם לסוף דעתי וכשמוע הפרנסים אמרי קודש אמרו להרב פר״ח ז״ל הדין עמך וכיונת אל האמת אשר לא תוכל
להיות רב בקהלתנו ובכן נסע נסע לש׳ עד כאן סיפר לי ר׳ דו[י]׳ד הנז׳ בהרחבה.

Sefer Ma-agal Tov ha-shalem, ed. Aron Freimann (Jerusalem: Mekize Nirdamim, 1934), 157. As
cited by S. Z. Havlin, "On the History of the Talmudic Academies in Jerusalem and Their Schol-

Figure 20. Romeyn de Hooghe, *De teba (bima) in de Portuguese Synagoge te Amster-dam*, ca. 1695. The Portuguese Synagogue as it appeared in a print roughly contemporary with the rebellion against Sasportas by the students of Ets Haim Yeshiva. Rijksmuseum, Amsterdam.

A number of points in this story can be verified. The first has to do with the nature of the source. Azulai's diary, which he kept on his person while traveling and survives in manuscript, was hardly a public document. While some evidence within the work suggests that he hoped to print it, and that he thought of *Ma-agal Tov* as an independent work, there is no reason to assume that he was fabricating the story.

The narrator within the story, David Meldola, was an actual historical personage and had served as the editor and corrector to *Ohel ya-akov* in 1737. Forty-one years earlier, when he was twenty-three years

ars at the End of the Seventeenth and Early Eighteenth Centuries" (Hebrew), *Shalem* 2 (1976): 146–147. Oded Cohen, "*Ma-agal Tov* by *HIDA*: A Meeting of Tradition and Modernity" (Hebrew) (MA thesis, Tel-Aviv University, 2010). On Azulai more generally, see Theodore Friedman, "The Life and Work of Hayyim Joseph David Azulai: A Study in Jewish Cultural History" (PhD diss., Columbia University, 1952); Meir Benayahu, *Rabi Hayim Yosef David Azulai* (Jerusalem: Rav Kook Institute, 1959).

old, he resided in Amsterdam. Meldola would have been in a position to have had such knowledge about the inner workings of Portuguese Jewish life in Amsterdam. Furthermore, Azulai had a somewhat strained relationship with Meldola. Azulai had first served as an emissary in the 1750s. In 1756 he had traveled with Meldola from Amersfort to Amsterdam. Meldola was seeking to sell his recently printed book *Divrei david*, and Azulai was seeking to raise funds for the Jewish communities of Palestine. Azulai thought that their competition had reduced the amount of funds he had been able to raise. He would probably not have repeated this story in Meldola's name if he had not thought it was accurate.[106]

This only supports the contention that Azulai believed what he wrote in his notebook in 1778; it does not prove that it actually happened in the late seventeenth century. Fortunately, a number of other details from the story can be corroborated. Hezekiah da Silva, the subject of Azulai's story, was born in Livorno in 1659. He studied in Jerusalem at the yeshiva of Moses Galante and was related by marriage to Moses Hagiz. Before he turned thirty, he embarked on the time-honored tradition of traveling to Europe to raise money for the Jews of Palestine.[107] Da Silva spent part of his four years in Europe in Amsterdam, where he befriended the Pereyra family. Jacob Pereyra, son of Sasportas's old enemy Abraham, donated funds to Da Silva to establish a yeshiva in Jerusalem called Beit ya-akov.[108] While he was in Amsterdam, Da Silva oversaw the printing of one volume of his commentary on Joseph Karo's *Shulhan arukh*, a book he entitled *Peri hadash*.[109] In transforming his manuscript into a printed book at a center for Hebrew printing in Europe, Da Silva continued a tradition of emissaries from Palestine. While in Amsterdam, he also preached a sermon that appeared as a printed Spanish pamphlet.[110]

---

[106] On Azulai's visit to Amsterdam in 1777, see Kaplan, "*Gente Politica*," 37.

[107] On Da Silva, see Abraham Yaari, *Sheluhei eretz yisrael* (Jerusalem: Rav Kook Institute, 1997), 1:295–298; on emissaries from Palestine to Europe, see Matthias B. Lehmann, *Emissaries from the Holy Land: The Sephardic Diaspora and the Practice of Pan-Judaism in the Eighteenth Century* (Stanford, CA: Stanford University Press, 2014).

[108] Yaari, "The Pereyra Yeshivot in Jerusalem and Hebron," 188.

[109] Hezekiah da Silva, *Sefer peri hadash* (Amsterdam: David Tartas, 1691).

[110] Hesqia da Silva, *Sermon, Moral del Fundamento de nuestra ley* (Amsterdam: Moseh Dias, 1691).

Da Silva was a younger and more successful version of Sasportas. He had come to Amsterdam from the outside, in his case Livorno and Jerusalem rather than Oran and Tlemcen; he had impressed the wealthy lay leaders to such an extent that they were willing to support his institution half a world away; he had sufficient self-regard and sufficient means to have his portrait painted; and he printed a major work of *halakha* that would go on to become a classic of modern Sephardic rabbinic literature. The *parnassim* could certainly have seen this young, charismatic outsider, with deep ties to one of the wealthiest families in Amsterdam, as a potentially fitting replacement for their rabbi.

But there is something even more revealing about Azulai's anecdote that highlights the elective affinities between Da Silva and Sasportas. If the report Meldola provided Azulai bears some relation to what transpired, one can easily imagine a scenario in which Sasportas would have told the *parnassim* of Amsterdam something very similar to what Meldola reported in the voice of Da Silva. The *parnassim* of Amsterdam had appointed Isaac Aboab da Fonseca as chief rabbi after the death of Saul Levi Morteira in 1660, a time when Sasportas was resident in Saleh. Had Sasportas been offered the job of chief rabbi in his late thirties rather than in his early eighties, one can imagine him positing a similar set of impossible stipulations as a precondition for his accepting the office. The position that Azulai and Meldola ventriloquized through Da Silva was extremely similar to that espoused by Sasportas throughout his writings: an indictment of a corrupt and self-satisfied elite who viewed the rabbinate as a figurehead rather than as a source of knowledge and power; a system predicated upon gift giving and favors rather than a respectable salary befitting a member of the clergy; a group of Jews whose leaders paid lip service to the Torah and its commandments but lived in sin and consistently violated the law. All of these criticisms one can imagine having been written by Sasportas. Some of them actually were.

Da Silva, of course, turned down the job and left Amsterdam. He died the same year as Sasportas, after having returned to Jerusalem. In 1692, around the same time that Da Silva had his exchange with the *parnassim* in Amsterdam, while Isaac Aboab da Fonseca was still alive, Jacob Sasportas inherited his son Samuel's estate. Samuel Sasportas had originally accompanied his father from Amsterdam to London in the summer of 1664. While Jacob served as *haham* to the congregation of roughly 250 Portuguese Jews, his son Samuel served as teacher, ritual slaughterer, and meat inspector.[111] Father and son fled London and the plague in the summer of 1665. While the father went to Hamburg, the son accepted assisted passage from the congregation to Barbados. By the summer of 1668 he had returned to London but quickly landed in Newgate Prison for "exercising the office of brokerage without admittance or allowance of the court of Aldermen."[112] In February 1671 he was confirmed in the office of broker along with one of his former fellow prisoners, Emanuel da Costa. At some point around the year 1672 Jacob visited Samuel in London. For the better part of the next decade, Samuel worked as a broker, until his dismissal from the Royal Exchange in October 1681 "for trading and Merchandizing to his owne use," an offense to which he pleaded guilty.[113] In 1687, he was naturalized.[114] In 1692, he was dead and his will named his father as his primary heir.

Samuel Sasportas drew up his will in London at the end of August 1692. He left a number of smaller legacies to the Ets Haim Yeshiva in London, to the Ets Haim Yeshiva in Amsterdam, and to the Jews of Safed and Hebron in the Holy Land. He also bequeathed personal gifts to rabbis such as Isaac Aboab da Fonseca in Amsterdam, as well as Selomoh Ailion and Jacob Fidanque in London. The bulk of his estate he left to his father, Jacob, "for my only and universall heir as of right he ought to be."[115] Two of his brothers made cameo appearances in his will. He charged Moseh Sasportas with the repayment of his debts, and Isaac Sasportas signed the will as one of the two witnesses, indicating his presence in London near the end of his brother's life.

Jacob Sasportas inherited the bulk of his son Samuel's estate. The most valuable asset held by Samuel and bequeathed to his father comprised shares in the Dutch East India Company (Vereenigde Oost-

[111] Samuel, "The Jews of London and the Great Plague (1665)," 11–12.

[112] Dudley Abrahams, "Jew Brokers of the City of London," *Miscellanies of the Jewish Historical Society of England* 3 (1937): 81

[113] Samuel, "The Jews of London and the Great Plague (1665)," 12; Lucien Wolf, "The First Stage of Anglo-Jewish Emancipation," in *Essays in Jewish History* (London: Jewish Historical Society of England, 1934), 133, as cited by Samuel.

[114] W. S. Samuel, "A List of Jewish Persons Endenized and Naturalised, 1609–1799," *TJHSE* 22 (1968–1969): 118, entry 113.

[115] London, PRO, Prob/11/411, Samuelis Saportas.

Figure 21. Portrait of Hezekiah da Silva. Hezekiah da Silva holds a closed book in his hands in a portrait painted of him during his visit to Amsterdam. Photo © The Israel Museum, Jerusalem by Ofrit Rosenberg.

Indische Compagnie, or VOC). Jacob Sasportas inherited shares issued by the Middelburg Chamber of the Dutch VOC, the second largest of the company's six chambers.[116] When Jacob Sasportas inherited his son's estate in 1692, he was an old man. His frailty and declining vision had already led him to seek a milder climate in Livorno. After that

[116]On Dutch VOC, see Lodewijk Petram, *The World's First Stock Exchange*, trans. Lynne Richards (New York: Columbia University Press, 2014), 9.

experiment ended in contentious dispute and he had returned to Amsterdam, his son Moses had emphasized his father's old age in his apologia. Soon after inheriting his son Samuel's estate, Jacob Sasportas had to confront the question of his own legacy. For roughly four years Sasportas does not appear to have done all that much about his estate apart from collecting the interest. During this period, from August 1692 until November 1696, Sasportas became the chief rabbi of the Portuguese Jews. He continued to issue approbations to the occasional Hebrew book printed in Amsterdam. One can reason with some degree of certainty that he fulfilled many, if not all of the functions as chief rabbi. On 13 November 1696, Jacob Sasportas appeared before a notary in Amsterdam along with three of his sons, Isaac, Moses, and Abraham. In the notary's presence he bequeathed to Isaac and Moses shares in the Middelburg Chamber of the Dutch VOC with a nominal value of 500 Flemish pounds each. This nominal value of 500 Flemish pounds was roughly equivalent to 3,000 guilders, but the shares were worth considerably more than their nominal value.[117] To Abraham he bequeathed shares totaling 250 Flemish pounds, and to Abraham's daughters, Rachel and Gratia, he bequeathed shares totaling 250 Flemish pounds.[118] These shares thus served as an extremely useful vehicle through which to transfer wealth from one generation to the next. In attempting to donate shares in the Dutch VOC to his children, Jacob Sasportas was behaving precisely like the upper-middle-class Sephardic Jews he had spent the previous five decades criticizing.[119] The notarial record was written in Dutch; at the conclusion of the act, the notary specifies that the deed had been read aloud in Spanish to Jacob Sasportas.[120] After living in the Dutch Republic for the better part of half a century, Jacob Sasportas continued to function in Spanish rather than learn Dutch. The next day Aaron Sasportas declared that he had received a sum of 200 guilders from his father-in-law, Jacob Sasportas, on behalf of his wife, Simha Sasportas.[121]

[117] For the financial history of shares in the Dutch VOC, see ibid., 17.

[118] SAA entry no. 5075, no. 5998, Not. P. Schabaelje, Acte van donatie van Jacob Saportas ten behoove van sijn Sonen, 13 November 1696.

[119] On VOC shares as a substantial part of the inherited wealth of Holland and Zeeland regent families, see Jonathan I. Israel, "Jews and the Stock Exchange: The Amsterdam Financial Crash of 1688," in Diasporas, 460.

[120] "Dat aldus passeerde binnen Amsterdam ter presentie van Jan Sonmans en Adriaen van Loons als getuijgen, ende is deeze door mij Notaris als spreeckende de Spaense en Neederduytsche tael aen de hr. Jacob Saportas in de Spaensche tael geinterpreteert geworden."

[121] SAA, entry no. 5075, no. 5998, Not. P. Schabaelje, 14 November 1696.

Fourteen months later, the principal partners gathered again before the same notary. On 20 January 1698, Jacob Sasportas granted power of attorney to Isaac Semah Ferro, a merchant in Middelburg who often served as a broker for the Portuguese Jews of Amsterdam, to transfer shares in the Middelburg Chamber of the Dutch VOC valued at 500 Flemish pounds to the *parnassim* of the Portuguese Jewish Nation, and the identical amount to Isaac Sasportas.[122] Four days later Isaac Sasportas directed Isaac Semah Ferro to transfer his shares to an Amsterdam merchant named Alvarez Nunes da Costa.[123] On 14 February 1698, Jacob Sasportas and his son Abraham appeared before the same notary. From this appearance it emerges that some unspecified difficulties had occurred in the transfer of property arranged in November 1696. As a result, both Jacob and Abraham agreed that Abraham's share as well as the share of his daughters would be held by the *maamad* of the Portuguese Jewish Nation in Amsterdam. Jacob had already transferred the funds to the *maamad* a month earlier and had informed them earlier of his plans, but both father and son agreed that they should inform them in writing, and once again the notary specified that he had read the deed to Jacob Sasportas in Spanish.[124] What had happened between November 1696 and the winter of 1698? Had the father fought with his sons or some of his sons over property?

On 7 March 1698, Jacob Sasportas made one final appearance before a notary. More precisely, the notary appeared before Jacob, who he specified was lying ill in his bed.[125] This time the Sasportas family switched notaries from P. Schabaelje to P. Padthuysen. Padthuysen recorded the will entirely in Spanish rather than recording it in Dutch and reading it aloud to Jacob in Spanish. The notary referred to Sasportas as "Predicador dela Nacion Judaica portuguesa en esta cuidad." A month before his death, Sasportas was described as a preacher, and the community that he served was not a community but the Portuguese Jewish Nation in the city of Amsterdam. The notary emphasized that although Sasportas was in poor health and as a consequence confined to his bed, he was of completely sound mind. The first section of Jacob's will reproduced his son Samuel's will in Spanish. Samuel's will had originally been composed in Spanish, and the English copy in the

---

[122] SAA, entry no. 5075, no. 6002, Not. P. Schabaelje, 20 January 1698.
[123] SAA, entry no. 5075, no. 6002, Not. P. Schabaelje, 24 January 1698.
[124] SAA, entry no. 5075, no. 6002, Not. P. Schabaelje, 14 February 1698.
[125] SAA, entry no. 5075, no. 2398, Not. P. Padthuysen, 7 March 1698.

Public Record Office specifies that it had been translated. It is unclear whether the Spanish version of Samuel's will that opened Jacob's was retranslated into Spanish or if it was the original. Given that Isaac Sasportas had served as a witness to his brother Samuel's will in London in 1692, he could have brought a copy of the original Spanish version from London to Amsterdam. After reproducing Samuel's will in its entirety, Jacob's will specified that he had fulfilled all of the terms of Samuel's will immediately after his death. Samuel's death had improved Jacob's financial position considerably; throughout the remainder of Jacob's will, a text that is roughly four times the length of Samuel's, the figure of the deceased son Samuel and his estate played a prominent role.

Jacob's will turned next to the dispersal of his own property. The will mentions the gifts he had given to his three living sons on 13 November 1696 and the succeeding attempts, in January and February of 1698, to ensure that they had indeed received the property. The next subject pertains to Jacob's married daughters. Jacob had three daughters who had married prior to Samuel's death: Sara Sasportas had married Elia de Costa Mesquita, Reina Sasportas had married Haim Toledano, and Simha Sasportas had married Aaron Sasportas. Reina and Simha may have married relatives, as Jacob's second wife was named Rachel Toledano, and Simha married someone with her father's last name. The will offers no information as to whether any of these daughters were born to Sasportas's first wife, whose name I have been unable to discover, or to his second wife. Jacob's will specified that each of his three daughters who married prior to Samuel's death had received a sum of 3,000 florins as a dowry, which indicates that Jacob was a man of some means even prior to Samuel's death. But Samuel's death had made a rich man even richer, and as a result each of his three married daughters received an additional 1,000 florins after their brother (or half brother) Samuel died. A fourth daughter, named Esther, married Samson da Costa Athias at some point between Samuel's death in 1692 and the composition of her father's will in March 1698. She and her husband received the sum of 9,500 florins del banco upon their marriage.

Sasportas had one other living daughter, Judica, at the time of his will's composition. His daughter Buenaventura, who was born in Livorno in 1679 and would have been nineteen at the time, does not appear in the will. She may have died as an infant or child, or she may have been married and no longer living in Amsterdam. Sasportas's will treated Judica's fate at some length. It specified that Jacob had put aside 10,000 florins del banco in a trust for her. She was to have access to the interest on those funds and was to receive an education overseen by her mother. She was required to choose a spouse who met the standards of her guardians, her mother, Rachel, and her brother Isaac. Having dealt with the dispersal of Samuel's estate and his five living daughters, Jacob's will next treated his wife, Rachel. It described the terms of their marriage: Rachel had brought a dowry of 4,000 florins, and Jacob had promised a sum of 6,000 florins in their *ketuba* in the event that he predeceased her. It specified the gold and silver plate that Jacob had bequeathed to his wife. The will concluded with a division of Jacob's estate between his wife and his three living sons, Isaac, Abraham, and Moses. At least two and probably three of Sasportas's children had predeceased him. His oldest son, Aaron, named as was customary among Sephardic Jews after his own father, died in Hamburg in 1670; his son Samuel died in London in 1692; his daughter Buenaventura appears to have died either in Livorno or in Amsterdam. Sasportas may well have had other children who predeceased him, about whose existence I am unaware. The will concludes in specifying that it was composed in Sasportas's home, which was situated right next to the Esnoga: "lo qual pass asi en la dha ciudad de Amsterdam en casa de dho otorgante cituada al lado dela Synagoga." It is not clear how long the Sasportas family had been living across from the Esnoga, whether this was an arrangement that began when he assumed the position of chief rabbi in 1693 or one that predated his appointment as chief rabbi.

The will offers almost no information about Sasportas as a thinker. Apart from the indication in the opening note that he had served as a preacher to the Portuguese Jewish Nation in Amsterdam, there is not a single reference to Sasportas's activities as a rabbi. His books do not appear as the subject of his inheritance; his writings are mentioned nowhere among his property to be disbursed among his heirs. From the fact that his son Abraham arranged and paid for the publication of his writings, it stands to reason that his sons maintained possession of their father's papers. But neither Sasportas nor the notary who recorded his will saw fit to mention either his activities or his writing. In short, although Jacob Sasportas's will was a document of considerable length, it is not a voluble document from which one can assess his worldview. In contrast to the tradition of Hebrew ethical wills, a category constructed by Israel Abrahams in the early twentieth century to refer to homiletic letters composed by rabbinic intellectuals prior to their death and addressed to their heirs, Sasportas's will focused almost entirely on the dispersal of his property.[126] Five weeks before his death Sasportas had come to resemble the rich merchants of the Portuguese Nation he had subjected to such withering scorn over the previous half a century. He lay in his bed in the courtyard of the Esnoga, surrounded by his living children, five daughters and three sons, counting his money and making sure each of them had received the correct sum. In one passage amid the technical discussion of dowries and legacies, one can still hear the voice of the same Sasportas who had waged decades of rabbinic combat pierce through the legalese of the Amsterdam notary: the fate of his daughter Judica. Four of Sasportas's daughters had already found husbands among the Portuguese Jewish Nation. His son Abraham had married and was father to two daughters. The will does not relate what became of either Moses's or Isaac's marriage prospects. But about Judica's fate, Sasportas showed considerable concern. In the passages about her care and future marriage settlement, one can sense both an anxious father leaving behind a young unmarried daughter and a man of iron will determined to control his family from beyond the grave.

On Tuesday, 15 April 1698, or the fourth day of the Hebrew month of Iyar of the year 5458, Jacob Sasportas died.[127] The Portuguese Nation may have treated the rabbi as an employee, but it knew how to hold a funeral. The members of the *maamad*, Sasportas's sons Isaac and Abraham, his friend the poet Daniel Levi de Barrios, and his successor as *haham*, Selomoh de Olivera accompanied his body to its final resting place in the Beth Haim, or cemetery, in the town of Ouderkerk aan de Amstel. Either at the funeral itself or some time shortly thereafter, Daniel Levi de Barrios delivered a eulogy for Sasportas that subsequently appeared in print with the imprimatur of the *maamad*. De Barrios described Sasportas as celebrated preacher and champion of Kabbalah (Spa. Eminente Preceptor y Campeon de la Cabala), reinforcing the

---

[126] *Hebrew Ethical Wills*, ed. Israel Abrahams (Philadelphia: JPS, 1976) [1926].
[127] De Barrios, *Monte Hermoso de la Ley Divina*, i.

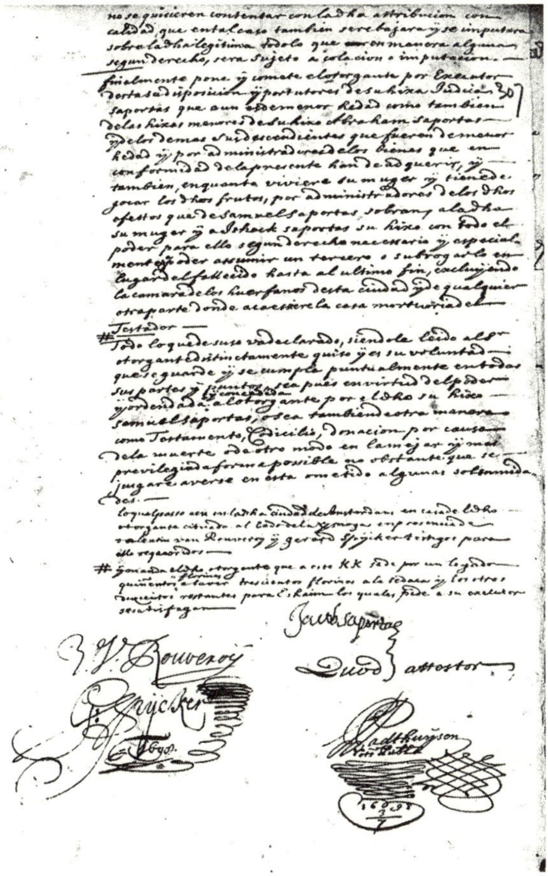

Figure 22. Will of Jacob Sasportas. Sasportas's signature appears to waver, indicating that he was in declining health. He died just over a month after composing this will. Amsterdam City Archives.

image Sasportas had of himself as a scholar and a kabbalist. In his brief summary of Sasportas's life, De Barrios mentioned his origins in Oran, his diplomatic service at the Spanish court, and the many different places he had served as rabbi: Tlemcen, Saleh, Hamburg, London, Livorno, and Amsterdam.[128] De Barrios occasionally included an ironic aside, as when he referred to Sasportas as "el gran Matuselah de Oran."[129] Yet in a sixteen-page eulogy delivered for a man who had spent the previous half century locked in rabbinic combat with all and sundry, De Barrios passed over the biliousness of his subject in deafening silence. The one comment I have been able to find that so much as gestures toward Sasportas's penchant for controversy occurs in a

[128] Ibid., 1.
[129] Ibid., 9.

passing reference to Sasportas's successor: "como en la eleccion del pacifico y docto Iaxam Selomoh de Olivera."[130] The description of Olivera as peaceful may well have been an implied contrast with Sasportas, who, as De Barrios well knew from his own experience, could hardly have been described as such.

Several months after his father's death, Isaac Sasportas composed a poetic elegy accompanied by a prose account of his own mourning. Unlike De Barrios's sermon, which appeared in print shortly after he had delivered it, Isaac Sasportas's elegy survives in a single manuscript that contains various writings by Isaac, his father, Jacob, and other authors.[131] The transcription of the elegy does not have any of the markings of a first or even a second draft; rather, it appears to have been the product of considerable reflection and revision. The text, which was written entirely in Hebrew, consists of three distinct sections: a thirty-three line elegy written in the default meter of Sephardic Hebrew poetry known as the *wafir*; a prose lamentation about the Sasportas family and their sorrow upon the death of their patriarch; and an imagined conversation between Isaac Sasportas and an otherworldly voice about the problem of suffering, with constant reference to the biblical Job.

In the first prose section of his lamentation, Isaac describes a family that had been visited repeatedly by death. Over and above the impetus for his writing provided by his father's death, Isaac mentions the death of his brothers Aaron and Samuel. He records that his brother Moses, who had been a regular recipient of their father's largesse in the previous decade, had died only recently, in the first year of his marriage, on his way to the Holy Land. Furthermore, his sister Sara had also died recently, and he was devastated to see her children as orphans.

In two instances over the course of the fourteen-page lamentation, Isaac Sasportas described his father. In the first instance he called him

> the rabbi, the pietist, the humble the divine kabbalist, the aged and honored, the great jurist, the universal sage, whom one cannot cease to praise, a plain man dwelling in tents (Gen. 25:26), known throughout

---

[130] Ibid., 3.
[131] Amsterdam, Ets Haim, MS 47_C_36, 4a–10b.

Figure 23. Pieter Stevens van Gunst, engraving of Jacob Sasportas. This engraving of Jacob Sasportas was made posthumously by the Dutch artist Pieter Stevens van Gunst. Rijksmuseum, Amsterdam.

the six gates, our teacher, and master Jacob Sasportas, may his memory be for a blessing.[132]

With all the allowance that one ought to make for the rhetorical flourishes added by a son grieving for his recently departed father, Isaac

[132] הרב החסיד והעניו המקובל האלקי היישיש הנכבד הדיין המצויין החכם הכולל אשר אין גומרין בו את ההלל איש תם יושב אהלים הנודע בשש שערים מהר"ר יעקב ששפורטש זצ"ל

Ibid., MS 47_C_36, 6a.

Sasportas's description of Jacob matches quite closely with that of De Barrios and, one might add, with Jacob's perception of himself in the second half of his life. Isaac described his father as a sage and a kabbalist; he emphasized his humility, a character trait that might seem rather foreign to a man who had spent the previous half century thundering about the lack of respect he had received from the lay leadership in the cities he served, and from the rabbinic colleagues with whom he corresponded. Jacob Sasportas may well have thought of himself as a humble man even as he projected the persona of a rabbi who refused to cede one iota of what he perceived as his due.

In the midst of his conversation with the heavenly voice about Job, Isaac Sasportas described his father in terms that offer some insight into the formation of his father's character:

> He was the only king, the philologist, the exegete, the allegorizer, the homilist, the prince, the lofty, the overflowing, the diffident, who remained from the lions of his land, a land blessed by God that raised up scholars, each one with a memory more phenomenal than the next, they sharpened one another's skills, battle after battle, as they fought the wars of the Lord over the meaning of the law, and each one illuminated the other like a flash of lightning in Oran. [133]

Sasportas himself wrote very little about his upbringing in Oran. Apart from the repeated refrain that when he had served as a rabbi and jurist in Oran and Tlemcen, he had been treated with respect, his surviving writings offer scant information about his training as a rabbi or his intellectual formation in the world of rabbinic learning. Sasportas emerged from a specific milieu that placed great emphasis on the use of rabbinic erudition as an instrument of intellectual combat. Sasportas had honed his skills in jousting with other scholars, but he remained the only surviving lion from the pride in which he was raised. This tantalizing hint was all that Isaac Sasportas provided in his eulogy. He indicated the names of neither his father's teachers nor his fellow students. Nor did he indicate whether he had studied in a yeshiva or a

---

[133] כי רק הוא מלך הבלשן הפשטן הרמזן הדרשן פרען הנשפן השופכן הבישן נשאר מיתר הלבאים בני ארצו מבורכת ה' היתה ארצו ארץ אשר בוניה בור סיד בבור סיד יחד כולם ככובשן היו מחדדים זה את זה בהלכה ומערכה מול מערכה נלחמו בספר מלחמות ה' ואיש אל עבר פניו האירו כברקים תבל באורן

Ibid., MS 47_C_36, 8b–9a.

hesger, an even more elitist institution that was open only to the very few.

This was as close as Isaac Sasportas would come to a description of his father's penchant for controversy: his skills in rabbinic argument had been well honed in his youth in Oran, and he had been the sole surviving literary lion. Both Daniel Levi de Barrios and Isaac Sasportas had been close to Jacob Sasportas over the last several decades of his life. During the time that they knew him, Jacob Sasportas repeatedly entered into disputes. Neither his close friend Daniel Levi de Barrios, a man Sasportas held very dear in spite of his continued belief in Sabbetai Zevi as the Messiah, nor his son Isaac Sasportas, whom he considered the most talented and learned of his surviving sons, chose to remember Jacob Sasportas's ordeals in their eulogies. In 1698 Sasportas was laid to rest as a grand old rabbi of an illustrious nation. The image of Sasportas as a zealot or as a Jewish inquisitor would take considerable work and time to forge. The former would be the product of the editorial brilliance of Jacob Emden and the latter of the historical imagination of Gershom Scholem. It is these figures and the worlds they made around Jacob Sasportas and his writings that the next two chapters describe.

SEVEN

∼

ZEALOT

One must have tradition in oneself to hate it properly.
—T. W. Adorno

Figure 24. Emden, *Kitzur zizath novel zvi* (Altona, 1754). Emden's edition of Sasportas effectively rescued Sasportas's writing from oblivion. Princeton University Library.

"LIKE A ZEALOT THE SON OF A ZEALOT." Thus Jacob Sasportas signed his letter to the rabbinate of Izmir, sent well after news of Sabbetai Zevi's conversion to Islam had reached him in Hamburg.[1] The phrase invokes a Talmudic description of Phineas son of Eleazar, who had ended a plague upon the Israelites by thrusting a spear through an Israelite man engaged in his own attempt to penetrate a Midianite woman.[2]

In the neighboring town of Altona, and eighty-eight years after Sasportas's letter, Jacob Emden used the identical phrase to describe himself on the title page of *Akitzat akrav* (Heb. The sting of a scorpion), a pamphlet printed in the name of a fictitious student as part of his assault on the alleged Sabbatianism of Jonathan Eibeschütz, chief rabbi of Altona-Hamburg-Wandsbek.[3] Like Sasportas, Emden emphasized both his zealotry and his sonship. Like the biblical Phineas, both men saw themselves as engaged in a battle to stop a plague that was ravaging Jewish life. In the early modern period, the plague was not the worship of Baal Peor, but the worship of a false Messiah, Sabbetai Zevi, whose followers had suspended the observance of the law. Phineas was a descendant of Levi, one the twelve sons of Jacob, remembered chiefly for having collaborated with his brother Simeon in slaughtering the

---

[1] כקנאי בן קנאי Sasportas, *ZNZ*, 169. Letter dated to Shevat 5427. Epigraph from T. W. Adorno, *Minima Moralia: Reflections from Damaged Life* (London: New Left Books, 1974), 52.

[2] BT, Sanhedrin 82b; Numbers 25.

[3] Jacob Emden, *Akitzat akrav* (Altona, 1752), t.p. As cited in Yehuda Liebes, "The Messianism of Rabbi Jacob Emden and Its Relationship to Sabbatianism" (Hebrew), in *Sod ha-emunah ha-shabtait*, 198n2. For evidence that Emden himself, rather than an anonymous disciple, wrote *Akitzat akrav*, see Shnayer Z. Leiman, "The Baal Teshuvah and the Emden-Eibeschuetz Controversy," *Judaic Studies* 1 (1985), 21.

male inhabitants of an entire city as recompense for the abduction of their sister Dinah.[4] Sasportas and Emden both invoked this lineage in legitimating zealotry as an appropriate response to the corruption of public life. Not only were they zealots; their ancestors had been zealots before them. Ancestry was crucial to Sasportas's self-image. In the next phrase of the concluding paragraph to the letter, Sasportas also took care to remind his correspondents in Izmir that he was an eleventh-generation descendant of Nahmanides. Emden tirelessly invoked his father, Hakham Zvi Ashkenazi, and devoted a substantial portion of his own life story, *Megillat sefer*, to the story his father's life.[5] He repeatedly dwelled on the lineage of potential marriage partners for members of his family and emphasized the importance of lineage over wealth.

The transmission of anti-Sabbatian ideas from Jacob Sasportas to Jacob Emden constitutes a crucial period in the formation of the early modern Jewish zealot. Indeed, Emden's relationship with Sasportas was far more substantial than the invocation of the identical Talmudic phrase. Five years after printing *Akitzat akrav*, as his battle with Eibeschütz continued to rage, Emden printed a new edition of Sasportas's *Kitzur zizath novel zvi*. This edition appeared at a particularly fraught time in Emden's life. He turned to Sasportas as a precedent in two of his primary battles: against the Eibeschütz party in Altona-Hamburg-Wandsbek and against the Frankist movement in Poland. On the title page of his edition, Emden left little room to doubt the magnitude of his self-imposed debt to his predecessor:

> My name is like his, his counsel is like my counsel, the name of his city, Perversity (Gen. 36:35), where that perverse event occurred is like the name of my city [Altona], where I was pursued by their multitude. This book soothed my pain when I saw that just like the heresy of the earlier ones, so too the heresy of the later ones.[6]

---

[4] On Phineas and the story of Dinah (Genesis 34), see Rashi's commentary BT Sanhedrin, 82b, s.v. ben kanai.

[5] Roughly one-fifth. See Emden, *MS*, 3–53.

[6] ושמי כשמו, ושם עצתו כשם עצתי, ושם עירו עו״ית בעת המאורע המעות הלז כשם עירי, מורדף מהמונם, ותהי זאת נחמתי בעניי בראות כמס״תה ראשונים כן מס״תה אחרונים.

Sasportas, *Kitzur*, ed. Emden, t.p. Nearly the identical statement had appeared a year earlier in Jacob Emden, *Edut be-ya-akov* (Altona, 1756), 37a. See below. The final phrase of this statement is an elaborate pun on a Talmudic passage in BT Ketubot 8b: "Just as the early ones drink [to assuage the pain of mourning], so too the later ones drink." Emden has changed the letter *shin* in

To these elective affinities with Sasportas—a common name, a common city, and a common enemy—one can add a few others: an acute sensitivity to the printed word, a pronounced sense of entitlement derived from a combination of lineage and learning, and a peripatetic lifestyle as a result of financial and communal difficulties.

Print, lineage, and geography formed a historical conjuncture that was constitutive of the early modern Jewish zealot, a new social type represented by Sasportas and Emden. In this context, rabbinic authority and social control loomed as critical problems. Both Sasportas and Emden departed from a similar premise: Sabbatianism posed a terrifying and fundamental threat to the maintenance of the Jewish social order. Sasportas had witnessed the Sabbatian movement as it unfolded, and had watched the abrogation of the law with horror. He also had a keen sense of the Jewish crowd as a powerful solvent of accepted social hierarchies. Emden too was a victim of popular religious enthusiasm. He had been denied a position as chief rabbi of Altona-Hamburg-Wandsbek to which he felt entitled by his learning and his family history. But the animus was not simply personal. He alleged that the rabbinic scholar Jonathan Eibeschütz, who had been hired in his stead, had written amulets replete with allusions to Sabbatian ideas and Sabbatian texts. One can grasp the urgency of these concerns for both figures through their respective discussions of Sabbatianism and Christianity, and through their respective engagements with the medium of print.

SABBATIANISM AND CHRISTIANITY

As Scholem first detected, Sasportas was unique among the contemporaries of Sabbetai Zevi in considering Sabbatianism as a new faith, *emunah hadasha*, and a new teaching, *torah hadasha*.[7] These terms appear frequently throughout *Zizath novel zvi*, particularly in the sections written after the apostasy. From his perspective, Sabbatians may have

---

mishteh (from the root *shin taf heh*, to drink) to a *samekh* in *misteh* (from the root *sin tet heh*, to stray). Emden's phrase becomes "just like the heresy of the earlier ones, so too the heresy of the later ones."

[7] Scholem, *Sabbatai Sevi*, 717–718; Goldish, *The Sabbatean Prophets*, chap. 5; Maciejko, *The Mixed Multitude*, 41–47.

continued to adhere to religious norms, but their transformation of traditional fast days into public holidays and their consumption of sacrificial meat beyond the legally mandated bounds of the Temple area were gross violations of rabbinic law. The new faith and the new teaching may have been popular innovations that resonated powerfully with the Jewish laity, but they decidedly violated the Jewish legal system as conceived and interpreted by the rabbis.

Sasportas made a historical analogy between contemporary Sabbatianism and ancient Christianity. Just as Christianity had been a new religion that was a corruption of Judaism, so too Sabbatianism. He drew a direct parallel between the new faith of Sabbatianism and the new faith of Jesus. In a narrative section of *Zizath novel zvi*, written in the summer of 1666 when the movement was at its height, he wrote:

> For some people, the beginning of their faith was accidental, but the conclusion was intentional so as to refute those who disputed them. I feared lest in order to prevent their honor from being replaced by disgrace, they would insist on their error, and this would lead to the creation of a new Law, Heaven forbid. How useful to us has the exile been! In this respect we can say that the exile is fitting for the Jews, for were it not so, those who follow the Messiah and [his] prophet would be like the followers of Jesus.[8]

Pride, ego, and shame had led Jews who had initially believed in Sabbetai Zevi as the Messiah to insist upon their faith rather than recant their error. Their stubbornness, Sasportas feared, would lead them to concoct an entirely new faith based upon their errors. He found cold comfort in the relative powerlessness of the Jews. Exile was suddenly a blessing, as these foolish and stubborn believers lacked any ability to coerce their fellow Jews to follow them into their new faith. Sasportas may also be offering an ironic reflection on his own sense of powerlessness. The Sabbatians could not force other Jews to follow them in

---

[8] ותחילת האמונה לקצתם היה בשוגג וסופה בזדון כדי לקנטר לבעלי ריבם, ומזה הייתי מתירא שמא לבעבור כבודם כדי שלא יומר בקלון יהיו עומדים בטעותם ותעשה ח"ו תורה חדשה. וכמה הועילה לנו היותנו במצב הגלות ועל זה נוכל לומר יא'[ה] גלותא לישראל שאם לא כן היו הנוטים אחר משיח ונביא כנוטים אחר ישו.

Sasportas, *ZNZ*, 123. The phrase "exile is fitting for the Jews" is a play on a rabbinic aphorism, "Poverty befits the Jews like a red strap for a white horse." See BT Hagigah 9b. The sense of the Talmudic passage is that poverty encourages the Jews to observe the commandments and avoid sin; Sasportas sarcastically implies that exile will ensure that most Jews will not flock to a Messiah, a point that the rest of his account seems to undermine.

their beliefs, but he was similarly unable to make the Sabbatians disappear. Thus he was reduced to resorting to the same weapon that the Sabbatians had used: an appeal to public opinion.

A few weeks later, after learning of Sabbetai Zevi's annulment of the fast on the ninth of Av, Sasportas made an explicit analogy between Sabbetai Zevi and Jesus:

> To accept upon themselves the commands of a divine being when he is a man and not a god, this is something shocking and terrifying to anyone who calls himself by the name of Israel and whoever is concerned for the respect of his creator. They should have also asked what relation the *musaf* prayer had to him, and what his birth had to do with the memory of the exodus from Egypt, and the [same goes for all] his [other] delusions. Just like a trickster, he has misled them into following him, setting for them a new Law and making himself like Jesus the Nazarene.[9]

Sabbetai Zevi had appealed to the Jewish laity as a demagogue. He and his followers had taken basic aspects of Jewish ritual—the additional prayer known as *musaf* recited on the Sabbath and on holidays, along with the repeated invocation of the exodus from Egypt in Jewish liturgy—and attempted to endow them with Sabbatian significance. These perversions reminded Sasportas of another man who had propounded a new faith against the legal standards set by contemporary rabbis. By raising the specter of Christianity, he hoped to shock his rabbinic colleagues into understanding what was as stake. The struggle over legal authority was a struggle over the social basis of Jewish collective life.

After the conversion of Sabbetai Zevi to Islam, Sasportas posited that the Sabbatians had begun to read scripture as if they were Christians. In his response to Nathan of Gaza's letter to Sabbetai Zevi's brother concerning the Messiah's conversion, Sasportas wrote:

> Look upon the words of this denier with the careful eye of Jewishness...
> [Nathan] further added falsehood by saying that apart from him [Sabbetai Zevi] there is no other redeemer for Israel, and that the verse "Be-

hold my servant shall deal prudently, he shall be exalted..." (Isa. 52:13) alluded to him. But this reveals aspects of prophecy that are untrue and renders it entirely false. This is precisely the belief of the Christians who explain [the verse] as a reference to Jesus the Nazarene. He has grasped their way of heresy, and has not moved from his wickedness to the point that they have called him God just like the believers in Jesus.[10]

To Sasportas, the Sabbatian exegesis of Isaiah was reminiscent of Christian understandings of the same passage. Sasportas warned his correspondents that the story of Sabbetai Zevi, although it was happening in real time, was not particularly new. It had already happened with Christianity. In his idiosyncratic interpretation of the Bible, Nathan of Gaza was repeating the exegetical errors made by the writers of the Gospels. Sasportas saw both Sabbetai Zevi and Jesus of Nazareth as demagogues who had seduced their constituents into following them into a new faith. Christianity and Sabbatianism were both forms of collective enthusiasm that disrupted the social order and deprived the rabbis of their sole authority to interpret the law.

Sasportas's understanding of Sabbatianism as a new religion and his analogy between Sabbatianism and Christianity fell largely on deaf ears. The Sabbatian prophets such as Nathan of Gaza, Abraham Miguel Cardozo, and others saw Sabbatianism as the realization of the messianic promise to the people of Israel. Most rabbinic authorities prior to the Messiah's conversion either agreed with them or remained silent; after the conversion, they usually preferred to pass over the episode in silence and dealt with individual Sabbatians as errant Jews. With the exception of Joseph Halevi in Livorno, none of Sasportas's correspondents or later readers appear to have understood Sabbatianism as a new religion. None, that is, until Emden. Throughout his writings, Emden repeatedly accepted and assimilated Sasportas's position, although he seems to have come to it independently. In discussing Selomoh Ailion, a man Scholem once described as a "discreet Sabbatian," Emden revealingly wrote, "Even though he had already distanced himself from them [the Sabbatians] and had returned to Jewish law [Heb. *dat yehudit*],

---

[10] יראה הרואה בעין יפה של יהדות בדברי הכופר הזה . . . עוד הוסיף סרה באומרו ובלעדיו אין גואל לישראל ועליו רמז הכתוב הנה ישכיל עבדי ירום וכו', והרי זה מגלה פנים בנבואה שלא כפי האמת ועושה אותה פלסתר, והיא ממש דעת הנוצרים המפרשים אותה על יש"ו הנוצרי ואחז דרכם דרך מינות ולא זז מרשעו עד שקראו ה' כמו מאמיני יש"ו.

Ibid., 201. The ellipsis following the biblical citation is Sasportas's.

nonetheless an impurity remained in his heart."[11] He referred to Ailion as having returned to the fold of Jewish law from Sabbatianism, an indication that he considered Sabbatianism something fundamentally different from Judaism.[12]

Emden thought of himself as uniquely qualified to establish the boundaries of Jewishness. More than any other dimension of life, the law stood at the center of his understanding of *dat yehudit*, a Hebrew phrase for which the English term "religion" cannot serve as an adequate translation.[13] The early modern Jewish zealot, Emden and Sasportas both, did not have terms for religion and heresy. Rather, they thought of Judaism, or more accurately Jewishness, as a legal system ruled by rabbis and violated by sinners, or, better yet, criminals. The valorization of transgression had put the Sabbatians beyond the boundaries of the Jewish legal system. In his "Resen mateh," which was printed as part of his *Sefer shimush*, Emden made this point with even greater force than had Sasportas:

> Christians would decree that the members of the sect of Sabbetai Zevi, may the name of the wicked rot, be burned. For it is a new and invented faith that has recently come.[14]

Emden did not cite Sasportas on this occasion, but he used a phrase, "a new and invented faith," that was quite similar to one used by Saspor-

---

[11] ואע"פ שכבר נפרד מהם וחזר לדת יהודית, מ"מ נשארה טינא בלבו

Scholem, "Leket Margoliyot," in *Mehkere shabtaut*, 701–702; Emden, *MS*, 31. Ailion's name appears in scholarly literature and library catalogs in various spellings; in a sermon printed in his lifetime it appears as Ailion. See *Sermon que predicó el doctissimo señor Haham Moreno a Rab R. Selomoh Ailion* (Amsterdam, 1723). On Ailion and Kabbalah, see Yael Nadav, "A Kabbalistic Treatise of R. Solomon Ailion" (Hebrew), *Sefunot* 3–4 (1960): 301–349, and 327 for the iterations of his name; on Sasportas and Ailion, see *Ohel ya-akov*, #64, 69b–70a; Tishby, "New Information on the 'Converso' Community in London," 495–496.

[12] Emden's assessment of Ailion may have been colored by the role he played in his father's departure from the Ashkenazi rabbinate in Amsterdam. See Carlebach, *Pursuit of Heresy*, chaps. 4–5; Matt Goldish, "An Historical Irony: Solomon Ailion's Court Tries the Case of a Repentant Sabbatean," *SR* 27 (1993): 5–12.

[13] On the phrase as it appears in the Mishnah (Ketubot 7:6), see Menahem Kister, " 'Like the Law of Moses and Yehudah': On the History of a Legal Religious Term" (Hebrew), in *Atarah le-hayim: Mehkarim ba-sifrut ha-talmudit ve-ha-rabanit li-khevod Profesor Hayim Zalman Dimitrovsky*, ed. Daniel Boyarin et al. (Jerusalem: Magnes Press, 2000), 202–208.

[14] כי הנוצרים היו דנין לאנשי כת ש"ץ שר"י בשרפה. לפי שהיא אמונה בדויה חדשה מקרוב באה

Lior Gottlieb, " 'Resen mateh' of Rabbi Jacob Emden: First and Second Editions with an Introduction, Textual Comparison and Notes" (Hebrew), in *Be-darkei shalom: iyunim be-hagut yehudit mugashim le-Shalom Rosenberg* ed. Benjamin Ish-Shalom (Jerusalem: Beit Morasha, 2007), 295–321, citation at 301. Hereafter Gottlieb, "Resen mateh."

tas, "a new faith," and alluded to the identical verse in Deuteronomy, "to new gods that came newly up" (Deut. 32:17), that Sasportas had alluded to in his description of Sabbatianism. Emden's invocation of what the Christians would do to the Sabbatians captures precisely the conundrum faced by the early modern Jewish zealot. As members of a religion with the power of the state behind it, Christians could declare the adherents of a new creed to be heretics and decree their death. As interpreters of a legal system, rabbis could define those who sinned as breakers of the law; but they could not outlaw the new faith. They could only castigate the Sabbatians for breaking the law; they lacked the political power to declare the members of this new faith to be beyond the boundaries of Jewishness. Where Sasportas had made an argument for the benefits of exile—the Sabbatians had no authority to force their enthusiasm upon all Jews—Emden lamented the fact that rabbis could not enforce their condemnation of Sabbatianism. If Sasportas and Emden expressed their grievances with slightly different accents, the impulse behind both of their polemics was similar. Both saw Sabbatianism as a threat to the Jewish social order and bemoaned the lack of rabbinic power to eliminate Sabbatianism from the Jewish corporate body.

When Emden turned from Sabbatianism to Christianity, he made a slightly different point from the one Sasportas had made. Where Sasportas saw the early followers of Jesus as enthusiasts who were seduced by a demagogue, like the contemporary Sabbatians who had been taken in by Sabbetai Zevi and Nathan of Gaza, Emden saw early Christianity as an effective form of social control. But for both, the threat of disorder remained the most terrifying problem posed by social enthusiasm. In "Resen mateh," Emden characterized Jesus as follows:

> From certain passages in the Gospels, learned Christians have understood that he [Jesus] came to give a new Torah in place of the Torah of Moses. If this were so, why did he explicitly say that he had come to fulfill it? Rather, this is as I have just explained: the authors of the Gospels did not think that the Nazarene had come to nullify the Jewish law [Heb. dat yehudit] entirely. Instead, he came to the nations, so as to establish a law [Heb. dat] for them. Furthermore, even that was not new, but old, for they are the seven Noahide commandments that the nations had forgotten.[15]

15 שבאיזה מקומות מאוונגליון משמע להו למלומדי הנוצרים שבא לתת תורה חדשה, במקום תורת משה. ואיך אם כן אמר בפירוש שלא בא אלא אלא לקיימה כנ'. אבל הוא הדבר אשר דברתי, שלא בא במחשבת כותבי האוונגליון. שבא

Where Sasportas saw Jesus as an ancient version of Sabbetai Zevi, Emden saw him as someone who had worked to ensure the maintenance of social order. Emden was willing to rehabilitate Jesus on precisely the same terms that Sasportas was prepared to dismiss him: the law. Emden saw Jesus as extending Noahide law, while Sasportas saw him as the object of uncritical popular belief.

Emden further underscored his position that Jesus had come as a Jewish lawgiver to the gentiles, a position largely consistent with Paul's argument in Romans:

> The Nazarene performed a double service for the world, as we can see with complete clarity in our own times. On the one hand, he strengthened and established the Torah of Moses with all his might, as I mentioned earlier... on the other hand, for the nations of the world whom he helped enormously (had they not misunderstood his intention as some of the madmen have done, who did not sufficiently understand the writings of the Gospels).[16]

Sasportas and Emden differed in the accents of their comparisons but not in the nature of their zealotry. Sasportas had sought to Christianize Sabbatianism, in order to discredit Sabbatianism; Emden sought to Judaize early Christianity, also in order to discredit Sabbatianism. Emden disagreed with learned Christians, here referred to as madmen, who had dismissed the Jewish roots of Christianity, because they were hostile to contemporary Judaism and, presumably, failed to understand and to follow the law. The difference between Sasportas's rejection of Jesus and Emden's acceptance was relatively trivial, and can probably be attributed to a combination of sensibility and time. Emden possessed a far more restless mind than Sasportas and had much broader intellectual interests. By the middle of the eighteenth century, Emden was prepared to accept and to argue for the Jewishness of ancient

---

הנוצרי לבטל דת יהודית לגמרי, אלא לאומות בא, לייסד דת מן אז והלאה, ואף היא לא חדשה כי אם ישנה, הלא הם שבע מצות בני נח ששכחום העמים.

Ibid., 304. On Emden and Christianity, see Maciejko, *The Mixed Multitude*, 47–62; Jacob J. Schacter, "Rabbi Jacob Emden, Sabbatianism, and Frankism: Attitudes toward Christianity in the Eighteenth Century," in *New Perspectives on Jewish-Christian Relations in Honor of David Berger*, ed. Elisheva Carlebach and Jacob J. Schacter (Leiden: Brill, 2012), 359–396. For earlier literature, see 373n40 and 376n52.

[16] שהנוצרי עשה טובה כפולה בעולם לפי הנראה ברור גלוי כיום הזה, במה שמצד אחד חזק וקיים תורת משה בכל עוז כנז"ל באר היטב,... . ומצד אחד לאו"ה, היטיב הרבה (אם לא יהפכו כונתו הרצויה אליהם, כדרך שעשו איזה משוגעים שלא ירדו לסוף דעת כותבי א"ג.)

Gottlieb, "Resen mateh," 307.

Christianity. Of far greater significance were the similarities between their positions with respect to the state of contemporary Jewry. Both valorized the Jewishness of the law. Both saw themselves as uniquely qualified by their learning and lineage to serve as spokesmen for the legal culture of the Jews.

Emden understood himself as sharing Sasportas's position on the Jewishness of the law. After having completed "Resen mateh," Emden wrote that someone had shown him a book entitled *Milhemet hovah*, a collection of medieval Jewish writings on Christianity printed in Constantinople in 1710. It included Nahmanides's disputation at Barcelona, works by Joseph and David Kimhi, and a lengthy responsum by Simeon ben Zemah Duran on Christianity. Writing in reference to Duran, Emden explained:

> After these words had appeared in print, I was shown the book *Milhemet hovah*, which was printed in Constantinople. Within it, one can find the writings of R. Simeon ben Zemah Duran on the Gospels... He proved decisively from the Gospels themselves exactly what I have said and proven here in my pamphlet of my own accord. He stated that the Christians perverted the intention of Jesus who never sought to nullify the Jewish law [Heb. *dat yehudit*] in respect of Israel, because he and his students fulfilled it. He came only to reinforce it and to bequeath the seven [Noahide] commandments to the nations of the world. These are his words of blessed memory. We have both written in exactly the same style. A short prophecy has fallen from my mouth and my pen. In this respect, we were born under the same star. But no two prophets ever prophesize in the same style. He, of blessed memory, expanded upon this issue at greater length. But I sufficed with my shorter proof, which was sufficient in this issue for my purpose... I have looked again and remembered that in the book *Zizath novel* as well, he [Sasportas] wrote exactly as I had written. Look at the second edition, printed in Altona, and you will see that all three of us [Simeon ben Zemah Duran, Sasportas, and Emden] agree with one another. In truth, these matters are simple, and they are compelling to those who examine them shrewdly and carefully.[17]

ואחר שיצאו דברי אלה לאור עולם בדפוס הראוני ס' מלחמת חובה שנדפס בקוסטאנטינה. בתוכו נמצאו דברי[17] תשובות הרשב"ץ ן ז"ל על אודות א"ג ... אמיתת מה שאמרתי והכרחתי אני בכאן בקונטרסי זה מדעתי. באמרו שהנוצרים החטיאו כונת ישו בזה. שלא כיון מעולם לבטל דת יהדות מישראל. כי הוא ותלמידיו קיימוה. לא בא אלא להחזיקה ולהניח שבע מצוות לאומות העולם. כך הם דבריו ז"ל. ממש סגנון אחד עלה עלה לנו. ונבואה קטנה נזרקה בפי ובקולמוסי.

Emden was aware of Sasportas's critical assessment of Jesus; some of the passages had appeared in his edition of the *Kitzur* mentioned in this very note.[18] Emden's appreciation of ancient Christianity seems, rather, to be a consequence of his reaction to Sabbatianism. Compared to Sabbatianism, a new religion that threatened the integrity of Judaism as a legal system—this was a point on which he and Sasportas were in agreement—Christianity, an ancient religion with roots in rabbinic culture itself, appeared to Emden to be an improvement. The Sabbatians who had turned hallowed fast days into public holidays were explicitly antinomian, and none more so than the Frankists, who were the subject of this pamphlet. Emden extended Sasportas's argument about the relationship between Sabbatianism and Christianity to its logical conclusion. Sasportas had condemned the Sabbatians because they reminded him of the followers of Jesus. Emden built upon Sasportas's comparison and claimed that the Sabbatians were even worse than Christians. The early followers of Jesus, according to Emden, had at least followed the Noahide commandments, a rudimentary form of the law that emerged out of rabbinic norms; the Sabbatians and the Frankists had thrown off the law entirely. Sasportas always confined his appeal to internal Jewish authorities, which is why his comparison served to shock. Emden's position, on the other hand, might have appealed to Christian authorities, who might otherwise have been inclined to ignore Sabbatianism as a Jewish problem.

PRINT

Both Sasportas and Emden were creatures of Hebrew print. Their zeal manifested itself as a call for a return to the classic texts of rabbinic literature. Both sought to harness print to focus reading on a set of key rabbinic texts such as the Mishnah and the Talmud that they felt had been unjustly neglected. In addition, both agonized over the relationship between Sabbatian enthusiasm and print. They saw print as a

---

בהך מילתא בר מזליה אנא. אלא שאין שני נביאים מתנבאים בסגנון אחד. הוא ז"ל אמנם הרחיב הענין יותר. ואנכי הסתפקתי במועט ההכרחי והמספיק בענין לפי כוונתי . . . שוב ראיתי ונזכרתי שגם בס' ציצת נובל כתב כדברי הנ"ל ממש. יעוין בדפוס שני (מד"א) והראה שדברי שלשתנו מכוונים בכך. ובאמת הדברים פשוטים הם ומוכרחים למי שיסתכל בעין פקוחה ובהשגחה.

Ibid., 309. See Schacter, "Rabbi Jacob Emden, Sabbatianism, and Frankism," 383–384.

[18] Sasportas, *ZNZ*, 131, and in Sasportas, *Kitzur*, ed. Emden, 26b.

medium with implications for the constitution and exercise of rabbinic authority. As with Jesus and Sabbatianism, however, the accents of their concerns were not always identical. Sasportas was relatively unconcerned with the relationship between print and authorship, whereas Emden was keenly aware and cultivated his own image in print.

Sasportas worked in the print shops of others while in his early to midforties; at roughly the same period in his life, at the age of forty-six, Emden established his own print shop with his own corrector, Aaron ben Elijah ha-Kohen.[19] Emden was not the first well-known Jewish author to run his own printing house. Menasseh ben Israel had preceded him a century earlier in this respect. Both presses operated for a considerable period of time: Menasseh's for twenty-eight years between 1627 and 1655, and Emden's for thirty between 1745 and 1775, the year before his death. Unlike Menasseh's, which produced books in a number of languages by a number of authors, Emden's printed thirty-eight books and twenty-eight pamphlets in Hebrew, all of them written or edited by Emden himself.[20]

Emden's first foray in print, *Lehem shamayim*, actually appeared in Wandsbek before he had established his own press in Altona.[21] *Lehem shamayim* contained his commentary on the first two orders of the Mishnah and should be seen as part of a larger focus on the Mishnah in the early modern period.[22] Figures as distant from one another as Yom-Tov Lipmann Heller in Prague and Abraham Azulai and Solomon Adeni in Hebron wrote commentaries on all or part of the Mishnah.[23] As other texts in a variety of genres poured forth from Hebrew presses, these scholars argued for a return to the Mishnah in and of itself. In

[19] Arthur Arnheim, "Hebrew Prints and Censorship in Altona," *Studies in Bibliography and Booklore* 21 (2001): 6.

[20] Emden, *MS*, 203–204; Arnheim, "Hebrew Prints and Censorship in Altona," 6.

[21] Isaac Raphael, "The Writings of Rabbi Jacob Emden" (Hebrew), *Areshet* 3 (1961): 242–243; Schacter, "Rabbi Jacob Emden: Life and Major Works," 159–173. Hereafter Schacter, "Rabbi Jacob Emden."

[22] Aaron Ahrend, "The Study of the Mishnah and Mishnah Circles in the Modern Period" (Hebrew), *Jewish Studies, an Internet Journal* 3 (2004): 19–53; Raz-Krakotzkin, "Persecution and the Art of Printing."

[23] Joseph Davis, *Yom-Tov Lipmann Heller: Portrait of a Seventeenth-Century Rabbi* (Oxford: Littman Library, 2004), chap. 4; Dov Zlotnick, "R. Abraham Azulai's Ahabath bat ta-anugim (Commentary to Tractate Eduyot)" (Hebrew), in *Mehkarim u-mekorot*, ed. H. Z. Dimitrovksy (New York: Jewish Theological Seminary, 1977), 1–122; Yehuda Ratzaby "Rabbi Solomon Adeni and His Work *Melekhet Shelomo*" (Hebrew), *Sinai* 106 (1990): 243–254; on the Mishnah in the Pereyra yeshiva, see Yaari, "The Pereyra Yeshivot in Jerusalem and Hebron," 193.

order to facilitate this study, they composed commentaries, printed the Mishnah as a separate book, and convened circles devoted to its study.[24] Both Emden and Sasportas fashioned themselves as masters of the rabbinic corpus and wrote commentaries on the very same text. Both saw the Mishnah as a separate book worthy of its own study and commentary independent of the Talmud.

In contrast to Sasportas, who consented to issue approbations, Emden was opposed to the genre in principle. Sasportas, his great predecessor, and Eibeschütz, his great rival, each issued over twenty approbations over the course of his life, while Emden himself issued only four.[25] One was of a work by Solomon Luria, whom, like Sasportas and so many other Talmudists in early modern Europe, Emden held in high esteem.[26] Another was to *Mikdash melekh*, a four-volume commentary on the *Zohar* by Shalom Buzaglo printed in Amsterdam between 1750 and 1752. In the approbation itself, Emden insisted that he had agreed to write it only at Buzaglo's urging. On two subsequent occasions he would repudiate it in print.[27] At the same time, the majority of Emden's own books, including his legal works *She-elat ya-avetz* and *Mor u-keziah*, appeared without approbation.[28] The few that did contain approbations appeared early in his career. Emden asserted his authorship, and thus declared his independence from the contemporary rabbinic establishment; by contrast, Sasportas had worked extraordinarily hard to break into its ranks. Once he had done so, he was prepared to join his colleagues and issue approbations. Elisheva Carlebach has noted that Moses Hagiz attempted to reclaim three instruments of rabbinic authority usurped by the Sabbatians and by powerful lay elites: the *herem* (ban), the *hebrah* (confraternity), and the *haskamah* (approbation). Concerning the *herem* and the *haskamah*, Hagiz thought that these standard avenues of rabbinic power had been corrupted by the

---

[24] Emden's Mishnah commentary appears to have grown out of a study circle convened in his home. See Emden, *MS*, 150. As cited by Schacter, "Rabbi Jacob Emden," 160.

[25] Shnayer Z. Leiman, "The Approbations of Rabbi Jonathan Eibeschütz and Rabbi Jacob Emden" (Hebrew), *Or ha-mizrah* 51 (2006): 169–203. Hereafter, Leiman, "The Approbations."

[26] Solomon Luria, *Yam shel shelomo al massekhet yevamot* (Altona, 1740), as cited and described in Leiman, "The Approbations," 196–198. On Luria, see Elchanan Reiner, "Changes in the Polish and Ashkenazi Academies in the Sixteenth and Seventeenth Centuries, and the Debate over Argumentation" (Hebrew), in *Ke-minhag Ashkenaz ve-Polin: Sefer yovel le-Chone Shmeruk*, ed. Israel Bartal et al. (Jerusalem: Zalman Shazar Center, 1993), 53–60, 68–80.

[27] Raphael, "The Writings of Rabbi Jacob Emden," 232; Leiman, "The Approbations," 199–201.

[28] Leiman, "The Approbations," 203n79.

excessive infringement of a powerful lay leadership.[29] Only a few decades later, Emden appears to have despaired of the power of the *haskamah* and shunned the genre almost entirely. In the course of his long fight with Eibeschütz, Emden seems to have despaired of much of the rabbinate as well.

Along with his edition of Sasportas, Emden repeatedly republished and reissued other early works. He reprinted the commentaries of Obadiah Bertinoro (d. ca. 1515) and Yom-Tov Lipmann Heller (d. 1654) alongside his own on the Mishnah on tractate Avot. He reissued *Seder olam*, a chronological text from rabbinic antiquity, with his own commentary.[30] Emden clearly saw the republication of earlier rabbinic texts as one of the central aspects of his intellectual life. In an extensive note concluding his edition of Sasportas's *Kitzur*, he apologized for having spent so much time on such a recent author:

> Thanks be to God who helped us to complete the book *Novel zvi*. Although this time I dealt with the editing (and correcting and explicating and publishing) of the book of this author who has but recently come (Deut. 32:17), and I was taken away from my labor and my craft that has already been well established, that is, to correct and comment upon our principal holy books and to stand them in their place.[31]

Emden seems to have thought of rabbinic literature as a separate concept. The modern Sasportas, as Emden would have it, was a distraction. His primary project was the republication and reedition of the central texts from the ancient rabbinic past.

In his long battle with Eibeschütz, Emden used his press in Altona as his bully pulpit. If the approbation was no longer an effective weapon in Sabbatian controversies, the printed word had hardly fallen into obsolescence. To the contrary, many of the books and the majority of the pamphlets he printed pertained to the conflict that dominated his life from 1751 until Eibeschütz's death, in 1764, and beyond. In addition to his own books on Sabbatianism, Emden published both Sabbatian and anti-Sabbatian literature in new editions. Thus references to the Yid-

[29] *Pursuit of Heresy*, 11–12.

[30] *Sefer etz avot* (Amsterdam, 1751); *Sefer seder olam rabah* (Hamburg, 1757). Entry 7 (p. 250) and entry 28 (p. 270) in Raphael, "The Writings of Rabbi Jacob Emden."

[31] וברוך ה' אשר עזרנו להשלים ס' נובל צבי, אך זה הפעם טפלתי בהגהה (ותקון ובאור והוצאה לאור) ספר של מחדש מקרוב, ובטלתי ממלאכת עצמי ומאומנתי המוחזקת בידי לעמוד על תקון והארת ספרינו הקדושים הראשיים להעמידם על מתכונתם

Sasportas, *Kitzur*, ed. Emden, 47a.

dish chronicle by the sexton of the Ashkenazi Jews in Amsterdam Leyb ben Ozer first appeared in print in Emden's *Torat ha-kenaot*.[32] Emden's edition of Sasportas should be seen within the framework of his attempt to harness past accounts about Sabbatianism for the present purpose of his campaign against Eibeschütz.

EMDEN'S EDITION

Emden's edition of the *Kitzur* differs from the first edition, published twenty years earlier as an appendix to *Ohel ya-akov*, in a number of ways. The most obvious has to do with the persistent textual presence of Emden himself. In his marginal notes and in his longer introductory and concluding statements, Emden corrected Sasportas's citations, explained obscure passages, pointed to other books, cited his own work with and without attribution, and alerted his audience to his forthcoming writing. Furthermore, the first edition appeared as a folio, the same as *Ohel ya-akov*, the second as a quarto. The respective sizes illustrate a larger thematic difference between the two editions. The first edition was both a literal and a figurative appendix to Sasportas's responsa. The monumentality of the folio corresponded to the monumentality of the law and of rabbinic literature. The second edition appeared as a work unto itself and was intended largely for polemical purposes.

A broadsheet that Emden printed twice offers a telling illustration of Emden's interest in Sasportas as a polemicist.[33] On one side, Emden issued a call for subscriptions to support the publication of a new edition of the Bible. On the other, he included "a list of works celebrated throughout the world by the rabbi from Emden and his students that have appeared in print." The list divided his and his ostensible students' work by size: folio, quarto, and octavo. Under each category, the titles appear along with short descriptions of the books and a mention of the author in the third person. The works in folio include his legal writings, such as *Lehem shamayim*, *She-elat ya-avetz*, and *Mor u-ketziah*. The works in quarto, by contrast, include his polemical writings, such as *Torat ha-kenaot*, *Akitzat akrav*, and *Sefer shimush*.[34] The third entry on the list reads:

[32] Zalman Shazar, introduction to Leyb ben Ozer, *Sippur ma-asei shabbtai sevi*, 13–17.
[33] Raphael, "The Writings of Rabbi Jacob Emden," 232–242.
[34] The division was not absolute. *Iggeret bikoret*, a largely polemical work not related to the

Figure 25. Emden, broadsheet with all of the books he printed for sale. This broadsheet advertised all of Emden's books that had appeared in print, including his new edition of *Kitzur zizath novel zvi*. The National Library of Israel.

Kitzur zizath novel zvi by Rabbi Jacob Sasportas, of blessed memory, printed a second time, carefully edited and cleared of the numerous mistakes that marred the first edition, explicated and annotated with

Eibeschütz controversy, appeared in folio; *Etz avot*, his commentary on Avot with the additions of Bertinoro and Yom-Tov Lipmann Heller, appeared in quarto. On *Iggeret bikoret*, see Maoz Kahana, "The Scientific Revolution and Encoding of Sources of Knowledge: Medicine, Halakha, and Alchemy, Hamburg-Altona, 1736" (Hebrew), *Tarbiz* 82 (2013): 165–212.

fitting glosses by the celebrated rabbi who composed the pure works mentioned above. In addition, it includes the responsa of Rabbi Jacob Sasportas, of blessed memory, the author of the above-mentioned work [*Zizath novel zvi*], edited from his work by the aforementioned craftsman; as well as a responsum by the rabbi who wrote these works with several innovative discussions of the law of the priestly blessing.[35]

As he indicated in his broadsheet, Emden's edition contained a substantial amount of material over and above his own notes that did not appear in the first edition. In an appendix to his *Kitzur*, Emden reprinted and commented on all of Sasportas's responsa pertaining to Sabbatianism that had appeared in *Ohel ya-akov*. The first two editions thus form mirror images of one another: in the first, *Ohel ya-akov* was the basic text and the *Kitzur* appeared as an appendix only after special pleading by the author's son; in the second, the *Kitzur* was the primary point of interest and *Ohel ya-akov* provided material for an appendix. Furthermore, Emden included a substantial responsum of his own on the recitation of the priestly blessing on the Sabbath, a subject over which Sasportas had engaged in a dispute with the Jews of Amsterdam. Finally, Emden's *Kitzur* contained indexes, one to the letters that appeared in his *Kitzur* and a second to his own *Torat ha-kenaot*. All of these bibliographic data serve to make a single point: Emden's *Kitzur* was a new book with a purpose fundamentally different from that of the first edition, printed two decades earlier.

At the start of the controversy in 1751, Emden was forced to leave Altona-Hamburg-Wandsbek and made his way to Amsterdam. On the title page of his edition, Emden declared, "I was like a guest for the night here in Amsterdam, when I found this book rescued from the fire."[36] Emden visited Amsterdam on a number of occasions.[37] But his description of himself as "pursued by the multitude" and as "a guest

---

[35] קצור ציצית נובל צבי להרב כמהו"רי ששפורטש זצ"ל מדפוס שנית מוגה היטב ממוקשי שבושי הטעיות הרבות שנפלו בדפוס ראשון מואר ומבואר בהגהות הראויות לתת לו ע"י הרב המפורסם מחבר חבורי טהרה הנ"ל ונוסף עליהם שו"ת ממהריש"פ ז"ל בה"ס נ"ל מזוקקים ע"י האומן הנ"ל ותשובתו הרמתה של הרב בעל החיבורים בכמה חידושי דינים בה"ל ב"כ

Jacob Emden, "A list of works celebrated throughout the world by the rabbi from Emden and his students that have appeared in print," Scholem Library, shelf mark 5385.1; Raphael, "The Writings of Rabbi Jacob Emden," 238.

[36] Sasportas, *Kitzur*, ed. Emden, t.p.

[37] Emden, *MS*, 99.

Figures 26 and 27. Pieter van Gunst, *A Prospect of the Portuguese and High German Jews Churches at Amsterdam*, eighteenth century. Daniel Crouch Rare Books. These engravings depict the Portuguese and German Jewish Synagogues in Amsterdam in the middle of the eighteenth century, the time and place in which Emden discovered Sasportas. The first engraving was printed around the year 1732 and the second

for the night" suggests that he read Sasportas only after having been expelled from Altona in 1751.[38] Although it had appeared in print fourteen years earlier, the first edition of the *Kitzur* does not seem to have reached Emden in Altona. Displeased by the way that Sasportas had portrayed them in the *Kitzur*, the leaders of the Portuguese Jews in Amsterdam systematically destroyed many of the copies.[39] The issue is not trivial: if Emden did encounter Sasportas at the beginning of his own controversy, then the *Kitzur* may have served as a generic precedent for his *Torat ha-kenaot*, one of the earliest of his polemical writings about Eibeschütz to appear in print at his own press in 1752, bearing the false imprint of Amsterdam.[40]

If Emden was personally invested in Sasportas the anti-Sabbatian, the first edition he encountered was the product of filial piety. Abra-

---

[38] For another description of his stay in Amsterdam as a period of exile, see *MS*, 150.

[39] Carlebach, *Pursuit of Heresy*, 150.

[40] Shnayer Z. Leiman, "Books Suspected of Sabbatianism: The List of Rabbi Jacob Emden" (Hebrew), *Sefer ha-zikaron le-rabi Moshe Lifshitz*, ed. R. Rosenbaum (New York, 1996), 885. Hereafter Leiman, "Books Suspected of Sabbatianism."

Vüe en perspective des Eglises des Juifs Portugais et Allemands a Amsterdam. A Prospect of the Portuges and High German Jews Churches at Amsterdam.

around 1752. In the later image, the series of smaller houses on the right-hand side has been replaced with a large and ornate building, the Neie Shul. This synagogue was completed in 1752, and its completion may have contributed to the publisher's decision to print a second edition of this engraving.

ham Sasportas, Jacob's son, had brought his father's manuscripts to press in 1737. He had hired David Meldola to transcribe the responsa from his father's manuscripts and paid for their printing at the press of Hertz Levi Rofe, an Ashkenazi printer who specialized primarily in Yiddish and Hebrew literature.[41] The first edition thus had little to do with Sabbatianism and merely fulfilled the time-honored tradition of a son collecting his father's writings and seeing them through to print.

Over a decade later, Meldola was still working in Amsterdam and editing rabbinic literature. At Rofe's press, between 1750 and 1752, he edited Buzaglo's *Mikdash melekh*, to which Emden had unwillingly contributed an approbation.[42] In his approbation, Emden had criticized

[41] On Rofe, see Berger, *Producing Redemption in Amsterdam*, 112–113, 128; on the Meldola family, see Nahon, "R. Rafael b. Eleazar Meldola in Bayonne, 1728–1741"; Francesca Bregoli, "Hebrew Printing in Eighteenth-Century Livorno: From Government Control to a Free Market," in *The Hebrew Book in Early Modern Italy*, ed. Joseph R. Hacker and Adam Shear (Philadelphia: University of Pennsylvania Press, 2011), 171–196.

[42] Shalom Buzaglo, *Mikdash melekh* (Amsterdam, 1750–1752), 4 vols. Emden's approbation appeared in vol. 3, printed in 1752. See Leiman, "Books Suspected of Sabbatianism," 891–894.

Figure 28. Frontispiece, *Ohel ya-akov* (Amsterdam: Hertz Levi Rofe, 1737). This collection of Sasportas's responsa did not appear in print until thirty-nine years after the author's death. Private collection.

Hemdat yamim, a work quoted by Buzaglo and suspected by Emden of Sabbatianism.[43] Four years later, at the height of the controversy,

[43] See Leiman, "The Approbations," 199–201. On *Hemdat yamim,* see Abraham Yaari, *Ta-alumat sefer: Sefer hemdat yamim, mi hibro, u-mah hayeta midat hashpa-ato* (Jerusalem: Rav Kook Institute, 1954); Gershom Scholem, "And the mystery still stands" (Hebrew), in *Mehkere shabtaut,* 250–288; Isaiah Tishby, "On the Study of the Sources of *Hemdat yamim*" and "Sources from the Early Eighteenth Century in the Book *Hemdat yamim*" (both in Hebrew), in *Netive emunah u-minut* (Jerusalem: Magnes Press, 1994), 108–168; Moshe Fogel, "The Sabbatian Character of *Hemdat yamim*: A Re-examination" (Hebrew), in *Ha-halom ve-shivro,* ed. Rachel Elior (Jerusalem: Magnes Press,

Emden retracted his approbation in print. In 1755 Eibeschütz issued his one response to the tide of polemical literature that had issued from Emden's press, a book printed in Altona entitled *Luhot edut* that contained letters from rabbis throughout Europe who had pledged their support of Eibeschütz.[44] The following year, Emden printed *Shevirat luhot ha-aven*, which provided a point-by-point rebuttal of Eibeschütz's anthology. In the midst of the work, Emden recounted a conversation between David Meldola and an emissary from Jerusalem named Abraham Israel that had taken place in Amsterdam.[45] When Israel had read Emden's criticism of *Hemdat yamim*, he expressed his horror to Meldola. He claimed that it would have been better not to have printed the approbation at all, a sentiment with which Emden was entirely in agreement.[46]

Emden's animus against Buzaglo was hardly limited to the approbation he had been talked into issuing or to Sabbatian allusions in *Hemdat yamim*. Like so much else in Emden's life after 1751, it was bound up with the controversy. In short, Emden seems to have thought of Buzaglo as an ally early on who had gone over to the opposing faction. The year after the controversy started, Emden published a pamphlet titled *Sefat emet*, which contained reproductions of Eibeschütz's amulets along with a number of letters by rabbinic colleagues commenting on the amulets. In a letter written to Eibeschütz, a copy of which had reached Emden via the rabbinate in Amsterdam, Buzaglo condemned

2001), 2:365–422; Liebes, "The Students of the Gra, Sabbatianism, and the Jewish Point," 142n104. Emden referred to *Hemdat yamim* in his edition of Sasportas's *Kitzur*; see 58b where he posited that the author was Nathan of Gaza. See Yaari, *Ta-alumat sefer*, 10, and Yehuda Liebes, "The Book *Zaddik yesod olam*: A Sabbatian Mythology" (Hebrew), in *Sod ha-emunah ha-shabtait*, 302n15. For further references to *Hemdat yamim* in Emden's writings, see Sasportas, *Kitzur zizath novel zvi* (Odessa, 1867), 103–104.

[44] Sid Z. Leiman, "When a Rabbi Is Accused of Heresy: The Stance of the Gaon of Vilna in the Emden-Eibeschuetz Controversy," in *Me'ah She'arim: Studies in Medieval Jewish Spiritual Life in Memory of Isadore Twersky*, ed. Ezra Fleischer et al. (Jerusalem: Magnes Press, 2001), 252–253.

[45] *Shevirat luhot ha-aven* (Altona, 1756), 45b. As cited by Leiman, "The Approbations," 199n53. On Abraham Israel (1708–1785) as an emissary, see Yaari, *Sheluhei eretz yisrael*, 1: 398–399.

[46] In the second volume of his responsa he pointed a correspondent to this reference in *Shevirat luhot ha-aven*. See *She-elat ya-avez* (Lemberg, 1884), vol. 2., no. 126, p. 39a. Reference to the photo-offset edition printed in New York, 1967. In *Iggeret Purim*, Emden explicitly mentioned Meldola. See Leiman, "Books Suspected of Sabbatianism," 892–894, which corrects Abraham Bik (Shauli) "Rabbi Jacob Emden's Apology for His Approbation to the Book *Mikdash melekh*" (Hebrew), *KS* 50 (1974): 154–156. On *Iggeret Purim*, see Jacob J. Schacter, "Rabbi Jacob Emden's '*Iggeret Purim*,'" in *Studies in Medieval Jewish History and Literature*, ed. Isadore Twersky (Cambridge, MA: Harvard University Press, 1984), 2:441–446.

the amulets as containing references to Sabbetai Zevi.[47] In September 1751 Buzaglo wrote to David Meldola from London with an apology. He again condemned the amulets for their references to Sabbetai Zevi but declared he would not denounce Eibeschütz any further, as the Sephardim in Hamburg had warned him not to get involved in an Ashkenazi controversy.[48] Evidently the following year, Buzaglo had changed his mind. In his *Edut be-ya-akov*, a collection he printed the same year as *Shevirat luhot ha-aven*, Emden recounted a story he had heard while he was in Amsterdam.[49] According to Emden, Buzaglo sought to use the services of Samuel Sumbal, a Jewish diplomat who had been sent by the Moroccan sultan to the king of Denmark.[50] On his way to Copenhagen, Sumbal had stopped in Altona-Hamburg-Wandsbek where he had met with Buzaglo and Eibeschütz. Two of Buzaglo's brothers were imprisoned at the time by the Moroccan sultan, and it stands to reason that he would have sought Sumbal's intercession on their behalf at the Danish court. Emden's sources in Amsterdam further indicated that Buzaglo and Eibeschütz both wanted Sumbal to arrange an audience for Eibeschütz with the king of Denmark in Copenhagen.[51] In short, Buzaglo had gone over to the opposing faction and was no longer to be trusted.

Elsewhere in *Edut be-ya-akov*, Emden described his first encounter with Sasportas's work in Amsterdam:

I was shown a copy of the book *Zizath novel* here in Amsterdam. My mind was settled and my original perplexity was relieved, because "if you threw a stick in the air, it will fall back on its place of origin" (Gen. Rabbah §33). I realize now that this very place had been readied for this catastrophe, as the rot began with its inhabitants. When the villain Sabbetai Zevi, may the name of the wicked rot, rose up, they were the ones

---

[47] *Sefat emet u-leshon zehorit* (Altona, 1752), sig. 8, i.

[48] Ibid., sig. 8, i–ii. As cited with reference to the 1877 Lvov reprint by H. J. Zimmels, "Note on 'Solomon ben Joseph Buzaglo,'" *TJHSE* 17 (1951–1952): 290–292.

[49] *Edut be-ya-akov*, 79a–79b. Through a printer's error, the pagination reads 58a–58b. As cited by Cecil Roth, "The Amazing Clan of Buzaglo," *TJHSE* 23 (1969–1970): 16n8.

[50] On Sumbal, see Daniel J. Schroeter, *The Sultan's Jew: Morocco and the Sephardi World* (Stanford, CA: Stanford University Press, 2002), 23–24; to the literature on Sumbal cited by Schroeter, one can add Cecil Roth, "Samuel Sumbal: A Forgotten Jewish Statesman" (Hebrew), in *Mehkarim u-peulot* 3 (Ben Zvi Institute: Jerusalem, 1960), 13–17.

[51] Jacob Emden, *Sefer hitavkut ish* (Altona, 1755) 105a; as cited by Zimmels, "Note on 'Solomon ben Joseph Buzaglo,'" 291. Zimmels refers to the second edition (Lemberg, 1877), 58a.

who rushed to him first, lusting after that forbidden meat, while abusing a righteous man, a pillar of the world, as I have seen with my own eyes [described] in the aforementioned book by the eminent and pious rabbi, Jacob Sasportas, may he rest in Eden, whose name is my name, whose city is my city, whose counsel is my counsel, the counsel of God [which] is the one that will stand (Ps. 33:11). He was hounded by the blinded masses, who wished to be free and liberated from the Torah and the commandments. They walked in darkness (Ps. 82:5) bending their tongues [like bows], their inkwells filled with lies (Jer. 9:2) at the time when this evil heresy of Sabbetai Zevi, may the name of the wicked rot, began to sprout... They repaid his kindness with wickedness, and persecuted him with intense hostility and anger. Exactly the same happened to me in this very place, the homeland of my forefathers, except that I had already come to expect it.[52]

With even greater intensity than in his introduction to the *Kitzur*, Emden here drew a direct analogy between his own experience and that of Sasportas. Both had been hounded by the ignorant masses for daring to challenge them in the open. Both met with grief for having dared to rebuke the people.

In his ever-escalating print war against the Eibeschütz faction, Emden found an ally in Sasportas. A year after issuing *Shevirat luhot ha-aven* and *Edut be-ya-akov*, he printed his edition of Sasportas's *Kitzur*. Meldola and Abraham Sasportas had both decried the messy and chaotic state of Sasportas's manuscripts in separate introductions to the first edition. It remains unclear whether they made this claim as an excuse to suppress some of the more radical aspects of Sasportas's polemic or because of the genuine difficulty of Sasportas's handwriting. Either way, Emden was unimpressed. In his own introduction, he recounted that he had corrected many of Meldola's mistakes. When one begins to read the book, this opening salvo seems mild. In his

---

[52] עד שהראוני פה אמשטרדם ספר ציצת נובל אז שקטה נחה דעתי וסרה תמיהתי מעיקרה, כי זרוק חוטרא באוירא אעיקריה קאי, הן עתה ידעתי כי זה המקום מוכן לפורענות זו. הן המה היו שהתחילו בקלקלה בעת שקם אדם רשע שב"ץ שר"י הם רצו אחריו בתחילה היו להוטים אחר הנבלה. והרעו לצדיק יסוד עולם. כאשר עתה ראיתי בעיני בספר הנ"ל שחיבר הגאון החסיד כמוהר"ר יעקב ששפורטש נ"ע ששמו כשמי ושם עירו כשם עירי ושם עצתו כעצתי עצת ה' תעמוד. והיה נרדף מהמון העם עורי לב. החפצים להיות בני חורין וחפשים מן התורה ומן המצות בחשכה יתהלכו וידרכו את לשונם קסתם שקר באותו הזמן שהתחילה להציץ המינות הרעה הזאת של שב"י שר"י ... ושלמו לו רעה תחת טובה לרדפו ולהדפו באיבה ובחימה רבה ככה ממש קרה לנו בזה המקום ארץ מגורי אבותי אלא שאני כבר הורגלתי בכך

Edut be-ya-akov, 37a. Through a printer's error, the pagination reads 36a.

discussion of Nathan of Gaza's wanderings after Sabbetai Zevi's apostasy, Sasportas referred to a letter that he had written in response to the prophecies of Abraham Miguel Cardozo. In a marginal gloss, Meldola added, "All of this appears in the third and fourth sections of the book *Zizath novel*, which remains in the possession of the author's son; but I did not have space to copy and print it." To Meldola's gloss, Emden added one of his own: "My anger and sorrow at this lack cannot be remediated: among these answers were wicked answers for fools"[53] (Job 34:36).

What had been only a spiteful comment erupted into unbounded rage several pages later when Emden composed his conclusion to Meldola's edition:

> Therefore, I do not find his [Meldola's] apology sufficient to justify the extent of his abridgment... for he should not have been cleverer than the author [Sasportas] who had worked very hard. This should not be done in Israel, to change the opinions of authors who have laid cornerstones (Job 38:6) and to remove from the work fundamental portions that the author had worked on and had gathered as sheaves unto the floor (Mic. 4:12). Nor did he work in vain, for all of his labor was done in truth (Ps. 33:4).[54]

Emden castigated Meldola for abridging and mutilating the work of an author who knew what he was doing. There may be something more than Sasportas's missing work in this outburst. At whatever juncture Emden encountered the *Kitzur*, he was unable to examine Sasportas's manuscripts. These manuscripts had at one point been in Meldola's possession and were to remain in Amsterdam until they were sold at public auction in 1811.[55] Meldola had been the editor of Buzaglo's *Mikdash melekh* and had played a role in soliciting Emden's approbation. Without pressing the evidence too far, one may speculate that Emden had little love for his colleague in the world of print. He expressed his fury with Meldola, whom he had met in Amsterdam at some point be-

---

[53] Sasportas, *Kitzur*, ed. Emden, 39b.

[54] לכן איגני רואה די התנצלות שלא מלא כפי קוצר, ולא היה לו התחכם יותר על המחבר שעמל בו הרבה, ולא יעשה כן בישראל לשנות מדעת בעלים אשר ירו אבני יסוד ופנה, לחסר מן החבור דברים עקריים שטרח בהם מחברו, וקבצם כעמיר גורנה, ולא לשוא עמל בו כי כל מעשהו באמונה

Ibid., 47a. For a description of Meldola's abridgment as the nullification of the words of Torah, see 52b.

[55] Isaiah Tishby, introduction to Sasportas, *ZNZ*, 39 (Hebrew pagination).

tween 1751 and 1752, in *Shevirat luhot ha-aven* and in his edition of the *Kitzur* printed, respectively, in 1756 and 1757.

Whatever the reasons for his anger at Meldola's abridgment—personal, intellectual, or some combination thereof—Emden proceeded to enumerate two basic imperatives for the preservation and publication of evidence that some might think portrayed past scholars in a negative light.

> This is either in order to demonstrate the righteousness and piety of the patriarchs who did not insist on what they had said [deceitfully] but rather admitted and were not ashamed to acknowledge their error once the truth had become clear to them, refraining from holding on to their deceit in order to cover their shame with lies and worthless vanities unlike the brazen accursed members of this sect of Sabbetai Zevi, may the name of the wicked rot, who stood harder than a rock to uphold their falsehood, setting it up on pillars of lies as an excuse ... Or else, in order that future generations should hear and learn and take heed, for they should not be so quick to believe anyone who makes false pretenses about such a weighty matter.[56]

Accounts that preserved past errors, thought Emden, would lead his contemporaries to exercise greater caution in their rush to embrace popular delusions. Whether or not this was true, this argument was very similar to the one that Sasportas had made when summoning up the mistakes of past Jewish sages, such as R. Akiva and his acceptance of Bar Kokhba as the Messiah. The past, provided it was recounted in its proper form and with accurate evidence, was a weapon for Emden and for Sasportas. They invoked it in their attempt to convince their Jewish coreligionists that the acceptance of a Messiah should come only as the result of sustained reflection and repeated proof of divine election.

Sasportas had lived through the events he had described; for Emden, his testimony as a living witness to Sabbatianism proved absolutely critical. In his introductory note, Emden explicitly invoked his own

[56] אם כדי להראות צדקתם וחסידותם של אבות העולם שלא עמדו על דבריהם הודו ולא בושו להכיר טעותם אחר שנתברר להם האמת ולא החזיקו בתרמית לכסות חרפתם בדברי שקר ותוהו ורעות רוח כענין החצופים הארורים הללו אנשי כת ש"ץ שר"י . . . למען ישמעו וילמדו דורות הבאים ויקחו מוסר, שלא למהר להאמין לכל המראה פנים בדבר גדול כזה

Sasportas, *Kitzur*, ed. Emden, 47a.

account of Sabbatianism, *Torat ha-kenaot*, and compared it with that of Sasportas:

> Even though I have already written the book *Torat ha-kenaot* about this, nevertheless, there is no comparison to one who hears it from the great rabbi in whose time this evil event occurred. He was a witness who either saw or knew all that happened. He girded his sword like Ishmael to wage the war of God against the instigator.[57]

Sasportas understood how to respond to fools, and this could be of great use to Emden in his current predicament. Lest there be any doubt that Emden wanted to press Sasportas and *Zizath novel zvi* into the controversy still raging in Altona-Hamburg-Wandsbek, he spelled it out:

> All things have I seen in the days of my vanity (Ecc. 7:15). There is a wicked man who has been practicing his wickedness for many days of anguish and pain. Would a ninety-year-old (the span of time since the days of Sabbetai Zevi, may the name of the wicked rot, when pride blossomed and heresy came forth) (Eze. 7:10) give birth (Gen. 17:17) to idolatrous children? For this reason, I decided that it was good to renew like an eagle (Ps. 103:5) the youth of this pleasing treatise.[58]

The imperative to reintroduce Sasportas to the public domain stemmed from the basic point that Sabbatianism continued to be a living and generative force within Jewish life. In republishing Sasportas's *Kitzur*, Emden sought to make a direct link between the Sabbatian movement in the seventeenth century and current events where he lived. The edition of Sasportas thus continued the work he had begun a few years earlier in *Torat ha-kenaot* and that would occupy much of his intellectual energy for the years to come. Emden clearly thought that the two periods, although separated by ninety years, could be located on a historical continuum.

In his extensive marginal notes throughout the *Kitzur*, Emden sought to construct a tradition of anti-Sabbatianism and position him-

---

[57] ועם שכבר יסדנו חבור תורת הקנאות מענין זה, מ״מ אינו דומה שומע מפי הרב הגדול ואשר בימיו אירע זה המאורע הרע והוא עד או ראה או ידע כל הנעשה וחגר חרבו כישמעאל ללחום מלחמות ה' נגד המסית ומדיח Ibid., 1a.

[58] את הכל ראיתי בימי הבלי יש רשע מאריך ברעתו ימים רבים של צער וצרה הבת תשעים שנה (הם מעת שב״ץ שר״י ציץ הזדון יצאה הכפירה) תלד בנים לעבודה זרה. לכן ראיתי כי טוב הוא לחדש כנשר נעוריו של חבור נחמד Ibid.

self as the intellectual heir to Sasportas. His notes served a number of purposes: bibliographic, critical, and explanatory. In his bibliographic notes, Emden repeatedly directed his reader to passages in *Torat ha-kenaot*, which had appeared five years earlier and to which Emden's edition of the *Kitzur* contained an index. Emden's *Kitzur* extended the work he had begun in his own *Torat ha-kenaot*, a work that contained a copious amount of writing by other individuals faithfully transcribed and acerbically annotated by Emden in the same typographic form as in his *Kitzur*. Emden may have imagined a reader of his *Kitzur* who would have had a copy of his *Torat ha-kenaot* close at hand. When, for example, Sasportas cited a passage from a responsum by Solomon ibn Adret that played a crucial role in his argument against Sabbatian prophecy, Emden added: "Look at what I have written in *Torat ha-kenaot*, 49b."[59] If one follows Emden's instructions, one discovers that he had reproduced the entirety of Ibn Adret's responsum along with his own glosses, followed by a short commentary.[60] In this way, Emden mobilized Ibn Adret's responsum in his own discussion of Moses Hayim Luzzatto's revelations from a *maggid*, or celestial mentor.[61] He used Ibn Adret's responsum to extend a note of caution to those, like Luzzatto, who claimed to communicate with otherworldly spirits. Only after a thorough and careful examination, the kind that Luzzatto himself had not undergone, could one be sure of direct revelation. Sasportas and Emden both sought to harness a medieval responsum on the question of prophecy for similar ends. To Sasportas, Ibn Adret had conclusively demonstrated that one should be wary of Sabbatian claims to prophecy; to Emden, of Sabbatian claims to celestial mentorship.

The further one delves into Emden's notes, the more one encounters a system of cross-references that few people other than Emden himself could have easily manipulated or understood. Sasportas had accused the Sabbatians of misunderstanding a passage in *Tikkunei Zohar*. In a note Emden added, "Look at *Torat ha-kenaot* page 66 and

[59] Ibid., 7a; Sasportas, *ZNZ*, 146.

[60] For Ibn Adret's responsum, see Emden, *Torat ha-kenaot* (Altona, 1752), 48b–49b; for Emden's comments, see 49b–50a. Elsewhere, Emden sharply criticized Ibn Adret. See *She-elat ya-avez*, 2: #146, 45a–47b. As cited by Charles Duschinsky, "Jacob Kimchi and Shalom Buzaglo," *TJHSE* 7 (1911–1914): 13.

[61] On Emden's position on Luzzatto in contrast to his elder colleague Moses Hagiz, see Carlebach, *Pursuit of Heresy*, 245n38.

page 67 where you shall find things dearer than gold."[62] There, Emden had adduced a series of passages from *Tikkunei Zohar* and criticized the Sabbatian reading much as Sasportas had. Both had rejected the Sabbatian use of *Tikkunei Zohar* to justify the conversion of Sabbetai Zevi. Emden had gone one step further and rejected the purported Sabbatian claim that Sabbetai Zevi himself had become a divinity, a claim Sasportas neither mentioned nor rejected in this context.[63]

Emden's annotations also referred to some of his own writing that had yet to appear in print. In a narrative passage of the *Kitzur*, Sasportas had detailed a number of the public transgressions committed by Sabbetai Zevi during his imprisonment in Gallipoli, such as the utterance of the divine name and the consumption of sacrificial meat at the improper time and place.[64] In a note to the passage, Emden added: "The author considered the lesser commandments as important as the greater ones. In terms of the utterance of the divine name, there is a reason. Look at what I have written, with the help of heaven, in *Lehem shamayim*, at the beginning of the chapter 'All of Israel has a portion,' in tractate Sanhedrin."[65] In fact, the second volume of *Lehem shamayim*, which included the passage in question, did not appear until 1768, over a decade after the commentary and edition of Sasportas's *Kitzur*. Emden referred to the opening Mishnah in that chapter of Sanhedrin, which recorded the opinion of Abba Saul: "He who utters the divine name has no share in the world to come." In his commentary, Emden indicated that the utterance of the divine name was not a severe prohibition but had been included in this Mishnah on account of the biblical verse about the name of God, "This is my name forever"[66] (Ex. 3:15).

In his annotations Emden paid careful attention to the accessibility of Sasportas's sources. He noted when Sasportas had cited a text that had yet to appear in print and was therefore likely unknown. Toward the conclusion of his letter to David de Mercado, Sasportas posited that it was forbidden to cite something in the name of the wicked. As a proof text, he cited a responsum written by David ibn abi Zimra, known in rabbinic literature by the acronym Radbaz or Ridbaz, who had lived

---

[62] Sasportas, *Kitzur*, ed. Emden, 42b.
[63] Emden, *Torat ha-kenaot*, 67a.
[64] Sasportas, *ZNZ*, 79.
[65] Sasportas, *Kitzur*, ed. Emden, 19a.
[66] Emden, *Lehem shamayim* (Altona, 1768), 38a.

in Egypt and Palestine in the sixteenth century. David ibn Zimra was an extremely prolific author of responsa, but they appeared in print in piecemeal fashion over the course of several centuries. The first book to appear, which would later constitute the fourth volume, was printed by Sasportas's correspondent Raphael Supino in Livorno in 1652. A further two volumes appeared in Venice in 1749.[67] Sasportas had written, "And our teacher Rabbi David ben Zimra proved in number 187 that it was forbidden to recount a statement in the name of a wicked man."[68] On this passage, Emden remarked: "There is no reason to derive this from Rabbi David ibn Zimra, for there are many places in the Talmud [that teach this] and we have already mentioned some of them earlier. Perhaps the author alluded to a responsum of David ibn Zimra that he possessed in manuscript that is unknown. But I looked in his responsum number 187 concerning the issue at hand. This requires an explanation so the reader does not stumble in his innocence."[69] A compulsive checker of other people's sources, Emden could not identify the passage Sasportas had cited in support of his statement. He appears to have been aware of the unusually large corpus of responsa left by Ridbaz, and allowed for the possibility that Sasportas had cited something in manuscript.

Emden was not always so generous in resolving his Talmudic disagreements with Sasportas. In a letter to his rabbinic colleagues in North Africa written well after Sabbetai Zevi's apostasy, Sasportas rebuked them for allowing their congregants to continue to suspend the traditional fast day on the ninth of Av and celebrate it as a holiday in honor of the new Messiah.[70] He chastised them for forgetting a Talmudic passage in tractate Megilah about an attempt by Rabbi Judah the Prince to suspend the ninth of Av and the refusal of the sages to acquiesce in his suggestion.[71] In the continuation of the passage, the Talmud modified Judah the Prince's original suggestion. He had referred

---

[67] On the publication history, see Israel L. Goldman, *The Life and Times of Rabbi David ibn abi Zimra: A Social, Economic, and Cultural Study of Jewish Life in the Ottoman Empire in the 15th and 16th Centuries as Reflected in the Responsa of the RDBZ* (New York: Jewish Theological Seminary, 1970).

[68] Sasportas, *ZNZ*, 236.

[69] Sasportas, *Kitzur*, ed. Emden, 55b. Emden's instincts appear to have been correct. The responsa of the Ridbaz cited by Sasportas did not appear in print until the nineteenth century. See Sasportas, *ZNZ*, 236n1.

[70] Sasportas, *ZNZ*, 317.

[71] BT Megilah, 5b.

only to a year when the ninth of Av had fallen on a Sabbath and the fast had already been deferred to the following day. Given that the fast had already been postponed by a day, he reasoned, why not suspend it altogether. In discussing this passage, Sasportas quoted the glosses of the Tosafot, a medieval commentary on the Talmud composed in northern France by a group of rabbis over several centuries.[72] The Tosafot wondered how Judah the Prince could have even thought to suspend the fast, given the Talmud's statement in tractate Taanit, "One who eats and drinks on the ninth of Av will never witness the comfort of Jerusalem."[73] Furthermore, the Tosafot continued, there is a legal principle whereby no court can nullify the ruling of another one unless it is greater in wisdom and size. The Tosafot had asked a second question, Sasportas claimed, because the first one had not sufficed. One could have dismissed the question brought from tractate Taanit by positing that it did not apply in a year when the fast had been deferred. To witness the comfort of Jerusalem pertained only to the issue of reward and punishment; with the deferral of the fast, one would simply receive no reward. In his marginal annotation to Sasportas's suggestion about a superfluous question in Tosafot, Emden exploded: "This is nonsense, may the Lord forgive him for his statement."[74] Emden's anger may simply have stemmed from a disagreement over how to interpret the proliferation of questions in Tosafot; it may also have derived from an intense Ashkenazi pride and what he perceived as encroachment by a Sephardic Talmudist on the Ashkenazi glosses.[75]

Emden edited the text of *Kitzur zizath novel zvi*, on some occasions silently emending an obscure reference and on others howling from the margins about errors committed by the previous editor or by Sasportas himself.[76] The republication of an earlier text in a new edition,

[72]BT Megilah, 5b, s.v. u-vikesh.

[73]BT Ta-anit, 30b, as cited by Tosafot.

[74]Sasportas, *Kitzur*, ed. Emden, 44b. Sasportas was not the only figure to whom Emden applied this phrase. For its use in reference to Jacob Joshua Falk, see Jacob Emden, *Mor u-ketziah* (Jerusalem: Makhon Jerusalem, 1996), par. 307, p. 339. On Falk and the controversy, see Sid Z. Leiman, "When a Rabbi Is Accused of Heresy: The Stance of Rabbi Jacob Joshua Falk in the Emden-Eibeschuetz Controversy," in *Rabbinic Culture and Its Critics*, ed. Daniel Frank and Matt Goldish (Detroit: Wayne State University Press, 2008), 435–456.

[75]Elsewhere Sasportas quoted Tosafot as supporting evidence for his own interpretation. See *ZNZ*, 235.

[76]For a silent emendation, see Sasportas, *ZNZ*, 221n5. The passage appears in Sasportas, *Kitzur*, ed. Emden, 51a, without any indication of the correction.

the citation of sources, and the explication of difficult passages: through these tasks Emden had appropriated Sasportas's own self-appointed role as a corrector of texts. Emden's edition seems to lie somewhere between the conventions of early modern rabbinic literature—enforced and promoted by Sasportas in his struggle for authority against the Sabbatian prophets—and those of modern scholarship, similarly informed by an elitist impulse to purify Jewish textuality.

As a work of rabbinic literature, Emden's *Kitzur* concludes with a long and argumentative responsum by Emden himself. The issue involved the priestly blessing on the Sabbath, the same one that had vexed Sasportas. In this respect, Emden placed himself within a generative tradition of Jewish law. Emden's marginal annotations also anticipate the conventions of the modern footnote that would come to dominate scholarship half a century later.[77] Like his medieval and early modern predecessors who composed countless *hasagot* and *hagahot*, Emden crafted notes that extended the legal issues raised in Sasportas's responsa.[78] Like modern scholars, Emden sifted and sorted through the sources of Sasportas's statements. This tension between the production of new rabbinic knowledge and the classification, preservation, and emendation of older rabbinic knowledge remains unresolved in Emden's edition of the *Kitzur*. It is not clear whether Emden saw himself as a traditionalist charged with the transmission of rabbinic authority or a scholarly author creating an accurate text. It is even less clear whether he would have made such a distinction.

Sasportas was never all that far from Emden's mind. Four years after issuing his new edition, Emden printed a long and harshly polemical book about the *Zohar* entitled *Mitpahat sefarim*.[79] Unlike many other early modern and modern works that treated the antiquity of the *Zohar*, Emden's combined a keen historical and philological sense of the relatively late origins of the work with a profound respect for and sacralization of its contents.[80] In the ninth chapter of the second section, Emden dealt with Moses Maimonides and Abraham ibn Ezra and their

[77] Anthony Grafton, *The Footnote: A Curious History* (Cambridge, MA: Harvard University Press, 1997).

[78] Spiegel, *Amudim be-toledot ha-sefer ha-ivri*.

[79] Isaiah Tishby, introduction to *The Wisdom of the Zohar* (Oxford: Littman Library, 1989), 38–43. Huss, *Zohar*.

[80] "Whoever compares his [Emden's] words with the book *Ari Nohem* [by Leon Modena] (which was unknown to him), shall see with complete clarity how much greater spiritual power

respective attitudes toward esotericism and mystical secrets. In a comment made as an aside to his larger discussion, Emden compared Ibn Ezra and Maimonides in terms of their respective lineages. Unlike Ibn Ezra, whose descendants appear to have vanished without a trace, Maimonides was fortunate to have founded a dynasty of scholars who perpetuated his legacy. Emden's assessment of Maimonides was quite mixed, and immediately beforehand he had repeated a claim he had made elsewhere that *The Guide of the Perplexed* was a forgery mistakenly attributed to Maimonides. Emden and Sasportas took different paths in their respective approaches to Maimonides. Sasportas made no attempt to distinguish between Maimonides the legalist and Maimonides the philosopher. He summoned both the *Code* and the *Guide*, either explicitly or implicitly, as he waged his epistolary war on the Sabbatians. Emden made a concerted effort to separate Maimonides as an authority on rabbinic law from Maimonides the philosopher.[81]

Not content to allow Maimonides the last word on the question of rabbinic dynasties, Emden continued:

> But even more than him, Nahmanides, of blessed memory, attained merit. For the secrets of true wisdom were revealed to him, and he did not immerse himself in the external sciences but established his tent in the house of study built by Shem and Ever.[82]

Comparisons between Maimonides and Nahmanides are nearly as old as study of medieval Judaism, and Emden indulged in the rather banal opposition between reason and faith that has marked so much of the writing on both figures.[83] Shortly thereafter he remarked favorably on Nahmanides's lineage, which was even more prominent than that of Maimonides:

---

this sage [Emden] possessed." Gershom Scholem, "Review of M. J. Cohen 'Jacob Emden: A Man of Controversy'" (Hebrew), in *Mehkere shabtaut*, 678.

[81]Jacob J. Schacter, "Rabbi Jacob Emden, Philosophy, and Maimonides," in *Be'erot Yitzhak: Studies in Memory of Isadore Twersky*, ed. Jay M. Harris (Cambridge, MA: Harvard University Press, 2005), 239–267.

[82]אבל יותר מזה זכה הרמב"ן ז"ל, שנגלו אליו גם תעלומות חכמה האמיתית, ולא עסק בדברי החיצונים בשקידה, אבל תקע אהלו בבתי מדרשות של שם ועבר

Jacob Emden, *Mitpahat sefarim* (Altona, 1768), 28a.

[83]Bernard Septimus, "'Open rebuke and concealed love': Nahmanides and the Andalusian Tradition," in *Rabbi Moses Nahmanides: Explorations in His Religious and Literary Virtuosity*, ed. Isadore Twersky (Cambridge, MA: Harvard University Press, 1983), 11.

This man Moses [ben Nahman] was very great and so worthy that his lineage continues to this day, for there are several sages even today in Barbary [who are his descendants]. Levi ben Gerson and Simeon ben Zemah Duran were the fruit of his loins, and the eminent Jacob Sasportas, close to our time, was an eleventh-generation descendant of Nahmanides, of blessed memory. Certainly his line shall continue forever. No one else in the diaspora has ever merited such a thing.[84]

Sasportas here appeared as an aside to an aside, but in a revealing context nonetheless. Sasportas's constant and repeated stress upon his own genealogy throughout his responsa and polemics on Sabbatianism had clearly made an impression on his like-minded reader. Emden never tired of invoking his father, whose testimony about the authenticity of certain letters attributed to Maimonides he had cited on the very same page.

Sasportas's ambivalence about print and his inability to print his chronicle of Sabbatianism in his lifetime were not without consequence. On the title page of his new edition of the *Kitzur*, Emden emphasized that he had come across the first edition only by accident. There is little reason to doubt this. In fact, the crucial figure who could have played a mediating role between Sasportas and Emden in the transmission of anti-Sabbatian ideas and in the formation of the early modern zealot did not engage with Sasportas's writings on Sabbatianism. Moses Hagiz was ideally placed to serve as a personal and intellectual link between Sasportas and Emden. His father, Jacob Hagiz, who exercised an outsized influence upon his formation as a rabbinic controversialist, had corresponded with Sasportas about the Sabbatian movement at the peak of the messianic enthusiasm. Moses Hagiz arrived in Amsterdam after Sasportas's death but would have been in a position to have had contact with Abraham Sasportas, who had preserved his father's papers. Elisheva Carlebach suggested that Hagiz may have known one of Sasportas's other sons, Moses, in his role as an emissary of Palestine.[85] In 1713–1714 Hagiz had collaborated with Emden's father, Hakham Zvi Ashkenazi, in the pursuit of Nehemiah

[84] וזה האיש משה גדול מאד, זכה שזרעו קיים עדיין בעולם, מהם נמצאים גם היום כמה ת"ח בברבריאה, הרלב"ג ורשב"ץן היו מי"ח והגאון מהר"י ששפורטש ז"ל קרוב לדורנו, הוא היה דור י"א לרמב"ן ז"ל, בודאי זרעו לעולם יהיה, כזה לא נודע עוד לשום אדם בגולה שזכה לכך.

Emden, *Mitpahat sefarim*, 28a.
[85] *Pursuit of Heresy*, 150.

Hayon for his alleged Sabbatian tendencies in Amsterdam. Furthermore, Moses Hagiz and Jacob Emden both lived among the Jews in Hamburg-Altona-Wandsbek after Emden returned to Altona and settled there in 1732.

Over and above the personal and geographic lines of filiation among these three figures, Hagiz shared Sasportas's experience of the western Sephardic Diaspora. He too came to the wealthy communities of Amsterdam and Hamburg as a mature rabbinic scholar with a keen sense of his own lineage. He too struggled to attain official recognition from his adopted communities and sought refuge in the world of Hebrew print. Like Sasportas, he believed in a return to a set of core rabbinic texts from antiquity that had been unjustly neglected, including and especially the Mishnah. Both emphasized and cited the very same passages of medieval rabbinic literature, such as *Sefer hasidim* and Solomon ibn Adret, in their polemical exchanges with real or alleged Sabbatians.[86] Hagiz, like Sasportas, opposed the introduction of novelty or innovation in ritual practice because of negative associations with Sabbatianism.[87] Both described Sabbatianism as a new Torah, or a new law.[88] If there were any other figure who could be classified as "a zealot the son of a zealot" along with Sasportas and Emden, it would seem to be Hagiz.[89] When one turns to Hagiz's writings, one finds a striking absence of reference to Sasportas's writings. Elisheva Carlebach has noted that Hagiz did not refer to Sasportas's anti-Sabbatian writings in any of his own polemical literature, and that his one reference to Sasportas appears in the context of his discussion of *Sefer heikhal hakodesh*, the kabbalistic commentary on the prayers by R. Moses b. Maimon (Elbaz) that Sasportas had printed at the Benveniste press in 1653.[90] Without pressing this lack of engagement too far, one could simply say that Hagiz may not have been aware of Sasportas's writings on Sabbatianism. All three of the campaigns he waged—against Nehemiah Hayon in Amsterdam, against the vestiges of Sabbatianism

---

[86] On Hagiz's citation of *Sefer hasidim*, see *R. Moshe Hayim Luzzatto u-venei doro*, ed. Ginzburg, 1:79; the reference *to Sefer Hasidim* is then repeated by Luzzatto's teacher Isaiah Bassan on 86. As cited by Carlebach, *Pursuit of Heresy*, 326–327n45.

[87] Carlebach, *Pursuit of Heresy*, 245.

[88] Hagiz, *Shever poshim* (London, 1714), 34a.

[89] The phrase "zealots sons of zealots" appears as part of a letter written by Hakham Zvi Ashkenazi and published by Hagiz. See *Shever poshim*, 39b.

[90] Carlebach, *Pursuit of Heresy*, 150.

in central Europe, and against Moses Hayim Luzzatto in Padua—had largely concluded before 1737, the year Sasportas's *Kitzur* first appeared in print.

In his study of Joseph Ashkenazi in sixteenth-century Poland, Elchanan Reiner cautions scholars against dismissing such thinkers as either sterile defenders of a well-worn past or as knee-jerk reactionaries rather than radical conservatives, a position that represents a different mode of creative engagement with the past.[91] Sasportas and Emden represent the modern genealogy of this position. Perhaps even more than Ashkenazi, Sasportas and Emden exemplify a new figure in Jewish life: the conservative who was excluded from social power, but whose learning and lineage led to a profound sense of entitlement. Their sense of expectancy and consequent rage produced not only self-pity and endless complaints about isolation and obscurity; they also served as the catalyst for an inventive fury. Sasportas, and Emden in his wake, introduced a new type of writing that had few specific precedents in medieval rabbinic literature. *Zizath novel zvi* and *Torat ha-kenaot* incorporated elements of the ordinance (*takanah*), the letter (*iggeret*), the gloss (*hasagah*), the responsum (*she-elah u-teshuvah*), the diary (a word for which there is no early modern Hebrew equivalent), and that rabbinic genre par excellence, the commentary (*perush*). The totality of these polemical writings far exceeded the sum of their inherited generic parts: with their careful attention to the recording of documents, keen sense of precedent, and powerful authorial voices, Sasportas and Emden stood at the brink of a revolution that had the power to turn rabbis into intellectuals.

THE RECEPTION OF EMDEN'S EDITION

Emden's edition turned Sasportas into a book. Without Emden, Sasportas might have languished in obscurity well into the twentieth century. Because of Emden, Sasportas was taken up by a number of later writers before Tishby reedited his work. A Jewish merchant in

---

[91]Elchanan Reiner, "'No Jew should learn anything but the Talmud alone': A Dispute over Books and Forbidden Books in Sixteenth-Century Ashkenaz" (Hebrew), in *Ta Shma: mehkarim be-madae ha-yahadut le-zikhro shel yisrael M. Ta-Shma*, ed. Avraham (Rami Reiner) et al. (Alon Shvut: Tevunot, 2011), 2:705–746.

eighteenth-century Poland, Dov Ber Bolechów, drew heavily on Emden's edition of Sasportas in his history of Jewish messianic movements entitled *Understanding Words* (Heb. *Divre binah*).[92] Over the next century, Jewish writers throughout the republic of Hebrew letters repeatedly referred to Sasportas. When they did, they frequently mentioned him in the same breath as Emden. Several decades after the completion of *Divre binah*, Emden and Sasportas appeared together in a footnote by Isaac Samuel Reggio (1784–1855). A rabbi and aspiring intellectual who lived in Habsburg Gorizia, Reggio had published a philosophical treatise on Torah and philosophy in 1827.[93] In the original publication, he had withheld a chapter on Kabbalah. When he discovered that this chapter had been circulating without his permission, he decided to include it in an anthology of his essays and research notes that he published in his hometown in 1854.[94] In an aside within this chapter, Reggio mentioned Sabbetai Zevi and the Sabbatian movement. He posited that Sabbetai Zevi would have been forgotten had a number of mistaken rabbis not seen fit to propagate his teachings in the century after his death. In a footnote, Reggio listed a series of rabbis suspected of Sabbatian leanings. "However," he added, "one who would like to discern the truth about these events should examine the book *Zizath novel zvi*, the book *Torat ha-kenaot*."[95] For Reggio, Sasportas and Emden constituted a repository of accurate historical knowledge that stood in contrast to the fantasies of clandestine Sabbatian rabbis.

A decade later, Sasportas and Emden appeared together in a short article by Salomon Rubin (1823–1910). A central figure in the Jewish revival of Spinoza, Rubin would later translate the *Ethics* into Hebrew.[96] In the German periodical *Ben-Chananja*, edited by Leopold Löw and printed in Hungary, Rubin published a short biographical notice of Sasportas.[97] He sketched the contours of Sasportas's life as he was

[92] Gershon David Hundert, "The Introduction to *Divre Binah* by Dov Ber Bolechów: An Unexamined Source for the History of Jews in the Lwów Region in the Second Half of the Eighteenth Century," *AJS Review* 33 (2009): 229n19.

[93] *Ha-torah veha-filosofiah: mehkar iyuni* (Vienna: Anton Schmid, 1827).

[94] *Yalkut yashar: Asefat hakirot al inyanim shonim* (Gorizia: Joh. Bap. Seitz, 1854).

[95] "Whether Reason Is Opposed to Kabbalah" (Hebrew), in ibid., 112–113n2. As cited by Shmuel Werses, "Frankists and *Maskilim* in Prague" (Hebrew), in *Haskalah ve-shabtaut: toldotav shel ma-avak* (Jerusalem: Zalman Shazar Center, 1988), 96n133.

[96] Daniel B. Schwartz, *The First Modern Jew: Spinoza and the History of an Image* (Princeton, NJ: Princeton University Press, 2012), chap. 4.

[97] "Biographisches: Jakob Saportas," *Ben-Chananja* 7 (1864): 711–714. As cited in Shmuel

able to deduce them from his writings in print. He mentioned Emden's edition and pointed to the similarities between the two figures, particularly in terms of the tone of their writing:

> Between these two zealous struggles for religious purity against Sabbatian sectarianism, we find the most conspicuous similarity in regard to attitude, character, and temperament: both devoted themselves to the Kabbalah, heart and soul, and nonetheless dealt it—precisely out of anxious care to keep it pure—the most staggering blows. Discursively both were at times modest and humble, to the point of self-denial; at other times, their dignity and merit were paraded excessively. When confronted with disputes, both quickly took up arms and then unloaded their witty sparks, full of sarcasm and bitterness.[98]

In a few sentences Rubin sketched the basic parallels between Emden and Sasportas, noting their penchant for disputation and their obsession with personal honor.

Three years later, Emden's edition reappeared in print at the press of Moses Eliezer Beilinson (1835–1908). A translator, editor, and writer, Beilinson took advantage of the relatively liberal censorship laws in Odessa and founded a printing house there in 1862.[99] Among the works published at his press was the Yiddish newspaper *Kol mevaser* and new editions of the seventeenth-century rabbinic polymath Joseph Solomon

---

Werses, "Sabbatianism and Frankism in the Light of Maskilic Historiography" (Hebrew), in *Haskalah ve-shabtaut*, 157n46; Jonatan Meir, "Jacob Frank: The Wondrous Charlatan" (Hebrew), *Tarbiz* 80 (2012): 464. On the journal, see Michael Jacoby, *Ben-Chananja: Eine deutschsprachige Zeitschrift von Leopold Löw; inhalte, autoren, rezipienten, 1858–1867* (Uppsala, 1997).

[98] "Wir finden zwischen diesen beiden eifrigen kämpen für Religionsreinheit gegen Sabbathätistche sektirerei, was Gesinnung, Character und Temperament betrifft, die auffallendste Aehnlichkeit: Beide waren der Kabbalah mit Leib und Seele ergeben, und verfetzen ihr nichtsdestoweniger, eben aus ängstlicher Sorgfalt, sie rein zu erhalten, die erschütterndsten Stösse. Beide waren in ihren Diskursen bald bescheiden und demüthig bis zur Selbstverleugnung, bald aber ihre Würde und Verdienste sasst über die Gebühr zur Schau tragend. Beide gereithen bei Disputationen leicht in harnisch und sprüheten sodann die geistreichsten Funken, vol Sarkasmus und Bitterheit."

Rubin, "Biographisches: Jakob Saportas," 713. See also his "Words of the Sages: On the History of the Sage and Kabbalist, R. Jacob Sasportas, of Blessed Memory" (Hebrew), *Ha-Melitz*, 2 March 1865, 6.

[99] Chone Shmeruk, "Yiddish Literature and the Beginnings of Modern Newspapers in Yiddish" (Hebrew), in *Sifrut yidish: Perakim le-toldoteha* (Tel Aviv: Porter Institute for Poetics and Semiotics, 1978), 261–293; Steven J. Zipperstein, *The Jews of Odessa: A Cultural History, 1794–1881* (Stanford, CA: Stanford University Press, 1985), 77; Alexander Orbach, *New Voices of Russian Jewry: A Study of the Russian-Jewish Press of Odessa in the Era of the Great Reforms, 1860–1871* (Leiden: Brill, 1980), 180.

Delmedigo. At the initiative of two rabbis, Meir Greenspan and Abraham Joshua Heschel Barsky, Beilinson reprinted Emden's *Kitzur zizath novel zvi* in 1867. Greenspan appears to have been the driving force behind the publication. In a short note he appended to the final page of the edition, he disavowed Barsky's involvement:

> I shall state in public that the man who appears with me on the book's title page removed himself from the printing after the first quire appeared. He has no claim against me. Owing to the expense of printing, however, I have not changed the title page.[100]

Another short notice, this one unsigned but possibly by Greenspan as well, indicates the particular circumstances that led to the reprint of Emden's edition:

> A few months ago, when I was in the city of Balta, the rabbi and maskil Menahem Nahum presented me with this book in an old printed edition. He gave it to me so that I would bring it to press and renew its youth like an eagle (Ps. 103:5). Given that it is so difficult to find, I girded my loins and spared no expense to print it.[101]

Greenspan had encountered Emden's *Kitzur* in Balta, a city roughly two hundred kilometers north of Odessa, and, at the urging of someone named Menahem Nahum, decided to do all within his power to reissue the work.[102] Greenspan and Beilinson reproduced Emden's edition and included the short introduction that had served as Emden's title page on the inside cover. However, they did not incorporate the extensive selections from *Ohel ya-akov* or Emden's responsum on the priestly blessing. Instead, the final two pages include a number of references to Sabbatianism and Sasportas that they had culled from Emden's other writings.

Over the next several decades, various writers referred to Sasportas in Hebrew periodicals.[103] Perhaps the most significant reference ap-

---

[100] Jacob Sasportas, *Kitzur zizath novel zvi* (Odessa: Beilinson, 1867), 104.

[101] Ibid., 2.

[102] In a later work printed at the same press, a Menahem Nahum Litinski published a document with a condemnation of the Sabbatians in Podoliya. See *Korot Podoliya ve-kadmoniyot ha-Yehudim sham* (Odessa: Beilinson, 1895), 64. However, library catalogs list him as having been born in 1851, which would have made him sixteen at the time of this exchange with Greenspan.

[103] David Cahana, *Ha-shahar* 3 (1872): 1; Hayim Gershon Gottdiener, "On the History of the Sage R. Jacob Sasportas and His Books" (Hebrew), *Ha-melitz*, 7 August 1894, 6; Samuel Viener, "R. Jacob Sasportas" (Hebrew), *Ha-melitz* 18 September 1894 and 19 November 1894. As cited by

peared in a novella by the writer Shmuel Yosef Agnon (1888–1970). Born in a small town in Habsburg Galicia named Buczacz, he lived there for the better part of his youth. In 1908 he made his way to Jaffa, Palestine, where he lived for four years and began to publish fiction. Shortly thereafter, he changed his name from Czaczkes to Agnon, the pseudonym under which his debut story had appeared. While in Palestine, Agnon wrote a literary fragment that appeared in *Ha-shiloah*, one of the literary journals published in Odessa, under the title "Aliyat neshamah" (Heb. The soul's ascent).[104] The fragment deals with the death of an unnamed young man who abandons the rigorous talmudism of his forefathers for the ecstatic pietism preached by a visiting preceptor referred to as *Ha-hozer* (Heb. he who repeats). The term came from the tradition of Habad Hasidim, where prominent students and often sons of the reigning rebbe would repeat his sermons to groups of Hasidim who might not have been present when the rebbe himself delivered them. In three highly compressed pages, Agnon traced the dramatic transition that took place when a young man who had been trained by his grandfather to revere the Talmudic novellas of Jacob Joshua Falk becomes entranced by a figure akin to a guru. The fragment concludes with the death of the young man and the ascent of his soul as he recites a verse from the Song of Songs.

"Aliyat neshamah" would eventually become the final chapter of a novella that Agnon worked on for a decade entitled *Ha-nidah* (The vanquished one). In 1912 Agnon moved to Germany, and, after short periods in Berlin and Lepizig, he settled in the Rhine Valley where he lived for much of World War I. In Germany, Agnon met a number of the figures who were to play critical roles in his subsequent literary development. These included his patron, Salman Schocken, and his correspondent and occasional editor Fischel Lachover. In a letter written to Schocken in June 1916, the year after he had first met him, Agnon declared: "I am sitting and copying my story *Ha-nidah* about the early flowering of Hasidism. I have copied this story more times than I can count. I doubt if it has as many letters as the times I have copied it."[105]

Werses, "Sabbatianism and Frankism in the Light of Maskilic Historiography," 176n126 (Cahana) and 190n190 (Gottdiener and Viener).

[104] S. Agnon, "Aliyat neshamah," *Ha-shiloah* 21 (1909–1910): 443–445. On this journal, see Ali Mohamed Abd El-Rahman Attia, *The Hebrew Periodical ha-Shiloah (1896–1919): Its Role in the Development of Modern Hebrew Literature* (Jerusalem: Magnes Press, 1991).

[105] *Shai Agnon-S.Z. Schocken: Hilufe igrot (1916–1959)* (Jerusalem: Schocken, 1991), 29. Letter dated 22 June 1916.

A postcard Agnon wrote to Fischel Lachover later that summer further underscores its importance: "I have worked on it [*Ha-nidah*] for nine years. Out of eighteen notebooks, I have reduced it to two. I think not a single word of it lacks life. Can you assure me that Frishman will not a change a single jot or tittle? If so, I am prepared to send it to *Ha-tekufah*."[106] Agnon referred to the literary journal funded by Abraham Joseph Stybel and edited at the time by David Frishman. At one point Agnon had intended to compose a considerably longer work based on the material that became *Ha-nidah*, but eventually abandoned this plan.[107] Lachover's efforts on Agnon's behalf were successful. The story appeared as the lead entry in the fourth volume of the journal, published in 1919.[108]

Ha-nidah deals with a dispute between Hasidim and Mitnagdim in early nineteenth-century Galicia. A Hasidic master named Rav Uriel arrives in the town of Shibush, a fictionalized version of Buczacz that is the setting for many of Agnon's stories. A number of commoners in the town assume he has come to heal Eideleh, the sick daughter of Rav Avigdor ha-Parnas. An elderly man of eighty-three, Rav Avigdor epitomizes the Talmudic erudition that characterized the opponents of the Hasidim known as Mitnagdim. He intercedes with the local authorities and prevents Rav Uriel from staying in the town. As he prepares to set up his court in a neighboring village, Rav Uriel counters with a malediction: *ki yidah mimenu nidah*. The Hebrew phrase alludes to 2 Samuel 14:14, *le-vilti yidah mi-menu nidah*, "that his banished be not expelled from him." In this somewhat cryptic curse, Rav Uriel wishes upon Rav Avigdor the banishment of one of his descendants. Rav Avigdor's son-in-law Meshulam approaches the Hasidic master and asks him to pray on behalf of his sick wife. Terrified that his community will transform into the Hasidim of Rav Uriel if the Hasid's prayer leads to Eideleh's recovery, Rav Avigdor entreats God to take his daughter

---

[106] *Mi-sod hakhamim: mikhtavim 1909–1970: Agnon, Brener, Bialik, Lachover, Katznelson, Sadan* (Jerusalem: Schocken, 2002), 101–102. Postcard dated 14 August 1918. On Agnon and *Ha-tekufah*, see Dania Amichay-Michlin, *Ahavat ish: Avraham Yosef Stybel* (Jerusalem: Bialik Institute, 2000), 195–199.

[107] Arnold J. Band, *Nostalgia and Nightmare: A Study in the Fiction of S. Y. Agnon* (Berkeley: University of California Press, 1968), 96–99; Uri D. Alter, "The Evolution of Worlds in *Ha-nidah* by S. Y. Agnon" (Hebrew), *Proceedings of the Fifth World Congress of Jewish Studies* (1969), 3:13–17. On the relationship between *Ha-nidah* and *Bilvav yamim*, see Shmuel Werses, "*Bilvav yamim* by S. Y. Agnon: Sources of the Story and Method of Composition" (Hebrew), in *Shai Agnon ki-feshuto* (Jerusalem: Bialik Institute, 2000), 156–158.

[108] *Ha-tekufah* 4 (Warsaw, 1919): 1–54.

immediately. Upon her subsequent and sudden death, her son Gershom remains distraught with grief. While in a yeshiva in another town, Gershom receives a letter from his grandfather Rav Avigdor warning him to stay away from the sect, a derisive term used to refer to the Hasidim. Gershom eventually returns home from yeshiva and falls sick. In the course of Gershom's illness, the figure referred to as *ha-hozer* in the earlier fragment draws Gershom under his spell. As a result of his influence, Gershom joins the Hasidim.

In the penultimate chapter, Agnon describes Gershom reading:

> In the course of his illness, he read war stories, works of history, and *Zizat novel zvi*, which told the story of Sabbetai Zevi and his adherents. These recalled to Gershom the sect of the Hasidim, and, when he remembered that he had gone to visit that Uriel, his eyes darkened in shame. He said to himself, had my sickness not taken hold of me along the way, I would have erred and strayed from the path. He justified divine judgment, and saw his illness as a great kindness, as a kindness of the Lord. He recited, in reference to himself, the verse "that he might humble thee [and that he might prove thee], to do thee good at thy latter end" (Deut. 8:16), for the Holy One, blessed be He, had chastised him in order to sweeten his end. From then on he would read scripture, study Mishnah, and engage in Talmudic dialectics like the disputatious scholars, until the preceptor returned and drew him back to his roots.[109]

The character of the preceptor, an impoverished translation of *ha-hozer*, appears to have emerged from Lubavitch sources.[110] He serves a living embodiment of Hasidism and has an almost mesmerizing hold on his young charge. Gershom abandons the study of Talmud and joins the Hasidim. In the final chapter, which follows immediately thereafter, Gershom recites a verse from the Song of Songs as his soul departs and ascends to heaven.

---

[109] בימי מחלתו קרא בספרי מלחמות ובדברי הימים ובציצת נובל צבי שכתוב בו מעשה שבתי צבי וסיעתו. מתוך הדברים נזכר גרשום בכת החסידים ונזכר שהלך אצל אותו אוריאל ועיניו חשכו מבושה. אמר בלבו אלמלא שתקפה אותי מחלתי בדרך הייתי טועה ויוצא חוץ לשיטה. הצדיק את הדין וראה את מחלתו כחסד מחסדי השם. קרא על עצמו למען ענותך להיטיבך באחריתך, שייסרו הקדוש ברוך הוא כדי להיטיב לו באחריתו. ומכאן ואילך היה קורא ושונה ומפלפל כדרך הלמדנים הפלגאים, עד שבא החוזר והחזירו לשרשו.

S. Y. Agnon, "Ha-nidah," in *Elu ve-elu* (Jerusalem: Schocken, 1998), 42.

[110] Yehoshua Levanon, "Lubavitch Motifs in *Ha-nidah* by S. Y. Agnon" (Hebrew), *Bikoret u-farshanut* 16 (1981) 135–153; Gedalyah Nigal, *Shai Agnon u-mekorotav ha-hasidiyim: iyun be-arba-ah mi-sipurav* (Ramat Gan: Kurzweil Institute of Bar-Ilan University, 1983), 3–11.

Upon the appearance of the story, Agnon took care to inform his colleagues how much it had meant to him. In his penultimate letter to Joseph Hayim Brenner, a Hebrew writer who had served as one of his early patrons upon his arrival in Palestine, Agnon concluded: "If *Ha-nidah* should make its way to you, please read it. I dealt with it for more than nine years. My mother, my [maternal] grandfather, and my father died in the course of the time I worked on it."[111] Agnon had dedicated the story to his father's memory. In an address he delivered at the house of Salman Schocken in the summer of 1938, he declared about his maternal grandfather, "Some of his stories and qualities you can find... in the character of R. Avigdor in *Ha-nidah*."[112]

Agnon continued to revise *Ha-nidah* even after its initial publication. In the 1920s, he planned a series of volumes that would include his collected stories and appear under Schocken's imprint. His correspondence with Schocken from this period includes repeated references to the story and to the order of its appearance in the planned volume. On one occasion, he informed Schocken: "Recently I have not written anything new, because for the last three months I have dealt with *Ha-nidah*. Now it seems to me that it has emerged as perfect. May it be [God's] will that the coming stories shall be like it."[113] Agnon had introduced substantial revisions into *Ha-nidah* when it reappeared as the lead story of *Me-az u-me-ata*, the third volume of his collected stories, published by Schocken in Berlin in 1931.[114] In the second edition of his collected writings, printed in Tel Aviv two decades later, Agnon included *Ha-nidah* as the first story of *Elu ve-elu*.[115] In its original publication in 1919, in Agnon's complete works in 1931, in the second version of his complete works in 1953, as well as in the posthumous edition of 1998, *Ha-nidah* includes the reference to Gershom reading *Zizath novel zvi*.[116]

[111] *Mi-sod hakhamim*, 30. Letter dated 16 February 1920.

[112] S. Y. Agnon, "At the Home of Salman Schocken" (Hebrew), *Mi-atzmi el atzmi* (Jerusalem: Schocken, 1976), 26.

[113] *Shai Agnon-S.Z. Schocken*, 189. Letter dated 8 June 1926; for a similar profession of exhaustion due to his intensive work on *Ha-nidah*, see Agnon's letter to Berl Katznelson dated 16 August 1926 in *Mi-sod hakhamim*, 169.

[114] *Kol sipurav shel Sh. Y. Agnon* (Berlin: Schocken, 1931), 3:9–69. Reference to *Zizath novel zvi* on 63. On these changes, see Judith Halevi-Zwick, "Tekufat Germanyah (1914–1924) bi-yetsirato shel S. Y. Agnon" (PhD diss., Hebrew University of Jerusalem, 1967).

[115] *Kol sipurav shel Sh. Y. Agnon* (Tel Aviv: Schocken, 1953), vol. 2. For the most recent edition, see Agnon *Elu ve-elu*, 5–45. Reference to *Zizath novel zvi* on 42.

[116] Elchanan Shilo, *Ha-kabalah bi-yetzirat Shai Agnon* (Ramat Gan: Bar-Ilan University Press,

In the context of Sasportas's afterlife, his appearance in *Ha-nidah* points to a particular and ironic transformation. Largely as a result of Emden's efforts, Sasportas had become a book. In the context of the story, Sasportas, or more precisely, *Zizath novel zvi*, plays a role similar to the one Sasportas had hoped the book would play in his debate with the Sabbatians. In his polemic against the Sabbatians, Sasportas had challenged them to come up with a single book that stated that they should believe in someone who had declared himself to be the Messiah. Mastery of a textual tradition served as a protective measure against messianic ardor. Sasportas upheld the authority of the written word as a response to the certainty of the messianic experience. In Agnon's story, *Zizath novel zvi* serves a function for Gershom similar to the one that medieval rabbinic literature had served for Sasportas. After Gershom reads *Zizath novel zvi*, the only book to be mentioned by name in the series of readings he undertakes during his illness, he realizes the folly of Hasidism. Reading Sasportas serves to convince Gershom of the foolishness of Hasidic enthusiasm, or *Schwärmerei* as contemporaries derisively referred to it.[117] Just as Sasportas described Sabbatian enthusiasm prior to the news of Sabbetai Zevi's conversion, so Gershom experienced Hasidism in Agnon's fictional world. The believers in Sabbetai Zevi pointedly ignored Sasportas's plea that they study the written word before leaping to conclusions about the arrival of the Messiah. The experience of lived religion proved so overwhelming to the Sabbatians that they had no interest in Sasportas or the many citations he hurled at them. Gershom was transformed by Sasportas's account of Sabbatianism and quickly realized its analogous application to contemporary Hasidism. All of his reading, whether it was the Talmud in yeshiva or Sasportas in his illness, was completely useless once the preceptor returned. He discarded the trenchant erudition of Sasportas for the ecstatic otherworldliness of the unnamed preceptor.

2011), 69, 137; Tzahi Weiss, "'Things that are better concealed than revealed': An Historical-Biographical Study of S. Y. Agnon's Attitude toward the Sabbatean Movement and the Traditional Jewish World," *AJS Review* 36 (2012): 112.

[117] Rachel Manekin, "Galician Haskalah and the Discourse of *Schwärmerei*," in *Secularism in Question: Jews and Judaism in Modern Times*, ed. Ari Joskowicz and Ethan Katz (Philadelphia: University of Pennsylvania Press, 2015).

EIGHT

~

ZION

None other than Scholem has instructed us that everything is possible in a Jewish sense in periods of plasticity. The decades after World War I were such a period of plasticity. Possibilities flashed up in them, which were later no longer visible: Leftists from the Right, rightists from the Left, Jewish Gnostics and Marcionites.

—Jacob Taubes

Figure 29. The Schocken Library, Jerusalem. This was the library of the Schocken Institute, in a building built for Salman Schocken designed by the expressionist architect Erich Mendelsohn. Gershom Scholem directed the Institute for the Study of Jewish Mysticism under whose auspices Isaiah Tishby edited Sasportas. Architectural Heritage Research Centre, Technion Haifa.

JACOB SASPORTAS DIED IN 1698. In the centuries after his death, his readers turned to him as an intellectual resource in the ideological battles they fought. Sasportas, his writing, or his image played a role in the polemics between Emden and Eibeschütz, Jacob Frank and the rabbis, Hasidim and Mitnagdim, Reform and Orthodox. In some of these controversies, such as that between Emden and Eibeschütz, his role was central to the substance of the polemic; in others, such as that between Reform and Orthodox in nineteenth-century Posen, his role was more peripheral. Over the course of the eighteenth and nineteenth centuries Sasportas served as a resource for rabbinic controversialists who used his writing to forge an image of tradition as immutable. Sasportas came to serve as a stand-in for a habit of mind that rejected novelty as such.

The most articulate exponent of this view was Gershom Scholem. In the second quarter of the twentieth century, between the 1930s and the 1950s, Scholem and his student Isaiah Tishby turned to Sasportas as a crucial source on the history of Sabbatianism. Under Scholem's supervision, Tishby prepared a critical edition of *Zizath novel zvi*. In turn, Scholem himself sketched a memorable portrait of Sasportas in his history of Sabbetai Zevi and the Sabbatian movement. Scholem's attitude toward Sasportas was one of profound ambivalence. He recognized the critical significance of Sasportas's account and supported Tishby's work on the edition for many years. Sasportas also served Scholem as a stand-in for a conservative approach to Jewish messianism, a posture he viewed as static and resistant to change. Sasportas occupied a particularly problematic juncture in the narrative Scholem recounted about his own rebellion, one that involved a turn toward an ostensibly new academic subject, Kabbalah, and that took place in an old-new land, Palestine. Sasportas did not conform to the series of oppositions that undergirded Scholem's intellectual edifice: he was both a halakhist and a kabbalist, a conservative and a radical, a critic of the rabbinate and the very instantiation of its ideals. In a certain sense, Scholem was well aware of Sasportas's import, and much, but not all, of his project on Sabbatianism in specific and messianism in general constituted a response to Sasportas and his writing. This chapter tracks Scholem's long and sustained engagement with Sasportas through the making of Tishby's critical edition, its circuitous path into print, the writing of *Sabbatai Sevi*, and the critical response to Scholem's two-volume Hebrew work. Scholem's treatment of Sasportas offers a case study in the history of intellectual ambivalence; that is, Scholem thought with, through, and against Sasportas throughout the long period he wrote on Sabbatianism.

Only two years after the appearance of Scholem's *Sabbatai Sevi* in Hebrew, another Jewish writer turned to Sasportas in the service of his own polemic: Joel Teitelbaum (1887–1979). Known to his followers as the Satmar Rebbe, Teitelbaum saw in Sasportas one of his own intellectual antecedents and turned to him repeatedly in his work *Sefer va-yo-el moshe*, a halakhic treatise on the subject of Zionism he published in 1959. Both Scholem and Teitelbaum read *Zizath novel zvi* carefully and passionately. Their respective readings serve as one index of the enduring importance that Jewish messianism in general and Sabbatianism in particular had in the twentieth century.

KINNUS AND COLLECTING THE JEWISH PAST

The story of Sasportas and Zion begins, like Zionism itself, in central Europe. More precisely, it begins in the city of Vienna, the adopted hometown of Theodor Herzl. Fin de siècle Vienna was home to a burgeoning Jewish population that served as a magnet for Jews throughout the Habsburg Empire.[1] In 1876 a learned member of a Warsaw-based banking family named Abraham Epstein settled in Vienna, where

---

[1] Carl E. Schorske, *Fin-de-siècle Vienna: Politics and Culture* (New York: Knopf, 1979), chap. 3; Marsha L. Rozenblit, *The Jews of Vienna, 1867–1914: Assimilation and Identity* (Albany: SUNY Press, 1983). Epigraph from Jacob Taubes, "Walter Benjamin—A Modern Marcionite? Scholem's Benja-

he lived until his death in 1918.[2] Over the course of several decades Epstein acquired an enormous library with a valuable collection of Hebrew manuscripts. He also contributed to a number of journals and published material from his library such as letters relating to Sabbatianism.[3] His manuscripts were eventually acquired by the Israelitische-Theologische Lehranstalt, a theological seminary in Vienna that served as a center of Jewish scholarship. In 1926 the central Jewish communal organization in interwar Vienna, the Israelitische Kultusgemeinde, acquired the library of the rabbinical seminary.[4] Beginning in 1914 and continuing for several decades, Arthur Zacharias Schwarz cataloged the collections of Hebrew manuscripts in Austria. In 1931 he published the first volume of his catalog of the Hebrew manuscripts in Austrian collections beyond the Nationalsbibliothek in Vienna. In contrast to the extensive descriptions of manuscripts that characterized his work throughout his career, Schwarz simply noted the existence of Hebrew manuscript 142 as *Zizath novel zvi* by Jacob Sasportas. This Vienna manuscript contained the text of Sasportas's chronicle in its entirety. Schwarz indicated that it had once been in the possession of Abraham Epstein and the Israelitische-Theologische Lehranstalt, and mentioned that he hoped to publish a more extensive description of the manuscript at another point.[5]

In fact, Schwarz planned for considerably more than a description of the manuscript. Schwarz's published writings do not give any indication as to the reasons why, but over the next eight years he worked assiduously to produce a new edition of *Zizath novel zvi*. For these purposes, Schwarz used the early modern printed editions of *Kitzur zizath novel zvi*, the Vienna manuscript, which contained a draft of the work in its entirety, as well as photographs of a manuscript in Berlin, which contained early drafts written by Sasportas of many of the letters he later included in *Zizath novel zvi*. Schwarz planned for his edition to

min Interpretation Reexamined," in *Walter Benjamin and Theology*, ed. Colby Dickinson and Stéphane Symons (New York: Fordham University Press, 2016), 175.

[2] *Sefer zikaron le-sofre yisrael ha-hayim itanu ka-yom*, ed. Nahum Sokolow (Warsaw, 1890), 162–166.

[3] Epstein, "Une lettre d'Abraham ha-Yakhini a Nathan Gazati," 209–219.

[4] Harriet Pass Freidenreich, *Jewish Politics in Vienna 1918–1938* (Bloomington: Indiana University Press, 1991), 18–21.

[5] *Die Hebräischen Handschriften in Österreich*, MS 142, p. 92. "Eine Analyse des Verhältnisses der Hs. zu den Drucken erfolgt an anderer Stelle." See Epstein, "Une lettre d'Abraham ha-Yakhini a Nathan Gazati," 218.

appear as part of a series produced by Mekize Nirdamim, a publishing venture and scholarly society that issued critical and semicritical editions of classical Hebrew texts.[6] Geopolitics, however, intervened. With the annexation of Austria by the Nazis in 1938, the library of the Kultusgemeinde in Vienna was requisitioned and shipped to the central library of the Reichssicherheitshauptamt in Berlin.[7] Schwarz fled Vienna and settled in Palestine, where he died in Jerusalem in February 1939. After his death his widow turned to Scholem, a scholar with whom Schwarz had corresponded, and who respected her late husband's codicological work.[8] She bequeathed Schwarz's material on Sasportas to him in the hope that he would find a suitable medium for its publication.

Over the next fifteen years, Scholem would work hard to see Schwarz's edition of Sasportas into print. The eventual publication of *Zizath novel zvi* constituted part of a larger enterprise known in Hebrew as *kinnus*, which can be rendered roughly as gathering or collecting. *Kinnus* conveyed an idea of identifying, editing, and preserving the cultural assets of a nation.[9] The notion emerged from European nationalism of the nineteenth century and the Haskalah, a form of Jewish romanticism that had spread to central and eastern Europe and nourished the proponents of Zionism. The idea of *kinnus* called for the rehabilitation of texts from the Jewish past and posited that cultural ideals had embedded themselves in these texts. The recuperation of these sources served to undergird the intellectual edifice of Zionism. Concurrent with their rehabilitation of a library of books, Zionist settlers in the early twentieth century established a physical library in Jerusalem that quickly became known as the Jewish National and University Library.[10] Upon his arrival in Jerusalem in 1923, sixteen years

[6] *Mi-tardemat ha-genazim le-aron ha-sefarim* (Jerusalem: Mekize Nirdamim, 2013).

[7] Richard Hacken, "The Jewish Community Library in Vienna: From Dispersion and Destruction to Partial Restoration," *Leo Baeck Institute Year Book* 47 (2002): 151–172.

[8] See his review of *Die Hebräischen Handschriften in Österreich*, in *KS* 8 (1931): 444; on their correspondence, see Gershom Scholem Papers, National Library of Israel, Jerusalem, 4o 1599 2370, File A. Z. Schwarz.

[9] Israel Bartal, "The *Kinnus* Project: *Wissenschaft des Judentums* and the Fashioning of a 'National Culture' in Palestine," in *Transmitting Jewish Traditions: Orality, Textuality and Cultural Diffusion*, ed. Yaakov Elman and Israel Gershoni (New Haven, CT: Yale University Press, 2000), 310–323.

[10] Dov Schidorsky, *Gevilim nisrafim ve-otiyot porhot: toldotehem shel osfei sefarim ve-sifriyot be Erets yisrael ve-nisyonot le-hatsalat seridehem le-ahar ha-shoah* (Jerusalem: Magnes Press, 2008), 13–58.

before he had received Schwarz's papers from his widow, Scholem had worked in this library.

Shortly after the construction of the library, Zionist settlers founded an Institute of Jewish Studies in December 1924 and the Hebrew University in April 1925.[11] The institute and the university constituted the physical manifestations of the idea of *kinnus,* an idea closely associated with the Hebrew poet Hayim Nahman Bialik (1873–1934). In the early decades of the twentieth century, Bialik had devoted much of his energy to this idea, as he edited the Hebrew poets of medieval Iberia and collaborated with Yeshoshua Ravnitzky in compiling a collection of narratives, folktales, and proverbs found in the Talmud and Midrash into a book called *Sefer ha-aggadah* (Heb. The book of legends). At the inauguration ceremony of the Hebrew University on Mount Scopus on 1 April 1925, Bialik evoked the idea of *kinnus* when he exhorted an audience of over seven thousand to gather the fragments of "our literature" and "connect and unify them, and make them whole in the nation's hands."[12]

Among the members of Bialik's audience was Gershom Scholem.[13] Just over three months later, Scholem addressed a letter to Bialik, whose essay "Halakha and Aggada" he had previously translated into German.[14] Scholem's letter to Bialik contained a précis of his research in Kabbalah up to that point and a manifesto for future research.[15] Written when he was twenty-seven years old, it laid out his scholarly trajectory for the next half a century, a trajectory in which he would be "almost monstrous in his consistency of purpose over the years."[16] One of the central ideas that undergirded Scholem's research plan and

[11] On the institute, see David N. Myers, *Re-inventing the Jewish Past: European Jewish Intellectuals and the Zionist Return to History* (New York: Oxford University Press, 1995), chap. 3; on the university see *Toledot ha-universitah ha-ivrit be-yerushalayim,* ed. Shaul Katz et al. (Jerusalem: Magnes Press, 1997–2013).

[12] For Bialik's address, see *Toledot ha-universitah ha-ivrit be-yerushalayim,* 1:350–354. As cited by Bartal, "The *Kinnus* Project," 310. On the size of the crowd, see Myers, *Re-Inventing the Jewish Past,* 57.

[13] Gershom Scholem, *From Berlin to Jerusalem: Memories of My Youth,* trans. Harry Zohn (Philadelphia: Paul Dry Books, 2012), 172–174.

[14] Chaim Nachman Bialik, "Halacha und Aggada," trans. Gerhard Scholem, *Der Jude* 4 (1919–1920): 61–77.

[15] "A Letter to H. N. Bialik" (Hebrew), in Gershom Scholem, *Devarim be-go* (Tel Aviv: Am Oved, 1976), 1:59–63. Letter dated 20 Tammuz 5685 (12 July 1925).

[16] Leon Wieseltier, preface to Walter Benjamin, *Illuminations,* trans. Harry Zohn (New York: Schocken Books, 2007), ix.

quite possibly the reason his programmatic statement took the form of a letter to Bialik was the concept of *kinnus*. Although he did not use the word explicitly, he called for the identification, the editing, and the publication of a library of kabbalistic texts. This included works such as the *Zohar* and the early commentaries on *Sefer yetzirah* as well as the writings of Abraham Abulafia, Isaac of Acre, and Moses de Leon. He stressed repeatedly that as long as most kabbalistic works remained in manuscript, scholars would have a limited understanding of the history of Kabbalah specifically and the history of Judaism more generally. Much of the letter he devoted to the bibliographic imperatives in the field. Toward its close, Scholem stressed the enormity of the task that he had outlined: "This is work that certainly cannot be undertaken by a single person but would require a team of assistants. Should the opportunity present itself, I would be willing to take upon myself the direction of this task."[17]

A little more than a week later, Bialik responded from Tel Aviv and affirmed Scholem's ambitious plan. He declared, "It would be an unpardonable sin for all of us, if we do not throw our gates wide open to your scholarship."[18] More to the point, Bialik declared that on his upcoming visit to Jerusalem he would put forth Scholem's plan to the university council and speak to Judah Magnes, chancellor of the Hebrew University. Bialik was as good as his word. After securing letters of reference for Scholem from two German scholars, Magnes appointed Scholem to the faculty of the newly founded university that very fall.[19]

At the time of his appointment Scholem was one of the younger faculty members of an institution whose nature was still in flux. Some hoped the Hebrew University would be a pure research institute, offering little or no instruction and conferring no degrees; others thought it should serve its students and by extension the larger society of Jewish colonists in Palestine.[20] The overwhelming demand for instruction

---

[17] אי-אפשר לה שתיעשה בידי איש אחד וצריך חבר עוזרים. ואם יזדמן, אהיה מוכן לקבל עלי הנהלת עבודה זו.

"A Letter to H. N. Bialik," 62. On Scholem and *kinnus*, see Noam Zadoff, "The Debate between Baruch Kurzweil and Gershom Scholem on the Study of Sabbatianism" (Hebrew), *Kabbalah* 16 (2007), 301–307.

[18] חטא לא יכופר יהי הדבר לכלנו, אם לא יפתחו לעבודתך שערים רחבים בגבולינו.

Letter #459, dated 20.7.25 in *Igrot Hayim Nahman Bialik*, ed. Fischel Lachover (Tel Aviv: Dvir, 1938), 3:48–49; on this exchange, Myers, *Re-Inventing the Jewish Past*, 159.

[19] Myers, *Re-Inventing the Jewish Past*, 58n18 and 159n40.

[20] Uri Cohen, "Governing Institutions of the Hebrew University: 1925–1948" (Hebrew), in *Toledot ha-universitah ha-ivrit be-yerushalayim*, 2:22–24.

and the economic pressures of a settler colonial movement both contributed to the resolution of this question. Within the first decade of
its existence, the Hebrew University began offering an increasing number of courses and granting degrees. One of the most popular lectur-
ers at the university, and a prolific writer who had been an early pro-
ponent of a Jewish university in Palestine, was Joseph Klausner
(1874–1958). A polymath who had studied at Heidelberg at the turn of
the twentieth century, Klausner had served as a magazine editor and
literary critic for decades prior to the founding of the Hebrew University. He had hoped for an appointment in classical Jewish history, but
the largely negative response to his 1922 study *Yeshu ha-notzri* (Heb.
Jesus the Nazarene) led to significant opposition to his appointment in
that field.[21] He joined the faculty as a professor of modern Hebrew literature, a field he taught for nearly two decades.[22]

Shortly after his appointment, however, he published a substantial
work on the classical period, entitled *Ha-ra-ayon ha-meshihi be-yisrael:
me-reshito ve-ad hatimat ha-mishnah* (Heb. The Messianic idea in Israel: from the beginnings until the close of the Mishnah).[23] Klausner
traced the idea of the Messiah from the period of the biblical prophets
through the Second Temple and up through the *tannaim*. Much of the
book assembled discussions of the Messiah in the primary sources from
the periods Klausner surveyed. The idea of Christianity hovers just
above the surface of Klausner's book, as he sought to set out the basis
for a Jewish messianic idea of earthly redemption that was prior to and
not dependent upon Christianity. At the beginning of the book, he emphasized that this was meant as the first installment of a multivolume
history of the messianic idea in Judaism from antiquity all the way to
the present. As a result, Klausner had little to say about the period after
the close of the Mishnah in the first volume of what he imagined would
be a longer work. Nonetheless, he made passing reference to "false
Messiahs" such as "Sabbetai Zevi who may have used practical Kabbalah to approach the heavenly kingdom but still sought, in the end,
for a kingdom on earth that would take root in the land of the

[21] Myers, *Re-Inventing the Jewish Past*, 53.

[22] Shmuel Werses, "Joseph Klausner and the Beginnings of Teaching Modern Hebrew Literature at the Hebrew University" (Hebrew), in *Toledot ha-universitah ha-ivrit be-yerushalayim*,
1:487–515.

[23] *Ha-ra-ayon ha-meshihi be-yisrael: me-reshito ve-ad hatimat ha-mishnah* (Jerusalem: ha-
Poalim, 1927).

forefathers."[24] In Klausner's telling, Sabbetai Zevi was a Zionist before his time. In case his readers had misinterpreted his point, Klausner continued: "In our own day and in the matter at hand, the national element that is entailed in the hope of redemption has returned to life alongside the spiritual component of Messianic time."[25] Klausner unabashedly celebrated the messianic idea and saw his own period and the larger project of Zionism as suffused with messianic import. For him, the fusion of nationalism with a cultural renaissance, a concept reflected in his use of the Hebrew word *tehiyah*, served as a cause for hope and for celebration. Not all of Klausner's readers were as enthused about the messianic idea as he would have liked. The dedicatee of the book, Judah Magnes, rebuked him in a letter for his identification with his subject: "Woe unto us if we begin with false messianism!"[26] Klausner's work took a radically different turn in the years following, and he never continued with a history of Jewish messianism in the medieval or modern periods.[27]

SCHOLEM, SABBETAI ZEVI, AND MAIMONIDES

In the decade following Klausner's book on the messianic idea, Scholem began to focus on the history of Jewish messianism.[28] In his early programmatic letter to Bialik, he had mentioned the subject only as an afterthought. Upon calling for a thorough analysis of the development of Kabbalah in all of its forms and throughout its history, he contin-

[24] אפילו משיחי שקר מעין דוד אלרואי ושבתי צבי, ששאפו למלכות שדי על ידי מסתורין וקבלה מעשית, רצו, סוף סוף שמלכתום תהא גם ארצית ותשתרע בארץ האבות דוקא.

Ibid., 9.

[25] ובימינו ולעינינו שב לתחיה החלק המדיני-הלאומי שבתקות הגאולה ביחד עם החלק הרוחני-העולמי שביעוד המשיחי.

Ibid., 9–10.

[26] Myers, *Re-inventing the Jewish Past*, 96n136.

[27] Beginning in 1930 and continuing for the next two decades, he wrote a multivolume history of modern Hebrew literature, *Historiyah shel ha-sifrut ha-ivrit ha-hadashah* (Jerusalem: Hebrew University, 1930–1950). On his significance as a literary critic, see Iris Parush, *Kanon sifruti ve-ideologyah leumit: bikoret ha-sifrut shel Frishman behasva-ah la-vikoret shel Klausner u-Brenner* (Jerusalem: Bialik Institute, 1992), 205–257.

[28] On the conjuncture between Scholem's study of messianism and the Nazi rise to power, see Amnon Raz-Krakotzkin, "Between 'Brit Shalom' and the Temple: The Dialectic of Redemption and Messianism in the Writings of Gershom Scholem" (Hebrew), *Theory and Critcisim* 20 (2002): 107.

ued, "And the same can be said for all that branches out from it, that is the messianic movements based upon esoteric wisdom and Hasidism."[29] Messianism appeared as a subject that, while important in its own right, was derivative of Kabbalah. In the decade that followed his letter to Bialik, Scholem discovered Sabbatianism and remembered his youthful dissatisfaction with Maimonides. These developments, which were bound up with one another, would eventually prove crucial for his understanding of Sasportas. In 1937 he turned to Sabbatianism directly in a Hebrew essay, "Redemption through Sin."[30] Scholem published the essay in the second volume of a serial that had been founded by Bialik and continued after his death as an annual publication dedicated to his memory. "Redemption though Sin" treats the history of Sabbatian theology after the conversion of Sabbetai Zevi to Islam. The essay had begun as a short article on the theology of Abraham Cardoso but gradually developed into one of Scholem's most ambitious attempts to grapple with a central problem in the history of Judaism: the failure of prophecy.[31] One of the primary avenues through which Scholem engaged this question was the notion of paradox, a notion that would remain central to his understanding of Sabbatianism in specific and messianism in general over the course of the next several decades.[32]

[29] והוא הדין לכל המסתעף ממנה, היינו התנועות המשיחיות המיוסדות על תורת הח"ן והחסידות. "A Letter to H. N. Bialik," 59.

[30] "Mitzvah ha-ba-ah ba-averah." One might render the title in English as "Fulfillment by transgression: toward an understanding of Sabbatianism." An English translation by Hillel Halkin appeared as "Redemption through Sin," in Scholem, *The Messianic Idea in Judaism*, 78–141. On Halkin's translation of the title, see Maciejko, *The Mixed Multitude*, 21. On this article, see Steven M. Wasserstrom, *Religion after Religion: Gershom Scholem, Mircea Eliade, and Henry Corbin at Eranos* (Princeton, NJ: Princeton University Press, 1999), chap. 14; Zadoff, "The Debate between Baruch Kurzweil and Gershom Scholem," 307–313; Benjamin Lazier, *God Interrupted: Heresy and the European Imagination between the World Wars* (Princeton, NJ: Princeton University Press, 2008), pt. 3; Amir Engel, *Gershom Scholem: An Intellectual Biography* (Chicago: University of Chicago Press, 2017), 141–147.

[31] Gershom Scholem, "Über die Theologie des Sabbatianismus im Lichte Abraham Cardozos," *Der Jude* 9 (1928): 123–139; on this essay as the basis for the early drafts of "Redemption through Sin," see the letters from Scholem to Walter Benjamin dated 18 December 1935 and 26 August 1936 in *The Correspondence of Walter Benjamin and Gershom Scholem 1932–1940*, ed. Gershom Scholem (New York: Schocken Books, 1989), 174, 184.

[32] For the centrality of paradox to Sabbatianism, see the epigraph taken from the correspondence of Count Paul York von Wartenburg and Wilhelm Dilthey to Scholem, *Sabbatai Sevi*, vii: "Paradox is a characteristic of truth. What *communis opinio* has of truth is surely no more than an elementary deposit of generalizing partial understanding, related to truth even as sulphurous fumes are to lightning." For its centrality to his overall approach to messianism, see "Response of Prof. Gershom Scholem" (Hebrew), in *Ha-ra-ayon ha-meshihi be-yisrael: yom iyun le-regel melot shemonim shanah le-Gershom Scholem* (Jerusalem: Israel Academy of Sciences, 1982), 254–255. On

In particular Scholem posited a relationship between paradox and truth. Sabbatian theologians had to explain first to themselves and then to their followers why the genuine Messiah whose redemptive mission had been experienced in public had decided to convert to Islam and forsake the religion of his faithful followers. Each of the Sabbatian theologians whom Scholem treated—Nathan of Gaza, Abraham Cardoso, and Jacob Frank—employed the notion of paradox as he articulated a theology of nihilism. Scholem was well aware of the article's importance as he was composing it. In a letter to Walter Benjamin, he recounted: "This work will bring me some notoriety as a Hebrew writer for the first time, for it is really good, and well suited to make an impression. Perhaps I will refashion it into an equivalent German after all; Schocken would like me to."[33]

Scholem referred to Salman Schocken, a figure who was to play a pivotal role in the twentieth-century recovery of Sasportas. Over the course of many decades Schocken functioned as a mercurial patron of Hebrew and German letters.[34] Scholem had known Schocken since his time in Germany, and maintained a long and difficult friendship with him that often took the form of a client soliciting a patron.[35] The year Scholem published "Redemption through Sin" he addressed a letter to Schocken on the occasion of his sixtieth birthday.[36] Like his earlier letter to Bialik, Scholem's letter to Schocken involved an elaborate and unspoken request for patronage from its addressee; however, unlike

the epigraph to *Sabbatai Sevi*, see Saverio Campanini, "Fulmini e vapori sulfurei: Storia di una citazione scholemiana," in *Energia e rappresentazione: Warburg, Panofsky, Wind*, ed. Alice Barale et al. (Milan: Mimesis, 2016), 133–148.

[33] Letter from Scholem to Benjamin dated 29 December 1936 in *The Correspondence of Walter Benjamin and Gershom Scholem 1932–1940*, 190.

[34] Anthony David, *The Patron: A Life of Salman Schocken 1877–1959* (New York: Metropolitan Books, 2003).

[35] On Scholem and Schocken, see Noam Zadoff, *Mi-Berlin le-Yerushalayim uva-hazarah: Gershom Scholem ben yisrael ve-Germanyah* (Jerusalem: Carmel, 2015), 77–90. Jonatan Meir and Shinichi Yamamoto, introduction to Gershom Scholem, *Toledot ha-tenuah ha-shabtait*, ed. Jonatan Meir and Shinichi Yamamoto (Tel Aviv: JTS-Schocken Institute, 2018), 11–43.

[36] Letter dated 29 October, 1937. First published as "A Birthday Letter from Gershom Scholem to Zalman Schocken," in David Biale, *Gershom Scholem: Kabbalah and Counter-History* (Cambridge, MA: Harvard University Press, 1979), Ger. 215–216; Eng. tr. 74–76; reprinted in a different translation as "A Candid Letter about My True Intentions in Studying Kabbalah," in Gershom Scholem, *On the Possibility of Jewish Mysticism in Our Time and Other Essays*, ed. Avraham Shapira, trans. Jonathan Chipman (Philadelphia: JPS, 1997), 3–5. On Biale's edition of the letter, see Saverio Campanini, "Some Notes on Gershom Scholem and Christian Kabbalah," in *Gershom Scholem: In Memoriam*, ed. Joseph Dan (Jerusalem: Hebrew University, 2007), 2:16n10.

the letter to Bialik, which mapped out a realm of scholarly inquiry, the letter to Schocken over a decade later took Scholem himself as its subject. Both letters have justifiably served scholars as critical points in Scholem's intellectual biography. For the purposes of understanding the twentieth-century reception of Sasportas, three aspects of this letter require consideration: the notion of paradox, the place of Maimonides, and the patronage of Schocken. Scholem closed the letter with a celebration of paradox, not the paradox of messianic theology, but the relationship between philological criticism and the "mystical totality of truth." In the final sentences, Scholem was at his most Delphic: "Today, as at the very beginning, my work lives in this paradox, in the hope of a true communication from the mountain, of that most invisible smallest fluctuation of history which causes truth to break forth from the illusions of 'development.' "[37] He invoked the notion of paradox to reject an idea of progress implied in the term "development."

Earlier in the letter, however, he was quite clear about one of the central reasons he had embarked upon the study of Kabbalah:

> I was struck by the impoverishment of what some like to call the Philosophy of Judaism. I was particularly incensed by the only three authors whom I knew, Saadia [Gaon], Maimonides, and Hermann Cohen, who conceived as their main task to construct antitheses to myth and pantheism, to refute them, although they should have concerned themselves with raising them to a higher level.[38]

In "Redemption through Sin," Scholem had articulated a similar reason:

> It is this paradox of a God of religion who is distinct from the First Cause that is the essence of true Judaism, that "faith of our fathers" which is

---

[37] "In diesem Paradox, aus solcher Hoffnung auf das richtige Angesprochenwerden aus dem Berge, auf jene unscheinbarste, kleinste Verschiebung der Historie, die aus dem Schein der 'Entwicklung' Wahrheit hervorbrechen lässt, lebt meine Arbeit, heute wie am ersten Tag." As cited and translated in Biale, *Gershom Scholem*, Ger. 216; Eng. tr. 76.

[38] "Ich stand unter dem Eindruck der Armseligkeit dessen, was man gern Philosophie des Judentums nennt. An den drei einzigen Autoren, die ich kannte, an Saadja, Maimonides und Hermann Cohen empörte mich, wie sie ihre Hauptaufgabe darin fanden. Antithesen gegen den Mythos und den Pantheismus aufzustellen, sie zu 'widerlegen', während es sich doch hätte darum handeln müssen, sie zu einer höheren Ordnung aufzuheben." As cited and translated in Biale, *Gershom Scholem*, Ger. 215; Eng. tr. 75. Translation slightly modified. On this passage, see James A. Diamond, *Maimonides and the Shaping of the Jewish Canon* (Cambridge: Cambridge University Press, 2014), 266–267.

concealed in the books of the Bible and in the dark sayings of the Aggadot and the Kabbalah. [A Gnostic approach with a reversal of values: The hidden God is not the good God. The hidden God has turned into the God of the rationalists that has no vitality in the realm of religion, and the God of Israel who creates the world and gives the Torah is the true God.] In the course of the confusion and demoralization brought on by the exile, this mystery (of which [according to Cardoso] even Christianity was nothing but a distorted expression) was forgotten and the Jewish people was mistakenly led to identify the impersonal First Cause with the personal God of the Bible, a spiritual disaster for which Saadiah Gaon, Maimonides, and the other philosophers will yet be held accountable![39]

Scholem again turned to the notion of paradox and indicted the entire philosophical tradition of Jewish rationalism for "a spiritual disaster" that was enabled by the political conditions of exile. He articulated his frustration with Saadia Gaon and Maimonides, who had sought to erase the "fundamental essence of true Judaism." In the letter to Schocken and in "Redemption through Sin," Scholem did not single out Maimonides but grouped him along with "Saadiah Gaon and Hermann Cohen" or "Saadiah Gaon and other philosophers."

Maimonides and his colleagues appear in these two texts as representatives of Jewish philosophy rather than Jewish law. As Scholem's thinking about the messianic idea continued to evolve over the course of the next two decades, his focus on the philosophical aspects of Maimonides's thought would change. Maimonides would become the sole focus of his intellectual ire. Maimonides's brief would also expand considerably. No longer would he serve simply as the bearer of the philosophical tradition; he would constitute the entirety and the distillation of the law. Sasportas may have played a role in this expansion of Mai-

---

[39] הפרדוכס הזה של ידיעת מציאות אלהי הדת שאינו הסבה הראשונה, זוהי מהות היהדות האמתית, זוהי 'אמונת' אבותינו' הגנוזה בספר התנ"ך ובגמגומי האגדות והמקובלים. [תפיסה גנוסטית בשנוי הערכים: האל הנסתר אינו האל הטוב. האל הנסתר נהפך לאלהי הרציונליסטים שאין לו חיים בתחומי הדת, ואלהי ישראל יוצר בראשית ונותן התורה הוא האל האמיתי.] אמונה זו (שמתוך סירוסיה נולדה לדעת קרדוזו גם הנצרות) נשכחה בגלות שהחשיכה את הלבבות ובלבלה את האמונה עד שנולדה גם בעמנו הטעות לחשוב שהסבה הראשונה הוא האלוה ועתידים רב סעדיה גאון והרמב"ם וחבריהם ליתן את הדין על בלבוליהם!

Passages in brackets reflect passages from the Hebrew that did not appear in Halkin's English translation in Scholem, "Redemption through Sin," in *The Messianic Idea in Judaism*, 105–106. The Hebrew text of this passage as it appears in the original publication in *Keneset*, p. 366, is identical to that in the later collected studies, Scholem, *Mehkarim*, p. 33.

monides's role in Scholem's reconstruction of the Jewish messianic tradition. By the late 1930s, however, two central themes had emerged in Scholem's developing approach to Jewish messianism: an emphasis on paradox as a hermeneutic key to understanding the issue of redemption. and a profound aversion to Maimonides and other bearers of a tradition of philosophical rationalism.

Scholem's letter to Schocken, however, had another purpose as well, one that was far more material and institutional. Over a decade earlier Scholem had emphasized to Bialik the enormity of the task he had outlined, and mentioned the possibility of assembling a group of scholars under his own supervision to carry out the necessary spadework. Collaborative research in the humanities had been a stated but somewhat elusive goal at the Hebrew University in the first decades of its existence.[40] During this period, however, Schocken founded the Research Institute for Medieval Hebrew Poetry under the direction of Hayim Brody. The institute was designed to publish new editions of medieval Hebrew poetry as part of a larger effort to preserve Jewish culture. The base of Schocken's cultural complex, which, in addition to the research institute, included a library as well as a German and Hebrew press, remained in Germany until 1933. With the Nazi seizure of power and the rapid increase in political anti-Semitism over the course of 1933, Schocken moved his library and primary residence into a specially commissioned building designed by the expressionist architect Erich Mendelsohn on Balfour Street in Jerusalem. His press, however, remained in Germany, where, under the direction of Lambert Schneider and Moses Spitzer, it issued an annual almanac, a series of short books on varied subjects of Judaica, and a range of other publications.[41] Schocken had been taken by the idea of *kinnus,* and he saw his press as an agent in the preservation and transmission of the Jewish past.

By the middle of the 1930s, Scholem and Schocken were effectively neighbors in Jerusalem, with Schocken's compound on Balfour Street a short walk from the apartments Scholem lived in on Ramban Street and Abarbanel Street. Schocken had been an early donor to the Jewish National and University Library and patron of the Hebrew University.

[40] Myers, *Re-inventing the Jewish Past,* 39, 67, 72.
[41] Stephen M. Poppel, "Salman Schocken and the Schocken Verlag: A Jewish Publisher in Weimar and Nazi Germany," *Harvard Library Bulletin* 21 (1973): 20–49. On Spitzer, see Ada Wardi, *Sefer Spitzer: pirke hayim ve-sifre Tarshish* (Jerusalem: Mineged, 2015).

Beginning in 1935 he played an increasingly powerful role at the university as the head of administration with control over the budget.[42] Scholem had extensive dealings with Schocken through the university and through his editors and publishers at Schocken's press. He contributed a series of articles, including one on Sabbatianism, to the annual Schocken Almanac and a volume on the *Zohar* to the Bücherei series. The give-and-take between Scholem and Schocken was subject to sudden shifts. Moses Spitzer expressed his frustration to Schocken about the difficulties in working with Scholem, an author who accepted commissions with alacrity and delivered his promised publications at a considerably slower pace.[43] Not all of Scholem's promises went unfulfilled. In 1937 he published a study of the Sabbatian Mordecai Ashkenazi and his dreams based on a manuscript in Schocken's library. He dedicated it to Schocken on the occasion of his sixtieth birthday, and Schocken was moved to publish it in a limited edition for bibliophiles.[44]

In the first half of 1938, Scholem delivered a series of lectures in New York at the Jewish Institute of Religion. These lectures constituted a general survey of Jewish mysticism from antiquity all the way up to the eighteenth century. When he returned to Jerusalem later that year, Scholem began to prepare the lectures for publication. In June 1939 he reached a tentative agreement with Schocken to publish the lectures in English, provided certain permissions could be obtained from Scholem's hosts in New York. As Scholem and Schocken worked out the details concerning the publication of what would become *Major Trends in Jewish Mysticism*, they began to discuss the possibility of another book on Sabbatianism. Scholem had decided to offer a course on Sabbatianism at the Hebrew University in 1939–1940, and at this stage in their discussions they planned for a book based on Scholem's lectures notes to the course.[45]

Several months later Scholem published an extensive review of Mortimer J. Cohen's study of Jacob Emden in *Kiryath sefer*, the bibliographic journal of the Jewish National and University Library.[46] The review reopened the vexed question of Jonathan Eibeschütz's Sabba-

---

[42] Cohen, "Governing Institutions of the Hebrew University: 1925–1948," 42–45.

[43] Zadoff, *Mi-Berlin le-Yerushalayim uva-hazarah*, 84–85.

[44] *Halomotav shel ha-Shabtai R. Mordecai Ashkenazi* (N.p.: Schocken, 1937).

[45] For the posthumous publication of the lectures, see Scholem, *Toledot ha-tenuah ha-shabtait.*

[46] *KS* 16 (1939): 320–338.

tianism through an excoriating attack on Cohen's use of sources and approach to Emden. In the final paragraph Scholem summoned his own studies of Mordecai Ashkenazi and "Redemption through Sin" as models for the unwritten history of Sabbatianism. The review found its way to Schocken's desk. Upon reading it, Schocken wrote to Scholem and declared that he was finally prepared to fund a scientific venture about the study of Sabbetai Zevi and Jacob Frank. At the conclusion of the letter, Schocken raised one other possibility. In the event that Mekize Nirdamim decided not to publish an edition of *Zizath novel zvi* based upon Schwarz's work, Schocken was prepared to consider it for publication.[47] On 19 November, Scholem proposed the foundation of a research institute to Schocken. On 4 December, Schocken and Scholem reached an agreement for a Programm Juedische Mystik. Under their agreement, they planned to publish a series of scholarly books on Jewish mysticism. The program would entail Scholem's supervision of two younger scholars, Chaim Wirszubski and Isaiah Tishby, who studied at the Hebrew University. Both would prepare scholarly editions of hitherto unpublished texts. Wirszubski would divide his time between two separate projects: an index of the Emden-Eibeschutz controversy and an edition of *Sefer ha-beriah* (Heb. The book of creation) by Nathan of Gaza, and Tishby would devote his time entirely to a new edition of *Zizath novel zvi*. Among the other proposed projects was a new edition and a Hebrew translation of Leyb ben Ozer's *Bashraybung fun shabsai svi* prepared by Zalman Rubaschoff. Schocken stipulated that he would pay for Rubaschoff to work on this edition only on the condition that he would cease his journalistic work at the same time.[48]

The summary of the agreement between Schocken and Scholem corresponded closely to Scholem's express wish to Bialik articulated over a decade earlier. Scholem was to have at his disposal a team of extraordinarily talented research assistants, a library well stocked with Judaica, funds to obtain photographs of manuscripts, and, most crucially, a publisher. There was, however, one significant difference between Scholem's plan outlined in his early letter to Bialik and the program of

[47] "Deshalb ist vielleicht eine Verlagsaenderung des bei Ihnen in Bearbeitung befindlichen 'Zizat Nowel Zwi' (wir haben daruber schon einmal gesprechen) von Wichtigkeit. Wenn aber die 'Mekize Nirdamim' sich dazu nicht entschliesen koennen ist das auch nich entscheidend." Letter from Schocken to Scholem, 1 November 1939. Jerusalem, Schocken Archives, 8 Privat 882/3.

[48] See "Salmann Schocken-Professor Gerhard Scholem: Programm 'Juedische Mystik,'" 4 December 1939. Schocken Archives, 8 Privat, 882/3.

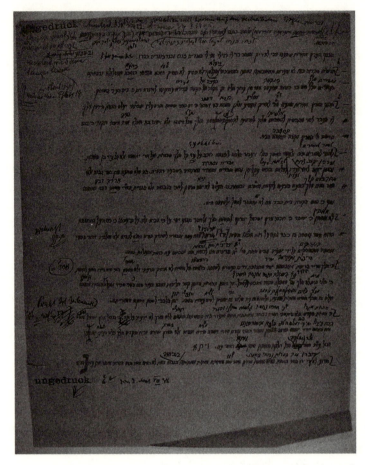

Figure 30. A. Z. Schwarz, typescript of lost manuscript. This typescript by Arthur Z. Schwarz contains a transcription of the complete text of Sasportas's *Zizath novel zvi* from a Hebrew manuscript in Vienna that was lost during World War II. Isaiah Tishby Archives, the National Library of Israel.

the research institute funded by Schocken. In Scholem's letter to Bialik, messianism appeared as an afterthought and Sabbatianism did not figure at all. The collective undertaking funded by Schocken bore a number of names. It began as Programm Juedische Mystik, was subsequently referred to as the Kabbala Forschungsunternehmens, and eventually took the name Ha-makhon le-heker ha-Kabbalah (Heb. The Research Institute for Kabbalah), which was parallel to Schocken's Research Institute for Medieval Hebrew Poetry. While nominally covering the entirety of the Jewish mystical tradition, the Research Institute for Kabbalah actually focused on two specific subfields: ancient Jewish mysticism and Sabbatianism. Scholem's own project at the institute involved an edition of Hekhalot texts, some of the earliest works of Jewish mysticism that describe heavenly journeys and ascents to the divine throne. The three major projects undertaken by his research assistants in the first year—editions of Sasportas and Nathan of Gaza, as well as an index of the Emden-Eibeschutz controversy—all bore directly on Sabbatianism. Furthermore, Scholem's planned book on Sabbatianism, variously referred to as "Buch ueber Sabbatianismus" or "Toldoth Tnuah Haschabtaith," appeared repeatedly in the progress reports of the research institute that Scholem dispatched to Schocken or to the members of his staff. Finally, the overwhelming majority of the funding was earmarked for Wirszubski and Tishby, who worked nearly full time, while Scholem himself continued to teach at the university and received considerably less in the form of an annual lump sum.[49] In the period between his initial appointment to the Hebrew University and the opening of the Research Institute for Kabbalah under Schocken's patronage, Scholem had made a decisive turn toward the study of messianism in general and Sabbatianism in specific.

TISHBY'S EDITION

On 31 December 1939 Scholem wrote to Tishby in Schocken's name and proposed terms for employment. Tishby was originally hired for a year under Scholem's supervision with the express purpose of preparing *Zizath novel zvi* for publication using the materials gathered by Schwarz. At the conclusion of the year, Schocken, and he alone, would decide whether he wanted Tishby to continue with his work "in the research field of Sabbatianism and Kabbalah."[50] A week later, Tishby responded to Scholem and accepted the conditions he had stipulated.[51]

---

[49]The work program stipulated that Wirszubski work five hours a day for a salary of LR 120 and Tishby six hours a day for a salary of 144. Scholem was given an annual stipend of LR 40/50. Rubaschoff was given LR 20 for a month's work. See "Salmann Schocken-Professor Gerhard Scholem: Programm Juedische Mystik'" 4 December 1939. Schocken Archives, 8 Privat, 882/3.

[50]Letter from Scholem to Tishby, 31 December 1939. Copies of the letter exist Schocken Archives, 8 Privat, 882/3 and Jerusalem, National Library of Israel, Isaiah Tishby Papers, Arc. 4o 1526, 01/27, File, Makhon Schocken.

[51]Letter from Tishby to Scholem, 8 January 1940, Jerusalem, Schocken Archives, 8 Privat, 882/3.

At this stage, Scholem planned for Tishby to establish the text of *Zizath novel zvi*, while he himself would write the historical introduction to the edition. For the entirety of the next year Tishby worked on the edition of Sasportas. In a report written half a year later, Tishby outlined the material on which he planned to base his edition. The Vienna manuscript copied by Schwarz contained the only complete text of *Zizath novel zvi*. Tishby did not have access to the Vienna manuscript or to photographs of it, and it appears to have disappeared during the Second World War. In addition to Schwarz's transcription, Tishby had photographs of one out of two volumes of a Berlin manuscript that had early drafts of many letters Sasportas included in *Zizath novel zvi*. Tishby was aware of the existence of a second volume to the Berlin manuscript but did not have photographs of it.[52] Tishby established the text of *Zizath novel zvi* on the basis of Schwarz's transcription of the Vienna manuscript and used the Berlin manuscript to provide variations between the early drafts of Sasportas's letters and the edited version of *Zizath novel zvi*. These variations would come to play a critical role in Scholem's portrait of Sasportas in *Sabbatai Sevi*.

Schocken funded the Research Institute for Kabbalah for the duration of the war, which Scholem and Tishby spent in Jerusalem and Schocken himself spent largely in the United States.[53] In October 1940 Scholem wrote a report on the institute's activities and described Tishby's progress on *Zizath novel zvi*, a work he defined as "the most important contemporary collection of documents about the Sabbatian movement in the years 1666–1667."[54] He predicted that the edition would be ready for publication by the first of January 1941, as had originally been stipulated. In a letter to Schocken nearly two years later, Scholem described the complete text of *Zizath novel zvi* as ready for press.[55] A paper shortage, however, made the publication of so long a work impossible during the war. In the same letter, Scholem described

---

[52] Both volumes of the Berlin manuscript resurfaced after the Second World War. They were subsequently acquired at public auction by Yeshiva University. For a description of the manuscripts, see Joseph Avivi, *Rabbinic Manuscripts: Mendel Gottesman Library Yeshiva University* (New York: Yeshiva University, 1998), catalog entry 374, pp. 134–135.

[53] David, *The Patron*, chaps. 16–18.

[54] "Dies ist die wichtigste zeitgenoessische Dokumentsammlung der sabbatianischen Bewegung in den Jaaren 1666/1667." Gershom Scholem, "Arbeitsprogramm," 1 October 1940, Schocken Archives, 8 Privat, 882/3.

[55] Letter from Scholem to Schocken 7 July 1942, in Schocken Archives, 8 Privat, 882/3.

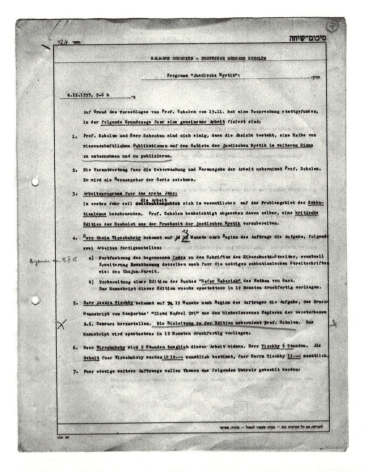

Figure 31. Scholem plan for Sasportas edition in the Research Institute for Kabbalah. At the early stages of the Institute for Research in Kabbalah, Scholem had planned a series of publications relating to Sabbatianism, including an edition of *Zizath novel zvi*. Scholem would write the introduction, while Tishby prepared the edition of the text. Schocken Institute for Jewish Research.

his own Hebrew book on the Sabbatian movement, which he was writing based on his teaching at the Hebrew University and on public lectures he had delivered at a theoretical seminar in Rehovot to the organization of Jewish workers known as the Histadrut. Gershom Schocken—Schocken's eldest son, who was in charge of the day-to-day operations of his father's concerns in Palestine during the war—had informed Scholem that the Schocken Press lacked the paper supplies to produce another big book after the printing of *Major Trends in*

Jewish Mysticism. For the first time, Scholem broached the possibility that his book on Sabbatianism would appear with another press, and he suggested that he would give it to the publishing house of the Histadrut. In a letter from the following year, however, Scholem continued to discuss the Sabbatianism book as a possible publication by Schocken and repeated that Tishby's edition of Sasportas had been completed.[56]

With the end of World War II, Schocken visited Jerusalem for the first time in several years. Schocken and Scholem had not seen one another for nearly the entirety of the time that Schocken had funded the Research Institute for Kabbalah. Scholem's letters and reports to Schocken during the war appear to have gone unanswered. Most of Scholem's dealings had been with Schocken's son Gershom, who lived in Tel Aviv and ran the newspaper *Ha-aretz*. Prior to Salman Schocken's arrival in Palestine, Scholem composed an extensive memo that described the activities of the Research Institute for Kabbalah between 1939 and 1945. He provided detailed descriptions of the work accomplished by Wirszubski and Tishby, as well as a third assistant, Joseph Weiss, who had joined the institute in 1943.[57] He indicated to Schocken that Wirszubski, who had been the first person hired by the research institute in 1939, planned to leave in October 1945, but that Tishby and Weiss were prepared to continue with their work. Scholem described his assistant to Schocken:

> In Tishby we have an independent, wide-ranging, outstanding scholar, from whom, if one provides him with the necessary bridle of sharp criticism, one can expect meaningful results. He is as good as it gets in the circle of Judaists, and may well be the greatest student that the university has produced.[58]

Scholem later described Tishby as a "bit of a nudnik" but made clear to Schocken that the scholars at his research institute were the best money

[56] Letter from Scholem to Schocken, 13 April 1943, in Schocken Archives, 8 Privat, 882/3.

[57] On Weiss and Scholem, *Gershom Scholem ve-Yosef Weiss: halifat mikhtavim, 1948–1964*, ed. Noam Zadoff (Jerusalem: Carmel, 2012).

[58] "In Tischby haben wir einen selbstandigen und weitgehend durchtrainierten Forscher, von den, wenn man ihm mit unter mit scharfer Kritik noetigenfalls am Zaume haelt, bedeutende Resultate zu erwarten sind. Er gilt mit Recht in Kreisen der Judaisten als ungefaehr der ausgezeichnetste Schueler, den die Universitaet her vorgebracht hat. " "Bemerkungen von Herrn Prof. Scholem an Herrn Schocken in Sachen des Kabbala-Forschungsunternehmens" 3 September 1945, Schocken Archives, 8 Privat 882/3.

could buy.[59] He proposed a significant alteration to the funding structure of the institute, asking him to fund it for a period of three to five years rather than renewing it annually. Furthermore, he stressed that Tishby's intellectual independence and relatively advanced age of thirty-eight merited a promotion to the position of senior assistant. The work at the research institute during the war had generated an entire library of books that had yet to be published, and Scholem listed those he thought should appear under its auspices.

As far as Scholem was concerned, the research institute had been a success. Wirszubski and Tishby had completed their work in a timely manner, and no fewer than four works relating to Sabbatianism awaited publication: the index to the Emden-Eibsechutz controversy, *Zizath novel zvi*, *Sefer ha-beriah*, and *Sefer zemir arisim*, the last two by Nathan of Gaza. Over the years of its activities, Scholem had been able to expand the chronological scope of the institute. Tishby had begun to work on medieval Kabbalah in Girona, which was the subject of his doctorate at the university, and Weiss on the Hasidic master Nahman of Bratzlav. Schocken had been deeply affected by Martin Buber's writings on Hasidism and would die clutching a volume of Nahman of Bratzlav's writings.[60] Scholem had every reason to imagine Schocken's delight at the possibility of Weiss working on Hasidism under his supervision at the research institute.

Schocken's response to Scholem's proposal was frigid. Over the course of September and October a series of exchanges ensued between Scholem and various employees of the Schocken enterprise. On 3 November, Salman Schocken wrote a letter to Scholem that directly confronted the basic issue: Scholem's book on Sabbetai Zevi. Almost immediately after the publication of "Redemption through Sin" in 1937, Scholem realized the potential for a large book-length study of Sabbatianism. Two crucial issues, however, led this to become a project that would span the better part of two decades. The first had to do with competing demands for Scholem's scholarly energies. Beginning with the writing and publication of the lectures that he had delivered in New York in 1938, Scholem understood the importance of composing syn-

[59] "Wahrend Tishby, um mich so auszudruecken, of a more ebullient nature, mit anderen Werten; ein Stueck von einem Nudnik ist . . ." in "Bemerkungen von Herrn Prof. Scholem an Herrn Schocken in Sachen des Kabbala-Forschungsunternehmens" 3 September 1945, Schocken Archives, 8 Privat 882/3.

[60] David, *The Patron*, 6.

thetic work at this point in his career and the considerable benefits to his scholarly reputation of its appearance in English. The second had to with the state of scholarship on Sabbatianism in 1935 as compared to 1955. Through the research institute, Scholem had been able to harness the talent of two young scholars to prepare critical editions of major Sabbatian sources. While not all of these works were to appear in print prior to Scholem's Sabbatianism book, Scholem had access to these materials as well as to Rubaschoff's manuscript of Leyb ben Ozer while he was writing his synthetic work. Concurrent with his work at the Schocken Institute, Scholem taught a course on Sabbetai Zevi and the Sabbatian movement at the Hebrew University in the academic year 1939–1940.

Scholem's correspondence with Schocken and his employees contained numerous references to his Sabbatianism book. There appears to have been a mutual understanding without any legal ramifications that Schocken would publish the work, much as he had published Scholem's earlier work. The dearth of materials during wartime had contributed to the backlog of publications that had been prepared but not published at the research institute. In 1942, the very year that Scholem had given a series of public lectures to the Histadrut in Rehovot about Sabbetai Zevi, Berl Katznelson founded a publishing house designed to produce books for the Zionist laborer. Katznelson served as founding editor of the press, which he called Am Oved (Heb. Working Nation), and suggested to Scholem that he publish his public lectures as a book with his new press. At the time, Scholem spoke with Gershom Schocken about this possibility before he agreed to terms with Am Oved.[61]

This is where matters stood when Schocken arrived in Palestine in the fall of 1945. Schocken was underwhelmed by Scholem's report of the research institute's wartime activities and greeted the list of works ready for publication prepared by Scholem and his assistants with a mixture of bemusement and frustration. A long-simmering tension between Schocken's desire to reach a mass Jewish audience through his publishing ventures and Scholem's quest to produce scholarship of the most rigorous quality boiled over into open dispute. The critical issue, however, pertained to Schocken's perceived betrayal by Scholem in the

[61]Letter from Scholem to Schocken 7 July 1942, in Schocken Archives, 8 Privat, 882/3. On Katznelson and Am Oved, see Anita Shapira, Berl: Biografiyah (Tel Aviv: Am Oved, 1980), 2:626–630, 649–663.

latter's agreeing to terms with Am Oved. Writing from Tel Aviv to his
father in Jerusalem in early November, Gershom Schocken denied all
responsibility for Scholem's defection:

> I cannot remember whether Scholem offered us this book. In any case,
> there is certainly no documentation in my files concerning it, but it is
> quite possible that Scholem had spoken of its publication on occasion
> and expressed his regret that Schocken Press would not be able to pub-
> lish it.[62]

Furthermore, he emphasized that Scholem's agreement with Am Oved,
which had been announced in the catalog published for the Jewish New
Year in 1942, had come at a time when the Schocken Press had not reopened owing to wartime scarcities.[63] Salman Schocken would have
none of this. In a letter to Scholem, he directly confronted the issue of
who would publish Scholem's book on Sabbatianism:

> I do not know whether a letter with such a question exists; I have no
> memory of having read a letter that posed a question about printing that
> required me to provide an answer. I have no memory of a negative de-
> cision. I am convinced that had I been posed a specific question, I would
> have found a way to respond affirmatively.[64]

Schocken was furious.

Much to Scholem's chagrin, Schocken took his time in deciding
the fate of the research institute.[65] Early in 1946 he finally informed

---

[62] "Ich kann mich nicht erinnern, dass Scholem uns dieses Buch angeboten hat. Jedenfalls gibt
es in meinen Akten darueber keinerlei Unterlagen, obwohl moeglich ist, dass Scholem mir
gelegntlich bei Gespraechen von der bevorstehenden Fertigstellung dieses Buches erzaehlt hat
und sein Bedauern darueber ausgedrueckt hat, dass der Schocken Verlag das Buch nicht bringen
kann." Letter from Gershom Schocken to Salman Schocken, 7 November 1945. Schocken Archives,
8 Privat, 882/3.

[63] "Jedenfalls war das zu einer Zeit als der Schockenverlag noch nicht reaktiviert war, und aus
der ersten Programmliste von Am Oved—wohl Rosch Haschanah 1942—erseh ich, dass dieses
Buch dort erscheinen wird." Gershom Schocken to Salman Schocken, 7 November 1945. Schocken
Archives, 8 Privat, 882/3.

[64] "Ich weiss nicht, ob Brief mit Anfragen an mich bestehen; ich habe keine Erinnerung, einen
Brief gelesen zu haben, der eine Frage wagen Drucklegung, die entscheiden werden musste, an
mich stellte. Ich habe keine negative Entscheidung im Gedachtnis. Ich bin ueberzeugt, dass, wenn
mir praesize Fragen vergelegt werdern waeren, ich einen Weg zu einer positive Antwort gefun-
den haette." Letter from Salman Schocken to Gershom Scholem, 8 November 1945. Schocken Archives, 8 Privat, 882/3.

[65] Scholem letter to Hannah Arendt, 16 December 1945, in *Hannah Arendt / Gershom Scholem:
Der Briefwechsel*, ed. Marie Luise Knott (Berlin: Suhrkamp Verlag, 2010), 85. As cited by David,

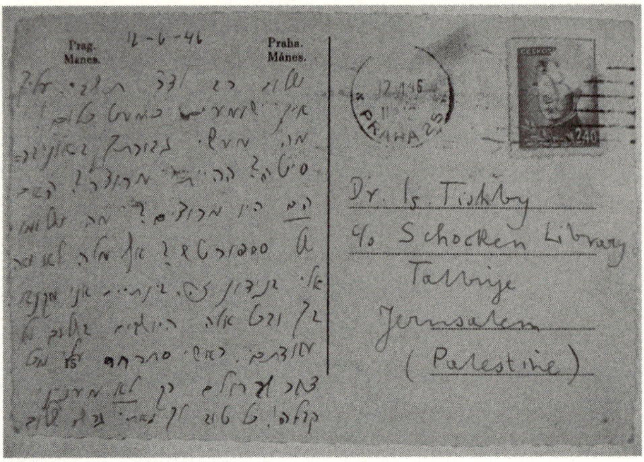

Figure 32. Scholem to Tishby, postcard from Prague, 1946. In the midst of a grueling trip to the Allied occupation zones of Europe, Scholem sent a postcard to Tishby from Prague inquiring about the progress of his work on Sasportas. Suhrkamp Verlag, Berlin.

Scholem that he could expect funding for only another five years, and on a considerably reduced scale at that.[66] Schocken's decision occurred on the eve of Scholem's departure to the Allied occupation zones to assess the fate of Jewish books in the aftermath of the Second World War.[67] On 8 April, two days before he left for what would be over four months of work in the ashes of postwar Europe, Scholem wrote a sternly worded missive to the rector of the Hebrew University about the fate of his prized student. He informed him that Tishby's work for Schocken would cease in a matter of months, and demanded suitable employment as an instructor for him: "I ask you, therefore, not to rely upon 'miracles' or 'influence,' as this shall not come to pass."[68] Scholem's memo did not fall upon deaf ears. A little more than a month later, the dean of the Hebrew University appointed Tishby to teach two courses for the upcoming academic year.[69]

The Patron, 341, with reference to its earlier publication in Gershom Scholem, *Briefe I: 1914–1947*, ed. Itta Shedletzky (Munich: Verlag C. H. Beck, 1994), 307–308.

[66] See David, *The Patron*, 334–335.

[67] Zadoff, *Mi-Berlin le-Yerushalayim uva-hazarah*, 208–261.

[68] אני מבקש ממך איפוא שלא תסמכו על "נסים" ו"השפעה" בעניין זה שלא יהיו ולא יבואו.

Gershom Scholem to the rector of the Hebrew University, 8 April 1946. Isaiah Tishby Papers, Arc. 4o 1526 02/97 File, Gershom Scholem. The unnamed rector was Michael Fekete, a mathematician. See Cohen, "Governing Institutions of the Hebrew University: 1925–1948," 37n123, and 69.

[69] M. Schwabe to Isaiah Tishby, 16 May 1946. Isaiah Tishby Papers, Arc. 4o 1526 02/97 File, Gershom Scholem.

The publication of *Zizath novel zvi* was another matter. In a postcard from Prague sent to Tishby care of the Schocken Library, Scholem asked: "What is going on with Sasportas? I have not heard a word about it."[70] Tishby's response a month later encapsulated all of the frustrations of a scholar working for a private patron:

> In terms of *Zizath novel zvi*: Quite some time ago I finished what was asked of me. The introduction—at a length of about 40–45 pages—is ready for press, but the question of publication has yet to be resolved. Mr. Schocken spoke with me prior to his depature for America, promised me that the book would be printed, but then left no instructions. After the submission of the introduction, Dr. Wilhelm wrote to him requesting urgent instructions but, as is customary in the world of Mr. Schocken, he did not receive any response. A few days ago G[ershom] Schocken asked for the manuscript along with the introduction, and perhaps he will decide to publish it at long last.[71]

Six months later, Leo Hermann, one of Schocken's employees, wrote from Tel Aviv to the aforementioned Kurt Wilhelm in Jerusalem with a publication outline and plan for the production of *Zizath novel zvi*. The memo concluded that as soon as Schocken gave his authorization, the manuscript would be sent to press in Jerusalem.[72]

Schocken eventually gave his authorization. Several months later Kurt Wilhelm wrote from Jerusalem to Schocken in New York about *Zizath novel zvi*:

> Mr. Hermann is at present in Jerusalem in order to arrange the printing of this book. You will receive samples of the paper and print next week. I saw the first unofficial samples and I think they are promising. I am sure that the procedure will be faster than we first assumed.[73]

[70] מה שלומו של ססְפורטש? אף מלה לא באה אלי בנידון זה.

Gershom Scholem to Isaiah Tishby, 12 June 1946, Isaiah Tishby Papers, Arc. 4o 1526 02/97 File, Gershom Scholem.

[71] בעניין "ציצת נובל צבי" גמרתי מזמן מה שמוטל עלי, המבוא מוכן לדפוס בהיקף של 45–40 עמוד, אבל שאלת ההדפסה לא נפתרה עדיין. מר שוקן שוחח אתי לפני נסיעתו לאמריקה, הבטיח שהספר יודפס, אבל לא השאיר שום הוראה. לאחר מסירת המבוא כתב לו ד״ר וילהם וביקש ממנו הוראה דחופה, אבל כנוהג שבעולמו של מר שוקן לא נתקבלה תשובה. בימים אלה ביקש ג. שוקן להמציא לו את כתב-היד בצירוף המבוא, ואולי יחליט לגשת סוף-סוף להדפסה.

Isaiah Tishby to Gershom Scholem, 10 July 1946, Isaiah Tishby Papers, Arc. 4o 1526 02/97 File, Gershom Scholem.

[72] Leo Hermann to Kurt Wilhelm, 8 December 1946, Schocken Archives, 8 Privat, 882/3.

[73] Letter in English. Kurt Wilhelm to Salman Schocken 13 May 1947, Schocken Archives, 8 Privat, 882/3.

In spite of Wilhelm's optimism, it would take the better part of the next year to print Schocken's edition of *Zizath novel zvi.*

If the Nazi occupation of Austria had abruptly ended Schwarz's work on his edition of Sasportas, the escalating violence in Palestine in 1948 would have a similar effect on Tishby's. Schocken's edition of *Zizath novel zvi* was to be printed in Jerusalem at the offices of the *Palestine Post* on Hasolel Street in the center of town. Around eleven o'clock on Sunday evening, 1 February 1948, a British army truck loaded with explosives blew up in front of the offices of the *Palestine Post.*[74] The following week Scholem reported to his colleague in Amsterdam Isaac Leo Seeligmann:

> In the meantime, something very tragic has occurred here: the bomb attacks on the printing press of the *Palestine Post* burned up all of the stock, which included the nearly completed typeset edition of the entirety of *Zizath novel zvi* by Sasportas upon which Tishby had worked. Thank God the printer's manuscript has been kept in its entirety.[75]

Scholem was not sanguine about the possibility of printing the book again in the near future. Schocken had left Palestine in late 1947 prior to the escalation of the conflict, and his relations with Scholem had frayed considerably. Nearly half a year later in a follow-up report to Seeligman, Scholem expressed his profound pessimism about the fate of Tishby's Sasportas. "Two hundred pages had just been typeset in their final galleys, while the remainder had already been proofread. Although the printer's manuscript has been preserved, no one can say when the printing will be resumed. It will certainly not happen this year. In the meantime, Schocken has shut down his publishing house, and the presses for *Ha-aretz* were seriously affected by the air raids on Tel Aviv."[76]

[74] "Palestine Post Press and Offices Destroyed," *Palestine Post,* 2 February 1948, 1.

[75] "Hier ist inzwischen etwas sehr Trauriges passiert, indem bei dem Bombenattentat auf die Druckerei der Palestine Post mit vielen anderen Beständen auch der fast beendete Satz des vollständigen Zizath Novel Zwi von Sasportas verbrannt ist, den Tishbi bearbeitet hat. Gott sei Dank ist das Druckmanuskript selbst vollständig erhalten." Scholem to Isaac Leo Seeligmann, 10 February 1948, in Gershom Scholem, *Briefe II: 1948–1970,* ed. Thomas Spaar (Munich: Verlag C. H. Beck, 1995), 5.

[76] "200 Seiten waren druckfertig in der letzten Korrektur, und das übrige schon aufgesetzt. Zwar ist das Manuskript erhalten, aber wann mit einer Neuaufnahme des Druckes zu rechnen ist, lässt sich nicht vorher sagen. In diesem Jahre sicher nicht mehr. Schocken hat inzwischen den Druck geschlossen und auch die Druckerei des Haaretz in Tel Aviv ist von einem der Luftbombardements

Early the following year Scholem wrote to the Bialik Institute, a publishing house founded in 1935. Scholem had long-standing ties with this press, which had joined with Dvir to publish *Keneset*. They were about to publish an anthology of writings extracted from the corpus of the *Zohar*, translated from medieval Aramaic into modern Hebrew, and preceded by a substantial introduction on the *Zohar* as a book. The project had started years earlier as a constitutive element of Bialik's efforts at *kinnus* and was entitled *Mishnat ha-Zohar* (Heb. The wisdom of the *Zohar*). When the editor of the project, Fischel Lachover, died in 1947, Scholem had been instrumental in steering the project toward completion by recommending Tishby to the Bialik Institute. In a letter acknowledging receipt of his advance copy of the first volume, Scholem heaped praise upon his student: "It seems to me that you entrusted the work into good hands, and I am delighted by this, just as I am delighted that I have been able to raise up such an extraordinary student as Dr. Tishby."[77]

Scholem was on his way to the United States for the first time in over a decade, where he was scheduled to deliver a lecture series, "Major Trends in Hasidism," similar in format to his lectures of 1938. While in the United States, Scholem met with Schocken. Writing about his meeting in a letter to his house sitter in Jerusalem, Shmuel Yosef Agnon, Scholem gave full vent to his frustration: "It is impossible to clarify anything with him [Schocken], because he lives in a world of fantasy."[78] Slightly over a month later, he reported about his meeting with Schocken to Tishby:

> I spoke with Schocken here and, as is his wont, he would not give an answer. In the meantime he has gone to Jerusalem, but I will not see him as he is scheduled to return here three days after we set sail. In my opin-

---

schwer in Mitleidenschaft gezogen worden." Scholem to Isaac Leo Seeligmann, 3 August 1948, in Scholem, *Briefe II*, 7. For a partial English translation of this letter, see *Gershom Scholem: A Life in Letters, 1914–1982*, ed. Anthony David Skinner (Cambridge, MA: Harvard University Press, 2002), 356–357. On Skinner's edition, see Anthony Grafton, "The Magician," *New Republic*, 3 March 2003, 38–45.

[77] נראה לי שמסרתם את העבודה בידיים נאמנות ומאומנות כראוי ואני שמח על כך כשם שאני שמח על שזכיתי להעמיד תלמיד מובהק כמו הד"ר תשבי.

Scholem to Bialik Institute, 16 February 1949, Isaiah Tishby Papers, Arc. 4o 1526 02/97 File, Gershom Scholem.

[78] Scholem to S. Y. Agnon, 6 May 1949. As cited in Dan Laor, *Haye Agnon: Biografiyah* (Jerusalem: Schocken Press, 1998), 421–422n88; Laor cited by David, *The Patron*, 362.

ion, you can inform him in writing of the situation, and explain that if he doesn't make formal arrangements to publish *Zizath novel zvi* by a certain date, you will feel free to publish the book in another way.[79]

A month later Tishby responded to Scholem:

I ran into Schocken on the street, and he stopped to congratulate me heartily on *Mishnat ha-Zohar*, which he was reading with great pleasure. He even indicated that he wanted to speak with me, but I have yet to be invited to see him. In the interim, however, I also met with Hermann from the Schocken Press. From what he said, I gathered that they have begun to prepare for the renewed publication of *Zizath novel zvi*.[80]

The invitation to speak with Schocken never arrived, and the plans to republish Sasportas came to naught. On 8 March 1950 the Schocken Press wrote an anonymous form letter to Tishby releasing him from his contract.[81]

For all of the stresses and strains of working under Schocken, Tishby had yet to see Sasportas through into print. The anonymously written note from Schocken's minions never arrived in Tishby's mailbox, and for another half a year he continued to hold out hopes that they would publish his edition.[82] When he finally understood the game was up, he turned to the Bialik Institute and offered them his edition of Sasportas. Unlike his negotiations with Schocken, where he was constantly in a position of supplicant, his dealings with the Bialik Institute were on somewhat more equal footing.[83] Tishby had completed Lachover's work on the first volume of *Mishnat ha-Zohar*, which had appeared the year before to considerable acclaim. A second volume of the work had

עם שוקן דברתי כאן והשתמטת כדרכו לתת תשובה. בינתיים היה בירושלים ולא אראה אותו עוד כי יחזור עוד[79] הנה ג' ימים אחר הפלגתנו. לדעתי תוכל עתה לכתוב לו מכתב ואחריות שבו תסביר בקיצור את המצב ותודיע לו שאם לא יועשו סידורים פורמליים להדפסת ס' ציצת נובל צבי עד תאריך קבוע, הרי אתה רואה אותך חפשי לדאוג לפרסום הספר באופן אחר.

Scholem to Tishby, 14 June 1949. Isaiah Tishby Papers, Arc. 4o 1526 02/97 File, Gershom Scholem.

בדרך מקרה נפגשתי עם שוקן ברחוב והוא עצרני ובירכני בידידות רבה למשנת הזוהר, שהוא קורא בו בהנאה[80] רבה. אף הודיעני שברצונו לשוחח אתי, אבל עד עתה לא הוזמנתי אצלו. בינתיים פגשתי גם את הרמן מהוצאת שוקן, ומתוך דבריו נודע לי, שהתחילו לטפל בהכנות לחידוש ההדפסה של ס' ציצת נובל צבי.

Tishby to Scholem, 10 July 1949. Isaiah Tishby Papers, Arc. 4o 1526 02.97 File, Gershom Scholem.

[81]Schocken Archives, 8 Privat, 882/3.

[82]Leo Hermann to Jacob Katzenstein, 19 October 1950. Schocken Archives, 8 Privat, 882/3.

[83]Contract between Isaiah Tishby and Bialik Institute, 9 August 1952. Isaiah Tishby Papers, Arc. 4o, 1526 04/80. File Bialik Institute.

been promised, and Moshe Gordon of the Bialik Institute was keen for it to appear. Tishby agreed to complete this second volume only on the condition that they first publish his edition of Sasportas. The following April, Moshe Gordon wrote a sternly worded letter to Tishby to inform him that *Zizath novel zvi* had been sent into production and to remind him of his obligations about the second volume of *Mishnat ha-Zohar*.[84] After some continued haggling about who would pay for the index and the design of the cover, *Zizath novel zvi* finally appeared in print in August 1954.

SCHOLEM'S SASPORTAS

A month later Scholem wrote from London to congratulate Tishby on his achievement. He informed him that he had reason to believe that the Vienna manuscript transcribed by Schwarz and presumed lost during the Second World War might have resurfaced at the Jewish Historical Institute in Warsaw. He concluded the letter with a short note about Sasportas:

> Those experts in physiognomy will recognize in the excellent portrait you included in the book Sasportas's unmistakable character, about which we have spoken several times. An irascible, cantankerous old man, whose talent and authority were not graced by the attribute of kindness. I looked for a long time at his face, and I understood a bit of his nature which overcame him, and led him to those astonishing forgeries in his book, which is really something that calls for attention![85]

Scholem referred to the frontispiece to Tishby's edition: an oil painting attributed to seventeenth-century Dutch portraitist Isaac Luttichuys that may have been a portrait of Sasportas. In this letter Scholem gave Sasportas's modern editor a preview of how he would describe Sasportas in the context of his larger history. Sasportas was one of a

---

[84] Moshe Gordon to Isaiah Tishby 10 April 1953. Isaiah Tishby Papers, Arc. 4o, 1526 04/80. File Bialik Institute.

[85] בעלי חכמת הפרצוף יכירו בתמונה המצויינת שציירפתם לספר את אופיו המיוחד של ששפורטש שדיברנו עליו כמה פעמים, זקן זועף וסכסכן שכשרונו וסמכותו לא נמתנו במדת החסד כל עיקר. הבטתי זמן רב בפנים אלו והבינותי גם מקצת מיצרו שנתגבר עליו והביאו לזיופים המופלאים שבספרו שהם באמת ענין לענות בו!

Scholem to Tishby 12 September 1954. Isaiah Tishby Papers, Arc. 4o 1526 02/97 File, Gershom Scholem.

handful of figures within Jewish history with whom Scholem genuinely struggled, and it was out of this struggle that his exhilarating story of Sabbatianism emerged. His ambivalence about Sasportas was the flip side of his ambivalence about Sabbetai Zevi.

Shabtai Tsevi veha-tenuah ha-shabta-it bi-yeme hayav (Heb. Sabbetai Zevi and the Sabbatian movement in his time) appeared with Am Oved in two volumes early in 1957. The first chapter, "The Background to the Sabbatian Movement," sought to establish the centrality of ideas to the history of Sabbatianism and concurrently argued strenuously for the immanence of the movement within Judaism. The expulsion of the Jews from Spain in 1492 served Scholem as a moment of profound rupture. Two generations after this national trauma, Isaac Luria and a group of kabbalists in Safed, Palestine, developed a myth that transposed exile and redemption from the historical experience of the Jews to the cosmic realm of divine creation. In the decades that elapsed between the end of the Safed renaissance and the beginning of the Sabbatian movement, Scholem argued that Lurianic kabbalah became the most accepted form of Jewish theology. To Scholem, the kabbalists of Safed emphasized the spiritual aspects of redemption. In so doing, they relegated the apocalyptic to the level of the symbolic and concealed the fact that they had inaugurated a radical new concept of the Messiah. Scholem also introduced a distinction in the messianic idea that he would later develop in an independent essay. He identified the messianic idea in Judaism with a dialectical tension between restorative and utopian tendencies in Jewish thought. In his reconstruction, a restorative approach to the messianic age was consistent with rabbinical political quiescence. Acute utopian messianism, by contrast, produced a form of apocalyptic thinking that undermined Jewish law and threatened rabbinic control over Jewish life: "From the point of view of the *halakha*, to be sure, Judaism appears as a well-ordered house, and it is a profound truth that a well-ordered house is a dangerous thing."[86]

Scholem mentioned an aspect of Jewish messianism that was opposed to the utopian and apocalyptic traditions: the rabbinic attenuation of active messianic speculation. In the later essay he would label

---

[86] "Toward an Understanding of the Messianic Idea in Judaism," in *The Messianic Idea in Judaism*, 21.

this a "conservative tendency," refusing to dignify it with the word "idea" or "concept." He explicitly identified this conservatism with the figure of Maimonides:

> Every utopia that is more than an abstract formula has a revolutionary sting. It hardly occasions surprise that Maimonides, the most extreme representative of the antiapocalyptic tendency, rejected all those myths that lived in the hearts of the believing masses, whom he contemptuously referred to as the "rabble."[87]

In his letter to Schocken and in "Redemption through Sin" written twenty years earlier, Scholem had indicted Maimonides as a philosopher of Judaism who had replaced the personal God of the Bible with the impersonal First Cause of the medieval philosophical tradition. In the late 1950s, both in his book on Sabbetai Zevi and in the essay on the messianic idea, Scholem similarly attacked Maimonides; however, the focus and tenor of his criticism had shifted. First, Maimonides appeared alone, independent of Saadia Gaon and of Hermann Cohen. Second, Scholem quoted the conclusion to Maimonides's *Mishneh Torah*, where Maimonides had discussed the figure of the Messiah in the Laws of Kings. Not only did Maimonides represent philosophical rationalism; he also personified legal codification. As Scholem glossed the passage from the Laws of Kings: "What Maimonides did succeed in doing was to suppress completely the apocalyptic moment."[88] The suppression of the apocalyptic tendency in the messianic idea deferred the arrival of the Messiah indefinitely. Scholem equated messianism—whether restorative or utopian—with change, and suppression with stasis. Rabbinic legalism, "the well-ordered house of the *halakha*," exemplified endless minute adjustments to religious regulation in the name of maintaining political quiescence. Maimonides, Scholem argued, was the great suppressor of popular Jewish craving for the Messiah.

The notion of Maimonides as someone who had suppressed a vital aspect of Judaism, outlined in the opening pages of *Sabbatai Sevi*, remained with Scholem until nearly the end of his life. At a conference on messianism held in honor of his eightieth birthday, Scholem delivered a closing statement that appeared in print the year of his death.

[87] Scholem, *Sabbatai Sevi*, 12.
[88] Ibid., 13.

He placed Maimonides at the center of his remarks and developed the idea mentioned at the outset of *Sabbatai Sevi*:

> Since Maimonides was so bold as to issue legal rulings that had no basis in the tradition, it comes as no surprise that he did not lack the audacity to sequester all that he did not like. Maimonides was a great sequesterer, and not only that, he was a successful one, for many generations, and even our own, the most recent one, were educated by this teaching of Maimonides, one that explains the Messianic idea as the law, a most bold law, at the conclusion of the Laws of Kings.[89]

Maimonides had adopted a modified and evolutionary scheme in his understanding of the Messiah. The realization of the messianic promise held out by the Hebrew Bible would develop only through the confines of the law. The coming of the Messiah would not depend upon the apocalyptic logic that amounted to a variation on the theory that the worse things became in the temporal realm of mundane reality, the higher the chances were that the Messiah would actually arrive. Variations of this apocalyptic logic could be found scattered throughout rabbinic literature from antiquity and the Middle Ages. As Scholem correctly observed, Maimonides chose not to emphasize these strands of apocalyptic thinking and adopted a muted approach to the coming of the Messiah. Scholem saw in the Maimonidean emphasis on the gradual nature of redemption an affinity with the nineteenth-century notion of progress. As he had indicated in his birthday letter to Schocken in 1937, he had thoroughly rejected this notion. Four decades later, Scholem continued to see himself as having been schooled in this idea only to rebel against it. The developmental gradualism of the rabbis took the shape of the law, or *halakha*. No figure represented this more than Maimonides, and no work encapsulated this more than the *Mishneh Torah*.

Throughout *Sabbatai Sevi* Scholem cast Sasportas in the role of a latter-day Maimonidean. Sasportas emerged in these pages as some-

---

[89] ולפי שהיה הרמב"ם בעל אומץ לב כה גדול לפסוק הלכות שאין להם שום יסוד במסורת, אין פלא, שלא נגרע מאומץ לבו גם בבואו לגנוז כל מה שלא חיבב. גונז גדול היה הרמב"ם, ולא זו בלבד, אלא גונז מצליח, שהרי דורות רבים, ואף אנו הצעירים, חונכו על משנה זאת של הרמב"ם, המפרשת את הרעיון המשיחי כהלכה, הלכה נועזת ביותר, בסוף הלכות מלכים.

"Response of Prof. Gershom Scholem" (Hebrew), in *Ha-ra-ayon ha-meshihi be-yisrael*, 256–257.

one whose response to Sabbatianism "caused him concern for the future of rabbinic Judaism." Nathan of Gaza's prophecies "opened the door to further departures from law and tradition."[90] In a comparison between Nehemiah Hacohen and Sasportas, Scholem expressed Sasportas's Maimonideanism quite succinctly. Sasportas "drew his anti-Sabbatian arguments from Scripture and from the writings of Maimonides."[91] If Scholem was later to accuse Maimonides of sequestering parts of the Jewish tradition, he took his criticism of Sasportas one step further and alleged that he doctored his own letters so as to appear more critical of Sabbatianism from the outset than he had actually been at the time. Drawing on Tishby's edition as well as a review by Rivkah Schatz, Scholem argued that comparison between the early drafts of the letters preserved in the Berlin manuscript and the later drafts in the Vienna manuscript "afford many examples of his [Sasportas] 'doctoring' his own letters and changing their original form in a manner that is often tantamount to falsification."[92] At a later point, he concluded that "letters which in their original form bespoke questioning doubt and diplomatic prudence were changed into fiercely pugnacious anti-Sabbatian manifestoes."[93]

The empirical evidence as established by Tishby and reviewed by Schatz established incontrovertibly that Sasportas edited the early drafts of his letters so as to express a more strenuous and acerbic critique of Sabbatianism from the start. The crucial question, however, has to do with what conclusions one draws from this editorial process about Sasportas and the nature of his writing. Scholem's assessment overlooks the role that initial doubt played in Sasportas's formulation of his criticism. Furthermore, the historical reconstruction of Sasportas's editorial process comes almost entirely from evidence provided by Sasportas himself. Sasportas preserved his early drafts among his own papers long after the Sabbatian movement had ceased to dominate his literary activity. Elsewhere Scholem noted that many Jews destroyed the evidence that had indicated their belief in Sabbetai Zevi as the Messiah. Sasportas, by contrast, kept a record of his own ambivalence; he did not destroy evidence of his own intial skepticism. Over

[90] Scholem, *Sabbatai Sevi*, 582.

[91] Ibid., 661.

[92] Ibid., 568. For Schatz's review, see *Behinot* 10 (1956): 50–67.

[93] Scholem, *Sabbatai Sevi*, 575.

and above this, the editorial changes seem considerably less dramatic when situated within the context of *Zizath novel zvi* as an entire book. *Zizath novel zvi* contains four parts, of which the first two constitute by far the largest portion of the work. Part 1 recounts the movement from the first reports of the Messiah's annunciation up until the news of his conversion to Islam, and part 2 recounts the movement after the conversion. Throughout nearly the entirety of part 1, Sasportas took great pains to preserve the possibility of Sabbetai Zevi as the Messiah and Nathan of Gaza as a prophet. He repeatedly emphasized the importance of his own doubt and contrasted it with the certainty of the believers. Both those letters he edited and those he left unedited show him in the throes of a struggle to establish the empirical facts themselves and the correct interpretation of them. In the initial months, roughly from December 1665 until April 1666, a considerable portion of the period covered by part 1, Sasportas repeatedly described himself as a possible believer in Sabbetai Zevi as the Messiah. The crucial period in the resolution of Sasportas's doubt seems to have been the spring and summer of 1666, as reports of Sabbetai Zevi's antinomian behavior increased both in their frequency and in their reliability. The tenor of Sasportas's prose changed dramatically after the conversion of Sabbetai Zevi to Islam. In part 1 he repeatedly referred to Sabbetai Zevi as a rabbi and attempted to understand his behavior; in parts 2 through 4, he appended imprecations to his name and condemned his character. Throughout part 1 Sasportas stressed the validity of doubt as a proper means to genuine repentance; after the conversion of the Messiah, he focused on the violation of the law perpetrated by the Sabbatians.

If the textual evidence of *Zizath novel zvi* served as one source for Scholem's description of Sasportas, an oil painting gave him an image of Sasportas's character. The Bezalel Art Museum in Jerusalem had acquired the painting through Bernard Houthakker of Amsterdam in 1951. Houthakker had obtained the painting from the Amsterdam art dealer Jacques Goudstikker, who perished in an attempt to flee the Nazis in 1940.[94] Both the artist and the subject of the painting have

---

[94]Pieter den Hollander, *Roofkunst: de zaak-Goudstikker* (Amsterdam: Meulenhoff, 2007); *Reclaimed: Paintings from the Collection of Jacques Goudstikker*, ed. Peter C. Sutton (New Haven, CT: Yale University Press, 2008).

been the focus of considerable debate. Goudstikker had received a certificate in 1928 that attributed the painting to Isaac Luttichuys. Bernd Ebert has rejected this attribution, stating that the painting bears none of the hallmarks of Luttichuys.[95]

The painting may not have been by Luttichuys, but did it depict Sasportas? Between 1928 and 1930 J. S. Da Silva Rosa, Houthakker, and Jac. Zwarts all discussed the image of Sasportas in seventeenth-century Dutch paintings and engravings and implied with varying degrees of certitude that the subject of this oil painting was indeed Sasportas. In 1999 Judy Schagen cast doubt on this possibility.[96]

Sasportas is the likely subject for two reasons. The first is the painting's date, and the second is the image itself. Ebert rejected the attribution to Luttichuys but dated the painting to 1671. Sasportas had returned to Amsterdam from Hamburg in the summer of 1671, and he was thus present in the city for at least part of the year in which the painting is thought to have been done. Moreover, there is the text depicted in the portrait: the book in the sitter's hands is open to chapter 28 of Ezekiel.[97] Repeatedly Sasportas described himself to Sabbatians as a "lacerating thorn" because of his persistent criticism of their belief.[98] He did so twice in *Zizath novel zvi* itself. The phrase "lacerating thorn" appears only once in the Bible: in Ezekiel 28:24. The figure in the painting, dressed like a cleric, holds a Bible open to the chapter that Sasportas used as the source of his own self-description.

From the standpoint of art historians, the attribution and the subject of the painting remain unresolved, but Scholem was absolutely certain that it depicted the seventeenth-century polemicist. The portrait gave Scholem an image corroborating his own judgment of Sasportas:

The portrait shows a stern and dour face, looking out with shrewd and unfriendly eyes: the face of a Jewish "Grand Inquisitor." The same basic

---

[95] Bernd Ebert, *Simon und Isaack Luttichuys: Monographie mit kritischem Werkverzeichnis* (Munich: Deutscher Kunstverlag, 2009), 622–623.

[96] J. S. da Silva Rosa, "Een geschilderd portret van Chagam Jacob Sasportas ontdekt," *De Vrijdagawond* 5 (1928): 131–134; Bernard Houthakker, "Bij de Portretten van Chagam Sa(s)portas," *De Vrijdagawond* 5 (1928): 134–136; Jac. Zwarts, "Een portret van Haham Jacob Sasportas door Nicolaas Maes," *Oude Kunst* (1930): 215–221; Judy Schagen, "Sasportas's Portraits: The Final Word!?" *SR* 33 (1999): 190–194.

[97] Safi Handler, *Musaf Ha-aretz*, 5 April 2013, 48–49.

[98] Sasportas, *ZNZ*, 70 and 131–132. For another instance, see Tishby, "Letters by Rabbi Jacob Sasportas," 156.

qualities of harshness, irascibility, arrogance, and fanaticism are much in evidence in his letters on the Sabbatian movement.[99]

The model of an inquisitor suggests a regime of clerical power. Although Scholem was well aware that Sasportas lacked an official position during the peak of the Sabbatian movement, he nonetheless associated him with the rabbinate that had the power to enforce the law.

Scholem despised Sasportas and had little trouble stating so unequivocally. It would be shortsighted to read his *Sabbatai Sevi* entirely as a condemnation of Sasportas. While one gets the sense that Scholem would spare no opportunity to criticize Sasportas and did not shy away from open assault, this pertains almost entirely to the places in *Sabbatai Sevi* where Scholem discussed Sasportas openly and directly. If one reads the entirety of the work with Sasportas's criticism of Sabbatianism in mind, a somewhat different and less one-sided picture emerges. One of Scholem's central insights in the work was the parallel he drew between Sabbatianism and early Christianity in general and the apostasy of Sabbetai Zevi and the crucifixion of Jesus in particular. Sasportas himself dwelled repeatedly on the parallels between Sabbatianism and Christianity. What is more, Scholem had a certain admiration for Sasportas's clarity of vision: "The same logic of paradox would serve to justify the Messiah's strange actions before his apostasy, as well as his subsequent apostasy. Sasportas saw the seed of schism and heresy long before the believers themselves suspected it."[100] Scholem seemed to want to have it both ways. On the one hand, Sasportas represented the intransigence of the law, the embodiment of rabbinic Orthodoxy that rejected all innovation as such; on the other hand, Scholem repeatedly wanted to show that Sasportas was in fact no such thing at all.

When *Sabbatai Sevi* appeared in print, it was subject to some of the most severe criticism Scholem would ever receive. Three critics—Baruch Kurzweil, R. J. Zwi Werblowsky, and Tishby—called attention to Scholem's depiction of Sasportas. In his wickedly titled review, Werblowsky accused Scholem of intellectual anarchism. In an aside to his larger criticism, Werblowsky posed a rhetorical question:

[99] Scholem, *Sabbatai Sevi*, 566–567.
[100] Ibid., 583.

And what about our evaluation of individuals, the "villains of the piece" such as Sasportas? Was he a simple dogmatist, just a quarrelsome and difficult man, or perhaps he had a bit of that spark of Jewish history which was enriched by history itself?[101]

Scholem had played a critical role in recruiting Werblowsky to the Hebrew University only a few years earlier, and they had already discussed the possibility of Werblowsky translating *Sabbatai Sevi* into English when this review appeared. Scholem did not respond publicly to Werblowsky. Instead, in a blistering letter that he never sent, Scholem rejected his defense of Sasportas wholeheartedly: "For example, I have enormous respect for Sasportas's foresight, and I said so explicitly, but this should not prevent me from expressing my opinion that I think he was a completely unsympathetic sage."[102]

In the pages of *Ha-aretz*, the literary critic Baruch Kurzweil wrote a two-part review of Scholem's *Sabbatai Sevi* that subsequently appeared in a volume of his essays.[103] Kurzweil had been an early critic of Agnon as well as a recipient of Schocken's patronage. His academic appointment was at Bar-Ilan University rather than the Hebrew University, and he remained somewhat apart from Scholem and his circle. In his review, Kurzweil saw through Scholem's claims to objectivity at the outset of *Sabbatai Sevi* and called him on it publicly. He declared that Scholem had applied a double standard in his treatment of Sasportas, whom he accused of falsifying his correspondence, as compared with Nathan of Gaza, whose rewriting Scholem refused to criticize, much

[101] "Reflections on 'Sabbetai Sevi' by G. Scholem" (Hebrew), *Molad* 112 (1957): 539–546. Citation at 545. The phrase "villains of the piece" appears in English in the original. The title alludes to Scholem's "Reflections on Jewish Studies" (Hebrew), *Luah ha-Aretz*, 1944, 94–112; reprinted in *Devarim bego* (Tel Aviv: Am Oved, 1976), 2:385–403.

[102] אני למשל מעריך מאוד, ואמרתי זאת בפירוש, את כוח ראיית הנולד של החכם ששפורטש, מה שלא מנע ממני להביע דעתי שעדיין אני מחזיק בה שזהו חכם בלתי סימפתי.

The letter appeared as an article, "The Faithful of Israel in Their Generation" (Hebrew), in Scholem, *Od Davar*, ed. Avraham Shapira (Tel Aviv: Am Oved, 1989), 98–104, citation at 101; and as a letter in Scholem, *Briefe II*, 38–45 (Ger.), and 242–250 (Heb.), German translation on 41, Hebrew on 246; in both publications, Werblowksy's name did not appear as the addressee. On Scholem's decision not to send the letter, see Zadoff, "The Debate between Baruch Kurzweil and Gershom Scholem," 347–348; on Werblowsky as a possible translator into English, see 345n206.

[103] "Notes on 'Sabbetai Sevi' by Gershom Scholem" (Hebrew), *Ha-aretz*, 25 September 1957, 2 October 1957, reprinted in *Ba-ma-avak al erkhe ha-yahadut* (Jerusalem: Schocken, 1969), 99–134. On this exchange, see, in addition to Zadoff's aforementioned article, David Myers, "The Scholem-Kurzweil Debate and Modern Jewish Historiography," *Modern Judaism* 6 (1986): 261–286.

less indict as forgery.[104] Kurzweil understood that Scholem's pose of neutrality masked a seething contempt for the law, and that Sasportas, more than any other figure in the history of Sabbatianism, represented the law. Toward Kurzweil's attack, Scholem maintained a contemptuous public silence. In a letter he wrote to Kurzweil a year and a half later, Scholem made no mention of Sasportas.[105]

If Werblowsky was a close colleague who had dared to criticize Scholem in public, and Kurzweil an intellectual who used the most important newspaper in Israel to do the same, Tishby had been Scholem's student. In a letter written in March 1957, Tishby described to Scholem his initial reading of *Sabbatai Sevi* and conveyed Agnon's congratulations on its appearance. He mentioned that he had disagreements, big and small, but that he would wait to share them until his review for *Tarbiz* had appeared.[106] Tishby's review, unlike Kurzweil's or even Werblowsky's, came from someone who had immersed himself in the sources of Sabbatianism. He was writing neither an opinion piece for the press nor a notice about the book for a literary journal. His review took the form of a substantial essay of over thirty pages. It appeared in 1959 and incorporated some of his own responses to the reviews by Kurzweil and Werblowsky.[107] Tishby conceded to Scholem that Sasportas was a difficult and even irascible figure who pursued honor beyond the veneer of humility. On the substantive issue of Sasportas's editorial practices, he took issue with Scholem, going so far as to retract one of his own arguments put forth in the introduction to *Zizath novel zvi*.[108] Upon closer examination of the evidence, Tishby concluded not only that Sasportas had never been a complete believer in Sabbeti Zevi, but also that even at the height of his confusion, he never completely overcame his doubt. Thus the editorial changes introduced into later versions of his letters did not amount so much to forgery as to a shift

---

[104] "Notes on 'Sabbetai Sevi' by Gershom Scholem," 131–132.

[105] Scholem to Kurzweil, 12 April 1959, in Scholem, *Briefe II*, 50–52 (Ger.), 252–254 (Heb.). On the lack of public response by Scholem to Kurzweil, see Zadoff, "The Debate between Baruch Kurzweil and Gershom Scholem," 340–351. In addition to the material discussed by Zadoff, see the footnote in the English translation of *Sabbatai Sevi*, 125n53.

[106] Tishby to Scholem, 29 March 1957, in Gershom Scholem Papers, Arc. 4o 1599 2654 file on Isaiah Tishby.

[107] "On Gershom Scholem's Approach to the Study of Sabbatianism" (Hebrew), *Tarbiz* 28 (1959): 101–133, reprinted in *Netive emunah u-minut* (Jerusalem: Magnes Press, 1964), 235–275.

[108] Tishby, "On Gershom Scholem's Approach to the Study of Sabbatianism," 258–262; and see 262n19 for his response to Schatz's review of his edition.

in accent and emphasis. Sasportas's planned trip to Palestine in the spring of 1666, of which Scholem had made so much, had been conceived after he concluded that Sabbetai Zevi was not the Messiah. Tishby posited that this aborted journey may have been Sasportas's attempt to gather information rather than, as Scholem had represented it, a pilgrimage to his Messiah. In short, Tishby both amplified Kurzweil's and Werblowsky's criticism of Scholem's Sasportas and substantively revised his own position. He did so with a thorough understanding of Sasportas's writing practices. Who better than Tishby, Sasportas's modern editor, was qualified to judge? Scholem's response appeared in a footnote to Werblowsky's English translation published in 1973: "In his review of the Hebrew edn. of the present book, Tishby has taken issue with some of the views expressed here; cf. *Ta[r]biz*, XXVIII (1958–1959), 119–123, trying to defend Sasportas. As I am not convinced of the validity of his strictures, I have not changed my presentation."[109] Scholem had made up his mind.

What explains Scholem's vitriol toward Sasportas? The English edition of *Sabbatai Sevi* contains numerous instances of Scholem revising his initial judgment or evaluation based on the appearance of new evidence or the reinterpretation of prior arguments. Throughout his career, Scholem repeatedly revised his own conclusions, perhaps most significantly on the question of the *Zohar*'s authorship. Why was Scholem so adamant in his indictment of Sasportas? To ask this question raises a number of critical issues: What did Sabbetai Zevi and the Sabbatian movement represent for Scholem, and where did Sasportas fit in within this schema? Any attempt to grapple with this question seems inevitably bound to fail. Scholem was far too ironic about his own project and far too self-conscious about his own scholarly practices to allow for any neat synthesis of what Sabbatianism meant to him. Nonetheless, a number of themes emerge. One is the antinomianism of Sabbatian messianism. Both the Messiah himself with his strange actions and his prophet Nathan with his elaborate and elegant theological explanations of Sabbetai Zevi's behavior provided Scholem with the "anarchic breeze" he found so intoxicating in Jewish messianism. One of Scholem's greatest achievements was his ability to write the history of Jewish mysticism independent of the law. Nearly all the protagonists

---

[109] Scholem, *Sabbatai Sevi*, 567n252.

in his history of the Jewish mystical tradition prior to the modern period were rabbis, and Scholem was still able to write about Kabbalah as if it were distinct from the law. The story of Sabbetai Zevi as Scholem told it was a triumphant and tragic rejection of the law.

Sabbatianism was also an assault on reason. The principal villains of Scholem's youth, Saadia Gaon, Maimonides, and Hermann Cohen, all subscribed to a religion of reason. They all also had a distinct dislike of disorder. Sabbetai Zevi and the messianic enthusiasm that spread in his name constituted a distinct threat to the intellectual and social order of early modern Jewish life. The Sabbatian prophets and ideologues from Nathan of Gaza at the height of the movement all the way to Jacob Frank in the eighteenth century had little interest in the elevation of reason as a guiding principle in Jewish public life. They valued their own experience of revelation rather than the heavy mantle of tradition. They celebrated the revolutionary present rather than the burdensome past.

The prophets of disorder were also ineluctably and irreducibly Jewish. In the long opening chapter of *Sabbatai Sevi*, Scholem mapped out the background and underlying causes of the messianic movement. With a wave of the hand he dismissed the notion that Sabbatianism was conditioned by social factors. He stressed that the enthusiasm cut across class lines and geographic borders. The one external factor that Scholem recognized, the expulsion of the Jews from Spain, triggered a revolution in the history of Jewish thinking about the apocalypse. Kabbalah and messianism, which had remained distinct spheres of life throughout the Middle Ages, suddenly became critical components of the best-articulated and most accepted form of Jewish theology: Lurianic Kabbalah. The spread of Luria's teachings, from a Safed that had declined in significance to the entirety of the Jewish world in the early decades of the seventeenth century, rendered it an interpretation of history that actually constituted a factor in history. On the penultimate page of the chapter, Scholem concluded decisively, "The messianic awakening was nourished from internal sources."[110] The immanence of Sabbatian messianism within the Jewish tradition remained a critical component of Scholem's argument. He cautioned against defining the

---

[110]Ibid., 101. On Scholem and immanence, see Amnon Raz-Krakotzkin, " 'Without regard for external considerations,' The Question of Christianity in Scholem and Baer's Writings" (Hebrew), *Jewish Studies* 38 (1998): 73–96.

"Jewishness" of a particular period in history in relation to any criteria dependent upon dogma. Rather, the "Jewishiness" should be evaluated "solely by what sincere Jews do, in fact, believe, or—at least—consider to be legitimate possibilities."[111]

Sasportas thus posed an extremely serious problem for the integrity of Scholem's history of Sabbatianism. His writing in *Zizath novel zvi* and his persona within the Sephardic Diaspora dissolved the binary between law and mysticism that was so critical for the construction of Scholem's scholarly edifice. Sasportas had a profound fear of disorder and chaos. He upheld Maimonides, both as the author of a law code and as a philosopher of reason, as the figure whose principles one ought to use to evaluate the validity of Sabbatianism. If Scholem was at pains to withhold his own scholarly judgment on the "Jewishness" of a particular phenomenon, Sasportas had no such qualms. He wrote from within the tradition and spoke in its name against Sabbetai Zevi.

TEITELBAUM'S SASPORTAS

If Scholem and Tishby had engaged in something akin to lower criticism in their editing and analysis of Sasportas, Joel Teitelbaum employed analysis similar to higher criticism in his use of Sasportas. If Scholem saw Sabbatianism as generative of a crisis and fundamental rupture in Jewish history and turned to Sasportas as a witness to this crisis, Teitelbaum experienced the middle decades of the twentieth century as a crisis in and of itself. To him, Sasportas was not an intellectual instrument with which to reconstruct the past; rather, he functioned as a moral resource that served as a guide for the proper rabbinic response to religious messianism in the present. Scholem's and Teitelbaum's readings of *Zizath novel zvi* thus placed Sasportas squarely at the heart of a central debate in modern Jewish life: Zionism.

Born into a Hasidic family in the town of Sziget in the Habsburg Empire, Teitelbaum received a thorough rabbinic education.[112] As his

---

[111] Scholem, *Sabbatai Sevi*, 283. See Paweł Maciejko, introduction to *Sabbatian Heresy: Writings on Mysticism, Messianism, and the Origins of Jewish Modernity* (Waltham, MA: Brandeis University Press, 2017), xi–xxxiii.

[112] On Teitelbaum, see Allan L. Nadler, "Piety and Politics: The Case of the Satmar Rebbe," *Judaism* 31 (1982): 135–152; Menachem Keren-Kratz, "R. Joel Teitelbaum, ha-Rebbe mi-Satmar (1887–1979): Biografiyah" (PhD diss., Tel Aviv University, 2013).

father's second son, he could not take up the family mantle as rebbe of Sziget. While still a relatively young man he moved to Szatamár, where he quickly established a reputation as a rabbinic firebrand but did not have an official position as a rabbi. In 1910 he was appointed rabbi of Ilsova, a small town roughly sixty miles away, but continued to maintain a residence in Szatamár, where he spent the duration of World War I. After the breakup of the Habsburg Empire, the town of Szatamár became Satu Mare, Romania. In 1926 Teitelbaum became rabbi of Carei, and in 1928 he was invited to become the rabbi of Satu Mare. Because of considerable opposition to his militant traditionalism, Teitelbaum did not take up the position until 1934. For the next decade Teitelbaum served the town as rabbi, for the first six years under Romanian rule and from 1940 until 1944 as part of Hungary. When the Nazis invaded Hungary in 1944, Teitelbaum was among the 1,685 Jews selected by Hungarian Zionist Rudolf Kastner to avoid deportation. While most of Teitelbaum's Hasidim were sent to Auschwitz, he spent several months in Bergen-Belsen before reaching safety in Switzerland in December 1944. After a brief period in Jerusalem, Teitelbaum immigrated to the United States and settled in Williamsburg, Brooklyn, in 1946. Through a combination of his immense learning, personal charisma, and radical sectarianism, Teitelbaum led the Brooklyn Satmars through a period of burgeoning growth and rapid expansion beyond its new center in Williamsburg. Over the last third of his long life, he succeeded in reestablishing Hungarian Hasidism in the United States.

Jewish Orthodoxy in modern Europe differed widely in time and place. One common feature shared by many of its varied strands and inherited from premodern tradition-bound Jewry was a persistent passivity with respect to planning the future of the Jewish life.[113] This manifested itself as a preference for political quietism and a resistance to Jewish involvement in politics. For many Orthodox rabbis of the nineteenth and twentieth centuries, the Jewish question that gnawed at Jews throughout Europe was simply not a question. They would continue to live their lives according to divine law. Only the Messiah's arrival, a prospect perpetually deferred to the distant and endlessly receding horizon of the future, would necessitate the formation of a Jewish commonwealth as a Jewish political entity. This too was a project deeply reactive to modernity rather than a simple continuation of

---

[113] Jacob Katz, "Orthodoxy in Historical Perspective," *Studies in Contemporary Jewry* 2 (1986): 9.

tradition as maintained by the Orthodox themselves.[114] This ideology of traditionalism presented deep-seated opposition to political Zionism. The language and the sources with which Orthodox rabbis in Europe articulated this opposition drew on the tradition of Jewish messianism. Zionism, in all of its varied forms, constituted a form of "hastening the end," or messianic activism. A political entity established by Jews under the godless aegis of secular nationalism was nothing short of anathema to traditionalist-minded rabbinic thinkers. When faced with the continuing success of political Zionism, the Orthodox rabbinate was forced to respond. Some adopted a form of political compromise and sought to negotiate a type of autonomy within the nascent Zionist entity even if they found the ideology of Zionism abhorrent. Others drew on the Jewish tradition itself and justified Zionism in theological terms. If the Jewish settlement in Palestine and the eventual establishment of a state did not constitute the arrival of the Messiah, then it served as "the beginnings of redemption." Still others viewed the history of modern Zionism through a typological reading of Jewish messianism.[115]

Teitelbaum was one of the most articulate exponents of this view. To him, modern political Zionism and the state it generated was the latest and most recent form of false messianism.[116] In 1959 at the age of seventy-two, Teitelbaum published *Va-yo-el moshe*, which consisted of a "treatise on the three oaths." Over the next two decades, he reissued and expanded the work a number of times until it eventually contained two other treatises: "the treatise on the settlement of the land of Israel" and "the treatise on the sacred tongue." *Va-yo-el moshe* contained elements of a textual commentary, legal monograph, and theological polemic. Teitelbaum used the word *ma-amar*, roughly equivalent to the term "treatise," to refer to the three constitutive parts that made up the later editions of the work, and *kuntres*, a word that has the connotation of a pamphlet, to refer to various sections of "the trea-

[114] Michael K. Silber, "The Emergence of Ultra-Orthodoxy: The Invention of a Tradition," in *The Uses of Tradition: Jewish Continuity in the Modern Era*, ed. Jack Wertheimer (Cambridge, MA: Harvard University Press, 1992), 23–84.

[115] Aviezer Ravitzky, *Messianism, Zionism, and Jewish Religious Radicalism* (Chicago: University of Chicago Press, 1996).

[116] David Sorotzkin, "Building the Earthly and Destroying the Heavenly: The Satmar Rabbi and the Radical Orthodox School of Thought" (Hebrew), in *Eretz yisrael ba-hagut ha-yehudit ba-meah ha-esrim*, ed. Aviezer Ravitzky (Jerusalem: Ben-Zvi Institute, 2004), 133–167; Eli Gurfinkel, "*Nezah yisrael* by the Maharal of Prague and the Satmar Rebbe's Concept of Redemption" (Hebrew), *Daat* 78 (2015): 77–91.

tise on the three oaths." *Va-yo-el moshe* contained elements of a legal ruling and rabbinic decision on matters of the law. At a number of points in the book, Teitelbaum essentially limited the scope of the work by stating, "I have come in this *kuntres* only to decide the essential law as it pertains to participation in government and in elections."[117] The legal nature of the work further manifested itself in the type of source material utilized. *Va-yo-el moshe* drew repeatedly on responsa literature and on legal codes. At the same time, Teitelbaum made a revealing statement in the introduction of the work when he stated, "I have come in this *kuntres* only to clarify the view of the Torah."[118] The phrase translated as "the view of the Torah" had equivalents in Hebrew, *Daat torah*, and in Yiddish, *Da-as toyre*, and was a technical term in the middle of the twentieth century that referred to the ability of rabbis to issue authoritative opinions on secular and political matters.[119] Teitelbaum's use of this term, which was associated with the political movement of Orthodox Jewry known as Agudas Yisroel, may well have been a polemical rejection of the attempt by other Orthodox Jews who had collaborated with the Zionists to appropriate the ability to issue such opinions.[120]

The title of the first treatise referred to a passage in the Babylonian Talmud in which God had made three oaths:

> What is the purpose of these three oaths? One that Israel shall not ascend the wall [of the Holy Land]; one that the Holy One, blessed be He, adjured Israel not to rebel against the nations of the world; and one that the Holy One, blessed be He, urged the idolaters not to oppress Israel overly much.[121]

---

[117] ולא באתי בקונטרס זה אלא לבאר עיקר ההלכה של השתתפות למלוכה ולבחירות.
Sefer va-yo-el moshe (Brooklyn, NY: Sander Deutsch, 1978), 146.

[118] ולא באתי בקונטרס זה אלא לברר דעת תורה.
Ibid., 8.

[119] Lawrence Kaplan, "*Daas Torah*: A Modern Conception of Rabbinic Authority," in *Rabbinic Authority and Personal Autonomy*, ed. Moshe Sokol (Northvale, NJ: J. Aronson, 1992), 1–60; Jacob Katz, "Da'at Torah: The Unqualified Authority Claimed for Halakhists," *Jewish History* 11 (1997): 41–50.

[120] Gershon C. Bacon, "Daat Torah and the Birth Pangs of the Messiah: On the Ideology of the *Agudas yisroel* in Poland" (Hebrew), *Tarbiz* 52 (1983): 497–508. For Teitelbaum's denunciation of Agudas Yisroel, see *Sefer va-yo-el moshe*, 111, 136, 144–145, and 147.

[121] ג' שבועות הללו למה שלא אחת שלא יעלו ישראל בחומה ואחת שהשביע הקדוש ברוך הוא את ישראל שלא ימרדו
באומות העולם ואחת שהשביע הקדוש ברוך הוא את העובדי כוכבים שלא ישתעבדו בהן בישראל יותר מדי
BT Ketubot 111a. See Ravitzky, *Messianism, Zionism, and Jewish Religious Radicalism*, 211–236; David N. Myers, "'Commanded War': Three Chapters in the 'Military' History of Satmar Hasidism," *Journal of the American Academy of Religion* 81 (2013): 311–356.

Teitelbaum used this Talmudic passage as his point of departure to make a specific argument about modern Jewish politics, one that rejected Zionism in all of its forms and argued for politically subservient pacifism. From his perspective, Jewish political activism that entailed the settlement of the Holy Land and the establishment of a Jewish political entity on its soil violated the first of the oaths: not to ascend the wall.

In *Va-yo-el moshe* Teitelbaum employed a typology of the Messiah that included Bar Kokhba, the Messiah in twelfth-century Yemen described in Maimonides's epistle, and Sabbetai Zevi. In order to construct this typology, Teitelbaum drew entirely on Jewish sources. For Bar Kokhba, whom he referred to as Ben Koziba, he cited the passages in rabbinic literature that described the rabbinic embrace and then rejection of the second-century rebel; for the Messiah in twelfth-century Yemen, he drew on Maimonides; for the history of Sabbetai Zevi, he turned to a number of sources, including Jacob Emden and Moses Hagiz. Teitelbaum had a keen sense of historical time, and much of his work depended on a negative response to the question of temporality in the history of Judaism. The modern period represented not a break with the past but the perpetuation of Jewish life in exile. One of his crucial points in his critique of Zionism was the difference in degree between the false messianism of mid-twentieth-century Zionism and prior episodes in Jewish history. To Teitelbaum, Ben Koziba "was an awesome and holy man who was worthy of prophecy in all of the attributes described by Maimonides, of blessed memory." Akiba, the great rabbinic sage described by much later rabbinic accounts as a believer in Bar Kokhba, required salvaging:

> When I stood at the grave of R. Akiba while visiting Tiberias this past summer (1959), an idea occurred to me that would explain R. Akiba's words and show that he did not err but rather, at that time, God had occasioned an important reason for interpreting the [Bar Kokhba event] as he did. I thought about a good way of explaining this but do not wish to elaborate on it now.[122]

Akiba's behavior, aberrant though it was, could still an induce an explanation that would render it normative.

<hr>

[122] ובעת שעמדתי על קברו של רבי עקיבא כשהייתי בקיץ הזה [תשי"ט] בטבריי' עלה בדעתי איזה רעיון לתרץ דברי ר"ע שלא טעה אלא הי' סיבה גדולה מן השמים לדרוש אז כן, וחשבתי טעם נכון בדבר, אלא שאין רצוני להאריך בזה כעת.

Sefer va-yo-el moshe, 50.

Akiba may have been wrong about Bar Kokhba, but he had not done away with the law. The same could not be said of Sabbetai Zevi, a figure who appeared in a number of discussions in *Va-yo-el moshe*. Fundamentally, Teitelbaum viewed Sabbetai Zevi as simply another instance in the history of false messiahs. In a discussion of repentance, Teitelbaum described him as follows:

> Although Sabbetai Zevi, may his name be erased, led several people to repent, and although it may have been many people, he permitted the violation of several biblical commandments and did not lead the majority of Israel to repentance, but rather only a certain number, and, in the end, it was all revealed as a lie, and all those who followed him fell into heresy.[123]

Sabbetai Zevi and his followers broke the law and did so publicly. To Teitelbaum it was no surprise that he and his followers came to a bad end.

At a later point in the treatise, Teitelbaum emphasized a different aspect of Sabbetai Zevi so as to set him in contrast to twentieth-century Zionists. He began the section by noting the pervasive character of Sabbatian messianism.

> When the great and awful confusion caused by the sect of Sabbetai Zevi, may his name be erased, began, it led nearly everyone astray, even great eminences who lived in those days. But Rabbi Jacob Sasportas, of blessed memory, who was then the great eminence of his age in wisdom and holiness—and I even saw that some scholars of his own generation described him using the attributes sacred and divine—he was the first and chief opponent to him [Sabbetai Zevi] and he risked his life against all those who rose against him for this reason, and afterward he composed the book *Zizath novel zvi* in four sections in which he described all the events that occurred about Sabbetai Zevi.[124]

---

[123] ואף שהש"ץ ימ"ש החזיר בתשובה כמה אנשים, ראשית דאף בעת שהחזיר בתשובה הרבה אנשים הי' איזה איסורי דאורייתא שהתיר, גם לא החזיר בתשובה את הכלל ישראל כ"א איזה סכום אנשים ולבסוף נתגלה שהכל הי' שקר ויצאו לתרבות רעה כל הנגררים אחריו.
Ibid., 101.

[124] וכאשר התחילה המבוכה הנוראה מכת ש"ץ ימ"ש בתחלה הטעה כמעט את כל העולם כולו, אף גדולים עצומים שהיו בימים ההם. והמהר"י ששפורטש ז"ל שהי' אז גדול הדור בגאונות וקדושה יתירה, וראיתי מחכמי דורו שמתארים אותו בתואר הקדוש האלקי, הוא הי' הראש והראשון שעמד במלחמה חזקה נגדו והפקיר את חייו נגד כל הקמים עליו בזה, וחיבר אח"כ ס' ציצת נובל צבי ד' חלקים, אשר בו יסופר כל המאורעות שעברו וחלפו בענין הש"ץ.
Ibid., 167. On Sasportas as a source for Teitelbaum, see Nadler, "Piety and Politics," 142; Aviezer Ravitzky, "Religious Radicalism and Political Messianism in Israel," in *Religious Radicalism and*

There follows a long citation from the opening pages of *Zizath novel zvi*. Teitelbaum upheld Sasportas as the lone voice of opposition in the upheaval generated by Sabbetai Zevi and his followers.

Teitelbaum's description of Sabbetai Zevi rendered Sasportas's opposition all the more impressive:

> The reason why the majority of the children of Israel were drawn toward him was that Sabbetai Zevi was well versed in the Talmud, the legal writings, and all the writings of Isaac Luria, all this was well known to him as a youth of fifteen. In addition, his worship by means of fasts, self-mortification, and songs of praise was truly amazing to all who saw him.[125]

The portrait of Sabbetai Zevi sketched by Teitelbaum combined various aspects of his persona well attested by historical sources, such as his love of song and penchant for theatricality, with a somewhat embellished description of his learning and erudition. Teitelbaum exaggerated in order to make a point: the people of Israel perpetually yearn to hear of the coming redemption. It was hardly surprising that news of a learned rabbi who had called upon them to repent and informed them that the Messiah had arrived had led them astray.

Teitelbaum praised Sabbetai Zevi's piety and learning only in the service of a polemical rejection of contemporary Zionism:

> The amazing thing is that even though this sect of redemption and falsehood in our own day did not begin with the rigor of Torah [study] and prayer or with the call on the people to repent, as did Sabbetai Zevi, not even in the slightest; but rather, from beginning to end, everything they do is designed to destroy the law, may the Lord have mercy. Furthermore, they fill the entire world with heresy and sectarianism, may the Lord have mercy; nonetheless the entire world strays after them.[126]

Politics in the Middle East, ed. Emmanuel Sivan and Menachem Friedman (Albany: SUNY Press, 1990), 17.

[125] והסיבה שנמשכו רוב בני ישראל הי' כי הש"ץ הי' בקי בכל הש"ס ופוסקים וכל כתבי האר"י הכל הי' רגיל על לשונו עוד בבחרותו בהיותו בן ט"ו שנים, גם עבודתו בתעניתים וסיגופים ושירות ותשבחות הי' עד להפליא בעיני כל רואיו.

Sefer va-yo-el moshe, 168.

[126] ולפלא שאותה הכת של גאולה של שקר בימינו לא התחילו כלל בכח תורה ועבודה ולעשות בעלי תשובה כמו הש"ץ, לא מיני' ולא מקצתו, אלא מתחלה ועד סוף כל מעשיהם להרס הדת ר"ל וממלאים את כל העולם במינות וכפירה נוראה ר"ל, ואעפי"כ טועין כל העולם אחריהם.

Ibid.

For Teitelbaum, modern political Zionism was a manifestation of false messianism, and a particularly virulent one at that. At the very least, Sabbetai Zevi had come from within the tradition. He was well versed in the writings of the law and had complete control over the corpus of Lurianic Kabbalah. Prior to his outburst of antinomian behavior, he had called upon the people of Israel to repent, which constituted a form of genuine piety. Political Zionism had no roots in the Jewish tradition, precisely the opposite of what Scholem had argued. It constituted the most noxious form of Jews imitating the behavior and customs of the gentiles. It sought to uproot the law.

Teitelbaum cited Sasportas as one of several rabbinic predecessors who articulated opposition to the premature hastening of the end. The most authoritative voice of rabbinic reserve about the messianic idea remained Maimonides, whose law code and "Epistle to Yemen" Teitelbuam drew upon throughout *Va-yo-el moshe*. To a certain extent, Teitelbaum viewed Sabbatianism as an epiphenomenon in the history of Jewish messianism. It served as a lesson about the consequences of public enthusiasm and mass hysteria. In this context, Sasportas was an ideal witness, as he had lived through the events he described; however, he was not the only articulate opponent of Sabbatianism. Teitelbaum adduced him in conjunction with Moses Hagiz and Jacob Emden. Teitelbaum appears to have cited Sasportas in the edition of *Zizath novel zvi* prepared by Emden and in *Ohel ya-akov*. To the extent that his citations allow one to identify his sources, Teitelbaum does not appear to have used Tishby's edition.[127] Nonetheless, one of Teitelbaum's statements should give pause. When he mentioned Sasportas, he referred to *Zizath novel zvi* as a work in four parts. Sasportas's editors prior to Tishby—namely, David Meldola and Jacob Emden—as well as the printers of the nineteenth-century reprint of Emden's edition, were all well aware of the fact that they were dealing with an abridged version of *Zizath novel zvi*. Meldola explicitly stated that the portions of the work he edited and published all came from the first section. Tishby's edition of Sasportas, which appeared five years prior to *Va-yo-el moshe*, printed all four sections of *Zizath novel zvi* for the first time.

[127] The reference to *Zizath novel zvi* in *Va-yo-el-moshe*, 167, appears in Emden's edition of *Zizath novel zvi* on 3b and in Tishby's edition on 17. Teitelbaum's other references to Sasportas in this work are to *Ohel ya-akov*, see *Va-yo-el moshe*, 125, 129.

One can assume, however, that Teitelbaum adduced Sasportas via Emden, an author he frequently mentioned in the same breath. One should not overestimate the importance Sasportas had for Teitelbaum. He could have, and almost certainly would have, made his theological polemic against Zionism without him. Nonetheless, it would be equally foolish to dismiss Sasportas as just another one of the sources that Teitelbaum cited for the sake of demonstrating his own erudition. Teitelbaum had clearly read Sasportas and, what is more, saw in him something of a kindred spirit. Sasportas had criticized Sabbetai Zevi and the messianic movement he inspired as it was occurring. Teitelbaum saw his own ongoing criticism of Zionism in a similar light. He too was an embattled lone voice in the chorus of Zionist enthusiasts. Over and above this, Teitelbaum continued to cite Sasportas and to draw upon him as a source of inspiration. In his "treatise on the sacred tongue," a polemic against the Zionist attitude toward the Hebrew language that appeared in later editions of *Va-yo-el moshe*, Teitelbaum turned to Sasportas.[128] In *Kuntres al ha-geulah ve-al ha-temurah*, a pamphlet written in response to the 1967 war that referred to Israel's military victories as demonic, Teitelbaum again turned to Sasportas.[129]

Teitelbaum considered the middle of the twentieth century a period of crisis in Jewish life. This crisis had been generated by political activism in the form of Zionism. It was decidedly not a crisis precipitated by the destruction of European Jewry, including many of his own followers. In the introduction to *Va-yo-el moshe*, Teitelbaum made a specific theological argument about the Final Solution. He explained:

> The essence of the matter: over and above the great sin of violating the oath [against the settlement of the land] they [the Zionists] further defiled the house of Israel with the impurity of heresy and sectarianism. It is no wonder that "wrath has gone forth from the Lord" (Num. 17:11), as scripture has warned in the pericope of "You stand this day" ["The Lord uprooted them from their soil in anger, fury, and great wrath, and

---

[128] *Va-yo-el moshe*, 429. Oded Schechter, "'Their impure language which they have called Hebrew': Between the Sacred Tongue and Aramaic, towards a Genealogy of the Hebrew" (Hebrew), *Mi-ta-am* 2 (2005): 123–138.

[129] *Kuntres al-ha-geulah ve-al ha-temurah* (Brooklyn, NY: Sander Deutsch, 1967), 22, 100, 141. In the first of these citations, Teitelbaum cites the same passage from *Zizath novel zvi* as he had in *Va-yo-el moshe*; in the second, he cites a passage from the opening of *Zizath novel zvi* that appears both in Emden's and Tishby's edition; in the third, he cites a passage from *Ohel ya-akov*.

cast them into another land, as is still the case" (Deut. 29:27)]. And even at the time of the destruction, many great Hasidim were killed as a result of the transgressions of those who sin and caused others to sin, in our great sins. And the anger was very great indeed.[130]

Teitelbaum gestured toward an argument that would emerge with even greater clarity in *Al ha-geulah ve-al ha-temurah*. The destruction of European Jewry was divine recompense for the activist role in politics played by the Zionists in the decades leading up to World War II.[131] Quietism, not activism, was the only response to the horrors of exile. In formulating his theology of quietism, Teitelbaum drew upon the long tradition of rabbinic messianic pacificism. He traced his intellectual genealogy all the way back to Maimonides and the rabbis of the Talmud. One of the central points in his usable past was the writing of Jacob Sasportas.

[130] *Sefer va-yo-el moshe,* 7.
[131] Nadler, "Piety and Politics," 149–150.

CODA

"The finest hour of Maimonides' theory came not in the Middle Ages but in the seventeenth century: the humanists recognized the affinity between their outlook and his."[1] Thus Amos Funkenstein described the reception of Maimonides in the writings of John Spencer and Benedict Spinoza. Jacob Sasportas was no less an attentive reader of Maimonides than these contemporary humanists. In the *Code of Law* and *The Guide of the Perplexed*, Maimonides articulated a relationship between writing and crisis. For Maimonides, the crisis that served as a stimulus to his own writing, both legal and philosophical, was one of transmission. The law in the twelfth century had become so diffuse and so varied that Maimonides considered it imperative to unify and codify the Jewish legal tradition in his *Code of Law*. Similarly, the philosophical secrets of creation that God had transmitted to Moses at Sinai had been lost over the passage of time. Through his own intellect, Maimonides thought he had been able to recover these secrets. *The Guide of the Perplexed* represented his attempt to preserve these secrets in writing for a philosophically inclined reader.

The chief subject of this book, Jacob Sasportas, as well as his three most intensive readers, Jacob Emden, Gershom Scholem, and Joel

[1] Amos Funkenstein, *Theology and the Scientific Imagination: From the Middle Ages to the Seventeenth Century* (Princeton, NJ: Princeton University Press, 1986), 241.

Teitelbaum, all perceived their worlds to be in crisis. For Sasportas, the crisis in the middle of the 1660s was one of order. This manifested itself as contempt for the law. The observance of fast days, traditionally marked by sorrow and lamentation, turned into a public celebration. Jews danced in the streets to mark the arrival of the Messiah. As Sasportas watched in horror, he articulated an epistemological problem in the writing of *Zizath novel zvi*: how does one know when the Messiah has actually arrived? For a considerable amount of time Sasportas did not know. *Zizath novel zvi* records his doubts, his anxieties, his anger, and his confusion over a single year of his long life. Sasportas used all the resources of the textual tradition he called his own to make sense of the world around him, a world that a Messiah whom he had never met and who lived half a world away had turned upside down. In his attempt to answer this question, Sasportas turned to the bookshelf, reached for Maimonides, and articulated his frustration. Maimonides had outlined a scenario for the messianic age; Sabbetai Zevi and his followers were not sticking to the script. Sasportas gestured toward a position that validated his own provisional skepticism as a better path to genuine repentance than the ardent and collective certainty of the Jewish crowd. His book constitutes a chapter in the history of seventeenth-century skepticism.

Sasportas's position had an elective affinity with a position historians of science have detected in the writings of Thomas Hobbes: the solution to the problem of order was coterminous with the solution to the problem of knowledge.[2] Sasportas had much in common with Hobbes: an unrelenting opposition to received wisdom, a deep-seated fear of anarchy and disorder, a thorough command of a textual tradition, an acute sense of personal honor, and a scathing wit. In one crucial respect, however, he differed from him. "For, at the deepest level of his intellectual character, Hobbes was a system builder: what was of consuming interest to him was not this or that new discovery but the overall theory into which all the phenomena could be fitted."[3] Sasportas thought the system had already been built. God's word as interpreted in the rabbinic tradition contained the overall theory into which

[2] Steven Shapin and Simon Schaffer, *Leviathan and the Air-Pump: Hobbes, Boyle, and the Experimental Life* (Princeton, NJ: Princeton University Press, 1985), 15.

[3] Noel Malcolm, "Hobbes and the European Republic of Letters," in *Aspects of Hobbes* (Oxford: Clarendon Press, 2002), 538–539.

all of life could be fitted. As he saw it, his task was to interpret and preserve that tradition, not to construct a new system. Most of the time, Sasportas did not need to write at great length to accomplish his task. He composed short texts that served a specific occasion: a sermon to mark the death of a young student, an index to the biblical citations in the Palestinian Talmud, a response to a legal query. In 1665–1666 the messianic movement around Sabbetai Zevi presented a crisis of epistemology and of order, and Sasportas wrote at extraordinary length in an attempt to work out solutions to these problems. The writing of *Zizath novel zvi* was overtaken by events. Once the Messiah converted to Islam, the mass movement fizzled out. Sasportas consigned his book to the drawer. The question Sasportas had posed—how does one know when the Messiah has arrived?—remained.

A half century after Sasportas died and nearly a century after he composed *Zizath novel zvi*, Jacob Emden discovered a severly truncated version of the book by chance. He too had arrived in Amsterdam after being sent into exile. Emden reedited and reprinted Sasportas, thereby forging an image of Sasportas as a heresy hunter. This image may have been ill suited to a dissident such as Sasportas, but it was pitch-perfect for Emden himself. If Sasportas lived through a messianic movement as it manifested itself in social chaos, Emden lived through a hollowing out of the rabbinate. In its specific form, this meant the appointment of Jonathan Eibeschütz, a clandestine Sabbatian, to serve as the rabbi of the Ashkenazi Jews in Hamburg-Altona-Wandsbek. The controversy that ensued soon engulfed the entire European rabbinate. It also served as the primary stimulus to Emden's astonishing literary production over the last two and a half decades of his life. As an editor, anthologist, exegete, and polemicist, Emden wrote his way through the controversy.

A century and a half after Emden's death, Gershom Scholem turned to Sabbetai Zevi and the messianic movement around him. Amnon Raz-Krakotzkin has argued that Scholem's discovery of Jewish messianism in general and Sabbatianism in specific emerged as a response to the rise of Nazism.[4] Scholem's engagement with Sabbatianism, which had its antecedents in a short study about Abraham Miguel Cardoso, took full form in his landmark 1937 article "Redemption through Sin." For

---

[4]Raz-Krakotzkin, " 'Without regard for external considerations.' "

the next two decades, as war raged first in Europe and then in Palestine, Scholem immersed himself in the world of Sabbetai Zevi. The result was a two-volume Hebrew work later translated into English as *Sabbatai Sevi: The Mystical Messiah*. Sabbetai Zevi and the messianic movement around him enabled Scholem to tell a story about Jewish immanence without the law. Scholem needed Sasportas, both for the data that he provided and for the foil that he presented to Sabbetai Zevi. "The enemy is the embodiment of your own question," the poet Theodor Däubler observed.[5] In *Zizath novel zvi*, one can discern the outline of Scholem's own question about exile and redemption. In Sasportas one can sense the mirror image of Scholem: a man of astonishing erudition and restrained passion; a scholar who retreated to his study as he watched the world around him in complete horror; a rationalist with night vision.[6]

Joel Teitelbaum lived through the same geopolitical catastrophe as Scholem but reached a different conclusion about it. Instead of the nation-state as Zion, Teitelbaum chose Williamsburg. In the immediate postwar period, Teitelbaum sought to reconstitute rabbinic authority neither in Europe nor in Palestine but in the United States of America. He settled in New York City, and through the combination of personal charisma, deep learning, and good luck, he turned the Satmar Hasidim into the largest Hasidic sect in the second half of the twentieth century. Teitelbaum may have lived as a Jew in New York, but he was not a New York Intellectual. In *Va-yo-el moshe*, Teitelbaum turned to Sasportas as part of his usable past. Just as Sasportas had the courage of his convictions to speak out against the Jews of his day, nearly all of whom had become believers in Sabbetai Zevi, Teitelbaum similarly rebuked the Jews of his own time, nearly all of whom had become Zionists.

Joel Teitelbaum, Gershom Scholem, and Hugh Trevor-Roper make for strange bedfellows. In the 1950s, the same decade that Trevor-Roper began to think about the middle of the seventeenth century as a period of crisis, Scholem and Teitelbaum each turned to Sasportas in their writings about Sabbatianism and Zionism. Scholem's history of Sabba-

---

[5] Theodor Däubler as cited in Horst Bredekamp, "From Walter Benjamin to Carl Schmitt, via Thomas Hobbes," *Critical Inquiry* 25 (1999): 248.

[6] Leon Wieseltier, introduction to Lionel Trilling, *The Moral Obligation to Be Intelligent* (New York: Farrar, Straus, and Giroux, 2000), xv.

tianism had as much to do with the middle of the twentieth century as it did with the seventeenth. Sasportas was both his source and his adversary. For Teitelbaum, Sasportas was a model rabbinic controversialist. As Europe had emerged from a second Thirty Years' War, one that began in 1914 and ended in 1945, historians, scholars, and controversialists turned to the period immediately following the first Thirty Years' War, the one that began in 1618 and ended in 1648, and found a period of crisis. Books written during a period of crisis, whether Maimonides's *The Guide of the Perplexed*, Emden's *Torat ha-kenaot*, Scholem's *Sabbatai Sevi*, or Teitelbaum's *Va-yo-el moshe*, are by necessity sui generis. Like these books, *Zizath novel zvi* stands as the record of one man's struggle to speak truth to the crowd.

ACKNOWLEDGMENTS

THE DEPARTMENT OF HISTORY, the Program in Judaic Studies, the University Committee on Research in the Humanities and Social Sciences, Princeton University; William C. Jordan; Martha Himmelfarb.

The Andrew W. Mellon Foundation Fellowship for assistant professors at the Institute for Advanced Study, Princeton; Jonathan I. Israel.

The Lady Davis Fellowship Trust at the Hebrew University in Jerusalem; Moshe Sluhovsky.

The Van Leer Institute in Jerusalem; Amnon Raz-Krakotzkin.

I am grateful to Carolyn Yerkes for the gift of her loving intellect.

Daniel Abrams, Bridget Alsdorf, James Amelang, Avishai Bar-Asher, Leora Batnitzky, Adam Beaver, David A. Bell, the late Shlomo Berger, Andrew Berns, Rachel Boerjtens, Jennifer Bradley, Betsy Brown, Peter Brown, Menachem Butler, Margot Canaday, Elisheva Carlebach, Javier Castaño, Lisa Cerami, Janet Y. Chen, D'Maris Coffman, Nicola Cooney, Angela N. H. Creager, Femke Deen, Joshua Dubler, Mitch Duneier, Theodor Dunkelgrün, Ed Eigen, Noam Elcott, Lucia Frattarelli, Rahel Fronda, Yonatan Garb, Mercedes García-Arenal Rodríguez, Matt Goldish, Michael Gordin, Anthony Grafton, Molly Greene, Joseph Hacker, Dirk Hartog, Sam Haselby, Richard Kagan, Maoz Kahana, Yosef Kaplan, David S. Katz, Michelle Komie, Stephen Kotkin, Shnayer Z. Leiman, Tirtsah Levie Bernfeld, Olga Litvak, Paweł Maciejko, Hugo Martins, Yakov Meir, Yitzhak Melamed, Naphtali Meshel, Dorothea von Moltke, Henk van Nierop, Phil Nord, Ekaterina Pravilova, Ted Rabb, Elchanan Reiner, Pinchas Roth, Ishay Rozen-Zvi, David Ruderman, Marina Rustow, Lena Salaymeh, Peter Schäfer, Shlomit Steinberg, Elli Stern, Yael Sternhell, Claude B. Stuczynski, Michael Studemund-Halévy, Francesca Trivellato, Moulie Vidas, Heide Warncke, Joanna Weinberg, James Weinberger, Sean Wilentz, the late Yosef Hayim Yerushalmi.

Anonymous reader #1.

Ada Rapoport-Albert.

Nicholas de Lange.

Fred Appel, Lauren Lepow, Thalia Leaf, Princeton University Press.

Leon Wieseltier.

Peter Ochs, Vanessa Ochs, Elizabeth Ochs, Taylor Ellowitz, Rochelle Dweck, Altoon Dweck, David Schorr, Irrit Dweck, Jeronimo Romero, Rachel Dweck, Moki Schwartz, Ezra Dweck, Chen Tiferet.

Natalie Dweck.

Juliana Ochs Dweck, Harry Dweck, Emanuella Dweck.

APPENDIX:
WILL OF JACOB SASPORTAS

~

Amsterdam City Archives
Entry no. 5075: Archives of Notaries in Amsterdam
No. 2398, Not. P. Padthuysen, 7 March 1698.

1 En el nombre de Dios todo poderoso Amen
2 oy en Siette dias del mes de Março, de mil
3 y seis cientos y noventa y ocho años, antemi
4 Pedro Padthuysen Notario publico, admitido
5 por la noble Corte de Holanda, residiente en
6 Amsterdam, y en presencia delos testigos
7 adelante nombrados parecio el Sr. Rabbi Jacob
8 Saportas Predicador dela nacion judaica portu
9 guesa en esta ciudad, aquien ÿo el notario
10 doy fee que conosco, estando algo achacoso
11 en su cama, pero enteramente capas para
12 losiguiente, segun claramente constava
13 y parecia.

7 Maart 1698
1 Ÿ declaro eldho otorgante que su hixo difunto Samuel Saportas, hombre
2 de negocios que fue en su vida en Londres dispuso de sus bienes que
3 dexo, en la manera siguiente.
4 en el nombre del Dios Bendito
5 Como en esta vida no ay cosa mas cierta quela muerte y el quando
6 por permision divina alos mortales oculto, deve cada qual
7 prepararse para como Dios disponer sus cosas para con elmundo.
8 porlo qual ÿo abaxo firmado, enpresencia de testigos, estando en mi
9 entero ÿ perfecto juizio, declaro quelo contenido aqui es mi ultima
10 voluntad, y postrer testamento, dando por nulos por invalidos y
11 deningun valor, todos los testamentos, codicilios y apuntamtos
12 hechos por mi, antes de agora, tanto los que hize notarialmente,
13 como de mi propria letra, o, de qualquier otra que sehallaren
14 entremis papeles, o que, esten enpoder ajeno, pues que mi
15 voluntad y gusto es que este mi testamento tenga todo vigor,

16 encargando y suplicando alos Executores abaxo nombrados, observen
17 lo contenido aqui, y que soliciten y ayuden a la cobrança de mis
18 effectos, que estan enpoder ajeno, como consta demis libros,
19 Mando y ordeno quedela mejor y mas bienparado de mi hazinda.
20 sepaguen todas mis deudas, cuya noticia, tiene hermano Moseh
21 saportas
22 item por un legado a este K.K. de Londres veinte livras esterlinas.
23 item por un legado a Hes Haim desta cuidad de Londres, dies livras
24 esterlinas.
25 item por un legado al K. K. de Amsterdam, florines mil y duzientos
26 item por un legado al medras de Hes Haim de o Amsterdam, florines
27 quinientos
28 item por legados a Saffet, tierra Sancta ÿ Hebron, livras veinte
29 esterlinas acada una.
30 item por un legado al Sr. H. R. Jshack Aboab de Amsterdam,
31 florines cinquenta
32 item por un legado al H. R. selomoh Ailion desta ciudad, livras
33 cinco.
34 item por un legado al Sr. H.R. Jahacob Fidanque desta ciudad, livras
35 cinco
36 item declaro ÿ dexo a mi Padre Sr. H.R. Jahacob Saportas por mi
37 solo y universal heredero, como de derecho letoca, despues de
38 satisfaser las mandas ariba mencionadas, de todo el resto de mis
39 bienes y hazienda, havida y por haver, para que en su vida ÿ por su
40 muerte que sea a largos años, le disponga entre mis hermanos en
41 laforma——que le tengo escrito, con esta adicion expressa
42 que a mis hermanos casados y a sus hixos, ni en vida de dho Sr. ni
43 por su muerte puede exceder a cada una mas que florines mil,
44 nombrando y constiteyendo onde a dho mi Padre y Sr. por Executor deste
45 mi testamento
46 item nombro y constituiyo a mi hermano Moseh Saportas por
47 Executor deste mi testamento.
48 item nombro y constitujo a mis amigos y SSres. Pedro Henriques junior
49 y Simon francia por Executores deste mi testamento, dexando
50 por um legado a cada uno de dhos SSres. livras veinte esterlinas
51 item que es mi gusto que se sastisfagan algunos legados a
52 differentes personas, como tiene por nota mi hermano Moseh
53 saportas

54 item dexo por un legado a cada una de mis hermanas de Termisen
55 florines quinentos encargando se remitan por la via de
56 Argel o de otra seguras Kensington 21 Agosto 1692—firmado—
57 Samuel Saportas—con un sello alli junto en laire vermejo—al
58 lado esta escrito—firmado, sellado ÿ publicado en presencia dos
59 testigos—y estan firmados—Jshack saportas—y con letras
60 hebraicas, Benjamin Bar Jahacob
61 declarando ansi mas que el dho Samuel Saportas lepidio y
62 encargo, tanto por cartas, como bocalmente, quando este
63 otorgante, algun tiempo antes de su fallecimiento
64 hablo con el largamente, diversas cosas, que juntamente
65 con su disposicion, que estava para hacer, ÿ en su virtud
66 queria se guardassen y cumpliessen, enconformidad de

301
1 todolo qual, el otorgante declaro y quiso lo que sigue
2 Porlo qual el otorgante en primer lugar declaro de aver
3 adido ÿ acetado la dha herencia de Samuel Saportas en
4 todas partes y puntos ala letra y enteramente, en
5 conformidad dela dha disposicion y lodemas ordenado
6 y que por el consiguiente el otorgante siempre avia
7 deseoso y aun deseiava en su consciencia jusgava
8 estar obligado a seguir y cumplir todo ello enteramente
9 y con puntualidad sin excepcion, limitacion ni cosas
10 en contrario
—
11 Asi como el otorgante declaro aun especialmente, de—
12 nunca aver sido de intencion, y de no serlo aun, para
13 pedir, pretender ni retener dela herencia del dho su
14 hixo alguna la minima cosa, sea por legitima,
15 trebellianica porcion, o por fintas pagadas del
16 penninquecenteno y duzenteno, o, semejantes cargos
17 ni para consentir que en su vida ni despues des su
18 muerte sepida, sepretende ni se retenga en raçon
19 de esso cosa alguna, pues, en quanto necessario sea, siempre
20 remitio a la dha herencia y aun remite a ella por
21 la presente las tales pretenciones o acciones.
22 Ademas de esso declaro el otorgante en virtud y en conformidad

22a   de aver hecho y otorgado

23 como ariba, y asimismo dela dha herencia y deaprobar aun,

24 y en quanto necessario sea, deconfirmar, tal auto de

25 donacion qual en trese de noviembre de mil y seiscientos

26 y noventa y seis se otorgo, ante el notario Pedro Schabaljie.

27 y que en siete de Diziembre primero siguiente se confirmo

28 y se aceto ante los señores Esclavines desta ciudad, y esto

29 respectivamente a favor des sus hixos Jsahack, Moseh

30 y Abraham Saportas y de Rachel y Gracia Saportas,

31 hixas demenor hedad del dho Abraham saportas juntos

32 respettivamente, que contiene la cantidad demil y

33 quiñentas livras degruesso de Capital, en aciones en la

34 Compania dela Yndia Oriental la Camara de Middel

35 burgo, contodas y tales condiciones, limitaciones y

36 obligaciones, quales mas largamente estan inxertas

37 en el dho auto, en cuya conformidad se traspassaron y

38 sequitaron entreinta de henero de mil y seiscientos y

39 noventa ÿ ocho, por respeto de Jshack Saportas,

40 quiñentas livras [sic] livras y por respeto de Abraham

41 saportas y delas dhas sus dos hixas respectivamente

42 tambien quiñentas livras desemjante acion enla

43 dha Camara, en nombre delos Señores Parnassims

44 dela nacion judaica portuguesa en esta ciudad, asi

45 como tambien, por respeto de Moseh Saportas y delos

46 que por su cabesa, o, parte tienen algun expectativo,

47 otras quiñentas livras como las de ariba se tras-

48 passaron y se quitaron en nombre delos dhos SSres

49 Parnassims desta ciudad, y de que por elconsiguiente

50 elotorgante passo ante los mismos señores un termo

51 o auto en veinte y cinco defebrero de mil y seis

52 siento y noventa y siete, al qual tambien por este

53 se refiere.

54 ansi mas declaro el otorgante, despues que en vida del

55 dho su hixo samuel Saportas, avia dado de sus propios

56 bienes en casamiento (: siendo comprehendido en eso

57 talporcion, qual aunque suplida por eldho hixo difunto

58 delotorgante Samuel Saportas, despues le fue otra

59 vez rebajda a elotorgante delo que el otorgante

60 anualmente venia agozar del mismo su hixo :) a
61 sus tres hixas, a saver, a sara Saportas quanto se caso

302
1 con Eliau da Costa mesquita, a Reina Saportas quando se
2 caso con Haim Toledano y a Simha Saportas quando se
3 caso con Aron Saportas, acada qual una suma de
4 tres milflorines poco mas, o, menos que hacen entodo
5 nueve mil florines poco mas, o, menos, y que el
6 otorgante despues delfallecimiento del dho su hixo
7 Samuel Saportas, dio aun, delo quel dexo el susdho
8 a ÿ en favor decada una delas dhas hixas una suma
9 de mil florines, cuÿas respettivas dadivas tambien
10 se apruevan por este, y que tambien despues dela
11 muerte del dho su hixo caso su quarta hixa Ester
12 Saportas con Simson da Costa Athias, ÿ dio con ella
13 en casamiento, delo que dexo al dho su hixo, la suma
14 de nueve mil y quiñentos florines dinero debanco,
15 segun consta del contratto antenupcial que passo
16 ante el notario Tixerandent a fuera delos gastos
17 hasta en cantidad de mil florines. Asi mas declaro
18 el otorgante, que siendo que sus quatro hixas que al
19 presente estan casadas, que sellaman Sara, Reina
20 {Simah} Ester y Simha Saportas respettivamente, vengan
21 a otorgar y a entregar, por respeto delas que al
22 tiempo del fallecimiento del otorgante sehallare
23 o se hallaren aqui, dentro deltermino de seis semanas
24 despues defallecido el otorgante, y dentro de seis
25 meses, despues de avido conocimiento desta disposicion,
26 por respeto delas que al tiempo de fallecimiento
27 desto otorgante estubieren fuera destos paises,
28 y por respeto delas que [entonces es] estubieren casadas, juntamente
29 con sus repettivos maridos y, en caso que alguna dellas
30 sea fallecida antes, los herederos dela tal, juntamente
31 conelos, para ello autorisa del que aqui adelante se
32 nombrara, por respeto del hixo o hixos menores
33 que hubierem que dado, un auto enla mejor forma,
34 por el qual se apruebe esta disposicion en todas

35 sus partes y puntos, con todo lo que es relativo a ella

36 o, delo qu en esta se hace mencion enteramente y

37 absolutamente, y en que, enquanto necessario sea,

38 se renuncia de todos los demas sosttenimientos o

39 pretenciones assi da legitima y falcidia como de

40 fideicomissos ÿ todos los demas autos pensados

41— y no pensados, ningunos ecetuados, y que despues

42 de aquella renunciacion "se diere" aun tambien dentro del

43 dho tiempo prefegido un auto suficiente a su viuda y

44 hixo "Jshack" corroborado con condenacion voluntaria del

45 Consejo supremo en Holanda, sin que de antes se aÿa

46 hecho ni pretendido mas avertura dela que en esta

47 esta dada, cujas respectivas aprobaciones este

48 otorgante deja encomendadas por esta alas dhas

49 quatro hixas y a sus maridos y sucessores respettiva

50 mente, sobre y con su bendicion paternal, qu en tal

51 caso y no de otro modo ni manera quiere el otorgante

52 se den aun ellas dhas hixas, o, siendo ellas fallacidas ante si

53 a su hixo o hixos respettivamente, de los bienes del dho su

54 hixo Samuel Saportas, es a saver a Sara, Reina, y

55 Ester Saportas a cada una duzientas libras esterlinas

56 de Capital en aciones en la Compania dela Yndia

304

1 oriental en Londres ÿ a Simha Saportas tres cientas livras

2 esterlinas de [capital en] aciones en la misma Compan que hacen en

3 todo, por respeto delas quatro hixas, nueve cienta

4 livras esterlinas, pidiendo el ortogranta muy encareci-

5 damente asus hixos de aprobabar [*sic*] especialmente y

6 las dhas mandas delas dhas respettivas sumas y dedar

7 efecto a ellas—

8 Ademas declaro el otorgante que siendo quela hixa del

9 otorgante que aun no esta casada, llamada Judica en

10 caso de su minoridad, el autorisado para ello, que

11 adelante se nombrara, viniere a otorgar y a entregar

12 dentro de seis semanas despues del falleicimiento deste

13 otorgante, un semejante auto de aprobacion y

14 renunciacion, como aqui ariba es requerido por

15 respeto dela[s] [*sic*] quatro hixas casadas (y elqual tambien
16 se encommienda ala dha. Judica, sobre y con la misma
17 bendicion paternal) que ental caso, y no de otro modo
18 ni manera, se pondra y tendra dela herencia del dho
19 Samuel Saportas, a satisfacion y eleccion del Executor
20 que aqui a delante se nombrarara, un Caudal de dies mil
21 florines [dinero debanco] queriendo por elconsiguiente el otorgante
22 quelos dhos, dies mil florines ayan de ser propios ala
23 dha, Judica Saportas en caso y al tiempo quando ella
24 viniere a casarse con bene placito dela esposa del
25 otorgante la Sra. Rachel Saportas, y del hixo mayor
26 del otorgante Ishack, o moriendose alguno dellos
27 antes deso, del que hubiere quedado,
28 o, siendo fallecidos esos ambos, de sus hermanos que
29 entonces estubieren en vida y no de otro modo ni
30 manera, y que los dhos, dies mil florines en el caso de
31 casarse como dicho es serviran para su propio y libre
32 dote y que dellos se devian hallar tambien los gastos
33 dela boda y vestidura y alajas queriendo aun mas
34 el otorgante quela dha. su hixa Judica Saportas,
35 mientras no fuere casada, aÿan de quedar a morar
36 con la dha. su madre, y que en el interim los frutos
37 liquidos delos dhos, dies mil florines se aÿan de—
38 entregar annualmente, y por final segun el
39 tiempo que hurbiere corrido, al dha su muger
40 delotorgante, para la educacion dela dha. su hixa
41 Judica Saportas, todo el tiempo que continuare
42 en morar con la dha. su madre y en ser le obediente,
43 como tambien para el alimento della y de su
44 muger, y siendo caso que ela dha su hixa Judica,
45 mientras no estubiere casada, se saliere dela
46 morada con su madre, o, serle
47 inobediente, que ental caso los dhos frutos aÿan de
48 ser y venir solamente a favor dela dha
49 su muger del otorgante, y en caso quela dha Judica
50 Saportas viniere a fallecer fuera de legitimo matri-
51 monio ental caso se repartira el dho. Caudal de dies mil
52 florines, como dinero libre, entre los hixos barones

53 del dho otorgante, o, aviendose fallecido alguno
54 de antes, sus legitimos descendientes.—
55 Aun declaro el otorgante de aver verdaderamente
56 recivido y goçado al tiempo de su casamiento de por
57 dote de su mujer, el monto o valor de quatro mil
58 florines y de aver ansi constituido a ella, en caso
59 que elotorgante falleciere antes della, una Ketuba
60 de seis mil florines, siendo ansi augmentados los dhos,
61 quatro mil florines con la mitad dellos, segunla,

305

1 costumbre ÿ que por el consiguente, siendo que el otorgante
2 fallecea antes della pertenicieran a ella los dhos seis mil
3 florines como una deuda y en virtud dela dha. Ketuba
4 acargo delos bienes del otorgante, y declaro ansi
5 mas que elotorgante tiene como hazienda propia, afuera
6 dela herencia desu hixo Samuel Saportas un
7 Caudal de siete cientos libras esterlinas de acciones en
8 la Compañia dela yndia oriental en Londres que
9 estan en nombre y de bajo dela direccion dele Sor.
10 Abraham Bernal hombre de negocios en aquella
11 ciudad, y que el otorgante tiene aun algun oro y
12 plata labrada y no monedada como tambien alajas
13 decasa muebles y libros que al presente paran enla
14 casa del otorgante (:a fuera delos que sehallaren ser
15 propios a su hixo Ishack:) pero que elotorgante, para
16 en contra de eso esta tambien para dejar algunas
17 deudas mortales y otras deudillas corrientes y que
18 portanto el otorgante quiere, siendo que fallecea antes
19 della que aÿan de seguir ala dha su mujer y a ser
20 suÿas propias las dhas acciones hasta en la cantidad
21 que al tiempo de su fallecimiento se hallaren valer
22 aprecio corriente y esto para en diminiucion
23 y rebaja delos dhos, seis mil florines y que para
24 ese efeto aÿan de ser devidamente tras passadas a ella
25 o a suorden por el dho Bernal a la primera demanda
26 y que sele aÿan de entregar las repartiones o frutos
27 que se hubieren de aver y que ansi mas para en satis-

28 facion del resto delos dhos, seis mil florines aÿan
29 deseguir asimismo ala dha. su mujer y venir a ser
30 propio a ella el dho oro y plata labrada y no
31 moneda como tambien las dhas. alajas decasa
32 muebles y libros, con calidad que la dha. su muger
33 para en contra de esso aÿa delastar y pagar las dhas.
34 deudas mortales y otras deudillas y ordeno ademas
35 tambien, en conformidad delo ordenado y dispuesto
36 por el dho. Samuel Saportas, quela dha su muger
37 aÿa detirar y goçar, durante toda su vida, todos los
38 frutos liquidos delo que aun restare y estubiere
39 en ser delo que dejo el dho. su hixo Samuel Saportas
40 ansimismo quiso y ordeno bien expressamente el
41 dho. otorgante que todo lo que a cada qual respettiva-
42 mente esta dado ÿ attribuido en la manera suso-
43 referida, ansi como por respetto de cada uno esta
44 extendido ÿ con las respettivas condiciones,
45 limitaciones ÿ obligaciones, aÿa de quedar finalmente
46 dado y attribuido y declaro ademas el otorgante
47 que de los effetos de su hixo Samuel Saportas
48 o, delo que por su muerte dejo no tiene mas ni otra
49 cosa de sobra, sino es lo que esta especificado en cierta
50 lista firmada por el otorgante y confirmada oÿ
51 por mi el notario, la qual se tiene aqui por
52 inxerta, y declaro tambien "en consciencia" que
53 a fuera delas dhas siette cientas livras
54 esterlinas de acciones Capitales, y delas reparticiones
55 o frutos dellas, como tambien del oro y plata
56 labrada ÿ no monedada, alajas de casa, muebles ÿ
57 libros, para en contra delo qual se deven lastar

306
1 las deudas mortales ÿ otras del otorgante, no tiene
2 propios ni otros bienes algunos directa ni indirectamte.
3 ni averse quedado tanpoco con algunos libros desus
4 medios o bien delos dejados por su hixo, y paradar
5 ansi seguidamente satisfacion ala intencion y
6 lo dispuesto del dho su hixo Samuel Saportas, al dho.

7 otorgante declaro derepartir y dexar los dhos. efetos

8 que sobran de su hixo Samuel Saportas, menos lo

9 dho dispuesto, en raçon delos frutos dello, en favor

10 de su muger del otorgante, igualmente ÿ por

11 porciones iguales a sus tres hixos Ishack Abraham

12 y Moseh Saportas, y si muriere alguno antes

13 a sus legitimos descendientes por representacion, pero

14 aviendose muerto alguno antes delotorgante sin/son legitima

15 generacion, alos hixos que quedaren o sus legitimos

16 descendientes tambien por representacion de tal calidad

17 contodo que acada uno delos dhos, hixos o sus legitimos

18 descendientes seles avra de abater o rebajar lo que se

19 hallare estarle deviendo, todo lo qual aunque este en

20 su nombre, estubieron y estan ellos debiendo verdaderamente por o en

21 raçon dela herencia de Samuel Saportas altiempo de

22 su fallecimiento, y es asaver Ishack Saportas dos mil

23 florines, Abraham saportas tres mil florines y

24 Moseh Saportas otros tres mil florines, y con eso se

25 avra de entender tambien estar enteramente fenecidos

26 y ajustados las quentas que, hubieren entre el otorgante y

27 sus respettivos hixos y señaladamente tambien

28 todo lo que entre el otorgante y su hixo Ishac

29 Saportas en manera alguna directa o indirectamte.

30 hubo en abierto sin reserva alguna en todo modo,

31 y ordeno ansimismo el otorgante que los dhos. sus tres

32 hixos aÿan de aprobar dentro del tiempo de seis

33 semanas despues del fallecimiento del otorgante

34 esta dispocision con todo a quello a que puede ser

35 tirada, o, de que en ella se hace mencion con un auto

36 en la mas bastante forma y en caso de fallacer

37 alguno delos dhos sus hixos y que el tal dexare

38 hixo o hixos legitimos ental caso se avra de hacer

39 la dha aprobacion departe de casos por quien nombraren

40 sus executores a quien

41 para eso se autorisa especialmente por la presente,

42 alqual tambien se autorisa para haser las respectivas

43 approbaciones, por respeto dela hixa menor del otorgante

44 Judica y delos hixos menores de todas las hixas del

45 otorgante detal manera como aqui atras esta

46 requerido.

47 Instituyendo el Sr. Testador a su tres hixos Ishack Abraham

48 y Moseh Saportas y a sus respectivos descendientes por

49 representacion por sus unicos y universales herederos

50 sobre el pie ÿ con las condiciones aqui atras mas largamte

51 mencionadas, y favoreciendo y dejando por via de

52 institucion a sus cinco hixas o a sus desciendientes por

53 representacion respettivamente lo que acada una ÿa

54 esta dado para su casamiento ÿ de otra manera o le avra

55 sido dado y esto

56 para en satisfacion de sus repettivas porciones

57 legitimas, en que se instituÿen solamente alas dhas sus

58 hixas y a sus descendientes por representacion en caso que

marginal note:

los que se hallaren

aqui presente y los que

no se hallaren aqui

altiempo quando aqui

llegaren

307

1 no se quisieren contentar con la dha attribucion con

2 calidad que ental caso tambien serebajara y se imputara

3 sobre la dha ilegitima todolo que en manera alguna

4 segun derecho, sera sujeto a colacion o imputacion,

5 Finalmente pone y comete el otorgante por Executor

6 desta su disposicion y por tutores de su hixa Judica

7 Saportas que aun esdemenorhedad como tambien

8 delas hixas menores de su hixo Abraham Saportas

9 y delos demas sus descendientes que fueren de menor

10 hedad y por administradores delos bienes que en

11 conformidad dela presente han de adquerir y

12 tambien, enquanto viviere su muger y tienede

13 goçar los dhos. frutos, por administradores delos dhos

14 ofertas que de Samuel Saportas sobran ala dha

15 su muger y a Ishack Saportas su hixo con todo el

16 poder para ello segun derecho necessario y especial-

17 mente poder assumir un tercereo o subrogar lo en

18 lugar del fallecido hasta al ultimo fin, excluyendo

19 la camara de los huerfanos desta ciudad y de qualquier

20 otra parte donde acaessiere la casa mortuoria del

21 Testador

22 #

23 Todo lo que de suso va declarado, siendole leido al Sr.

24 otorgante distinctamente quiso ÿ es su voluntad

25 que se guarde y se cumpla puntualmente en todas

26 sus partes y puntos sea pues en virtud del poder

27 y orden dada y concedida al otorgante por el dho. su hixo

28 Samuel Saportas, o sea tambien de otra manera

29 como Testamento, Codicilio, donacion por causa

30 dela muerte o de otro modo en la mejor y mas

31 previlegiada forma possible no obstante que se

32 jusagare averse en esta ometido algunas solemnida

33 des—

34 lo qual passo asi en la dha ciudad de Amsterdam en casa del dho.

35 otorgante cituada al lado dela Ysnoga en presencia de

36 Valentin van Rouveroy y Gerard Spÿcker testigos para

37 ello requeridos

38 # y manda al dho. otorgante que a este KK sede por un legado

39 quiñentos florines a saver trescientos florines a la sedaca y los otros

40 duzientos restantes para Es haim los quales pide a su executor

41 sesatisfagan

42 Jacob Saportas

43 quod attestor

44 B.G. Rouveroy

45 G. Spÿcker

46 P. Padthuysen

47 1698

48 3

49 7

BIBLIOGRAPHY

~

ARCHIVAL SOURCES

Amsterdam City Archives (Stadsarchief Amsterdam, SAA)
 Entry no. 334: Amsterdam Portuguese Jewish Community
 Kahal Kados de Talmud Torah
  Nos. 19–22 *Escamot*
  Nos. 172–177 *Manual* 1639–1718 (5399–5478)
 Entry no. 5075: Archives of Notaries in Amsterdam (Archief van de Notarissen ter standplaats Amsterdam)
  No. 2205, Not. A. Lock, pp. 466, 23 September 1658
  No. 5998, Not. P. Schabaelje, Acte van donatie van Jacob Saportas ten behoove van sijn Sonen. 13 November 1696
  No. 5998, Not. P. Schabelje, 14 November 1696
  No. 6002, Not. P. Schabelje, 20 January 1698
  No. 6002, Not. P. Schabalje, 24 January 1698
  No. 6002, Not. P. Schabalje, 14 February 1698
  No. 2398, Not. P. Padthuysen, 7 March 1698
Hamburg City Archives (Staatsarchiv Hamburg, SAH)
 Jüdische Gemeinden, 993/I
 Jüdische Gemeinden, 993/II Verträge zwischen den deutsch-jüdischen gemeinden in Hamburg und Altona 1669, 9 Adar II 429
Jerusalem, National Library of Israel
 Gershom Scholem Papers, 4o 1599
  2370 A.Z. Schwarz
  2654 Isaiah Tishby
 Isaiah Tishby Papers, 4o 1526
  01/27 Makhon Schocken
  02/97 Gershom Scholem
  04/80 Bialik Institute
Jerusalem, Schocken Archives, Schocken Institute
 8 Privat 882/3
Livorno, Archivio della Communità Ebraica
 Registro de Ketubot D, 1672–1679
 Registro de Ketubot, 1678–1686
 Registro dei nati dal 1668–1740
 Repertorio delle nascite dal'anno 1668
London, Public Record Office
 Prob/11/411 Samuelis Saportas

MANUSCRIPT SOURCES

Amsterdam
    Biblioteca Rosenthaliana
        HS Ros. 281
    Ets Haim Library
        Sasportas, Isaac. MS 47_ C_ 36
New York
    Yeshiva University Library
        Sasportas, Jacob. MS 1251–1252
Oxford
    Bodleian Library
        Perlhefter, Berl. Neubauer, MS 1416

BOOKS PRINTED PRIOR TO 1800

Aaron of Pesaro. *Sefer toledot aharon.* Amsterdam: Menasseh Ben Israel, 1652.

Ailion, Selomoh. *Sermon que predicó el doctissimo señor Haham Moreno a Rab. R. Selomoh Ailion.* Amsterdam, 1723.

Ashkenazi, Samuel Yafe. *Yefe mareh.* Venice, 1567.

De Barrios, Daniel Levi. *Monte Hermoso de Lay Divina: Sermon Exemplar.* Amsterdam, 1698.

———. *Triumpho del govierno popular.* Amsterdam, 1683.

Bedersi, Yedaiah. *Behinat olam.* Ferrara, 1552.

Ben Israel, Menasseh. *Nishmat hayim.* Amsterdam: Menasseh Ben Israel, 1651.

Buzaglo, Shalom. *Mikdash melekh.* Amsterdam, 1750–1752.

Delmedigo, Joseph Solomon. *Ta-alumot hokhmah.* Hanau, 1629–1631.

Elbaz, Moses b. Maimon. *Sefer heikhal ha-kodesh.* Amsterdam: Benveniste, 1653.

Emden, Jacob. *Akitzat akrav.* Altona, 1752.

———. *Edut be-ya-akov.* Altona, 1756.

———. *Lehem shamayim.* Altona, 1768.

———. *Mitpahat sefarim.* Altona, 1768.

———. *Sefat emet u-leshon zehorit.* Altona, 1752.

———. *Sefer etz avot.* Amsterdam, 1751.

———. *Sefer hitavkut ish.* Altona, 1755.

———. *Sefer seder olam rabah.* Hamburg, 1757.

———. *She-elat ya-avetz.* Lemberg, 1884.

———. *Shevirat luhot ha-aven.* Altona, 1756.

———. *Torat ha-kenaot.* Altona, 1752.

Hagiz, Moses. *Shever poshim.* London, 1714.

Halevi, Samuel ben David. *Sefer nahalat shivah.* Amsterdam: Uri Phoebus, 1667–1668.

Ibn Adret, Solomon. *She-elot u-teshuvot.* Venice: Giustiniani, 1545–1546.

Ibn Verga, Solomon. *Shevet yehudah.* Amsterdam, 1648.

Lida, David. *Be-er eshek.* Amsterdam: Uri Phoebus Halevi, 1680.

——. *Migdal David.* Amsterdam: Uri Phoebus Halvi, 1680.

Likutim shonim. Constantinople, 1519.

Luria, Solomon. *Hokhmat shelomo.* Amsterdam, Joseph Athias, 1691.

——. *Yam shel shelomo al massekhet yevamot.* Altona, 1740.

Maimonides, Moses. *Sefer ha-mitzvot.* Amsterdam: Joseph Athias, 1660.

De Mercado, Moses. *Perush sefer kohelet ve-tehilim.* Amsterdam: Benveniste, 1653.

Milhemet hovah, Constantinople, 1710.

Morteira, Saul Levi. *Givat shaul.* Amsterdam: Benveniste, 1645.

Mussaphia, Benjamin. *Shtem esreh she-elot.* Amsterdam: Uri Phoebus, 1672.

Perlhefter, Beer. *Ma-ase hoshen u-ketoret.* Prague, 1686.

Raphael, Sabbetai. *Sefer ta-alumot u-mekorot ha-hokhmah.* Venice, 1662.

Sefer ha-yalqut: helek sheni. Livorno, 1650.

Sasportas, Jacob. *Eleh divre ya-akov Sasportas.* Amsterdam: Benveniste, 1652.

——. *Va-yakem edut be-ya-akov.* Amsterdam: Uri Phoebus, 1672.

Sefer hasidim. Bologna, 1538.

Da Silva, Hezekiah. *Sefer peri hadash.* Amsterdam: David Tartas, 1691.

——. *Sermon, Moral del Fundamento de nuestra ley.* Amsterdam: Moseh Dias, 1691.

De Vidas, Elijah. *Tratado del temor divino.* Amsterdam, 1633.

Wagenseil, Johann Christoph. *Tela ignea Satane: hoc est arcani & horribiles Judaeorum adversus Christum.* Altdorf, 1681.

Wolf, Benjamin Zeev. *Nahalat Binyamin.* Amsterdam: Uri Phoebus Halevi, 1682.

Zalman, Solomon. *Marat ha-zedek.* Amsterdam: Uri Phoebus Halevi, 1682.

BOOKS AND ARTICLES PRINTED AFTER 1800

Abrahams, Dudley. "Jew Brokers of the City of London." *Miscellanies of the Jewish Historical Society of England* 3 (1937): 80–94.

Abrahams, Israel. *Hebrew Ethical Wills.* Philadelphia: JPS, 1976. [1926]

Abrams, Daniel. *Kabbalistic Manuscripts and Textual Theory: Methodologies of Textual Scholarship and Editorial Practice in the Study of Jewish Mysticism.* Jerusalem: Magnes Press, 2010.

Acero, Beatriz Alonso. *Orán-Mazalquivir, 1589–1639: una sociedad española en la frontera Berbería.* Madrid: Consejo Superior de Investigaciones Científicas, 2000.

Agnon, S. "Aliyat neshamah" *Ha-shiloah* 21 (1909–1910): 443–445.

——. "At the Home of Salman Schocken" (Hebrew). In *Mi-atzmi el atzmi,* 23–31. Jerusalem: Schocken, 1976.

——. *Elu ve-elu.* Jerusalem: Schocken, 1998.

——. "*Ha-nidah.*" *Ha-tekufah* 4 (Warsaw, 1919): 1–54.

——. *Kol sipurav shel Sh.Y. Agnon.* Berlin: Schocken, 1931.

Agnon, S. *Kol sipurav shel Sh.Y. Agnon.* Tel Aviv: Schocken, 1953.

——. *Mi-sod hakhamim: mikhtavim 1909–1970: Agnon, Brener, Bialik, Lachover, Katznelson, Sadan.* Jerusalem: Schocken, 2002.

Agnon, S. Y., and Salman Schocken. *Shai Agnon-S.Z. Schocken: Hilufe igrot (1916–1959).* Jerusalem: Schocken, 1991.

Ahrend, Aaron. "Approbations to Sacred Books in Our Era" (Hebrew). *Alei Sefer* 18 (1996): 157–170.

——. "The Study of the Mishnah and Mishnah Circles in the Modern Period" (Hebrew). *Jewish Studies, an Internet Journal* 3 (2004): 19–53.

Albert, Anne Oravetz. "The Rabbi and the Rebels: A Pamphlet on the *Herem* by Rabbi Isaac Aboab da Fonseca." *JQR* 104 (2014): 171–191.

Alter, Uri D. "The Evolution of Worlds in *Ha-nidah* by S. Y. Agnon" (Hebrew). *Proceedings of the Fifth World Congress of Jewish Studies* (1969), 3:13–17.

——. "Where's Esther?" *London Review of Books* 35.17, 12 September 2013, 29–30.

Amarillo, Abraham. "Sabbatian Documents from the Collection of Rabbi Saul Amarillo" (Hebrew). *Sefunot* 5 (1961): 237–274.

Amelang, James. *Historias paralelas: judeoconversos y moriscos en la España moderna.* Madrid: Ediciones Akal, 2011.

Amichay-Michlin, Dania. *Ahavat ish: Avraham Yosef Stybel.* Jerusalem: Bialik Institute, 2000.

Aminoah, Noah. *R. Yosef Sasportas ve-sefer teshuvotav.* Tel Aviv: Tel Aviv University Press, 1994.

Armstrong, Elizabeth. *Before Copyright: The French Book-Privilege System, 1498–1526.* Cambridge: Cambridge University Press, 1990.

Arnheim, Arthur. "Hebrew Prints and Censorship in Altona." *Studies in Bibliography and Booklore* 21 (2001): 3–9.

Assis, Yom Tov, and Yosef Kaplan, eds. *Dor Gerush Sefarad.* Jerusalem: Zalman Shazar Center, 1999.

Aston, Margaret. "The Fiery Trigon Conjunction: An Elizabethan Astrological Prediction." *Isis* 61 (1970): 159–187.

Attia, Ali Mohamed Abd El-Rahman. *The Hebrew Periodical ha-shiloah (1896–1919): Its Role in the Development of Modern Hebrew Literature.* Jerusalem: Magnes Press, 1991.

Attias, Moshe, and Gershom Scholem. *Shirot ve-tishbahot shel ha-Shabetaim.* Tel Aviv: Dvir, 1947.

Avivi, Joseph. *Rabbinic Manuscripts: Mendel Gottesman Library Yeshiva University.* New York: Yeshiva University, 1998.

Azevedo, João Lúcio. *História dos Christãos-Novos Portugueses.* Lisbon: Livraria clássica editora de A. M. Teixeira, 1921.

Azulai, Hayim Joseph David. *Sefer Ma-agal Tov ha-shalem.* Edited by Aron Freimann. Jerusalem: Mekize Nirdamim, 1934.

Bacon, Gershon C. "Daat Torah and the Birth Pangs of the Messiah: On the Ideology of the *Agudas yisroel* in Poland" (Hebrew). *Tarbiz* 52 (1983): 497–508.

Baer, Marc David. *The Dönme: Jewish Converts, Muslim Revolutionaries, and Secular Turks.* Stanford, CA: Stanford University Press, 2010.

Baer, Yitzhak. *A History of the Jews in Christian Spain*. Philadelphia: JPS, 1966.

Balberg, Mira, and Moulie Vidas. "Impure Scholasticism: The Study of Purity Laws and Rabbinic Self-Criticism in the Babylonian Talmud." *Prooftexts* 32 (2012): 312–356.

Band, Arnold J. *Nostalgia and Nightmare: A Study in the Fiction of S. Y. Agnon*. Berkeley: University of California Press, 1968.

Bar Hiyya, Abraham. *Megilat ha-megaleh*. Edited by A. Poznanski. Berlin, 1924.

Barnai, Jacob. "Rabbi Joseph Escafa and the Rabbinate in Izmir" (Hebrew). *Sefunot* 18 (1985): 53–81.

Barnett, Lionel D. *El libro de los acuerdos, being the records and accompts of the Spanish and Portuguese synagogue of London from 1663 to 1681*. Oxford: Oxford University Press, 1931.

Baroja, Julio Caro. *Los Judios en la España moderna y contemporánea*. Madrid: Ediciones Arión, 1962.

Baron, Salo W. *A Social and Religious History of the Jews*. 2nd ed. Vol. 15. New York: Columbia University Press, 1973.

Bartal, Israel. "The *Kinnus* Project: *Wissenschaft des Judentums* and the Fashioning of a 'National Culture' in Palestine." In *Transmitting Jewish Traditions*, edited by Yaakov Elman and Israel Gershoni, 310–323. New Haven, CT: Yale University Press, 2000.

Baumgarten, Jean. *Le peuple des livres: les ouvrages populaire dans la société ashkénaze, XVI–XVIIIe siècle*. Paris: Albin Michel, 2010.

Becker, Hans-Jürgen. " 'Epikureer' im Talmud Yerushalmi." In *The Talmud Yerushalmi and Graeco-Roman Culture*, edited by Peter Schäfer, 1:397–421. Tübingen: Mohr Siebeck, 1998.

Beinart, Haim. "Conversos of Chillón and Siruela and the Prophecies of Mari Gómez and Inés, daughter of Juan Esteban" (Hebrew). *Zion* 48 (1983): 241–272.

———. "The Conversos of Halia and the Movement of the Prophetess Inés of Herrera" (Hebrew). *Zion* 53 (1988): 13–52

———. *Conversos on Trial: The Inquisition of Ciudad Real*. Jerusalem: Magnes Press, 1981.

———. *The Expulsion of the Jews from Spain*. Oxford: Littman Library, 2002.

———. *The Sephardi Legacy*. Edited by Haim Beinart. Jerusalem: Magnes Press, 1992.

Benayahu, Meir. *Dor ehad ba-aretz: Igrot R. Shmuel Aboab ve-R. Moshe Zaku be-inyene eretz yisrael*. Jerusalem: Yad ha-Rav Nisim, 1988.

———. *Haskamah u-reshut bi-defuse Venetzyah*. Jerusalem: Ben Zvi Institute, 1971.

———. *Marbits Torah: samkhuyotav, tafkidav, ve-helko be-mosdot ha-kehilah bi-Sefarad, be-Turkiyah uve-artsot ha-mizrah*. Jerusalem: Rav Kook Institute, 1953.

———. "News from Italy and Holland on the Beginning of Sabbatianism" (Hebrew). *Erez yisrael* 4 (1956): 194–205.

———. *Rabi Hayim Yosef David Azulai*. Jerusalem: Rav Kook Institute, 1959.

Bentov, Haim. "The Siriro Family" (Hebrew). In *Fez ve-arim aherot be-Morocco*, edited by Moshe Bar-Asher, Moshe Amar, and Shimon Sharvit, 337–348. Ramat Gan: Bar-Ilan University Press, 2013.

Berger, David. "The Barcelona Disputation." In *Persecution, Polemic, and Dialogue: Essays in Jewish-Christian Relations*, 199–208. Boston: Academic Studies Press, 2010.

Berger, David. "Judaism and General Culture in Medieval and Early Modern Times." In *Cultures in Collision and Conversation: Essays in the Intellectual History of the Jews*, 21–116. Boston Academic Studies Press, 2011.

——. "On the Uses of History in Medieval Jewish Polemic against Christianity: The Quest for the Historical Jesus." In *Persecution, Polemic, and Dialogue: Essays in Jewish-Christian Relations*, 139–157. Boston: Academic Studies Press, 2010.

——. "Sephardic and Ashkenazi Messianism in the Middle Ages: An Assessment of the Historiographical Controversy" (Hebrew). In *Rishonim ve-ahronim: mehkarim be-toledot yisrael mugashim le-Avraham Grossman*, edited by Joseph Hacker, B. Z. Kedar, and Yosef Kaplan, 11–28. Jerusalem: Zalman Shazar Center, 2010.

——. "Some Ironic Consequences of Maimonides' Rationalist Approach to the Messianic Age" (Hebrew). *Maimonidean Studies* 2 (1991): 1–8. Reprinted and translated into English in David Berger, *Cultures in Collision and Conversation: Essays in the Intellectual History of the Jews*, 278–288. Boston: Academic Studies Press, 2011.

——. "Three Typological Themes in Early Jewish Messianism: Messiah Son of Joseph, Rabbinic Calculations, and the Figure of Armilus." In *Cultures in Collision and Conversation: Essays in the Intellectual History of the Jews*, 253–277. Boston: Academic Studies Press, 2011.

Berger, Shlomo. *Producing Redemption in Amsterdam: Early Modern Yiddish Books in Paratextual Perspective*. Leiden: Brill, 2013.

Bernheimer, Carlo. "Some New Contributions to Abraham Cardoso's Biography." *JQR* 18 (1927): 97–129.

Bethencourt, Francisco. *The Inquisition: A Global History, 1478–1834*. Cambridge: Cambridge University Press, 2009.

Biale, David. *Gershom Scholem: Kabbalah and Counter-History*. Cambridge, MA: Harvard University Press, 1979.

Bialik, Chaim Nachman. "Halacha und Aggada." Translated by Gerhard Scholem. *Der Jude* 4 (1919–1920): 61–77.

Bik (Shauli), Abraham. "Rabbi Jacob Emden's Apology for His Approbation to the Book *Mikdash melekh*" (Hebrew). *KS* 50 (1974): 154–156.

Bodian, Miriam. "Biblical Hebrews and the Rhetoric of Republicanism: Seventeenth-Century Portuguese Jews on the Jewish Community." *AJS Review* 22 (1997): 199–221.

——. *Hebrews of the Portuguese Nation: Conversos and Community in Early Modern Amsterdam*. Bloomington: Indiana University Press, 1997.

——. "'Men of the Nation': The Shaping of Converso Identity in Early Modern Europe." *P&P* 143 (1994): 48–76.

——. "The Portuguese Jews of Amsterdam and the Status of Christians." In *New Perspectives on Jewish-Christian Relations in Honor of David Berger*, edited by Elisheva Carlebach and Jacob J. Schacter, 329–357. Leiden: Brill, 2012.

Bouza, Fernando. *Corre manuscrito: una historia cultural del Siglo de Oro*. Madrid: Marcial Pons, 2001.

Bowersock, G. W. "A Roman Perspective on the Bar Kochba War." In *Approaches to An-*

cient Judaism, edited by William Scott Green, 2:131–141. Missoula, MT: Scholars Press, 1980.

Brady, Thomas A., Jr. "Confessionalization: The Career of a Concept." In *Confessionalization in Europe, 1555–1700: Essays in Honor and Memory of Bodo Nischan*, edited by John M. Headley et al., 1–20. Aldershot, UK: Ashgate, 2004.

Bredekamp, Horst. "From Walter Benjamin to Carl Schmitt, via Thomas Hobbes." *Critical Inquiry* 25 (1999): 247–266.

Bregoli, Francesca. "Hebrew Printing in Eighteenth-Century Livorno: From Government Control to a Free Market." In *The Hebrew Book in Early Modern Italy*, edited by Joseph R. Hacker and Adam Shear, 171–196. Philadelphia: University of Pennsylvania Press, 2011.

Brik, Avraham. "Rabbi Meir Ashkenazi and Rabbi Jacob Sasportas, First Rabbis of the Congregation Atlona, Wandsbek, Hamburg" (Hebrew). *Moriah* 8 (1978): 72–78.

Bromwich, David. *The Intellectual Life of Edmund Burke: From the Sublime and Beautiful to American Independence*. Cambridge, MA: Belknap Press of Harvard University Press, 2014.

Campanini, Saverio. "Fulmini e vapori sulfurei: Storia di una citazione scholemiana." In *Energia e rappresentazione: Warburg, Panofsky, Wind*, edited by Alice Barale et al., 133–148. Milan: Mimesis, 2016.

———. "Some Notes on Gershom Scholem and Christian Kabbalah." In *Gershom Scholem: In Memoriam*, edited by Joseph Dan, 2:13–33. Jerusalem: Hebrew University, 2007.

Caputo, Nina. *Nahmanides in Medieval Catalonia: History, Community, and Messianism*. Notre Dame, IN: University of Notre Dame Press, 2007.

Carlebach, Elisheva. "Between History and Hope: Jewish Messianism in Ashkenaz and Sepharad." *Third Annual Lecture of the Victor J. Selmanowitz Chair of Jewish History*. New York: Touro College, 1998.

———. "Die messianische Haltung der deutschen Juden im Spiegl von Glikls 'Zikhroynes.'" In *Die Hamburger Kauffrau Glikl: jüdische Existenz in der Frühen Neuzeit*, edited by Monika Richarz, 238–253. Hamburg: Christians, 2001.

———. *The Pursuit of Heresy: Rabbi Moses Hagiz and the Sabbatian Controversies*. New York: Columbia University Press, 1990.

———. "The Sabbatian Posture of German Jewry." In *Ha-halom ve-shivro*, edited by Rachel Elior, 2:1–29. Jerusalem: Hebrew University, 2001.

Chajes, J.H. *Between Worlds: Dybbuks, Exorcists and Early Modern Judaism*. Philadelphia: University of Pennsylvania Press, 2003.

Chakrabarty, Dipesh. *Provincializing Europe: Postcolonial Thought and Historical Difference*. Princeton, NJ: Princeton University Press, 2000.

Chartier, Roger. *The Order of Books: Readers, Authors, and Libraries in Europe between the Fourteenth and Eighteenth Centuries*. Stanford, CA: Stanford University Press, 1994.

Chazan, Robert. *Barcelona and Beyond: The Disputation of 1263 and Its Aftermath*. Berkeley: University of California Press, 1992.

Cohen, Gerson D. "Messianic Postures of Ashkenazim and Sephardim." In *Studies in the Variety of Rabbinic Cultures*, 271–297. Philadelphia: JPS, 1991.

———. "Review of B. Netanyahu's *The Marranos of Spain*." *Jewish Social Studies* 29 (1967): 178–184.

Cohen, Jeremy. "Rationales for Conjugal Sex in RaBaD's *Ba'alei ha-nefesh*." *Jewish History* 6 (1992): 65–78.

Cohen, Oded. "*Ma-agal tov* by *HIDA*: A Meeting of Tradition and Modernity." MA thesis, Tel Aviv University, 2010.

Cohen, Uri. "Governing Institutions of the Hebrew University: 1925–1948" (Hebrew). In *Toledot ha-universitah ha-ivrit be-yerushalayim*, edited by Hagit Lavsky, 2:3–70. Jerusalem: Magnes Press, 2005.

Coppenhagen, J. H. *Menasseh ben Israel: A Bibliography*. Jerusalem: Misgav Yerushalayim, 1990.

Crome, Andrew. "English National Identity and the Readmission of the Jews, 1650–1656." *Journal of Ecclesiastical History* 66 (2015): 280–301.

Dahm, Volker *Das jüdischen Buch im Dritten Reich: Salmon Schocken und sein Verlag*. Frankfurt am Main: Buchhändler Vereiningung, 1979.

Dan, Joseph. *Ha-sippur ha-ivri bi-yemei ha-beinayim*. Jerusalem: Keter, 1974.

Da Silva Rosa, J. S. "Een geschilderd portet van Chagam Jacob Sasportas ontdekt." *De Vrijdagawond* 5 (1928): 131–134.

David, Anthony. *The Patron: A Life of Salman Schocken 1877–1959*. New York: Metropolitan Books, 2003.

Davidson, Herbert A. *Moses Maimonides: The Man and His Works*. New York: Oxford University Press, 2005.

Davis, Joseph. *Yom-Tov Lipmann Heller: Portrait of a Seventeenth-Century Rabbi*. Oxford: Littman Library, 2004.

Diamond, James A. *Maimonides and the Shaping of the Jewish Canon*. Cambridge: Cambridge University Press, 2014.

Dienstag, Jacob I. "Maimonides' *Guide for the Perplexed*: A Bibliography of Editions and Translations." In *Occident and Orient: A Tribute to the Memory of Alexander Scheiber*, edited by Robert Dán, 95–128. Budapest: Akadémiai Kiadó;Leiden: Brill, 1988.

Driver, Samuel R., and Adolf Neubauer, trans. *The Fifty-Third Chapter of Isaiah according to the Jewish Interpreters*. Oxford: James Parker, 1876. Reprint, New York: Hermon Press, 1969.

Dunkelgrün, Theodor. " 'Like a Blind Man Judging Colors': Joseph Athias and Johannes Leusden Defend Their 1667 Hebrew Bible." *SR* 44 (2012): 79–115.

Duckesz, Eduard. *Iwoh lemoschaw*. Krakow: Josef Fischer, 1903.

Duschinsky, Charles. "Jacob Kimchi and Shalom Buzaglo." *TJHSE* 7 (1911–1914): 272–290.

Ebert, Bernd. *Simon und Isaack Luttichuys: Monographie mit kritischem Werkverzeichnis*. Munich: Deutscher Kunstverlag, 2009.

Einbinder, Susan L. *No Place of Rest: Jewish Literature, Expulsion and the Memory of Medieval France*. Philadelphia: University of Pennsylvania Press, 2009.

Eisner, Adolf A. *Toledot ha-gaon rabbi David Lida*. Breslau, 1938.

Elbaum, Jacob. *Teshuvat ha-lev ve-kabalat yisurim: iyunim be-shitot ha-teshuvah shel hakhme Ashkenaz u-Polin, 1348–1648*. Jerusalem: Magnes Press, 1992.

Elliott, J. H. *Imperial Spain, 1469–1716*. London: Penguin Books, 2002.

———. "Revolution and Continuity in Early Modern Europe." *P&P* 42 (1969): 35–56.

Elqayam, Avraham. *Ha-masa le-ketz ha-yamin: besorat he-ge-ulah ha-shabtait la-meshorer Moshe ben Gideon Abudiente*. Los Angeles: Cherub Presss, 2014.

———. "The Rebirth of the Messiah: New Revelations about R. Isaachar Beer Perlhefter" (Hebrew). *Kabbalah* 1 (1996): 85–166.

———. " 'To Know the Messiah': The Dialectics of Sexual Discourse in the Messianic Thought of Nathan of Gaza" (Hebrew). *Tarbiz* 65 (1996): 637–670.

Emanuel, Simcha. "Manuscripts of the Responsa by Ibn Adret in the Writings of Scholars between the Fifteenth and Nineteenth Centuries." (Hebrew). *Jewish Studies, an Internet Journal* 13 (2015): 1–46.

Emden, Jacob. *Megillat sefer*. Edited by David Cahana. Warsaw, 1897.

———. *Mor u-ketziah*. Jerusalem: Makhon Jerusalem, 1996.

Endelman, Todd M. *The Jews of Britain, 1656–2000*. Berkeley: University of California Press, 2002.

Engel, Amir. *Gershom Scholem: An Intellectual Biography*. Chicago: University of Chicago Press, 2017.

Epstein, Abraham. "Une lettre d'Abraham ha-Yakhini a Nathan Gazati." *REJ* 26 (1893): 209–219.

Ettinger, Shmuel. "The Emden-Eibeschütz Controversy in the Light of Jewish Historiography" (Hebrew). *Kabbalah* 9 (2003): 329–392.

Even-Shmuel, Yehudah. *Midreshe geulah*. Tel Aviv: Bialik Institute, 1943.

Fine, Lawrence. "Penitential Practices in a Kabbalistic Mode." In *Seeking the Favor of God*, edited by Mark J. Boda et al., 3:127–148. Atlanta, GA: Society of Biblical Literature, 2008.

Finkelstein, Louis. *Akiba: Scholar, Saint, and Martyr*. New York: Atheneum, 1970. [1936]

Fishbane, Michael. "Midrash and Messianism: Some Theologies of Suffering and Salvation." In *Toward the Millenium: Messianic Expectations from the Bible to Waco*, edited by Peter Schäfer and Mark Cohen, 57–71. Leiden: Brill, 1998.

Fisher, Benjamin. "Opening the Eyes of the *Novos Reformados*: Rabbi Saul Levi Morteira, Radical Christianity, and the Jewish Reclamation of Jesus, 1620–1660." *SR* 44 (2012): 117–148.

Fishman, Talya. "Changing Early Modern Jewish Discourse about Christianity: The Efforts of Rabbi Leon Modena." In *The Lion Shall Roar*, edited by David Malkiel, 159–194. Jerusalem: Magnes Press, 2003.

Fogel, Moshe. "The Sabbatian Character of *Hemdat yamim*: A Re-examination" (Hebrew). In *Ha-halom ve-shivro*, edited by Rachel Elior, 2:365–422. Jerusalem: Magnes Press, 2001.

Franco Mendes, David. *Memorias do estabelecimento e progresso dos Judeos Portuguezes e Espanhoes nesta famosa citade de Amsterdam*. Edited by L. Fuks and R. G. Fuks Mansfeld. Special Issue of *SR* 9 (1975).

Freidenreich, Harriet Pass. *Jewish Politics in Vienna 1918–1938*. Bloomington: Indiana University Press, 1991.

Freimann, Aron. *Inyene shabetai tsevi*. Berlin: Mekize Nirdamim, 1912.

———. "R. David Lida and His Justification in *Be-er eshek*" (Hebrew). In *Sefer ha-yovel shai li-khevod Nahum Sokolov*, 455–480. Warsaw: Shuldberg, 1904.

Friedman, Mordechai Akiva. *Ha-rambam, ha-mashiah be-teman ve-ha-shemad*. Jerusalem: Ben Zvi Institute, 2002.

Friedman, Theodore. *The Life and Work of Hayyim Joseph David Azulai: A Study in Jewish Cultural History*. PhD diss., Columbia University, 1952.

Fuks, L. "De Amsterdamse Opperabbijn David Lida en de Vierlandensynode (1680–1684)." *SR* 6 (1972): 166–179.

———. "Disharmony between the 'Council of Four Lands' and the Ashkenazi Kehilla of Amsterdam during the Rabbinate of R. David Lida (1680–1684)" (Hebrew). *Michael* 6 (1980): 170–176.

———. "Jewish Libraries in Amsterdam in 1640." In *Aspects of Jewish Life in the Netherlands: A Selection from the Writings of Leo Fuks*, edited by Renate G. Fuks Mansfeld, 38–57. Assen: Van Gorcum, 1995.

———. "Nieuwe Gegevens over de Amsterdamse Opperabbijn David Lida en de Vierlandensynode." *SR* 10 (1976): 189–194.

———. "Sabatianisme in Amsterdam in het Begin van de 18 Eeuw. Enkele Beschouwingen over Reb Leib Oizers en zijn Werk." *SR* 14 (1980): 20–28.

Fuks, L., and R. G. Fuks-Mansfeld. *Hebrew Typography in the Northern Netherlands, 1585–1815: Historical Evaluation and Descriptive Bibliography*. Leiden: Brill, 1984–1987.

———. "The Inauguration of the Portuguese Synagogue of Amsterdam, Netherlands, in 1675." *Arquivos do Centro Cultural Português* 14 (1979): 489–507.

Funkenstein, Amos. "Maimonides: Political Theory and Realistic Messianism." In *Perceptions of Jewish History*, 131–155. Berkeley: University of California Press, 1993.

———. *Theology and the Scientific Imagination: From the Middle Ages to the Seventeenth Century*. Princeton, NJ: Princeton University Press, 1986.

Gampel, Benjamin R. *Anti-Jewish Riots in the Crown of Aragon and the Royal Response, 1391–1392*. New York: Cambridge University Press, 2016.

———. *The Last Jews on Iberian Soil: Navarrese Jewry 1479/1498*. Berkeley: University of California Press, 1989.

García-Arenal, Mercedes, and Gerard Wiegers. *A Man of Three Worlds: Samuel Pallache, a Moroccan Jew in Catholic and Protestant Europe*. Baltimore: Johns Hopkins University Press, 2003.

Ginzburg, Simon, ed. *R. Moshe Hayim Luzzatto u-venei doro*. Tel Aviv: Dvir, 1937.

Glaser, Amelia M., ed. *Stories of Khmelnytsky: Competing Legacies of the 1648 Ukranian Cossack Uprising*. Stanford, CA: Stanford University Press, 2015.

Glickl. *Zikhronos, 1691–1719*. Edited and translated by Chava Turniansky. Jerusalem: Zalman Shazar Center and Ben-Zion Dinur Center, 2006.

Goldgar, Anne. *Impolite Learning: Conduct and Community in the Republic of Letters, 1680–1750*. New Haven, CT: Yale University Press, 1995.

Goldin, Judah. "Of Midrash and the Messianic Theme." In *Studies in Midrash and Related Literature*, edited by Barry L. Eichler and Jeffrey H. Tigay, 359–379. Philadelphia: JPS, 1988.

———. "Towards a Profile of the Tanna, Aqiba ben Joseph." In *Studies in Midrash and Related Literature*, edited by Barry L. Eichler and Jeffrey H. Tigay, 299–323. Philadelphia, JPS, 1988.

Goldish, Matt. "Hakham Jacob Sasportas and the Former Conversos." *SR* 44 (2012): 149–172.

———. "An Historical Irony: Solomon Ailion's Court Tries the Case of a Repentant Sabbatean." *SR* 27 (1993): 5–12.

———. "Rabbi Jacob Sasportas: Defender of Torah Authority in an Age of Change." MA thesis, Hebrew University of Jerusalem, 1991.

———. *The Sabbatean Prophets*. Cambridge, MA: Harvard University Press, 2004.

Goldman, Israel L. *The Life and Times of Rabbi David ibn abi Zimra: A Social, Economic, and Cultural Study of Jewish Life in the Ottoman Empire in the 15th and 16th Centuries as Reflected in the Responsa of the RDBZ*. New York: Jewish Theological Seminary, 1970.

Goshen-Gottstein, Alon. " 'The Sage Is Superior to the Prophet': The Conception of the Torah through the Prism of the History of Exegesis" (Hebrew). In *Study and Knowledge in Jewish Thought*, edited by Howard Kreisel, 37–77. Beer Sheva: Ben Gurion University Press, 2006.

———. *The Sinner and the Amnesiac: The Rabbinic Invention of Elisha ben Abuya and Eleazar ben Arach*. Stanford, CA: Stanford University Press, 2000.

Gottlieb, Lior. " 'Resen mateh' of Jacob Emden: First and Second Editions with an Introduction, Textual Comparison and Notes" (Hebrew). In *Be-darkei shalom: iyunim be-hagut yehudit mugashim le-Shalom Rosenberg*, edited by Benjamin Ish-Shalom, 295–321. Jerusalem: Beit Morasha, 2007.

Grafton, Anthony. *Cardano's Cosmos: The Worlds and Works of a Renaissance Astrologer*. Cambridge, MA: Harvard University Press, 1999.

———. *The Culture of Correction in Renaissance Europe*. London: The British Library, 2011.

———. *The Footnote: A Curious History*. Cambridge, MA: Harvard University Press, 1997.

———. *Humanists with Inky Fingers: The Culture of Correction in Renaissance Europe*. Florence: L. S. Olschki, 2011.

———. "The Magician." *New Republic*. 3 March 2003, 38–45.

Graizbord, David. "Religion and Ethnicity among 'Men of the Nation': Toward a Realistic Interpretation." *Jewish Social Studies* 15 (2008): 32–65.

———. *Souls in Dispute: Converso Identities in Iberia and the Jewish Diaspora, 1580–1700*. Philadelphia: University of Pennsylvania Press, 2004.

Grunwald, Max. *Hamburgs deutsche Juden bis zur Auflösung der drei Gemeinden*. Hamburg: A. Janssen, 1904.

Gurfinkel, Eli. "Maimonides and Kabbalah: An Annotated Bibliography" (Hebrew). *Daat* 64–66 (2009): 417–485.

Gurfinkel, Eli. "*Nezah yisrael* by the Maharal of Prague and the Satmar Rebbe's Concept of Redemption" (Hebrew). *Daat* 78 (2015): 77–91.

Habermann, A. M. *Ha-madpis Daniel Bomberg u-reshimat sifre bet defuso.* Safed: Museum for the Art of Printing, 1978.

Hacken, Richard. "The Jewish Community Library in Vienna: From Dispersion and Destruction to Partial Restoration." *Leo Baeck Institute Year Book* 47 (2002): 151–172.

Hacker, Joseph R. "The Connections of Spanish Jewry with Eretz Israel between 1391 and 1492" (Hebrew). *Shalem* 1 (1974): 105–156.

——. "Israel among the Nations as Described by Solomon LeBeit Halevi of Salonika" (Hebrew). *Zion* 34 (1969): 43–89.

Halbertal, Moshe. *Al derekh ha-emet: ha-Ramban vi-yetsiratah shel masoret.* Jerusalem: Shalom Hartman Institute, 2006.

——. *Maimonides: Life and Thought.* Princeton, NJ: Princeton University Press, 2014.

——. "What Is the *Mishneh Torah*? On Codification and Its Ambivalence." In *Maimonides after 800 Years: Essays on Maimonides and His Influence*, edited by Jay M. Harris, 81–111. Cambridge, MA: Harvard University Press, 2007.

Halevi-Zwick, Judith. "Tekufat Germanyah (1914–1924) bi-yetsirato shel S. Y. Agnon." PhD diss., Hebrew University of Jerusalem, 1967.

Halkin, A. S. "Yedaiah Bedershi's Apology." In *Jewish Medieval and Renaissance Studies*, edited by Alexander Altmann, 165–184. Cambridge, MA: Harvard University Press, 1967.

Halperin, David J. *Abraham Miguel Cardozo: Selected Writings.* Mahwah, NJ: Paulist Press, 2001.

——. *Sabbatai Zevi: Testimonies to a Fallen Messiah.* Oxford: Littman Library, 2007.

——. "The Son of the Messiah: Ishmael Zevi and the Sabbatian Aqedah." *HUCA* 67 (1996): 143–219.

Handler, Safi. *Musaf ha-aretz,* 5 April 2013, 48–49.

Hathaway, Jane. "The Grand Vizier and the False Messiah: The Sabbatai Sevi Controversy and the Ottoman Reform in Egypt." *Journal of the American Oriental Society* 117 (1997): 665–671.

Havlin, S. Z. "On the History of the Talmudic Academies in Jerusalem and Their Scholars at the End of the Seventeenth and Early Eighteenth Centuries" (Hebrew). *Shalem* 2 (1976): 113–192.

Heinemann, Joseph. "The Messiah of Ephraim and the Premature Exodus of the Tribe of Ephraim." *Harvard Theological Review* 68 (1975): 1–15.

Heller, Marvin J. "Benjamin ben Immanuel Mussafia: A Study in Contrasts." *Gutenberg Jahrbuch* 89 (2014): 208–218.

——. *Printing the Talmud: A History of the Earliest Printed Editions of the Talmud.* Brooklyn, NY: Im hasefer, 1992.

Herculano, Alexandre. *History of the Origin and Establishment of the Inquisition in Portugal.* Prolegomenon by Yosef Hayim Yerushalmi. New York: Ktav Publishing House, 1972.

Heschel, Abraham Joshua. *Prophetic Imagination after the Prophets: Maimonides and Other Medieval Authorities.* Edited by Morris M. Faierstein. Hoboken, NJ: Ktav, 1996.

Heyd, Michael. *"Be Sober and Reasonable": The Critique of Enthusiasm in the Seventeenth and Early Eighteenth Centuries.* Leiden: Brill, 1995.

Himmelfarb, Martha. *Jewish Messiahs in a Christian Empire: A History of the Book of Zerubbabel.* Cambridge, MA: Harvard University Press, 2017.

———. "Sefer Zerubbabel." In *Rabbinic Fantasies: Imaginative Narratives from Classical Hebrew Literature*, edited by David Stern and Mark J. Mirsky, 67–90. New Haven, CT: Yale University Press, 1990.

———. "*Sefer Zerubbabel* and Popular Religion." In *A Teacher for All Generations: Essays in Honor of James C. VanderKam*, edited by Eric F. Mason et al., 2:621–634. Leiden: Brill, 2012.

Hirschberg, H. Z. *A History of the Jews of North Africa.* Leiden: Brill, 1974–1981.

Hobsbawm, E. J. "The General Crisis of the European Economy in the 17th Century." *P&P* 5 (1954): 33–53.

Hollander, Pieter den. *Roofkunst: de zaak-Goudstikker.* Amsterdam: Meulenhoff, 2007.

Horbury, William. *Jewish War under Trajan and Hadrian.* Cambridge: Cambridge University Press, 2014.

Houthakker, Bernard. "Bij de Portretten van Chagam Sa(s)portas." *De Vrijdagawond* 5 (1928): 134–136.

Hsia, R. Po-chia, and Henk van Nierop, eds. *Calvinisim and Religious Toleration in the Dutch Golden Age.* New York: Cambridge University Press, 2002.

Hundert, Gershon David. "The Introduction to *Divre Binah* by Dov Ber Bolechów: An Unexamined Source for the History of Jews in the Lwów Region in the Second Half of the Eighteenth Century." *AJS Review* 33 (2009): 225–269.

———. *Jews in Poland-Lithuania in the Eighteenth Century: A Genealogy of Modernity.* Berkeley: University of California Press, 2004.

Huss, Boaz. "'A Sage Is Better than a Prophet': R. Simeon bar Yohai and Moses in the *Zohar*" (Hebrew). *Kabbalah* 4 (1999):103–139.

———. *The Zohar: Reception and Impact.* Oxford: Littman Library, 2016.

Idel, Moshe. "R. Nehemiah ben Shlomo the Prophet on the Star of David and the Name *Taftatfia*: From Jewish Magic to Practical and Theoretical Kabbalah" (Hebrew). In *Ta-shma: mehkarim be-madae ha-yahadut le-zikhro shel yisrael M. Ta-Shma*, edited by Avraham (Rami) Reiner et al., 1:1–76. Alon Shvut: Tevunot, 2011.

———. "Rabbi Solomon ibn Adret and Abraham Abulafia: History of a Submerged Controversy about Kabbalah" (Hebrew). In *Atarah le-hayim: Mehkarim ba-sifrut ha-talmudit ve-ha-rabanit li-khevod Profesor Hayim Zalman Dimitrovsky*, edited by Daniel Boyarin et al., 235–251. Jerusalem: Magnes Press, 2000.

———. *Saturn's Jews: On the Witches' Sabbat and Sabbateanism.* London: Continuum, 2011.

Israel, Jonathan I. *Diasporas within a Diaspora: Jews, Crypto-Jews and the World Maritime Empires (1540–1740).* Leiden: Brill, 2002.

———. *The Dutch Republic: Its Rise, Greatness, and Fall, 1477–1806.* Oxford: Clarendon Press, 1995.

———. *European Jewry in the Age of Mercantilism 1550–1750.* London: Littman Library, 1988.

Israel, Jonathan I. "Jews and the Stock Exchange: The Amsterdam Financial Crash of 1688." In *Diasporas within a Diaspora: Jews, Crypto-Jews, and the World Maritime Empires (1540–1740)*, 449–487. Leiden: Brill, 2002.

———. "The Jews of Spanish North Africa." In *Diasporas within a Diaspora: Jews, Crypto-Jews and the World Maritime Empires (1540–1740)*, 151–184. Leiden: Brill, 2002.

———. "Menasseh ben Israel and the Dutch Sephardi Colonization Movement of the Mid-17th Century." In *Diasporas within a Diaspora: Jews, Crypto-Jews, and the World Maritime Empires (1540–1740)*, 385–420. Leiden: Brill, 2002.

———. "Piracy, Trade and Religion: The Jewish Role in the Rise of the Muslim Corsair Republic of Saleh (1624–1666)." In *Diasporas within a Diaspora: Jews, Crypto Jews, and the World Maritime Empires (1540–1740)*, 291–311. Leiden: Brill, 2002.

———. "Sephardic Immigration into the Dutch Republic, 1595–1672." *SR* 23 (1989): 45–53.

———. "The Sephardi Diaspora and the Struggle for Portuguese Independence from Spain (1640–1668). In *Diasporas within a Diaspora: Jews, Crypto-Jews, and the World Maritime Empires (1540–1740)*, 313–354. Leiden: Brill, 2002.

———. "Venice, Salonika, and the Founding of the Sephardi Diaspora in the North (1574–1621)." In *Diasporas within a Diaspora: Jews, Crypto-Jews and the World Maritime Empires (1540–1740)*, 67–96. Leiden: Brill, 2002.

Jacoby, Michael. *Ben-Chananja: Eine deutschsprachige Zeitschrift von Leopold Löw; inhalte, autoren, rezipienten, 1858–1867*. Uppsala, 1997.

Jastrow, Marcus. *A Dictionary of the Targumim, the Talmud Babli, and Yerushalmi and the Midrashic Literature*. New York: Judaica Press, 1992.

Johns, Adrian. *The Nature of the Book: Print and Knowledge in the Making*. Chicago: University of Chicago Press, 1998.

Jütte, Daniel. "Interfaith Encounters between Jews and Christians in the Early Modern Period and Beyond: Toward a Framework." *AHR* 118 (2013): 378–400.

Kahana, Maoz. "The Allure of Forbidden Knowledge: The Temptation of Sabbatean Literature for Mainstream Rabbis in the Frankist Moment, 1756–1761." *JQR* 102 (2012): 589–616.

———. "The Hatam Sofer: The Authority in His Own Eyes" (Hebrew). *Tarbiz* 76 (2007): 519–556.

———. "How Did the Hatam Sofer Seek to Trump Spinoza? Text, Hermeneutics and Romanticism in the Writings of R. Moses Sofer" (Hebrew). *Tarbiz* 79 (2011): 557–585.

———. "Sabbetai Zevi—the Halakhic Man" (Hebrew). *Zion* 81 (2016): 391–433.

———. "The Scientific Revolution and Encoding of Sources of Knowledge: Medicine, Halakha, and Alchemy, Hamburg-Altona, 1736" (Hebrew). *Tarbiz* 82 (2013): 165–212.

Kamen, Henry. "The Mediterranean and the Expulsion of Spanish Jews in 1492." *P&P* 119 (1988): 30–55.

———. *The Spanish Inquisition: A Historical Revision*. 4th ed. New Haven CT: Yale University Press, 2014.

Kanarfogel, Ephraim. "Dreams as a Determinant of Jewish Law and Practice in Northern Europe during the High Middle Ages." In *Studies in Medieval Jewish Intellectual and Social History: Festschrift in Honor of Robert Chazan*, edited by David Engel et al., 111–143. Leiden: Brill, 2012.

———. "Medieval Rabbinic Conceptions of the Messianic Age: The View of the Tosafists." In *Me'ah She'arim: Studies in Medieval Jewish Spiritual Life in Memory of Isadore Twersky*, edited by Ezra Fleischer et al., 147–169. Jerusalem: Magnes Press, 2001.

Kaplan, Benjamin J. *Divided by Faith: Religious Conflict and the Practice of Toleration in Early Modern Europe.* Cambridge, MA: Belknap Press of Harvard University Press, 2007.

Kaplan, Debra. " 'To Immerse their Wives': Communal Identity and the 'Kahalishe' Mikveh of Altona." *AJS Review* 36 (2012): 257–279.

Kaplan, Lawrence. "*Daas Torah*: A Modern Conception of Rabbinic Authority." In *Rabbinic Authority and Personal Autonomy*, edited by Moshe Sokol, 1–60. Northvale, NJ: J. Aronson, 1992.

Kaplan, Yosef. *An Alternative Path to Modernity: The Sephardi Diaspora in Western Europe.* Leiden: Brill, 2000.

———. "Amsterdam and the Ashkenazi Migration in the Seventeenth Century." In *An Alternative Path to Modernity*, 78–107. Leiden: Brill, 2000.

———. "The Attitude of the Sephardi Leadership in Amsterdam to the Sabbatian Movement, 1665–1671." In *An Alternative Path to Modernity*, 211–233. Leiden: Brill, 2000.

———. "Attitudes toward Circumcision among Early Modern Western Sephardim" (Hebrew). In *Rishonim ve-Aharonim: Mehkarim be-toledot yisrael Mugashim le-Avraham Grossman*, edited by Joseph Hacker, B. Z. Kedar, and Yosef Kaplan, 353–389. Jerusalem: Zalman Shazar Center, 2010.

———. "Between Cristóbal Méndes and Abraham Franco de Silveyra: The Odyssey of a Converso in the Seventeenth Century" (Hebrew). In *Asupah le-Yosef: Kovetz mehkarim shai le-Yosef Hacker*, edited by Yaron Ben-Naeh et al., 406–440. Jerusalem: Zalman Shazar Center, 2014.

———. "Deviance and Excommunication in the Eighteenth Century." In *An Alternative Path to Modernity*, 143–154. Leiden: Brill, 2000.

———. *From Christianity to Judaism: The Story of Isaac Orobio de Castro*, translated by Raphael Loewe. Oxford: Littman Library and Oxford University Press, 1989.

———. "*Gente Política*: The Portuguese Jews of Amsterdam vis-à-vis Dutch Society." In *Dutch Jews as Perceived by Themselves and by Others*, edited by Chaya Brasz and Yosef Kaplan, 21–40. Leiden: Brill, 2001.

———. "The Jewish Profile of the Spanish-Portuguese Community of London during the Seventeenth Century." In *An Alternative Path to Modernity*, 155–167. Leiden: Brill, 2000.

———, ed. *Jews and Conversos: Studies in Society and the Inqusition.* Jerusalem: Magnes Press, 1985.

———. "Jews and Judaism in the Hartlib Circle." *SR* 38–39 (2006): 186–215.

———. "The Jews in the Republic until about 1750: Religious, Cultural, and Social Life."

In *The History of the Jews in the Netherlands*, edited by J.C.H. Blom et al., 116–163. Oxford: Littman Library, 2002.

Kaplan, Yosef. "The Libraries of Three Sephardi Rabbis in Early Modern Western Europe" (Hebrew). In *Sifriyot ve-osfe sefarim*, edited by Moshe Sluhovsky and Yosef Kaplan, 225–260. Jerusalem: Zalman Shazar Center, 2006.

———. *Mi-notsrim hadashim li-yehudim hadashim*. Jerusalem: Zalman Shazar Center, 2003.

———. *Les Nouveaux-Juifs d'Amsterdam*. Paris: Chandeigne, 1999.

———. "Order and Discipline in the Portuguese Synagogue of Amsterdam." In *Jewish Studies and the European Academic World*, edited by Albert van der Heide and Irene E. Zwiep, 1–14. Paris and Louvain: Peeters, 2005.

———. "The Place of the *Herem* in the Sephardi Community of Hamburg." In *An Alternative Path to Modernity*, 168–195. Leiden: Brill, 2000.

———. "R. Saul Levi Morteira and His Treatise 'Arguments against the Christian Religion'" (Hebrew). In *Dutch Jewish History* 1, edited by Joseph Michman, 9–31. Jerusalem: Magnes Press, 1975.

———. "Relations between Spanish and Portuguese Jews and Ashkenazim in Seventeenth-Century Amsterdam" (Hebrew). In *Temurot ba-historyah ha-yehudit ha-hadasha: kovetz maamrim shai li-Shmuel Ettinger*, edited by Shmuel Almog, 389–412. Jerusalem: Historical Society of Israel and Zalman Shazar Center, 1988.

———. "Secularising the Portuguese Jews: Integration and Orthodoxy in Early Modern Judaism." *Simon Dubnow Institute Yearbook* 6 (2007): 99–110.

———. "The Self-Definition of the Sephardi Jews of Western Europe and Their Relation to the Alien and the Stranger." In *An Alternative Path to Modernity*, 51–77. Leiden: Brill, 2000.

———. "Sephardi Students at the University of Leiden." In *An Alternative Path to Modernity*, 196–210. Leiden: Brill, 2000.

———. "The Social Functions of the *Herem*." In *An Alternative Path to Modernity*, 108–142. Leiden: Brill, 2000.

———. "Spinoza in the Library of an Early Modern Dutch Sephardic Rabbi." In *La centralità del dubbio: Un progetto di Antonio Rotondò*, edited by C. Hermanin and L. Simonutti, 2:641–664. Florence: Leo S. Olschki Editore, 2011.

———. "The Travels of Portuguese Jews from Amsterdam to the 'Lands of Idolatry' (1644–1724)." In *Jews and Conversos: Studies in Society and the Inquisition*, edited by Yosef Kaplan, 197–224. Jerusalem: Magnes Press, 1985.

———. *Zwischen 'Neuchristen' und 'Neuen Juden': Die verschlungenen Wege von Kryptojuden und westlichen Sefarden in der Frühen Neuzeit*. Trier: Kliomedia, 2014.

Kaplan, Yosef, Henry Méchoulan, and Richard H. Popkin. *Menasseh ben Israel and His World*. Leiden: Brill, 1989.

Katchen, Aaron L. *Christian Hebraists and Dutch Rabbis: Seventeenth Century Apologetics and the Study of Maimonides' Mishneh Torah*. Cambridge, MA: Harvard University Press, 1984.

Katz, David S. *The Jews in the History of England, 1485–1850*. New York: Clarendon Press, 1994.

Katz, David S., and Yosef Kaplan. *Gerush ve-shivah: yehude angliyah be-hilufe zemanim.* Jerusalem: Zalman Shazar Center, 1993.

Katz, Jacob. "Da'at Torah: The Unqualified Authority Claimed for Halakhists." *Jewish History* 11 (1997): 41–50.

———. "Orthodoxy in Historical Perspective." In *Studies in Contemporary Jewry* 2 (1986): 3–17.

———. "Towards a Biography of the Hatam Sofer." In *Divine Law in Human Hands: Case Studies in Halakhic Flexibility* 403–443. Jerusalem: Magnes Press, 1998.

Katz, Shaul, ed. *Toledot ha-universitah ha-ivrit be-yerushalayim.* Jerusalem: Magnes Press, 1997–2013.

Kaufmann, David, ed. *Die Memorien der Glückel von Hameln (1645–1719).* Frankfurt, 1896.

Kayserling, Meyer. *Sephardim: Romanische Poesien der Juden in Spanien: Ein Beitrag zur Literatur und Geschichte der Spanisch-Portugiesischen Juden.* Leipzig, 1859. Reprint, Hildesheim, Georg Olms Verlag, 1972.

Kellenbenz, Hermann. *Sephardim an der unteren Elbe: ihre wirtschaftliche und politische Bedeutung vom Ende des 16. bis zum begin des 18. Jahrhunderts.* Wiesbaden: Franz Steiner Verlag, 1958.

Keren-Kratz, Menachem. "R. Joel Teitelbaum, ha-Rebbi mi-Satmar (1887–1979): Biografiyah." PhD diss., Tel Aviv University, 2013.

Kister, Menahem. " 'Like the Law of Moses and Yehudah': On the History of a Legal Religious Term" (Hebrew). In *Atarah le-hayim: Mehkarim ba-sifrut ha-talmudit ve-ha-rabanit li-khevod Profesor Hayim Zalman Dimitrovsky*, edited by Daniel Boyarin et al., 202–208. Jerusalem: Magnes Press, 2000.

Klausner, Joseph. *Ha-ra-ayon ha-meshihi be-yisrael: me-reshito ve-ad hatimat ha-mishnah.* Jerusalem: ha-Poalim, 1927.

———. *Historiyah shel ha-sifrut ha-ivrit ha-hadashah.* Jerusalem: Hebrew University, 1930–1950.

Klibansky, Raymond, Erwin Panofsky, and Fritz Saxl. *Saturn and Melancholy: Studies in the History of Natural Philosophy, Religion and Art.* New York: Basic Books, 1964.

Knohl, Israel. *Be-ikvot ha-mashiah.* Tel Aviv: Schocken, 2000.

Knott, Marie Luise, ed. *Hannah Arendt / Gershom Scholem: Der Briefweschel.* Berlin: Suhrkamp Verlag, 2010.

Koselleck, Reinhart. "Crisis." *JHI* 67 (2006): 357–400.

Kraemer, Joel L. "On Maimonides' Messianic Postures." In *Studies in Medieval Jewish History and Literature*, edited by Isadore Twersky, 2:109–142. Cambridge, MA: Harvard University Press, 1984.

Kreisel, Howard. *Prophecy: The History of an Idea in Medieval Jewish Philosophy.* Dordrecht: Kluwer Academic Publishers, 2001.

Kurzweil, Baruch. *Ba-ma-avak al erkhe ha-yahadut.* Jerusalem: Schocken, 1969.

Labendz, Jenny R. " 'Know What to Answer the Epicurean': A Diachronic Study of the 'Apiqoros in Rabbinic Literature." *HUCA* 74 (2003): 175–214.

Lachover, Fischel, ed. *Igrot Hayim Nahman Bialik.* Tel Aviv: Dvir, 1938.

Laor, Dan. *Haye Agnon: Biografiyah.* Jerusalem: Schocken Press, 1988.

Lapin, Hayim. *Rabbis as Romans: The Rabbinic Movement in Palestine, 100–400 CE.* New York: Oxford University Press, 2012.

Lazier, Benjamin. *God Interrupted: Heresy and the European Imagination between the World Wars.* Princeton, NJ: Princeton University Press, 2008.

Lehmann, Matthias B. *Emissaries from the Holy Land: The Sephardic Diaspora and the Practice of Pan-Judaism in the Eighteenth Century.* Stanford, CA: Stanford University Press, 2014.

Leicht, Reimund. "Toward a History of Hebrew Astrological Literature: A Bibliographical Survey." In *Science in Medieval Jewish Cultures,* edited by Gad Freudenthal, 255–291. Cambridge: Cambridge University Press, 2011.

Leiman, Shnayer Z. "The Approbations of Rabbi Jonathan Eibeschütz and Rabbi Jacob Emden" (Hebrew). *Or ha-mizrah* 51 (2006): 169–203.

———. "The Baal Teshuvah and the Emden-Eibeschuetz Controversy." *Judaic Studies* 1 (1985).

———. "Books Suspected of Sabbatianism: The List of Rabbi Jacob Emden" (Hebrew). In *Sefer ha-zikaron le-rabi Moshe Lifshitz,* edited by R. Rosenbaum, 885–894. New York: 1996.

———. "Rabbi Ezekiel Landau's 'Iggeret shelomim'" (Hebrew). In *Lo yasur shevet mi-yehudah: hanhaga, rabanut, ve-kehila be-toledot yisrael mehkarim mugashim le-Professor Simon Schwarzfuchs,* edited by Joseph R. Hacker and Yaron Harel, 317–331. Jerusalem: Bialik Institute, 2011.

———. "When a Rabbi Is Accused of Heresy: The Stance of the Gaon of Vilna in the Emden-Eibeschuetz Controversy." In *Me'ah She'arim: Studies in Medieval Jewish Spiritual Life in Memory of Isadore Twersky,* edited by Ezra Fleischer et al., 251–263. Jerusalem: Magnes Press, 2001.

———. "When a Rabbi Is Accused of Heresy: The Stance of Rabbi Jacob Joshua Falk in the Emden-Eibeschuetz Controversy." In *Rabbinic Culture and Its Critics,* edited by Daniel Frank and Matt Goldish, 435–456. Detroit: Wayne State University Press, 2008.

Leiman, Sid Z., and Simon Schwarzfuchs. "New Evidence on the Emden-Eibeschuetz Controversy: The Amulets from Metz." *REJ* 165 (2006): 229–249.

Levanon, Yehoshua. "Lubavitch Motifs in *Ha-nidah* by S. Y. Agnon" (Hebrew). *Bikoret u-farshanut* 16 (1981): 135–153.

Lévi, Israël. *Le Ravissement du Messie à sa naissance et autres essais.* Edited by Evelyne Patlagean. Paris: Peeters, 1994.

Levie Bernfeld, Tirtsah. *Poverty and Welfare among the Portuguese Jews in Early Modern Amsterdam.* Oxford: Littman Library, 2012.

Leyb ben Ozer. *La beauté du diable: Portrait de Sabbataï Zevi.* Edited and translated by Nathan Weinstock. Paris: Honoré Champion, 2011.

———. *Sippur ma-asei shabbtai sevi: Bashraybung fun shabsai tsvi.* Translated by Zalman Shazar. Edited by Shlomo Zucker and Rivka Plesser. Jerusalem: Zalman Shazar Center, 1978.

Lewis, Bernard. *The Assassins: A Radical Sect in Islam.* New York: Octagon Books, 1980.

Lieberman, Julia R. "Academias literarias y de estudios religiosos en Amsterdam en el siglo XVII." In *Los judaizantes en Europa y la litteratura castellana del Siglo de Oro*, edited by Fernando Díaz Esteban, 247–260. Madrid: Letrúmero, 1994.

Liebes, Yehuda. "The Attitude of Sabbetai Zevi to His Conversion" (Hebrew). In *Sod ha-emunah ha-Shabtait*, 20–34. Jerusalem: Bialik Institute, 1995.

———. "The Book *Zaddik yesod olam*: A Sabbatian mythology" (Hebrew). In *Sod ha-emunah ha-shabtait*, 53–69. Jerusalem: Bialik Institute, 1995.

———. "Elijah of Vilna's Self-Image and Its Relationship to Sabbatianism" (Hebrew). In *Le-tzvi u-le-gaon: mi-shabtai zvi el ha-gaon mi-vilna*, 95–119. Tel Aviv: Idra, 2017.

———. *Heto shel Elisha*. Jerusalem: Akademon, 1990.

———. "Jonah ben Amitai as Messiah ben Joseph" (Hebrew). In *Mehkarim ba-kabalah be-filosofiyah yehudit uve-sifrut ha-musar vehegahut mugashim le-Yishayahu Tishby*, edited by Joseph Dan and Joseph Hacker, 269–311. Jerusalem: Magnes Press, 1986.

———. *Le-tzvi u-le-gaon: mi-shabtai zvi el ha-gaon mi-vilna*. Tel Aviv: Idra, 2017.

———. "The Messianism of Rabbi Jacob Emden and Its Relationship to Sabbatianism" (Hebrew). In *Sod ha-emunah ha-shabtait*, 198–211. Jerusalem: Bialik Institute, 1995.

———. "The Prophecy of the Sabbatian R. Heschel Zoref of Vilna in the Writings of Menahem Mendel of Shklov, Student of the Gaon of Vilna and Founder of the Ashkenazi Settlement in Jerusalem" (Hebrew). In *Le-tzvi u-le-gaon: mi-shabtai zvi el ha-gaon mi-vilna*, 285–360. Tel Aviv: Idra, 2017.

———. "The Students of the Gra, Sabbatianism, and the Jewish Point" (Hebrew). In *Le-tzvi u-le-gaon: mi-shabtai zvi el ha-gaon mi-vilna*, 123–173. Tel Aviv: Idra, 2017.

Long, Pamela O. *Artisan/Practitioners and the Rise of the New Sciences, 1400–1600*. Corvallis: Oregon State University Press, 2011.

Löwenstein, Leopold. *Mafteah ha-haskamot*. Frankfurt a.m.: J. Kauffmann, 1923.

Lowry, Martin. *The World of Aldus Manutius: Business and Scholarship in Renaissance Venice*. Ithaca, NY: Cornell University Press, 1979.

Maciejko, Paweł. *The Mixed Multitude: Jacob Frank and the Frankist Movement, 1755–1816*. Philadelphia: University of Pennsylvania Press, 2011.

———. *Sabbatian Heresy: Writings on Mysticism, Messianism, and the Origins of Jewish Modernity*. Waltham, MA: Brandeis University Press, 2017.

Maier, Ingrid, and Winfried Schumacher. "Ein Medien-Hype im 17 Jahrhundert? Fünf illustrierte Drucke aus dem Jahre 1666 über die angebliche Hinrichtung von Sabbatai Zwi." *Quaerendo* 39 (2009): 133–167.

Maimonides, Moses. *The Guide of the Perplexed*. Translated by Shlomo Pines. Chicago: University of Chicago Press, 1963.

———. *Epistle to Yemen*. Edited by Abraham S. Halkin. New York: American Academy of Jewish Research, 1952.

Malcolm, Alistair. *Royal Favouritism and the Governing Elite of the Spanish Monarchy, 1640–1665*. Oxford: Oxford University Press, 2017.

Malcolm, Noel. "Hobbes and the European Republic of Letters." in *Aspects of Hobbes*, 457–545. Oxford: Clarendon Press, 2002.

Manekin, Rachel. "Galician Haskalah and the Discourse of *Schwärmerei*." in *Secularism in Question: Jews and Judaism in Modern Times*, edited by Ari Joskowicz and Ethan Katz, 189–207. Philadelphia: University of Pennsylvania Press, 2015.

Manor, Dan. "R. Moses b. Maimon (Elbaz): Kabbalistic Commentary and Its Sources" (Hebrew). *Kabbalah* 7 (2002): 199–223.

Marciano, Yoel. "The Messianic Movement in Ávila in 1295. MA thesis. Bar-Ilan University, 2001.

Marcus, Ivan G. *Sefer Hasidim and the Ashkenazic Book in Medieval Europe*. Philadelphia: University of Pennsylvania Press, 2018.

Marks, Richard G. *The Image of Bar Kokhba in Traditional Jewish Literature: False Messiah and National Hero*. University Park: Pennsylvania State University Press, 1994.

Marriott, Brandon. *Transnational Networks and Cross-Religious Exchange in the Seventeenth Century Mediterranean and Atlantic Worlds: Sabbatai Sevi and the Lost Tribes of Israel*. Burlington, VT: Ashgate, 2015.

Martínez, María Elena. *Genealogical Fictions: Limpieza de sangre, Religion, and Gender in Colonial Mexico*. Stanford, CA: Stanford University Press, 2008.

Marx, Alexander. "The Correspondence between the Rabbis of Southern France and Maimonides about Astrology." *HUCA* 3 (1926): 311–358.

Méchoulan, Henry. "Abraham Pereyra, juge des marranes et censeur des ses coreligionnaires à Amsterdam au temps de Spinoza." *REJ* 138 (1979): 391–400.

———. *Hispanidad y judaismo en tiempos de Espinoza: estudio y edicion anotada de La Certeza del Camino de Abraham Pereyra, Amsterdam, 1666*. Salamanca: Ediciones Universidad de Salamanca, 1987.

———. "La Pensée d'Abraham Pereyra dans *La Certeza del Camino*." *Dutch Jewish History*, edited by Joseph Michman, 2:69–85. Jerusalem: Magnes Press, 1989.

Meijer, Jaap. "Sabetai Rephael in Hamburg: Korte bidrage tot de geschiedenis van de Joodse wereld na Sabetai Tswi." In *Weerklank op het wer van Jan Romein: Liber Amicorum*, 103–108. Amsterdam: Wereldbibliotheek, 1953.

Meir, Jonatan. "Jacob Frank: The Wondrous Charlatan" (Hebrew). *Tarbiz* 80 (2012): 463–474.

Midrash Ekha Rabba. Edited by Salomon Buber. Vilna, 1899.

Mill, J. S. *Mill on Bentham and Coleridge*. Edited by F. R. Leavis. London: Chatto and Windus, 1950.

Miller, Michael Laurence. "Rabbi David Oppenheim on Trial: Turks, Titles, and Tribute in Counter-Reformation Prague." *JQR* 106 (2016): 42–75.

Moote, A. Lloyd, and Dorothy C. Moote. *The Great Plague: The Story of London's Most Deadly Year*. Baltimore: Johns Hopkins University Press, 2004.

Mortera, Saul Levi. *Tratado de verdade de lei de Moisés*. Edited by H. P. Salomon. Coimbra: Coimbra University Press, 1988.

Moyal, Elie. *Ha-tenuah ha-shabtait be-Morocco: toldoteha u-mekoroteha*. Tel Aviv: Am Oved, 1984.

———. *Rabbi Yaakov Sasportas: meholel ha-pulmus neged ha-tenuah ha-shabtait u-maavakav le-ma-an shilton ha-halakah*. Jerusalem: Rav Kook Institute, 1992.

Muchnik, Natalia. "Des intrus en pays d'inquisition: présence et activités des juifs dans l'Espagne du xvii siècle," *REJ* 164 (2005): 119–156.

Myers, David N. " 'Commanded War': Three Chapters in the 'Military' History of Satmar Hasidism." *Journal of the American Academy of Religion* 81 (2013): 311–356.

———. *Re-inventing the Jewish Past: European Jewish Intellectuals and the Zionist Return to History.* New York: Oxford University Press, 1995.

———. "The Scholem-Kurzweil Debate and Modern Jewish Historiography." *Modern Judaism* 6 (1986): 261–286.

Nadav, Yael. "A Kabbalistic Treatise of R. Solomon Ailion" (Hebrew). *Sefunot* 3–4 (1960): 301–349.

Nadler, Allan L. "Piety and Politics: The Case of the Satmar Rebbe." *Judaism* 31 (1982): 135–152.

Nahon, Gérard. "Les institutions éducatives au XVIIe siècle: trois paradigms—Palestine, Amsterdam, Maroc." In *Le Monde Sépharade*, edited by Shmuel Trigano, 2:302–318. Paris: Seuil, 2006.

———. "Les Marranes espagnols et portugais et les communautés juives issues du marranisme dans l'historiographie récente." *REJ* 136 (1977): 297–367.

———. *Les "Nations" Juives Portugaises du Sud-Oest de la France (1684–1791): Documents.* Paris: Fundãço Calouste Gulbenkian Centro Cultural Portugês, 1981.

———. "R. Rafael b. Eleazar Meldola in Bayonne, 1728–1741" (Hebrew). In *Lo yasur shevet mi-yehuda: hanhaga, rabanut, ve-kehila be-toledot yisrael mehkarim mugashim le-Profesor Simon Schwarzfuchs*, edited by Joseph R. Hacker and Yaron Harel, 271–299. Jerusalem: Bialik Institute, 2011.

Netanyahu, Benzion. *The Marranos of Spain: From the Late XIVth to the Early XVIth Century according to Contemporary Hebrew Sources.* New York: American Academy of Jewish Research, 1966.

Newman, Hillel I. "Dating *Sefer Zerubavel*: Dehistoricizing and Rehistoricizing a Jewish Apocalypse of Late Antiquity." *Admantius* 19 (2013): 324–336.

Nigal, Gedalyah. *Shai Agnon u-mekorotav ha-hasdiyim: iyun be-arba-ah mi-sipurav.* Ramat Gan: Kurzweil Institute of Bar-Ilan University, 1983.

Novenson, Matthew V. "Why Does R. Akiba Acclaim Bar Kokhba as Messiah?" *Journal for the Study of Judaism* 40 (2009): 551–572.

Nusteling, Hurbert P. H. "The Jews in the Republic of the United Provinces: Origin, Numbers, and Dispersion." In *Dutch Jewry: Its History and Secular Culture (1500–2000)*, edited by Jonathan Israel and Reinier Salverda, 43–62. Leiden: Brill, 2002.

Offenberg, A. K. *Menasseh ben Israel 1604–1657: A Biographical Sketch.* Amsterdam: Menasseh ben Israel Instituut, 2015.

Orbach, Alexander. *New Voices of Russian Jewry: A Study of the Russian-Jewish Press of Odessa in the Era of the Great Reforms, 1860–1871.* Leiden: Brill, 1980.

Pachter, Mordechai. "Hazut Kasha of Rabbi Moses Alshekh" (Hebrew). *Shalem* 1 (1974): 157–195.

Panofsky, Erwin. *Early Netherlandish Painting: Its Origin and Character.* Cambridge, MA: Harvard University Press, 1966.

Paraira, M. C., and J. S. da Silva Rosa. *Gedenkschrift uitgegeven ter gelegenheid van het 300-jarig bestaan der onderwijisnrichtingen Talmud Tora en Ets Haïm.* Amsterdam: Roeloffzen-Hübner, 1916.

Parush, Iris. *Kanon sifruti ve-ideologyah leumit: bikoret ha-sifrut shel Frishman behasva-ah le-vikoret shel Klausner u-Brenner.* Jerusalem: Bialik Institute, 1992.

Pedaya, Haviva. *Ha-Ramban: hit-alut, zeman mahzori ve-tekst kadosh.* Tel Aviv: Am Oved, 2003.

Penkower, Jordan S. "Jacob ben Hayyim and the Rise of the Biblia Hebraica." PhD diss., Hebrew University of Jerusalem, 1982.

Petram, Lodewijk. *The World's First Stock Exchange.* Translated by Lynne Richards. New York: Columbia University Press, 2014.

Phillips, Derek. *Well-Being in Amsterdam's Golden Age.* Amsterdam: Pallas Publications, 2008.

Pieterse, Wilhelmina C. *Daniel Levi de Barrios als geschiedschrijver van de Portugees-Israelitische gemeente te Amsterdam in zijn "Triumpho del govierno popular".* Amsterdam: Scheltema and Holkema, 1968.

Poppel, Stephen M. "Salman Schocken and the Schocken Verlag: A Jewish Publisher in Weimar and Nazi Germany." *Harvard Library Bulletin* 21 (1973): 20–49.

Radensky, Paul Ira. "Leyb ben Ozer's 'Bashraybung fun Shabsai Tsvi': An Ashkenazic Appropriation of Sabbatianism." *JQR* 88 (1997):43–56.

Rakover, Nahum. *Zekhut ha-yotsrim ba-mekorot ha-yehudiyim.* Jerusalem: Moreshet ha-mishpat be-yisrael, 1991.

Raphael, Isaac. "The Writings of Rabbi Jacob Emden" (Hebrew). *Areshet* 3 (1961): 231–277.

Rapoport-Albert, Ada. "On the Position of Women in Sabbatianism" (Hebrew). In *Ha-halom ve-shivro,* edited by Rachel Elior, 1:143–327. Jerusalem: Magnes Press, 2001.

———. *Women and the Messianic Heresy of Sabbatai Zevi 1666–1816.* Oxford: Littman Library, 2011.

Ratzaby, Yehuda. "Rabbi Solomon Adeni and Iis Work *Melekhet Shelomo*" (Hebrew). *Sinai* 106 (1990): 243–254.

Rauschenbach, Sina. *Judentum für Christen: Vermittlung und Selbstbehauptung Menasseh ben Israels in den gelehrten Debatten des 17. Jahrhunderts.* Berlin: De Gruyter, 2012.

Ravitzky, Aviezer. *Messianism, Zionism, and Jewish Religious Radicalism.* Chicago: University of Chicago Press, 1996.

———. "Religious Radicalism and Political Messianism in Israel." In *Religious Radicalism and Politics in the Middle East,* edited by Emmanuel Sivan and Menachem Friedman, 11–37. Albany: SUNY Press, 1990.

Raz-Krakotzkin, Amnon. "Between 'Brit Shalom' and the Temple: The Dialectic of Redemption and Messianism in the Writings of Gershom Scholem" (Hebrew). *Theory and Criticism* 20 (2002): 87–112.

———. *The Censor, the Editor, and the Text: The Catholic Church and the Shaping of the Jewish Canon in the Sixteenth Century.* Philadelphia: University of Pennsylvania Press, 2007.

———. "Law and Censure: The Printing of the *Shulhan Arukh* as the Commencement of Jewish Modernity" (Hebrew). In *Tov Elem: Memory, Community, and Gender in Medieval and Early Modern Jewish Societies; Essays in Honor of Robert Bonfil,* edited by Elisheva Baumgarten et al., 306–335. Jerusalem: Bialik Institute, 2011.

———. "Persecution and the Art of Printing: Hebrew Books in Italy in the 1550s." In

Jewish Culture in Early Modern Europe: Essays in Honor of David B. Ruderman, edited by Richard I. Cohen et al., 97–108. Cincinnati, OH: HUC Press; Pittsburgh, PA: University of Pittsburgh Press, 2014.

——. "'Without regard for external considerations': The Question of Christianity in Scholem and Baer's Writings" (Hebrew). *Jewish Studies* 38 (1998): 73–96.

Reggio, Isaac. *Ha-torah veha-filosofiah: mehkar iyuni.* Vienna: Anton Schmid, 1827.

——. *Yalkut yashar: Asefat hakirot al inyanim shonim.* Gorizia: Joh. Bap. Seitz, 1854.

Reiner, Elchanan. "Beyond the Realm of the Haskalah: Changing Learning Patterns in Jewish Traditional Society" (Hebrew). In *Yashan mi-pene hadash: Shai le-Emanuel Etkes*, edited by David Assaf and Ada Rapoport-Albert, 2:289–311. Jerusalem: Zalman Shazar Center, 2009.

——. "Changes in the Polish and Ashkenazi Academies in the Sixteenth and Seventeenth Centuries, and the Debate over Argumentation" (Hebrew). In *Ke-minhag Ashkenaz ve-Polin: Sefer yovel le-Chone Shmeruk*, edited by Israel Bartal et al., 9–80. Jerusalem: Zalman Shazar Center, 1993.

——. "An Itinerant Preacher Publishes His Books: An Untold Chapter in the Cultural History of European Jewry in the Seventeenth Century" (Hebrew). In *Hut shel hen: shai le-Chava Turniansky*, edited by Israel Bartal et al., 1:123–156. Jerusalem: Zalman Shazar Center, 2013.

——. "'No Jew should learn anything but the Talmud alone': A Dispute over Books and Forbidden Books in Sixteenth-Century Ashkenaz" (Hebrew). In *Ta-Shma: mehkarim be-madae ha-yahadut le-zikhro shel yisrael M. Ta-Shma*, edited by Avraham (Rami) Reiner et al., 2:705–746. Alon Shvut: Tevunot, 2011.

——. "Wealth, Social Status, and Talmud Torah: The *Kloyz* in Jewish Society in Eastern Europe in the Seventeenth and Eighteenth Centuries" (Hebrew). *Zion* 58 (1993): 287–328.

Revah, Israel S. "Les Écrivains Manuel de Pina et Miguel de Barrios et la censure de la communauté judéo-portugaise d'Amsterdam." *Tesoro de los Judïos Sefardies* 8 (1965): lxxiv–xci.

——. "Les Marranes." *REJ* 118 (1959–1960): 29–77.

Richler, Benjamin. *Guide to Hebrew Manuscript Collections.* Jerusalem: Israel Academy of Sciences and Humanities, 2014.

Riemer, Nathaniel. "Zwischen christlichen Hebraisten und Sabbatianern—der Lebensweg von R. Beer und Bila Perlhefter." *Aschkenas* 14 (2004): 163–201.

Riemer, Nathaniel, and Sigrid Senkbeil, eds. *'Beer Sheva' by Beer and Bella Perlhefter: An Edition of a Seventeenth-Century Encyclopedia.* Wiesbaden: Harrassowitz, 2011.

Rohrbacher, Stefan. "Die Drei Gemeinden Altona, Hamburg Wandsbek zur Zeit der Glikl." *Aschkenas* 8 (1998): 105–124.

Van Rooden, Peter T., and Jan Wim Wesselius. "Two Early Cases of Publication by Subscription in Holland and Germany: Jacob Abendana's *Mikhlal Yophi* (1661) and David Cohen de Lara's *Keter Kehunna* (1668)." *Quarendo* 16 (1986): 110–130.

Rose, Mark. *Authors and Owners: The Invention of Copyright.* Cambridge, MA: Harvard University Press, 1993.

Rosman, Moshe. "Authority of the Council of Four Lands beyond Poland" (Hebrew). *Bar-Ilan* 24–25 (1989): 11–30.

Roth, Cecil. "The Amazing Clan of Buzaglo." *TJHSE* 23 (1969–1970): 11–21.

———. *A Life of Menasseh ben Israel: Rabbi, Printer, and Diplomat.* Philadelphia: JPS, 1945.

———. "Samuel Sumbal: A Forgotten Jewish Statesman" (Hebrew). *Mehkarim u-peulot*, 3:13–17.

Roth, Norman. *Conversos, Inquisition and the Expulsion of the Jews from Spain.* Madison: University of Wisconsin Press, 1995.

Rozenblit, Marsha L. *The Jews of Vienna, 1867–1914: Assimilation and Identity.* Albany: SUNY Press, 1983.

Rubenstein, Jeffrey L. *Talmudic Stories: Narrative Art, Composition and Culture.* Baltimore: Johns Hopkins University Press, 1999.

Rubin, Salomon. "Biographisches: Jakob Saportas." *Ben-Chananja* 7 (1864): 711–714.

———. "Words of the Sages: On the History of the Sage and Kabbalist, R. Jacob Sasportas, of Blessed Memory" (Hebrew). *Ha-melitz*, 2 March 1865.

Ruderman, David B. *Early Modern Jewry: A New Cultural History.* Princeton, NJ: Princeton University Press, 2010.

———. "The Impact of Science on Jewish Culture and Society in Venice (with Special Reference to Jewish Graduates of Padua's Medical School." In *Essential Papers on Jewish Culture in Renaissance and Baroque Italy*, edited by David B. Ruderman, 519–553. New York: New York University Press, 1992.

———. *Jewish Thought and Scientific Discovery in Early Modern Europe.* New Haven, CT: Yale University Press, 1995.

———, ed. *Preachers of the Italian Ghetto.* Berkeley: University of California Press, 1992.

Samuel, Wilfred S. "The Jews of London and the Great Plague (1665)." *Miscellanies of the Jewish Historical Society of England* 3 (1937): 7–15.

———. "A List of Jewish Persons Endenized and Naturalised, 1609–1799." *TJHSE* 22 (1968–1969): 111–144.

Saperstein, Marc. *Exile in Amsterdam: Saul Levi Morteira's Sermons to a Congregation of "New Jews."* Cincinnati, OH: Hebrew Union College Press, 2005.

———. *Jewish Preaching, 1200–1800: An Anthology.* New Haven, CT: Yale University Press, 1989.

Sárraga, Marian, and Ramón F. Sárraga. "The Poet Moses Gideon Abudiente and His Family in Amsterdam and Hamburg: Echoes of 1666 Sabbatian Polemics in Hamburg Epitaphs." *SR* 35 (2001): 214–240.

Sasportas, Jacob. *Kitzur zizath novel zvi.* Odessa: Beilinson, 1867.

Saunders, J. W. "The Stigma of Print: A Note on the Social Bases of Tudor Poetry." *Essays in Criticism* 1 (1951): 139–164.

Schacter, Jacob J. "Motivations for Radical Anti-Sabbatianism: The Case of Hakham Zevi Ashkenazi." In *Ha-halom ve-shivro*, edited by Rachel Elior, 2:31–55. Jerusalem: Hebrew University, 2001.

———. "Rabbi Jacob Emden: Life and Major Works." PhD diss., Harvard University, 1988.

———. "Rabbi Jacob Emden, Philosophy, and Maimonides." In *Be'erot Yitzhak: Studies in Memory of Isadore Twersky*, edited by Jay M. Harris, 239–267. Cambridge, MA: Harvard University Press, 2005.

———. "Rabbi Jacob Emden, Sabbatianism, and Frankism: Attitudes toward Christianity in the Eighteenth Century." In *New Perspectives on Jewish-Christians Relations in Honor of David Berger*, edited by Elisheva Carlebach and Jacob J. Schacter, 359–396. Leiden: Brill, 2012.

———. "Rabbi Jacob Emden's '*Iggeret Purim.*" In *Studies in Medieval Jewish History and Literature*, edited by Isadore Twersky, 2:441–446. Cambridge, MA: Harvard University Press, 1984.

Schäfer, Peter. "Bar Kokhba and the Rabbis." In *The Bar Kokhba War Reconsidered: New Perspectives on the Second Jewish Revolt against Rome*, edited by Peter Schäfer, 1–22. Tübingen: Mohr Siebeck, 2003.

———. *Der Bar Kokhba-Aufstand: Studien zum zweiten jüdischen Krieg gegen Rome.* Tübingen: Mohr, 1981.

———. *The Jewish Jesus: How Judaism and Christianity Shaped Each Other.* Princeton, NJ: Princeton University Press, 2012.

Schagen, Judy. "Sasportas's Portraits: The Final Word!?" *SR* 33 (1999): 190–194.

Schatz, Rivkah. "Review of *Zizath novel zvi*" (Hebrew). *Behinot* 10 (1956): 50–67.

Schaub, Jean-Frédéric. *Les juifs du roi d'Espagne: Oran 1509–1669.* Paris: Hachette, 1999.

Schechter, Oded. " 'Their impure language which they have called Hebrew': Between the Sacred Tongue and Aramaic, towards a Genealogy of the Hebrew" (Hebrew). *Mi-ta-am* 2 (2005): 123–138.

Schidorsky, Dov. *Gevilim nisrafim ve-otiyot porhot: toldotehem shel osfei sefarim ve-sifriyot be Erets yisrael ve-nisyonot le-hatsalat seridehem le-ahar ha-shoah.* Jerusalem: Magnes Press, 2008.

Schmelzer, Menahem. "Poems in Praise of Books by David ben Joseph ibn Yahya" (Hebrew). In *Asupah le-Yosef: kovetz mehkarim shai le-Yosef Hacker*, edited by Yaron Ben-Naeh et al., 322–335. Jerusalem: Zalman Shazar Center, 2014.

Scholberg, Kenneth R. "Miguel de Barrios and the Amsterdam Sephardic Community." *JQR* 53 (1962): 120–159.

Scholem, Gershom. *Be-ikvot mashiah.* Jerusalem: Tarshish, 1944.

———. *Briefe I: 1914–1947.* Edited by Itta Shedletzky. Munich: Verlag C. H. Beck, 1994.

———. *Briefe II: 1948–1970.* Edited by Thomas Spaar. Munich: Verlag C. H. Beck, 1995.

———. "A Candid Letter about My True Intentions in Studying Kabbalah." In *On the Possibility of Jewish Mysticism in Our Time and Other Essays*, edited by Avraham Shapira, translated by Jonathan Chipman, 3–5. Philadelphia: JPS, 1997.

———. "A Commentary to the Psalms from the Circle of Sabbetai Zevi in Adrianople" (Hebrew). In *Mehkere shabtaut*, edited by Yehuda Liebes, 89–141. Tel Aviv: Am Oved, 1991.

———, ed. *The Correspondence of Walter Benjamin and Gershom Scholem, 1932–1940.* Edited by Gershom Scholem. New York: Schocken Books, 1989.

———. "The Crypto-Jewish Sect of the Dönmeh (Sabbatians) in Turkey." In *The Messi-*

anic Idea in Judaism and Other Essays on Jewish Spirituality, 142–166. New York: Schocken Books, 1971.

Scholem, Gershom. "The Faithful of Israel in their Generation" (Hebrew). In *Od davar*, edited by Avraham Shapira, 98–104. Tel Aviv: Am Oved, 1989.

——. *From Berlin to Jerusalem: Memories of My Youth*. Translated by Harry Zohn. Philadelphia: Paul Dry Books, 2012.

——. *Halomotav shel ha-Shabtai R. Mordecai Ashkenazi*. N.p.: Schocken, 1937.

——. "Leket Margoliyot." In *Mehkere shabtaut*, edited by Yehuda Liebes, 686–706. Tel Aviv: Am Oved, 1991.

——. "The Letter of Abraham Miguel Cardoso to the Judges of Izmir" (Hebrew). In *Mehkarim u-mekorot le-toledot ha-shabtaut ve-gilguleha*, 298–331 Jerusalem: Bialik Institute, 1974.

——. "The Letter of the Shield of Abraham from the Land of the West, Written Apparently by Abraham Miguel Cardoso" (Hebrew). In *Mehkere shabtaut*, edited by Yehuda Liebes, 142–179. Tel Aviv: Am Oved, 1991.

——. "A Letter to H. N. Bialik" (Hebrew). In *Devarim be-go*, 1:59–63. Tel Aviv: Am Oved, 1976.

——. *Major Trends in Jewish Mysticism*. Jerusalem: Schocken Books, 1941.

——. *Mehkarim u-mekorot le-toledot ha-shabtaut ve-gilguleha*. Jerusalem: Bialik Institute, 1974.

——. *Mehkere shabtaut*. Edited by Yehuda Leibes. Tel Aviv: Am Oved, 1991.

——. "Mitzvah ha-ba-ah ba-averah: le-havanat ha-shabtaut." *Keneset* 2 (1937): 347–392.

——. "And the mystery still stands" (Hebrew). In *Mehkere shabtaut*, edited by Yehuda Leibes, 250–288. Tel Aviv: Am Oved, 1991.

——. "Nathan of Gaza's Letter on Sabbetai Zevi and His Conversion." In *Mekharim u-mekorot le-toledot ha-shabtaut ve-gilguleha*, 233–273. Jerusalem: Bialik Institute, 1974.

——. "New Information on Abraham Cardoso" (Hebrew). In *Mehkere shabtaut*, edited by Yehuda Liebes, 393–424. Tel Aviv: Am Oved, 1991.

——. "New Sabbatian Documents from the Book *To-ei Ruah*" (Hebrew). In *Mehkere shabtaut*, edited by Yehuda Liebes, 26–53. Tel Aviv: Am Oved, 1991.

——. "Redemption through Sin." In *The Messianic Idea in Judaism and Other Essays on Jewish Spirituality*, 78–141. New York: Schocken Books, 1971.

——. "Reflections on Jewish Studies" (Hebrew). In *Devarim be-go*, 2:385–403. Tel Aviv: Am Oved, 1976.

——. "Response of Prof. Gershom Scholem" (Hebrew). In *Ha-ra-ayon ha-meshihi be-yisrael: yom iyun le-regel melot shemonim shanah le-Gershom Scholem*, 254–262. Jerusalem: Israel Academy of Sciences, 1982.

——. "Review of M. J. Cohen 'Jacob Emden: A Man of Controversy'" (Hebrew). In *Mehkere shabtaut*, edited by Yehuda Liebes, 655–680. Tel Aviv: Am Oved, 1991.

——. "The Sabbatian Movement in Poland." In *Mekkarim u-mekorot le-toledot ha-shabtaut ve-gilguleha*, 68–140. Jerusalem: Bialik Institute, 1974.

———. *Sabbatai Sevi: The Mystical Messiah.* Translated by R. J. Zwi Werblowsky. Princeton, NJ: Princeton University Press, 1973.

———. *Shabbetai Sevi ve-ha-tenuah ha-shabetait bi-yeme hayav.* Tel Aviv: Am Oved, 1957.

———. *Toledot ha-tenuah ha-shabtait.* Edited by Jonatan Meir and Shinichi Yamamoto. Tel Aviv: JTS-Schocken Institute, 2018.

———. "Toward an Understanding of the Messianic Idea in Judaism." In *The Messianic Idea in Judaism and Other Essays on Jewish Spirituality,* 1–36. New York: Schocken Books, 1971.

———. "Tradition and New Creation in the Ritual of the Kabbalists." In *On the Kabbalah and Its Symbolism,* 118–157. New York: Schocken Books, 1965.

———. "Über die Theologie des Sabbatianismus im Lichte Abraham Cardozos." *Der Jude* 9 (1928): 123–139.

———. "Works on Sabbetai Zevi, the Majority from the Writings of Nathan of Gaza in MS Adler, 494" (Hebrew). In *Mehkere shabtaut,* edited by Yehuda Liebes, 17–25. Tel Aviv: Am Oved, 1991.

Schorsch, Ismar. "From Messianism to Realpolitik: Menasseh ben Israel and the Readmission of the Jews to England." *Proceedings of the American Academy for Jewish Research* 45 (1978): 187–208.

Schorske, Carl E. *Fin-de-siècle Vienna: Politics and Culture.* New York: Knopf, 1979.

Schroeter, Daniel J. *The Sultan's Jew: Morocco and the Sephardi World.* Stanford, CA: Stanford University Press, 2002.

Schwartz, Daniel B. *The First Modern Jew: Spinoza and the History of an Image.* Princeton, NJ: Princeton University Press, 2012.

Schwartz, Seth. *Imperialism and Jewish Society, 200 B.C.E. to 640 C.E.* Princeton, NJ: Princeton University Press, 2001.

Schwarz, A. Z. *Die Hebräischen Handschriften in Österreich (Ausserhalb der Nationalbibliothek in Wien).* Leipzig: Verlag Karl W. Hiersemann, 1931.

Sclar, David. "Books in the Ets Haim Yeshivah: Acquisition, Publishing and a Community of Scholarship in Eighteenth-Century Amsterdam." *Jewish History* 30 (2016): 207–232.

Sefer hasidim. Edited by Jehuda Wistinetzki with an introduction and index by Jacob Freimann. Frankfurt: M. A. Wahrmann, 1924.

Sela, Shlomo. "Abraham bar Hiyya's Astrological Work and Thought." *Jewish Studies Quarterly* 13 (2006): 128–158.

Septimus, Bernard. " 'Open rebuke and concealed love': Nahmanides and the Andalusian Tradition." In *Rabbi Moses Nahmanides: Explorations in His Religious and Literary Virtuousity,* edited by Isadore Twersky, 11–34. Cambridge, MA: Harvard University Press, 1983.

———. "What Did Maimonides Mean by *Madda*?" In *Me'ah She'arim: Studies in Medieval Jewish Spiritual Life in Memory of Isadore Twersky,* edited by Ezra Fleischer et al., 83–110. Jerusalem: Magnes Press, 2001.

Shapin, Steven, and Simon Schaffer. *Leviathan and the Air-Pump: Hobbes, Boyle, and the Experimental Life.* Princeton, NJ: Princeton University Press, 1985.

Shapira, Anita. *Berl: Biografiyah.* Tel Aviv: Am Oved, 1980.

Shapira-Meir, Irit. "Historiography and Autobiography in Leyb ben Ozer's 'Bashray-bung fun Shabsai Tsvi'" (Hebrew). MA thesis. Hebrew University of Jerusalem, 2014.

Shilo, Elchanan. *Ha-kabalah bi-yetzirat Shai Agnon.* Ramat Gan: Bar-Ilan University Press, 2011.

Shmeruk, Chone. "Yiddish Literature and the Beginnings of Modern Newspapers in Yiddish" (Hebrew). In *Sifrut yidish: perakim le-toldoteha,* 261–293. Tel Aviv: Porter Institute for Poetics and Semiotics, 1978.

Shmidman, Michael A. "Rashba as Halakhic Critic of Maimonides." In *Turim: Studies in Jewish History and Literature Presented to Dr. Bernard Lander,* edited by Michael A. Shmidman, 257–273. New York: Touro College Press, 2007.

Sicroff, Albert. *Les Controverses de "pureté de sang" en Espange du XVe au XVIIe siècle.* Paris: Didier, 1960.

Silber, Michael K. "The Emergence of Ultra-Orthodoxy: The Invention of a Tradition." In *The Uses of Tradition: Jewish Continuity in the Modern Era,* edited by Jack Wertheimer, 23–84. Cambridge, MA: Harvard University Press, 1992.

Şişman, Cengiz. "A Jewish Messiah from Tartaria in 1671: A New Source of the Lives of the Sabbatean Prophets, Sabbatai Raphael and/or Shilo Sabbatai." *Kabbalah* 9 (2003): 63–75.

Skinner, Anthony David, ed.. *Gershom Scholem: A Life in Letters, 1914–1982.* Cambridge, MA: Harvard University Press, 2002.

Sokolow, Nahum, ed. *Sefer zikaron le-sofre yisrael ha-hayim itanu ka-yom.* Warsaw, 1890.

Soloveitchik, Haym. "*Minhag Ashkenaz ha-Kadmon:* An Assessment." In *Collected Essays,* 2:29–69. Oxford: Littman Library, 2014.

———. "Piety, Pietism, and German Pietism: 'Sefer Hasidim I' and the Influence of Hasidei Ashkenaz." *JQR* 92 (2002): 455–493.

———. "Rabad of Posquières: A Programmatic Essay." In *Studies in the History of Jewish Society in the Middle Ages and in the Modern Period Presented to Jacob Katz on His Seventy-Fifth Birthday,* edited E. Etkes and Y. Salmon, 7–40. Jerusalem: Magnes Press, 1980.

———. "Three Themes in the *Sefer Hasidim.*" *AJS Review* 1 (1976): 311–357.

Sonne, Isaiah. "On the History of Sabbatianism in Italy" (Hebrew). In *Sefer ha-yovel le-Alexander Marx,* 89–103. New York, 1943.

———. "Sabbatian Issues in the Notebook of R. Abraham Rovigo" (Hebrew). *Sefunot* 3–4 (1960): 41–69.

Sorotzkin, David. "Building the Earthly and Destroying the Heavenly: The Satmar Rabbi and the Radical Orthodox School of Thought" (Hebrew). In *Eretz yisrael ba-hagut ha-yehudit ba-meah ha-esrim,* edited by Aviezer Ravitzky, 133–167. Jerusalem: Ben Zvi Institute, 2004.

Spiegel, Yaakov S. *Amudim be-toledot ha-sefer ha-ivri: hagahot u-megihim.* Ramat Gan: Bar-Ilan University Press, 1996.

———. *Amudim be-toledot ha-sefer ha-ivri: ketivah ve-ha-taka.* Ramat Gan: Bar-Ilan University Press, 2005.

Sprang, Felix. " 'I was told they were all Iewes': Mentalities and Realities of Segregation, Sephardi and Ashkenazi Jews in Early Modern Hamburg and Altona." In *Frühneutzeitliche Ghettos in Europa im Vergleich,* edited by Fritz Backhaus et al., 399–416. Berlin: Trafo, 2012.

Stanislawski, Michael. "The Yiddish Shevet Yehudah: A Study in the 'Ashkenization' of a Spanish Jewish Classic." In *Jewish History and Jewish Memory: Essays in Honor of Yosef Hayim Yerushalmi,* edited by Elisheva Carlebach, John M. Efron, and David N. Myers, 135–149. Hanover, NH: Brandeis University Press, 1998.

Starn, Randolph. "Historians and 'Crisis.' " *P&P* 52 (1971): 3–22.

Stern, David. *The Jewish Bible: A Material History.* Seattle: University of Washington Press, 2017.

———. "The Rabbinic Bible in Its Sixteenth-Century Context." In *The Hebrew Book in Early Modern Italy,* edited by Joseph R. Hacker and Adam Shear, 76–108. Philadelphia: University of Pennsylvania Press, 2011.

Stow, Kenneth, and Adam Teller, eds. "The Chmielnitzky Massacres, 1648–1649: Jewish, Polish, and Ukranian Perspectives." Special Issue of *Jewish History* 17 (2003).

Stroumsa, Sarah. *Maimonides in His World: Portrait of a Mediterranean Thinker.* Princeton, NJ: Princeton University Press, 2009.

Studemund-Halévy, Michael, ed. *Die Sefarden in Hamburg: zur Geschichte einer Minderheit.* Hamburg: Buske, 1994–1997.

———. "*Senhores* versus *criados da Nação*: Portugueses, asquenasías y tudescos en el Hamburgo del siglo xvii." *Sefarad* 60 (2000): 349–368.

———. "What Happened in Izmir Was Soon the Talk of Hamburg: Sabbatai Sevi in Contemporary German Press Reports." *El Presente* 10 (2016): 155–172.

Sussmann, Yaacov. "The Scholarly Oeuvre of Professor Ephraim Elimelech Urbach" (Hebrew). In *Ephraim Elimelech Urbach: Bio-biliyografit mehkarit,* 7–116. Supplement to *Madae yahadut,* edited by David Assaf. Jerusalem: World Union of Jewish Studies, 1993.

Sutton, Peter C., ed. *Reclaimed: Paintings from the Collection of Jacques Goudstikker.* New Haven, CT: Yale University Press, 2008.

Swetschinski, Daniel M. "Kinship and Commerce: The Foundations of Portuguese Jewish Life in Seventeenth-Century Holland." *SR* 15 (1981): 52–74.

———. *Reluctant Cosmopolitans: The Portuguese Jews of Seventeenth-Century Amsterdam.* London: Littman Library, 2000.

Talmud Yerushalmi. Jerusalem: Academy of Hebrew Language, 2001.

Ta-Shma, Israel. "German Pietism in Sepharad: Rabbi Jonah Gerondi, the Man and His Work." (Hebrew). In *Keneset mehkarim iyunim be-sifrut ha-rabanit be-yeme ha-benayim: Sepharad,* 2:109–148. Jerusalem: Bialik Institute, 2004.

Teitelbaum, Joel. *Kuntres al-ha-geulah ve-al ha-temurah.* Brooklyn, NY: Sander Deutsch, 1967.

———. *Sefer va-yo-el moshe.* Brooklyn, NY: Sander Deutsch, 1978.

Teller, Adam. "Rabbis without a Function? The Polish Rabbinate and the Council of Four Lands in the 16th–18th Centuries." In *Jewish Religious Leadership: Image and Reality*, edited by Jack Wertheimer, 1:371–400. New York: Jewish Theological Seminary, 2004.

Tishby, Isaiah. "The First Sabbatian *Magid* in R. Abraham Rovigo's House of Study" (Hebrew). In *Netive emunah u-minut*, 81–107. Jerusalem: Magnes Press, 1994.

———. "Letters by Rabbi Jacob Sasportas against the *Parnassim* of Livorno from 1681" (Hebrew). *Kovez al yad* 4 (1946): 143–160.

———. "New Information on the 'Converso' Community in London according to the Letters of Sasportas from 1664/1665" (Hebrew). In *Galut ahar golah: mehkarim be-toledot am yisrael mugashim le-Professor Haim Beinart li-melot lo shivim shana*, edited by Aharon Mirsky, Avraham Grossman, and Yosef Kaplan, 470–496. Jerusalem: Ben Zvi Institute, 1988.

———. "On Gershom Scholem's Approach to the Study of Sabbatianism" (Hebrew). *Tarbiz* 28 (1959): 101–133.

———. "On the Study of the Sources of *Hemdat yamim*" (Hebrew). In *Netive emunah u-minut*, 108–142. Jerusalem: Magnes Press, 1994.

———. "The Penitential Rituals of Nathan of Gaza" (Hebrew). In *Netive emunah u-minut*, 30–51. Jerusalem: Magnes Press, 1994.

———. "Sources from the Early Eighteenth Century in the Book *Hemdat yamim*" (Hebrew). In *Netive emunah ve-minut*, 143–168. Jerusalem: Magnes Press, 1994.

———. *The Wisdom of the Zohar*. Oxford: Littman Library, 1989.

Toaff, Alfredo S. "The Controversy between R. Sasportas and the Jewish Community in Leghorn, (1681)" (Hebrew). *Sefunot* 9 (1964): 169–191.

Trevor-Roper, H. R. "The General Crisis of the Seventeenth Century." *P&P* 16 (1959): 31–64.

Trivellato, Francesca. *The Familiarity of Strangers: The Sephardic Diaspora, Livorno and Cross-Cultural Trade in the Early Modern Period*. New Haven, CT: Yale University Press, 2009.

Turniansky, Chava. "Review of Leyb b. Oyzer, *Sippur ma-asei shabbtai sevi*." *KS* 54 (1979): 161–167.

Tzarfati, Isaac ben Vidal. *Toledot Yitzhak*. Jerusalem: Sephardic Community in Beit ha-Kerem, 1996.

Urbach, Ephraim E. *Hazal: Pirke emunot ve-deot*. Jerusalem: Magnes Press, 1969.

———. "The Religious Meaning of the Law" (Hebrew). In *Al yahadut ve-hinukh*, 127–139. Jerusalem: School of Education of the Hebrew University, 1966.

Urbani, Rossana, and Guido Nathan Zazzu, eds. *The Jews in Genoa*. Leiden: Brill, 1999.

Vidas, Moulie. *Tradition and the Formation of the Talmud*. Princeton, NJ: Princeton University Press, 2014.

Vinograd, Isaiah. *Otzar ha-sefer ha-ivri*. Jerusalem: Institute for Computerized Hebrew Bibliography, 1993–1995.

Wachtel, Nathan. *Entre Moïse et Jésus: Etudes Marranes(xve–xxie siècle)*. Paris: CNRS Editions, 2013.

——. *The Faith of Remembrance: Marrano Labyrinths*. Translated by Nikki Halpern. Philadelphia: University of Pennsylvania Press, 2013.

Wardi, Ada. *Sefer Spitzer: pirke hayim ve-sifre Tarshish*. Jerusalem: Mineged, 2015.

Wasserstrom, Steven M. *Religion after Religion: Gershom Scholem, Mircea Eliade, and Henry Corbin at Eranos*. Princeton, NJ: Princeton University Press, 1999.

Weiss, Tzahi. "'Things that are better concealed than revealed': An Historical-Biographical Study of S. Y. Agnon's Attitude toward the Sabbatean Movement and the Traditional Jewish World." *AJS Review* 36 (2012): 103–120.

Werblowsky, R. J. Zwi. "Reflections on 'Sabbetai Sevi' by G. Scholem" (Hebrew). *Molad* 112 (1957): 539–546.

Werses, Shmuel. "*Bilvav yamim* by S. Y. Agnon: Sources of the Story and Method of Composition" (Hebrew). In *Shai Agnon ki-feshuto*, 153–188. Jerusalem: Bialik Institute, 2000.

——. "Frankists and *Maskilim* in Prague" (Hebrew). In *Haskalah ve-shabtaut: toldotav shel ma-avak*, 63–98. Jerusalem: Zalman Shazar Center, 1988.

——. "Joseph Klausner and the Beginnings of Teaching Modern Hebrew Literature at the Hebrew University" (Hebrew). In *Toledot ha-universitah ha-ivrit be-yerushalayim*, edited by Shaul Katz, 1:487–515. Jerusalem: Magnes Press, 1997.

——. "Sabbatianism and Frankism in the Light of Maskilic Historiography" (Hebrew). In *Haskalah ve-shabtaut: toldotav shel ma-avak*, 146–190. Jerusalem: Zalman Shazar Center, 1988.

Wertheimer, Solomon. *Batei midrashot*. Jerusalem: Rav Kook Institute, 1954.

Whaley, Joachim. *Religious Toleration and Social Change in Hamburg: 1529–1819*. Cambridge: Cambridge University Press, 1985.

Wieseltier, Leon. Introduction to Lionel Trilling, *The Moral Obligation to Be Intelligent*, ix–xvii. New York: Farrar, Straus, and Giroux, 2000.

——. "A Passion for Waiting: Liberal Notes on Messianism and the Jews." In *For Daniel Bell*, edited by Mark Lilla and Leon Wieseltier, 131–155. N.p., 2005.

——. Preface to Walter Benjamin *Illuminations*, translated by Harry Zohn, vii–x. New York: Schocken Books, 2007.

Wijk, Jetteke van. "The Rise and Fall of Sabbatai Zevi as Reflected in Contemporary Press Reports." *SR* 33 (1999): 7–27.

Wilke, Carsten L. "Le 'Messie mystique' et la Bourse d'Amsterdam, le 3 mai 1666." *Sefarad* 67 (2007): 191–211.

——. "*Midrashim from Bordeaux*: A Theological Controversy inside the Portuguese Jewish Diaspora at the Time of Spinoza's Excommunication." *European Journal of Jewish Studies* 6 (2012): 207–247.

Wirszubski, Chaim. "The Sabbatian Ideology of the Messiah's Conversion" (Hebrew). In *Ben ha-shitin*, 121–151. Jerusalem: Magnes Press, 1990.

Wittkower, Rudolf, and Margot Wittkower. *Born under Saturn: The Character and Conduct of Artists*. New York: Random House, 1963.

Wiznitzer, Arnold. "The Merger Agreement and Regulations of Congregation Talmud Torah of Amsterdam (1638–1639)." *Historia Judaica* 20 (1958): 109–132.

Wolf, Lucien. "The First Stage of Anglo-Jewish Emancipation." In *Essays in Jewish History*. London: Jewish Historical Society of England, 1934.

———. *Jews in the Canary Islands: being a calendar of Jewish cases extracted from the records of the Canariote Inquisition in the collection of the Marquess of Bute*. London, 1926. Reprint, Toronto: University of Toronto Press, 2001.

Wolfson, Elliot R. "Constructions of the Shekinah in the Messianic Theosophy of Abraham Cardoso." *Kabbalah* 3 (1998): 11–143.

———. " 'Sage Is Preferable to Prophet': Revisioning Midrashic Imagination." In *Scriptural Exegesis: The Shapes of Culture and the Religious Imagination; Essays in Honour of Michael Fishbane*, edited by Deborah A. Green and Laura S. Lieber, 186–210. Oxford: Oxford University Press, 2009.

Woudhuysen, H. R. *Sir Philip Sidney and the Circulation of Manuscripts 1558–1640*. New York: Clarendon Press, 1996.

Yaari, Abraham. "The Pereyra Yeshivot in Jerusalem and Hebron" (Hebrew). In *Yerushalayim: mehkere erez yisrael*, edited by M. Benayahu et al., 185–202. Jerusalem, 1953.

———. *Sheluhe erez yisrael*. Jerusalem: Rav Kook Institute, 1997.

———. *Ta-alumat sefer: Sefer hemdat yamim, mi hibro, u-mah hayeta midat haspha-ato*. Jerusalem: Rav Kook Institute, 1954.

Yadin, Azzan. "Rabban Gamliel, Aprhodite's Bath, and the Question of Pagan Monotheism." *JQR* 96 (2006): 149–179.

Yadin-Israel, Azzan. *Scripture and Tradition: Rabbi Akiva and the Triumph of Midrash*. Philadelphia: University of Pennsylvania Press, 2015.

Yerushalmi, Yosef Hayim. "Assimilation and Racial Anti-Semitism: The Iberian and the German Models." In *The Faith of Fallen Jews: Yosef Hayim Yerushalmi and the Writing of Jewish History*, edited by David N. Myers and Alexander Kaye, 176–209. Hanover, NH: Brandeis University Press, 2014.

———. *From Spanish Court to Italian Ghetto: Isaac Cardoso; A Study in Seventeenth-Century Marranism and Jewish Apologetics*. New York: Columbia University Press, 1971.

———. "Professing Jews in Post-Expulsion Spain and Portugal." In *Salo Wittmayer Baron Jubilee Volume*, edited by Saul Lieberman, 2:1023–1058. Jerusalem: American Academy of Jewish Research, 1974.

———. "The Re-education of Marranos in the Seventeenth Century." In *The Faith of Fallen Jews: Yosef Hayim Yerushalmi and the Writing of Jewish History*, edited by David N. Myers and Alexander Kaye, 159–174. Hanover, NH: Brandeis University Press, 2014.

Yosha, Nissim. "The Philosophical Background of Sabbatian Theology: Guidelines toward an Understanding of Abraham Michael Cardoso's Theory of the Divine" (Hebrew). In *Galut ahar golah: Mehkarim be-toledot am yisrael mugashim le-Professor Haim Beinart li-melot lo shivim shana*, edited by Aharon Mirsky, Avraham Grossman, and Yosef Kaplan, 541–572. Jerusalem: Ben Zvi Institute, 1988.

———. "Time and Space: A Theological Philosophical Controversy between Miguel Cardoso and Nathan of Gaza" (Hebrew). *JSJT* 12 (1996): 259–284.

Yuval, Israel Jacob. "*Moses Redivius*: Maimonides as the Messiah's Helper" (Hebrew). *Zion* 72 (2007): 161–188.

———. *Two Nations in Your Womb: Perceptions of Jews and Christians in Late Antiquity and the Middle Ages*. Translated by Barbara Harshav and Jonathan Chipman. Berkeley: University of California Press, 2006.

Zadoff, Noam. "The Debate between Baruch Kurzweil and Gershom Scholem on the Study of Sabbatianism" (Hebrew). *Kabbalah* 16 (2007): 299–360.

———, ed. *Gershom Scholem ve-Yosef Weiss: halifat mikhtavim, 1948–1964*. Jerusalem: Carmel, 2012.

———. *Mi-Berlin le-Yerushalayim uva-hazarah: Gershom Scholem ben yisrael ve-Germanyah*. Jerusalem: Carmel, 2015.

Zafran, Eric. "Saturn and the Jews." *Journal of the Warburg and Courtauld Institutes* 42 (1979): 16–27.

Zimmels, H. J. "Note on Solomon ben Joseph Buzaglo." *TJHSE* 17 (1951–1952): 290–292.

Zimmer, Yitzhak (Eric). "The Times of the Priestly Blessing" (Hebrew). In *Olam ke-minhago noheg: perakim be-toledot ha-minhagim, hilkhotehem, ve-giluglehem*, 132–151. Jerusalem: Zalman Shazar Center, 1996.

Zipperstein, Steven J. *The Jews of Odessa: A Cultural History, 1794–1881*. Stanford, CA: Stanford University Press, 1985.

Zlotnick, Dov. "R. Abraham Azulai's Ahabath bat ta-anugim (Commentary on Tractate Eduyot)" (Hebrew). In *Mehkarim u-mekorot*, edited by H. Z. Dimitrovsky, 1–122. New York: Jewish Theological Seminary, 1977.

Zwarts, Jac. "Een portret van Haham Jacob Sasportas door Nicolaas Maes." *Oude Kunst* (1930): 215–221.

INDEX

Note: Page numbers in italic type indicate illustrations.